T0205786

Lecture Notes in Artificial Intelligence   12941

Subseries of Lecture Notes in Computer Science

More information about this subseries at http://www.springer.com/series/1244

Boris Konev · Giles Reger (Eds.)

Frontiers of Combining Systems

13th International Symposium, FroCoS 2021
Birmingham, UK, September 8–10, 2021
Proceedings

 Springer

Editors
Boris Konev
University of Liverpool
Liverpool, UK

Giles Reger
The University of Manchester
Manchester, UK

ISSN 0302-9743   ISSN 1611-3349 (electronic)
Lecture Notes in Artificial Intelligence
ISBN 978-3-030-86204-6   ISBN 978-3-030-86205-3 (eBook)
https://doi.org/10.1007/978-3-030-86205-3

LNCS Sublibrary: SL7 – Artificial Intelligence

This Springer imprint is published by the registered company Springer Nature Switzerland AG
The registered company address is: Gewerbestrasse 11, 6330 Cham, Switzerland

Preface

These proceedings contain the papers selected for presentation at the 13th International Symposium on Frontiers of Combining Systems (FroCoS 2021). The symposium was held during September 8–10, 2021 in Birmingham, UK, at Birmingham University. It was co-located with the 30th International Conference on Automated Reasoning with Analytic Tableaux and Related Methods (TABLEAUX 2021).

FroCoS is the main international event for research on the development of techniques and methods for the combination and integration of formal systems, their modularization and analysis. Previous FroCoS meetings were organized in Munich (Germany, 1996), Amsterdam (The Netherlands, 1998), Nancy (France, 2000), Santa Margherita Ligure (Italy, 2002), Cork (Ireland, 2004, as part of the International Joint Conference on Automated Reasoning, IJCAR), Vienna (Austria, 2005), Seattle (USA, 2006, as part of IJCAR), Liverpool (UK, 2007, co-located with the International Workshop on First-Order Theorem Proving, FTP), Sydney (Australia, 2008, as part of IJCAR), Trento (Italy, 2009), Edinburgh (UK, 2010, as part of IJCAR), Saarbrücken (Germany, 2011), Manchester (UK, 2012, as part of IJCAR), Nancy (France, 2013, co-located with TABLEAUX), Vienna (Austria, 2014, as part of IJCAR), Wrocław (Poland, 2015, co-located with TABLEAUX), Coimbra (Portugal, 2016, as part of IJCAR), Brasilia (Brazil, 2017, co-located with TABLEAUX), Oxford (UK, 2018, as part of IJCAR), London (UK 2019, co-located with TABLEAUX) and Paris (France 2020, as part of IJCAR).

FroCoS 2021 received 23 high-quality paper submissions, which were evaluated by the Program Committee on the basis of their significance, novelty, technical soundness, and appropriateness for the FroCoS audience. Reviewing was single-blind and each paper was subject to at least three reviews, followed by a discussion within the Program Committee. In the end, 16 papers were selected for presentation at the symposium and publication. We have grouped them in this volume according to the following topic classification: (1) calculi and unification, (2) description logics, (3) interactive theorem proving, (4) machine learning, (5) satisfiability modulo theories, and (6) verification.

We were delighted to have four outstanding invited speakers.

- Michael Benedikt, University of Oxford (joint with TABLEAUX 2021)
- Vijay Ganesh, University of Waterloo
- Chantal Keller, Université Paris-Sud
- Renate Schmidt, University of Manchester (joint with TABLEAUX 2021)

We would like to thank all the people who contributed to making FroCoS 2021 a success. In particular, we thank the invited speakers for their inspiring talks, the authors for providing their high-quality contributions, and the Program Committee members and the external reviewers for their careful, competent reviewing and discussion of the submissions on quite a tight schedule. We extend our thanks to the University of Birmingham for hosting FroCoS, especially to Anupam Das.

We gratefully acknowledge financial support from Springer and the University of Birmingham. Finally, we are grateful to EasyChair for allowing us to use their excellent conference management system.

September 2021   Boris Konev
                                                                    Giles Reger

Organization

Program Committee Chairs

Boris Konev   University of Liverpool, UK
Giles Reger   University of Manchester, UK

Steering Committee

Franz Baader (chair)	TU Dresden, Germany
Clare Dixon	University of Manchester, UK
Marcelo Finger	University of Sao Paulo, Brazil
Andreas Herzig	IRIT, Université Paul Sabatier, France
Carsten Lutz	Universität Bremen, Germany
Andrei Popescu	University of Sheffield, UK
Silvio Ranise	University of Trento and Fondazione Bruno Kessler, Italy

Program Committee

Takahito Aoto	Niigata University, Japan
Carlos Areces	Universidad Nacional de Córdoba, Argentina
Alessandro Artale	Free University of Bozen-Bolzano, Italy
Franz Baader	TU Dresden, Germany
Peter Baumgartner	CSIRO, Australia
Christoph Benzmüller	Freie Universität Berlin, Germany
Jasmin Blanchette	Vrije Universiteit Amsterdam, The Netherlands
Clare Dixon	University of Manchester, UK
Pascal Fontaine	Université de Liège, Belgium
Didier Galmiche	LORIA, Université de Lorraine, France
Silvio Ghilardi	Università degli Studi di Milano, Italy
Jürgen Giesl	RWTH Aachen University, Germany
Andreas Herzig	IRIT, Université Paul Sabatier, France
Jean Christoph Jung	Universität Bremen, Germany
Roman Kontchakov	Birkbeck, University of London, UK
Aina Niemetz	Stanford University, USA
Andrei Popescu	University of Sheffield, UK
Silvio Ranise	University of Trento and Fondazione Bruno Kessler, Italy
Andrew Reynolds	University of Iowa, USA
Christophe Ringeissen	LORIA, Université de Lorraine, France
Philipp Ruemmer	Uppsala University, Sweden
Uli Sattler	University of Manchester, UK

Roberto Sebastiani	University of Trento, Italy
Viorica Sofronie-Stokkermans	University of Koblenz-Landau, Germany
Martin Suda	Czech Technical University in Prague, Czech Republic
Christoph Weidenbach	Max Planck Institute for Informatics, Germany

Additional Reviewers

Alessandro Gianola
Alexander Bentkamp
Andrea Mazzullo
Chencheng Liang
Filip Bártek
Florian Rabe
Haniel Barbosa

Joseph Scott
Manfred Schmidt-Schauss
Martin Bromberger
Petar Vukmirović
Santiago Escobar
Yannick Chevalier

Abstracts of Invited Talk

The Strange Career of Interpolation and Definability

Michael Benedikt

University of Oxford
michael.benedikt@gmail.com

Beth Definability, Craig Interpolation, and their variants have long been seen as an important topic in commputational logic, telling us something about logical simplification. But the rationale for their significance has varied over time, and it is not even clear whether they should be best seen as a property of a logic or of a proof system. In this talk I will look back at the somewhat twisty evolution of the topic, highlighting some issues that have been underexplored. I'll also present some current work (joint with Pierre Pradic) aimed at filling some of the gaps. No background on interpolation or definability will be assumed in the talk.

On the Unreasonable Effectiveness of SAT Solvers

Vijay Ganesh

University of Waterloo
vganesh@uwaterloo.ca

Over the last two decades, software engineering (broadly construed to include testing, analysis, synthesis, verification, and security) has witnessed a silent revolution in the form of Boolean SAT and SMT solvers. These solvers are now integral to many testing, analysis, synthesis, and verification approaches. This is largely due to a dramatic improvement in the scalability of these solvers vis-a-vis large real-world formulas. What is surprising is that the Boolean satisfiability problem is NP-complete, believed to be intractable, and yet these solvers easily solve industrial instances containing millions of variables and clauses in them. How can that be?

In my talk, I will address this question of why SAT solvers are so efficient through the lens of machine learning (ML) as well as ideas from (parameterized) proof complexity. While the focus of my talk is almost entirely empirical, I will show how we can leverage theoretical ideas to not only deepen our understanding but also to build better SAT solvers. I will argue that SAT solvers are best viewed as proof systems, composed of two kinds of sub-routines, ones that implement proof rules and others that are prediction engines that optimize some metric correlated with solver running time. These prediction engines can be built using ML techniques, whose aim is to structure solver proofs in an optimal way. Thus, two major paradigms of AI, namely machine learning and logical deduction, are brought together in a principled way in order to design efficient SAT solvers. A result of my research is the MapleSAT solver that has been the winner of several recent international SAT competitions and is widely used in industry and academia.

General Automation in Coq Through Modular Transformations and SMT Solving

Chantal Keller

Université Paris-Sud
Chantal.Keller@lri.f

The subject of the SMTCoq project is to significantly enhance automation in the Coq proof assistant. At the heart of SMTCoq is a Coq plugin that offers a way to use automatic provers with the same degree of trust as Coq itself. On top of it, we define a framework called Sniper to progressively encode Coq's logic into first-order logic, through modular and fine-grained logical transformations that can be composed. Our objective is to obtain automatic while expressive tactics for Coq.

In this talk, I will concisely introduce the communication between Coq and external provers, before presenting the new framework of logical transformations. I will report on work in progress of examples of transformations in this framework.

This is a collaboration with Valentin Blot, Louise Dubois de Prisque, and Pierre Vial.e

Forgetting and Subontology Generation for the Medical Ontology SNOMED CT

Renate A. Schmidt◉

Department of Computer Science, The University of Manchester, UK
Renate.Schmidt@manchester.ac.uk

In this talk I discuss efforts in developing systems to provide automated support for content extraction for the medical ontology SNOMED CT. SNOMED CT is a large knowledge base of standardised, precise definitions of clinical terms and medical codes for use in electronic health records to allow consistent data capture at the point of care and meaningful processing of data across health care sectors. Since SNOMED CT is so large, it has long been an aim to have the capability to compute smaller extracts of the ontology that are self-contained but restricted to a narrow focus, for example, kidney diseases, dentistry or vocabulary relevant for nursing. Such subontologies would make it easier to reuse and share content, to assist with new ontology creation, quality assurance, ontology update, and debugging. In addition, reasoning tasks such as querying and classification take less time to execute over a smaller extract than over the original ontology.

The aim of our research is to compute extracts that are semantically complete in that they faithfully capture the knowledge in an ontology about a user-specified focus signature. This is a challenging problem, because the knowledge of an ontology is not only given by the explicitly stated axioms in the ontology but also all implicit knowledge that can be inferred from these axioms. Forgetting creates a compact representation of the implicit knowledge of an ontology over specified focus concepts and relations by performing inferences on the non-focus (forgetting) signature. A number of PhD projects in our group have developed a series of forgetting tools and adaptations for use in applications such as logical difference computation and abduction in the context of description logic-based ontologies. These tools provided the basis for a series of industry projects in which we applied and further developed these for use cases of the medical ontology SNOMED CT. A workflow of different modularisation and forgetting methods was devised and thoroughly evaluated. With this workflow, we managed to significantly improve the performance and success rates of our tools and provide a feasible way to compute faithful extracts of SNOMED CT.

Building on these experiences, in a current joint project with SNOMED Intl., we have developed a new bespoke approach and prototype for computing subontologies of SNOMED CT. This approach is definition, driven and returns concise encodings of descriptions of the specified focus concepts in a normal form according to modelling guidelines of SNOMED Intl. These can be efficiently computed and are significantly smaller than both forgetting solutions and subontologies computed by modularisation methods.

The talk will give an overview of this research spanning several years, focussing on key ideas, findings, experiences, and practical challenges encountered.

Contents

Calculi and Unification

A Datalog Hammer for Supervisor Verification Conditions Modulo Simple Linear Arithmetic

Martin Bromberger[1(✉)], Irina Dragoste[2], Rasha Faqeh[2], Christof Fetzer[2], Markus Krötzsch[2], and Christoph Weidenbach[1]

[1] Max Planck Institute for Informatics, Saarland Informatics Campus, Saarbrücken, Germany
{mbromber,weidenb}@mpi-inf.mpg.de
[2] TU Dresden, Dresden, Germany

Abstract. The Bernays-Schönfinkel first-order logic fragment over simple linear real arithmetic constraints BS(SLR) is known to be decidable. We prove that BS(SLR) clause sets with both universally and existentially quantified verification conditions (conjectures) can be translated into BS(SLR) clause sets over a finite set of first-order constants. For the Horn case, we provide a Datalog hammer preserving validity and satisfiability. A toolchain from the BS(LRA) prover SPASS-SPL to the Datalog reasoner VLog establishes an effective way of deciding verification conditions in the Horn fragment. This is exemplified by the verification of supervisor code for a lane change assistant in a car and of an electronic control unit for a supercharged combustion engine.

1 Introduction

Modern dynamic dependable systems (e.g., autonomous driving) continuously update software components to fix bugs and to introduce new features. However, the safety requirement of such systems demands software to be safety certified before it can be used, which is typically a lengthy process that hinders the dynamic update of software. We adapt the *continuous certification* approach [15] of variants of safety critical software components using a *supervisor* that guarantees important aspects through challenging, see Fig. 1. Specifically, multiple processing units run in parallel – *certified* and *updated not-certified* variants that produce output as *suggestions* and *explications*. The supervisor compares the behavior of variants and analyses their explications. The supervisor itself consists of a rather small set of rules that can be automatically verified and run by a *reasoner*. The reasoner helps the supervisor to check if the output of an updated variant is in agreement with the output of a respective certified variant. The absence of discrepancy between the two variants for a long-enough period of running both variants in parallel allows to dynamically certify it as a safe software variant.

While supervisor safety conditions formalized as existentially quantified properties can often already be automatically verified, conjectures about invariants

© Springer Nature Switzerland AG 2021
B. Konev and G. Reger (Eds.): FroCoS 2021, LNAI 12941, pp. 3–24, 2021.
https://doi.org/10.1007/978-3-030-86205-3_1

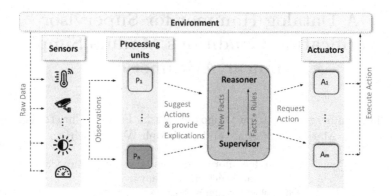

Fig. 1. The supervisor architecture.

formalized as universally quantified properties are a further challenge. In this paper we show that supervisor safety conditions and invariants can be automatically proven by a Datalog hammer. Analogous to the Sledgehammer project [7] of Isabelle [30] translating higher-order logic conjectures to first-order logic (modulo theories) conjectures, our Datalog hammer translates first-order Horn logic modulo arithmetic conjectures into pure Datalog programs, equivalent to Horn Bernays-Schönfinkel clause fragment, called HBS.

More concretely, the underlying logic for both formalizing supervisor behavior and formulating conjectures is the hierarchic combination of the Bernays-Schönfinkel first-order fragment with real linear arithmetic, BS(LRA), also called *Superlog* for Supervisor Effective Reasoning Logics [15]. Satisfiability of BS(LRA) clause sets is undecidable [13,21], in general, however, the restriction to simple linear real arithmetic BS(SLR) yields a decidable fragment [17,20]. Our first contribution is decidability of BS(SLR) with respect to universally quantified conjectures, Sect. 3, Lemma 10.

Inspired by the test point method for quantifier elimination in arithmetic [25] we show that instantiation with a finite number of first-order constants is sufficient to decide whether a universal/existential conjecture is a consequence of a BS(SLR) clause set.

For our experiments of the test point approach we consider two case studies: verification conditions for a supervisor taking care of multiple software variants of a lane change assistant in a car and a supervisor for a supercharged combustion engine, also called an ECU for Electronical Control Unit. The supervisors in both cases are formulated by BS(SLR) Horn clauses, the HBS(SLR) fragment. Via our test point technique they are translated together with the verification conditions to Datalog [1] (HBS). The translation is implemented in our Superlog reasoner SPASS-SPL. The resulting Datalog clause set is eventually explored by the Datalog engine VLog [11]. This hammer constitutes a decision procedure for both universal and existential conjectures. The results of our experiments show that we can verify non-trivial existential and universal conjectures in the range of seconds while state-of-the-art solvers cannot solve all problems in reasonable time. This constitutes our second contribution, Sect. 5.

Related Work: Reasoning about BS(LRA) clause sets is supported by SMT (Satisfiability Modulo Theories) [28, 29]. In general, SMT comprises the combination of a number of theories beyond LRA such as arrays, lists, strings, or bit vectors. While SMT is a decision procedure for the BS(LRA) ground case, universally quantified variables can be considered by instantiation [34]. Reasoning by instantiation does result in a refutationally complete procedure for BS(SLR), but not in a decision procedure. The Horn fragment HBS(LRA) out of BS(LRA) is receiving additional attention [6, 18], because it is well-suited for software analysis and verification. Research in this direction also goes beyond the theory of LRA and considers minimal model semantics in addition, but is restricted to existential conjectures. Other research focuses on universal conjectures, but over non-arithmetic theories, e.g., invariant checking for array-based systems [12] or considers abstract decidability criteria incomparable with the HBS(LRA) class [33]. Hierarchic superposition [2] and Simple Clause Learning over Theories [9] (SCL(T)) are both refutationally complete for BS(LRA). While SCL(T) can be immediately turned into a decision procedure for even larger fragments than BS(SLR) [9], hierarchic superposition needs to be refined by specific strategies or rules to become a decision procedure already because of the Bernays-Schönfinkel part [19]. Our Datalog hammer translates HBS(SLR) clause sets with both existential and universal conjectures into HBS clause sets which are also subject to first-order theorem proving. Instance generating approaches such as iProver [23] are a decision procedure for this fragment, whereas superposition-based [2] first-order provers such as E [37], SPASS [41], Vampire [35], have additional mechanisms implemented to decide HBS. In our experiments, Sect. 5, we will discuss the differences between all these approaches on a number of benchmark examples in more detail.

The paper is organized as follows: after a section on preliminaries, Sect. 2, we present the theory of our new Datalog hammer in Sect. 3. Section 4 introduces our two case studies followed by experiments on respective verification conditions, Sect. 5. The paper ends with a discussion of the obtained results and directions for future work, Sect. 6. Binaries of our tools and all benchmark problems can be found under https://github.com/knowsys/eval-datalog-arithmetic and an extended version of this paper including proofs on arXiv [8].

2 Preliminaries

We briefly recall the basic logical formalisms and notations we build upon. We use a standard first-order language with *constants* (denoted a, b, c), without non-constant function symbols, *variables* (denoted w, x, y, z), and *predicates* (denoted P, Q, R) of some fixed *arity*. *Terms* (denoted t, s) are variables or constants. We write $\bar{x}$ for a vector of variables, $\bar{a}$ for a vector of constants, and so on. An *atom* (denoted A, B) is an expression $P(\bar{t})$ for a predicate P of arity n and a term list $\bar{t}$ of length n. A *positive literal* is an atom A and a *negative literal* is a negated atom $\neg A$. We define $\mathrm{comp}(A) = \neg A$, $\mathrm{comp}(\neg A) = A$, $|A| = A$ and $|\neg A| = A$. Literals are usually denoted L, K, H.

A *clause* is a disjunction of literals, where all variables are assumed to be universally quantified. C, D denote clauses, and N denotes a clause set. We write atoms(X) for the set of atoms in a clause or clause set X. A clause is *Horn* if it contains at most one positive literal, and a *unit clause* if it has exactly one literal. A clause $A_1 \vee \ldots \vee A_n \vee \neg B_1 \vee \ldots \vee \neg B_m$ can be written as an implication $A_1 \wedge \ldots \wedge A_n \rightarrow B_1 \vee \ldots \vee B_m$, still omitting universal quantifiers. If Y is a term, formula, or a set thereof, vars(Y) denotes the set of all variables in Y, and Y is *ground* if vars$(Y) = \emptyset$. A *fact* is a ground unit clause with a positive literal.

Datalog and the Bernays-Schönfinkel Fragment: The *Bernays-Schönfinkel fragment* (BS) comprises all sets of clauses. The more general form of BS in first-order logic allows arbitrary *formulas* over atoms, i.e., arbitrary Boolean connectives and leading existential quantifiers. However, both can be polynomially removed with common syntactic transformations while preserving satisfiability and all entailments that do not refer to auxiliary constants and predicates introduced in the transformation [31]. Sometimes, we still refer explicitly to formulas when it is more beneficial to apply these transformations after some other processing steps. BS theories in our sense are also known as *disjunctive Datalog programs* [14], specifically when written as implications. A set of Horn clauses is also called a *Datalog program*. (Datalog is sometimes viewed as a second-order language. We are only interested in query answering, which can equivalently be viewed as first-order entailment or second-order model checking [1]). Again, it is common to write clauses as implications in this case.

Two types of *conjectures*, i.e., formulas we want to prove as consequences of a clause set, are of particular interest: *universal* conjectures $\forall \bar{x} \phi$ and *existential* conjectures $\exists \bar{x} \phi$, where ϕ is any Boolean combination of BS atoms that only uses variables in $\bar{x}$.

A *substitution* σ is a function from variables to terms with a finite domain dom$(\sigma) = \{x \mid x\sigma \neq x\}$ and codomain codom$(\sigma) = \{x\sigma \mid x \in \text{dom}(\sigma)\}$. We denote substitutions by σ, δ, ρ. The application of substitutions is often written postfix, as in $x\sigma$, and is homomorphically extended to terms, atoms, literals, clauses, and quantifier-free formulas. A substitution σ is *ground* if codom(σ) is ground. Let Y denote some term, literal, clause, or clause set. σ is a *grounding* for Y if $Y\sigma$ is ground, and $Y\sigma$ is a *ground instance* of Y in this case. We denote by gnd(Y) the set of all ground instances of Y, and by gnd$_B(Y)$ the set of all ground instances over a given set of constants B. The *most general unifier* mgu(Z_1, Z_2) of two terms/atoms/literals Z_1 and Z_2 is defined as usual, and we assume that it does not introduce fresh variables and is idempotent.

We assume a standard first-order logic model theory, and write $\mathcal{A} \models \phi$ if an interpretation $\mathcal{A}$ satisfies a first-order formula ϕ. A formula ψ is a logical consequence of ϕ, written $\phi \models \psi$, if $\mathcal{A} \models \psi$ for all $\mathcal{A}$ such that $\mathcal{A} \models \phi$. Sets of clauses are semantically treated as conjunctions of clauses with all variables quantified universally.

BS with Linear Arithmetic: The extension of BS with linear arithmetic over real numbers, BS(LRA), is the basis for the formalisms studied in this paper. For simplicity, we assume a one-sorted extension where all terms in BS(LRA) are of arithmetic sort LA, i.e., represent numbers. The language includes free first-order logic constants that are eventually interpreted by real numbers, but we only consider initial clause sets without such constants, called *pure* clause sets. Satisfiability of pure BS(LRA) clause sets is semi-decidable, e.g., using *hierarchic superposition* [2] or *SCL(T)* [9]. Impure BS(LRA) is no longer compact and satisfiability becomes undecidable, but it can be made decidable when restricting to ground clause sets [16], which is the result of our grounding hammer.

Example 1. The following BS(LRA) clause from our ECU case study compares the values of speed (Rpm) and pressure (KPa) with entries in an ignition table (IgnTable) to derive the basis of the current ignition value (IgnDeg1):

$$x_1 < 0 \ \lor \ x_1 \geq 13 \ \lor \ x_2 < 880 \ \lor \ x_2 \geq 1100 \ \lor \ \neg KPa(x_3, x_1) \ \lor$$
$$\neg Rpm(x_4, x_2) \ \lor \ \neg IgnTable(0, 13, 880, 1100, z) \ \lor \ IgnDeg1(x_3, x_4, x_1, x_2, z) \tag{1}$$

Terms of sort LA are constructed from a set $\mathcal{X}$ of *variables*, a set of *first-order arithmetic constants*, the set of integer constants $c \in \mathbb{Z}$, and binary function symbols $+$ and $-$ (written infix). Atoms in BS(LRA) are either *first-order atoms* (e.g., IgnTable$(0, 13, 880, 1100, z)$) or *(linear) arithmetic atoms* (e.g., $x_2 < 880$). Arithmetic atoms may use the predicates $\leq, <, \neq, =, >, \geq$, which are written infix and have the expected fixed interpretation. Predicates used in first-order atoms are called *free*. *First-order literals* and related notation is defined as before. *Arithmetic literals* coincide with arithmetic atoms, since the arithmetic predicates are closed under negation, e.g., comp$(x_2 \geq 1100) = x_2 < 1100$.

BS(LRA) clauses and conjectures are defined as for BS but using BS(LRA) atoms. We often write clauses in the form $\Lambda \parallel C$ where C is a clause solely built of free first-order literals and Λ is a multiset of LRA atoms. The semantics of $\parallel$ is implication where Λ denotes a conjunction, e.g., the clause $x > 1 \lor y \neq 5 \lor \neg Q(x) \lor R(x, y)$ is also written $x \leq 1, y = 5 \parallel \neg Q(x) \lor R(x, y)$. For Y a term, literal, or clause, we write ints(Y) for the set of all integers that occur in Y.

A clause or clause set is *pure* if it does not contain first-order arithmetic constants, and it is *abstracted* if its first-order literals contain only variables. Every clause C is equivalent to an abstracted clause that is obtained by replacing each non-variable term t that occurs in a first-order atom by a fresh variable x while adding an arithmetic atom $x \neq t$ to C. We assume abstracted clauses for theory development, but we prefer non-abstracted clauses in examples for readability,e.g., a fact $P(3, 5)$ is considered in the development of the theory as the clause $x = 3, x = 5 \parallel P(x, y)$, this is important when collecting the necessary test points.

The semantics of BS(LRA) is based on the standard model $\mathcal{A}^{LRA}$ of linear arithmetic, which has the domain $LA^{\mathcal{A}^{LRA}} = \mathbb{R}$ and which interprets all arithmetic predicates and functions in the usual way. An interpretation of BS(LRA) coincides with $\mathcal{A}^{LRA}$ on arithmetic predicates and functions, and freely interprets free predicates and first-order arithmetic constants. For pure clause sets this is well-defined [2]. Logical satisfaction and entailment is defined as usual, and uses similar notation as for BS.

Simpler Forms of Linear Arithmetic: The main logic studied in this paper is obtained by restricting BS(LRA) to a simpler form of linear arithmetic. We first introduce a simpler logic BS(SLR) as a well-known fragment of BS(LRA) for which satisfiability is decidable [17,20], and then present the generalization BS(LRA) PP of this formalism that we will use.

Definition 2 *The* Bernays-Schönfinkel fragment over simple linear arithmetic, BS(SLR), *is a subset of* BS(LRA) *where all arithmetic atoms are of form* $x \triangleleft c$ *or* $d \triangleleft c$, *such that* $c \in \mathbb{Z}$, d *is a (possibly free) constant,* $x \in \mathcal{X}$, *and* $\triangleleft \in \{ \leq, <, \neq, =, >, \geq \}$.

Example 3 The ECU use case leads to BS(LRA) clauses such as

$$
\begin{aligned}
x_1 < y_1 \ \lor \ x_1 \geq y_2 \ \lor \ x_2 < y_3 \ \lor \ x_2 \geq y_4 \ \lor \ \neg \text{KPa}(x_3, x_1) \ \lor \\
\neg \text{Rpm}(x_4, x_2) \ \lor \ \neg \text{IgnTable}(y_1, y_2, y_3, y_4, z) \ \lor \ \text{IgnDeg1}(x_3, x_4, x_1, x_2, z).
\end{aligned}
\tag{2}
$$

This clause is not in BS(SLR), e.g., since $x_1 > x_5$ is not allowed in BS(SLR). However, clause (1) of Example 1 is a BS(SLR) clause that is an instance of (2), obtained by the substitution $\{y_1 \mapsto 0, y_2 \mapsto 13, y_3 \mapsto 880, y_4 \mapsto 1100\}$. This grounding will eventually be obtained by resolution on the IgnTable predicate, because it occurs only positively in ground unit facts.

Example 3 shows that BS(SLR) clauses can sometimes be obtained by instantiation. Relevant instantiations can be found by *resolution*, in our case by *hierarchic resolution*, which supports arithmetic constraints: given clauses $\Lambda_1 \| L \lor C_1$ and $\Lambda_2 \| K \lor C_2$ with $\sigma = \text{mgu}(L, \text{comp}(K))$, their *hierarchic resolvent* is $(\Lambda_1, \Lambda_2 \| C_1 \lor C_2)\sigma$. A *refutation* is the sequence of resolution steps that produces a clause $\Lambda \| \bot$ with $\mathcal{A}^{\text{LRA}} \models \Lambda\delta$ for some grounding δ. *Hierarchic resolution* is sound and refutationally complete for pure BS(LRA), since every set N of pure BS(LRA) clauses N is *sufficiently complete* [2], and hence *hierarchic superposition* is sound and refutationally complete for N [2,5]. Resolution can be used to eliminate predicates that do not occur recursively:

Definition 4 (Positively Grounded Predicate). *Let* N *be a set of* BS(LRA) *clauses. A free first-order predicate* P *is a* positively grounded predicate *in* N *if all positive occurrences of* P *in* N *are in ground unit clauses (also called facts).*

For a positively grounded predicate P in a clause set N, let $\text{elim}(P, N)$ be the clause set obtained from N by resolving away all negative occurrences of P in N and finally eliminating all clauses where P occurs negatively. We need to keep the P facts for the generation of test points. Then N is satisfiable iff $\text{elim}(P, N)$ is satisfiable. We can extend elim to sets of positively grounded predicates in the obvious way. If n is the number of P unit clauses in N, m the maximal number of negative P literals in a clause in N, and k the number of clauses in N with a negative P literal, then $|\text{elim}(P, N)| \leq |N| + k \cdot n^m$, i.e., $\text{elim}(P, N)$ is exponential in the worst case.

We further assume that elim simplifies LRA atoms until they contain at most one integer number and that LRA atoms that can be evaluated are reduced to true and false and the respective clause simplified. For example, given the pure and abstracted BS(LRA) clause set $N = \{$IgnTable$(0, 13, 880, 1100, 2200), x_1 \leq x_2 \vee z_2 \geq z_1 \parallel \neg$IgnTable$(x_1, x_2, y_1, y_2, z_1) \vee$ R$(z_2)\}$, the predicate IgnTable is positively grounded. Then elim(IgnTable, N) $= \{z_2 \geq 2200 \parallel$ R$(z_2)\}$ where the unifier $\sigma = \{x_1 \mapsto 0, x_2 \mapsto 13, y_1 \mapsto 880, y_2 \mapsto 110, z_1 \mapsto 2200\}$ is used to eliminate the literal $\neg$IgnTable$(x_1, x_2, y_1, y_2, z_1)$ and $(x_1 \leq x_2)\sigma$ becomes true and can be removed.

Definition 5 (Positively Grounded BS(SLR): BS(SLR) P). *A clause set N is out of the fragment* positively grounded BS(SLR), BS(SLR) P *if* elim(S, N) *is out of the* BS(SLR) *fragment, where S is the set of all positively grounded predicates in N.*

Pure BS(SLR) P clause sets are called BS(SLR) PP and are the starting point for our Datalog hammer.

3 The Theory of the Hammer

We define two hammers that help us solve BS(SLR) PP clause sets with both universally and existentially quantified conjectures. Both are equisatisfiability preserving and allow us to abstract BS(SLR) PP formulas into less complicated logics with efficient and complete decision procedures.

The first hammer, also called *grounding hammer*, translates any BS(SLR) PP clause set N with a universally/existentially quantified conjecture into an equi-satisfiable ground and no longer pure BS(SLR) clause set over a finite set of first-order constants called *test points*. This means we reduce a quantified problem over an infinite domain into a ground problem over a finite domain. The size of the ground problem grows worst-case exponentially in the number of variables and the number of numeric constants in N and the conjecture. For the Horn case, HBS(SLR) PP, we define a Datalog hammer, i.e. a transformation into an equi-satisfiable Datalog program that is based on the same set of test points but does not require an overall grounding. It keeps the original clauses almost one-to-one instead of greedily computing all ground instances of those clauses over the test points. The Datalog hammer adds instead a finite set of Datalog facts that correspond to all theory atoms over the given set of test points. With the help of these facts and the original rules, the Datalog reasoner can then derive the same conclusions as it could have done with the ground HBS(SLR) clause set, however, all groundings that do not lead to new ground facts are neglected. Therefore, the Datalog approach is much faster in practice because the Datalog reasoner wastes no time (and space) on trivially satisfied ground rules that would have been part of the greedily computed ground HBS(SLR) clause set. Moreover, Datalog reasoners are well suited to the resulting structure of the problem, i.e. many facts but a small set of rules.

Note that we never compute or work on $\text{elim}(S, N)$ although the discussed clause sets are positively grounded. We only refer to $\text{elim}(S, N)$ because it allows us to formulate our theoretical results more concisely. We avoid working on $\text{elim}(S, N)$ because it often increases the number of non-fact clauses (by orders of magnitude) in order to simplify the positively grounded theory atoms to variable bounds. This is bad in practice because the number of non-fact clauses has a high impact on the performance of Datalog reasoners. Our Datalog hammer resolves this problem by dealing with the positively grounded theory atoms in a different way that only introduces more facts instead of non-fact clauses. This is better in practice because Datalog reasoners are well suited to handling a large number of facts. Since the *grounding hammer* is meant primarily as a stepping stone towards the Datalog hammer, we also defined it in such a way that it avoids computing and working on $\text{elim}(S, N)$.

Hammering BS(SLR) Clause Sets with a Universal Conjecture: Our first hammer, takes a BS(SLR) PP clause set N and a universal conjecture $\forall \bar{y}.\phi$ as input and translates it into a ground BS(SLR) formula. We will later show that the cases for no conjecture and for an existential conjecture can be seen as special cases of the universal conjecture. Since ϕ is a universal conjecture, we assume that ϕ is a quantifier-free pure BS(SLR) formula and $\text{vars}(\phi) = \text{vars}(\bar{y})$. Moreover, we denote by S the set of positively grounded predicates in N and assume that none of the positively grounded predicates from S appear in ϕ. There is not much difference developing the hammer for the Horn or the non-Horn case. Therefore, we present it for the general non-Horn case, although our second Datalog hammer is restricted to Horn. Note that a conjecture $\forall \bar{y}.\phi$ is a consequence of N, i.e. $N \models \forall \bar{y}.\phi$, if $\forall \bar{y}.\phi$ is satisfied by every interpretation $\mathcal{A}$ that also satisfies N, i.e. $\forall \mathcal{A}.(\mathcal{A} \models N \rightarrow \forall \bar{y}.\phi)$. Conversely, $\forall \bar{y}.\phi$ is not a consequence of N if there exists a counter example, i.e. one interpretation $\mathcal{A}$ that satisfies N but does not satisfy $\forall \bar{y}.\phi$, or formally: $\exists \mathcal{A}.(\mathcal{A} \models N \wedge \exists \bar{y}.\neg\phi)$.

Our hammer is going to abstract the counter example formulation into a ground BS(SLR) formula. This means the hammered formula will be unsatisfiable if and only if the conjecture is a consequence of N. The abstraction to the ground case works because we can restrict our solution space from the infinite reals to a finite set of test points and still preserve satisfiability. To be more precise, we partition $\mathbb{R}$ into intervals such that any variable bound in $\text{elim}(S, N)$ and ϕ either satisfies all points in one such interval I or none. Then we pick $m = \max(1, |\text{vars}(\phi)|)$ test points from each of those intervals because any counter example, i.e. any assignment for $\neg\phi$, contains at most m different points per interval.

We get the interval partitioning by first determining the necessary set of interval borders based on the variable bounds in $\text{elim}(S, N)$ and ϕ. Then, we sort and combine the borders into actual intervals. The interval borders are extracted as follows: We turn every variable bound $x \triangleleft c$ with $\triangleleft \in \{\leq, <, >, \geq\}$ in $\text{elim}(S, N)$ and ϕ into two interval borders. One of them is the interval border implied by the bound itself and the other its negation, e.g., $x \geq 5$ results in the interval border $[5$ and the interval border of the negation $5)$. Likewise, we turn every variable bound $x \lhd c$ with $\lhd \in \{=, \neq\}$ into all four possible interval borders for c, i.e. $c)$, $[c, c]$, and $(c$. The set of interval endpoints $\mathcal{C}$ is then defined as follows:

$$\mathcal{C} = \{c], (c \mid x \lhd c \in \text{atoms}(\text{elim}(S, N)) \cup \text{atoms}(\phi) \text{ where } \lhd \in \{\leq, =, \neq, >\}\} \cup$$
$$\{c), [c \mid x \lhd c \in \text{atoms}(\text{elim}(S, N)) \cup \text{atoms}(\phi) \text{ where } \lhd \in \{\geq, =, \neq, <\}\} \cup \{(-\infty, \infty)\}$$

It is not necessary to compute $\text{elim}(S, N)$ to compute $\mathcal{C}$. It is enough to iterate over all theory atoms in N and compute all of their instantiations in $\text{elim}(S, N)$ based on the facts in N for predicates in S. This can be done in $O(n_t \cdot n_A \cdot n_S^{n_v})$, where n_v is the maximum number of variables in any theory atom in N, n_A is the number of theory atoms in N, n_S is the number of facts in N for predicates in S, and n_t is the size of the largest theory atom in N with respect to the number of symbols.

The intervals themselves can be constructed by sorting $\mathcal{C}$ in an ascending order such that we first order by the border value—i.e. $\delta < \epsilon$ if $\delta \in \{c), [c, c], (c\}$, $\epsilon \in \{d), [d, d], (d\}$, and $c < d$—and then by the border type—i.e. $c) < [c < c] < (c$. The result is a sequence $[\ldots, \delta_l, \delta_u, \ldots]$, where we always have one lower border δ_l, followed by one upper border δ_u. We can guarantee that an upper border δ_u follows a lower border δ_l because $\mathcal{C}$ always contains $c)$ together with $[c$ and $c]$ together with $(c$ for $c \in \mathbb{Z}$, so always two consecutive upper and lower borders. Together with $(-\infty$ and $\infty)$ this guarantees that the sorted $\mathcal{C}$ has the desired structure. If we combine every two subsequent borders δ_l, δ_u in our sorted sequence $[\ldots, \delta_l, \delta_u, \ldots]$, then we receive our partition of intervals $\mathcal{I}$. For instance, if $x < 5$ and $x = 0$ are the only variable bounds in $\text{elim}(S, N)$ and ϕ, then $\mathcal{C} = \{5), [5, 0), [0, 0], (0, (-\infty, \infty)\}$ and if we sort it we get $\{(-\infty, 0), [0, 0], (0, 5), [5, \infty)\}$.

Corollary 6. *Let* $\lhd \in \{<, \leq, =, \neq, \geq, >\}$. *For each interval* $I \in \mathcal{I}$, *every two points* $a, b \in I$, *and every variable bound* $x \lhd c \in \text{atoms}(\text{elim}(S, N)) \cup \text{atoms}(\phi)$, $a \lhd c$ *if and only if* $b \lhd c$.

The above Corollary states that two points $a, b \in I$ belonging to the same interval $I \in \mathcal{I}$ satisfy the same theory atoms in $\text{elim}(S, N)$ and ϕ. However, two points $a, b \in I$ do not necessarily satisfy the same non-theory atom under an arbitrary interpretation $\mathcal{A}$; not even if $\mathcal{A}$ satisfies $N \wedge \exists \bar{y}.\neg\phi$. E.g., $\mathcal{A}$ may evaluate $P(a)$ to true and $P(b)$ to false. Sometimes this is even necessary or we would be unable to find a counter example:

Example 7. Let $\phi = (0 \leq x, x \leq 1, 0 \leq y, y \leq 1 || \neg P(x) \vee P(y))$ be our conjecture and $N = \emptyset$ be our clause set. Informally, the property $\forall x, y.\phi$ states that P must be uniform over the interval $[0, 1]$, i.e. either all points in the interval $[0, 1]$ satisfy P or none do. As a result, all interpretations that are uniform over $[0, 1] \in \mathcal{I}$ also satisfy $\forall x, y.\phi$. However, there still exist counter examples that are not uniform, e.g., $P^{\mathcal{A}} = \{0\}$, which satisfies N but not $\forall x, y.\phi$ because it evaluates $P(0)$ to true and $P(a)$ to false for all $a \in [0, 1] \backslash \{0\}$.

To better understand the above example, let us look again at the counter example formulation $N \wedge \exists \bar{y}.\neg\phi$. This formula is satisfiable, i.e. we have a counter example to our conjecture $\forall \bar{y}.\phi$ if there exists an interpretation $\mathcal{A}$ and a grounding ρ for ϕ (also called an assignment for ϕ) such that $\mathcal{A}$ satisfies N and $\neg\phi\rho$. In the worst case, the assignment ρ maps to $m = |\text{vars}(\phi)|$ different points in one of the intervals $I \in \mathcal{I}$. Each of those m points may "act" differently in the interpretation $\mathcal{A}$ although it belongs to the same interval. On the one hand, this means that we need in the worst case $m = |\text{vars}(\phi)|$ different test points for each interval in $\mathcal{I}$. On the other hand, we will show in the proof of Lemma 9 that we can always find a counter example, where (i) no more than m points per interval act differently and (ii) the actual value of a point does not matter as long as it belongs to the same interval $I \in \mathcal{I}$. This is owed mainly to Corollary 6, i.e. that the points in an interval act at least the same in the theory atoms. We ensure that a test point a belongs to a certain interval I by adding a set of variable bounds to our formula. We define these bounds with the functions ilbd and iubd that turn intervals into lower and upper bounds: $\text{ilbd}((-\infty, u), x) = \emptyset$, $\text{ilbd}((-\infty, u], x) = \emptyset$, $\text{ilbd}((l, u), x) = \{l < x\}$, $\text{ilbd}((l, u], x) = \{l < x\}$, $\text{ilbd}([l, u), x) = \{l \leq x\}$, $\text{ilbd}([l, u], x) = \{l \leq x\}$ for $l \neq -\infty$; $\text{iubd}((l, \infty), x) = \emptyset$, $\text{iubd}([l, \infty), x) = \emptyset$, $\text{iubd}((l, u), x) = \{x < u\}$, $\text{iubd}((l, u], x) = \{x \leq u\}$, $\text{iubd}([l, u), x) = \{x < u\}$, $\text{iubd}([l, u], x) = \{x \leq u\}$ for $u \neq \infty$.

Note that this test point scheme would no longer be possible if we were to allow general inequalities. Even allowing difference constraints, i.e., inequalities of the form $x - y \leq c$, would turn the search for a counter example into an undecidable problem [13, 21], because variables can now interact both on the first-order and the theory side.

As a result of these observations, we construct the hammered formula ψ, also called the *finite abstraction* of $N \wedge \exists \bar{y}.\neg\phi$, as follows. First we fix the following notations for the remaining subsection: $\mathcal{I}$ is the interval partition for N and ϕ; $\mathcal{I}_{=} = \{I \in \mathcal{I} \mid I = [l, l]\}$ is the set of all intervals from $\mathcal{I}$ that are just points; $\mathcal{I}_{\infty} = \mathcal{I} \setminus \mathcal{I}_{=}$ is the set of all intervals that are not just points and therefore contain infinitely many values; $m = \max(1, |\text{vars}(\phi)|)$ is the number of test points needed per interval with infinitely many values; $B = \{a_{I,1} \mid I \in \mathcal{I}_{=}\} \cup \{a_{I,j} \mid I \in \mathcal{I}_{\infty} \text{ and } j = 1, \ldots, m\}$ is the set of test points for our abstraction such that we have one test point per interval $I \in \mathcal{I}_{=}$ and m different test points for each interval $I \in \mathcal{I}_{\infty}$; $\text{idef}(B) = \bigcup_{a_{I,i} \in B} \text{ilbd}(I, a_{I,i}) \cup \bigcup_{a_{I,i} \in B} \text{iubd}(I, a_{I,i})$ is a set of bounds that defines to which interval each constant belongs; and $\psi = \text{gnd}_B(N) \cup \text{idef}(B) \wedge (\bigvee_{\rho:\text{vars}(\phi) \to B} \neg\phi\rho)$ is the finite abstraction of $N \wedge \exists \bar{y}.\neg\phi$.

The hammered formula ψ contains $\text{gnd}_B(N)$, i.e. a ground clause $(\Lambda \parallel C)\sigma$ for every clause $(\Lambda \parallel C) \in N$ and every assignment $\sigma : \text{vars}(\Lambda \parallel C) \to B$. This means any deduction over the tests points B we could have performed with the set of clauses N can also be performed with the set of clauses $\text{gnd}_B(N)$ in ψ. Similarly, $\bigvee_{\rho:\text{vars}(\phi) \to B} \neg\phi\rho$ is a big disjunction over all assignments of ρ for ϕ that assign its variables to test points. Hence, ψ is satisfiable if there exists a counter example for $N \wedge \exists \bar{y}.\neg\phi$ that just uses the test points B. Although the finite abstraction is restricted to the test points B, it is easy to extend any of its interpretations to all of $\mathbb{R}$ and our original formula. We just have to interpret all values in an interval that are not test points like one of the test points:

Lemma 8. *Let $\mathcal{A}'$ be an interpretation satisfying the finite abstraction ψ of $N \wedge \exists \bar{y}.\neg\phi$. Moreover, let $\rho : \mathrm{vars}(\phi) \to B$ be a substitution such that $\mathcal{A}'$ satisfies $\neg\phi\rho$. Then the interpretation $\mathcal{A}$ satisfies $N \wedge \exists \bar{y}.\neg\phi$ if it is constructed as follows: $P^{\mathcal{A}} = \{\bar{a} \in \mathbb{R}^n \mid P(\bar{a}) \in N\}$ if $P \in S$ and $P^{\mathcal{A}} = \{\bar{a} \in \mathbb{R}^n \mid \bar{a}\sigma \in P^{\mathcal{A}'}\}$ if $P \notin S$ and $\sigma = \{a \mapsto a_{I,1}^{\mathcal{A}'} \mid I \in \mathcal{I}$ and $a \in I \backslash \{a_{I,2}^{\mathcal{A}'}, \ldots, a_{I,m}^{\mathcal{A}'}\}\}$.*

Similarly, we can extend any interpretation $\mathcal{A}$ satisfying $N \wedge \exists \bar{y}.\neg\phi$ into an interpretation satisfying ψ. We just have to pick one assignment $\rho' : \mathrm{vars}(\phi) \to \mathbb{R}$ such that $\mathcal{A}$ satisfies $\neg\phi\rho'$ and pick one test point B for each point in $\mathrm{codom}(\rho')$ and interpret it as its corresponding point in $\mathrm{codom}(\rho')$.

Lemma 9. *Let $\mathcal{A}$ be an interpretation satisfying the formula $N \wedge \exists \bar{y}.\neg\phi$. Then we can construct an interpretation $\mathcal{A}'$ that satisfies its finite abstraction ψ.*

If we combine both results, we get that $N \wedge \exists \bar{y}.\neg\phi$ is equisatisfiable to ψ:

Lemma 10. *$N \wedge \exists \bar{y}.\neg\phi$ has a satisfying interpretation if and only if its finite abstraction ψ has a satisfying interpretation.*

The finite abstraction for the case with a universal conjecture can also be used to construct a finite abstraction for the case without a conjecture and the case with an existential conjecture. Let N be a BS(SLR) PP clause set and let S be the set of all positively grounded predicates in N. N is satisfiable if and only if $N \not\models \bot$. Hence, we get a finite abstraction for N if we build one for $N \models \bot$, which can be treated as a universal conjecture because all variables in $\bot$ are universally quantified. The existential case works similarly: $N \models \exists \bar{y}.\phi$ if and only if $N \cup N' \models \bot$, where N' is the universal BS(SLR) clause set we get from applying a CNF transformation [31] to $\forall \bar{y}.\neg\phi$.

A Datalog Hammer for HBS(SLR) PP: The set $\mathrm{gnd}_B(N)$ grows exponentially with regard to the maximum number of variables n_C in any clause $(\Lambda \parallel C) \in N$, i.e. $O(|\mathrm{gnd}_B(N)|) = O(|N| \cdot |B|^{n_C})$. Since B is large for realistic examples (e.g., in our examples the size of B ranges from 15 to 1609 constants), the finite abstraction is often too large to be solvable in reasonable time. As an alternative approach, we propose a Datalog hammer for the Horn fragment of BS(SLR) PP clause sets, called HBS(SLR)PP. This hammer exploits the ideas behind the finite abstraction and will allow us to make the same ground deductions, but instead of grounding everything, we only need to (i) ground the negated conjecture over our test points and (ii) provide a set of ground facts that define which theory atoms are satisfied by our test points. As a result, the hammered formula is much more concise and we need no actual theory reasoning to solve the formula. In fact, we can solve the hammered formula by greedily resolving with all facts (from our set of clauses and returned as a result of this process) until this produces the empty clause—which would mean the conjecture is implied—or no more new facts—which would mean we have found a counter example. (In practice, greedily applying resolution is not the best strategy and we recommend to use more advanced techniques for instance those used by a state-of-the-art Datalog reasoner.)

The Datalog hammer takes as input (i) a HBS(SLR)PP clause set N (where S is the set of all positively grounded predicates in N) and (ii) optionally a universal conjecture $\forall \bar{y}.P(\bar{y})$ where $P \notin S$. Restricting the conjecture to a single positive literal may seem like a drastic restriction, but we will later show that we can transform any universal conjecture into this form if it contains only positive atoms. Given this input, the Datalog hammer first computes the same interval partition $\mathcal{I}$ and test point/constant set B needed for the finite abstraction. Then it computes an assignment β for the constants in B that corresponds to the interval partition, i.e. $a_{I,i}\beta \in I$ and $a_{I,i}\beta \neq a_{I,j}\beta$ if $i \neq j$. Next, it computes three clause sets that will make up the Datalog formula. The first set $\mathrm{tren}_N(N)$ is computed out of N by replacing each theory atom A in N with a literal $P_A(\bar{x})$, where $\mathrm{vars}(A) = \mathrm{vars}(\bar{x})$ and P_A is a fresh predicate. This is necessary to eliminate all non-constant function symbols (e.g., $+, -$) in positively grounded theory atoms because Datalog does not support non-constant function symbols. (It is possible to reduce the number of fresh predicates needed, e.g., by reusing the same predicate for two theory atoms that are equivalent up to variable renaming.) The second set is empty if we have no universal conjecture or it contains the ground and negated version ϕ of our universal conjecture $\forall \bar{y}.P(\bar{y})$. Since we restricted the conjecture to a single positive literal, ϕ has the form $C_\phi \rightarrow \bot$, where C_ϕ contains all literals $P(\bar{y})\rho$ for all groundings $\rho : \mathrm{vars}(\bar{y}) \rightarrow B$. We cannot skip this grounding but the worst-case size of C_ϕ is $O(\mathrm{gnd}_B(N)) = O(|B|^{n_\phi})$, where $n_\phi = |\bar{y}|$, which is in our applications typically much smaller than the maximum number of variables n_C contained in any clause in N. The last set is denoted by $\mathrm{tfacts}(N, B)$ and contains a fact $\mathrm{tren}_N(A)$ for every ground theory atom A contained in the theory part Λ of a clause $(\Lambda \parallel C) \in \mathrm{gnd}_B(N)$ such that $A\beta$ simplifies to true. (Alternatively, it is also possible to use a set of axioms and a smaller set of facts and let the Datalog reasoner compute all relevant theory facts for itself.) The set $\mathrm{tfacts}(N, B)$ can be computed without computing $\mathrm{gnd}_B(N)$ if we simply iterate over all theory atoms A in all constraints Λ of all clauses $(\Lambda \parallel C) \in N$ and compute all groundings $\tau : \mathrm{vars}(A) \rightarrow B$ such that $A\tau\beta$ simplifies to true. This can be done in time $O(\mu(n_v) \cdot n_L \cdot |B|^{n_v})$ and the resulting set $\mathrm{tfacts}(N, B)$ has worst-case size $O(n_A \cdot |B|^{n_v})$, where n_L is the number of literals in N, n_v is the maximum number of variables $|\mathrm{vars}(A)|$ in any theory atom A in N, n_A is the number of different theory atoms in N, and $\mu(x)$ is the time needed to simplify a theory atom over x variables to a variable bound. Please note that already satisfiability testing for BS clause is NEXPTIME-complete in general, and DEXPTIME-complete for the Horn case [24, 32]. So when abstracting to a polynomially decidable clause set (ground HBS) an exponential factor is unavoidable.

Lemma 11. $N \wedge \exists \bar{y}.\neg P(\bar{y})$ *is equisatisfiable to its hammered version* $N_D = \mathrm{tren}_N(N) \cup \mathrm{tfacts}(N, B) \cup \{\phi\}$. N *is equisatisfiable to its hammered version* $\mathrm{tren}_N(N) \cup \mathrm{tfacts}(N, B)$.

Note that $\mathrm{tren}_N(N) \cup \mathrm{tfacts}(N, B) \cup \{\phi\}$ is actually a HBS clause set over a finite set of constants B and not yet a Datalog input file. It is well known that such a formula can be transformed easily into a Datalog problem by adding a nullary predicate Goal and adding it as a positive literal to any clause without a positive literal. Querying for the Goal atom returns true if the HBS clause set was unsatisfiable and false otherwise.

Positive Conjectures: One of the seemingly biggest restrictions of our Datalog hammer is that it only accepts universal conjectures over a single positive literal $\forall \bar{y}.P(\bar{y})$. We made this restriction because it is the easiest way to guarantee that our negated and finitely abstracted goal takes the form of a Horn clause. However, there is a way to express any positive universal conjecture—i.e. any universal conjecture where all atoms have positive polarity—as a universal conjecture over a single positive literal. (Note that any negative theory literal can be turned into a positive theory literal by changing the predicate symbol, e.g., $\neg(x \leq 5) \equiv (x > 5)$). Similarly as in a typical first-order CNF transformation [31], we can simply rename all subformulas, i.e. recursively replace all subformulas with some fresh predicate symbols and add suitable Horn clause definitions for these new predicates to our clause set N. A detailed algorithm for this flattening process and a proof of equisatisfiability can be found in the extended version of this paper. Using the same technique, we can also express any positive existential conjecture—i.e. any existential conjecture where all atoms have positive polarity—as additional clauses in our set of input clauses N.

4   Two Supervisor Case Studies

We consider two supervisor case studies: a lane change assistant and the ECU of a supercharged combustion engine; both using the architecture in Fig. 1.

Lane Assistant: This use case focuses on the lane changing maneuver in autonomous driving scenario *i.e.*, the safe *lane* selection and the *speed*. We run two variants of software processing units (updated and certified) in parallel with a supervisor. The variants are connected to different sensors that capture the state of the freeway such as video or LIDAR signal sensors. The variants process the sensors' data and suggest the safe lanes to change to in addition to the evidence that justify the given selection. The supervisor is responsible for the selection of which variant output to forward to other system components *i.e.*, the execution units (actuators) that perform the maneuver. Variants categorize the set of available actions for each time frame into *safe/unsafe* actions and provide *explications*. The supervisor collects the variants output and processes them to reason about (a) if enough evidence is provided by the variants to consider actions safe (b) find the actions that are considered safe by all variants.

Variants formulate their explications as *facts* using first-order predicates. The supervisor uses a set of logical *rules* formulated in BS(SLR) PP to reason about the suggestions and the explications (see List 1.1). In general, the rules do not belong to the BS(SLR) PP fragment, e.g., the atom $= (xh1, -(xes, 1))$ includes even an arithmetic calculation. However, after grounding with the facts of the formalization, only simple bounds remain.

```
1  ## Exclude actions per variant if safety disproved or declared unsafe.
2  SuggestionDisproven(xv, xa), VariantName(xv) -> ExcludedAction(xv, xa).
3  VariantName(xv), LaneNotSafe(xv, xl, xa)       -> ExcludedAction(xv, xa).
4  ## Exclude actions for all variants if declared unsafe by the certified
5  CertifiedVariant(xv1), UpdatedVariant(xv2), LaneNotSafe(xv1, xl, xa)
6    -> ExcludedAction(xv2,xa).
7
8  ## A safe action is disproven
9  SafeBehindDisproven(xv, xenl, xecl, xecs, xes, xa), LaneSafe(xv, xl, xa),
10   SuggestedAction(xv, xa)  -> SuggestionDisproven(xv, xa).
11 SafeFrontDisproven(xv, xenl, xecl, xecs, xes, xa),  LaneSafe(xv, xl, xa),
12   SuggestedAction(xv, xa)  -> SuggestionDisproven(xv, xa).
13
14 ## Unsafe left lane: speed decelerated and unsafe distance front
15 >(xh1, xfd), !=(xecl, xenl),  =(xh1,-(xes,1)) ||
16   LaneSafe(xv, xenl, adecelerateleft), EgoCar(xv, xecl, xecs, xes),
17   DistanceFront(xv, xenl, xofp, xfd, adecelerateleft),
18   SpeedFront(xv, xenl, xofp, xofs, adecelerateleft)
19   -> SafeFrontDisproven(xv, xenl, xecl, xecs, xes, adecelerateleft).
```

List. 1.1. The rules snippets for the lane changing use case in BS(SLR) PP.

Variants Explications: The `SuggestedAction` predicate encodes the actions suggested by the variants. `LaneSafe` and `LaneNotSafe` specify the lanes that are safe/unsafe to be used with the different actions. `DistanceFront` and `DistanceBehind` provide the explications related to the obstacle position, while their speeds are `SpeedFront` and `SpeedBehind`. `EgoCar` predicate reports the speed and the position of the ego vehicle.

Supervisor reasoning: To select a safe action, the supervisor must exclude all unsafe actions. The supervisor considers actions to be excluded per variant (`ExcludedAction`) if (a) `SuggestionDisproven`; the variant fails to prove that the suggested action is safe (line 2), or (b) the action is declared unsafe (line 3). The supervisor declares an action to be excluded cross all variants if the certified variant declares it unsafe (lines 5–6). To consider an action as `SuggestionDisproven`, the supervisor must check for each `LaneSafe` the existence of unsafe distances between the ego vehicle in the given lane and the other vehicles approaching either from behind (`SafeBehindDisproven`) or in front (`SafeFrontDisproven`). The rule `SafeFrontDisproven` (lines 15–19) checks in the left lane, if using the ego vehicle decelerated speed (`=(xh1,-(xes,1))`) the distance between the vehicles is not enough (`>(xh1, xfd)`). The supervisor checks `ExcludeAction` for all variants. If all actions are excluded, the supervisor uses an emergency action as no safe action exists. Otherwise, selects a safe action from the not-excluded actions suggested by the updated variant, if not found, by the certified.

ECU: The GM LSJ Ecotec engine (https://en.wikipedia.org/wiki/GM_Ecotec_engine) is a supercharged combustion engine that was almost exclusively deployed in the US, still some of those run also in Europe. The main sensor inputs of the LSJ ECU consist of an inlet air pressure and temperature sensor (in KPa and in degree Celsius), a speed sensor (in Rpm), a throttle pedal sensor, a throttle sensor, a coolant temperature sensor, oxygen sensors, a knock sensor, and its main actuators controlling the engine are ignition and injection timing, and throttle position. For the experiments conducted in this paper we have taken the routines of the LSJ ECU that compute ignition and injection timings out of inlet air pressure, inlet air temperature, and engine speed. For this part of the ECU this is a two stage process where firstly, basic ignition and injection timings are computed out of engine speed and inlet air pressure and secondly, those are adjusted with respect to inlet air temperature. The properties we prove are safety properties, e.g., certain injection timings are never generated and also invariants, e.g., the ECU computes actuator values for all possible input sensor data and they are unique. Clause 2, page 5, is an actual clause from the ECU case study computing the base ignition timing.

5   Implementation and Experiments

We have implemented the Datalog hammer into our BS(LRA) system SPASS-SPL and combined it with the Datalog reasoner Rulewerk. The resulting toolchain is the first implementation of a decision procedure for HBS(SLR) with positive conjectures.

SPASS-SPL is a new system for BS(LRA) based on some core libraries of the first-order theorem prover SPASS [41] and including the CDCL(LA) solver SPASS-SATT [10] for mixed linear arithmetic. Eventually, SPASS-SPL will include a family of reasoning techniques for BS(LRA) including SCL(T) [9], hierarchic superposition [2,5] and hammers to various logics. Currently, it comprises the Datalog hammer described in this paper and hierarchic UR-resolution [26] (Unit Resulting resolution) which is complete for pure HBS(LRA). The Datalog hammer can produce the clause format used in the Datalog system *Rulewerk* (described below), but also the SPASS first-order logic clause format that can then be translated into the first-order TPTP library [38] clause format. Moreover, it can be used as a translator from our own input language into the SMT-LIB 2.6 language [4] and the CHC competition format [36].

Note that our implementation of the Datalog hammer is of prototypical nature. It cannot handle positively grounded theory atoms beyond simple bounds, unless they are variable comparisons (i.e., $x \triangleleft y$ with $\triangleleft \in \{\leq, <, \neq, =, >, \geq\}$). Moreover, positive universal conjectures have to be flattened until they have the form $\Lambda \parallel P(\bar{x})$. On the other hand, we already added some improvements, e.g., we break/eliminate symmetries in the hammered conjecture and we exploit the theory atoms Λ in a universal conjecture $\Lambda \parallel P(\bar{x})$ so the hammered conjecture contains only groundings for $P(\bar{x})$ that satisfy Λ.

Rulewerk (formerly *VLog4j*) is a rule reasoning toolkit that consists of a Java API and an interactive shell [11]. Its current main reasoning back-end is the rule engine *VLog* [39], which supports Datalog and its extensions with stratified

Problem	Q	Status	X	Y	B	Size	t-time	h-time	p-time	r-time	vampire	spacer	z3	cvc4
lc_e1	∃	true	9	3	19	12/30	0.2	0.0	0.1	0.1	0.0	0.0	0.0	0.0
lc_e2	∃	false	9	3	17	13/27	0.2	0.0	0.1	0.1	0.0	0.1	timeout	timeout
lc_e3	∃	false	9	3	15	12/22	0.2	0.0	0.1	0.1	0.0	0.0	timeout	timeout
lc_e4	∃	true	9	3	21	12/35	0.2	0.0	0.1	0.1	0.0	0.0	0.0	0.1
lc_u1	∀	false	9	2	29	12/25	0.2	0.0	0.1	0.1	0.0	N/A	timeout	timeout
lc_u2	∀	false	9	2	26	12/25	0.2	0.0	0.1	0.1	0.0	N/A	timeout	timeout
lc_u3	∀	true	9	2	23	12/22	0.2	0.0	0.1	0.1	0.0	N/A	0.0	0.1
lc_u4	∀	false	9	2	32	12/33	0.2	0.0	0.1	0.1	0.0	N/A	timeout	timeout
ecu_e1	∃	false	10	6	311	27/649	1.1	0.1	0.3	0.7	0.5	0.1	timeout	timeout
ecu_e2	∃	true	10	6	311	27/649	1.1	0.1	0.3	0.7	0.5	0.1	2.4	0.4
ecu_u1	∀	true	11	1	310	27/651	1.1	0.1	0.3	0.7	94.6	N/A	145.2	0.3
ecu_u2	∀	false	11	1	310	27/651	1.1	0.1	0.3	0.7	80.7	N/A	timeout	timeout
ecu_u3	∀	true	9	2	433	27/1291	1.0	0.1	0.5	0.4	12.0	N/A	209.7	0.1
ecu_u4	∀	true	9	2	1609	26/20459	12.4	2.9	3.2	6.3	526.5	N/A	167.7	0.1
ecu_u5	∀	true	10	3	629	28/17789	22.6	0.7	2.1	19.8	timeout	N/A	timeout	timeout
ecu_u6	∀	false	10	3	618	27/15667	11.6	0.7	1.7	9.1	timeout	N/A	timeout	timeout

Fig. 2. Benchmark results and statistics

negation and existential quantifiers, respectively. VLog is an in-memory reasoner that is optimized for efficient use of resources, and has been shown to deliver highly competitive performance in benchmarks [40].

We have not specifically optimized VLog or Rulewerk for this work, but we have tried to select Datalog encodings that exploit the capabilities of these tools. The most notable impact was observed for the encoding of universal conjectures. A direct encoding of (grounded) universal claims in Datalog leads to rules with many (hundreds of thousands in our experiments) ground atoms as their precondition. Datalog reasoners (not just VLog) are not optimized for such large rules, but for large numbers of facts. An alternative encoding in plain Datalog would therefore specify the expected atoms as facts and use some mechanism to iterate over all of them to check for goal. To accomplish this iteration, the facts that require checking can be endowed with an additional identifier (given as a parameter), and an auxiliary binary successor relation can be used to specify the iteration order over the facts. This approach requires only few rules, but the number of rule applications is proportional to the number of expected facts.

In Rulewerk/VLog, we can encode this in a simpler way using negation. Universal conjectures require us to evaluate ground queries of the form $entailed(\bar{c}_1) \wedge \ldots \wedge entailed(\bar{c}_\ell)$, where each $entailed(\bar{c}_i)$ represents one grounding of our conjecture over our set of test points. If we add facts $expected(\bar{c}_i)$ for the constant vectors $\bar{c}_1, \ldots, \bar{c}_\ell$, we can equivalently use a smaller (first-order) query $\forall \bar{x}.(expected(\bar{x}) \rightarrow entailed(\bar{x}))$, which in turn can be written as $\neg(\exists \bar{x}.(expected(\bar{x}) \wedge \neg entailed(\bar{x})))$. This can be expressed in Datalog with negation and the rules $expected(\bar{x}) \wedge \neg entailed(\bar{x}) \rightarrow missing$ and $\neg missing \rightarrow Goal$, where $Goal$ encodes that the query matches. This use of negation is *stratified*, i.e., not entwined with recursion [1]. Note that stratified negation is a form of non-monotonic negation, so we can no longer read such rules as first-order formulae over which we compute entailments. Nevertheless, implementation is simple and stratified negation is a widely supported feature in Datalog engines, including Rulewerk. The encoding is particularly efficient since the rules using negation are evaluated only once.

Benchmark Experiments: To test the efficiency of our toolchain, we ran benchmark experiments on the two real world HBS(SLR) PP supervisor verification conditions. The two supervisor use cases are described in Sect. 4. The names of the problems are formatted so the lane change assistant examples start with lc and the ECU examples start with ecu. The lc problems with existential conjectures test whether an action suggested by an updated variant is contradicted by a certified variant. The lc problems with universal conjectures test whether an emergency action has to be taken because we have to exclude all actions for all variants. The ecu problems with existential conjectures test safety properties, e.g., whether a computed actuator value is never outside of the allowed safety bounds. The ecu problems with universal conjectures test whether the ecu computes an actuator value for all possible input sensor data. Our benchmarks are prototypical for the complexity of HBS(SLR) reasoning in that they cover all abstract relationships between conjectures and HBS(SLR) clause sets. With respect to our two case studies we have many more examples showing respective characteristics. We would have liked to run benchmarks from other sources too, but we could not find any suitable HBS(SLR) problems in the SMT-LIB or CHC-COMP benchmarks.

For comparison, we also tested several state-of-the-art theorem provers for related logics (with the best settings we found): the satisfiability modulo theories (SMT) solver *cvc4-1.8* [3] with settings `--multi-trigger-cache --full-saturate-quant`; the SMT solver *z3-4.8.10* [27] with its default settings; the constrained horn clause (CHC) solver *spacer* [22] with its default settings; and the first-order theorem prover *vampire-4.5.1* [35] with settings `--memory_limit 8000 -p off`, i.e., with memory extended to 8 GB and without proof output.

For the experiments, we used a Debian Linux server with 32 Intel Xeon Gold 6144 (3.5 GHz) processors and 754 GB RAM. Our toolchain employs no parallel computing, except for the java garbage collection. The other tested theorem provers employ no parallel computing at all. Each tool got a time limit of 40 min for each problem.

The table in Fig. 2 lists for each benchmark problem: the name of the problem (Problem); the type of conjecture (Q), i.e., whether the conjecture is existential $\exists$ or universal $\forall$; the status of the conjecture (Status), i.e., true if the conjecture is a consequence and false otherwise; the maximum number of variables in any clause (X); the number of variables in the conjecture (Y); the number of test points/constants introduced by the Hammer (B); the size of the formula in kilobyte before and after the hammering (Size); the total time (in s) needed by our toolchain to solve the problem (t-time); the time (in s) spent on hammering the input formula (h-time); the time (in s) spent on parsing the hammered formula by Rulewerk (p-time); the time (in s) Rulewerk actually spent on reasoning (r-time). The remaining four columns list the time in s needed by the other tools to solve the benchmark problems. An entry "N/A" means that the benchmark example cannot be expressed in the tools input format, e.g., it is not possible to encode a universal conjecture (or, to be more precise, its negation) in the CHC format. An entry "timeout" means that the tool could not solve the problem in the given time limit of 40 min. Rulewerk is connected to SPASS-SPL via a file interface. Therefore, we show parsing time separately.

The experiments show that only our toolchain solves all the problems in reasonable time. It is also the only solver that can decide in reasonable time whether a universal conjecture is not a consequence. This is not surprising because to our knowledge our toolchain is the only theorem prover that implements a decision procedure for HBS(SLR). On the other types of problems, our toolchain solves all of the problems in the range of seconds and with comparable times to the best tool for the problem. For problems with existential conjectures, the CHC solver spacer is the best, but as a trade-off it is unable to handle universal conjectures. The instantiation techniques employed by cvc4 are good for proving some universal conjectures, but both SMT solvers seem to be unable to disprove conjectures. Vampire performed best on the hammered problems among all first-order theorem provers we tested, including iProver [23], E [37], and SPASS [41]. We tested all provers in default theorem proving mode, but adjusted the memory limit of Vampire, because it ran out of memory on ecu_u4 with the default setting. The experiments with the first-order provers showed that our hammer also works reasonably well for them, e.g., they can all solve all lane change problems in less than a second, but they are simply not specialized for the HBS fragment.

6   Conclusion

We have presented several new techniques that allow us to translate BS(SLR) PP clause sets with both universally and existentially quantified conjectures into logics for which efficient decision procedures exist. The first set of translations returns a finite abstraction for our clause set and conjecture, i.e., an equisatisfiable ground BS(LRA) clause set over a finite set of test points/constants that can be solved in theory by any SMT solver for linear arithmetic. The abstraction grows exponentially in the maximum number of variables in any input clause. Realistic supervisor examples have clauses with 10 or more variables and the basis of the growth exponent is also typically large, e.g., in our examples it ranges from 15 to 1500, so this leads immediately to very large clause sets. An exponential growth in grounding is also unavoidable, because the abstraction reduces a NEXPTIME-hard problem to an NP-complete problem (ground BS, i.e., SAT). As an alternative, we also present a Datalog hammer, i.e., a translation to an equisatisfiable HBS clause set without any theory constraints. The hammer is restricted to the Horn case, i.e., HBS(SLR) PP clauses, and the conjectures to positive universal/existential conjectures. Its advantage is that the formula grows only exponentially in the number of variables in the universal conjecture. This is typically much smaller than the maximum number of variables in any input clause, e.g., in our examples it never exceeds three.

We have implemented the Datalog hammer into our BS(LRA) system SPASS-SPL and combined it with the Datalog reasoner Rulewerk. The resulting toolchain is an effective way of deciding verification conditions for supervisors if the supervisors can be modeled as HBS(SLR) clause sets and the conditions as positive BS(SLR) conjectures. To confirm this, we have presented two use cases for real-world supervisors: (i) the verification of supervisor code for the electrical control unit of a super-charged combustion engine and (ii) the continuous certification of lane assistants. Our experiments show that for these use cases our toolchain is overall superior to existing solvers. Over existential conjectures, it is comparable with existing solvers (e.g., CHC solvers). Moreover, our toolchain is the only solver we are aware of that can proof and disproof universal conjectures for our use cases.

For future work, we want to further develop our toolchain in several directions. First, we want SPASS-SPL to produce explications that prove that its translations are correct. Second, we plan to exploit specialized Datalog expressions and techniques (e.g., aggregation and stratified negation) to increase the efficiency of our toolchain and to lift some restrictions from our input formulas. Third, we want to optimize the selection of test points. For instance, we could partition all predicate argument positions into independent sets, i.e., two argument positions are dependent if they are assigned the same variable in the same rule. For each of these partitions, we should be able to create an independent and much smaller set of test points because we only have to consider theory constraints connected to the argument positions in the respective partition. In many cases, this would lead to much smaller sets of test points and therefore also to much smaller hammered and finitely abstracted formulas.

Acknowledgments. This work was funded by DFG grant 389792660 as part of TRR 248 (CPEC), by BMBF in project ScaDS.AI, and by the Center for Advancing Electronics Dresden (cfaed). We thank Pascal Fontaine, Alberto Griggio, Andrew Reynolds, Stephan Schulz and our anonymous reviewers for discussing various aspects of this paper.

References

1. Abiteboul, S., Hull, R., Vianu, V.: Foundations of Databases. Addison Wesley, Reading (1994)
2. Bachmair, L., Ganzinger, H., Waldmann, U.: Refutational theorem proving for hierarchic first-order theories. Appl. Algebra Eng. Commun. Comput. (AAECC) 5(3/4), 193–212 (1994). https://doi.org/10.1007/BF01190829
3. Barrett, C., et al.: CVC4. In: Gopalakrishnan, G., Qadeer, S. (eds.) CAV 2011. LNCS, vol. 6806, pp. 171–177. Springer, Heidelberg (2011). https://doi.org/10.1007/978-3-642-22110-1_14
4. Barrett, C., Fontaine, P., Tinelli, C.: The SMT-LIB standard: version 2.6. Technical report, Department of Computer Science, The University of Iowa (2017). http://www.SMT-LIB.org/
5. Baumgartner, P., Waldmann, U.: Hierarchic superposition revisited. In: Lutz, C., Sattler, U., Tinelli, C., Turhan, A.-Y., Wolter, F. (eds.) Description Logic, Theory Combination, and All That. LNCS, vol. 11560, pp. 15–56. Springer, Cham (2019). https://doi.org/10.1007/978-3-030-22102-7_2
6. Bjørner, N., Gurfinkel, A., McMillan, K., Rybalchenko, A.: Horn clause solvers for program verification. In: Beklemishev, L.D., Blass, A., Dershowitz, N., Finkbeiner, B., Schulte, W. (eds.) Fields of Logic and Computation II. LNCS, vol. 9300, pp. 24–51. Springer, Cham (2015). https://doi.org/10.1007/978-3-319-23534-9_2

7. Böhme, S., Nipkow, T.: Sledgehammer: judgement day. In: Giesl, J., Hähnle, R. (eds.) IJCAR 2010. LNCS (LNAI), vol. 6173, pp. 107–121. Springer, Heidelberg (2010). https://doi.org/10.1007/978-3-642-14203-1_9

8. Bromberger, M., Dragoste, I., Faqeh, R., Fetzer, C., Krötzsch, M., Weidenbach, C.: A datalog hammer for supervisor verification conditions modulo simple linear arithmetic. CoRR abs/2107.03189 (2021). https://arxiv.org/abs/2107.03189

9. Bromberger, M., Fiori, A., Weidenbach, C.: Deciding the Bernays-Schoenfinkel fragment over bounded difference constraints by simple clause learning over theories. In: Henglein, F., Shoham, S., Vizel, Y. (eds.) VMCAI 2021. LNCS, vol. 12597, pp. 511–533. Springer, Cham (2021). https://doi.org/10.1007/978-3-030-67067-2_23

10. Bromberger, M., Fleury, M., Schwarz, S., Weidenbach, C.: SPASS-SATT. In: Fontaine, P. (ed.) CADE 2019. LNCS (LNAI), vol. 11716, pp. 111–122. Springer, Cham (2019). https://doi.org/10.1007/978-3-030-29436-6_7

11. Carral, D., Dragoste, I., González, L., Jacobs, C., Krötzsch, M., Urbani, J.: VLog: a rule engine for knowledge graphs. In: Ghidini, C., et al. (eds.) ISWC 2019. LNCS, vol. 11779, pp. 19–35. Springer, Cham (2019). https://doi.org/10.1007/978-3-030-30796-7_2

12. Cimatti, A., Griggio, A., Redondi, G.: Universal invariant checking of parametric systems with quantifier-free SMT reasoning. In: Proceedings of CADE-28 (2021, to appear)

13. Downey, P.J.: Undecidability of presburger arithmetic with a single monadic predicate letter. Technical report, Center for Research in Computer Technology, Harvard University (1972)

14. Eiter, T., Gottlob, G., Mannila, H.: Disjunctive datalog. ACM Trans. Database Syst. **22**(3), 364–418 (1997)

15. Faqeh, R., et al.: Towards dynamic dependable systems through evidence-based continuous certification. In: Margaria, T., Steffen, B. (eds.) ISoLA 2020. LNCS, vol. 12477, pp. 416–439. Springer, Cham (2020). https://doi.org/10.1007/978-3-030-61470-6_25

16. Fiori, A., Weidenbach, C.: SCL with theory constraints. CoRR abs/2003.04627 (2020). https://arxiv.org/abs/2003.04627

17. Ge, Y., de Moura, L.: Complete instantiation for quantified formulas in satisfiabiliby modulo theories. In: Bouajjani, A., Maler, O. (eds.) CAV 2009. LNCS, vol. 5643, pp. 306–320. Springer, Heidelberg (2009). https://doi.org/10.1007/978-3-642-02658-4_25

18. Grebenshchikov, S., Lopes, N.P., Popeea, C., Rybalchenko, A.: Synthesizing software verifiers from proof rules. In: Vitek, J., Lin, H., Tip, F. (eds.) ACM SIGPLAN Conference on Programming Language Design and Implementation, PLDI 2012, Beijing, China, 11–16 June 2012, pp. 405–416. ACM (2012)

19. Hillenbrand, T., Weidenbach, C.: Superposition for bounded domains. In: Bonacina, M.P., Stickel, M.E. (eds.) Automated Reasoning and Mathematics. LNCS (LNAI), vol. 7788, pp. 68–100. Springer, Heidelberg (2013). https://doi.org/10.1007/978-3-642-36675-8_4

20. Horbach, M., Voigt, M., Weidenbach, C.: On the combination of the Bernays–Schönfinkel–Ramsey fragment with simple linear integer arithmetic. In: de Moura, L. (ed.) CADE 2017. LNCS (LNAI), vol. 10395, pp. 77–94. Springer, Cham (2017). https://doi.org/10.1007/978-3-319-63046-5_6

21. Horbach, M., Voigt, M., Weidenbach, C.: The universal fragment of presburger arithmetic with unary uninterpreted predicates is undecidable. CoRR abs/1703.01212 (2017)

22. Komuravelli, A., Gurfinkel, A., Chaki, S.: SMT-based model checking for recursive programs. In: Biere, A., Bloem, R. (eds.) CAV 2014. LNCS, vol. 8559, pp. 17–34. Springer, Cham (2014). https://doi.org/10.1007/978-3-319-08867-9_2

23. Korovin, K.: iProver – an instantiation-based theorem prover for first-order logic (system description). In: Armando, A., Baumgartner, P., Dowek, G. (eds.) IJCAR 2008. LNCS (LNAI), vol. 5195, pp. 292–298. Springer, Heidelberg (2008). https://doi.org/10.1007/978-3-540-71070-7_24

24. Lewis, H.R.: Complexity results for classes of quantificational formulas. J. Comput. Syst. Sci. **21**(3), 317–353 (1980)

25. Loos, R., Weispfenning, V.: Applying linear quantifier elimination. Comput. J. **36**(5), 450–462 (1993)

26. McCharen, J., Overbeek, R., Wos, L.: Complexity and related enhancements for automated theorem-proving programs. Comput. Math. Appl. **2**, 1–16 (1976)

27. de Moura, L., Bjørner, N.: Z3: an efficient SMT solver. In: Ramakrishnan, C.R., Rehof, J. (eds.) TACAS 2008. LNCS, vol. 4963, pp. 337–340. Springer, Heidelberg (2008). https://doi.org/10.1007/978-3-540-78800-3_24

28. de Moura, L.M., Bjørner, N.: Satisfiability modulo theories: introduction and applications. Commun. ACM **54**(9), 69–77 (2011)

29. Nieuwenhuis, R., Oliveras, A., Tinelli, C.: Solving SAT and SAT modulo theories: from an abstract Davis-Putnam-Logemann-Loveland procedure to DPLL(T). J. ACM **53**, 937–977 (2006)

30. Nipkow, T., Wenzel, M., Paulson, L.C. (eds.): Isabelle/HOL—A Proof Assistant for Higher-Order Logic. LNCS, vol. 2283. Springer, Heidelberg (2002). https://doi.org/10.1007/3-540-45949-9

31. Nonnengart, A., Weidenbach, C.: Computing small clause normal forms. In: Handbook of Automated Reasoning, pp. 335–367. Elsevier and MIT Press (2001)

32. Plaisted, D.A.: Complete problems in the first-order predicate calculus. J. Comput. Syst. Sci. **29**, 8–35 (1984)

33. Ranise, S.: On the verification of security-aware e-services. J. Symb. Comput. **47**(9), 1066–1088 (2012)

34. Reynolds, A., Barbosa, H., Fontaine, P.: Revisiting enumerative instantiation. In: Beyer, D., Huisman, M. (eds.) TACAS 2018. LNCS, vol. 10806, pp. 112–131. Springer, Cham (2018). https://doi.org/10.1007/978-3-319-89963-3_7

35. Riazanov, A., Voronkov, A.: The design and implementation of VAMPIRE. AI Commun. **15**(2–3), 91–110 (2002)

36. Rümmer, P.: Competition report: CHC-COMP-20. In: Fribourg, L., Heizmann, M. (eds.) Proceedings of the 8th International Workshop on Verification and Program Transformation and 7th Workshop on Horn Clauses for Verification and Synthesis, VPT/HCVS@ETAPS 2020, Dublin, Ireland, 25–26 April 2020, vol. 320, pp. 197–219. EPTCS (2020)

37. Schulz, S., Cruanes, S., Vukmirović, P.: Faster, higher, stronger: E 2.3. In: Fontaine, P. (ed.) CADE 2019. LNCS (LNAI), vol. 11716, pp. 495–507. Springer, Cham (2019). https://doi.org/10.1007/978-3-030-29436-6_29

38. Sutcliffe, G.: The TPTP problem library and associated infrastructure - from CNF to TH0, TPTP v6.4.0. J. Autom. Reason. **59**(4), 483–502 (2017)

39. Urbani, J., Jacobs, C., Krötzsch, M.: Column-oriented Datalog materialization for large knowledge graphs. In: Schuurmans, D., Wellman, M.P. (eds.) Proceedings of the 30th AAAI Conference on Artificial Intelligence (AAAI 2016), pp. 258–264. AAAI Press (2016)

40. Urbani, J., Krötzsch, M., Jacobs, C., Dragoste, I., Carral, D.: Efficient model construction for horn logic with VLog. In: Galmiche, D., Schulz, S., Sebastiani, R. (eds.) IJCAR 2018. LNCS (LNAI), vol. 10900, pp. 680–688. Springer, Cham (2018). https://doi.org/10.1007/978-3-319-94205-6_44

41. Weidenbach, C., Dimova, D., Fietzke, A., Kumar, R., Suda, M., Wischnewski, P.: SPASS version 3.5. In: Schmidt, R.A. (ed.) CADE 2009. LNCS (LNAI), vol. 5663, pp. 140–145. Springer, Heidelberg (2009). https://doi.org/10.1007/978-3-642-02959-2_10

Non-disjoint Combined Unification and Closure by Equational Paramodulation

Serdar Erbatur[1], Andrew M. Marshall[2], and Christophe Ringeissen[3]

[1] University of Texas at Dallas, Richardson, USA
[2] University of Mary Washington, Fredericksburg, USA
[3] Université de Lorraine, CNRS, Inria, LORIA, 54000 Nancy, France
`Christophe.Ringeissen@loria.fr`

Abstract. Closure properties such as forward closure and closure via paramodulation have proven to be very useful in equational logic, especially for the formal analysis of security protocols. In this paper, we consider the non-disjoint unification problem in conjunction with these closure properties. Given a base theory E, we consider classes of theory extensions of E admitting a unification algorithm built in a hierarchical way. In this context, a hierarchical unification procedure is obtained by extending an E-unification algorithm with some additional inference rules to take into account the rest of the theory. We look at hierarchical unification procedures by investigating an appropriate notion of E-constructed theory, defined in terms of E-paramodulation. We show that any E-constructed theory with a finite closure by E-paramodulation admits a terminating hierarchical unification procedure. We present modularity results for the unification problem modulo the union of E-constructed theories sharing only symbols in E. Finally, we also give sufficient conditions for obtaining terminating (combined) hierarchical unification procedures in the case of regular and collapse-free E-constructed theories.

1 Introduction

Unification plays a central role in all logic-based tools using the resolution principle, for instance to perform new deductions using superposition and paramodulation inferences implemented in equational provers. Both superposition and paramodulation aim at deducing a new equality from two equalities that can overlap via (syntactic) unification. In this context, a syntactic unification algorithm computing a most general unifier is ubiquitous. More generally, we may consider equational unification, where the problem is defined modulo an equational theory E, such as the famous example of Associativity-Commutativity. Equational unification, called E-unification, is undecidable in general, but unification algorithms are known for particular classes, like for instance: (1) the class SH of shallow theories [8] defined by axioms whose variables can occur at depth at most 1; (2) the class PC of theories with a finite paramodulation closure [21]; (3) the class FVP of theories defined by convergent term rewrite systems with the Finite Variant Property [9,17]. FVP and PC can be related

© Springer Nature Switzerland AG 2021
B. Konev and G. Reger (Eds.): FroCoS 2021, LNAI 12941, pp. 25–42, 2021.
https://doi.org/10.1007/978-3-030-86205-3_2

since *FVP* coincides with the class *FC* of theories with a finite forward closure [6], a particular closure similar to paramodulation closure but dedicated to convergent terms rewrite systems. *SH*, *PC*, and *FVP* are particular classes of syntactic theories (see respectively [8], [21], [11]). When a theory is syntactic [20,25], it is possible to apply a rule-based unification procedure extending the one known for syntactic unification with some additional mutation rules. In general, being syntactic is not a sufficient condition to ensure the termination of this unification procedure. Fortunately, *SH*, *PC*, and *FVP* admit terminating instances of this mutation-based unification procedure (see respectively [8], [21], [11]).

In many practical applications, E is a component in a union of theories, say $F \cup E$. In that case, it is quite natural to solve the $F \cup E$-unification problem in a modular way thanks to the unification algorithms known for F and for E. There are terminating and complete combination procedures when F and E have disjoint signatures [3,27]. These combination procedures can be extended to some non-disjoint unions of theories sharing only constructor symbols, but it is quite difficult to identify particular cases where these procedures terminate [10,26]. A terminating case has been identified in [5] by investigating a notion of *bounded* theory over the constructor symbols. More recently, a hierarchical unification approach [11,12,15] has been initiated when $F \cup E$-unification can be considered as a conservative extension of E-unification while some symbols of E may occur as constructors in F. In that scenario, hierarchical unification consists in using an E-unification algorithm plus some mutation-based unification procedure to manage the remaining part of $F \cup E$. In [15], we have shown that the hierarchical unification approach is particularly well-suited to tackle E-convergent term rewrite systems in which all the symbols in E are constructors. In particular, it is possible to get a terminating hierarchical unification procedure when such constructed-based rewrite system has a finite forward closure [11].

In this paper, we investigate the possible use of hierarchical unification for a class of theories defined via an E-paramodulation closure, where E-paramodulation generalizes the classical paramodulation inference by replacing syntactic unification with E-unification. In that direction, we introduce the notion of E-syntacticness, a useful property to study a possible mutation-based unification procedure modulo the base theory E. To obtain a complete hierarchical unification procedure, it is required that the E-unification algorithm is applicable without loss of completeness to solve any $F \cup E$-unification problem expressed over the signature of E. To fulfill this requirement, we introduce the class of E-constructed theories. These theories are defined using E-paramodulation and generalize the E-convergent term rewrite systems for which all the symbols of E are constructors. The class of E-constructed theories is particularly interesting in the context of non-disjoint combination. Actually, a union of E-constructed theories sharing only E is a union of non-disjoint theories without any overlap between the component theories. We study two classes of E-constructed theories: (i) a class of regular collapse-free E-constructed theories F such that $F \cup E$ admits a hierarchical unification algorithm; (ii) the class of E-constructed theories closed by E-paramodulation. We show the following modularity result: let $\mathcal{C}$ be any class (i) or (ii), if F_1 and F_2 are two theories in $\mathcal{C}$ sharing only the symbols in E, then $F_1 \cup F_2$ is a theory in $\mathcal{C}$. In both cases, there exists a hierarchical unification algorithm for $F_1 \cup F_2 \cup E$. Compared to [15], we consider equational theories that are not necessarily presented by E-convergent term rewrite systems, and we go beyond the subterm collapse-free assumption of [15]. For example, in the class (i) the combined hierarchical unification algorithm applies without loss of completeness to theories that are assumed to be regular and collapse-free but not necessarily subterm collapse-free. The regularity and the collapse-freeness of a theory is trivially checked by examining its axioms, while the subterm collapse-freeness is a property that can be difficult to check.

Motivating Examples from Security Protocols. Let us consider a theory used in practice to model a group messaging protocol [7]. For this protocol, the theory modeling the intruder can be defined [24] as a combination $R_{ENC}^{=} \cup K$ where $K = \{keyexch(x, pk(x'), y, pk(y')) = keyexch(x', pk(x), y', pk(y))\}$, and

$$R_{ENC}^{=} = \left\{ \begin{array}{ll} adec(aenc(m, pk(sk)), sk) = m & getmsg(sign(m, sk)) = m \\ checksign(sign(m, sk), m, pk(sk)) = ok & sdec(senc(m, k), k) = m \end{array} \right\}$$

The equational theories $R_{ENC}^{=}$ and K share the absolutely free constructor pk and they are both closed by paramodulation. Thanks to a modularity result developed in this paper, we can show that $R_{ENC}^{=} \cup K$ is closed by paramodulation too. Thus, $R_{ENC}^{=} \cup K$ admits a (hierarchical) unification algorithm.

Let us now consider a theory for dealing with member keys in a group of users and an overall group key [22]. Member keys can be kept in a tree like structure with the group key being the root. A *pick* function is included to retrieve the group key. In [22], the group is modeled thanks to a constructor with some equational properties, ideally a set union operator. Here, we consider $E_1 = \{pick(x, tree(y, x \cup m)) = y, add(x, tree(y, m)) = tree(y, x \cup m)\}$ where $\cup$ is an AC-constructor used to build multisets. This theory is closed by AC-paramodulation, and so it admits a hierarchical unification algorithm built over an AC-unification algorithm. To model homomorphic encryption or exponentiation, we can use axioms such as $e(x * y, z) = e(x, z) * e(y, z)$ and $e(e(x, y), z) = e(x, y \circledast z)$, where $\circledast$ is an AC-symbol. In [15], it has been shown that two distributive theories including these axioms admit a hierarchical unification algorithm. These regular and collapse-free theories satisfy the assumptions needed to get a terminating combined unification procedure.

Outline. After this introduction and the next section on preliminaries, the paper is organized as follows. Section 3 presents the E-paramodulation closure and then the E-constructed theories. In Sect. 4, we introduce the notion of E-syntacticness. In Sect. 5, a hierarchical unification procedure is given as a rule-based system including some classical purification rules, an E-unification algorithm encapsulated in a solving rule, plus a couple of mutation rules.

The unification problem and the related modularity properties are investigated in Sect. 6 for the class (i) and in Sect. 7 for the class (ii). Omitted proofs can be found in [16].

2 Preliminaries

We use the standard notation of equational unification [4] and term rewriting systems [1]. Given a first-order signature Σ and a (countable) set of variables V, the set of Σ-terms over variables V is defined in the usual way. The set of variables in a term t is denoted by $Var(t)$. A term t is *ground* if $Var(t) = \emptyset$. For any position p in a term t (including the root position ϵ), $t(p)$ is the symbol at position p, $t|_p$ is the subterm of t at position p, and $t[u]_p$ is the term t in which $t|_p$ is replaced by u. A substitution is an endomorphism of the Σ-structure of terms over V such that only finitely many variables are not mapped to themselves, denoted by $\sigma = \{x_1 \mapsto t_1, \dots, x_m \mapsto t_m\}$, where the domain and the range of σ are respectively $Dom(\sigma) = \{x_1, \dots, x_m\}$ and $Ran(\sigma) = \{t_1, \dots, t_m\}$. Application of a substitution σ to t is written $t\sigma$.

Equational Theories. Given a set E of Σ-axioms (i.e., pairs of Σ-terms, denoted by $l = r$), the *equational theory* $=_E$ is the congruence closure of E under the law of substitutivity (by a slight abuse of terminology, E is often called an equational theory). Equivalently, $=_E$ can be defined as the reflexive transitive closure $\leftrightarrow_E^*$ of an equational step $\leftrightarrow_E$ defined as follows: $s \leftrightarrow_E t$ if there exist a position p of s, $l = r$ (or $r = l$) in E, and substitution σ such that $s|_p = l\sigma$ and $t = s[r\sigma]_p$. An axiom $l = r$ is *regular* if $Var(l) = Var(r)$. An axiom $l = r$ is *collapse-free* if l and r are non-variable terms. An equational theory is *regular* (resp., collapse-free) if all its axioms are regular (resp., collapse-free). A term t is *subterm collapse-free modulo E* if it is not the case that $t =_E u$ where u is any strict subterm of t. An equational theory E is *subterm collapse-free* if for any term t, t is subterm collapse-free modulo E.

A theory E is *syntactic* if it has a finite *resolvent presentation* S, defined as a finite set of axioms S such that each equality $t =_E u$ has an equational proof $t \leftrightarrow_S^* u$ with at most one equational step $\leftrightarrow_S$ applied at the root position. One can easily check that $C = \{x * y = y * x\}$ (Commutativity) and $AC = \{x * (y * z) = (x * y) * z, \ x * y = y * x\}$ (Associativity-Commutativity) are regular, collapse-free, and linear (variables occur only once). Moreover, C and AC are syntactic [20]. An axiom $l = r$ is *shallow* if variables can only occur at a position at depth at most 1 in both l and r. An equational theory is *shallow* if all its axioms are shallow. For example, C is shallow, but A is not. It has been shown in [8] that shallow theories are syntactic.

Equational Unification. A Σ-equation is a pair of Σ-terms denoted by $s =^? t$ or simply $s = t$ when it is clear from the context that we do not refer to an axiom. A *flat* Σ-equation is either an equation between variables or a *non-variable flat Σ-equation* of the form $x_0 = f(x_1, \dots, x_n)$ where $x_0, x_1, \dots, x_n$ are variables and

f is a function symbol in Σ. An E-unification problem is a set of Σ-equations, $G = \{s_1 =^? t_1, \ldots, s_n =^? t_n\}$, or equivalently a conjunction of Σ-equations. The set of variables in G is denoted by $Var(G)$. A solution to G, called an E-unifier, is a substitution σ such that $s_i\sigma =_E t_i\sigma$ for all $1 \leq i \leq n$, written $E \models G\sigma$. A substitution σ is more general modulo E than θ on a set of variables V, denoted as $\sigma \leq_E^V \theta$, if there is a substitution τ such that $x\sigma\tau =_E x\theta$ for all $x \in V$. $\sigma|_V$ denotes the substitution σ restricted to the set of variables V. A Complete Set of E-Unifiers of G, denoted by $CSU_E(G)$, is a set of substitutions such that each $\sigma \in CSU_E(G)$ is an E-unifier of G, and for each E-unifier θ of G, there exists $\sigma \in CSU_E(G)$ such that $\sigma \leq_E^{Var(G)} \theta$. An E-unification algorithm is an algorithm that computes a finite $CSU_E(G)$ for all E-unification problems G. An inference rule $G \vdash G'$ for E-unification is sound if each E-unifier of G' is an E-unifier of G; and complete if for each E-unifier σ of G, there exists an E-unifier σ' of G' such that $\sigma' \leq_E^{Var(G)} \sigma$. An inference system for E-unification is sound if all its inference rules are sound; and complete if for each E-unification problem G on which an inference applies and each E-unifier σ of G, there exist an E-unification problem G' inferred from G and an E-unifier σ' of G' such that $\sigma' \leq_E^{Var(G)} \sigma$. Thus, the set of E-unifiers is preserved by a sound and complete inference system for E-unification. The definition of complete inference system adopted here allows us to take into account the rules that need to be applied with a don't know nondeterministic choice in order to preserve the set of E-unifiers. When a don't know nondeterminism is necessary to apply some rules, we mention it explicitly. By default, the inference rules are applied using a don't care nondeterminism: when several rules are applicable, it is sufficient to apply one of them.

A set of equations $G = \{x_1 =^? t_1, \ldots, x_n =^? t_n\}$ is said to be in tree solved form if each x_i is a variable occurring once in G. Given an idempotent substitution $\sigma = \{x_1 \mapsto t_1, \ldots, x_n \mapsto t_n\}$ (such that $\sigma\sigma = \sigma$), $\hat{\sigma}$ denotes the corresponding tree solved form. A set of equations is said to be in dag solved form if they can be arranged as a list $x_1 =^? t_1, \ldots, x_n =^? t_n$ where (a) each left-hand side x_i is a distinct variable, and (b) $\forall 1 \leq i \leq j \leq n$: x_i does not occur in t_j. A set of equations $\{x_1 =^? t_1, \ldots, x_n =^? t_n\}$ is a cycle if for any $i \in [1, n-1], x_{i+1} \in Var(t_i), x_1 \in Var(t_n)$, and there exists $j \in [1, n]$ such that t_j is not a variable. Given two disjoint signatures Σ_0 and Σ_1 and any $i = 1, 0$, Σ_i-terms (including the variables) and Σ_i-equations (including the equations between variables) are called Σ_i-pure. A term t is called a Σ_i-rooted term if its root symbol is in Σ_i. An alien subterm of a Σ_i-rooted term t is a Σ_j-rooted subterm s of t ($i \neq j$) such that all superterms of s are Σ_i-rooted. Given a Σ_0-theory E, a theory $F \cup E$ is a conservative extension of E if $=_{F\cup E}$ and $=_E$ coincide on Σ_0-terms. When $F \cup E$ is a conservative extension of E, E-unification is said to be complete for solving the Σ_0-fragment of $F \cup E$-unification if for any Σ_0-pure $F \cup E$-unification problem G, any $CSU_E(G)$ is a $CSU_{F\cup E}(G)$. If F and E have disjoint signatures, E-unification is known to be complete for solving the Σ_0-fragment of $F \cup E$-unification.

Equational Rewrite Relations. Given a signature Σ, an oriented Σ-axiom is called a rewrite rule of the form $l \to r$ if l is not a variable and $Var(r) \subseteq Var(l)$. Given a set R of rewrite rules and an Σ-equational theory E, A term s R, E-*rewrites* to a term t, denoted by $s \to_{R,E} t$, if there exist a position p of s, $l \to r \in R$, and substitution σ such that $s|_p =_E l\sigma$ and $t = s[r\sigma]_p$. The term s is said to be R, E-*reducible*, and $s|_p$ is called a *redex*. The symmetric relation $\leftarrow_{R,E} \cup \to_{R,E} \cup =_E$ is denoted by $\longleftrightarrow_{R \cup E}$. The rewrite relation $\to_{R,E}$ is Church-Rosser modulo E if $\longleftrightarrow^*_{R \cup E}$ is included in $\to^*_{R,E} \circ =_E \circ \leftarrow^*_{R,E}$. When $=_E \circ \to_{R,E} \circ =_E$ is terminating, the following properties are equivalent [18]: (1) $\to_{R,E}$ is Church-Rosser modulo E; (2) for any terms t, t', $t \longleftrightarrow^*_{R \cup E} t'$ if and only if $t \downarrow =_E t' \downarrow$, where $t \downarrow$ (resp., $t' \downarrow$) denotes any normal form w.r.t $\to_{R,E}$ of t (resp., t'). The rewrite relation $\to_{R,E}$ is E-*convergent* if $=_E \circ \to_{R,E} \circ =_E$ is terminating and $\to_{R,E}$ is Church-Rosser modulo E. A function symbol that does not occur in $\{l(\epsilon) \mid l \to r \in R\}$ is called a *constructor* for R. Let Σ_0 be the subsignature of Σ that consists of all function symbols occurring in the axioms of E. An E-convergent rewrite relation $\to_{R,E}$ is said to be E-*constructed* if all symbols in Σ_0 are constructors for R. When $\to_{R,E}$ is clear from the context, a normal form w.r.t $\to_{R,E}$ is said to be *normalized*. A substitution σ is *normalized* if, for every variable x in the domain of σ, $x\sigma$ is normalized. An instance $l\sigma \to r\sigma$ of a rule $l \to r \in R$ is a *right-reduced* instance if $\sigma_{|Var(r)}$ is normalized. A term t is an *innermost redex* if no subterm of t is a redex. An E-convergent $\to_{R,E}$ is *IR1* if every innermost redex is R, E-reducible to a normal form in one step.

When R is a finite set of rules, the pair (R, E) is called an *equational term rewrite system* (TRS). We say that a property is satisfied by an equational TRS (R, E) if this property is satisfied by $\to_{R,E}$. Given a TRS (R, E), $R^=$ denotes the set of equalities $\{l = r \mid l \to r \in R\}$, and $R^= \cup E$ is the *equational theory of* (R, E). For sake of brevity, we may use $R \cup E$ instead of $R^= \cup E$.

To simplify the notation, we often use tuples of terms, like $\bar{u} = (u_1, \ldots, u_n)$, $\bar{v} = (v_1, \ldots, v_n)$. Applying a substitution σ to $\bar{u}$ is the tuple $\bar{u}\sigma = (u_1\sigma, \ldots, u_n\sigma)$. The tuples $\bar{u}$ and $\bar{v}$ are said to be E-*equal*, denoted by $\bar{u} =_E \bar{v}$, if $u_1 =_E v_1, \ldots, u_n =_E v_n$. Similarly, $\bar{u} \to^*_R \bar{v}$ if $u_1 \to^*_R v_1, \ldots, u_n \to^*_R v_n$, $\bar{u}$ is normalized if $u_1, \ldots, u_n$ are normalized, and $\bar{u} =^? \bar{v}$ is $\{u_1 =^? v_1, \ldots, u_n =^? v_n\}$.

3   Closure by Equational Paramodulation

From now on, let E be a regular and collapse-free Σ_0-theory, and F a Σ-theory such that $\Sigma_0 \subseteq \Sigma$. We assume a reduction ordering $>$ on terms such that $>$ is E-compatible, meaning that $s' =_E s > t =_E t'$ implies $s' > t'$. It is important to note that a single reduction ordering $>$ is used even in the context of a union of theories. In that case, $>$ is assumed to be defined on terms built over the combined signature. Given a set of equalities F, $Gr(F)$ denotes the set of ground instances of F. A set F of ground equalities is $>$-*orientable* if each equality in F can be oriented into a rule $l \to r$ such that $l > r$ and l is $\Sigma \backslash \Sigma_0$-rooted. A set F of equalities is $>$-*orientable* if $Gr(F)$ is $>$-orientable. A ground equality $s = t$ is *optimally joinable* w.r.t a $>$-orientable set F of ground equalities if for $F^> = \{l \to r \mid l > r, l = r$ or $r = l$ in $F\}$ there exists a rewrite proof $s \to^*_{F^>,E} s' =_E t' \leftarrow^*_{F^>,E} t$ for which each rewrite step $u \to_{F^>,E} v$ in $s \to^*_{F^>,E} s'$ and in $t \to^*_{F^>,E} t'$ is applied at a position p such that $u|_p$ is an innermost redex and $v|_p$ is in normal form w.r.t $\to_{F^>,E}$. An equality $s = t$ is *optimally joinable* w.r.t a $>$-orientable set F of equalities if each ground instance of $s = t$ is optimally joinable w.r.t $Gr(F)$. Given a finite set of equalities F, the *E-paramodulation closure* of F is inductively defined as follows as a partial function:

- If F is $>$-orientable, then $PC^0(F) = F$; otherwise $PC^0(F)$ is undefined.
- For any $k \geq 0$, assume $PC^k(F)$ is defined. Let PE be the set of all equalities e obtained by:

> **E-Paramodulation** $g = d[l'], \; l = r \vdash (g = d[r])\sigma$
> where l' is not a variable, $\sigma \in CSU_E(l' =^? l)$, and $l\sigma \not< r\sigma$

using premises in $PC^k(F)$ and such that e is not optimally joinable w.r.t $PC^k(F)$. If PE is $>$-orientable, then $PC^{k+1}(F) = PC^k(F) \cup PE$; otherwise $PC^{k+1}(F)$ is undefined. If $PC^k(F)$ is defined for any $k \geq 0$, then $PC(F) = \bigcup_{k \geq 0} PC^k(F)$; otherwise $PC(F)$ is undefined.

Example 1. Consider the equational theory $E_2 = \{rm(x, x \cup m) = m\}$ where $\cup$ is an AC-symbol. Notice that the left-to-right orientation of E_2 provides an AC-compatible reduction ordering for which we have $PC(E_2) = E_2$ because there is no non-variable overlap between a left-hand side of a rule and a right-hand side.

Definition 1 (E-constructed theory). *Let E be a regular and collapse-free theory. A finite set of equalities F is said to be an E-constructed theory if there exists an E-compatible reduction ordering $>$ such that $PC(F)$ is defined; F is closed by E-paramodulation if $PC(F) = F$.*

Given an E-constructed theory F and $Gr = Gr(PC(F))$, we define the following sets of ground rules for any $s = t$ or $t = s$ in Gr such that $s > t$:

- $I^{s=t} = \begin{cases} \emptyset, & \text{if } s \text{ or } t \text{ is } R^{<s=t}, E\text{-reducible} \\ \{s \to t\}, & \text{otherwise} \end{cases}$
- $R^{<s=t} = \bigcup_{(u=v) < (s=t)} I^{u=v}$, *where the equalities are ordered by treating them as multisets of terms: $(u = v) < (s = t)$ iff $\{s, t\}$ is strictly greater than $\{u, v\}$ w.r.t the multiset extension of $>$,*
- $R_F = \bigcup_{s=t \in Gr} I^{s=t}$.

Theorem 1. *Let R_F be the set of ground rules introduced in Definition 1 for an E-constructed theory F. Then, all the symbols of E are constructors for R_F, the rewrite relation $\to_{R_F,E}$ is E-convergent on ground terms and for any ground terms s, t, $s =_{F \cup E} t$ iff $s \downarrow_{R_F,E} =_E t \downarrow_{R_F,E}$.*

Proof (Sketch). Assume $\to_{R_F,E}$ is not Church-Rosser modulo E on ground terms. In that case, there exists a non-joinable critical pair possibly generated by *E*-**Paramodulation**, provided that it is not optimally joinable. This critical pair cannot be optimally joinable, otherwise it would be joinable. Thus *E*-**Paramodulation** applies, and this contradicts the definition of R_F.   □

Note that we overlap with non-maximal sides in E-**Paramodulation**. This allows us to build a rewrite relation $\rightarrow_{R_F,E}$ which is both E-convergent and $IR1$. The next lemma is a direct consequence of Definition 1.

Lemma 1. *Let (R, E) be any E-constructed TRS and $>$ the reduction ordering defined by $s > t$ if $s \rightarrow_{R,E}^+ t$. Then, $R^=$ is an E-constructed theory. If $\rightarrow_{R,E}$ is IR1, then $R^=$ is an E-constructed theory closed by E-paramodulation.*

Lemma 1 provides us a way to get an E-constructed theory closed by E-paramodulation starting from any forward-closed E-constructed TRS since any E-constructed TRS is forward-closed iff it is $IR1$ [15,19].

Lemma 2. *If F is an E-constructed theory, then E-unification is complete for solving the Σ_0-fragment of $F \cup E$-unification.*

A proof of Lemma 2 is developed in [16].

Example 2. Consider the Group Keys example from Sect. 1. Since E_1 is closed by AC-paramodulation $E_1 = PC(E_1)$. In addition, since $\Sigma_0 = \{\cup\}$, the conditions of Definition 1 are satisfied. Orienting the rule of E_1 from left to right we obtain a ground AC-convergent system $\rightarrow_{E_1,AC}$. Finally, from Lemma 1 we have an AC-constructed theory.

4   Equational Syntacticness

In this section, we introduce an equational extension of the classical notion of syntactic theory.

Definition 2 (E-syntactic theory). *Consider a Σ_0-theory E and a Σ-theory $F \cup E$. Let S be a finite set of $F \cup E$-equalities $l = r$ such that l or r is $\Sigma \backslash \Sigma_0$-rooted. The set S is said to be an E-resolvent presentation of $F \cup E$ if for any $F \cup E$-equality $t =_{F \cup E} t'$ there exists an equational proof $t \leftrightarrow^*_{S \cup E} t'$ with the following property: if there is an S-equational step applied at the root position, then it is the only $S \cup E$-equational step applied at the root position. The equational theory $F \cup E$ is said to be E-syntactic if there exists an E-resolvent presentation of $F \cup E$.*

When E is the empty theory over an empty signature Σ_0, an E-syntactic theory (resp., an E-resolvent presentation) corresponds to the classical definition of a syntactic theory (resp., a resolvent presentation) [20,25].

Lemma 3. *Assume $F \cup E$ is E-syntactic. Consider any terms $\bar{s}, \bar{t}$ and any function symbols f, g such that $f(\bar{s})$ or $g(\bar{t})$ is $\Sigma \backslash \Sigma_0$-rooted. Then, $f(\bar{s}) =_{F \cup E} g(\bar{t})$ iff either $f, g \in \Sigma \backslash \Sigma_0$, $f = g$ and $\bar{s} =_{F \cup E} \bar{t}$, or there exist $f(\bar{l}) = g(\bar{r}) \in S$ and a substitution σ such that $\bar{s} =_{F \cup E} \bar{l}\sigma$ and $\bar{t} =_{F \cup E} \bar{r}\sigma$.*

Proof. This follows from Definition 2. Consider the proof of $f(\bar{s}) =_{S \cup E} g(\bar{t})$ where S is the E-resolvent presentation of $F \cup E$. Since S is an E-resolvent presentation and $f(\bar{s})$ or $g(\bar{t})$ is $\Sigma \backslash \Sigma_0$-rooted, there can only be one or no S-equational steps at the root position and no E-equational steps. If there is no S-equational step at the root position, then $f = g$ and $\bar{s} =_{S \cup E} \bar{t}$ which implies $\bar{s} =_{F \cup E} \bar{t}$. If there is an S-equational step at the root position, then it is the only step applied at the root position. Thus, there exist $f(\bar{l}) = g(\bar{r}) \in S$ and a substitution σ such that $\bar{s} =_{S \cup E} \bar{l}\sigma$ and $\bar{t} =_{S \cup E} \bar{r}\sigma$, which implies the result. $\square$

The following lemma states the connection between syntacticness and the partial form of syntacticness represented by E-syntacticness.

Lemma 4. *Let F be any E-constructed theory. Then, $F \cup E$ is syntactic iff $F \cup E$ is E-syntactic and E is syntactic.*

Proof. For both directions, we proceed by induction on the size of $F \cup E$-equalities, where the size of an equality is defined as the number of function symbols occurring in the equality.

For the only-if direction, consider $S_{F \cup E}$ is a resolvent presentation of a theory $F \cup E$ such that F is E-constructed. Let $S_E = \{l = r \mid l = r \in S_{F \cup E}, \text{ and } l, r \text{ are } \Sigma_0\text{-terms}\}$. By induction on the size of $F \cup E$-equalities between Σ_0-terms, we can prove that, for any $t =_{F \cup E} t'$ where t and t' are Σ_0-terms, there exists an equational proof $t \longleftrightarrow^*_{S_E} t'$ with at most one step applied at the root position. Since $=_E$ and $=_{F \cup E}$ coincide on Σ_0-terms, S_E is resolvent presentation of E. Let $S = \{l = r \mid l = r \in S_{F \cup E}, \{l(\epsilon), r(\epsilon)\} \cap (\Sigma \backslash \Sigma_0) \neq \emptyset\}$. Since F is E-constructed, there exist some particular $F \cup E$-equational proofs (cf. [16]) which permit us to prove the following statement by induction on the size of $F \cup E$-equalities: for any $t =_{F \cup E} t'$ there exists an equational proof $t \longleftrightarrow^*_{S \cup E} t'$ such that any S-equational step applied at the root position is necessarily the unique $S \cup E$-equational step applied at the root position. Therefore, S is an E-resolvent presentation of $F \cup E$.

For the if-direction, consider S_E is a resolvent presentation of E and S is an E-resolvent presentation of a theory $F \cup E$ such that F is E-constructed. Let $S_{F \cup E} = S \cup S_E$. Thanks to the same particular $F \cup E$-equational proofs as the ones used above (cf. [16]), we can prove the following statement by induction on the size of $F \cup E$-equalities: for any $t =_{F \cup E} t'$ there exists an equational proof $t \longleftrightarrow^*_{S_{F \cup E}} t'$ with at most one step applied at the root position. Therefore, $S_{F \cup E}$ is a resolvent presentation of $F \cup E$. $\square$

5   Hierarchical Unification

We present a general result to build a hierarchical unification procedure for E-syntactic theories. The rules in Fig. 1 provide the skeleton of the type of hierarchical procedure we are looking for. The procedure is parameterized by an E-unification algorithm and an inference system U like the one given in

Fig. 2. The rules, **Coalesce**, **Split**, **Flatten**, and **VA** are used to separate the equations, U is used to simplify the $\Sigma \backslash \Sigma_0$-equations, and finally, **Solve**, is used to apply the E-unification algorithm on Σ_0-equations.

Coalesce $\{x = y\} \cup G \vdash \{x = y\} \cup (G\{x \mapsto y\})$
where x and y are distinct variables occurring both in G.

Split $\{f(\bar{v}) = t\} \cup G \vdash \{x = f(\bar{v}), x = t\} \cup G$
where $f \in \Sigma \backslash \Sigma_0$, t is a non-variable term and x is a fresh variable.

Flatten $\{v = f(\ldots, u, \ldots)\} \cup G \vdash \{v = f(\ldots, x, \ldots), x = u\} \cup G$
where $f \in \Sigma \backslash \Sigma_0$, v is a variable, u is a non-variable term, and x is a fresh variable.

VA $\{s = t[u]\} \cup G \vdash \{s = t[x], x = u\} \cup G$
where t is Σ_0-rooted, u is an alien subterm of t, and x is a fresh variable.

Solve $G \cup G_0 \vdash G \cup \hat{\sigma}_0$
where G is a set of $\Sigma \backslash \Sigma_0$-equations, G_0 is a set of Σ_0-equations, G_0 is E-unifiable and not in tree solved form, $\hat{\sigma}_0$ is the tree solved form associated to $\sigma_0 \in CSU_E(G_0)$, and w.l.o.g for any $x \in Dom(\sigma_0)$, $x\sigma_0 \in Var(G_0)$ if $x\sigma_0$ is a variable.

Fig. 1. H_E rules

Dec $\{x = f(\bar{v}), x = f(\bar{w})\} \cup G \vdash \{x = f(\bar{v}), \bar{v} = \bar{w}\} \cup G$
where $f \in \Sigma \backslash \Sigma_0$.

Mut$_S$ $\{x = f(\bar{v}), x = g(\bar{w})\} \cup G \vdash \{x = f(\bar{v}), \bar{v} = \bar{l}, \bar{w} = \bar{r}\} \cup G$
where $f(\bar{l}) = g(\bar{r}) \in S$.

Fig. 2. DM_S rules

Definition 3 (Hierarchical unification procedure). *Assume a Σ_0-theory E, an E-unification algorithm computing a finite $CSU_E(G_0)$ for all E-unification problems G_0, a Σ-theory $F \cup E$ for which E-unification is complete for solving the Σ_0-fragment of $F \cup E$-unification, and an inference system U satisfying the following assumptions: U transforms only non-variable flat $\Sigma \backslash \Sigma_0$-equations; U is sound and complete for $F \cup E$-unification; U is parameterized by some finite set S of $F \cup E$-equalities such that the soundness of each inference $\vdash_U$ follows from at most one equality in S. Under these assumptions, $H_E(U)$ is the inference system defined as the repeated application of some inference from H_E (cf. Fig. 1) or U, using the following order of priority:* **Coalesce**, **Split**, **Flatten**, **VA**, U, **Solve**. *An $F \cup E$-unification problem is* separate, *also called in* separate form, *if it is a normal form w.r.t $H_E \backslash \{$**Solve**$\}$. $H_E(U)$ is a hierarchical unification procedure for $F \cup E$ if the $F \cup E$-unifiable normal forms w.r.t $H_E(U)$ are the separate dag solved forms.*

Note that when we speak of an inference system, U, this is not just a set of rules but also a strategy for apply those rules, for instance to avoid non-termination [13]. The theory-specific rules in $\{\textbf{Solve}\} \cup U$ are applied using a don't know nondeterminism. From now on, an inference system $H_E(U)$ always denotes a hierarchical unification procedure.

Lemma 5. *Any hierarchical unification procedure for $F \cup E$ is a sound and complete $F \cup E$-unification procedure.*

Proof. Let $H_E(U)$ be a hierarchical unification procedure as given in Definition 3. All the rules in $H_E \backslash \{\textbf{Solve}\}$ are always sound and complete, independently from the underlying equational theory. By assumption on $F \cup E$ and U, $H_E(U)$ is sound and complete. Since the $F \cup E$-unifiable normal forms w.r.t $H_E(U)$ are assumed to be the separate dag solved forms, collecting all the separate dag solved forms reached by $H_E(U)$ provides a complete set of $F \cup E$-unifiers.   □

It will now be useful to consider an E-syntactic theory $F \cup E$ for which all the $\Sigma \backslash \Sigma_0$-rooted terms are subterm collapse-free modulo $F \cup E$. This allows us to get a possible instantiation of the hierarchical unification procedure.

Lemma 6. *Assume a Σ_0-theory E, an E-unification algorithm, a Σ-theory $F \cup E$ such that F is E-constructed, $F \cup E$ is E-syntactic with an E-resolvent presentation S, and all the $\Sigma \backslash \Sigma_0$-rooted terms are subterm collapse-free modulo $F \cup E$. Given E, $F \cup E$ and DM_S the inference system from Fig. 2, all the assumptions of Definition 3 are satisfied to get a hierarchical unification procedure $H_E(DM_S)$, and $H_E(DM_S)$ is a sound and complete $F \cup E$-unification procedure.*

Proof. By Lemma 2, **Solve** is sound and complete. By Lemma 3, DM_S is sound and complete. Moreover, the soundness of each inference rule in DM_S follows from at most one equality in S.

Consider any separate form $G_1 \wedge G_0$ containing a cycle with at least one equation in G_1. By assumption, this cycles has no solution in $F \cup E$. Consequently, the separate dag solved forms are the $F \cup E$-unifiable normal forms w.r.t $H_E(DM_S)$. Hence, all the assumptions of Definition 3 are satisfied and Lemma 5 applies.   □

In Lemma 6, one can notice that E is necessarily collapse-free and E-unification is finitary. So, E is syntactic according to [20]. By Lemma 4, $F \cup E$ is not only E-syntactic but syntactic when Lemma 6 applies.

In the following, we focus on combinations of E-constructed theories admitting terminating hierarchical unification procedures. The case of regular and collapse-free E-constructed theories is studied in Sect. 6. The class of E-constructed theories closed by E-paramodulation is considered in Sect. 7.

6   Combination of Regular Collapse-Free Theories

In this section we extend the approach initiated in [15] moving from the restricted case of subterm collapse-free theories to the less restrictive regular and collapse-free theories. Let us consider a union $F_1 \cup F_2 \cup E$ of regular collapse-free theories such that F_1 and F_2 are E-constructed theories. The signatures of E, F_1 and F_2 are respectively denoted by Σ_0, Σ_1 and Σ_2. The theories F_1 and F_2 are assumed to share only the symbols of E, meaning that $\Sigma_0 = \Sigma_1 \cap \Sigma_2$. We can show that, for any $i = 1, 2$, $F_i \cup E$-unification is complete for solving the Σ_i-fragment of $F_1 \cup F_2 \cup E$-unification (cf. [16]). This paves the way of building a combined procedure for $F_1 \cup F_2 \cup E$, but some additional restrictions on $F_1 \cup F_2 \cup E$ are needed. The theory $F_1 \cup F_2 \cup E$ is said to be a *simple combination* if the following two conditions hold: First, for any $\Sigma_1 \backslash \Sigma_0$-rooted term t_1 and any $\Sigma_2 \backslash \Sigma_0$-rooted term t_2, t_1 cannot be equal to t_2 modulo $F_1 \cup F_2 \cup E$. Second, for any term t and any position p in t such that $\bigcup_{q \leq p} \{t(q)\}$ contains at least both a symbol in $\Sigma_1 \backslash \Sigma_0$ and a symbol in $\Sigma_2 \backslash \Sigma_0$, t cannot be equal to $t|_p$ modulo $F_1 \cup F_2 \cup E$. These two conditions mean that there are no solutions to conflicts of theories and no solutions to compound cycles. Let us now introduce a technical lemma which is useful to get a hierarchical unification procedure for $F_1 \cup F_2 \cup E$.

Lemma 7. *Let Σ_1 and Σ_2 be two signatures such that $\Sigma_0 = \Sigma_1 \cap \Sigma_2$. Consider E is a Σ_0-theory and for $i = 1, 2$, F_i is an E-constructed Σ_i-theory such that $F_i \cup E$ admits a sound and complete unification procedure of the form $H_E(U_i)$. If $F_1 \cup F_2 \cup E$ is a simple combination, then we have that*

- *$H_E(U_1 \cup U_2)$ is a sound and complete $F_1 \cup F_2 \cup E$-unification procedure,*
- *if for $i = 1, 2$, S_i is an E-resolvent presentation of $F_i \cup E$, then $S_1 \cup S_2$ is an E-resolvent presentation of $(F_1 \cup F_2) \cup E$.*

Proof. According to the assumptions, any normal form w.r.t $H_E(U_1 \cup U_2)$ is $F_1 \cup F_2 \cup E$-unifiable iff it is in dag solved form. Then, Lemma 5 applies.

Assume now S_i is an E-resolvent presentation of $F_i \cup E$ for $i = 1, 2$. In that case, $S_1 \cup S_2$ is an E-resolvent presentation of $(F_1 \cup F_2) \cup E$ since by assumption it is not possible to have $t_1 =_{F_1 \cup F_2 \cup E} t_2$ for some $\Sigma_1 \backslash \Sigma_0$-rooted term t_1 and some $\Sigma_2 \backslash \Sigma_0$-rooted term t_2.   □

We study below a possible way to satisfy the assumptions of Lemma 7, thanks to a property on the shape of normal forms.

Definition 4 (E-capped theory). *Let F be an E-constructed theory over the signature Σ. A Σ-term t is said to be E-capped if there exist a constant-free Σ_0-term u and a substitution σ such that $t = u\sigma$, $Dom(\sigma) = Var(u)$ and $Ran(\sigma)$ is a set of $\Sigma \backslash \Sigma_0$-rooted terms. The E-constructed theory F is said to be E-capped if any normal form w.r.t $\to_{R_F, E}$ of any $\Sigma \backslash \Sigma_0$-rooted ground term is E-capped.*

In Definition 4, the term u can be a variable, to take into account the case where the normal form of a $\Sigma \backslash \Sigma_0$-rooted ground term remains $\Sigma \backslash \Sigma_0$-rooted.

Example 3. Consider $\Sigma_0 = \{*\}$ and the Σ_0-theory E defined by an emptyset of Σ_0-axioms.

First, let $(R_{\mathcal{D}}, E)$ be the E-constructed TRS where $R_{\mathcal{D}} = \{h(x*y) \rightarrow h(x)*h(y)\}$. The term $h(x)*h(y)$ is E-capped because $h(x)*h(y) = u\sigma$ for the Σ_0-term with no constants $u = v*w$ and the substitution $\sigma = \{v \mapsto h(x), w \mapsto h(y)\}$. Notice that $h(x)$ is also E-capped since $h(x) = u\sigma$ for $u = v$ and $\sigma = \{v \mapsto h(x)\}$. By induction on the length of outermost derivations, we can show that any normal form w.r.t $(R_{\mathcal{D}}, E)$ of any term rooted by h is E-capped. Thus, $R_{\mathcal{D}}^=$ is E-capped.

Second, let $(R_{\mathcal{D}1}, E)$ be the E-constructed TRS where $R_{\mathcal{D}1} = \{f(x*y, z) \rightarrow f(x, z)*f(y, z)\}$. In a way similar to $R_{\mathcal{D}}^=$, we can show that $R_{\mathcal{D}1}^=$ is E-capped.

Lemma 8. *Assume E is a Σ_0-theory. If for $i = 1, 2$, F_i is a regular collapse-free E-capped Σ_i-theory, and $\Sigma_1 \cap \Sigma_2 = \Sigma_0$, then $F_1 \cup F_2$ is a regular collapse-free E-capped $\Sigma_1 \cup \Sigma_2$-theory such that $F_1 \cup F_2 \cup E$ is a simple combination.*

Proof (Sketch). Let us consider the *height of layers* of a term t, inductively defined as follows: $ht(t) = 0$ if t is a variable; $ht(t) = 1$ if t is a non-variable pure term; $ht(t) = 1 + \max\{ht(u) \mid u$ is an alien subterm of $t\}$ if t is not pure.

By contradiction, assume there exist a term t and a position p such that $t =_{F_1 \cup F_2 \cup E} t|_p$ and the path from ϵ to p contains both a symbol in $\Sigma_1 \backslash \Sigma_0$ and a symbol in $\Sigma_2 \backslash \Sigma_0$. Let $u = t|_p$ and let t' and u' be the respective normal forms w.r.t $\rightarrow_{R_{F_1} \cup R_{F_2}, E}$ of t and u (viewed as ground terms). Since $t' =_E u'$ and E is regular collapse-free, t' and u' have the same height of layers. By the E-capped assumption, t and t' have the same height of layers, as well as u and u'. Thus t and u have the same height of layers, which leads to a contradiction since the path from ϵ to p includes both a symbol in $\Sigma_1 \backslash \Sigma_0$ and a symbol in $\Sigma_2 \backslash \Sigma_0$.

Assume there exist some $\Sigma_1 \backslash \Sigma_0$-rooted term t_1 and some $\Sigma_2 \backslash \Sigma_0$-rooted term t_2 such that $t_1 =_{F_1 \cup F_2 \cup E} t_2$. Then, $t'_1 =_E t'_2$ where t'_1 and t'_2 are the respective normal forms w.r.t $\rightarrow_{R_{F_1} \cup R_{F_2}, E}$ of t_1 and t_2 (viewed as ground terms). The E-capped assumption implies that t'_i must still contain a symbol in $\Sigma_i \backslash \Sigma_0$ for $i = 1, 2$. Since E is regular collapse-free, it is impossible to have $t'_1 =_E t'_2$. □

By Lemma 8, the two assumptions of Lemma 7 can be satisfied, and this leads to the following hierarchical unification procedure.

Corollary 1. *Assume E is a Σ_0-theory; for $i = 1, 2$, F_i is a regular collapse-free E-capped Σ_i-theory, all the $\Sigma_i \backslash \Sigma_0$-rooted terms are subterm collapse-free modulo $F_i \cup E$, S_i is an E-resolvent presentation of $F_i \cup E$; and $\Sigma_1 \cap \Sigma_2 = \Sigma_0$. Then $F_1 \cup F_2$ is a regular collapse-free E-capped theory, $S_1 \cup S_2$ is an E-resolvent presentation of $F_1 \cup F_2 \cup E$, and $H_E(DM_{S_1} \cup DM_{S_2})$ is a sound and complete $F_1 \cup F_2 \cup E$-unification procedure.*

Proof. By Lemmas 8, 7, 6 and the fact that $H_E(DM_{S_1 \cup S_2})$ coincides with $H_E(DM_{S_1} \cup DM_{S_2})$. □

Example 4. (Example 3 continued) There exists an E-resolvent presentation $S_{\mathcal{D}}$ (resp., $S_{\mathcal{D}1}$) of $R_{\mathcal{D}} \cup E$ (resp., $R_{\mathcal{D}1} \cup E$). By Corollary 1, $H_E(DM_{S_{\mathcal{D}}} \cup DM_{S_{\mathcal{D}1}})$ is a sound and complete $R_{\mathcal{D}} \cup R_{\mathcal{D}1} \cup E$-unification procedure.

To study the termination of the combined hierarchical unification procedure given in Lemma 7, we reuse the notion of decreasingness initiated in [15].

Definition 5 (Decreasingness). *Consider a complexity measure defined as a mapping C from separate forms to natural numbers. A $H_E(U)$ inference system is said to be C-decreasing if for any separate form $G \cup G_0$ we have that*

- *for any G' such that $G \cup G_0 \vdash_U G' \cup G_0$, the separate form of $G' \cup G_0$ does not increase C;*
- *for any G_0' such that $G \cup G_0 \vdash_{Solve} G \cup G_0'$, then either the separate form of $G \cup G_0'$ is in normal form w.r.t $H_E(U)$, or it decreases C.*

$H_E(U)$ *is terminating if there exists some C such that $H_E(U)$ is C-decreasing.*

Theorem 2. *Assume a theory E, an E-unification algorithm, and a complexity measure C defined on separate forms. Let F_1 and F_2 be two regular collapse-free E-capped theories sharing only symbols in E such that, for $i = 1, 2$, $F_i \cup E$ admits a C-decreasing unification algorithm of the form $H_E(U_i)$. Then $F_1 \cup F_2$ is a regular collapse-free E-capped theory such that $F_1 \cup F_2 \cup E$ admits a C-decreasing unification algorithm of the form $H_E(U_1 \cup U_2)$.*

Proof. $F_1 \cup F_2$ is a regular collapse-free E-capped theory by Lemma 8. In addition, Lemma 7 and Lemma 5 can be applied. Hence, $H_E(U_1 \cup U_2)$ provides a sound and complete $F_1 \cup F_2 \cup E$-unification procedure. Moreover, $H_E(U_1 \cup U_2)$ is C-decreasing and so it is terminating.   □

This theorem subsumes a similar result from [15]. The advantage now is that we don't need to check the subterm-collapse freeness property, which can be a difficult task. Rather, we need only to check regularity and collapse-freeness, and this can be trivially achieved by examining the axioms. For example, Theorem 2 allows us to obtain a combined hierarchical unification algorithm for the exponentiation theories from Sect. 1.

7   Combination of Theories Closed by E-Paramodulation

In this section, we focus on E-constructed theories F such that $PC(F) = F$. The next lemma follows from a very similar argument to Lemma 3.

Lemma 9. *Let F be an E-constructed theory closed by E-paramodulation. For each ground equality $u =_{F \cup E} v$ such that u is $\Sigma \backslash \Sigma_0$-rooted and v is normalized w.r.t $\to_{R_F, E}$, one of the following is true: (1) $u = f(\bar{u})$, $v = f(\bar{v})$ and $\bar{u} =_{F \cup E} \bar{v}$; (2) $u = f(\bar{u})$, there exist $f(\bar{s}) = t \in F$ and a substitution σ normalized w.r.t $\to_{R_F, E}$ such that $\bar{u} =_{F \cup E} \bar{s}\sigma$, $v =_E t\sigma$ and $\bar{s}\sigma, t\sigma$ are normalized w.r.t $\to_{R_F, E}$.*

The inference system BSM_F given in Fig. 3 can be used to show the existence of a hierarchical unification algorithm for the class of E-constructed theories closed by E-paramodulation. One can notice that each inference rule in BSM_F generates some boxed terms. This particular annotation of terms, detailed in [11, 21], allows us to control the rule applications, disregarding needless inferences on boxed terms in such a way that the termination is guaranteed.

Imit $\bigcup_i \{x = f(\bar{v}_i)\} \cup G \vdash \{x = \boxed{f(\bar{y})}\} \cup \bigcup_i \{\bar{y} = \bar{v}_i\} \cup G$

where $f \in \Sigma \backslash \Sigma_0$, $i > 1$, $\bar{y}$ are fresh variables and there are no more equations $x = f(\dots)$ in G.

MutConflict$_F$ $\{x = f(\bar{v})\} \cup G \vdash \{x = \boxed{t}, \boxed{\bar{s}} = \bar{v}\} \cup G$
where $f \in \Sigma \backslash \Sigma_0$, $f(\bar{s}) = t$ is a fresh instance of an equality in F, $f(\bar{v})$ is unboxed, and (there is another equation $x = u$ in G with a non-variable term u or $x = f(\bar{v})$ occurs in a cycle).

ImitCycle $\{x = f(\bar{v})\} \cup G \vdash \{x = \boxed{f(\bar{y})}, \bar{y} = \bar{v}\} \cup G$
where $f \in \Sigma \backslash \Sigma_0$, $f(\bar{v})$ is unboxed, $\bar{y}$ are fresh variables and $x = f(\bar{v})$ occurs in a cycle.

Fig. 3. BSM_F rules

Theorem 3. *Consider any E-constructed theory F closed by E-paramodulation and the inference system BSM_F given in Fig. 3. Then, $F \cup E$ is an E-syntactic theory admitting a unification algorithm of the form $H_E(BSM_F)$.*

Proof. $F \cup E$ is E-syntactic since an E-resolvent presentation of $F \cup E$ is $F \cup \{l\sigma = g\sigma \mid l = r, g = d \in F, l\sigma \not< r\sigma, g\sigma \not< d\sigma, \sigma \in CSU_E(r =^? d), l\sigma \neq g\sigma\}$. By Lemma 9, BSM_F satisfies the assumption of Definition 3. Since the separate dag solved forms are the $F \cup E$-unifiable normal forms w.r.t $H_E(BSM_F)$, Lemma 5 applies and so $H_E(BSM_F)$ is a sound and complete $F \cup E$-unification procedure. Moreover $H_E(BSM_F)$ can be proved terminating using the same proof as the one developed in [11,15] for forward-closed E-constructed TRSs. Thus, $H_E(BSM_F)$ is a sound and complete terminating $F \cup E$-unification procedure. □

Theorem 4. *If F_1 and F_2 are two E-constructed theories closed by E-paramodulation and sharing only symbols in E, then $F_1 \cup F_2$ is an E-constructed theory closed by E-paramodulation.*

Proof (Sketch). The maximal sides of equalities in F_i are necessarily $\Sigma_i \backslash \Sigma_0$-rooted for $i = 1, 2$. Therefore, it is impossible to apply E-**Paramodulation** with one premise in F_1 and the other one in F_2. □

Corollary 2. *If for $i = 1, 2$, F_i is an E-constructed Σ_i-theory closed by E-paramodulation, and $\Sigma_1 \cap \Sigma_2 = \Sigma_0$, then $F_1 \cup F_2 \cup E$ is an E-syntactic theory admitting a unification algorithm of the form $H_E(BSM_{F_1} \cup BSM_{F_2})$.*

Proof. By Theorems 4, 3, and the fact that $H_E(BSM_{F_1 \cup F_2})$ coincides with $H_E(BSM_{F_1} \cup BSM_{F_2})$. □

Example 5. Continuing Example 2 and Example 1, we can notice that E_1 and E_2 are both AC-constructed and closed by AC-paramodulation. By Theorem 4, $E_1 \cup E_2$ is closed by AC-paramodulation. Furthermore, $E_1 \cup E_2$ is an AC-syntactic theory admitting a unification algorithm of the form $H_{AC}(BSM_{E_1} \cup BSM_{E_2})$.

Theorem 4 can be applied to *IR1* E-constructed TRSs combined with some particular shallow theories.

Definition 6 (Shallow extension). *Let* (R, E) *be an E-constructed TRS over the signature* Σ, *and* Σ' *a signature extension of* Σ. *A shallow extension of* (R, E) *is an equational* Σ'-*theory* $F \cup R^=$ *where* F *is a finite set of shallow* Σ'-*equalities* $l = r$ *such that* $l(\epsilon), r(\epsilon) \in (\Sigma' \backslash \Sigma) \cup X$ *and all the ground terms occurring in* F *are* Σ-*terms in normal form w.r.t* (R, E).

A shallow extension $F \cup R^=$ of (R, E) can be viewed as a union of two E-constructed theories sharing only symbols in E (plus, some additional constants). The first theory, say F', is obtained from F by performing a constant abstraction of maximal ground terms rooted by symbols defined by R. The second theory is given by a set of rules, say R', defined as R plus all the rules $t \to c$ for each abstracted ground term t, c being the constant that abstracts t. We can show that F' admits a finite closure by E-paramodulation. If (R, E) is an *IR1* E-constructed TRS, then so is (R', E), and $R'^=$ is closed by E-paramodulation according to Lemma 1. Then, Theorem 4 can be applied to get:

Theorem 5. *Assume* (R, E) *is any E-constructed TRS such that* $\to_{R,E}$ *is IR1,* $F \cup R^=$ *is any shallow extension of* (R, E), *and* $>$ *is a reduction ordering including* $\to_{R,E}$ *such that* $PC(F)$ *is defined. Then,* $PC(F \cup R^=)$ *is finite.*

8   Conclusion

Assuming a regular collapse-free theory E and an E-unification algorithm, we have studied the (combined) unification problem in (unions of) E-constructed theories. Our notion of constructor seems to be closely related to the one used in [5] but this remains to be formally shown.

As future work, it would be interesting to apply our hierarchical approach to unification in order-sorted equational theories, to handle for instance order-sorted AC-convergent rewrite systems with the Finite Variant Property that can be used for homomorphic encryption [28]. In the near future, we plan to reuse the notion of E-constructed theory in order to investigate the possible extension of the combination methods developed in [14] for two knowledge problems of particular interest in the analysis of protocols. These combination methods have been initially developed for the case of theories sharing only absolutely free constructors and we believe that the framework above will be useful to lift these methods to the case of theories sharing only constructors modulo E.

In a longer term, we envision to study the possible development of a hierarchical approach to solve the disunification problem modulo theories closed by E-paramodulation. The disunification problem has been already successfully considered for forward-closed rewrite systems [23]. Since paramodulation-closed theories bear similarities with forward-closed rewrite systems, investigating a hierarchical approach to solve the disunification problem [2,23] appears to be a promising research direction.

References

1. Baader, F., Nipkow, T.: Term Rewriting and All That. Cambridge University Press, Cambridge (1998)
2. Baader, F., Schulz, K.U.: Combination techniques and decision problems for disunification. Theor. Comput. Sci. **142**(2), 229–255 (1995)
3. Baader, F., Schulz, K.U.: Unification in the union of disjoint equational theories: combining decision procedures. J. Symb. Comput. **21**(2), 211–243 (1996)
4. Baader, F., Snyder,W.: Unification theory. In: Robinson, J.A., Voronkov, A. (eds.) Handbook of Automated Reasoning (in 2 volumes), pp. 445–532. Elsevier and MIT Press (2001)
5. Baader, F., Tinelli, C.: Combining decision procedures for positive theories sharing constructors. In: Tison, S. (ed.) RTA 2002. LNCS, vol. 2378, pp. 352–366. Springer, Heidelberg (2002). https://doi.org/10.1007/3-540-45610-4_25
6. Bouchard, C., Gero, K.A., Lynch, C., Narendran, P.: On forward closure and the finite variant property. In: Fontaine, P., Ringeissen, C., Schmidt, R.A. (eds.) FroCoS 2013. LNCS (LNAI), vol. 8152, pp. 327–342. Springer, Heidelberg (2013). https://doi.org/10.1007/978-3-642-40885-4_23
7. Cohn-Gordon, K., Cremers, C., Garratt, L., Millican, J., Milner, K.: On ends-to-ends encryption: asynchronous group messaging with strong security guarantees. In: Lie, D., Mannan, M., Backes, M., Wang, X. (eds.) Proceedings of the 2018 ACM SIGSAC Conference on Computer and Communications Security, CCS 2018, Toronto, ON, Canada, 15–19 October 2018, pp. 1802–1819. ACM (2018)
8. Comon, H., Haberstrau, M., Jouannaud, J.-P.: Syntacticness, cycle-syntacticness, and shallow theories. Inf. Comput. **111**(1), 154–191 (1994)
9. Comon-Lundh, H., Delaune, S.: The finite variant property: how to get rid of some algebraic properties. In: Giesl, J. (ed.) RTA 2005. LNCS, vol. 3467, pp. 294–307. Springer, Heidelberg (2005). https://doi.org/10.1007/978-3-540-32033-3_22
10. Domenjoud, E., Klay, F., Ringeissen, C.: Combination techniques for non-disjoint equational theories. In: Bundy, A. (ed.) CADE 1994. LNCS, vol. 814, pp. 267–281. Springer, Heidelberg (1994). https://doi.org/10.1007/3-540-58156-1_19
11. Eeralla, A.K., Erbatur, S., Marshall, A.M., Ringeissen, C.: Rule-based unification in combined theories and the finite variant property. In: Martín-Vide, C., Okhotin, A., Shapira, D. (eds.) LATA 2019. LNCS, vol. 11417, pp. 356–367. Springer, Cham (2019). https://doi.org/10.1007/978-3-030-13435-8_26
12. Erbatur, S., Kapur, D., Marshall, A.M., Narendran, P., Ringeissen, C.: Hierarchical combination. In: Bonacina, M.P. (ed.) CADE 2013. LNCS (LNAI), vol. 7898, pp. 249–266. Springer, Heidelberg (2013). https://doi.org/10.1007/978-3-642-38574-2_17
13. Erbatur, S., Marshall, A.M., Kapur, D., Narendran, P.: Unification over distributive exponentiation (sub)theories. J. Autom. Lang. Comb. **16**(2–4), 109–140 (2011)
14. Erbatur, S., Marshall, A.M., Ringeissen, C.: Notions of knowledge in combinations of theories sharing constructors. In: de Moura, L. (ed.) CADE 2017. LNCS (LNAI), vol. 10395, pp. 60–76. Springer, Cham (2017). https://doi.org/10.1007/978-3-319-63046-5_5
15. Erbatur, S., Marshall, A.M., Ringeissen, C.: Terminating non-disjoint combined unification. In: Fernández, M. (ed.) LOPSTR 2020. LNCS, vol. 12561, pp. 113–130. Springer, Cham (2021). https://doi.org/10.1007/978-3-030-68446-4_6
16. Erbatur, S., Marshall, A.M., Ringeissen, C.: Non-disjoint combined unification and closure by equational paramodulation (extended version). Research report (2021). http://hal.inria.fr

17. Escobar, S., Sasse, R., Meseguer, J.: Folding variant narrowing and optimal variant termination. J. Log. Algebr. Program. **81**(7–8), 898–928 (2012)
18. Jouannaud, J.-P., Kirchner, H.: Completion of a set of rules modulo a set of equations. SIAM J. Comput. **15**(4), 1155–1194 (1986)
19. Kim, D., Lynch, C., Narendran, P.: Reviving basic narrowing modulo. In: Herzig, A., Popescu, A. (eds.) FroCoS 2019. LNCS (LNAI), vol. 11715, pp. 313–329. Springer, Cham (2019). https://doi.org/10.1007/978-3-030-29007-8_18
20. Kirchner, C., Klay, F.: Syntactic theories and unification. In: Proceedings of the Fifth Annual Symposium on Logic in Computer Science (LICS 1990), Philadelphia, Pennsylvania, USA, 4–7 June 1990, pp. 270–277. IEEE Computer Society (1990)
21. Lynch, C., Morawska, B.: Basic syntactic mutation. In: Voronkov, A. (ed.) CADE 2002. LNCS (LNAI), vol. 2392, pp. 471–485. Springer, Heidelberg (2002). https://doi.org/10.1007/3-540-45620-1_37
22. Lynch, C., Morawska, B.: Faster *Basic Syntactic Mutation* with sorts for some separable equational theories. In: Giesl, J. (ed.) RTA 2005. LNCS, vol. 3467, pp. 90–104. Springer, Heidelberg (2005). https://doi.org/10.1007/978-3-540-32033-3_8
23. Meseguer, J.: Variant-based satisfiability in initial algebras. Sci. Comput. Program. **154**, 3–41 (2018)
24. Nguyen, K.: Formal verification of a messaging protocol. Internship report (2019). Work done under the supervision of Vincent Cheval and Véronique Cortier
25. Nipkow, T.: Proof transformations for equational theories. In: Proceedings of the Fifth Annual Symposium on Logic in Computer Science (LICS 1990), Philadelphia, Pennsylvania, USA, 4–7 June 1990, pp. 278–288. IEEE Computer Society (1990)
26. Ringeissen, C.: Unification in a combination of equational theories with shared constants and its application to primal algebras. In: Voronkov, A. (ed.) LPAR 1992. LNCS, vol. 624, pp. 261–272. Springer, Heidelberg (1992). https://doi.org/10.1007/BFb0013067
27. Schmidt-Schauß, M.: Unification in a combination of arbitrary disjoint equational theories. J. Symb. Comput. **8**(1/2), 51–99 (1989)
28. Yang, F., Escobar, S., Meadows, C.A., Meseguer, J., Narendran, P.: Theories of homomorphic encryption, unification, and the finite variant property. In: Chitil, O., King, A., Danvy, O. (eds.) Proceedings of the 16th International Symposium on Principles and Practice of Declarative Programming, Kent, Canterbury, United Kingdom, 8–10 September 2014, pp. 123–133. ACM (2014)

Symbol Elimination and Applications to Parametric Entailment Problems

Dennis Peuter and Viorica Sofronie-Stokkermans[✉]

University Koblenz-Landau, Koblenz, Germany
{dpeuter,sofronie}@uni-koblenz.de

Abstract. We analyze possibilities of second-order quantifier elimination for formulae containing parameters – constants or functions. For this, we use a constraint resolution calculus obtained from specializing the hierarchical superposition calculus. If saturation terminates, we analyze possibilities of obtaining weakest constraints on parameters which guarantee satisfiability. If the saturation does not terminate, we identify situations in which finite representations of infinite saturated sets exist. We identify situations in which entailment between formulae expressed using second-order quantification can be effectively checked. We illustrate the ideas on a series of examples from wireless network research.

1 Introduction

The main motivation for this work was a study of models for graph classes naturally occurring in wireless network research – in which nodes that are close are always connected, nodes that are far apart from each other are never connected and any other node pairs can, but do not need to be connected. Transformations can be applied to such graphs to make them symmetric; this way we can define further graph classes. When checking inclusion between graph classes described using transformations we need to check entailment of second-order formulae. In addition, many such graph class descriptions are parametric in nature, so the goal is, in fact, to obtain (weakest) conditions on the parameters used in such descriptions that guarantee that graph classes are non-empty or that inclusions hold. This can be achieved by eliminating "non-parametric" constants or function symbols used in the description of such classes.

In this paper we combine methods for general symbol elimination (which we use for eliminating existentially quantified predicates) with methods for property-directed symbol elimination (which we use for obtaining conditions on "parameters" under which formulae are satisfiable or second-order entailment holds). For general second-order quantifier elimination we use a form of ordered resolution similar to that proposed in [19]. For property-directed symbol elimination we use a method we proposed in [40]. The advantage of using such a two-layered approach is that it avoids non-termination that might occur if using only general symbol elimination methods. The main application area we consider in this paper is the analysis of inclusions between graph classes arising in wireless network research. Our main contributions are:

B. Konev and G. Reger (Eds.): FroCoS 2021, LNAI 12941, pp. 43–62, 2021.
https://doi.org/10.1007/978-3-030-86205-3_3

- We analyze theories used in modeling graph classes and prove locality of theories of "distances" occurring in this context.
- We analyze possibilities of general symbol elimination, using a simple specialization $HRes_\succ^P$ of the hierarchical superposition calculus (a form of ordered resolution) for eliminating a predicate symbol P.
- If saturation terminates, we analyze possibilities of obtaining weakest constraints on parameters occurring in the clauses which guarantee satisfiability, using methods for property-directed symbol elimination.
- If the saturation does not terminate, we study possibilities of representing an (infinite) saturated set as a set of constrained clauses in which the constraints are interpreted in the minimal model of a set of constrained Horn clauses.
- We analyze possibilities of effectively checking entailment between formulae expressed using second-order quantification.
- We illustrate the ideas on examples related to the study of wireless networks.

Related Work. The study of second-order quantifier elimination goes back to the beginning of the 20th century (cf. [10] and [2,3]). Most of its known applications are in the study of modal logics or knowledge representation [20,21]; in many cases second-order quantifier elimination is proved only for very restricted fragments (cf. e.g. [41]). In [19], Gabbay and Ohlbach proposed a resolution-based algorithm for second-order quantifier elimination which is implemented in the system SCAN. In [5], Bachmair et al. mention that hierarchical superposition (cf. [8,9] for further refinements) can be used for second-order quantifier elimination modulo a theory. In [33] and [23], Hoder et al. study possibilities of symbol elimination in inference systems (e.g. the superposition calculus and its extension with ground linear rational arithmetic and uninterpreted functions). The main challenge when using saturation approaches for symbol elimination is the fact that the saturated sets might be infinite. Sometimes finite representations of possibly infinite sets of clauses exist: for this, Horbach and Weidenbach introduced a melting calculus [26], later used in [24,25] and [17]. Similar aspects were explored in the study of *acceleration* for program verification modulo Presburger arithmetic by Boigelot, Finkel and Leroux [14,18], in relationship with array systems by [4], or in the study of constrained Horn clauses (cf. [12]). We analyze possibilities of representing infinite saturated sets as sets of constrained clauses in which the constraints are interpreted in the minimal model of a set of constrained Horn clauses.

Orthogonal to this direction of study is what we call "property-directed" symbol elimination: There, given a theory $\mathcal{T}$ and a ground formula G satisfiable w.r.t. $\mathcal{T}$, the goal is to derive a (weakest) universal formula Γ over a subset of the signature, such that $\Gamma \wedge G$ is unsatisfiable w.r.t. $\mathcal{T}$. We devised methods for solving such problems in [40] and used them for interpolant computation [40], and invariant generation [37]. We here use these results in a different context.

We are not aware of other similar approaches to the area of computational (geometric) graph theory. Existing approaches use a logical representation of graphs based on monadic second-order logic (cf. e.g. [15]) or higher-order theorem provers like Isabelle/HOL (cf. e.g. [1]). Our approach is orthogonal; it allows a reduction of many problems to satisfiability modulo a suitable theory.

Structure of the Paper. In Sect. 1.1 we present the motivation for our research. In Sect. 2 we introduce the results on (local) theory extensions needed in the paper and prove the locality of theories of distance functions. In Sect. 3 we present the $HRes^P_\succ$ calculus we use for eliminating predicate P, and analyze possibilities of giving finite representations for infinite saturated sets and of investigating the satisfiability of the saturated sets. In Sect. 4 we use these ideas for checking entailment. In Sect. 5 we present conclusions and plans for future work. The details of the proofs and additional examples can be found in the extended version of the paper [36].

1.1   Motivation

Graph classes important in wireless network research are: The class **UDG** of *unit disk graphs* (two nodes are connected iff they are different and their distance is ≤ 1); the class **QUDG(r)** of quasi unit disk graphs, for $\mathbf{r} \in (0,1]$ (two distinct nodes with distance $\leq \mathbf{r}$ are always connected and nodes with distance > 1 are never connected); the class **DTG**$(r, \mathbf{r})$ of *directed transmission graphs* for $\mathbf{r} > 0$ (every node v has a maximum communication distance $r(v) \leq \mathbf{r}$; an edge from v to w exists iff $v \neq w$ and the distance between v and w is $\leq r(v)$).

Many graph classes $\mathbf{C}(\bar{p})$ (where $\bar{p}$ is a sequence of symbols denoting *parameters*) can be described using *inclusion, exclusion* and *transfer* axioms. The *inclusion axioms* specify under which conditions an edge from u to v has to exist; the conditions are described by a formula $\pi^i_C(u, v)$; inclusion axioms have the form:

$$(1) \qquad \forall u, v \; (\pi^i_C(u, v) \to E(u, v)).$$

The *exclusion axioms* specify under which condition an edge from u to v is not allowed to exist; the conditions are described by a formula $\pi^e_C(u, v)$, so exclusion axioms have the form:

$$(2) \qquad \forall u, v \; (\pi^e_C(u, v) \to \neg E(u, v)).$$

The *transfer axioms* specify under which conditions an edge from u to w must exist as a consequence of the existence of an edge from u to v; the conditions are described by a formula $\pi^t_C(u, v, w)$, so the transfer axioms we consider here have the form:

$$(3) \qquad \forall u, v, w \; (\pi^t_C(u, w, v) \wedge E(u, v) \to E(u, w)).$$

We can define more general versions of the classes **MinDG**(r), **MaxDG**(r) and **CRG** used in the literature, in which we assume that every vertex v has a maximum communication distance $r(v)$, using axioms:

- MinDG(r): axiom (1), where $\pi^i_r(u, v)$ is the formula $u \neq v \wedge d(u, v) \leq r(u)$;
- MaxDG(r): axiom (2), where $\pi^e_r(u, v)$ is the formula $d(u, v) > r(u)$;
- CRG: axiom (3), where $\pi^t(u, w, v)$ is the formula $u \neq w \wedge d(u, w) \leq d(u, v)$.

In the case when $r(v) = \mathbf{r}$ for all v, where $\mathbf{r} \in \mathbb{R}$, we use the constant $\mathbf{r}$ when describing the classes instead of the function r. For instance, $\mathbf{UDG} = \mathbf{MinDG}(1) \cap \mathbf{MaxDG}(1)$ is axiomatized by $\mathsf{MinDG}(1) \wedge \mathsf{MaxDG}(1)$. We may want to check whether a graph class $\mathbf{C}(\overline{p})$ has non-empty models, or determine (weakest) conditions on the parameters $\overline{p}$ under which this is the case.

We can define transformations γ on graphs that transform the edges, and form classes $\gamma(\mathbf{C}) = \{\gamma(G) \mid G \in \mathbf{C}\}$. Two examples of transformations are $\cdot^+$ and $\cdot^-$: Given a graph $G = (V, E)$, we can build the symmetric supergraph $G^+ = (V, E^+)$ resp. symmetric subgraph $G^- = (V, E^-)$, defined by:

$$\forall x, y(E^+(x,y) \leftrightarrow (E(x,y) \vee E(y,x))) \text{ and } \forall x, y(E^-(x,y) \leftrightarrow (E(x,y) \wedge E(y,x))).$$

We can thus define the classes $\mathbf{C}^+$ and $\mathbf{C}^-$. The class of quasi unit disk graphs [7,34] can be described as $\mathbf{QUDG}(r) = (\mathbf{MinDG}(r) \cap \mathbf{MaxDG}(1))^-$. We might want to obtain an axiomatization for $\mathbf{QUDG}(r)$ that depends only on the predicates $\pi_r^i(x,y), \pi_1^e(x,y)$ or test whether the class is the same as the class described by $(\mathbf{MinDG}(r) \cap \mathbf{MaxDG}(1))^+$.

To find an axiomatization of a graph class $\gamma(\mathbf{C})$, where γ is a transformation, we need to find a first-order formula equivalent to $\exists E'(\mathsf{N}_{E'} \cap \mathsf{Tr}(E', E))$, where $\mathsf{N}_{E'}$ is a class of clauses describing class $\mathbf{C}$ and Tr is a formula describing the way the edges of the graph $(V, E) = \gamma(V, E')$ can be obtained from the description of the graph (V, E'). If we can find such formulae for two graph classes, then we can also check containment (provided the formulae belong to decidable theory fragments). In this paper we analyze situations in which this is possible.

2   Local Extensions; Hierarchical Symbol Elimination

We assume known the basic notions in (many-sorted) first-order logic. We consider signatures of the form $\Pi = (S, \Sigma, \mathsf{Pred})$, where S is a set of sorts, Σ is a family of function symbols and Pred a family of predicate symbols, such that for every function symbol f (resp. predicate symbol p) their arity $a(f) = s_1 \ldots s_n \to s$ (resp. $a(p) = s_1 \ldots s_m$), where $s_1, \ldots, s_n, s \in S$, is specified. If C is a fixed countable set of fresh constants, we denote by Π^C the extension of Π with constants in C. We assume known standard definitions from first-order logic such as Π-structure, model, satisfiability, unsatisfiability. If $\Pi \subseteq \Pi'$ and $\mathcal{A}$ is a Π'-structure, we denote its reduct to Π by $\mathcal{A}_{|\Pi}$.

Notation. We will denote with (indexed versions of) x, y, z variables and with (indexed versions of) a, b, c, d constants; $\overline{x}$ will stand for a sequence of variables $x_1, \ldots, x_n$, and $\overline{c}$ for a sequence of constants $c_1, \ldots, c_n$.

Theories. Theories can be defined by specifying a set of axioms, or by specifying a class of structures (the models of the theory). If F and G are formulae we write $F \models G$ (resp. $F \models_{\mathcal{T}} G$ – also written as $\mathcal{T} \cup F \models G$) to express the fact that every model of F (resp. every model of F which is also a model of $\mathcal{T}$) is a model of G. We denote "falsum" with $\bot$. $F \models \bot$ means that F is unsatisfiable; $F \models_{\mathcal{T}} \bot$ means that there is no model of $\mathcal{T}$ in which F is true.

A theory $\mathcal{T}$ over a signature Π *allows quantifier elimination* (QE) if for every formula ϕ over Π there exists a quantifier-free formula ϕ^* over Π which is equivalent to ϕ modulo $\mathcal{T}$. Examples of theories which allow quantifier elimination are rational and real linear arithmetic ($\mathsf{LI}(\mathbb{Q})$, $\mathsf{LI}(\mathbb{R})$), the theory of real closed fields, and the theory of absolutely-free data structures.

Sometimes, in order to define more complex theories we can consider theory extensions and combinations thereof. Let $\Pi_0 = (\Sigma_0, \mathsf{Pred})$ be a signature, and $\mathcal{T}_0$ be a "base" theory with signature Π_0. We consider extensions $\mathcal{T} := \mathcal{T}_0 \cup \mathcal{K}$ of $\mathcal{T}_0$ with new function symbols Σ (*extension functions*) whose properties are axiomatized using a set $\mathcal{K}$ of (universally closed) clauses in the extended signature $\Pi = (\Sigma_0 \cup \Sigma, \mathsf{Pred})$, such that each clause in $\mathcal{K}$ contains function symbols in Σ. Especially well-behaved are the Ψ-*local theory extensions*, i.e. theory extensions $\mathcal{T}_0 \subseteq \mathcal{T}_0 \cup \mathcal{K}$ as defined above, in which checking ground satisfiability can be done using a finite instantiation scheme described by a suitable closure operator Ψ, without loss of completeness. We express this with the following condition:

(Loc_f^Ψ) For every finite set G of ground Π^C-clauses (for an additional set C of constants) it holds that $\mathcal{T}_0 \cup \mathcal{K} \cup G \models \perp$ if and only if $\mathcal{T}_0 \cup \mathcal{K}[\Psi_\mathcal{K}(G)] \cup G$ is unsatisfiable.

where, for every set G of ground Π^C-clauses, $\mathcal{K}[\Psi_\mathcal{K}(G)]$ is the set of instances of $\mathcal{K}$ in which the terms starting with a function symbol in Σ are in $\Psi_\mathcal{K}(G) = \Psi(\mathsf{est}(\mathcal{K}, G))$, where $\mathsf{est}(\mathcal{K}, G)$ is the set of ground terms starting with a function in Σ occurring in G or $\mathcal{K}$. Ψ-local extensions can be recognized by showing that certain partial models embed into total ones [29,38]. Especially well-behaved are theory extensions with the property (Comp_f^Ψ) which requires that every partial model of $\mathcal{T}$ whose reduct to Π_0 is total and the "set of defined terms" is finite and closed under Ψ embeds into a total model of $\mathcal{T}$ *with the same support* (cf. [27,29]). If Ψ is the identity, we denote Loc_f^Ψ by Loc_f and Comp_f^Ψ by Comp_f.

Theorem 1 [27]. *The following theory extensions have property* (Comp_f), *so are local: (i) The extension of a theory $\mathcal{T}_0$ with uninterpreted function symbols. (ii) The extension of a theory $\mathcal{T}_0$ (containing a predicate $\leq$ which is reflexive) with a function f satisfying the axioms $\mathcal{K} = \{\forall \overline{x}\ \phi_i(\overline{x}) \rightarrow L_i(\overline{x}) \mid i = 1, \ldots, n\}$ where ϕ_i are Π_0-formulae with $\phi_i(\overline{x}) \wedge \phi_j(\overline{x}) \models \perp$ if $i \neq j$ (n can be 1 and ϕ_1 can be $\top$), and $L_i(\overline{x})$ has the form (1) $s_i \leq f(\overline{x})$ or (2) $f(\overline{x}) \leq t_i$ or (3) $s_i \leq f(\overline{x}) \leq t_i$, where s_i, t_i are Π_0-terms and in case (3) $\phi_i \models_{\mathcal{T}_0} s_i \leq t_i$.*

Theorem 2 [38]. *Let $\mathcal{K}$ be a set of clauses. Assume that $\mathcal{T}_0 \subseteq \mathcal{T}_1 = \mathcal{T}_0 \cup \mathcal{K}$ is a Ψ-local theory extension. For any finite set G of ground Π^C-clauses, let $\mathcal{K}_0 \cup G_0 \cup \mathsf{Def}$ be obtained from $\mathcal{K}[\Psi_\mathcal{K}(G)] \cup G$ by introducing, in a bottom-up manner, new constants $c_t \in C$ for subterms $t = f(c_1, \ldots, c_n)$ where $f \in \Sigma$ and c_i are constants, together with definitions $c_t = f(c_1, \ldots, c_n)$ (included in Def) and replacing the corresponding terms t with the constants c_t in $\mathcal{K}$ and G. Then $\mathcal{T}_1 \cup G \models \perp$ if and only if $\mathcal{T}_0 \cup \mathcal{K}_0 \cup G_0 \cup \mathsf{Con}_0 \models \perp$, where $\mathsf{Con}_0 = \{ \bigwedge_{i=1}^{n} c_i \approx d_i \rightarrow c \approx d \mid \begin{smallmatrix} f(c_1, \ldots, c_n) \approx c \in \mathsf{Def} \\ f(d_1, \ldots, d_n) \approx d \in \mathsf{Def} \end{smallmatrix} \}$.*

Algorithm 1. Symbol elimination in theory extensions [39][40]

Input: Theory extension $\mathcal{T}_0 \cup \mathcal{K}$ with signature $\Pi = \Pi_0 \cup \Sigma_1$, where $\Sigma_1 = \Sigma \cup \Sigma_{\mathsf{par}}$
where Σ_{par} is a set of parameters
G: set of ground Π^C-clauses; T: set of ground Π^C-terms with $\Psi_{\mathcal{K}}(G) \subseteq T$
Output: $\forall \overline{y} \Gamma_T(\overline{y})$ (universal $\Pi_0 \cup \Sigma_{\mathsf{par}}$-formula)

Step 1 Purify $\mathcal{K}[T] \cup G$ as described in Theorem 2 (with set of extension symbols Σ_1).
Let $\mathcal{K}_0 \cup G_0 \cup \mathsf{Con}_0$ be the set of Π_0^C-clauses obtained this way.

Step 2 Let $G_1 = \mathcal{K}_0 \cup G_0 \cup \mathsf{Con}_0$. Among the constants in G_1, we identify
  (i) the constants c_f, $f \in \Sigma_{\mathsf{par}}$, where c_f is a constant parameter or c_f is introduced
  by a definition $c_f \approx f(c_1, \ldots, c_k)$ in the hierarchical reasoning method,
  (ii) all constants $\overline{c}_p$ occurring as arguments of functions in Σ_{par} in such definitions.
Replace all the other constants $\overline{c}$ with existentially quantified variables $\overline{x}$ (i.e.
replace $G_1(\overline{c}_p, \overline{c}_f, \overline{c})$ with $\exists \overline{x} G_1(\overline{c}_p, \overline{c}_f, \overline{x})$).

Step 3 Construct a formula $\Gamma_1(\overline{c}_p, \overline{c}_f)$ equivalent to $\exists \overline{x} G_1(\overline{c}_p, \overline{c}_f, \overline{x})$ w.r.t. $\mathcal{T}_0$ using a
method for quantifier elimination in $\mathcal{T}_0$.

Step 4 Replace each constant c_f introduced by definition $c_f = f(c_1, \ldots, c_k)$ with
the term $f(c_1, \ldots, c_k)$ in $\Gamma_1(\overline{c}_p, \overline{c}_f)$. Let $\Gamma_2(\overline{c}_p)$ be the formula obtained this way.
Replace $\overline{c}_p$ with existentially quantified variables $\overline{y}$.

Step 5 Let $\forall \overline{y} \Gamma_T(\overline{y})$ be $\forall \overline{y} \neg \Gamma_2(\overline{y})$.

Property-Directed Symbol Elimination. In [40] we proposed a method for property-directed symbol elimination described in Algorithm 1. We present a slight generalization (the proof is similar to the proof in [40]; it is presented in detail in the extended version of this paper [36]).

Theorem 3 [39,40]. *Let $\mathcal{T}_0$ be a Π_0-theory allowing quantifier elimination[1], Σ_{par} be a set of parameters (function and constant symbols) and $\Pi = (S, \Sigma, \mathsf{Pred})$ be such that $\Sigma \cap (\Sigma_0 \cup \Sigma_{\mathsf{par}}) = \emptyset$. Let $\mathcal{K}$ be a set of clauses in the signature $\Pi_0 \cup \Sigma_{\mathsf{par}} \cup \Sigma$ in which all variables occur also below functions in $\Sigma_1 = \Sigma_{\mathsf{par}} \cup \Sigma$. Assume $\mathcal{T} \subseteq \mathcal{T}_0 \cup \mathcal{K}$ satisfies condition (Comp_f^{Ψ}) for a suitable closure operator Ψ with $\mathsf{est}(G) \subseteq \Psi_{\mathcal{K}}(G)$ for every set G of ground Π^C-clauses. Then, for $T = \Psi_{\mathcal{K}}(G)$, Algorithm 1 yields a universal $\Pi_0 \cup \Sigma_{\mathsf{par}}$-formula $\forall \overline{x} \Gamma_T(\overline{x})$ such that $\mathcal{T}_0 \cup \forall \overline{x} \Gamma_T(\overline{x}) \cup \mathcal{K} \cup G \models \bot$ which is entailed by every universal formula Γ with $\mathcal{T}_0 \cup \Gamma \cup \mathcal{K} \cup G \models \bot$.*

2.1   Locality of Theories of Distances

The theories related to wireless networks used in Sect. 1.1 refer to cost or distance functions. Axiomatizations for such functions define local theory extensions.

---

[1] If $\mathcal{T}_0$ does not allow QE but has a model completion $\mathcal{T}_0^*$ which does, and if we use QE in $\mathcal{T}_0^*$ in Alg. 1, $\mathcal{T}_0 \wedge \forall \overline{x} \Gamma_T(\overline{x}) \cup G \models \bot$, but $\forall \overline{x} \Gamma_T(\overline{x})$ might not the weakest universal formula Γ with the property that $\mathcal{T}_0 \cup \Gamma \cup \mathcal{K} \models \bot$.

Theorem 4. *Let T_0 be the disjoint combination of the theory $\mathcal{E}$ of pure equality (sort p) and linear real arithmetic (sort num). The following extensions of T_0 with a function d (sort $p \times p \to$ num) are Ψ-local for a suitable closure operator Ψ:*

(1) $T_d^m = T_0 \cup \mathcal{K}_m$, where $\mathcal{K}_m$ are axioms of a metric, is Ψ_m-local, where $\Psi_m(T) = T \cup \{d(a,b) \mid a, b \text{ constants of sort } p \text{ occurring in } T\}$.

(2) $T_d^n = T_0 \cup \mathcal{K}_n$, where $\mathcal{K}_n$ contains all axioms of a metric except for the triangle inequality, is Ψ_n-local, where $\Psi_n(T) = T \cup \{d(b,a) \mid d(a,b) \in T\} \cup \{d(a,a) \mid a \text{ constant of sort } p \text{ occurring in } T\}$.

(3) T_d^u, the extension of T_0 with an uninterpreted function d, and $T_d^p = T_0 \cup \mathcal{K}_p$, where $\mathcal{K}_p = \forall x, y \; d(x,y) \geq 0$, are Ψ-local, where $\Psi(T) = T$.

Proof: For proving locality, it is sufficient to prove that the theory extensions satisfy condition Comp_f^{Ψ}, where Ψ is the corresponding closure operator. Due to the form of the closure operators, the non-linearity of the symmetry axiom or of the triangle inequality is not problematic for guaranteeing Ψ-locality. A detailed proof is given in the extended version of this paper [36]. □

3   Second-Order Quantifier Elimination

Let $\mathcal{T}$ be a theory with signature $\Pi = (S, \Sigma, \mathsf{Pred})$ and $P_1, \ldots, P_n, Q_1, \ldots, Q_m$ be predicate symbols which are not in Pred. Let $\Pi' = (S, \Sigma, \mathsf{Pred} \cup \{P_1, \ldots, P_n\})$ and $\Pi'' = (S, \Sigma, \mathsf{Pred} \cup \{Q_1, \ldots, Q_m\})$; F be a Π'-formula and G a Π''-formula.

A Π-structure $\mathcal{A}$ is a model of $\exists P_1 \ldots P_n \; F$ (notation: $\mathcal{A} \models \exists P_1 \ldots P_n \; F$) if there exists a Π'-structure $\mathcal{B}$ such that $\mathcal{B} \models F$ and $\mathcal{B}_{|\Pi} = \mathcal{A}$.

We say that $\exists P_1 \ldots P_n \; F$ entails $\exists Q_1 \ldots Q_m \; G$ w.r.t. $\mathcal{T}$ (and use the notation: $\exists P_1 \ldots P_n \; F \models_{\mathcal{T}} \exists Q_1 \ldots Q_m \; G$) iff for every Π-structure $\mathcal{A}$ which is a model of $\mathcal{T}$, if $\mathcal{A} \models \exists P_1 \ldots P_n \; F$ then $\mathcal{A} \models \exists Q_1 \ldots Q_m \; G$.

If there exists a first-order formula F_0 over the signature Π such that for every model $\mathcal{A}$ of $\mathcal{T}$, $\mathcal{A} \models F_0$ iff $\mathcal{A} \models \exists P_1 \ldots P_n \; F$, we say that F_0 and $\exists P_1 \ldots P_n \; F$ are equivalent w.r.t. $\mathcal{T}$ (and write $F_0 \equiv_{\mathcal{T}} \exists P_1 \ldots P_n \; F$).

We consider here only the elimination of one predicate; for formulae of the form $\exists P_1 \ldots P_n \; F$ the process can be iterated. Let $\mathcal{T}$ be a theory with signature $\Pi = (S, \Sigma, \mathsf{Pred})$ and let $\Pi' = (S, \Sigma, \mathsf{Pred} \cup \{P\})$, where $P \notin \mathsf{Pred}$.

Let F be a universal first-order Π'-formula. Our goal is to compute, if possible, a first-order Π-formula G such that $G \equiv_{\mathcal{T}} \exists P \; F$. We adapt the hierarchical superposition calculus proposed in [8,9] to this case.

We consider theories $\mathcal{T}$ over many-sorted signatures $\Pi = (S, \Sigma, \mathsf{Pred})$, where the set of sorts $S = S_i \cup S_u$, consists of a set S_i of interpreted sorts and a set S_u of uninterpreted sorts. The models of the theories are Π-structures $\mathcal{A} = (\{A_s\}_{s \in S}, \{f_{\mathcal{A}}\}_{f \in \Sigma}, \{p_{\mathcal{A}}\}_{p \in \mathsf{Pred}})$, where each support of interpreted sort is considered to be fixed. Following the terminology used in [8,9], we will refer to elements in the fixed domain of sort $s \in S_i$ as *domain elements of sort s*.

Let F be a universal first-order formula over signature $\Pi' = (S, \Sigma, \mathsf{Pred} \cup \{P\})$. We can assume, without loss of generality, that F is a set of clauses of the form $\forall \overline{x} \, D(\overline{x}) \vee C(\overline{x})$, where $D(\overline{x})$ is a clause over the signature Π and $C(\overline{x})$ is a clause containing literals of the form $(\neg)P(x_1, \ldots, x_n)$, where $x_1, \ldots, x_n$ are variables[2]. Such clauses can also be represented as *constrained clauses* in the form $\forall \overline{x} \, \phi(\overline{x}) \, || \, C(\overline{x})$, where $\phi(\overline{x}) := \neg D(\overline{x})$. We will refer to clauses of this form as constrained P-clauses.

Let $\succ$ be a strict, well-founded ordering on terms that is compatible with contexts and stable under substitutions. As in [9] we assume that $\succ$ has the following properties[3]: (i) $\succ$ is total on ground terms, (ii) $t \succ d$ for every domain element d of interpreted sort s and every ground term t that is not a domain element. Let $HRes_\succ^P$ be the calculus containing the following ordered resolution and factorization rules for constrained P-clauses:

$$\frac{\phi_1 \, || \, P(\overline{x}) \vee C \qquad \phi_2 \, || \, \neg P(\overline{y}) \vee D}{(\phi_1 \wedge \phi_2)\sigma \, || \, (C \vee D)\sigma} \qquad\qquad \frac{\phi \, || \, P(\overline{x}) \vee P(\overline{y}) \vee C}{\phi\sigma \, || \, (P(\overline{x}) \vee C)\sigma}$$

where (i) $\sigma = \mathsf{mgu}(P(\overline{x}), P(\overline{y}))$ \qquad (i) $\sigma = \mathsf{mgu}(P(\overline{x}), P(\overline{y}))$
(ii) $P(\overline{x})\sigma$ is strictly maximal in $(P(\overline{x}) \vee C)\sigma$ \quad (ii) $P(\overline{x})\sigma$ is maximal in
(iii) $\neg P(\overline{y})\sigma$ is maximal in $(\neg P(\overline{y}) \vee D)\sigma$. \qquad $(P(\overline{x}) \vee C)\sigma$

Redundancy. The inference rules are supplemented by a redundancy criterion $\mathcal{R} = (\mathcal{R}_c, \mathcal{R}_i)$ meant to specify a set $\mathcal{R}_c$ of redundant clauses (which can be removed) and a set $\mathcal{R}_i$ of redundant inferences (which do not need to be computed). We say that a set of clauses N^* is saturated up to $\mathcal{R}$-redundancy w.r.t. $HRes_\succ^P$ if every $HRes_\succ^P$ inference with premises in N^* is redundant (i.e. in $\mathcal{R}_i$).

The following notion of redundancy $\mathcal{R}_c^0$ for clauses is often used: A (constrained) clause is redundant w.r.t. a set N of clauses if all its ground instances are entailed w.r.t. $\mathcal{T}$ by ground instances of clauses in N which are strictly smaller w.r.t. $\succ$. We will use the following notion of redundancy for inferences: If $\mathcal{R}_c$ is a redundancy criterion for clauses, we say that an inference ι on ground clauses is redundant w.r.t. N if either one of its premises is redundant w.r.t. N and $\mathcal{R}_c$ or, if C_0 is the conclusion of ι then there exist clauses $C_1, \ldots, C_n \in N$ that are smaller w.r.t. $\succ$ than the maximal premise of ι and $C_1, \ldots, C_n \models C_0$. A non-ground inference is redundant if all its ground instances are redundant.

Example 1 (Semantic $\mathcal{T}$-entailment; redundancy criterion $\mathcal{R}_\mathcal{T}$). A constrained P-clause $\forall \overline{x} \, (\phi(\overline{x}) \, || \, C(\overline{x}))$ is $\mathcal{T}$-*semantically entailed* by $\forall \overline{x} \, (\psi(\overline{x}) \, || \, D(\overline{x}))$ if (i) $C = D$, (ii) $\mathcal{T} \models \forall \overline{x} \, \phi(\overline{x}) \rightarrow \psi(\overline{x})$ and (iii) $\neg\phi(\overline{x})\sigma \succ \neg\psi(\overline{x})\sigma$ for every ground substitution σ. We say that a clause C is $\mathcal{R}_\mathcal{T}$-*redundant w.r.t. a set N of clauses* if it is $\mathcal{T}$-semantically entailed by a clause in N. (If $C_1 = (\phi(\overline{x}) || C(\overline{x}))$ is $\mathcal{T}$-semantically entailed by $C_2 = (\psi(\overline{x}) || D(\overline{x}))$

---

[2] We can bring the clauses to this form using variable abstraction.

[3] These conditions are satisfied by an LPO with an operator precedence in which the predicate symbol P (which can be regarded as function symbol with output sort bool) is larger than the other operators and domain elements are minimal w.r.t. $\succ$ which is supposed to be well-founded on the domain elements.

then $C_1\sigma \succ C_2\sigma$ and $C_2\sigma \models_\mathcal{T} C_1\sigma$ for every ground substitution σ, so $\mathcal{R}_\mathcal{T}$-redundant clauses are $\mathcal{R}_c^0$-redundant.) We call the notion of redundancy induced on inferences also $\mathcal{R}_\mathcal{T}$-redundancy. ∎

Let $\mathcal{R} = (\mathcal{R}_c, \mathcal{R}_i)$ be a redundancy criterion with $\mathcal{R}_c \subseteq \mathcal{R}_c^0$.

Theorem 5. *Let N be a set of constrained P-clauses over background theory $\mathcal{T}$, N^* its saturation (up to $\mathcal{R}$-redundancy) under $HRes^P_\succ$, and N_0^* the set of clauses in N^* not containing P. For every model $\mathcal{A}$ of $\mathcal{T}$ the following are equivalent:*

(1) $\mathcal{A}$ is a model of N_0^*.
(2) There exists a Π'-structure $\mathcal{B}$ with $\mathcal{B} \models N$ and $\mathcal{B}_{|\Pi} = \mathcal{A}$.

Proof: Note that for constrained P-clauses the hierarchical superposition calculus specializes to $HRes^P_\succ$: With the terminology used in [5,8,9], the background signature is Π; the only foreground symbol is P. Since there are no "background"-sorted terms starting with a "foreground" function symbol and no foreground terms, sets of P-clauses are sufficiently complete and all substitutions are simple.
$(2) \Rightarrow (1)$ follows from the soundness of the hierarchical superposition calculus.
$(1) \Rightarrow (2)$ is proved with a model construction similar to the one used for proving completeness of hierarchical superposition. For details cf. [36]. □

Case 1: Saturation is Finite. If the saturation N^* of N under $HRes^P_\succ$ (up to $\mathcal{R}$-redundancy) is finite and N_0^* is the set of clauses in N^* not containing P then, by Theorem 5, the universal closure of the conjunction of the clauses in N_0^* is equivalent to $\exists P\ N$.

Example 2. Consider a class of graphs described by the following set N of constrained E-clauses:

$$\{(1)\pi^i(u,v)||E(u,v),\quad (2)\pi^t(u,w,v)||E(u,v) \to E(u,w),\quad (3)\pi^e(u,v)||\neg E(u,v)\}$$

For arbitrary predicates π^i, π^e and π^t we can generate with $HRes^E_\succ$ an infinite set of clauses including, e.g., all clauses of the form:

$(4_n)\ \pi^i(u,v) \wedge \pi^t(u,w_1,v) \wedge \pi^t(u,w_2,w_1) \wedge \cdots \wedge \pi^t(u,w_n,w_{n-1})\ ||\ E(u,w_n)$

If we assume that π^i, π^e, π^t satisfy the additional axioms defining a theory $\mathcal{T}_\pi$:

(c1) $\forall u,v,w$ $\pi^i(u,v) \wedge \pi^t(u,w,v) \to \pi^i(u,w)$
(c2) $\forall u,v,w$ $\pi^e(u,w) \wedge \pi^t(u,w,v) \to \pi^e(u,v)$
(c3) $\forall u,v,w,x$ $\pi^t(u,w,v) \wedge \pi^t(u,x,w) \to \pi^t(u,x,v)$

then all inferences by resolution between clauses (1) and (2), (2) and (3) are $\mathcal{T}_\pi$-redundant. The inferences between (2) and (2) are also $\mathcal{T}_\pi$-redundant: Consider a ground instance of such an inference (the maximal literals are underlined):

$$\frac{\pi^t(c_1,c_2,c_3)||\underline{E(c_1,c_3)} \to E(c_1,c_2) \quad \pi^t(c_1,c_3,c_4)||E(c_1,c_4) \to \underline{E(c_1,c_3)}}{\pi^t(c_1,c_2,c_3), \pi^t(c_1,c_3,c_4)||E(c_1,c_4) \to E(c_1,c_2)}$$

The ground instance C of (2) $\pi^t(c_1, c_2, c_4) \| E(c_1, c_4) \rightarrow E(c_1, c_2)$ differs from the conclusion of the inference above only in the background part and is smaller than the first premise of the inference. If $(c3)$ holds then C entails the conclusion of the inference above, which makes the inference redundant w.r.t. $\mathcal{T}_\pi$.

Thus, only the inference of clauses (1) and (3) yields a non-redundant resolvent:

(4) $\pi^i(u, v) \wedge \pi^e(u, v) \| \perp$

so $N^* = N \cup \{(4)\}$ is saturated up to $\mathcal{T}_\pi$-redundancy. By Theorem 5, N is satisfiable iff $\forall u, v(\pi^i(u, v) \wedge \pi^e(u, v) \rightarrow \perp)$ is satisfiable w.r.t. $\mathcal{T}_\pi$.   ∎

When modelling concrete situations, the predicates π^i, π^e and π^t might not be arbitrary, but might have definitions using other symbols with given properties.

Example 3. The theory $\mathcal{T}_\pi$ might be actually described in a detailed way. Let $\mathsf{C}(r_1, r_2)$ be a graph class described by the set N of axioms in Example 2, where π^i, π^e, π^t are defined by the axioms:

$$\mathsf{Def}_\pi(r_1, r_2) = \{\; \forall u, v\; \pi^i(u, v) \leftrightarrow u \neq v \wedge d(u, v) \leq r_1(u),$$
$$\forall u, v\; \pi^e(u, v) \leftrightarrow d(u, v) > r_2(u),$$
$$\forall u, v, w\; \pi^t(u, w, v) \leftrightarrow u \neq w \wedge d(u, w) \leq d(u, v)\},$$

where d is a distance or cost function. We can regard the theory extension $\mathcal{T} \subseteq \mathcal{T}_\pi = \mathcal{T} \cup UIF_{\{r_1, r_2\}} \cup \mathsf{Def}_\pi$, where $\mathcal{T}$ is one of the theories $\mathcal{T}_d^u, \mathcal{T}_d^p, \mathcal{T}_d^n$ or $\mathcal{T}_d^m$ introduced in Theorem 4 and $UIF_{\{r_1, r_2\}}$ indicates that r_1, r_2 are regarded as uninterpreted function symbols, so $\mathcal{T} \cup UIF_{\{r_1, r_2\}}$ can be represented as a local extension of the disjoint combination of a theory of real numbers and of pure equality. We can use the hierarchical reduction in Theorem 2 to check that $(c1), (c2)$ and $(c3)$ are valid w.r.t. $\mathcal{T}$.   ∎

In applications we might not be interested in checking the satisfiability of N or the satisfiability of $\forall u, v(\pi^i(u, v) \wedge \pi^e(u, v) \rightarrow \perp)$ w.r.t. $\mathcal{T}_\pi$, but in a *specific model* $\mathcal{A}$ satisfying $\mathcal{T}_\pi$ (we refer to it as "canonical model").

This is the case, for instance, in the applications in wireless network theory analyzed in Sect. 1.1: The vertices of the graphs considered in this context are very often points in the Euclidean space, and the distance is a concrete function which can be, for instance, the Euclidean metric, or a concrete cost function which might satisfy additional properties (for instance positivity or symmetry). If we want to analyze such graph classes in full generality, we might assume that the properties of some of the functions are not fully specified.

Let $\mathcal{A}$ be a model of a theory $\mathcal{T}$ describing properties of function symbols in a set Σ we want to model. We assume that Σ contains a set of "parameters" Σ_{par} (function symbols whose properties are "underspecified" in $\mathcal{T}$). If we are given a set N of constrained clauses, we might be interested in obtaining (weakest) universal conditions Γ on Σ_{par} such that for *every* fixed model $\mathcal{A}$ of $\mathcal{T}$ which also satisfies Γ, there exists an interpretation for P in $\mathcal{A}$ for which N is satisfied, i.e. $\mathcal{A} \models \exists P\, N$. We present a situation in which this is possible.

Theorem 6. *Let $\mathcal{T}$ be a theory with signature $\Pi = (S, \Sigma, \mathsf{Pred})$, N a set of constrained P-clauses. Assume that the saturation N^* of N up to $\mathcal{T}$-redundancy w.r.t. $\mathsf{HRes}^P_{\succeq}$ is finite; let N^*_0 be the set of clauses in N^* not containing P.*
    Let $\Sigma_{\mathsf{par}} \subseteq \Sigma$ be a set of parameters. If (i) $\mathcal{T}$ allows quantifier elimination or (ii) $\mathcal{T}_0 \subseteq \mathcal{T} = \mathcal{T}_0 \cup \mathcal{K}$ is a local theory extension satisfying condition (Comp^{ψ}_f) and $\mathcal{T}_0$ allows quantifier elimination, then we can use Algorithm 1 to obtain a (weakest) universal constraint Γ on the parameters such that every model $\mathcal{A}$ of $\mathcal{T} \cup \Gamma$ is a model of (the universal closure of) N^*_0, hence $\mathcal{A} \models \exists P\ N$.

Proof: Follows from Theorem 5 and Theorem 3. A proof is given in [36]. □

Example 4. Consider again the situation described in Example 3. We show how one can use Theorem 3 and Algorithm 1 to derive constraints Γ on the parameters r_1, r_2 under which for every model $\mathcal{A}$ of $\mathcal{T}^u_d \cup UIF_{\{r_1, r_2\}} \cup \Gamma$

$$\pi^i(u, v) \wedge \pi^e(u, v) = (u \neq v \wedge d(u, v) \leq r_1(u)) \wedge (d(u, v) > r_2(u))$$

is unsatisfiable in $\mathcal{A}$ (we consider the case in which d is an uninterpreted function; other axioms for d can be analyzed as well). The formula above is unsatisfiable in any model $\mathcal{A}$ of $\mathcal{T}^u_d \cup UIF_{\{r_1, r_2\}}$ whose support of sort p has cardinality 1. If we only consider models $\mathcal{A}$ with $|A_p| \geq 2$ then we can proceed as follows:

Step 1: We purify the formula by introducing new constants: $c_d := d(u, v), c_1 = r_1(u), c_2 = r_2(u)$ and obtain: $(u \neq v \wedge c_d \leq c_1 \wedge c_d > c_2)$.

Step 2: We quantify existentially all constants not denoting terms starting with $-$ or used as arguments of $- r_1, r_2$ and obtain: $\exists v, \exists c_d (u \neq v \wedge c_d \leq c_1 \wedge c_d > c_2)$.

Step 3: After quantifier elimination in a combination of $\mathsf{LI}(\mathbb{R})$ and the theory of equality with models with ≥ 2 elements [37] we obtain $\Gamma_1(c_1, c_2, u) : c_2 < c_1$.[4]

Step 4: We replace the constants c_1, c_2 with the terms they denote and quantify the arguments existentially and obtain: $\exists u(r_2(u) < r_1(u))$.

Step 5: We negate this condition and obtain: $\forall u(r_1(u) \leq r_2(u))$. ∎

Example 5. We find an axiomatization for the graph class $\mathbf{C}^- = \{G^- \mid G \in \mathbf{C}\}$, when class $\mathbf{C}$ is described by the set N of constrained clauses in Example 2 and π^i, π^e and π^t satisfy conditions $(c1), (c2), (c3)$. Let $N^* = N \cup \{(4)\}$ be obtained by saturating N under $\mathsf{HRes}^E_{\succeq}$ up to redundancy. A graph $H = (V, F) \in \mathbf{C}^-$ iff there exists a graph $G = (V, E) \in \mathbf{C}$ such that $H = G^-$. This condition can be described by $M = N^* \cup \mathsf{Tr}(E, F)$, where $\mathsf{Tr}(E, F) = \{\forall x, y\ (F(x, y) \leftrightarrow E(x, y) \wedge E(y, x))\}$, which can be written in the form of constrained clauses as:

$$\mathsf{Tr}(E, F) = \{F(x, y)\|E(x, y),\ F(x, y)\|E(y, x),\ \neg F(x, y)\|\neg E(x, y) \vee \neg E(y, x)\}$$

The base theory is $\mathcal{T} \cup UIF_F$, the extension of $\mathcal{T}$ with the uninterpreted symbol F, with signature $\Pi_F = (\Sigma, \mathsf{Pred} \cup \{F\})$. We can saturate M under

---

[4] We can consider only models $\mathcal{A}$ whose support of sort p is infinite. The theory that formalizes this is the model completion of the theory $\mathcal{E}$ of pure equality which allows quantifier elimination. We can then use the method for quantifier elimination in combinations of theories with QE described in [37].

$HRes_{\succ}^{E}$ up to redundancy (we used SCAN [19] cf. also Sect. 5 and [36]). The set of clauses not containing E in M^* is $N^* \cup N_F^-$, where

$$N_F^- = \{ \ F(x,y) \to F(y,x), \quad F(y,x) \wedge \pi^e(x,y) \to \bot, \quad F(x,y) \wedge \pi^e(x,y) \to \bot,$$
$$\pi^i(x,y) \wedge \pi^i(y,x) \to F(y,x), \quad \pi^i(x,y) \wedge \pi^t(y,x,z) \wedge F(y,z) \to F(x,y),$$
$$\pi^t(x,y,z) \wedge F(x,z) \wedge \pi^t(y,x,u) \wedge F(y,u) \to F(y,x)\}.$$

The universal closure G of the conjunction of these clauses is equivalent w.r.t. $\mathcal{T} \cup UIF_F$ to the formula $\exists E(N^* \cup \mathrm{Tr}(E,F))$, and thus axiomatizes $\mathbf{C}^-$.   ∎

Case 2: Finite Representation of Possibly Infinite Saturated Sets. The saturation of a set N of constrained P-clauses up to redundancy under $HRes_{\succ}^{P}$ might be infinite. We here consider a very special case under which a finite set of constrained P-clauses $N = \{\phi_i(\overline{x}) \ || \ C_i(\overline{x}) \mid i = 1, \ldots, n\}$ can have a saturation that can be finitely described: The situation in which the set of clauses $\{C_1, \ldots, C_n\}$ can be finitely saturated under ordered resolution.

Theorem 7. *Let $N = \{\phi_i(\overline{x})||C_i(\overline{x}) \mid i = 1, \ldots, n\}$ be a finite set of constrained P-clauses and $N_P = \{C_1, \ldots, C_n\}$. Assume that the saturation of N_P under ordered resolution is finite, $N_P^* = \{C_1, \ldots, C_n, C_{n+1}, \ldots, C_{n+k}\}$, and the set $\mathcal{I}_P$ of all possible inferences used for deriving these clauses is finite and can be effectively described. If $\bot \notin N_P^*$, then $\exists P \ N \equiv_{\mathcal{T}} \top$. Assume now that $\bot \in N_P^*$. Let $\mathcal{A}$ be a model of $\mathcal{T}$, $\mathcal{T}_A$ the theory with $\mathcal{A}$ as canonical model (i.e. $\mathcal{T}_A = Th(\mathcal{A})$). Let N_A be the set of all instances of N in which the variables are replaced with elements in $\mathcal{A}$ (seen as constants). Then:*

(1) The saturation N_A^* of N_A up to $\mathcal{R}_{\mathcal{T}}$-redundancy can be described as $N_A^* = \{\mu_i^{\mathcal{A}}(\overline{a}) \ || \ C_i(\overline{a}) \mid i = 1, \ldots, n+k, \overline{a} \text{ elements of } \mathcal{A}\}$, where $(\mu_i^{\mathcal{A}})_{i=1,n+k}$ are given by the minimal model of the constrained Horn clauses CH_N w.r.t. $\mathcal{T}_A$:

$$CH_N = \{ \ \phi_i(\overline{x}) \to \mu_i(\overline{x}) \mid i \in \{1, \ldots, n\}\}$$
$$\cup\{ \ (\mu_i(\overline{x}) \wedge \mu_j(\overline{y}))\sigma \to \mu_k(\overline{z}) \mid C_k(\overline{z}) \text{ is obtained by a resolution}$$
$$\text{inference in } \mathcal{I}_P \text{ from } C_i(\overline{x}) \text{ and } C_j(\overline{y}) \text{ with m.g.u. } \sigma\}$$
$$\cup\{ \ \mu_i(\overline{x})\sigma \to \mu_k(\overline{z}) \mid C_k(\overline{z}) \text{ is obtained by a factorization inference}$$
$$\text{in } \mathcal{I}_P \text{ from } C_i(\overline{x}) \text{ with m.g.u. } \sigma\}.$$

(2) Let $\mathcal{A}^\mu$ be the extension of $\mathcal{A}$ with predicates $(\mu_i)_i$ whose interpretation is given by $(\mu_i^{\mathcal{A}})_i$. Let j be such that $\bot = C_j$. Then $\mathcal{A} \models \exists P \ N$ iff $CH_N \cup \{\neg\mu_j(\overline{x})\}$ is satisfiable w.r.t. $\mathcal{T}_A$.

Proof: (Idea): (1) follows from the fact that the computation of the minimal model of CH_N using a canonical model construction (cf. e.g. [12]) parallels the saturation process for the ground instances of the clauses in N_A^*.

(2) follows from (1) and the fact $\mathcal{A} \models \exists P \ N$ iff $\mathcal{A}$ is a model of the set N_0^* of clauses in N^* not containing P iff $\mathcal{A}^\mu \models \forall \overline{x} \neg \mu_j(\overline{x})$ iff $\mathcal{A}^\mu \models CH_N \cup \{\neg\mu_j(\overline{x})\}$. To check this, it is sufficient to check whether $CH_N \cup \{\neg\mu_j^{\mathcal{A}}(\overline{x})\}$ is satisfiable w.r.t. $\mathcal{T}_A$. For a detailed proof cf. [36].   □

If T has only one (canonical) model and is supported by μZ [22], we can use μZ for checking whether N is satisfiable[5].

Example 6. Consider the set N consisting of the following constrained P-clauses:

(1) $x = y||P(x,y)$,   (2) $y = x + 1||P(y,z) \rightarrow P(x,z)$,   (3) $n(x,y)||\neg P(x,y)$

over the theory of integers without multiplication with model $\mathbb{Z}$. Saturating N without any simplification strategy yields the infinite set N^* consisting of:

$(1_k) \bigwedge_{i=1}^{k} x_i = x_{i-1}+1 \ || \ P(x_0, x_k)$
$\qquad\qquad (2_k) \bigwedge_{i=1}^{k} x_i = x_{i-1}+1 \ || \ P(x_k, z) \rightarrow P(x_0, z)$

$(3_k) \ n(x_0, y) \wedge \bigwedge_{i=1}^{k} x_i = x_{i-1}+1 \ || \ \neg P(x_k, y)$ $(4_k) \bigwedge_{i=1}^{k} x_i = x_{i-1}+1 \wedge n(x_0, x_k) \ || \ \bot, k \in \mathbb{N}$

(i) We first show how Theorem 7 can be used in this case. Let $N_P = \{C_1, C_2, C_3\}$, where $C_1 = P(x_1, y_1), C_2 = P(y_2, z_1) \rightarrow P(x_1, z_1)$, and $C_3 = \neg P(x_3, y_3)$. We can saturate N_P as follows: From C_1 and C_3 we can derive $C_4 = \bot$; from C_1 and C_2 we can derive a clause of type C_1, from C_2 and C_2 a clause of type C_2 and from C_2 and C_3 a clause of type C_3. We obtain $N_P^* = \{C_1, C_2, C_3, C_4\}$. By Theorem 7, the saturation of N is N^*:

$$\{\mu_1(x,y)||P(x,y), \ \mu_2(x,y,z)||P(y,z) \rightarrow P(x,z), \ \mu_3(x,y)||\neg P(x,y), \ \mu_4(x,y)|| \bot\},$$

where $\mu_1, \mu_2, \mu_3, \mu_4$ are given by the minimal model M of CH_N:

$$CH_N = \{x = y \rightarrow \mu_1(x,y), \quad y = x + 1 \rightarrow \mu_2(x,y,z), \quad n(x,y) \rightarrow \mu_3(x,y),$$
$$\mu_1(x,y) \wedge \mu_2(u,x,y) \rightarrow \mu_1(u,y), \quad \mu_3(x,y) \wedge \mu_2(x,u,y) \rightarrow \mu_3(u,y),$$
$$\mu_2(x,y,z) \wedge \mu_2(u,x,z) \rightarrow \mu_2(u,y,z), \quad \mu_1(x,y) \wedge \mu_3(x,y) \rightarrow \mu_4(x,y)\}$$

μZ cannot check whether this set of Horn constraints is satisfiable because of the parameter n. If we replace $n(x,y)$ with $x > y$ μZ yields the following solution:

$$\mu_1(x,y) = x \leq y, \ \mu_2(x,y,z) = (y > z) \vee (x < z), \ \mu_3(x,y) = x > y, \ \mu_4 = \bot.$$

(ii) Alternatively, note that if we use the fact that $\exists x_1 \ldots x_{k-1} \bigwedge_{i=1}^{k} x_i = x_{i-1}+1$ is equivalent to $x_k = x_0 + k$ we obtain an infinite set of clauses consisting of:

$(1'_k) \ y = x + k||P(x,y)$ $\qquad\qquad (2'_k) \ y = x + k||P(y,z) \rightarrow P(x,z)$
$(3'_k) \ n(x,y) \wedge z = x + k||\neg P(z,y)$ $(4'_k) \ y = u + k \wedge n(u,y)|| \bot$ $\qquad k \in \mathbb{N}$

If we regard k in each clause as a universally quantified variable (with additional condition $k \geq 0$) we obtain:

$$N' = \{ \ y = x + k \wedge k \geq 0||P(x,y), \ y = x + k \wedge k \geq 0||P(y,z),$$
$$n(x,y) \wedge z = x + k \wedge k \geq 0||\neg P(z,y), \ y = u + k \wedge k \geq 0 \wedge n(u,y)|| \bot\}.$$

If $\mathcal{A} = (\mathbb{Z}, n_A)$, $\mathcal{A} \models \exists_P N'$ iff $\mathcal{A} \models \forall u, y, k \ (k \geq 0 \wedge y = u + k \rightarrow \neg n(u,y))$.

---

[5] If the set N of constrained P-clauses (hence the set of constrained Horn clauses CH_N) contains at least one parameter then μZ often returns "unknown". In addition, if μZ can prove satisfiability of $CH_N \cup \{\neg \mu_j(\overline{x})\}$ for a non-parametric problem, the model it returns is not guaranteed to be minimal in general, and cannot be used for representing the saturated set of clauses. By Theorem 7 (2), satisfiability of $CH_N \cup \{\neg \mu_j(\overline{x})\}$ is sufficient for proving the satisfiability of N in this case.

Note that the interpretations of $(\mu_i)_{1 \le i \le 4}$ in the minimal model of CH_N w.r.t. the model $\mathcal{A} = (\mathbb{Z}, n_A)$, for a fixed interpretation of n (say as $n_A(x, y) = (x > y)$) are: $\mu_1(x, y) = \mu_2(x, y, z) = \exists k (k \ge 0 \wedge y = x + k)$, $\mu_3(x, y) = \exists z \exists k(n(z, y) \wedge x = z + k)$ and $\mu_4(x, y) = \mu_1(x, y) \wedge \mu_3(x, y)$. This shows the link to (i). ∎

Example 6(ii) uses acceleration techniques, in particular the following result:

Theorem 8 [14,18]. *Let N be a set of constrained clauses of the form:*

$$N = \{\phi_0(\overline{x}) \parallel R(\overline{x}), \quad \phi(\overline{x}) \wedge \overline{y} = M \cdot \overline{x} + \overline{v} \parallel R(\overline{x}) \to R(\overline{y})\}$$

where $\overline{x}, \overline{y}$ describe vectors of n variables, $\overline{v}$ a vector of n constants in $\mathbb{Z}$, ϕ_0 is a condition expressible in Presburger arithmetic and $M = (m_{i,j})_{1 \le i,j \le n}$ is a $n \times n$ matrix over $\mathbb{Z}$, and $\phi(x_1, \ldots, x_n) = \bigwedge_{i=1}^{k}(\sum_{j=1}^{n} a_{ij}x_j \le b_i)$, where $a_{ij}, b_i \in \mathbb{Z}$.

The interpretation of R in the minimal model of N is Presburger definable if $\langle M \rangle = \{M^n \mid n \in \mathbb{N}\}$ is finite. If $\phi = \top$ then the interpretation of R in the minimal model of N is Presburger definable iff $\langle M \rangle = \{M^n \mid n \in \mathbb{N}\}$ is finite.

Acceleration techniques have been investigated e.g. for fragments of theories of arrays with read and write in the presence of iterators and selectors in [4]. Similar ideas are used in the superposition calculus in [17,26], and in approaches which combine superposition and induction [30] or use solutions for recurrences in loop invariant generation [31,32]. We plan to analyze such aspects in future work.

4   Checking Entailment

Let $\mathcal{T}$ be a theory with signature $\Pi = (S, \Sigma, \mathsf{Pred})$, and let $\overline{P}_1 = P_1^1, \ldots, P_{n_1}^1$ and $\overline{P}_2 = P_1^2, \ldots, P_{n_2}^2$ be finite sequences of different predicate symbols with $P_j^i \notin \mathsf{Pred}$, and $\Pi_i = (\Sigma, \mathsf{Pred} \cup \{P_j^i \mid 1 \le j \le n_i\})$ for $i = 1, 2$. Let F_1 be a universal Π_1-formula and F_2 be a universal Π_2-formula. We analyze the problem of checking whether "$\exists \overline{P}_1 \, F_1$ entails $\exists \overline{P}_2 \, F_2$ w.r.t. $\mathcal{T}$" holds.

Example 7. Such questions arise in the graph-theoretic problems discussed in Sect. 1.1. Let $\mathbf{A}$ be a class of graphs described by axioms Ax_A and $\mathbf{B}$ be a class of graphs described by axioms Ax_B. Let $\mathcal{T}$ be a theory used for expressing these axioms. Consider the $\cdot^+$ and $\cdot^-$ transformations described in Sect. 1.1. Then $\mathbf{A}^+ \subseteq \mathbf{B}^-$ (i.e. for every graph $H = (V, F) \in \mathbf{A}^+$ we have $H \in \mathbf{B}^-$) if and only if $\exists E_A \, (\mathsf{Ax}_A \wedge Tr^+(E_A, F)) \models_{\mathcal{T}} \exists E_B \, (\mathsf{Ax}_B \wedge Tr^-(E_B, F))$. ∎

Assume that there exist Π-formulae G_1 and G_2 such that $G_1 \equiv_{\mathcal{T}} \exists \overline{P}_1 F_1$ and $G_2 \equiv_{\mathcal{T}} \exists \overline{P}_2 F_2$. Such formulae can be found either by saturation[6] by successively eliminating $P_1, \ldots, P_n$, or by using acceleration techniques or other methods. In this case, $\exists \overline{P}_1 \, F_1 \models_{\mathcal{T}} \exists \overline{P}_2 \, F_2$ iff $G_1 \models_{\mathcal{T}} G_2$ (which is the case iff $G_1 \wedge \neg G_2 \models_{\mathcal{T}} \bot$).

---

[6] We can iterate the application of $HRes^P_{\succ}$ for variables $P_1^i, \ldots, P_n^i$ (in this order). This corresponds to a variant of ordered resolution which we denote by $HRes_{\succ}^{P_1^i, \ldots, P_n^i}$; if saturation terminates the conjunction of clauses not containing $P_1^i, \ldots, P_n^i$ is equivalent to $\exists P_1^i, \ldots, P_n^i \, N_{F_i}$, where N_{F_i} is the clause form of F_i.

The problem of checking whether $G_1 \wedge \neg G_2 \models_{\mathcal{T}} \bot$ is in general undecidable, even if G_1 and G_2 are universal formulae and $\mathcal{T}$ is the extension of Presburger arithmetic or real arithmetic with a new function or predicate symbol (cf. [42]).

If $G_1 \wedge \neg G_2$ is in a fragment of $\mathcal{T}$ for which checking satisfiability is decidable, then we can effectively check whether $\exists \overline{P}_1 \, F_1 \models_{\mathcal{T}} \exists \overline{P}_2 \, F_2$. This is obviously the case when $\mathcal{T}$ is a decidable theory. We will show that a similar condition can be obtained for local theory extensions of theories allowing quantifier elimination if G_1 and G_2 are universal formulae and the extensions satisfy a certain "flatness property" which allows finite complete instantiation and that in both cases we can also generate constraints on "parameters" under which entailment holds.

Theorem 9. *Assume that there exist Π-formulae G_1 and G_2 such that $G_1 \equiv_{\mathcal{T}}$ $\exists \overline{P}_1 F_1$ and $G_2 \equiv_{\mathcal{T}} \exists \overline{P}_2 F_2$. If $\mathcal{T}$ is a decidable theory then we can effectively check whether $\exists \overline{P}_1 \, F_1 \models_{\mathcal{T}} \exists \overline{P}_2 \, F_2$. If $\mathcal{T}$ has quantifier elimination and the formulae F_1, F_2 contain parametric constants, we can use quantifier elimination in $\mathcal{T}$ to derive conditions on these parameters under which $\exists \overline{P}_1 F_1 \models_{\mathcal{T}} \exists \overline{P}_2 F_2$.*

Theorem 10. *Assume that there exist* universal *Π-formulae G_1 and G_2 such that $G_1 \equiv_{\mathcal{T}} \exists \overline{P}_1 F_1$ and $G_2 \equiv_{\mathcal{T}} \exists \overline{P}_2 F_2$, and that $\mathcal{T} = \mathcal{T}_0 \cup \mathcal{K}$, where $\mathcal{T}_0$ is a decidable theory with signature $\Pi_0 = (S_0, \Sigma_0, \mathsf{Pred}_0)$ where S_0 is a set of interpreted sorts and $\mathcal{K}$ is a set of (universally quantified) clauses over $\Pi = (S_0 \cup S_1, \Sigma_0 \cup \Sigma_1, \mathsf{Pred}_0 \cup \mathsf{Pred}_1)$, where (i) S_1 is a new set of uninterpreted sorts, (ii) $\Sigma_1, \mathsf{Pred}_1$ are sets of new function, resp. predicate symbols which have only arguments of uninterpreted sort $\in S_1$, and all function symbols in Σ_1 have interpreted output sort $\in S_0$. Assume, in addition, that all variables and constants of sort $\in S_1$ in $\mathcal{K}, G_1$ and $\neg G_2$ occur below function symbols in Σ_1. Then:*

(1) We can use the decision procedure for $\mathcal{T}_0$ to effectively check whether $G_1 \wedge \neg G_2 \models_{\mathcal{T}} \bot$ (hence if $\exists \overline{P}_1 \, F_1 \models_{\mathcal{T}} \exists \overline{P}_2 \, F_2$).

(2) If $\mathcal{T}_0$ allows quantifier elimination and the formulae F_1, F_2 (hence also G_1, G_2) contain parametric constants and functions, we can use Algorithm 1 for obtaining constraints on the parameters under which $\exists \overline{P}_1 \, F_1 \models_{\mathcal{T}} \exists \overline{P}_2 \, F_2$.

Proof: Let C be the set of constants of uninterpreted sort $s \in S_1$ occurring in $\mathcal{K}, G_1$ and $\neg G_2$. Note that $G_1 \wedge \neg G_2$ is satisfiable w.r.t. $\mathcal{T} = \mathcal{T}_0 \cup \mathcal{K}$ iff $(\mathcal{K} \wedge G_1)^{[C]} \wedge \neg G_2$ is satisfiable, where $(\mathcal{K} \wedge G_1)^{[C]}$ is the set of all instances of $\mathcal{K} \wedge G_1$ in which the variables of sort $s \in S_1$ are replaced with constants of sort s in C. (1) The hierarchical reasoning method in Theorem 2 allows us to reduce testing whether $G_1 \wedge \neg G_2 \models_{\mathcal{T}} \bot$ to a satisfiability test w.r.t. $\mathcal{T}_0$. (2) If $\mathcal{T}_0$ allows QE we can use Theorem 3. □

We illustrate how Theorem 10 can be used for checking one of the class inclusions mentioned in Sect. 1.1.

Example 8. Let $\mathbf{QUDG}(r) = (\mathbf{MinDG}(r) \cap \mathbf{MaxDG}(1))^-$, be axiomatized by $\mathsf{MinDG}(r) \wedge \mathsf{MinDG}(1) \wedge \mathsf{Tr}^-(E, F)$, where r is a function symbol (where $r(v)$ models the maximum communication distance of node v), and:

$\mathsf{MinDG}(r) : \forall x, y\ \pi_r^i(x, y) \rightarrow E(x, y)$ where $\pi_r^i(x, y) = x \neq y \wedge d(x, y) \leq r(x)$
$\mathsf{MaxDG}(1) : \forall x, y\ \pi^e(x, y) \rightarrow \neg E(x, y)$ where $\pi^e(x, y) = d(x, y) > 1$
$\mathsf{Tr}^-(E, F) : \forall x, y\ (F(x, y) \leftrightarrow E(x, y) \wedge E(y, x))$.

We want to check[7] whether $\mathbf{A}(r) \subseteq \mathbf{B}(r)$, where $\mathbf{A}(r) = \mathbf{QUDG}(r)$ and $\mathbf{B}(r) = (\mathbf{MinDG}(r) \cap \mathbf{MaxDG}(1))^+$ is described by $\mathsf{MinDG}(r) \wedge \mathsf{MinDG}(1) \wedge \mathsf{Tr}^+(E, F)$. We obtain axiomatizations $G_1 \equiv \exists E(\mathsf{MinDG}(r) \wedge \mathsf{MinDG}(1) \wedge \mathsf{Tr}^-(E, F))$ for $\mathbf{A}(r)$ and $G_2 \equiv \exists E(\mathsf{MinDG}(r) \wedge \mathsf{MinDG}(1) \wedge \mathsf{Tr}^+(E, F))$ for $\mathbf{B}(r)$ by eliminating E:

G_1		
$\forall x, y\ \pi_r^i(x, y) \wedge \pi^e(x, y) \rightarrow$	$\bot$
$\forall x, y\ \pi_r^i(x, y) \wedge \pi_r^i(y, x) \rightarrow$	$F(y, x)$
$\forall x, y\ \pi^e(x, y)$	$\rightarrow \neg F(x, y)$
$\forall x, y\ \pi^e(x, y)$	$\rightarrow \neg F(y, x)$
$\forall x, y\ F(x, y)$	$\rightarrow F(y, x)$

G_2		
$\forall x, y\ \pi_r^i(x, y) \wedge \pi^e(x, y) \rightarrow$	$\bot$
$\forall x, y\ \pi^e(x, y) \wedge \pi^e(y, x) \rightarrow \neg F(y, x)$
$\forall x, y\ \pi_r^i(x, y)$	$\rightarrow F(x, y)$
$\forall x, y\ \pi_r^i(x, y)$	$\rightarrow F(y, x)$
$\forall x, y\ F(x, y)$	$\rightarrow F(y, x)$
$\forall x\ \pi^e(x, x)$	$\rightarrow \neg F(x, x)$

We check whether $G_1 \models_{\mathcal{T}} G_2$, i.e. whether $G_1 \wedge \neg G_2$ is unsatisfiable w.r.t. $\mathcal{T}$, where $\neg G_2$ is the disjunction of the following ground formulae (we ignore the negation of the first clause obviously implied by G_1):

(g_1) $\pi^e(a, b) \wedge \pi^e(b, a) \wedge F(b, a)$ (g_2) $\pi^e(a, a) \wedge F(a, a)$ (g_3) $F(a, b) \wedge \neg F(b, a)$
(g_4) $\pi_r^i(a, b) \wedge \neg F(a, b)$ (g_5) $\pi_r^i(a, b) \wedge \neg F(b, a)$

By Theorem 10 (2), we can consider the set of all instances of G_1 in which the variables of sort p are replaced with the constants a, b, then use a method for checking ground satisfiability of $G_1[T] \wedge g_i$ w.r.t. $\mathcal{T}_d \cup UIF_r$, where $\mathcal{T}_d \in \{\mathcal{T}_d^u, \mathcal{T}_d^p, \mathcal{T}_d^s, \mathcal{T}_d^m\}$. For this, we use H-PILoT [28]. This allows us to check that $G_1[T] \wedge g_i$ is unsatisfiable for $i \in \{1, 2, 3\}$, but satisfiable for $i \in \{4, 5\}$ (this is so for all four theories). For cases 4 and 5 we can use Algorithm 1 to derive conditions on parameters under which $G_1[T] \wedge g_i$ is unsatisfiable. If e.g. we consider d and r to be parameters, for $\mathcal{T}_d^m$ we obtain condition $C^{d,r} = \forall x, y (x \neq y \wedge d(x, y) \leq 1 \wedge d(x, y) \leq r(x) \rightarrow d(y, x) \leq r(y))$. For further details cf. [36]. ∎

5   Conclusions

In this paper, we analyzed possibilities of combining general second-order symbol elimination and property-directed symbol elimination for analyzing the satisfiability of formulae w.r.t. models in a theory $\mathcal{T}$ and for checking entailment between formulae expressed using second-order quantification. In particular, these methods proved useful for obtaining (weakest) constraints Γ on "parameters" used in the description of the theory $\mathcal{T}$ such that satisfiability or entailment is guaranteed in models satisfying Γ. We tested the methods we proposed on several examples. Since the implementations of the hierarchical superposition calculus

---

[7] To check that the inclusion holds in one given model $\mathcal{A}$ we can choose $\mathcal{T} = \mathsf{Th}(\mathcal{A})$.

we are aware of have as background theory linear arithmetic and in our examples we had more complex theories, we used a form of abstraction first: We renamed the constraints over more complex theories with new predicate symbols, and used SCAN [19] for second-order quantifier elimination. For satisfiability checking we used H-PILoT [28] with Z3 [11,13] and Redlog [16] as external provers; for obtaining the constraints on parameters we used Algorithm 1 [40], implemented in an extension of H-PILoT, sehpilot, by P. Marohn [35]. Some tests can be found in [36]. H-PILoT uses eager instantiation, so provers like CVC4 [6] or Z3 [11,13] are in general faster in proving unsatisfiability. The advantage of using H-PILoT is that knowing the instances needed for a complete instantiation allows us to correctly detect satisfiability (and generate models) in situations in which e.g. CVC4 returns "unknown", and use property-directed symbol elimination to obtain additional constraints on parameters which ensure unsatisfiability. For checking the satisfiability of families of constrained Horn clauses we used the fixpoint package of Z3 [22]. In future work we would like to identify other situations in which second-order quantifier elimination yields finite formulae. We would like to analyze possibilities of checking entailment when the second-order quantifier elimination method returns a fixpoint and not a formula. (The main obstacle when working on this problem was that μZ returns "unknown" in the presence of parameters.)

Acknowledgments. We thank Hannes Frey and Lucas Böltz for the numerous discussions we had on the problems in wireless networks discussed in Sect. 1.1, Renate Schmidt for maintaining a website where one can run SCAN online and for sending us the executables and instructions for running them, and to the anonymous reviewers for their helpful comments.

References

1. Abdulaziz, M., Mehlhorn, K., Nipkow, T.: Trustworthy graph algorithms (invited talk). In: Rossmanith, P., Heggernes, P., Katoen, J. (eds.) Proceedings 44th International Symposium on Mathematical Foundations of Computer Science (MFCS 2019), volume 138 of LIPIcs, pp. 1:1–1:22. Schloss Dagstuhl - Leibniz-Zentrum für Informatik (2019)

2. Ackermann, W.: Untersuchungen über das Eliminationsproblem der mathematischen Logik. Mathematische Annalen **110**, 390–413 (1935)

3. Ackermann, W.: Zum Eliminationsproblem der mathematischen Logik. Mathematische Annalen **111**, 61–63 (1935)

4. Alberti, F., Ghilardi, S., Sharygina, N.: Definability of accelerated relations in a theory of arrays and its applications. In: Fontaine, P., Ringeissen, C., Schmidt, R.A. (eds.) FroCoS 2013. LNCS (LNAI), vol. 8152, pp. 23–39. Springer, Heidelberg (2013). https://doi.org/10.1007/978-3-642-40885-4_3

5. Bachmair, L., Ganzinger, H., Waldmann, U.: Refutational theorem proving for hierarchic first-order theories. Appl. Algebra Eng. Commun. Comput. **5**, 193–212 (1994)

6. Barrett, C.W., et al.: CVC4. In: Gopalakrishnan, G., Qadeer, S. (eds.) CAV 2011. LNCS, vol. 6806, pp. 171–177. Springer, Heidelberg (2011). https://doi.org/10.1007/978-3-642-22110-1_14

7. Barrière, L., Fraigniaud, P., Narayanan, L., Opatrny, J.: Robust position-based routing in wireless ad hoc networks with irregular transmission ranges. Wirel. Commun. Mobile Comput. **3**(2), 141–153 (2003)

8. Baumgartner, P., Waldmann, U.: Hierarchic superposition with weak abstraction. In: Bonacina, M.P. (ed.) CADE 2013. LNCS (LNAI), vol. 7898, pp. 39–57. Springer, Heidelberg (2013). https://doi.org/10.1007/978-3-642-38574-2_3

9. Baumgartner, P., Waldmann, U.: Hierarchic superposition revisited. In: Lutz, C., Sattler, U., Tinelli, C., Turhan, A.-Y., Wolter, F. (eds.) Description Logic, Theory Combination, and All That. LNCS, vol. 11560, pp. 15–56. Springer, Cham (2019). https://doi.org/10.1007/978-3-030-22102-7_2

10. Behmann, H.: Beiträge zur Algebra der Logik, insbesondere zum Entscheidungsproblem. Mathematische Annalen **86**(3–4), 163–229 (1922)

11. Bjørner, N., de Moura, L., Nachmanson, L., Wintersteiger, C.M.: Programming Z3. In: Bowen, J.P., Liu, Z., Zhang, Z. (eds.) SETSS 2018. LNCS, vol. 11430, pp. 148–201. Springer, Cham (2019). https://doi.org/10.1007/978-3-030-17601-3_4

12. Bjørner, N., Gurfinkel, A., McMillan, K., Rybalchenko, A.: Horn clause solvers for program verification. In: Beklemishev, L.D., Blass, A., Dershowitz, N., Finkbeiner, B., Schulte, W. (eds.) Fields of Logic and Computation II. LNCS, vol. 9300, pp. 24–51. Springer, Cham (2015). https://doi.org/10.1007/978-3-319-23534-9_2

13. Bjørner, N., Nachmanson, L.: Navigating the universe of Z3 theory solvers. In: Carvalho, G., Stolz, V. (eds.) SBMF 2020. LNCS, vol. 12475, pp. 8–24. Springer, Cham (2020). https://doi.org/10.1007/978-3-030-63882-5_2

14. Boigelot, B.: Symbolic Methods for Exploring Infinite State Spaces. Ph.D. thesis, Université de Liège (1998)

15. Courcelle, B.: The expression of graph properties and graph transformations in monadic second-order logic. In: Rozenberg, G. (ed.) Handbook of Graph Grammars and Computing by Graph Transformations, Volume 1: Foundations, pp. 313–400. World Scientific (1997)

16. Dolzmann, A., Sturm, T.: REDLOG: computer algebra meets computer logic. SIGSAM Bull. **31**(2), 2–9 (1997)

17. Fietzke, A., Kruglov, E., Weidenbach, C.: Automatic generation of invariants for circular derivations in SUP(LA). In: Bjørner, N., Voronkov, A. (eds.) LPAR 2012. LNCS, vol. 7180, pp. 197–211. Springer, Heidelberg (2012). https://doi.org/10.1007/978-3-642-28717-6_17

18. Finkel, A., Leroux, J.: How to compose Presburger-accelerations: applications to broadcast protocols. In: Agrawal, M., Seth, A. (eds.) FSTTCS 2002. LNCS, vol. 2556, pp. 145–156. Springer, Heidelberg (2002). https://doi.org/10.1007/3-540-36206-1_14

19. Gabbay, D.M., Ohlbach, H.J.: Quantifier elimination in second-order predicate logic. In: Nebel, B., Rich, C., Swartout, W. (eds.) Principles of Knowledge Representation and Reasoning (KR92), pp. 425–435. Morgan Kaufmann. Also published as a Technical Report MPI-I-92-231, Max-Planck-Institut für Informatik, Saarbrücken, and in the South African Computer Journal (1992)

20. Gabbay, D.M., Schmidt, R.A., Szalas, A.: Second-Order Quantifier Elimination - Foundations, Computational Aspects and Applications, volume 12 of Studies in logic: Mathematical logic and foundations. College Publications (2008)

21. Goranko, V., Hustadt, U., Schmidt, R.A., Vakarelov, D.: SCAN is complete for all Sahlqvist formulae. In: Berghammer, R., Möller, B., Struth, G. (eds.) RelMiCS 2003. LNCS, vol. 3051, pp. 149–162. Springer, Heidelberg (2004). https://doi.org/10.1007/978-3-540-24771-5_13

22. Hoder, K., Bjørner, N., de Moura, L.: μZ– an efficient engine for fixed points with constraints. In: Gopalakrishnan, G., Qadeer, S. (eds.) CAV 2011. LNCS, vol. 6806, pp. 457–462. Springer, Heidelberg (2011). https://doi.org/10.1007/978-3-642-22110-1_36

23. Hoder, K., Kovács, L., Voronkov, A.: Interpolation and symbol elimination in Vampire. In: Giesl, J., Hähnle, R. (eds.) IJCAR 2010. LNCS (LNAI), vol. 6173, pp. 188–195. Springer, Heidelberg (2010). https://doi.org/10.1007/978-3-642-14203-1_16

24. Horbach, M., Sofronie-Stokkermans, V.: Obtaining finite local theory axiomatizations via saturation. In: Fontaine, P., Ringeissen, C., Schmidt, R.A. (eds.) FroCoS 2013. LNCS (LNAI), vol. 8152, pp. 198–213. Springer, Heidelberg (2013). https://doi.org/10.1007/978-3-642-40885-4_14

25. Horbach, M., Sofronie-Stokkermans, V.: Locality transfer: from constrained axiomatizations to reachability predicates. In: Demri, S., Kapur, D., Weidenbach, C. (eds.) IJCAR 2014. LNCS (LNAI), vol. 8562, pp. 192–207. Springer, Cham (2014). https://doi.org/10.1007/978-3-319-08587-6_14

26. Horbach, M., Weidenbach, C.: Deciding the inductive validity of ∀∃* queries. In: Grädel, E., Kahle, R. (eds.) CSL 2009. LNCS, vol. 5771, pp. 332–347. Springer, Heidelberg (2009). https://doi.org/10.1007/978-3-642-04027-6_25

27. Ihlemann, C., Jacobs, S., Sofronie-Stokkermans, V.: On local reasoning in verification. In: Ramakrishnan, C.R., Rehof, J. (eds.) TACAS 2008. LNCS, vol. 4963, pp. 265–281. Springer, Heidelberg (2008). https://doi.org/10.1007/978-3-540-78800-3_19

28. Ihlemann, C., Sofronie-Stokkermans, V.: System description: H-PILoT. In: Schmidt, R.A. (ed.) CADE 2009. LNCS (LNAI), vol. 5663, pp. 131–139. Springer, Heidelberg (2009). https://doi.org/10.1007/978-3-642-02959-2_9

29. Ihlemann, C., Sofronie-Stokkermans, V.: On hierarchical reasoning in combinations of theories. In: Giesl, J., Hähnle, R. (eds.) IJCAR 2010. LNCS (LNAI), vol. 6173, pp. 30–45. Springer, Heidelberg (2010). https://doi.org/10.1007/978-3-642-14203-1_4

30. Kersani, A., Peltier, N.: Combining superposition and induction: A practical realization. In: Fontaine, P., Ringeissen, C., Schmidt, R.A. (eds.) FroCoS 2013. LNCS (LNAI), vol. 8152, pp. 7–22. Springer, Heidelberg (2013). https://doi.org/10.1007/978-3-642-40885-4_2

31. Kovács, L.: Invariant generation for P-solvable loops with assignments. In: Hirsch, E.A., Razborov, A.A., Semenov, A., Slissenko, A. (eds.) CSR 2008. LNCS, vol. 5010, pp. 349–359. Springer, Heidelberg (2008). https://doi.org/10.1007/978-3-540-79709-8_35

32. Kovács, L.: Reasoning algebraically about P-solvable loops. In: Ramakrishnan, C.R., Rehof, J. (eds.) TACAS 2008. LNCS, vol. 4963, pp. 249–264. Springer, Heidelberg (2008). https://doi.org/10.1007/978-3-540-78800-3_18

33. Kovács, L., Voronkov, A.: Interpolation and symbol elimination. In: Schmidt, R.A. (ed.) CADE 2009. LNCS (LNAI), vol. 5663, pp. 199–213. Springer, Heidelberg (2009). https://doi.org/10.1007/978-3-642-02959-2_17

34. Kuhn, F., Wattenhofer, R., Zollinger, A.: Ad hoc networks beyond unit disk graphs. Wirel. Networks 14(5), 715–729 (2008)

35. Marohn, P.: Verifikation und Constraint-Generierung in parametrisierten Systemen. BSC Thesis, University Koblenz-Landau (2021)

36. Peuter, D., Marohn, P., Sofronie-Stokkermans, V.: Symbol elimination for parametric second-order entailment problems (with applications to problems in wireless network theory) (2021). https://arxiv.org/abs/2107.02333

37. Peuter, D., Sofronie-Stokkermans, V.: On invariant synthesis for parametric systems. In: Fontaine, P. (ed.) CADE 2019. LNCS (LNAI), vol. 11716, pp. 385–405. Springer, Cham (2019). https://doi.org/10.1007/978-3-030-29436-6_23

38. Sofronie-Stokkermans, V.: Hierarchic reasoning in local theory extensions. In: Nieuwenhuis, R. (ed.) CADE 2005. LNCS (LNAI), vol. 3632, pp. 219–234. Springer, Heidelberg (2005). https://doi.org/10.1007/11532231_16

39. Sofronie-Stokkermans, V.: On interpolation and symbol elimination in theory extensions. In: Olivetti, N., Tiwari, A. (eds.) IJCAR 2016. LNCS (LNAI), vol. 9706, pp. 273–289. Springer, Cham (2016). https://doi.org/10.1007/978-3-319-40229-1_19

40. Sofronie-Stokkermans, V.: On interpolation and symbol elimination in theory extensions. Log. Methods Comput. Sci. **14**(3) (2018)

41. Voigt, M.: Towards elimination of second-order quantifiers in the separated fragment. In: Koopmann, P., Rudolph, S., Schmidt, R.A., Wernhard, C. (eds.) Proceedings of the Workshop on Second-Order Quantifier Elimination and Related Topics (SOQE 2017), Dresden, Germany, 6–8 December, 2017, volume 2013 of CEUR Workshop Proceedings, pp. 67–81. CEUR-WS.org (2017)

42. Voigt, M.: Decidable fragments of first-order logic and of first-order linear arithmetic with uninterpreted predicates. Ph.D. thesis, Saarland University, Saarbrücken, Germany (2019)

On the Copy Complexity of Width 3 Horn Constraint Systems

K. Subramani[1(✉)], P. Wojciechowski[1], and Alvaro Velasquez[2]

[1] LDCSEE, West Virginia University, Morgantown, WV, USA
k.subramani@mail.wvu.edu, pwojciec@mix.wvu.edu
[2] Air Force Research Laboratory, Rome, NY, USA
alvaro.velasquez.1@us.af.mil

Abstract. In this paper, we analyze the copy complexity of unsatisfiable width 3 Horn constraint systems, under the ADD refutation system. Recall that a linear constraint of the form $\sum_{i=1}^{n} a_i \cdot x_i \geq b$, is said to be a Horn constraint if all the $a_i \in \{0, 1, -1\}$ and at most one of the a_is is positive. A conjunction of such constraints is called a Horn constraint system (HCS). An HCS is said to have width 3, if there are at most 3 variables with non-zero coefficients per constraint. Horn constraints arise in a number of domains including but not limited to program verification, power systems, econometrics, and operations research. The ADD refutation system is both **sound** and **complete**. Additionally, it is the simplest and most natural refutation system for refuting the feasibility of a system of linear constraints. The copy complexity of an infeasible linear constraint system (not necessarily Horn) in a refutation system is the minimum number of times each constraint needs to be replicated, in order to obtain a read-once refutation. In this paper, we analyze width 3 HCSs from the perspective of copy complexity.

1 Introduction

This paper is concerned with the problem of determining bounds on the **copy complexity** of Horn constraint systems (HCSs) under the ADD refutation system [10]. A linear constraint of the form $\sum_{i=1}^{n} a_i \cdot x_i \geq b$, $b \in \mathbb{Z}$, is said to be Horn, if $\forall i, a_i \in \{0, 1, -1\}$ and at most one of the $a_i = 1$. A conjunction of such constraints is called a Horn constraint system (HCS). Horn constraints arise in a number of application domains such as program verification [2,3], lattice programming [9] and econometrics. The ADD refutation system is a refutation system with a single inference rule, viz., if two constraints l_1 and l_2 are part of the HCS or can be inferred from the HCS, then so can their sum. It is well-known that the ADD refutation system is both sound and complete from the perspective of establishing infeasibility in polyhedral constraint systems [10]. Furthermore,

K. Subramani—This research was supported in part by the Air-Force Office of Scientific Research through Grant FA9550-19-1-0177 and in part by the Air-Force Research Laboratory, Rome through Contract FA8750-17-S-7007.

© Springer Nature Switzerland AG 2021
B. Konev and G. Reger (Eds.): FroCoS 2021, LNAI 12941, pp. 63–78, 2021.
https://doi.org/10.1007/978-3-030-86205-3_4

this system enables the extraction of the actual refutation. When it comes to establishing infeasibility, the goal is clearly to find "short" certificates, since such certificates can be effectively verified. However, not all constraint systems have compact certificates in the ADD refutation system. In our quest for compactness, we attempt to minimize the number of times a constraint can be used by the refutation system, in order to infer a contradiction. This leads to the notion of copy complexity of a constraint system under the ADD refutation system. For the rest of the paper, we will assume that the constraint system under consideration is Horn and that the refutation system is the ADD refutation system (see Sect. 2). Accordingly, we will use the phrase "copy complexity" without reference to the accompanying refutation system.

The problem of determining the copy complexity of an HCS is known to be **NP-hard** [8].

In this paper, we investigate width 3 HCSs. In most program verification applications, the width of Horn clauses or constraints is bounded by a small constant. Accordingly, this investigation is well-motivated.

2   Statement of Problems

In this section, we define the problems studied in this paper.

Definition 1. *A system of constraints* $\mathbf{A} \cdot \mathbf{x} \geq \mathbf{b}$ *is said to be a Horn Constraint system (HCS) if:*

1. *The entries in* $\mathbf{A}$ *belong to the set* $\{0, 1, -1\}$.
2. *Each row of* $\mathbf{A}$ *contains at most one positive entry.*
3. $\mathbf{x}$ *is a real valued vector.*
4. $\mathbf{b}$ *is an integral vector.*

In the constraint $\mathbf{a} \cdot \mathbf{x} \geq b_j$, b_j is called the **defining constant**. If a Horn constraint has at most w non-zero coefficients, then it is called a width w Horn constraint. A system of width w Horn constraints is known as a width w HCS. In a Horn constraint we refer to the terms x_i and $-x_i$ as literals.

If a Horn constraint has only one non-zero coefficient, then it is called an absolute constraint. If that coefficient is 1, then it is called a positive absolute constraint.

We are interested in certificates of infeasibility. In this paper, we utilize an inference rule known as the **ADD rule** [10]. This inference rule derives a new constraint by summing a pair of constraints (either from the original system or derived by previous inferences) and is defined as follows:

$$\text{ADD} : \frac{\sum_{i=1}^{n} a_i \cdot x_i \geq b_1 \qquad \sum_{i=1}^{n} a_i' \cdot x_i \geq b_2}{\sum_{i=1}^{n} (a_i + a_i') \cdot x_i \geq b_1 + b_2} \tag{1}$$

This inference rule plays a similar role to the role played by resolution in clausal formulas.

Using Rule (1), we can now define a linear refutation.

Definition 2. *A linear refutation is a sequence of applications of the ADD rule that results in a contradiction of the form $0 \geq b$, $b > 0$.*

The form of refutation defined in Definition 2 is both sound and complete when used as a proof system for linear feasibility. It is sound since any assignment that satisfies the constraints used by an application of the ADD rule also satisfies the constraint derived by that application. Additionally, ADD rule based linear refutation is **complete**. This means that repeated application of the ADD rule will eventually result in a contradiction of the form: $0 \geq b$, $b > 0$ for any linearly infeasible system. The completeness of ADD rule based linear refutations was established by Farkas [4], in a lemma that is famously known as Farkas' Lemma for systems of linear inequalities [12].

Of particular interest is a restricted form of refutation known as read-once refutation.

Definition 3. *A* **read-once** *refutation is a refutation in which each constraint, l, can be used in only one inference. This applies to constraints present in the original systems and those derived as a result of previous inferences.*

Example 1. Consider the HCS **H** defined by System (2).

$$l_1 : x_1 - x_2 - x_3 \geq 0 \quad l_2 : x_2 - x_3 \geq -1$$
$$l_3 : x_3 - x_1 \geq 1 \quad l_4 : x_3 \geq 1 \tag{2}$$

System (2) has the following read-once refutation:

1. Apply the ADD rule to l_1 and l_2 to get $l_5 : x_1 - 2 \cdot x_3 \geq -1$.
2. Apply the ADD rule to l_5 and l_3 to get $l_6 : -x_3 \geq 0$.
3. Apply the ADD rule to l_6 and l_4 to get the contradiction $0 \geq 1$.

We can now define copy complexity in terms of read-once refutations.

Definition 4. *A HCS **H** has* **copy complexity** *k if k is the smallest integer for which there exists a multi-set of Horn constraints, **H**′ such that:*

1. *Every constraint in **H** appears at most k times in **H**′.*
2. *Every constraint in **H**′ appears in **H**.*
3. ***H**′ has a read-once refutation using the ADD rule.*

In this paper, we examine the following problems related to copy complexity:

Definition 5. *The copy complexity (CC_D) problem: given an HCS **H** and an integer k, is the copy complexity of **H** at most k?*

Definition 6. *The optimal copy complexity (CC_{Opt}) problem: given an HCS **H**, what is the smallest k such that the copy complexity of **H** is at most k?*

In this paper, we focus on these problems in width 3 HCSs, for the most part. The principal contributions of this paper are as follows:

1. Establishing a lower bound on the copy complexity of bounded width HCSs (Theorem 2).
2. Establishing that the CC_D problem for width 3 HCSs is **NP-complete** (Theorem 4).
3. Establishing that no algorithm for the CC_D problem for width 3 HCSs can run in time $2^{o(n)}$ unless the Exponential Time Hypothesis (**ETH**) fails (Theorem 6).
4. Establishing that the CC_{Opt} problem for width 3 HCSs is **NPO-complete** [7] (Theorem 7).

3   Observations on Copy Complexity

In this section, we observe several properties of the copy complexity of bounded width HCSs.

First, we show that the copy complexity of a width w HCS with $((w-1) \cdot n' + 1)$ variables can be as large as $2^{(w-2) \cdot n'}$.

Theorem 1. *For each integer $n' \geq 0$, there exists a width w HCS $\mathbf{H}$ with $((w-1) \cdot n' + 1)$ variables such that $\mathbf{H}$ has copy complexity $2^{(w-2) \cdot n'}$.*

Proof. Let $\mathbf{H}$ be the HCS constructed as follows:

1. The constraint l_1 is $-x_1 \geq 1$.
2. For $r = 2, \ldots, (w-1) \cdot n' + 1$, the constraint l_r is

$$x_{r-1} - \sum_{j=r}^{\left\lceil \frac{r-1}{w-1} \right\rceil \cdot (w-1) + 1} x_j \geq 0.$$

3. The constraint $l_{(w-1) \cdot n' + 2}$ is $x_{(w-1) \cdot n' + 1} \geq 0$.

We will show that for each $i = 0 \ldots n'$, the constraint $l_{(w-1) \cdot i + 2}$ must be used at least $2^{(w-2) \cdot i}$ times by any linear refutation of $\mathbf{H}$.

Note that constraint l_1 is the only constraint in $\mathbf{H}$ that has a positive defining constant. Thus, l_1 must be in any linear refutation of $\mathbf{H}$. Additionally, the only constraint in $\mathbf{H}$ with the literal x_1 is l_2. Thus, the constraint l_2 must be used at least 2^0 times by any linear refutation of $\mathbf{H}$.

Now assume that the constraint $l_{(w-1) \cdot i + 2}$ must be used at least $2^{(w-2) \cdot i}$ times by any linear refutation of $\mathbf{H}$. Note that this constraint contains the literal $-x_{(w-1) \cdot i + 2}$ and that this is the only constraint in $\mathbf{H}$ containing that literal. The only constraint in $\mathbf{H}$ with the literal $x_{(w-1) \cdot i + 2}$ is $l_{(w-1) \cdot i + 3}$. Thus, this constraint must also be used at least $2^{(w-2) \cdot i}$ times by any linear refutation of $\mathbf{H}$.

Both constraints $l_{(w-1) \cdot i + 2}$ and $l_{(w-1) \cdot i + 3}$ contain the literal $-x_{(w-1) \cdot i + 3}$ and these are the only constraints in $\mathbf{H}$ containing that literal. Thus, the literal $-x_{(w-1) \cdot i + 3}$ is used by at least $2^{(w-2) \cdot i + 1}$ constraints in any linear refutation of $\mathbf{H}$.

For each $j = 1 \dots w - 1$, the constraints $l_{(w-1) \cdot i + 2}$ through $l_{(w-1) \cdot i + j + 1}$ contain the literal $-x_{(w-1) \cdot i + j + 1}$ and these are the only constraints in $\mathbf{H}$ containing that literal. Thus, the literal $-x_{(w-1) \cdot i + j + 1}$ is used by at least $2^{(w-2) \cdot i + j - 1}$ constraints in any linear refutation of $\mathbf{H}$.

Note that the only constraint in $\mathbf{H}$ with the literal $x_{(w-1) \cdot i + w} = x_{(w-1) \cdot (i+1) + 1}$ is $l_{(w-1) \cdot (i+1) + 2}$. Thus, any linear refutation of $\mathbf{H}$ must use the constraint $l_{(w-1) \cdot (i+1) + 2}$ at least $2^{(w-2) \cdot (i+1)}$ times as desired.

Thus, for each $i = 0 \dots n'$, the constraint $l_{(w-1) \cdot i + 2}$ must be used at least $2^{(w-2) \cdot i}$ times by any linear refutation of $\mathbf{H}$. In particular, the constraint $l_{(w-1) \cdot n' + 2}$ must be used at least $2^{(w-2) \cdot n'}$ times by any linear refutation of $\mathbf{H}$.

We can construct a linear refutation of $\mathbf{H}$ by using each constraint l_r, $2^{r-1-\lfloor \frac{r-1}{w-1} \rfloor}$ times. $\qquad \square$

From, Theorem 1, there is a width w HCS $\mathbf{H}$ with $n \equiv 1 \mod (w-1)$ variables such that $\mathbf{H}$ has copy complexity at least $2^{(w-2) \cdot \frac{n-1}{w-1}}$. Utilizing a different construction, we can obtain a tighter bound based on a generalization of the Fibonacci Sequence.

Recall that the Fibonacci Sequence F_n is the sequence in which each element is the sum of the two previous elements. More formally, the Fibonacci Sequence is defined as follows: $F_0 = 0$, $F_1 = 1$, and $F_n = F_{n-1} + F_{n-2}$ for $n \geq 2$. We can generalize this definition by having each element depend on more than just the previous two elements. Our result on width w HCSs utilizes the following generalization of the Fibonacci Sequence.

For each $w \geq 1$, the width w Fibonacci Sequence $F_{w,n}$ is defined as follows: $F_{w,0} = 0$, $F_{w,1} = 1$, $F_{w,n} = \sum_{i=\max\{0, n-w\}}^{n-1} F_{w,i}$ for $n \geq 2$. Thus, in the width w Fibonacci Sequence each element depends on the sum of the previous w elements, not just the previous 2 elements. Note that the width 2 Fibonacci Sequence is simply the regular Fibonacci Sequence.

We now make a structural observation about $F_{w,n}$.

Lemma 1. *For $w \geq 1$ and $2 \leq n \leq w + 1$, $F_{w,n} = 2^{n-2}$.*

Proof. Let w be a positive integer. By definition, $F_{w,0} = 0$ and $F_{w,1} = 1$. Additionally, for $n = 2 \dots w$, $F_{w,n} = \sum_{i=0}^{n-1} F_{w,i}$. Since $F_{w,0} = 0$, we have that for $n = 2 \dots w + 1$, $F_{w,n} = \sum_{i=1}^{n-1} F_{w,i}$.
When $n = 2$, we have

$$F_{w,n} = F_{w,2} = F_{w,0} + F_{w,1} = 1 = 2^{n-2}.$$

Let n be an integer such that $2 \leq n \leq w + 1$. Assume that $F_{w,i} = 2^{i-2}$ for $2 \leq i < n$. Recall that,

$$F_{w,n} = \sum_{i=1}^{n-1} F_{w,i} = 1 + \sum_{i=2}^{n-1} 2^{i-2} = 1 + (2^{n-2} - 1) = 2^{n-2}.$$

Thus, for $w \geq 1$ and $2 \leq n \leq w + 1$, $F_{w,n} = 2^{n-2}$. $\qquad \square$

We will now utilize width w Fibonacci Sequences to establish a stronger lower bound on the copy complexity of HCSs with bounded constraint width.

Theorem 2. *For each $w \geq 2$ and $n \geq 2$, there exists a width w HCS $\mathbf{H}_{w,n}$ with n variables such that the copy complexity of $\mathbf{H}_{w,n}$ is $2 \cdot F_{(w-1),n}$.*

Proof. For each $w \geq 2$ and $n \geq 2$, Let $\mathbf{H}_{w,n}$ be the HCS constructed as follows:

1. The constraint l_0 is $-x_1 - x_2 - \ldots - x_w \geq 1$.
2. For $r = 1, \ldots, n-1$, the constraint l_r is $x_r - \sum_{j=r+1}^{\min\{r+w-1,n\}} x_j \geq 0$.
3. The constraint l_n is $x_n \geq 0$.

Let R be a linear refutation of $\mathbf{H}_{w,n}$ and let $C(l_i)$ be the number of times the constraint l_i is used by R. We will show that for any refutation R of $\mathbf{H}_{w,n}$, $C(l_i) \geq 2 \cdot F_{(w-1),i}$ for $i = 2 \ldots n$.

We make the following observations about R and the structure of $\mathbf{H}_{w,n}$:

1. l_0 is the only constraint with positive defining constant. Thus, l_0 must be used by R and $C(l_0) \geq 1$
2. For each $i = 1 \ldots n$, the constraint l_i is the only constraint to use the literal x_i. Additionally, the constraints l_{i-w+1} through l_{i-1} are the only constraints in $\mathbf{H}_{w,n}$ to use the literal $-x_i$. The only exception to this is the literal $-x_w$ which also appears in the constraint l_0.
   Since R is a refutation of $\mathbf{H}_{w,n}$, the number of constraints in R that use the literal x_i and the number of constraints in R that use the literal $-x_i$ are equal. Thus, for $i = 1 \ldots n$, $i \neq w$ we have that $C(l_i) = \sum_{j=\max\{0,i-w+1\}}^{i-1} C(l_j)$ and $C(l_w) = \sum_{j=0}^{w-1} C(l_j)$.
3. For $i = 1 \ldots w$, $C(l_i) = \sum_{j=0}^{i-1} C(l_j)$. Thus, $C(l_i) \geq 2^{i-1}$. From Lemma 1, we have that for $i = 2 \ldots w$, $F_{(w-1),i} = 2^{i-2}$. Thus, for $i = 2 \ldots w$, $C(l_i) \geq 2 \cdot F_{(w-1),i}$.
4. Let i be an integer such that $w < i \leq n$. Assume that for each $j = 2 \ldots i-1$, $C(l_j) \geq 2 \cdot F_{(w-1),j}$. We have that $C(l_i) = \sum_{j=i-w+1}^{i-1} C(l_j)$. Since $(i-w+1) \geq 2$, $\sum_{j=i-w+1}^{i-1} C(l_j) \geq \sum_{j=i-w+1}^{i-1} 2 \cdot F_{(w-1),j} = 2 \cdot F_{(w-1),i}$. Thus, $C(l_i) \geq 2 \cdot F_{(w-1),i}$ as desired.

From the above observations, for each $i = 2 \ldots n$, $C(l_i) \geq 2 \cdot F_{(w-1),i}$. In particular, $C(l_n) \geq 2 \cdot F_{(w-1),n}$. Thus, the copy complexity of $\mathbf{H}_{w,n}$ is at least $2 \cdot F_{(w-1),n}$.

Let R be such that $C(l_0) = 1$, $C(l_1) = 1$, and for each $i = 2 \ldots n$, $C(l_i) = 2 \cdot F_{(w-1),i}$. It can be algebraically verified that R is a linear refutation of $\mathbf{H}_{w,n}$. Thus, copy complexity of $\mathbf{H}_{w,n}$ is $2 \cdot F_{(w-1),n}$ as desired. $\square$

Let S_l be the following set of constraints:

$$l_1 : x_{2 \cdot l+1} - x_{2 \cdot l} - x_{2 \cdot l-1} \geq 0 \qquad l_2 : x_{2 \cdot l} - x_{2 \cdot l-1} \geq 0$$
$$l_3 : x_{2 \cdot l-1} - x_{2 \cdot l-2} - x_{2 \cdot l-3} \geq 0 \qquad l_4 : x_{2 \cdot l-2} - x_{2 \cdot l-3} \geq 0 \qquad \ldots$$
$$l_{2 \cdot l-1} : x_3 - x_2 - x_1 \geq 0 \qquad l_{2 \cdot l} : x_2 - x_1 \geq 0 \qquad l_{2 \cdot l+1} : x_1 \geq 0$$

Theorem 1, when applied to width 3 HCSs, can be extended to the following result which will be utilized later in the paper.

Theorem 3. *Let $\mathbf{H}$ be an HCS and let $\{x_1, \ldots, x_{2 \cdot l+1}\}$ be a subset of the variables in $\mathbf{H}$ such that for each $i = 1 \ldots (2 \cdot l + 1)$, the only constraint in $\mathbf{H}$ that uses the literal x_i belongs to the set S_l. If a linear refutation R of $\mathbf{H}$ uses a constraint $x - \sum_{i \in S} x_i \geq b$ for some set $S \subseteq \{1, 3, \ldots, 2 \cdot l + 1\}$, then R must use the constraint $x_1 \geq 0$ at least $\sum_{2 \cdot i+1 \in S} 2^i$ times.*

Proof. Let $\mathbf{H}$ be an appropriately constructed HCS. For some subset $S \subseteq \{1, 3, \ldots, 2 \cdot l + 1\}$ let $x - \sum_{i \in S} x_i \geq b$ be a constraint in $\mathbf{H}$ used by a linear refutation R of $\mathbf{H}$.

Let x_i be a variable such that $2 \cdot i + 1 \in S$. By the definition of $\mathbf{H}$, the only constraint in $\mathbf{H}$ with the literal $x_{2 \cdot i+1}$ is $x_{2 \cdot i+1} - x_{2 \cdot i} - x_{2 \cdot i-1} \geq 0$. Thus, this constraint must be used by R. Observe the following:

1. The constraint $x_{2 \cdot i} - x_{2 \cdot i-1} \geq 0$ is the only constraint with the literal $x_{2 \cdot i}$. Thus, it needs to be in R. Consequently, R has at least 2 constraints with the literal $-x_{2 \cdot i-1}$.
2. The constraint $x_{2 \cdot i-1} - x_{2 \cdot i-2} - x_{2 \cdot i-3} \geq 0$ is the only constraint with the literal $x_{2 \cdot i-1}$. Thus, R needs to use this constraint at least 2 times. Consequently, R has at least 2 constraints with the literal $-x_{2 \cdot i-2}$.
3. The constraint $x_{2 \cdot i-2} - x_{2 \cdot i-3} \geq 0$ is the only constraint with the literal $x_{2 \cdot i-2}$. Thus, R needs to use this constraint at least 2 times. Consequently, R has at least 4 constraints with the literal $-x_{2 \cdot i-3}$.
4. For each r, R uses at least 2^r constraints with the literal $-x_{2 \cdot (i-r)+1}$. Thus, the constraint $x_{2 \cdot (i-r)+1} - x_{2 \cdot (i-r)} - x_{2 \cdot (i-r-1)+1} \geq 0$ needs to be in the refutation at least 2^r times. Consequently, R uses at least 2^r constraints with the literal $-x_{2 \cdot (i-r)}$.
5. For each r, R uses at least 2^r constraints with the literal $-x_{2 \cdot (i-r)}$. Thus, the constraint $x_{2 \cdot (i-r)} - x_{2 \cdot (i-r-1)+1} \geq 0$ needs to be in the refutation at least 2^r times. Consequently, R uses at least 2^{r+1} constraints with the literal $-x_{2 \cdot (i-r-1)+1}$.
6. The constraint $x_1 \geq 0$ needs to be used at least 2^i times by R.

Thus, for each $2 \cdot i + 1 \in S$, R must use the constraint $x_1 \geq 0$ at least 2^i times. Consequently, R must use the constraint $x_1 \geq 0$ at least $\sum_{2 \cdot i+1 \in S} 2^i$ times. $\square$

4   Computational Complexity of the CC_D Problem

In this section, we explore the computational and approximation complexities of the copy complexity problem for width 3 HCSs.

First, we show that the problem of determining the copy complexity of an HCS is **NP-complete** even when each constraint in the HCS has at most 3 non-zero coefficients.

Let Φ be a 3-CNF formula with m' clauses over n' variables and let $\mathbf{H}$ be the HCS constructed as follows:

1. For each variable x_i of Φ, create the variables x_i and y_i. Create the constraints $-x_1 - y_1 \geq 0$, $y_1 - x_2 - y_2 \geq 0, \ldots, y_{n'-2} - x_{n'-1} - y_{n'-1} \geq 0$, $y_{n'-1} - x'_n \geq 1 - m'$. These constraints are equivalent to the constraint $-\sum_{i=1}^{n'} x_i \geq 1 - m'$.

2. For each clause $\phi_j \in \Phi$, create the variable c_j. Additionally, create the constraints $c_j \geq 1$, $c_j \geq 0$, and $c_j \geq 0$.
3. For each clause $\phi_j \in \Phi$ and each variable x_i in clause ϕ_j, create the variable $z_{i,j}$. Since each clause has at most 3 literals, there are at most $3 \cdot m'$ such variables.
4. For each variable x_i, let $Pos(i) = \{\phi_{j_1}, \ldots, \phi_{j_{|Pos(i)|}}\}$ be the set of clauses containing the literal x_i. Create the constraints $x_i - z_{i,j_1} \geq 0$, $z_{i,j_1} - c_{j_1} - z_{i,j_2} \geq 0, \ldots, z_{i,j_{|Pos(i)|}} - c_{j_{|Pos(i)|}} \geq 0$. This is equivalent to the constraint $x_i - \sum_{\phi_j \in Pos(i)} c_j \geq 0$.
5. For each variable x_i, let $Neg(i) = \{\phi_{j'_1}, \ldots, \phi_{j'_{|Neg(i)|}}\}$ be the set of clauses containing the literal $\neg x_i$. Create the constraints $x_i - z_{i,j'_1} \geq 0$, $z_{i,j'_1} - c_{j'_1} - z_{i,j'_2} \geq 0, \ldots, z_{i,j'_{|Neg(i)|}} - c_{j'_{|Neg(i)|}} \geq 0$. This is equivalent to the constraint $x_i - \sum_{\phi_j \in Neg(i)} c_j \geq 0$.

Note that $\mathbf{H}$ has $n \leq (4 \cdot m' + 2 \cdot n')$ variables.

We now show that a 3-CNF formula Φ has a solution if and only if the HCS $\mathbf{H}$ has a copy complexity of 1.

Lemma 2. *Let Φ be a 3-CNF formula and let $\mathbf{H}$ be the HCS constructed from Φ. Φ has a solution if and only if $\mathbf{H}$ has a copy complexity of 1.*

Proof. First, assume that Φ has a solution $\mathbf{x}$. We will show that $\mathbf{H}$ has copy complexity 1 by showing that $\mathbf{H}$ has a read-once linear refutation R.

We construct R as follows:

1. Add the constraints $-x_1 - y_1 \geq 0, \ldots, y_{n'-1} - x'_n \geq 1 - m'$ to R. Note that summing these constraints results in the constraint $-\sum_{i=1}^{n'} x_i \geq 1 - m'$.
2. For each variable x_i, if x_i is assigned **true** by $\mathbf{x}$, then add the constraints $x_i - z_{i,j_1} \geq 0, \ldots, z_{i,j_{|Pos(i)|}} - c_{j_{|Pos(i)|}} \geq 0$ to R. If x_i is assigned **false** by $\mathbf{x}$, then add the constraints $x_i - z_{i,j'_1} \geq 0, \ldots, z_{i,j'_{|Neg(i)|}} - c_{j'_{|Neg(i)|}} \geq 0$ to R.
3. For each clause $\phi_r \in \Phi$, let $C(r)$ be the number of times the literal $-c_r$ is used by a constraint in R so far. Since ϕ_r has at most 3 literals, $C(r) \leq 3$. Additionally, since $\mathbf{x}$ satisfies Φ, the clause ϕ_r must contain a literal $T(r)$ set to **true** by $\mathbf{x}$.
4. If $T(r)$ is the literal x_i, then the variable x_i is assigned **true** by $\mathbf{x}$. Thus, by construction, R contains the equivalent of the constraint $x_i - \sum_{\phi_r \in Pos(i)} c_r \geq 0$. Since $\Phi_r \in Pos(i)$, the literal $-c_r$ is used by a constraint in R. Thus, $C(r) \geq 1$.
5. If $T(r)$ is the literal $\neg x_i$, then the variable x_i is assigned **false** by $\mathbf{x}$. Thus, by construction, R contains the equivalent of the constraint $x_i - \sum_{\phi_r \in Neg(i)} c_r \geq 0$. Since $\Phi_r \in Neg(i)$, the literal $-c_r$ is used by a constraint in R. Thus, $C(r) \geq 1$. Consequently, for each clause $\phi_r \in \Phi$, $1 \leq C(r) \leq 3$.
6. For each clause $\phi_r \in \Phi$, add the constraint $c_r \geq 1$ and $(C(r) - 1)$ copies of the constraint $c_r \geq 0$ to R. Note that $\mathbf{H}$ has 2 copies of the constraint $c_r \geq 0$ and that $0 \leq C(r) - 1 \leq 2$.

It is easy to see that summing all of the constraints in R results in a contradiction of the form $0 \geq 1$. Thus, R is a read-once refutation of $\mathbf{H}$.

Now assume that $\mathbf{H}$ has a refutation R that uses no constraint more than once. We construct an assignment $\mathbf{x}$ to Φ as follows: for each variable x_i, if R contains a constraint of the form $x_i - z_{i,j_1} \geq 0$ such that $\phi_{j_1} \in Pos(x_i)$, then set x_i to **true**. Otherwise set x_i to **false**.

We make the following observations about R:

1. If the constraint $-x_1 - y_1 \geq 0$ is removed from $\mathbf{H}$, then $\mathbf{H}$ is feasible. Thus, this constraint must be used by R. To cancel each y_i variable, all of the constraints $-x_1 - y_1 \geq 0, \ldots, y_{n'-1} - x'_n \geq 1 - m'$ must be in R. These constraints are equivalent to the constraint $-\sum_{i=1}^{n'} x_i \geq 1 - m'$.
2. To get a contradiction, the defining constant of the derived constraint must be positive. Note that the only constraints with positive defining constant in $\mathbf{H}$ are of the form $c_r \geq 1$. There are m' such constraints, thus they must all be used by R.
3. Consider the constraint $c_r \geq 1$. The only constraints with $-c_r$ in $\mathbf{H}$ are of the form $z_{i,r} - c_r - z_{i,r'} \geq 0$ where $\phi_r \in Pos(i)$ or $\phi_r \in Neg(i)$. Thus, R must contain a constraint of this form.
4. If R contains a constraint of the form $z_{i,r} - c_r - z_{i,r'} \geq 0$ where $\phi_r \in Pos(i)$, then to cancel all the $z_{i,r}$ variables R must contain the constraints $x_i - z_{i,j_1} \geq 0, \ldots, z_{i,j_{|Pos(i)|}} - c_{j_{|Pos(i)|}} \geq 0$. Thus, x_i is set to **true** by $\mathbf{x}$. Note that $\phi_r \in Pos(i)$ if and only if ϕ_r contains the literal x_i. Thus, ϕ_r is satisfied by $\mathbf{x}$.
5. If R contains a constraint of the form $z_{i,r} - c_r - z_{i,r'} \geq 0$ where $\phi_j \in Neg(i)$, then to cancel all the $z_{i,r}$ variables R must contain the constraints $x_i - z_{i,j'_1} \geq 0, \ldots, z_{i,j'_{|Neg(i)|}} - c_{j'_{|Neg(i)|}} \geq 0$. By construction, $\mathbf{H}$ has only one constraint with the literal $-x_i$. Thus, R cannot contain both the constraint $x_i - z_{i,j'_1} \geq 0$ and a constraint of the form $x_i - z_{i,j_1} \geq 0$ such that $\phi_{j_1} \in Pos(x_i)$. Consequently, x_i is set to **false** by $\mathbf{x}$. Note that $\phi_r \in Neg(i)$ if and only if ϕ_r contains the literal $\neg x_i$. Thus, ϕ_r is satisfied by $\mathbf{x}$.

Note that $\mathbf{x}$ satisfies every clause in Φ. Thus, Φ is satisfiable.   □

Theorem 4. *The CC_D problem for width 3 HCSs is* **NP-complete**.

Proof. For each integer k we can establish that the copy complexity of a width 3 HCS is at most k by providing a Farkas vector $\mathbf{y}$ such that $\|\mathbf{y}\|_\infty \leq k$. Note that $\|\mathbf{y}\|_\infty$ is the largest element of $\mathbf{y}$ and is called the L_∞ norm of $\mathbf{y}$. Thus, the CC_D problem for width 3 HCSs is in **NP**.

From Lemma 2, we have that given a 3-CNF formula Φ, we can construct a width 3 HCS $\mathbf{H}$ such that $\mathbf{H}$ has copy complexity 1 if and only if Φ is feasible. Thus, the CC_D problem for width 3 HCSs is **NP-complete**.   □

The result in Theorem 4, relies on the fact that the problem of determining if a width 3 HCS has copy complexity 1 is **NP-complete**. However, this result can be extended to any fixed positive integer C.

Theorem 5. *Let C be a positive integer. The problem of determining if a width 3 HCS has copy complexity at most C is* **NP-complete**.

Proof. Let Φ be a 3-CNF formula and let $\mathbf{H}$ be the HCS constructed from Φ. From Lemma 2, we know that $\mathbf{H}$ has copy complexity 1 if and only if Φ is satisfiable.

We can construct an HCS $\mathbf{H'}$ from $\mathbf{H}$ as follows:

1. Initially, $\mathbf{H'} = \mathbf{H}$.
2. Let $E \subseteq \mathbb{N}$ be such that $\sum_{i \in E} 2^i = C$. For each $k = 1 \ldots |E|$, let $E(k)$ be the kth element of E.
3. For each constraint l_j of $\mathbf{H}$:
   (a) Create the variables $g_{j,1}$ through $g_{j,2 \cdot \lfloor \log C \rfloor + 1}$ and the constraint $g_{j,1} \geq 0$. Additionally, create the constraints
   $$g_{j,2 \cdot l + 1} - g_{j,2 \cdot l} - g_{j,2 \cdot l - 1} \geq 0 \text{ and } g_{j,2 \cdot l} - g_{j,2 \cdot l - 1} \geq 0 \text{ for } l = 1 \ldots \lfloor \log C \rfloor.$$
   Let S_j denote this set of constraints.
   (b) Create the variables $e_{j,k}$ for $k = 0 \ldots |E|$. Additionally, create the constraints $e_{j,0} - e_{j,1} \geq 0$, $e_{j,1} - g_{j,2 \cdot E(1) + 1} - e_{j,2} \geq 0, \ldots, e_{j,|E|-1} - g_{j,2 \cdot E(|E|-1)+1} - e_{j,|E|} \geq 0$, and $e_{j,|E|} - g_{j,2 \cdot E(|E|)+1} \geq 0$.
   (c) Add the literal $-e_{j,0}$ to the constraint l_j.

We will now show that $\mathbf{H'}$ has copy complexity at most C if and only if $\mathbf{H}$ has copy complexity 1.

First assume that $\mathbf{H}$ has copy complexity 1. Let R be a read-once refutation of $\mathbf{H}$. We construct a refutation R' of $\mathbf{H'}$ as follows:

1. Add each constraint used by R to R'.
2. For each constraint l_j used by R, add the constraints $e_{j,0} - e_{j,1} \geq 0, \ldots, e_{j,|E|} - g_{j,2 \cdot E(|E|)+1} \geq 0$ to R'. Additionally, add enough copies of the constraints in S_j to cancel all of the $g_{j,l}$ variables. From Theorem 3, this requires $\sum_{i \in E} 2^i = C$ copies of the constraint $g_{j,1} \geq 0$.

Note that R' is a refutation of $\mathbf{H'}$ that uses each constraint at most C times. Thus, $\mathbf{H'}$ has copy complexity at most C.

Now assume that $\mathbf{H'}$ has a refutation that uses no constraint more than C times. We construct a read-once refutation R of $\mathbf{H}$ as follows: for each constraint l_j in $\mathbf{H'}$ used by R' add the corresponding constraint l_j from $\mathbf{H}$ to R. By construction, the remaining constraints in R' are used to eliminate the variable $e_{j,0}$ from each constraint l_j. Since these variables do not exist in $\mathbf{H}$, R is a refutation of $\mathbf{H}$. All that remains is to show that no constraint l_j is used more than once by R'.

Assume that for some j, the constraint l_j is used $r > 1$ times by R'. Thus, by construction, the constraint $e_{j,0} - e_{j,1} \geq 0$ must also be used r times by R'. From Theorem 3, this means that the constraint $g_{j,1} \geq 0$ needs to be used at least $r \cdot C > C$ times by R'. This contradicts the fact that R used no constraint more than C times. Thus, each constraint l_j is used at most once. Consequently, R is a read-once refutation of H. □

Since the CC_D problem is in **NP**, there exists a $2^{p(m,n)}$ algorithm for this problem, where $p(m,n)$ is some polynomial in m and n. We now show that there cannot be a $2^{o(n)}$ algorithm for the CC_D problem for width 3 HCSs unless the Exponential Time Hypothesis (**ETH**) fails [5,6].

The ETH states that for each $k \geq 3$, there exists a constant $s_k > 0$ such that k-SAT cannot be solved in time less than $O(2^{s_k \cdot n})$. In particular, this precludes a $2^{o(n)}$ time algorithm for 3-SAT. We now utilize the reduction used by Lemma 2 to establish a likely lower bound on the running time on any algorithm for solving the copy complexity problem for width 3 HCSs.

Theorem 6. *There cannot be a $2^{o(n)}$ algorithm for the CC_D problem for width 3 HCSs unless the ETH fails.*

Proof. From Lemma 2, if there is a $2^{o(n)}$ time algorithm for the copy complexity problem for HCSs, then there is a $2^{o(n'+m')}$ algorithm for 3-CNF feasibility. This violates the ETH [5,6]. Thus, it is unlikely that a $2^{o(n)}$ time algorithm exists for the CC_D problem for HCSs. □

We now show that the problem of finding the copy complexity of a width 3 HCS is **NPO complete** [1]. We do this by a reduction from the Weighted Min-Ones problem.

The Weighted Min-Ones problem is defined as follows: Given a 3CNF formula Φ and positive integer valued variable weight function w, what is the satisfying assignment to Φ with least weight of variables set to **true**. This problem is known to be **NPO-complete** [11].

Let Φ be a CNF formula with m clauses over n variables where each variable x_i has weight $w(i)$. Additionally, let W be the target weight. We construct the corresponding HCS **H** as follows:

1. Let w_{max} be the largest weight of any variable x_i of Φ. Additionally let $f = \lfloor \log w_{max} \rfloor$.
2. For each variable x_i of Φ, create the variables x_i, t_i and y_i^+.
3. Create the constraints $-x_1 - t_1 \geq 0, t_1 - x_2 - t_2 \geq 0, \ldots, t_{n-2} - x_{n-1} - t_{n-1} \geq 0$, and $t_{n-1} - x_n \geq 1 - m$. Let S be the set containing these constraints. Note that these constraints are the only constraints to use the variables t_i for $i = 1 \ldots (n-1)$. If any constraint in S is used more times by a refutation R of **H** than any other constraint in S, then there would be a variable t_i left over in the resultant constraint. Thus, any refutation of **H** must use all of these constraints an equal number of times. Note that together these constraints are equivalent to the constraint $- \sum_{i=1}^{n} x_i \geq m - 1$.
4. For each variable x_i, let $P(i)$ be the number of clauses in Φ containing the literal x_i, and let $N(i)$ be the number of clauses in Φ containing the literal $\neg x_i$. Create the variables $z_{i,l}^+$ and $t_{i,l}^+$ for $l = 1 \ldots P(i)$ and the variables $z_{i,l}^-$ and $t_{i,l}^-$ for $l = 1 \ldots N(i)$.

5. For each variable x_i of Φ, create the constraints $x_i \geq 0$, $x_i - t_{i,1}^- \geq 0$, $t_{i,1}^- - z_{i,1}^- \geq 0$, $t_{i,1}^- - z_{i,1}^- - t_{i,2}^- \geq 0, \ldots, t_{i,N(i)-1}^- - z_{i,N(i)-1}^- \geq 0$, $t_{i,N(i)-1}^- - z_{i,N(i)-1}^- - t_{i,N(i)}^- \geq 0$, and $t_{i,N(i)}^- - z_{i,N(i)}^- \geq 0$. For each $l = 0 \ldots N(i)$, let $S_{i,l}^-$ be the set:

$$\{x_i - t_{i,1}^- \geq 0, t_{i,1}^- - z_{i,1}^- - t_{i,2}^- \geq 0, \ldots, t_{i,l}^- - z_{i,l}^- \geq 0\}.$$

Note that the constraints in $S_{i,l}^-$ are equivalent to the constraint

$x_i - \sum_{j=1}^{l} z_{i,j}^- \geq 0$.

6. For each variable x_i of Φ, create the constraints $x_i - y_i^+ \geq 0$, $x_i - y_i^+ - t_{i,1}^+ \geq 0$, $t_{i,1}^+ - z_{i,1}^+ \geq 0$, $t_{i,1}^+ - z_{i,1}^+ - t_{i,2}^+ \geq 0, \ldots, t_{i,P(i)-1}^+ - z_{i,P(i)-1}^+ \geq 0$, $t_{i,P(i)-1}^+ - z_{i,P(i)-1}^+ - t_{i,P(i)}^+ \geq 0$, and $t_{i,P(i)}^+ - z_{i,P(i)}^+ \geq 0$. For each $l = 0 \ldots P(i)$, let $S_{i,l}^+$ be the set:

$$\{x_i - y_i^+ - t_{i,1}^+ \geq 0, t_{i,1}^+ - z_{i,1}^+ - t_{i,2}^+ \geq 0, \ldots, t_{i,l}^+ - z_{i,l}^+ \geq 0\}.$$

Note that the constraints in $S_{i,l}^+$ are equivalent to the constraint $x_i - y^+ - \sum_{j=1}^{l} z_{i,j}^+ \geq 0$.

7. For each clause $\phi_j \in \Phi$, create the variables c_j and d_j. Additionally, create the constraint $c_j - d_j \geq 1$.

8. For each clause $\phi_j \in \Phi$, create the variables $d_{j,1}$ through $d_{j,2 \cdot \lfloor \log W \rfloor + 1}$ and the constraint $d_{j,1} \geq 0$. Additionally, create the constraints $d_{j,2 \cdot l+1} - d_{j,2 \cdot l} - d_{j,2 \cdot l-1} \geq 0$ and $d_{j,2 \cdot l} - d_{j,2 \cdot l-1} \geq 0$ for $l = 1 \ldots \lfloor \log W \rfloor$. Let S_j' denote this set of constraints.

9. Let $E_W \subseteq \mathbb{N}$ be such that $\sum_{j \in E_W} 2^j = W$. For each $k = 1 \ldots |E_W|$, let $E(W, k)$ be the kth element of E_W. For each clause ϕ_j, create the variables $h_{j,k}$ for $k = 1 \ldots |E_W|$. Additionally, create the constraints $d_j - h_{j,1} \geq 0$, $h_{j,1} - d_{j,2 \cdot E(W,1)+1} - h_{j,2} \geq 0, \ldots, h_{j,|E_W|-1} - d_{j,2 \cdot E(W,|E_W|-1)+1} - h_{j,|E_W|} \geq 0$, and $h_{j,|E_W|} - d_{j,2 \cdot E(W,|E_W|)+1} \geq 0$.

10. For each clause $\phi_j \in \Phi$ and each variable x_i, if the literal x_i appears in the clause ϕ_j, add the constraints $z_{i,l}^+ - c_j \geq 0$ for $l = 1 \ldots P(i)$ to $\mathbf{H}$. If the literal $\neg x_i$ appears in the clause ϕ_j, add the constraints $z_{i,l}^- - c_j \geq 0$ for $l = 1 \ldots N(i)$ to $\mathbf{H}$.

11. Create the variables g_1 through $g_{2 \cdot f+1}$ and the constraint $g_1 \geq 0$. Additionally, create the constraints $g_{2 \cdot l+1} - g_{2 \cdot l} - g_{2 \cdot l-1} \geq 0$ and $g_{2 \cdot l} - g_{2 \cdot l-1} \geq 0$ for $l = 1 \ldots f$. Let S_f denote this set of constraints.

12. For each variable x_i of Φ, let $E_i \subseteq \mathbb{N}$ be such that $\sum_{j \in E_i} 2^j = w(i)$. For each $k = 1 \ldots |E_i|$, let $E(i, k)$ be the kth element of E_i. Create the variables $e_{i,k}$ for $k = 1 \ldots |E_i|$. Additionally, create the constraints $y_i^+ - e_{i,1} \geq 0$, $e_{i,1} - g_{2 \cdot E(i,1)+1} - e_{i,2} \geq 0, \ldots, e_{i,|E_i|-1} - g_{2 \cdot E(i,|E_i|-1)+1} - e_{i,|E_i|} \geq 0$, and $e_{i,|E_i|} - g_{2 \cdot E(i,|E_i|)+1} \geq 0$.

We now show that a CNF formula Φ has a solution in which the total weight of **true** variables is at most W if and only if the HCS $\mathbf{H}$ has a copy complexity of at most W.

Lemma 3. *Let Φ be a CNF formula with weighted variables and let $\mathbf{H}$ be the HCS constructed from Φ. Φ has a solution in which the total weight of **true** variables is at most W if and only if $\mathbf{H}$ has a copy complexity of at most W.*

Proof. First, assume that Φ has a solution $\mathbf{x}$ such that $W^* = \sum_{x_i : x_i = \text{true}} w(i) \leq W$. We will show that $\mathbf{H}$ has copy complexity at most W by showing that $\mathbf{H}$ has a refutation R that uses each constraint at most W^* times. We construct R as follows:

1. Add the constraints in S to R. Recall that these constraints are equivalent to $-\sum_{i=1}^{n} x_i \geq 1 - m$.
2. For each clause $\phi_j \in \Phi$ let $T(j)$ be a literal in ϕ_j set to **true** by $\mathbf{x}$.
3. For each variable x_i, let $Pos(i) = \{\phi_j : T(j) = x_i\}$, and let $Neg(i) = \{\phi_j : T(j) = \neg x_i\}$.
4. For each variable x_i, if x_i is assigned **true** by $\mathbf{x}$, then add the constraints in $S^+_{i,|Pos(i)|}$ to R. If x_i is assigned **false** by $\mathbf{x}$, then add the constraints in $S^-_{i,|Neg(i)|}$ to R.
5. For each variable x_i set to **true** by $\mathbf{x}$, add the constraints $y_i^+ - e_{i,1} \geq 0, \ldots, e_{i,|E_i|} - g_{2 \cdot E(i,|E_i|)+1} \geq 0$ to R. Additionally, add enough copies of the constraints in S_f to cancel all of the g_l variables. From Theorem 3, this requires $\sum_{j \in E_i} 2^j = w(i)$ copies of the constraint $g_1 \geq 0$.
6. For each variable x_i set to **true** by $\mathbf{x}$ and for each $l = 1 \ldots |Pos(i)|$, let ϕ_j be the lth element of $Pos(i)$. Add the constraint $z_{i,l}^+ - c_j \geq 0$ to R.
7. For each variable x_i set to **false** by $\mathbf{x}$ and for each $l = 1 \ldots |Neg(i)|$, let ϕ_j be the lth element of $Neg(i)$. Add the constraint $z_{i,l}^- - c_j \geq 0$ to R.
8. Add the constraints $c_1 - d_1 \geq 1$ through $c_m - d_m \geq 1$ to R.
9. For each clause ϕ_j, add the constraints $d_j - h_{j,1} \geq 0, \ldots, h_{j,|E_W|} - d_{j,2 \cdot E(W,|E_W|)+1} \geq 0$ to R. Additionally, add enough copies of the constraints in S'_j to cancel all of the $d_{j,l}$ variables. From Theorem 3, this requires $\sum_{l \in E_W} 2^l = W$ copies of the constraint $d_{j,1} \geq 0$.

It is easy to see that summing all of the constraints in R results in a contradiction of the form $0 \geq 1$. Thus, R is a refutation of $\mathbf{H}$. Note that the constraints reused by R belong to the sets S_f and S'_j for $j = 1 \ldots m$. From Theorem 3, the constraints reused the most are the constraint $g_1 \geq 0$ and the constraints $d_{j,1} \geq 0$ for $j = 1 \ldots m$. These constraints are each used at most W times as desired.

Now assume that $\mathbf{H}$ has a refutation that uses no constraint more than W times. Thus, $\mathbf{H}$ has a refutation R such that the constraint $g_1 \geq 0$ is used $W^* \leq W$ times. We construct an assignment $\mathbf{x}$ to Φ as follows: for each variable x_i, if R contains the constraint $x_i - y_i^+ \geq 0$ or $x_i - y_i^+ - t_{i,1}^+ \geq 0$, then set x_i to **true**. Otherwise set x_i to **false**.

We make the following observations about R:

1. If the constraints in S are removed from $\mathbf{H}$, then $\mathbf{H}$ is feasible, thus these constraints must be used by R. Recall that these constraints are equivalent to $-\sum_{i=1}^{n} x_i \geq 1 - m$.

2. To get a contradiction, the defining constant of the derived constraint must be positive. Note that the only constraints with positive defining constant in $\mathbf{H}$ are of the form $c_j - d_j \geq 1$. As noted previously, eliminating d_j from each of these constraints requires W copies of the constraint $d_{j,1} \geq 0$. Thus, each of these constraints is used at most once by R. There are m such constraints, thus they must all be used by R. Consequently, the constraints in S can be each used at most once by R.

3. Consider the constraint $c_j - d_j \geq 1$. The only constraints with $-c_j$ in $\mathbf{H}$ are of the form $z_{i,l}^- - c_j \geq 0$ and $z_{i,l}^+ - c_j \geq 0$. Thus, R must contain a constraint of this form.

4. If R contains a constraint of the form $z_{i,l}^- - c_j \geq 0$, then it must contain the constraint $t_{i,l}^- - z_{i,l}^- \geq 0$ or $t_{i,l}^- - z_{i,l}^- - t_{i,l+1}^- \geq 0$. To cancel the $t_{i,l}^-$ variables, R must include the constraint $x_i - t_{i,1}^- \geq 0$. This constraint cancels the variable x_i from the constraint $-\sum_{i=1}^n x_i \geq 1 - m$. Thus, the constraints $x_i - y_i^+ \geq 0$ and $x_i - y_i^+ - t_{i,1}^+ \geq 0$ cannot be in R. This means that x_i is set to **false** by $\mathbf{x}$. Note that the constraint $z_{i,l}^- - c_j \geq 0$ is in $\mathbf{H}$ if and only if ϕ_j contains the literal $\neg x_i$. Thus, ϕ_j is satisfied by $\mathbf{x}$.

5. If R contains a constraint of the form $z_{i,l}^+ - c_j \geq 0$, then it must contain the constraint $t_{i,l}^+ - z_{i,l}^+ \geq 0$ or $t_{i,l}^+ - z_{i,l}^+ - t_{i,l+1}^+ \geq 0$. To cancel the $t_{i,l}^+$ variables, R must include the constraint $x_i - y_i^+ - t_{i,1}^+ \geq 0$. This means that x_i is set to **true** by $\mathbf{x}$. Note that the constraint $z_{i,l}^- - c_j \geq 0$ is in $\mathbf{H}$ if and only if ϕ_j contains the literal $\neg x_i$. Thus, ϕ_j is satisfied by $\mathbf{x}$.

6. As observed previously, canceling y_i^+ from the constraint $x_i - y_i^+ - z_{i,1}^+ \geq 0$ takes at least $w(i)$ uses of the constraint $g_1 \geq 0$. Thus, $\sum_{x_i : x_i = \mathbf{true}} w(i) \leq W^* \leq W$ as desired.   □

Using Lemma 3, we now show that the CC_{Opt} problem for width 3 HCSs is **NPO-complete**.

Theorem 7. *The CC_{Opt} problem for width 3 HCSs is* **NPO-complete**.

Proof. The copy complexity of an HCS can be verified in polynomial time by providing the Farkas vector. Thus, the CC_{Opt} problem is in **NPO**. All that remains is to show **NPO-hardness**.

Let Φ be a CNF formula with m clauses over n variables where each variable x_i has weight $w(i)$. Using the construction in this section, we can construct a corresponding width 3 HCS $\mathbf{H}$. From Theorem 3, this HCS has a copy complexity of at most W if and only if Φ has a solution in which the total weight of **true** variables is at most W. This is a strict (and hence) PTAS reduction [11]. Consequently, the CC_{Opt} problem for width 3 HCSs is **NPO-complete**.   □

Since the CC_{Opt} problem for width 3 HCSs is **NPO-complete**, this problem cannot be approximated to within a polynomial factor unless $\mathbf{P} = \mathbf{NP}$ [7].

5   Conclusion

In this paper, we analyzed the problem of determining bounds on the copy complexity bounds of HCSs. We showed that for any HCS, the copy complexity cannot exceed 2^{n-1}, where n is the number of variables in the HCS. We also showed that for each n, there exists a family of width 3 HCSs with copy complexity $2^{\lfloor \frac{n}{2} \rfloor}$. Additionally, we showed that the CC_D problem for width 3 HCSs is **NP-complete**.

From our perspective, the following avenues are worth pursuing:

1. The focus of this paper has been copy complexity with respect to the ADD refutation system. However, additional inference rules exist which allow for constraints to be multiplied by and divided by positive integers. We hope to replicate the analysis in this paper when we allow for the use of these additional inference rules.
2. The goal of this paper was to focus on the copy complexity of HCSs. In some refutation models, the goal is not so much to minimize the copy complexity, but to minimize the total number of **distinct** constraint replications. In other words, the first replication has a cost associated with it, but all other replications are gratis. It would be interesting to study HCSs in this model.

References

1. Ausiello, G., Crescenzi, P., Gambosi, G., Kann, V., Marchetti-Spaccamela, A., Protasi, M.: Complexity and Approximation: Combinatorial Optimization and their Approximability Properties, 1st edn. Springer, Cham (1999). https://doi.org/10.1007/978-3-642-58412-1
2. Bakhirkin, A., Monniaux, D.: Combining forward and backward abstract interpretation of horn clauses. In: Ranzato, F. (ed.) SAS 2017. LNCS, vol. 10422, pp. 23–45. Springer, Cham (2017). https://doi.org/10.1007/978-3-319-66706-5_2
3. Bjørner, N., Gurfinkel, A., McMillan, K., Rybalchenko, A.: Horn clause solvers for program verification. In: Beklemishev, L.D., Blass, A., Dershowitz, N., Finkbeiner, B., Schulte, W. (eds.) Fields of Logic and Computation II. LNCS, vol. 9300, pp. 24–51. Springer, Cham (2015). https://doi.org/10.1007/978-3-319-23534-9_2
4. Farkas, G.: Über die Theorie der Einfachen Ungleichungen. J. für die Reine und Angewandte Mathematik **124**(124), 1–27 (1902)
5. Impagliazzo, R., Paturi, R.: Complexity of k-sat. In: Proceedings. Fourteenth Annual IEEE Conference on Computational Complexity, pp. 237–240 (1999)
6. Impagliazzo, R., Paturi, R., Zane, F.: Which problems have strongly exponential complexity? J. Comput. Syst. Sci. **63**(4), 512–530 (2001)
7. Kann, V.: On the Approximability of NP-complete Optimization Problems. PhD thesis, Royal Institute of Technology Stockholm (1992)
8. Kleine Büning, H., Wojciechowski, P.J., Subramani, K.: New results on cutting plane proofs for Horn constraint systems. In: 39th IARCS Annual Conference on Foundations of Software Technology and Theoretical Computer Science, FSTTCS 2019, 11–13 December, 2019, Bombay, India, pp. 43:1–43:14 (2019)
9. LiCalzi, M., Veinott, A.: Subextremal functions and lattice programming. SSRN Electron. J. **10**, 367 (2005)

10. Nemhauser, G.L., Wolsey, L.A.: Integer and Combinatorial Optimization. John Wiley & Sons, New York (1999)
11. Orponen, P., Mannila, H.: On approximation preserving reductions: Complete problems and robust measures. Technical Report, Department of Computer Science, University of Helsinki (1987)
12. Schrijver, A.: Theory of Linear and Integer Programming. John Wiley and Sons, New York (1987)

Description Logics

Restricted Unification in the DL $\mathcal{FL}_0$

Franz Baader[1]([⊠])[ID], Oliver Fernández Gil[1][ID], and Maryam Rostamigiv[2][ID]

[1] Theoretical Computer Science, TU Dresden, Dresden, Germany
{franz.baader,oliver.fernandez}@tu-dresden.de
[2] Département d'Informatique, Paul Sabatier University, Toulouse, France
Maryam.Rostamigiv@irit.fr

Abstract. Unification in the Description Logic (DL) $\mathcal{FL}_0$ is known to be ExpTime-complete and of unification type zero. We investigate whether a lower complexity of the unification problem can be achieved by either syntactically restricting the role depth of concepts or semantically restricting the length of role paths in interpretations. We show that the answer to this question depends on whether the number formulating such a restriction is encoded in unary or binary: for unary coding, the complexity drops from ExpTime to PSpace. As an auxiliary result, we prove a PSpace-completeness result for a depth-restricted version of the intersection emptiness problem for deterministic root-to-frontier tree automata. Finally, we show that the unification type of $\mathcal{FL}_0$ improves from type zero to unitary (finitary) for unification without (with) constants in the restricted setting.

1 Introduction

Unification of concept patterns has been proposed as an inference service in Description Logics that can, for example, be used to detect redundancies in ontologies. For the DL $\mathcal{FL}_0$, which has the concept constructors conjunction ($\sqcap$), value restriction ($\forall r.C$), and top concept ($\top$), unification was investigated in detail in [6]. It was shown there that unification in $\mathcal{FL}_0$ corresponds to unification modulo the equational theory $ACUIh$ since (modulo equivalence) conjunction is associative (A), commutative (C), idempotent (I) and has top as a unit (U), and value restrictions behave like homomorphisms for conjunction and top (h). For this equational theory, it had already been shown in [1] that it has unification type zero, which means that a solvable unification problem need not have a minimal complete set of unifiers, and thus in particular not a finite one. From the DL point of view, the decision problem is, however, more interesting than the unification type. Since $ACUIh$ is a commutative/monoidal theory [1,14], solvability of $ACUIh$ unification problems (and thus of unification problems in $\mathcal{FL}_0$) can be reduced to solvability of systems of linear equations in a certain semiring, which for the case of $ACUIh$ consists of finite languages over a finite alphabet, with union as semiring addition and concatenation as semiring multiplication [6]. By a reduction to the emptiness problem for root-to-frontier tree automata (RFAs), it was then shown in [6] that solvability of the language

© Springer Nature Switzerland AG 2021
B. Konev and G. Reger (Eds.): FroCoS 2021, LNAI 12941, pp. 81–97, 2021.
https://doi.org/10.1007/978-3-030-86205-3_5

equations corresponding to an $\mathcal{FL}_0$ unification problem can be decided in exponential time. In addition, ExpTime-hardness of this problem was proved in [6] by reduction from the intersection emptiness problem for deterministic RFAs (DRFAs) [16].

In the present paper, we investigate two kinds of restrictions on unification in $\mathcal{FL}_0$. On the one hand, we *syntactically restrict the role depth* (i.e., the maximal nesting of value restrictions) in the concepts obtained by applying a unifier to be bounded by a natural number $k \geq 1$. This restriction was motivated by a similar restriction used in research on least common subsumers (lcs) [15], where imposing a bound on the role depth guarantees existence of the lcs also in the presence of a (possibly cyclic) terminology. Also note that such a restriction was used in [11] for the theory ACh, for which unification is known to be undecidable [13]. It is shown in [11] that the problem becomes decidable if a bound on the maximal nesting of applications of homomorphisms is imposed. On the other hand, we consider a *semantic restriction* where only interpretations for which the length of role paths is bounded by a given number k are considered when defining the semantics of concepts. A similar restriction (for $k = 1$) was employed in [9] to improve the unification type for the modal logic $\mathbf{K}$ from type zero [10] to unitary or finitary for $\mathbf{K} + \Box\Box\bot$.

In the present paper we show that both the syntactic and the semantic restriction ensures that the unification type of $\mathcal{FL}_0$ (and equivalently, of the theory $ACUIh$) improves from type zero to unitary for unification without constants and finitary for unification with constants. Regarding the decision problem, we can show that the complexity depends on whether the bound k is assumed to be encoded in unary or binary[1]. For binary encoding of k, the complexity stays ExpTime, whereas for unary coding it drops from ExpTime to PSpace. This is again the case both for the syntactic and the semantic restriction. As an auxiliary result we prove that a depth-restricted variant of the intersection emptiness for DRFAs is PSpace-complete.

Showing these results requires combining methods and results from knowledge representation, unification theory, and automata theory. Due to space restrictions, we cannot give detailed proofs here. They can be found in [3].

2   The DL $\mathcal{FL}_0$ and Restrictions

Starting with mutually disjoint countably infinite sets N_C and N_R of concept and role names, respectively, the set of $\mathcal{FL}_0$ concepts is inductively defined as follows:

- $\top$ (top concept) and every concept name $A \in N_C$ is an $\mathcal{FL}_0$ concept,
- if C, D are $\mathcal{FL}_0$ concepts and $r \in N_R$ is a role name, then $C \sqcap D$ (conjunction) and $\forall r.C$ (value restriction) are $\mathcal{FL}_0$ concepts.

---

[1] For unary coding, the size of the input k is the number k, whereas for binary coding it is the size of its binary encoding, i.e., $\log k$.

The *semantics* of $\mathcal{FL}_0$ concepts is defined using first-order interpretations $\mathcal{I} = (\mathcal{D}^{\mathcal{I}}, \cdot^{\mathcal{I}})$ consisting of a non-empty domain $\mathcal{D}^{\mathcal{I}}$ and an interpretation function $\cdot^{\mathcal{I}}$ that assigns a set $A^{\mathcal{I}} \subseteq \mathcal{D}^{\mathcal{I}}$ to each concept name A, and a binary relation $r^{\mathcal{I}} \subseteq \mathcal{D}^{\mathcal{I}} \times \mathcal{D}^{\mathcal{I}}$ to each role name r. This function is extended to $\mathcal{FL}_0$ concepts as follows:

$$\top^{\mathcal{I}} = \mathcal{D}^{\mathcal{I}} \quad \text{and} \quad (C \sqcap D)^{\mathcal{I}} = C^{\mathcal{I}} \cap D^{\mathcal{I}},$$

$$(\forall r.C)^{\mathcal{I}} = \{x \in \mathcal{D}^{\mathcal{I}} \mid \forall y \in \mathcal{D}^{\mathcal{I}} \colon (x,y) \in r^{\mathcal{I}} \Rightarrow y \in C^{\mathcal{I}}\}.$$

Given two $\mathcal{FL}_0$ concepts C and D, we say that C is subsumed by D (written $C \sqsubseteq D$) if $C^{\mathcal{I}} \subseteq D^{\mathcal{I}}$ holds for all interpretations $\mathcal{I}$, and that C is equivalent to D (written $C \equiv D$) if $C \sqsubseteq D$ and $D \sqsubseteq C$. It is well known that subsumption (and thus also equivalence) of $\mathcal{FL}_0$ concepts can be decided in polynomial time [12].

Note that, up to equivalence, conjunction is associative, commutative, and idempotent, and has the unit element $\top$. In addition, the following equivalences hold for value restrictions: $\forall r.\top \equiv \top$ and $\forall r.(C \sqcap D) \equiv \forall r.C \sqcap \forall r.D$. Due to these equivalences, one can transform $\mathcal{FL}_0$ concepts into a normal form that uses formal languages over the alphabet of role names to represent value restrictions that end with the same concept name. In fact, using these equivalences as rewrite rules from left to right, every $\mathcal{FL}_0$ concept can be transformed into an equivalent one that is either $\top$ or a conjunction of concepts of the form $\forall r_1. \cdots \forall r_n.A$, where $r_1, \ldots, r_n$ are role names and A is a concept name. Such a concept can be abbreviated as $\forall w.A$, where $w = r_1 \ldots r_n$ is a word over the alphabet N_R. Note that $n = 0$ means that w is the empty word ε, and thus $\forall \varepsilon.A$ corresponds to A. Furthermore, a conjunction of the form $\forall w_1.A \sqcap \ldots \sqcap \forall w_m.A$ can be written as $\forall L.A$ where $L \subseteq N_R^*$ is the finite language $\{w_1, \ldots, w_m\}$. We use the convention that $\forall \emptyset.A$ corresponds to the top concept $\top$. Thus, any two $\mathcal{FL}_0$ concepts C, D containing only the concept names $A_1, \ldots, A_\ell$ can be represented as

$$C \equiv \forall K_1.A_1 \sqcap \ldots \sqcap \forall K_\ell.A_\ell \quad \text{and} \quad D \equiv \forall L_1.A_1 \sqcap \ldots \sqcap \forall L_\ell.A_\ell, \qquad (1)$$

where $K_1, L_1, \ldots, K_\ell, L_\ell$ are finite languages over the alphabet of role names N_R. We call this representation the *language normal form (LNF)* of C, D. If C, D have the LNF shown in (1), then $C \equiv D$ holds iff $L_1 = K_1, \ldots, L_\ell = K_\ell$ (see Lemma 4.2 of [6]).

2.1   Syntactically Restricting the Role Depth

The role depth of an $\mathcal{FL}_0$ concept is the maximal nesting of value restrictions in this concept. Since occurrences of $\top$ within value restrictions can increase the role depth artificially, we assume without loss of generality that $\mathcal{FL}_0$ concepts different from $\top$ do not contain any occurrences of $\top$. We will make this assumption in the rest of the paper without mentioning it explicitly.

The role depth $rd(C)$ of an $\mathcal{FL}_0$ concept C is defined by induction:

- $rd(\top) = rd(A) = 0$ for all $A \in N_C$,
- $rd(C \sqcap D) = \max(rd(C), rd(D))$ and $rd(\forall r.C) = 1 + rd(C)$.

It is easy to see that (under the above assumption) the role depth of $\mathcal{FL}_0$ concepts is preserved under equivalence.

We are now ready to define our first restricted version of subsumption and equivalence in $\mathcal{FL}_0$. For an integer $k \geq 1$ and $\mathcal{FL}_0$ concepts C and D, we define subsumption and equivalence restricted to concepts of role depth $\leq k$ as follows:

- $C \sqsubseteq_{syn}^k D$ if $C \sqsubseteq D$ and $\max(rd(C), rd(D)) \leq k$,
- $C \equiv_{syn}^k D$ if $C \sqsubseteq_{syn}^k D$ and $D \sqsubseteq_{syn}^k C$.

The effect of this definition is that subsumption and equivalence can only hold for concepts that satisfy the restriction of the role depth by k. For concepts satisfying this syntactic restriction, the relations $\sqsubseteq_{syn}^k$ and $\equiv_{syn}^k$ coincide with the classical subsumption and equivalence relations on $\mathcal{FL}_0$ concepts. Using the language normal form of $\mathcal{FL}_0$ concepts, the equivalence $\equiv_{syn}^k$ can be characterized as follows: if C, D have the LNF shown in (1), then $C \equiv_{syn}^k D$ iff $L_1 = K_1 \subseteq N_R^{\leq k}, \ldots, L_\ell = K_\ell \subseteq N_R^{\leq k}$, where $N_R^{\leq k}$ denotes the set of words over N_R of length at most k.

2.2 Semantically Restricting the Length of Role Paths

For an integer $n \geq 1$ and a given interpretation $\mathcal{I} = (\mathcal{D}^\mathcal{I}, \cdot^\mathcal{I})$, a role path of length n is a sequence $d_0, r_1, d_1, \ldots, d_{n-1}, r_n, d_n$, where $d_0, \ldots, d_n$ are elements of $\mathcal{D}^\mathcal{I}$, $r_1, \ldots, r_n$ are role names, and $(d_{i-1}, d_i) \in r_i^\mathcal{I}$ holds for all $i = 1, \ldots, n$. The interpretation $\mathcal{I}$ is called k-restricted if it does not contain any role paths of length $> k$.

For an integer $k \geq 1$ and $\mathcal{FL}_0$ concepts C and D, we define subsumption and equivalence restricted to interpretations with role paths of length $\leq k$ as follows:

- $C \sqsubseteq_{sem}^k D$ if $C^\mathcal{I} \subseteq D^\mathcal{I}$ holds for all k-restricted interpretations $\mathcal{I}$,
- $C \equiv_{sem}^k D$ if $C \sqsubseteq_{sem}^k D$ and $D \sqsubseteq_{sem}^k C$.

The effect of this notion of equivalence is that all concepts occurring at a role depth $> k$ can be replaced by $\top$. To be more precise, we define the restriction of a concept C to role depth $n \geq 0$ by induction on n as follows:

- $A|_n = A$ for $A \in N_C \cup \{\top\}$ and $(C \sqcap D)|_n = C|_n \sqcap D|_n$ for all $n \geq 0$;
- $(\forall r.C)|_0 = \top$ and $(\forall r.C)|_n = \forall r.(C|_{n-1})$ for all $n \geq 1$.

For example, $(\forall r.\forall r.\forall r.A)|_4 = \forall r.\forall r.\forall r.A = (\forall r.\forall r.\forall r.A)|_3$ and $(\forall r.\forall r.\forall r.A)|_2 = \forall r.\forall r.\top \equiv \top$. In the language normal form, restricting to role depth n means that all words that are longer than n can simply be removed.

It is easy to see that $C \equiv_{sem}^k D$ iff $C|_k \equiv D|_k$, which yields the following characterization of the equivalence $\equiv_{sem}^k$: if C, D have the LNF shown in (1), then $C \equiv_{sem}^k D$ iff $L_1 \cap N_R^{\leq k} = K_1 \cap N_R^{\leq k}, \ldots, L_\ell \cap N_R^{\leq k} = K_\ell \cap N_R^{\leq k}$.

3   Unification in $\mathcal{FL}_0$

In unification, we consider concepts that may contain variables, which can be replaced by concepts. More formally, we introduce a countably infinite set N_V of concept variables, which is disjoint with N_C and N_R. An $\mathcal{FL}_0$ concept pattern is an $\mathcal{FL}_0$ concept that is constructed using $N_C \cup N_V$ as concept names. The semantics of concept patterns is defined as for concepts, i.e., concept variables are treated like concept names when defining the semantics. This way, the notions of subsumption and equivalence (both in the restricted and in the unrestricted setting) transfer from concepts to concept patterns in the obvious way.

A substitution σ is a mapping from N_V into the set of all $\mathcal{FL}_0$ concept patterns such that $dom(\sigma) := \{X \in N_V \mid \sigma(X) \neq X\}$ is finite. This mapping is extended to concept patterns in the obvious ways:

- $\sigma(A) := A$ for all $A \in N_C \cup \{\top\}$,
- $\sigma(C \sqcap D) := \sigma(C) \sqcap \sigma(D)$ and $\sigma(\forall r.C) := \forall r.\sigma(C)$.

An $\mathcal{FL}_0$ *unification problem* is an equation of the form $C \overset{?}{\equiv} D$ where C, D are $\mathcal{FL}_0$ concept patterns. A unifier of this equation is a substitution σ such that $\sigma(C) \equiv \sigma(D)$.

It was shown in [6] that the question of whether a given $\mathcal{FL}_0$ unification problem has a unifier or not can be reduced to solving linear language equations, i.e., equations of the form

$$S_0 \cup S_1 \cdot X_1 \cup \cdots \cup S_n \cdot X_n = T_0 \cup T_1 \cdot X_1 \cup \cdots \cup T_n \cdot X_n, \tag{2}$$

where $S_0, \ldots, S_n, T_0, \ldots, T_n$ are finite languages of words over an alphabet $\Delta = \{1, \ldots, \rho\}^2$ and $X_1, \ldots, X_n$ are variables that can be replaced by finite languages over Δ. A solution of the Eq. (2) is an assignment θ of finite languages $\theta(X_i)$ to the variables X_i (for $i = 1, \ldots, n$) such that

$$S_0 \cup S_1 \cdot \theta(X_1) \cup \cdots \cup S_n \cdot \theta(X_n) = T_0 \cup T_1 \cdot \theta(X_1) \cup \cdots \cup T_n \cdot \theta(X_n), \tag{3}$$

where $\cup$ is interpreted as union and $\cdot$ as concatenation of languages. Strictly speaking, a given $\mathcal{FL}_0$ unification problem yields one such language equation for every concept name occurring in the problem. But since these equations do not share variables, they can be solved separately. Also note that solvability of language equations of the form (2) can in turn be reduced in polynomial time to $\mathcal{FL}_0$ unification.

A word $w = i_1 \ldots i_\ell$ occurring in a solution of the form (3) corresponds to a conjunct $\forall r_{i_1}. \cdots \forall r_{i_\ell}.A$ in the unified concept $\sigma(C) \equiv \sigma(D)$. Thus, the length of the word w is equal to the role depth of the corresponding sequence of value restrictions.

---

[2] Intuitively, ρ is the number of different role names occurring in the unification problem and each letter $i, 1 \leq i \leq \rho$, stands for a role name r_i.

Example 1. Consider the $\mathcal{FL}_0$ unification problem $\forall r_1.\forall r_1.A \sqcap \forall r_1.\forall r_1.X \overset{?}{\equiv} X \sqcap \forall r_1.\forall r_1.\forall r_1.Y$. The substitution σ with $\sigma(X) = \forall r_1.\forall r_1.A$ and $\sigma(Y) = \forall r_1.A$ is one of the unifiers of this problem. The language equation induced by this unification problem is $\{11\} \cup \{11\}\cdot X = \{\varepsilon\}\cdot X \cup \{111\}\cdot Y$. The unifier σ corresponds to the following solution θ of this problem: $\theta(X) = \{11\}$ and $\theta(Y) = \{1\}$.

3.1 Syntactically Restricted Unification in $\mathcal{FL}_0$

For an integer $k \geq 1$, a syntactically k-restricted unification problem is an equation of the form $C \overset{?}{\equiv}{}^k_{syn} D$, where C, D are $\mathcal{FL}_0$ concept patterns. A unifier of this equation is a substitution σ such that $\sigma(C) \equiv^k_{syn} \sigma(D)$.

Due to the LNF characterization of $\equiv^k_{syn}$ and the correspondence between role depth and word length mentioned above, solvability of a given syntactically k-restricted unification problem can be reduced to checking whether language equations of the form (2) have solutions θ such that

$$S_0 \cup S_1\cdot\theta(X_1) \cup \cdots \cup S_n\cdot\theta(X_n) = T_0 \cup T_1\cdot\theta(X_1) \cup \cdots \cup T_n\cdot\theta(X_n) \subseteq \Delta^{\leq k}, \quad (4)$$

where $\Delta^{\leq k}$ denotes the set of words over Δ of length at most k.

The unifier σ of the $\mathcal{FL}_0$ unification problem in Example 1 is not a syntactically 3-restricted unifier of this problem since the unified concept $\sigma(\forall r_1.\forall r_1.A \sqcap \forall r_1.\forall r_1.X) = \forall r_1.\forall r_1.A \sqcap \forall r_1.\forall r_1.\forall r_1.\forall r_1.A = \sigma(X \sqcap \forall r_1.\forall r_1.Y)$ has role depth 4. This is reflected on the language equation side by the fact that $\{11\} \cup \{11\}\cdot\{11\} = \{11, 1111\} = \{\varepsilon\}\cdot\{11\} \cup \{111\}\cdot\{1\} \not\subseteq \Delta^{\leq 3}$. In fact, it is easy to see that this problem does not have a syntactically 3-restricted unifier.

3.2 Semantically Restricted Unification in $\mathcal{FL}_0$

For an integer $k \geq 1$, a semantically k-restricted unification problem is an equation of the form $C \overset{?}{\equiv}{}^k_{sem} D$, where C, D are $\mathcal{FL}_0$ concept patterns. A unifier of this equation is a substitution σ such that $\sigma(C) \equiv^k_{sem} \sigma(D)$.

Whereas in the syntactically restricted case a sequence of value restrictions of depth $> k$ (a word of length $> k$) destroys the property of being a unifier (solution), in the semantically restricted case one can simply ignore such sequences (words). Thus, one can reduce the question of whether a given semantically k-restricted unification problem has a unifier or not to checking whether, for language equations of the form (2), there is an assignment θ such that

$$(S_0 \cup S_1\cdot\theta(X_1) \cup \cdots \cup S_n\cdot\theta(X_n)) \cap \Delta^{\leq k}$$
$$= (T_0 \cup T_1\cdot\theta(X_1) \cup \cdots \cup T_n\cdot\theta(X_n)) \cap \Delta^{\leq k}. \quad (5)$$

Note that, in general, such an assignment need not be a solution of (2), but clearly any solution θ of (2) satisfying (3) also satisfies (5).

Example 2. The $\mathcal{FL}_0$ unification problem $\forall r_1.A \sqcap \forall r_1.\forall r_1.X \overset{?}{\equiv} X$ induces the language equation $\{1\} \cup \{11\}\cdot X = \{\varepsilon\}\cdot X$. This language equation does not have a solution in the classical sense, but it has a semantically 3-restricted solution. In fact, for the assignment θ with $\theta(X) = \{1, 111\}$ we have $\{1\} \cup \{11\} \cdot \theta(X) = \{1, 111, 11111\}$ and $\{\varepsilon\} \cdot \theta(X) = \{1, 111\}$. Intersecting these two sets with $\Delta^{\leq 3}$ yields the same set $\{1, 111\}$. Thus, the above unification problem does not have a unifier, but it has a semantically 3-restricted unifier.

4   Root-to-Frontier Tree Automata

It was shown in [6] that checking solvability of linear language equations can be reduced to testing emptiness of tree automata. More precisely, the tree automata employed in [6] work on finite node-labelled trees, going from the root to the leaves. Such automata are called root-to-frontier tree automata (RFAs) in [6]. Basically, given a linear language equation, one can construct an RFA whose size is exponential in the size of the language equation, and which accepts some tree iff the language equation has a solution. Since the emptiness problem for RFAs is polynomial, this yields an ExpTime upper bound for solvability of linear language equations. The matching ExpTime lower bound was proved in [6] by reduction from the intersection emptiness problem for deterministic RFAs (DRFAs). In this section, we formally introduce (D)RFAs and the trees they accept, and recall the ExpTime-completeness result for the intersection emptiness problem for DRFAs from [16]. We then state our new result that a depth-restricted version of this problem is PSpace-complete.

We consider trees with labels in a ranked alphabet Σ, where the number of successors of a node is determined by the rank of its label.

Definition 1. *Let Σ be a finite alphabet, where each $f \in \Sigma$ is associated with a rank, denoted as $rank(f)$, such that $rank(f) \geq 0$, and let ρ be the maximal rank of the elements of Σ. A (finite) Σ-tree is a mapping $t : dom(t) \to \Sigma$ such that $dom(t)$ is a finite subset of $\{1, \ldots, \rho\}^*$ such that*

– *the empty word ε belongs to $dom(t)$;*
– *for all $u \in \{1, \ldots, \rho\}^*$ and $i \in \{1, \ldots, \rho\}$, we have $ui \in dom(t)$ iff $u \in dom(t)$ and $i \leq rank(t(u))$.*

The elements of $dom(t)$ are the nodes of the tree t, and $t(u)$ is called the label of node u. The empty word ε is the root of t, and the nodes u such that $ui \notin dom(t)$ for all $i = 1, \ldots, \rho$ are the leaves of t. By the above definition, the leaves are the nodes labeled with a symbol of rank zero, i.e., $rank(t(u)) = 0$ iff u is a leaf of t. We denote the set of symbols of rank 0 by $\Sigma_0 := \{f \in \Sigma \mid rank(f) = 0\}$. We always assume $\Sigma_0 \neq \emptyset$ since otherwise there is no finite Σ-tree. Nodes of t that are not leaves are called inner nodes. The *depth of a node* $u \in dom(t)$ is just the length of the word u. The *depth of the tree* t, denoted as $depth(t)$, is the maximal depth of a node in $dom(t)$.

Definition 2. *A (non-deterministic) root-to-frontier tree automaton (RFA) that works on Σ-trees is a 5-tuple $\mathcal{A} = (\Sigma, Q, I, T, F)$, where*

- Σ is a finite, ranked alphabet,
- Q is a finite set of states,
- $I \subseteq Q$ is the set of initial states,
- T assigns to each $f \in \Sigma \setminus \Sigma_0$ of rank n a transition relation $T(f) \subseteq Q \times Q^n$,
- $F : \Sigma_0 \to 2^Q$ assigns to each $c \in \Sigma_0$ a set of final states $F(c) \subseteq Q$.

A run of $\mathcal{A}$ on the tree t is a mapping $r : dom(t) \to Q$ such that

- $(r(u), r(u1), \ldots, r(un)) \in T(t(u))$ for all inner nodes u of rank n.

The run r is called successful if

- $r(\varepsilon) \in I$ (root condition),
- $r(u) \in F(t(u))$ for all leaves u (leaf condition).

The tree language accepted by $\mathcal{A}$ is defined as

$$\mathcal{L}(\mathcal{A}) := \{t \mid \text{there exists a successful run of } \mathcal{A} \text{ on } t\}.$$

The emptiness problem for $\mathcal{A}$ is the question whether $\mathcal{L}(\mathcal{A}) = \emptyset$.

These automata are called root-to-frontier automata since they start at the root with an initial state, and then label successor nodes with states according to the transition relation, until they reach the leaves (also called the frontier), which must be labeled by final states to yield a successful run. Frontier-to-root automata (FRAs) work in the other direction. It is well-known that both types of automata accept the same class of tree languages, but only FRAs can be determinized, i.e., deterministic RFAs are weaker than general ones, whereas deterministic FRAs accept the same class of tree languages as general FRAs.

It is well-known that the emptiness problem for RFAs is decidable in polynomial time (see, e.g., [17]). It is also known that, if an RFA $\mathcal{A}$ accepts a tree, then it also accepts one of depth at most q, where q is the number of states of $\mathcal{A}$. In contrast to the emptiness problem, the intersection emptiness problem is ExpTime-complete even for deterministic RFAs [16].

Definition 3. The RFA $\mathcal{A} = (\Sigma, Q, I, T, F)$ is a deterministic root-to-frontier automaton (DRFA) if

- the set I of initial states consists of a single initial state q_0,
- for all states $q \in Q$ and all symbols f of rank $n > 0$ there exists exactly one n-tuple $(q_1, \ldots, q_n)$ such that $(q, q_1, \ldots, q_n) \in T(f)$.

For deterministic automata it is often more convenient to use a transition function δ in place of the (functional) transition relations. This function is defined as $\delta(q, f) := (q_1, \ldots, q_n)$, where $(q_1, \ldots, q_n)$ is the unique tuple satisfying $(q, q_1, \ldots, q_n) \in T(f)$.

Given a collection $\mathcal{A}_1, \ldots, \mathcal{A}_n$ of DRFAs, the intersection emptiness problem asks whether $L(\mathcal{A}_1) \cap \ldots \cap L(\mathcal{A}_n) = \emptyset$. For a natural number k, the k-restricted intersection emptiness problem asks, for given DFRAs $\mathcal{A}_1, \ldots, \mathcal{A}_n$, whether there is a tree t with $depth(t) \leq k$ such that $t \in L(\mathcal{A}_1) \cap \ldots \cap L(\mathcal{A}_n)$.

The complexity of the k-restricted intersection emptiness problem depends on the encoding of the number k. A proof of the following theorem can be found in [3]. The most challenging task is proving PSpace-hardness for the unary case.

Theorem 1. *The k-restricted intersection emptiness problem for DRFAs is ExpTime-complete if the number k is encoded in binary, and PSpace-complete if the number k is encoded in unary.*

5   Solving Linear Language Equations Using RFAs

As mentioned in Sect. 3, checking solvability of linear language equations was reduced in [6] to testing emptiness of RFAs. However, this approach cannot directly treat equations of the form (2). It needs equations where the variables X_i are in front of the coefficients S_i. Fortunately, such equations can easily be obtained from the ones of the form (2) by considering the mirror images of the involved languages. For a word $w = i_1 \dots i_\ell \in \Delta^*$, its mirror image is defined as $w^{mi} := i_\ell \dots i_1$, and for a finite set of words $L = \{w_1, \dots, w_m\}$, its mirror image is $L^{mi} := \{w_1^{mi}, \dots, w_m^{mi}\}$. Obviously, the assignment θ with $\theta(X_1) = L_1, \dots, \theta(X_n) = L_n$ is a solution of (2) iff θ^{mi} with $\theta^{mi}(X_1) = L_1^{mi}, \dots, \theta^{mi}(X_n) = L_n^{mi}$ is a solution of the corresponding mirrored equation

$$S_0^{mi} \cup X_1 {\cdot} S_1^{mi} \cup \dots \cup X_n {\cdot} S_n^{mi} = T_0^{mi} \cup X_1 {\cdot} T_1^{mi} \cup \dots \cup X_n {\cdot} T_n^{mi}. \qquad (6)$$

Finite languages over the alphabet $\Delta = \{1, \dots, \rho\}$ can be represented by Σ-trees for the ranked alphabet $\Sigma = \{f_0, f_1, c_0, c_1\}$, where f_0, f_1 are ρ-ary and c_0, c_1 nullary symbols. A given Σ-tree t represents the finite language

$$L_t = \{u \in dom(t) \mid t(u) \in \{c_1, f_1\}\}.$$

Given an equation of the form (6), it is shown in [6] how to construct an RFA $\mathcal{A} = (\Sigma, Q, I, T, F)$ of size exponential in the size of the equation that satisfies the following property.

Lemma 1 (Lemma 6.3 in [6]). *For a Σ-tree t, the following are equivalent:*

1. *The tree t is accepted by $\mathcal{A}$.*
2. *There are finite sets of words $\theta(X_1), \dots, \theta(X_n)$ such that*

$$S_0^{mi} \cup \theta(X_1) {\cdot} S_1^{mi} \cup \dots \cup \theta(X_n) {\cdot} S_n^{mi} = L_t$$
$$= T_0^{mi} \cup \theta(X_1) {\cdot} T_1^{mi} \cup \dots \cup \theta(X_n) {\cdot} T_n^{mi}.$$

Consequently, Eq. (2) has a solution iff equation (6) has a solution iff the RFA $\mathcal{A}$ constructed from (6) accepts some tree. Since the size of $\mathcal{A} = (\Sigma, Q, I, T, F)$ is exponential in the size of (2), and the emptiness problem for RFAs is decidable in polynomial time, this yields an ExpTime decision procedure for solvability of equations of the form (2), and thus for unifiability in $\mathcal{FL}_0$. As mentioned in Sect. 4, it is also shown in [6] by reduction from the intersection emptiness problem for DRFAs, that these problems are actually ExpTime-hard.

Theorem 2 [6]. *Unifiability in $\mathcal{FL}_0$ as well as solvability of language equations of the forms (2) and (6) are ExpTime-complete problems.*

In the restricted setting, we consider equations of the form (2) and are looking for solutions θ satisfying (4) for the syntactically restricted setting or satisfying (5) for the semantically restricted setting. Since clearly $(\Delta^{\leq k})^{mi} = \Delta^{\leq k}$, the respective restrictions apply unchanged to the mirrored equation (6).

5.1 The Syntactically Restricted Case

In this case we are thus looking for solutions θ of (6) satisfying

$$S_0^{mi} \cup \theta(X_1) \cdot S_1^{mi} \cup \cdots \cup \theta(X_n) \cdot S_n^{mi}$$
$$= T_0^{mi} \cup \theta(X_1) \cdot T_1^{mi} \cup \cdots \cup \theta(X_n) \cdot T_n^{mi} \subseteq \Delta^{\leq k}. \tag{7}$$

Intuitively, for the trees accepted by the automaton $\mathcal{A}$ this means that we want to check whether $\mathcal{A}$ accepts a tree of depth $\leq k$. This can be achieved by adding a counter that is decremented whenever we go from a node in the tree to a successor node. As soon as the counter reaches 0, no more transitions are possible.

To be more precise, let $\mathcal{A} = (\Sigma, Q, I, T, F)$ be the RFA constructed from (6), as described in [6]. For an integer $k \geq 1$, we define the automaton $\mathcal{A}_{syn}^k = (\Sigma, Q_{syn}^k, I_{syn}^k, T_{syn}^k, F_{syn}^k)$ as follows:

- $Q_{syn}^k = Q \times \{0, 1, \ldots, k\}$,
- $I_{syn}^k = I \times \{k\}$,
- $T_{syn}^k(f) = \{((q, i), (q_1, i-1), \ldots, (q_\rho, i-1)) \mid (q, q_1, \ldots, q_\rho) \in T(f) \text{ and } i \geq 1\}$ for $f \in \{f_0, f_1\}$,
- $F_{syn}^k(c) = F(c) \times \{0, 1, \ldots, k\}$ for $c \in \{c_0, c_1\}$.

Basically, $\mathcal{A}_{syn}^k$ works like $\mathcal{A}$, but once it has reached a node at depth k in the tree, it cannot make any transition. Thus, it accepts exactly the trees that have depth at most k and are accepted by $\mathcal{A}$. Since nodes at a depth i correspond to words of this length i, we obtain the following lemma.

Lemma 2. *The automaton $\mathcal{A}_{syn}^k$ accepts a tree t iff (6) has a solution θ that satisfies (7).*

Proof. If (6) has a solution θ that satisfies (7), then there is a tree t of depth at most k that represents this solution in the sense that it satisfies 2. of Lemma 1. The tree t then also satisfies 1. of Lemma 1, i.e., it is accepted by $\mathcal{A}$. Since t has depth at most k, it is then also accepted by $\mathcal{A}_{syn}^k$.

Conversely, if the tree t is accepted by $\mathcal{A}_{syn}^k$, then it is also accepted by $\mathcal{A}$ and has depth at most k. The former implies, by Lemma 1, that 2. of Lemma 1 holds, and the latter yields that $L(t) \subseteq \Delta^{\leq k}$. Thus, the sets $\theta(X_1), \ldots, \theta(X_n)$ provided by 2. of Lemma 1 satisfy (7). □

As an easy consequence of this lemma and the connection between syntactically k-restricted unification and the problem of finding solutions of (6) that satisfy (7), we obtain the following complexity results (see [3] for detailed proofs).

Theorem 3. *Given an integer $k \geq 1$ and $\mathcal{FL}_0$ concepts C, D as input, the problem of deciding whether the syntactically k-restricted unification problem $C \stackrel{?}{\equiv}_{syn}^{k} D$ has a unifier or not is ExpTime-complete if the number k is assumed to be encoded in binary, and PSpace-complete if k is assumed to be encoded in unary.*

The ExpTime upper bound is an immediate consequence of the fact that the size of $\mathcal{A}_{syn}^{k}$ is exponentially bounded by the size of the input equation and the binary representation of k. The ExpTime lower bound can be shown using the fact that the automaton $\mathcal{A}$ accepts a tree iff it accepts one of depth linear in the size of $\mathcal{A}$ (which is exponential in the size of the input equation). Regarding the PSpace upper bound, one cannot construct the exponentially large modified automaton $\mathcal{A}_{syn}^{k}$ before testing it for emptiness, but rather constructs the relevant parts of $\mathcal{A}_{syn}^{k}$ while doing the emptiness test on-the-fly. This needs only polynomial space since the depth of the run to be constructed is linear in the size of the unary representation of k. The PSpace lower bound can be shown by reduction of the k-restricted intersection emptiness problem for DRFAs, based on the reduction for the unrestricted case given in [6].

5.2   The Semantically Restricted Case

In this case, to solve the mirrored equation (6), we are looking for assignments θ satisfying

$$
\begin{aligned}
&(S_0^{mi} \cup \theta(X_1) \cdot S_1^{mi} \cup \cdots \cup \theta(X_n) \cdot S_n^{mi}) \cap \Delta^{\leq k} \\
&= (T_0^{mi} \cup \theta(X_1) \cdot T_1^{mi} \cup \cdots \cup \theta(X_n) \cdot T_n^{mi}) \cap \Delta^{\leq k}.
\end{aligned}
\tag{8}
$$

The existence of such a solution can again be tested by building an RFA that extends the automaton $\mathcal{A} = (\Sigma, Q, I, T, F)$ constructed from (6), as described in [6], by a counter. But now, we allow the automaton to make transitions where the value of the counter becomes -1. States that have counter value -1 are final states since they indicate that the word represented by this node of the tree is longer than k, and thus it is not relevant for deciding whether the tree represents a solution or not. To be more precise, for an integer $k \geq 1$, we define the automaton $\mathcal{A}_{sem}^{k} = (\Sigma, Q_{sem}^{k}, I_{sem}^{k}, T_{sem}^{k}, F_{sem}^{k})$ as follows:

- $Q_{sem}^{k} = Q \times \{-1, 0, 1, \ldots, k\}$,
- $I_{sem}^{k} = I \times \{k\}$,
- $T_{sem}^{k}(f) = \{((q, i), (q_1, i-1), \ldots, (q_\rho, i-1)) \mid (q, q_1, \ldots, q_\rho) \in T(f) \text{ and } i \geq 0\}$
  for $f \in \{f_0, f_1\}$,
- $F_{sem}^{k}(c) = (F(c) \times \{0, 1, \ldots, k\}) \cup \{(q, -1) \mid q \in Q\}$ for $c \in \{c_0, c_1\}$.

The following lemma, whose proof can be found in [3], states correctness of this construction.

Lemma 3. *The automaton $\mathcal{A}_{sem}^{k}$ accepts a tree t iff there is an assignment θ that satisfies (8).*

Based on this lemma, the complexity upper bounds stated in the following theorem can be shown analogously to the proof of Theorem 3. The PSpace lower bound can be shown by reduction from syntactically k-restricted unification (see [3] for a proof).

Theorem 4. *Given an integer $k \geq 1$ and $\mathcal{FL}_0$ concepts C, D as input, the problem of deciding whether the semantically k-restricted unification problem $C \stackrel{?}{\equiv}_{sem}^{k} D$ has a unifier or not is in ExpTime if the number k is assumed to be encoded in binary, and PSpace-complete if k is assumed to be encoded in unary.*

If k is encoded in binary, then the reduction used for the unary case is no longer polynomial. It is an open problem whether, for the case of binary coding, the ExpTime upper bound in Theorem 4 is tight.

6   The Unification Type

Until now, we were mainly interested in the complexity of deciding solvability of unification problems. For this, it is sufficient to consider ground unifiers. Now, we want to investigate the question of whether all unifiers of a given unification problem can be represented as instances of a finite set of (non-ground) unifiers.

In the unrestricted setting, the instance relation between $\mathcal{FL}_0$ unifiers is defined as follows. Let $C \stackrel{?}{\equiv} D$ be an $\mathcal{FL}_0$ unification problem, V the set of concept variables occurring in C and D, and σ, θ two unifiers of this problem. We define

$$\sigma \trianglelefteq \theta \text{ if there is a substitution } \lambda \text{ such that } \theta(X) \equiv \lambda(\sigma(X)) \text{ for all } X \in V.$$

If $\sigma \trianglelefteq \theta$, then we say that θ is an *instance* of σ.

Definition 4. *Let $C \stackrel{?}{\equiv} D$ be an $\mathcal{FL}_0$ unification problem. The set of substitutions M is called a* complete set of unifiers *for $C \stackrel{?}{\equiv} D$ if it satisfies*

1. *every element of M is a unifier of $C \stackrel{?}{\equiv} D$;*
2. *if θ is a unifier of $C \stackrel{?}{\equiv} D$, then there exists a unifier $\sigma \in M$ such that $\sigma \trianglelefteq \theta$.*

The set M is a minimal complete set of unifiers *for $C \stackrel{?}{\equiv} D$ if it additionally satisfies*

3. *if $\sigma, \theta \in M$, then $\sigma \trianglelefteq \theta$ implies $\sigma = \theta$.*

The unification type of a given unification problem is determined by the existence and cardinality of such a minimal complete set.

Definition 5. *Let $C \stackrel{?}{\equiv} D$ be an $\mathcal{FL}_0$ unification problem. This problem has type* unitary *(finitary, infinitary) if it has a minimal complete set of unifiers of cardinality 1 (finite cardinality, infinite cardinality). If $C \stackrel{?}{\equiv} D$ does not have a minimal complete set of unifiers, then it is of type* zero.

The unification types can be ordered as follows:

$$\text{unitary} < \text{finitary} < \text{infinitary} < \text{type zero}.$$

Basically, the unification type of $\mathcal{FL}_0$ is the maximal type of an $\mathcal{FL}_0$ unification problem. However, in unification theory, one usually distinguishes between unification with and without constants [8]. In an $\mathcal{FL}_0$ unification problem with constants, no restrictions are put on the concepts C and D to be unified. In an $\mathcal{FL}_0$ unification problem without constants, C and D must not contain concept names from N_C. The unification type of $\mathcal{FL}_0$ for unification with (without) constants is the maximal type of an $\mathcal{FL}_0$ unification problem with (without) constants.

It was shown in [6] that equivalence of $\mathcal{FL}_0$ concepts can be axiomatized by the equational theory

$$ACUIh := \{ \ (x \wedge y) \wedge z = x \wedge (y \wedge z), \ x \wedge y = y \wedge x, \ x \wedge x = x, \ x \wedge 1 = x \ \}$$
$$\cup \{ \ h_r(x \wedge y) = h_r(x) \wedge h_r(y), \ h_r(1) = 1 \mid r \in N_R \ \},$$

where $\wedge$, h_r, and 1 in the terms respectively correspond to $\sqcap$, $\forall r.$, and $\top$ in the concepts. These identities say that $\wedge$ is associative (A), commutative (C), and idempotent (I) with unit 1 (U), and that the unary function symbols behave like homomorphisms (h) for $\wedge$ and 1.

The unification type of an equational theory is defined analogously to the definitions given above for $\mathcal{FL}_0$ (see [8] for details). It was shown in [1] that the unification type of the theory $ACUIh$ (called $AIMH$ in [1]) is zero, even if one has only one homomorphism h and considers unification without constants. Thus, unification in $\mathcal{FL}_0$ is also of type zero for unification without constants, and thus also for unification with constants. We will show in this section that this is no longer the case if we consider restricted unification. For the semantically restricted case, this is an easy consequence of general results about commutative/monoidal theories [1,14].

6.1   The Semantically Restricted Case

The equivalence $\equiv_{sem}^k$ can be axiomatized by adding identities to $ACUIh$ that say that nesting of homomorphisms of depth $> k$ produces the unit. Given a word $u = r_1 r_2 \dots r_n \in N_R^*$, we denote a term of the form $h_{r_1}(h_{r_2}(\cdots h_{r_n}(t)\cdots))$ as $h_u(t)$. It is now easy to see that $\equiv_{sem}^k$ is axiomatized by

$$ACUIh^k := ACUIh \cup \{h_u(x) = 1 \mid u \in N_R^* \text{ with } |u| = k + 1\}.$$

Both $ACUIh$ and $ACUIh^k$ are so-called commutative/monoidal theory [1,7,14], for which unification can be reduced to solving linear equations over a corresponding semiring. For $ACUIh$ this semiring consists of finite languages over the alphabet Δ with union as addition and concatenation as multiplication [6]. As shown in [3], the semiring corresponding to $ACUIh^k$ consists of the subsets of $\Delta^{\leq k}$, with union as addition and the following multiplication: $L_1 \cdot_k L_2 = (L_1 \cdot L_2) \cap \Delta^{\leq k}$.

According to [14], unification without constants in a monoidal theory E is unitary if the semiring S_E corresponding to E is finite. In [1], the same result is shown for commutative theories E under the assumption that the finitely generated E-free algebras are finite. It is easy to see that these two conditions actually coincide for commutative theories [7]. In addition to unification without constants, also unification with constants is considered in [1], and it is shown that, if the finitely generated E-free algebras are finite, then unification with constants in the commutative theory E is at most finitary (i.e., unitary or finitary). The following theorem is an easy consequence of these results.

Theorem 5. *Unification in $ACUIh^k$, and thus also semantically k-restricted unification in $\mathcal{FL}_0$, is unitary for unification without constants and finitary for unification with constants.*

Proof. It is easy to see that the semiring corresponding to $ACUIh^k$ is finite since its elements are all the subsets of the finite set $\Delta^{\leq k}$. Thus, the results in [1,14] yield that $ACUIh^k$ is unitary for unification without constants and at most finitary for unification with constants. The following example shows that the theory is not unitary for unification with constants: if x is a variable and a a constant, then the terms $x \wedge a$ and a have (restricted to x) exactly two $ACUIh^k$ unifiers $\{x \mapsto 1\}$ and $\{x \mapsto a\}$, which are not in any instance relationship.   □

6.2 The Syntactically Restricted Case

To deal with the syntactically restricted case, the results on the unification type for commutative/monoidal theories cannot be applied directly, but we can show the same results as for the semantically restricted case, using the ideas underlying the proofs in [1,14]. We will formulate our proof using the syntax of $\mathcal{FL}_0$ rather than the equational theory variant.

Let C, D be $\mathcal{FL}_0$ concepts and σ a syntactically k-restricted unifier of C and D. Let $X_1, \ldots, X_n$ be the concept variables occurring in C, D and $A_1, \ldots, A_\ell$ the concept constants. First, note that we can assume that σ does not introduce new concept constants since otherwise one could get a more general unifier by replacing such a constant by a new variable. Let $Y_1, \ldots, Y_m$ be the concept variables in the range of σ, where we assume without loss of generality that they are different from the variables $X_1, \ldots, X_n$. For $i = 1, \ldots, n$, the LNF of the concept $\sigma(X_i)$ is of the form

$$\sigma(X_i) = K_i \sqcap \forall L_{i,1}.Y_1 \sqcap \ldots \sqcap \forall L_{i,m}.Y_m, \tag{9}$$

where K_i is a concept of role depth $\leq k$ not containing concept variables and only concept constants in $\{A_1, \ldots, A_\ell\}$ and the $L_{i,j}$ are subsets of $\Delta^{\leq k}$. Recall that $\forall L_{i,j}.Y_j$ abbreviates the conjunction of the value restrictions $\forall w.Y_j$ for $w \in L_{i,j}$, which in turn is an abbreviation for $\forall r_1. \cdots \forall r_\nu.Y_j$ if $w = r_1 \ldots r_\nu$.

Now, consider for every variable $Y_j, 1 \leq j \leq m$, the tuple of languages $L(Y_j) = (L_{1,j}, \ldots, L_{n,j})$, and assume that there are indices $j \neq j'$ such that $L(Y_j) = L(Y_{j'})$. Let $\theta_{j'}$ be the substitution that replaces $Y_{j'}$ with $\top$ and leaves all other variable Y_μ unchanged. Then $\sigma_{j'} = \sigma\theta_{j'}$ is an instance of σ, which is still a syntactically k-restricted unifier of C and D, but introduces one variable less. Conversely, using the substitution $\lambda_{j,j'} = \{Y_j \mapsto Y_j \sqcap Y_{j'}\}$, we obtain σ as an instance of $\sigma_{j'}$ since $\sigma = \sigma_{j'}\lambda_{j,j'}$.

Let c denote the (finite) cardinality of $\Delta^{\leq k}$. Then there are at most $2^{c \cdot n}$ different n-tuples of subsets of $\Delta^{\leq k}$. Thus, if a syntactically k-restricted unifier of C and D introduces more than $2^{c \cdot n}$ variables, it is an instance of a syntactically k-restricted unifier of C and D that introduces at least one variable less. This observation can be used to show the following lemma.

Lemma 4. *There is a complete set of syntactically k-restricted unifiers of C and D that consists of unifiers whose range contains at most the variables $Y_1, \ldots, Y_m$ for $m = 2^{c \cdot n}$.*

Once we have restricted the unifiers in the complete set to ones using only finitely many variables, we know that there can be only finitely many unifiers in this set. In fact, if we consider (9), then we see that the K_i and $L_{i,j}$ range over finite sets. This proves the following theorem.

Theorem 6. *Syntactically k-restricted unification with constants in $\mathcal{FL}_0$ is finitary.*

To show that unification with constants is not unitary, we can use the same example as in the semantically restricted case. Unification without constants is again unitary.

Corollary 1. *Syntactically k-restricted unification without constants in $\mathcal{FL}_0$ is unitary.*

Proof. By the previous theorem, there is a finite complete set $\{\sigma_1, \ldots, \sigma_\kappa\}$ of syntactically k-restricted unifiers of C, D. Without loss of generality, we can assume that the variables occurring in the ranges of these unifiers are disjoint and that no concept constant occurs in the range. The latter assumption can be made since the unification problem itself does not contain such constants. Under these assumptions, the substitution σ defined as

$$\sigma(X_i) = \sigma_1(X_i) \sqcap \ldots \sqcap \sigma_\kappa(X_i) \quad \text{for } i = 1, \ldots, n$$

is also a syntactically k-restricted unifier of C, D, and it has the substitutions $\sigma_1, \ldots, \sigma_\kappa$ as instances (see [3] for a proof of these two claims). This shows that $\{\sigma\}$ is a complete set of unifiers. $\square$

7   Conclusion

We have investigated both a semantically and a syntactically restricted variant of unification in $\mathcal{FL}_0$, where either the role depth of concepts or the length of role paths in interpretations is restricted by a natural number $k \geq 1$. These restrictions lead to a considerable improvement of the unification type from the worst possible type to unitary/finitary for unification without/with constants. For the complexity of the decision problem, we only obtain an improvement if k is assumed to be encoded in unary.

While these results are mainly of (complexity) theoretic interest, they could also have a practical impact. In fact, in our experiments with the system UEL, which implements several unification algorithms for the DL $\mathcal{EL}$ [4], we have observed that the algorithms usually yield many different unifiers, and it is hard to choose one that is appropriate for the application at hand (e.g., when generating new concepts using unification [2]). For this reason, we added additional constraints to the unification problem to ensure that the generated concepts are of a similar shape as the concepts already present in the ontology [2]. It makes sense also to use a restriction on the role depth as such an additional constraint since the role depth of the (unfolded) concepts occurring in real-world ontologies is usually rather small. This claim is supported by our experiments with the medical ontology SNOMED CT[3], which has a maximal role depth of 10, and the acyclic ontologies in Bioportal 2017[4], where a large majority also has a role depth of at most 10.

As future work, we will investigate whether the ExpTime upper bound in Theorem 4 for the case of binary coding of k is tight. In addition, we will consider similar restrictions for other DLs. For example, the unification type of the DL $\mathcal{EL}$ is also known to be zero, and the decision problem is NP-complete [5]. We conjecture that, for $\mathcal{EL}$, the restricted variants will not lead to an improvement of unification type or complexity.

In [11], a syntactically restricted version of unification in the theory ACh was shown to be decidable, but neither the unification type nor the complexity of the decision problem was determined. It would be interesting to investigate these problems and also consider a semantically restricted variant. Note that, with the exception of the missing unit, ACh is commutative/monoidal, but the main difference to $ACUIh$ is that already the semiring corresponding to the subtheory without homomorphisms is infinite, whereas the semiring corresponding to $ACUI$ is finite.

Acknowledgements. Franz Baader was partially supported by DFG TRR 248 (cpec, grant 389792660), Oliver Fernández Gil by DFG in project number 335448072, and Maryam Rostamigiv by a DAAD Short-Term Grant, 2021 (57552336). The authors should like to thank Patrick Koopmann for determining the maximal role depth of concepts in ontologies from Bioportal 2017 and in SNOMED CT.

---

[3]   https://www.snomed.org/.
[4]   https://zenodo.org/record/439510.

References

1. Baader, F.: Unification in commutative theories. J. Symbolic Comput. **8**(5), 479–497 (1989)
2. Baader, F., Borgwardt, S., Morawska, B.: Constructing SNOMED CT concepts via disunification. LTCS-Report 17–07, Chair for Automata Theory, Institute for Theoretical Computer Science, Technische Universität Dresden, Dresden, Germany (2017). https://lat.inf.tu-dresden.de/research/reports/2017/BaBM-LTCS-17-07.pdf
3. Baader, F., Fernández Gil, O., Rostamigiv, M.: Restricted unification in the DL $\mathcal{FL}_0$ (extended version). LTCS-Report 21–02, Chair of Automata Theory, Institute of Theoretical Computer Science, Technische Universität Dresden, Dresden, Germany (2021). https://lat.inf.tu-dresden.de/research/reports/2021/BaGiRo21.pdf
4. Baader, F., Mendez, J., Morawska, B.: UEL: unification solver for the description logic $\mathcal{EL}$ – system description. In: Gramlich, B., Miller, D., Sattler, U. (eds.) IJCAR 2012. LNCS (LNAI), vol. 7364, pp. 45–51. Springer, Heidelberg (2012). https://doi.org/10.1007/978-3-642-31365-3_6
5. Baader, F., Morawska, B.: Unification in the description logic $\mathcal{EL}$. Logical Methods Comput. Sci. **6**(3), 350–364 (2010)
6. Baader, F., Narendran, P.: Unification of concept terms in description logics. J. Symbolic Comput. **31**(3), 277–305 (2001)
7. Baader, F., Nutt, W.: Combination problems for commutative/monoidal theories: how algebra can help in equational reasoning. J. Appl. Algebra Eng. Commun. Comput. **7**(4), 309–337 (1996)
8. Baader, F.: Unification theory. In: Schulz, K.U. (ed.) IWWERT 1990. LNCS, vol. 572, pp. 151–170. Springer, Heidelberg (1992). https://doi.org/10.1007/3-540-55124-7_5
9. Balbiani, P., Gencer, C., Rostamigiv, M., Tinchev, T.: About the unification type of $K + \Box\Box\bot$. In: Proceedings of the 34th International Workshop on Unification (UNIF 2020), pp. 4:1–4:6. RISC-Linz (2020)
10. Jerabek, E.: Blending margins: the modal logic K has nullary unification type. J. Logic Comput. **25**(5), 1231–1240 (2015)
11. Ajay Kumar Eeralla and Christopher Lynch: Bounded ACh unification. Math. Struct. Comput. Sci. **30**(6), 664–682 (2020)
12. Levesque, H.J., Brachman, R.J.: Expressiveness and tractability in knowledge representation and reasoning. Comput. Intell. **3**, 78–93 (1987)
13. Narendran, P.: Solving linear equations over polynomial semirings. In: Proceedings of the 11th Annual IEEE Symposium on Logic in Computer Science (LICS 1996), pp. 466–472. IEEE Computer Society (1996)
14. Nutt, W.: Unification in monoidal theories. In: Stickel, M.E. (ed.) CADE 1990. LNCS, vol. 449, pp. 618–632. Springer, Heidelberg (1990). https://doi.org/10.1007/3-540-52885-7_118
15. Peñaloza, R., Turhan, A.-Y.: A practical approach for computing generalization inferences in $\mathcal{EL}$. In: Antoniou, G., et al. (eds.) ESWC 2011. LNCS, vol. 6643, pp. 410–423. Springer, Heidelberg (2011). https://doi.org/10.1007/978-3-642-21034-1_28
16. Seidl, H.: Haskell overloading is DEXPTIME-complete. Inf. Process. Lett. **52**, 57–60 (1994)
17. Thomas, W.: Automata on infinite objects. In: Handbook of Theoretical Computer Science, volume B, chapter 4, pp. 134–189. Elsevier Science Publishers (North-Holland), Amsterdam (1990)

Combining Event Calculus and Description Logic Reasoning via Logic Programming

Peter Baumgartner[✉]

Data61/CSIRO and The Australian National University, Canberra, Australia
Peter.Baumgartner@data61.csiro.au

Abstract. The paper introduces a knowledge representation language that combines the event calculus with description logic in a logic programming framework. The purpose is to provide the user with an expressive language for modelling and analysing systems that evolve over time. The approach is exemplified with the logic programming language as implemented in the Fusemate system. The paper extends Fusemate's rule language with a weakly DL-safe interface to the description logic $\mathcal{ALCIF}$ and adapts the event calculus to this extended language. This way, time-stamped ABoxes can be manipulated as fluents in the event calculus. All that is done in the frame of Fusemate's concept of stratification by time. The paper provides conditions for soundness and completeness where appropriate. Using an elaborated example it demonstrates the interplay of the event calculus, description logic and logic programming rules for computing possible models as plausible explanations of the current state of the modelled system.

1 Introduction

This paper presents an expressive logical language for modelling systems that evolve over time. The language is intended for model computation: given a history of events until "now", what are the system states at these times, in particularly "now", expressed as logical models. This is a useful reasoning service in application areas with only partially observed events or incomplete domain knowledge. By making informed guesses and including its consequences, the models are meant to provide plausible explanations for helping understand the current issues, if any, as a basis for further decision making.

For example, transport companies usually do not keep detailed records of what goods went on what vehicle for a transport on a particular day. Speculating the whereabouts of a missing item can be informed by taking known locations of other goods of the same batch on that day into account; problems observed with goods on delivery site, e.g., low quality of fresh goods, may or may not be related to the transport conditions, and playing through different scenarios may lead to plausible explanations while eliminating others (truck cooling problems? tampering?).

There are numerous approaches for modelling and analysing systems that evolve over time. They are often subsumed under the terms of stream processing, complex event recognition, and situational awareness, temporal verification

© Springer Nature Switzerland AG 2021
B. Konev and G. Reger (Eds.): FroCoS 2021, LNAI 12941, pp. 98–117, 2021.
https://doi.org/10.1007/978-3-030-86205-3_6

among others, see [1–4,14] for some logic-based methods. Symbolic event recognition, for instance, accepts as input a stream of time-stamped low-level events and identifies high-level events – collections of events that satisfy some pattern [1]. See [36] for a recent sophisticated event calculus. Other approaches utilize description logics in a temporalized setting of ontology-based data access (OBDA) [30]. For instance, [29] describes a method for streaming data into a sequence of ABoxes, which can be queried in an SQL-like language with respect to a given ontology.

The knowledge representation language put forward in this paper combines Kowalski's event calculus (EC) with description logics (DL) in a logic programming framework. The rationale is, DLs have a long history of developments for representing structured domain knowledge and for offering reliable (decidable) reasoning services. The EC provides a structured way of representing actions and their effects, represented as fluents that may change their truth value over time. For the intended model computation applications mentioned above, the EC makes it easy to take snapshots of the fluents at any time. The full system state at a chosen time then is derived from the fluent snapshot and DL reasoning. The logic programming rules orchestrate their integration and serve other purposes, such as diagnosis.

This paper uses the Fusemate logic programming language and system [11,12]. Fusemate computes possible models of stratified disjunctive logic programs [33,34], see Sect. 2 for details. Fusemate was introduced in [11] with the same motivation as here. In [12] it was extended with novel language operators improved with a weaker form of stratification. Their usefulness in combination was demonstrated by application to description logic reasoning. In [12] it was shown how to transform an $\mathcal{ALCIF}$[1] knowledge base into a set of Fusemate rules and facts that is satisfiable if and only if the knowledge base is $\mathcal{ALCIF}$-satisfiable. All of that is used in this paper.

Paper Contributions. This paper builds on the Fusemate developments summarized above and extends them in the following ways:

1. Integration of the description logic reasoner of [12] as a subroutine callable from Fusemate rules. Section 3 details the semantics of the combination and conditions for its soundness and completeness. This is an original contribution in its own right which exploits advantages of a stratified setting.
2. A version of the event calculus [20] that fits Fusemate's model computation and notion of stratification. Details are in Sect. 4.
3. Integrating DL and EC by means of rules, and utilizing rules for KR aspects not covered by either. Details in particular in Sect. 5
4. Providing an elaborated example the integrated EC/DL/rules language. It is included in the Fusemate distribution which is available at https://bitbucket.csiro.au/users/bau050/repos/fusemate/.

To the best of my knowledge, a combination of DL with EC has not been considered before. Given the long history of applying DL reasoning (also) for time

---

[1] $\mathcal{ALCIF}$ is the well-known description logic $\mathcal{ALC}$ extended with inverse roles and functional roles. See [5] for background on description logics.

evolving systems, I find this surprising. From that perspective, a main contribution of this paper is to fill the gap and to argue that the proposed combination makes sense.

There is work is on integrating DLs into the situation calculus (SitCalc) and similar methods [8–10, 15]. SitCalc [23] is a first-order logic formalism for specifying state transitions in terms of pre- and post-conditions of actions. Its is mostly used for planning and related applications that require reachability reasoning for state transitions. Indeed, the papers [9] and [15] investigate reasoning tasks (executability and projection, ABox updates) that are relevant in that context. Both approaches are restricted to acyclic TBoxes. In [10], actions are specified as sets of conditional effects, where conditions are based on epistemic queries over the knowledge base (TBox and ABox), and effects are expressed in terms of new ABoxes. The paper investigates verification of temporal properties. As a difference to the EC, none of these approaches supports a *quantitative* notion of time.

2   Stratified Logic Programs and Model Computation

This paper uses the extended "Fusemate" rule language introduced in [12] without the earlier belief revision operator introduced in [11]. This section complements the earlier paper [12] with a rigorous definition of the semantics of the extended language. It also provides soundness and completeness arguments, under certain conditions, wrt. abstract fixpoint iteration and wrt. Fusemate's procedure more concretely.

Terms and atoms of a given first-order signature with "free" *ordinary* function and predicate symbols are defined as usual. Let $\mathbb{T}$ be a countably infinite discrete set of *time points* equipped with a well-founded total strict ordering $<$ (strictly earlier), e.g., the natural numbers. Assume that the time points, comparison operators $=$, $\leq$ (earlier), and a next time function $+1$ are also part of the signature and interpreted in the obvious way. A *time term* is a (possibly non-ground) term over the sub-signature $\mathbb{T} \cup \{+1\}$. The signature may contain other "built-in" interpreted predicate and function symbols for predefined types such as strings, arithmetic data types, sets, etc. We only informally assume that all terms are built in a well-sorted way, and that interpreted operators over ground terms can be evaluated effectively to a value represented by a term.

Let $var(e)$ denote the set of variables occurring in a term or atom e. We say that e is *ground* if $var(e) = \emptyset$. We write $e\sigma$ for applying a substitution σ to e. The domain of σ is denoted by $dom(\sigma)$. A substitution γ is a *grounding substitution for a finite set of variables* X iff $dom(\gamma) = X$. In the following, the letters x, y, z stand for variables, *time* for a time term variable, s, t for terms, and tt for a time term, possibly indexed. Lists of terms or other expressions are written as vectors, e.g., $\vec{t}$ is a list of terms $t_1, \ldots, t_n$ for some $n >= 0$. A *(Fusemate) rule* is an implication written in Prolog-like syntax as

$$H :- b_1, \ldots, b_k, \textbf{not } \vec{b}_1, \ldots, \textbf{not } \vec{b}_n. \tag{1}$$

In (1), the rule *head* H is either (a) *ordinary*, a disjunction $h_1 \vee \cdots \vee h_m$ of ordinary atoms, for some $m \geq 1$, or (b) the expression **fail**.[2] In case (a) the rule is *ordinary* and in case (b) it is a *fail rule*. The list to the right of :- is the rule *body*. Bodies are defined by recursion as follows, along with associated sets *fvar* (free variables).

Name	Form	fvar	Comment
Ordinary atom	$p(tt, \vec{t})$	$var(tt, \vec{t})$	tt time term, p free predicate
Comprehension with time term x	$p(x \circ tt, \vec{t})$ **sth** B	$\{x\} \cup var(tt, \vec{t})$	$\circ \in \{<, \leq, >, \geq\}$, B is a body
Built-in call	$p(\vec{t})$	$var(\vec{t})$	p is built-in predicate
Time comparison	$s \circ t$	$var(s, t)$	s, t time terms, $\circ \in \{<, \leq, >, \geq\}$
Let special form	**let**(x, t)	$\{x\} \cup var(t)$	
Choose special form	**choose**(x, ts)	$\{x\} \cup var(ts)$	ts is a set of terms
Collect special form	**collect**$(x, t$ **sth** $B)$	$\{x\}$	
Positive body $\vec{b}$	$b_1, \ldots, b_k$	$\cup_{i=1..k} fvar(b_i)$	$k \geq 0$, b_i is one of above
Negative body literal	**not** $\vec{b}$	$\emptyset$	$\vec{b}$ is non-empty positive body
Body B	$\vec{b}, \textbf{not } \vec{b}_1, \ldots, \textbf{not } \vec{b}_n$	$fvar(\vec{b})$	$n \geq 0$, and $\vec{b}$, $\vec{b}_j$ positive bodies

A *positive body literal* is of one of the forms up to **collect**. Examples are below.

Note 1 (Implicit quantification). In a body B, the variables $fvar(B)$ are implicitly existentially quantified in front of that B.[3] Rules may contain extra variables in negative body literals. An example is the rule $\mathsf{p}(time, x)$:- $\mathsf{q}(time, x, y), \textbf{not}(z < time, \mathsf{r}(x, y, z))$ which corresponds to the (universal quantification of the) formula $\mathsf{q}(time, x, y) \wedge \neg \exists z.(z < time \wedge \mathsf{r}(x, y, z)) \rightarrow \mathsf{p}(time, x)$. The extra variable z will be picked up for existential quantification after ground instantiating the rule body's *fvars* $\{time, x, y\}$. If γ is such a grounding substitution then indeed $fvar((z < time, \mathsf{r}(x, y, z))\gamma) = \{z\}$ as desired. The formal definition of the possible model semantics below will make this precise.   □

A *normal rule* is an ordinary rule with one head literal ($m = 1$ in (1)). A *Horn rule* is a normal rule or a fail rule. A *fact* is an ordinary rule with empty body ($k, n = 0$ in (1)) and is simply written as H. A rule H :- B is *range-restricted* iff $var(H) \subseteq fvar(B)$. A *(Fusemate) program* is a finite set of range-restricted and *stratified* rules.

Stratification. The standard notion of stratification ("by predicates") means that the call graph of a program has no cycles going through negative body literals [31]. Every strongly connected component of the call graph is called a *stratum* and contains the predicates that are defined (in rule heads) mutually

---

[2] This definition of head is actually simplified as Fusemate offers an additional head operator for belief revision, see [11]. This is ignored here.

[3] The variables $var(t)$ in the **collect** special form have to be excluded from that because they are quantified within their "**sth** B" body scope. To avoid name conflicts, we assume that $var(t) \cap fvar(B') = \emptyset$ for all bodies B' such that $B = B'$ or B occurs in B'.

recursive with each other. All head predicates of the same rule are put into the same stratum. Fusemate employs a weaker *stratification by time and by predicates (SBTP)* [12]. With SBTP, every ordinary non-fact rule (1) must have an ordinary body literal b_i, for some $1 \leq i \leq k$, with a *pivot* variable *time*, such that every other time term in the head (body) is syntactically constrained to $\geq$ ($\leq$, respectively) than *time*, and the literals within negative body literals are syntactically constrained to be (a) $<$ than *time* or (b) $\leq$ than *time* and must be in a stratum strictly lower than the head stratum. For example, the rule $p(time, x) :- q(time, x), \mathbf{not}(r(t, y), t \leq time)$ is SBTP if r is in a strictly lower stratum than p, and $p(time, x) :- q(time, x), \mathbf{not}(r(t, y), t < time)$ is SBTP even if r is in the same stratum as p. This has the effect that model computation can be done in time/stratum layers in increasing (lexicographic) order using only already derived atoms.

Comprehension and **collect** must be stratified for the same reason. For the purpose of SBTP, a comprehension $p(x \circ tt, \vec{t}) \, \mathbf{sth} \, B$ is taken as if $p(x, \vec{t})$ and B were negative body literals, and $\mathbf{collect}(x, t \, \mathbf{sth} \, B)$ is taken as if B were a negative body literal.

2.1 Possible Models

We need some preliminaries pertaining to the semantics of rules before formally defining "possible models". A *(rule) closure* is a pair $(H :- B, \beta)$ such that β is a grounding substitution for $fvar(B)$ called *body matcher* in this context. For a program P, its *full closure* $cl(P)$ is the set of all closures of all rules in P.

Full closures supplant the usual full ground instantiation of programs. They make it easy to define rule semantics in presence of the special forms, comprehension operators, and implicit existential quantification without full grounding. This works as follows.

An *interpretation I* is a (possibly infinite) set of ordinary atoms. Let I be an interpretation and β a grounding substitution for some set of variables. Let B be a body as in (1). If $fvar(B\beta) = \emptyset$ define $I, \beta \models B$ iff $I, \beta \models b_i$ for all $i = 1..k$ and $I, \beta \models \mathbf{not} \, \vec{b}_j$ for all $j = 1..n$, where the following table provides the definitions for body literals:

Name	Form	Def
Ordinary atom	$I, \beta \models p(tt, \vec{t})$	iff $p(tt, \vec{t})\beta \in I$
Comprehension with time term x	$I, \beta \models p(x < tt, \vec{t}) \, \mathbf{sth} \, B$	iff $x\beta$ is the maximal (latest) time point s.th. $x\beta < tt\beta$, $I, \beta \models p(x, \vec{t})$ and $I, \beta \models \exists B$. Accordingly for $\geq, <, \leq$
Built-in call	$I, \beta \models p(\vec{t})$	iff $p(\vec{t})\beta$ evaluates to true
Time comparison	$I, \beta \models s \circ t$	iff $s\beta \circ t\beta$
Let special form	$I, \beta \models \mathbf{let}(x, t)$	iff $x\beta = t\beta$
Choose special form	$I, \beta \models \mathbf{choose}(x, ts)$	iff $x\beta \in ts\beta$
Collect special form	$I, \beta \models \mathbf{collect}(x, t \, \mathbf{sth} \, B)$	iff $x\beta = \{t\gamma \mid I, \beta\gamma \models B$ for some grounding substitution γ for $fvar(B\beta)\}$

In that table, define $I, \beta \models \exists B$ iff there is a grounding substitution γ for $fvar(B\beta)$ such that $I, \beta\gamma \models B$ ($\beta\gamma$ is β extended with bindings for the implicitly

existentially quantified variables in $B\beta$). For closures define $I \models (H :- B, \beta)$
iff $I, \beta \not\models B$ or else H is an ordinary head $h_1 \vee \cdots h_m$ and $h_i\beta \in I$ for some
$1 \le i \le m$. In this case we say that I *satisfies* $(H :- B, \beta)$. An interpretation I
is a *model of a set C of closures*, written as $I \models C$ iff I satisfies every closure
in C. It is *minimal* iff $J \not\models C$ for every $J \subsetneq I$. It is *supported* iff for every $a \in I$
there is a $(h :- B, \beta) \in C$ such that $a = h\beta$ and $I, \beta \models B$.

Note 2 (Fixpoint iteration for DLPs [33]). The possible model semantics [33,34]
assigns to a disjunctive logic program sets of Horn programs and takes their
intended models as the possible models of the disjunctive program. The Horn
programs represent all possible ways of making one or more head literals true,
for every disjunctive rule. As a propositional example, the disjunctive program
$\{a :- b, \ a \vee c :- b, \ b :- \mathbf{not}\, d\}$ is split into the Horn programs $\{a :- b, \ b :- \mathbf{not}\, d\}$
and $\{a :- b, \ c :- b, \ b :- \mathbf{not}\, d\}$. The possible models are $\{a, b\}$ and $\{a, b, c\}$.
Non-ground programs have to be fully ground-instantiated using the program's
(possibly infinite) Herbrand base first.

As explained in [33], the possible models of such ground-instantiated *stratified* programs can be constructed by iterated fixpoint computation along the
program's stratification. For each stratum, in ascending order, the rules with a
head predicate from that stratum are evaluated in the model so far, up to that
stratum, and, only if necessary, made true by adding the head to the model,
until fixpoint. In general this construction requires transfinite induction with a
limit ordinal at each stratum.   □

From a practical (Fusemate) perspective we are mostly interested in finite fixpoints for making model computation effective. We start with a definition for
the possible models splitting operator in terms of closures.

Definition 1 (Split program closure). *Let P be a program and $cl(P)$ its
full closure. A* split program closure *of P is obtained from $cl(P)$ by replacing
every closure $(h_1 \vee \cdots \vee h_m \leftarrow B, \beta)$ in $cl(P)$ by the* split closures $(h \leftarrow B, \beta)$,
for every $h \in S$, where S is some non-empty subset of $\{h_1, \ldots, h_m\}$.

Definition 2 (Possible model, adapted from [33]). *An interpretation I is
a possible model of P if I is a minimal supported model of some split program
closure of P.*

2.2 Fusemate Soundness and Completeness

We wish to apply the fixpoint model construction (Note 2) to Fusemate programs. For this to work, rules must be *monotonic* and *compact*.

Definition 3. *Let $(H :- B, \beta)$ be an ordinary rule closure. It is monotonic iff
for all I and $J \supseteq I$ such that every atom in $J \setminus I$ is in the same stratum as $H\beta$,
if $I, \beta \models B$ then $J, \beta \models B$. It is compact iff for all I, if $I, \beta \models B$ then $J, \beta \models B$
for some finite $J \subseteq I$.*

In general, monotonicity of an operator guarantees the existence of a least fixpoint, and compactness guarantees that it can be found by fixpoint iteration. For satisfiable Horn programs, monotonicity entails the "model intersection property" which entails the existence of a unique minimal model. These are all well-known standard results [24], and the above definitions are formulated in a way to make these results applicable.

Fusemate rules are always monotonic. For comprehension and **collect** this is due to stratification. However **collect** is not always compact. Given a body literal **collect**$(x, t \text{ sth } B)$, there could be infinitely many substitutions γ in the comprehension $\{t\gamma \mid I, \beta\gamma \models B$ for some grounding substitution γ for $fvar(B\beta)\}$. Because infinite sets have no term representation, such a **collect** literal renders its rule body always unsatisfied, resulting in incompleteness. One possible way out is to make sure that the variables in t range only over finite domains, e.g., sets of constants. With this fix, it follows that fixpoint iteration (Note 2) wrt. SBTP is sound and complete for possible models of Fusemate programs (Definition 2). The proof is an adaptation of the corresponding one in [33].

Soundness and completeness of fixpoint iteration holds in particular for *finite* models. This suggests another "fix": thanks to stratification, the mentioned incompleteness can occur only when I itself is infinite at a limit step in the fixpoint iteration. Because computing (rather, finitely representing) infinite models is out of scope anyway, it is safe to ignore the compactness problem for finite model computation.

Fusemate. Fusemate implements a bottom-up model computation procedure in the style of hyper tableaux [13] in a stratified way (SBTP). The Fusemate main loop computes body matchers β of bodies B of program rules $H :- B$ against a current branch (a model candidate) and closes it or branches out according to possible models splitting. Each new branch is for a set S in Definition 1 and receives all $h\beta$ for $h \in S$.[4] This constructs tableau in a depth-first left-to-right order. Body matcher computation is made more practical by guaranteed left-to-right evaluation of bodies. This helps to avoid unexpected undefinedness of comprehensions and special forms. For example, in the body of $r(time, xs) :-$ $q(time, y), \textbf{collect}(xs, x \text{ sth}(p(time, x), x > y))$ the **collect** special form binds the variable xs to the list of all x such that $p(time, x)$ and $x > y$ hold, where y has *already* been bound by the preceding $q(time, y)$. See [12] for a formal definition of left-to-right body matcher computation.

Other than that, Fusemate model computation follows the abstract fixpoint computation procedure (see Note 2) for finite interpretations. This entails *finite model soundness*: if Fusemate terminates on a program P with an open exhausted branch then this branch contains a finite possible model of P. It also entails *finite model completeness*: if every possible model of P is finite then Fusemate will compute each of them in its open exhausted branches. A formal

---

[4] Body matcher are represented internally in the Scala runtime system without explicit grounding.

theorem for these results could be given but is not stated here because it would require more formalization.

Fusemate's termination behavior could be improved with a breadth-first strategy, however at the expense of one-branch-at-a-time space efficiency. In the programs below this is not a problem.

3   Description Logic Interface

Fusemate can be used as a description logic (DL) reasoner by mapping a DL knowledge base into a logic program and running that program for satisfiability [12]. This section makes that reasoner callable from rules, but other DL reasoners could be coupled, too. It describes the syntax, semantics, and soundness and completeness properties of the coupling, and it discusses related work.

The DL terminology follows [5]. To summarize, a DL knowledge base KB consists of a TBox and an ABox. A TBox T is a set of GCIs (general concept inclusions), each of the form $C \sqsubseteq D$ where C and D are DL *concept expressions*, or just *concepts*. An ABox A is a set of *ABox assertions*, i.e., concept assertions and role assertions of the forms $a : C$ and $(a, b) : r$, respectively, where a and b are individuals and r is a role. Fusemate currently implements $\mathcal{ALCIF}$, which is $\mathcal{ALC}$ extended with inverse roles and functional roles. A *role*, hence, is either a role name n or an inverse role name n^{-1}. Roles can be declared as functional (right-unique). As usual, KB-satisfiability is assumed to be decidable and concept formation must be closed under negation, so that query entailment can be reduced to KB unsatisfiability as follows. Given a KB (A, T) and an ABox Q, the *(ground) query*, define $(A, T) \models_{\mathsf{DL}} Q$ iff the KB entails Q wrt. the usual first-order logic semantics of description logics, or, equivalently: for all $a : C \in Q$ the KB $(A \cup \{a : \neg C\}, T)$ is unsatisfiable and for all $(a, b) : r \in Q$ the KB $(A \cup \{a : \forall r . \neg B,\ b : B\}, T)$ is unsatisfiable, where B is a fresh concept name.

The coupling between the rules and the DL reasoner is *two-way* and *dynamic*: it is two-way in the sense that rules can not only *call* the DL reasoner wrt. a fixed ABox and a TBox, the rules can also *construct* ABoxes during model computation, individually in each possible model. It is *dynamic* in the sense that ABox assertions are time-stamped, like ordinary atoms, and also all earlier ABoxes are accessible by the rules.

Syntax. Concepts and roles are treated as constants by the rule language while any free ground term can be a DL individual. More precisely, assume a DL signature whose concept and role names are disjoint with the signature of the rule language. Let t, t_1, t_2 be free possibly non-ground terms, C a concept, r a role and tt a time term. An *untimed DL-atom* is of the form $t : C$ or $(t_1, t_2) : r$. Let IsAAt/3 and HasAAt/4 be distinguished ordinary predicate symbols. A *timed DL-atom* is an ordinary atom IsAAt(t, C, tt) or HasAAt(t_1, r, t_2, tt), usually written as $t : C @ tt$ or $(t_1, t_2) : r @ tt$, respectively. Timed DL-atoms can appear in heads (and bodies) of ordinary rules. This allows to create time-stamped ABoxes initially as sets of facts and dynamically during program execution. For calling the DL reasoner, the rule language is extended by the following *DL-call* special forms, where T is a TBox, A is an ABox, and $\vec{q}$ ("query") is a list of untimed DL-atoms.

$$T \models \vec{q} \qquad \textsf{DLISSAT}(T) \qquad \textsf{DLISUNSAT}(T)$$
$$(A, T) \models \vec{q} \qquad \textsf{DLISSAT}(A, T) \qquad \textsf{DLISUNSAT}(A, T)$$

The free variables are $fvar(\vec{q})$ in the left column cases, otherwise empty.

Semantics. Logic programming considers syntactically different terms as unequal. This is not enforced in DLs. Indeed, e.g., if $A = \{(\mathsf{a}, \mathsf{c}) : \mathsf{r}, (\mathsf{a}, \mathsf{b}) : \mathsf{r}\}$ and r is a functional role then A is satisfiable by making b and c *equal*. To avoid such discrepancies, DL individuals are explicitly equipped with a unique name assumption, as follows.

Given an ABox A, let $K(A) = \{a_1, \ldots a_n\}$ be the set of all ("known") individuals mentioned in A and define $UNA(A) = \{a_i : N_{(a_i, a_j)}, a_j : \neg N_{(a_i, a_j)} \mid a_i, a_j \in K(A) \text{ and } 1 \leq i < j \leq n\}$. In that, $N_{(a_i, a_j)}$ are fresh concept names. The set $UNA(A)$ specifies that all individuals in A must be pairwise unequal (a, b and c in the example).

The definition of rule semantics in Sect. 2 is extended by DL-calls as follows: $I, \beta \models ((A, T) \models \vec{q})$ iff $(A \cup UNA(A) \cup UNA(\vec{q}\beta), T) \models_{\mathsf{DL}} \vec{q}\beta$ ($\vec{q}\beta$ as a set); $I, \beta \models \textsf{DLISSAT}(A, T)$ iff $(A \cup UNA(A), T)$ is satisfiable; $I, \beta \models \textsf{DLISUNSAT}(A, T)$ iff $(A \cup UNA(A), T)$ is unsatisfiable.

For the DL-calls on the first line, let *time* be the pivot variable of the rule containing the DL-call and take $A = abox(I, time\,\beta)$ for the corresponding definition with explicit A, where $abox(I, d) = \{t : C \mid t : C @ d \in I\} \cup \{(t_1, t_2) : r \mid (t_1, t_2) : r @ d \in I\}$ is the *induced ABox from I at time d*. Intuitively, such a DL-call gets its ABox from the current interpretation by projection from its timed DL-atoms at the current time.

Notice the implicit dependency of an induced ABox on timed DL-atoms at pivot time. This is why for the purpose of stratification every line one DL-call stands for the two subgoals $\textsf{IsAAt}(\_, \_, time)$ and $\textsf{HasAAt}(\_, \_, \_, time)$. For constant ABoxes on the second line stratification is not an issue. (As such they are not very useful - but see Example 2 and the example in Sect. 5 below.)

With all that in place, the possibly model semantics for stratified programs defined in Sect. 2.1 carries over to the DL coupling without change. Notice that the semantics of the coupling is agnostic of the notion of (un)satisfiability and entailment in the DL part. This way, the coupling respects the usual open world semantics of DL reasoning. Notice also that it is possible that a program has a possible model I whose induced ABox is unsatisfiable with some TBox T. If this is not desirable it is easy to reject such a model with a **fail** rule utilising a $\textsf{DLISUNSAT}(T)$ call.

Soundness and Completeness. Soundness and completeness carries over from Sect. 2.2 with some caveats. Incompleteness can arise due to potentially infinite ABoxes induced at limit ordinals. With an interest in finite models only, this issue can safely be ignored, as before. A more relevant issue is monotonicity (Definition 3). **DLISSAT** calls can be non-monotonic because first-order logic satisfiability is, of course, not always preserved when a KB grows. This can lead to both incompleteness/unsoundness, depending on a positive/negative call context. The other two forms are based on unsatisfiability, hence monotonic, and cause no problem. With those only, iterated fixpoint computation and Fusemate model computation are both sound and complete for finite possible models.

Related Work. According to the classification in [16], ours is a hybrid approach with a loose coupling between the description logic and the rule reasoner. The coupling is done in a DL-safe way [27], in fact, essentially, in a *weakly* DL-safe [32] way as in DL+Log. DL+log [32] is among the most expressive languages that combines rules with ontologies. DL+log rules can query a DL reasoner by taking concept/role names as unary/binary predicates and using (in our terms) extra existentially quantified variables in queries. With Fusemate rules one would equivalently use existential role restrictions. Unlike DL+log, Fusemate allows DL-calls within default negation, cf. Example 2. Most other hybrid languages, like the one in [27] and dl+Programs [17] do not allow DL atoms in the head. Unlike as in the other approaches, concepts and roles are *terms* here and, hence, can be quantified over in rules. This is advantageous for writing domain independent rules involving concepts and roles, such as the event calculus in Sect. 4.

3.1   Example

As a running example we consider a highly simplified transport scenario. Boxes containing goods are loaded onto a truck, moved to a destination, and unloaded again. The boxes can contain perishable goods that require cooling, fruits, or non-perishable goods, toys. Boxes of the former kind (and only those) can be equipped with temperature sensors and provide a temperature value, which is classified as low (unproblematic) or high (problematic). A part of this domain is modelled in the description logic $\mathcal{ALC}$ extended with functional roles. The following KB has a TBox on box properties (left), and an ABox on temperature classes (middle) and box properties (right):

$Box \sqsubseteq \forall\, Temp.TempClass$	$Low : TempClass$	$Box_0 : FruitBox$
$FruitBox \sqsubseteq \exists\, Temp.TempClass$	$High : TempClass$	$Box_1 : FruitBox$
$ToyBox \sqsubseteq \neg\exists\, Temp.TempClass$		$Box_2 : Box$
$FruitBox \sqsubseteq Box$		$Box_3 : ToyBox$
$ToyBox \sqsubseteq Box$		$Box_4 : Box \sqcap \forall\, Temp.\neg TempClass$
$Temp$ is a functional role		$Box_5 : Box \sqcap \exists\, Temp.TempClass$

Example 1. The ABox assertions can be represented as a program with facts timed at, say, 0 ("beginning of time"), e.g., $Box(5) : Box \sqcap \exists\, Temp.TempClass@0$.[5] Let tbox denote the TBox above. Some example rules with DL-calls are

---

[5] The concrete Fusemate syntax is IsAAt(Box(5), And(Box,Exists(Temp,TempClass)), 0) but we stick with the better readable ":"-syntax. TBoxes have similar syntax and are typically bound to (Scala) variables like tbox in the example. In concrete syntax, free constant, function and predicate symbols start with a capital letter, variables with a lower case letter. An underscore _ is an anonymous variable.

1 x : Box @ time :– x : _ @ time, tbox ⊨ x : Box
2 TempBox(time, box) :– box : Box @ time, tbox ⊨ box : (∃ Temp.TempClass)
3 KnownTempBox(time, box) :–
4   box : Box @ time, **choose**(temp, List(Low, High)), tbox ⊨ (box, temp) : Temp

The first rule materializes the Box concept. Any known individual at a given time that is provable a Box will explicitly become a Box individual at time. While this is redundant for DL-reasoning, it comes in handy for rules. For example, the second rule applies to explicitly given Boxes at time that provably have a Temp attribute. Thanks to the first rule, TempBox(0,Box(i)) is derivable for $i \in \{0, 1, 5\}$. (Recall that the ABox in the DL-call is formed from the timed DL-atoms at pivot time.) The third rule is a variation of the second rule and tests if a box has a *concrete* Temp attribute Low or High instead of *some*.   □

Example 2. This is an example for a stratified DL-call within default negation and explicit ABox:

1 ColdBox(time, box) :–
2   box : Box @ time,
3   **not** (t < time, (l.aboxAt(t), tbox) ⊨ box : Box, (box, High) : Temp)

According to this rule, a box is a ColdBox at a given time if it never provably was a Box in the past with a High temperature. The (Scala) expression l.aboxAt(t) can be used in Fusemate to retrieve the induced abox at time t from the current interpretation I.[6] Notice that t is strictly earlier than time which renders the DL-call stratified.

An example for the DLISUNSAT DL-call is in the rule **fail** :- Now(time), DLISUNSAT(tbox). This rule abandons a current model candidate if its induced abox at the current time "Now" is inconsistent with tbox.   □

4   Event Calculus Embedding

The event calculus (EC) is a logical language for representing and reasoning about actions and their effects [20, 35]. At its core, effects are fluents, i.e., statements whose truth value can change over time, and the event calculus provides a framework for specifying the effects of actions in terms of initiating or terminating fluents.

Many versions of the EC exists, see [26] for a start. The approach below makes do with a basic version that is inspired by the discrete event calculus in [28] with integer time. The event calculus of [28] is operationalized by translation to propositional SAT. Its implementation in the "decreasoner" is geared for efficiency and can be used to solve planning and diagnosis tasks, among others. The version below is tailored for the model computation tasks mentioned

---

[6] Access to I is unusual for logic programming systems. See [12] for a discussion of this features.

in the introduction, where a fixed sequence of events at given timepoints can be supposed.[7] It rests on minimal model semantics and stratified default negation. Most of it is not overly specific to Fusemate, and answer set programming encodings of the event calculus, e.g. [21], should be applicable as well.

The rest of this section explains the EC/DL integration grouped into "axiom sets":

- Domain independent EC axioms: principles of actions initiating/terminating fluents
- Domain independent EC/DL integration axioms: ABox assertions as fluents
- Domain dependent axioms: initial situation and concrete actions effects
- Concrete actions: events driving the model computation
- Fusemate specific rules

Domain Independent Axioms. The EC main syntactic categories are *Fluents* and *Actions*, both given via designated sub-signatures of the term signature. They are used with *EC-predicates* in intended sorting as follows:

$$\text{Initiates} : \mathbb{T} \times \text{Action} \times \text{Fluent} \qquad \text{Initiated} : \mathbb{T} \times \text{Fluent}$$

$$\text{Terminates} : \mathbb{T} \times \text{Action} \times \text{Fluent} \qquad \text{Terminated} : \mathbb{T} \times \text{Fluent}$$

$$\text{StronglyTerminates} : \mathbb{T} \times \text{Action} \times \text{Fluent} \qquad \text{StronglyTerminated} : \mathbb{T} \times \text{Fluent}$$

$$\text{HoldsAt} : \mathbb{T} \times \text{Fluent} \qquad \text{Happens} : \mathbb{T} \times \text{Action}$$

The EC was originally introduced as a Prolog logic program. The following *domain independent rules* are similar but modified for stratified bottom-up model computation. Some rules use a "strong negation" operator **neg** which can be applied to ordinary atoms in the body or the head. Fusemate implements the usual semantic [18] which amounts to adding the rules **fail** :- $p(time, \vec{x}), \mathbf{neg}\, p(time, \vec{x})$ for every ordinary predicate p.

1 Initiated(time+1, f) :- Happens(time, a), Initiates(time, a, f) // *H1*
2 Terminated(time+1, f) :- Happens(time, a), Terminates(time, a, f) // *H2*
3 StronglyTerminated(time+1, f) :- Happens(time, a), StronglyTerminates(time, a, f) // *H3*
4 Terminated(time, f) :- StronglyTerminated(time, f) // *H4*

6 HoldsAt(time, f) :- Initiated(time, f), **not** Terminated(time, f) // *EC3*
7 **neg**(HoldsAt(time, f)) :- StronglyTerminated(time, f), **not** Initiated(time, f) // *EC4*

9 HoldsAt(time, f) :- Step(time, prev), HoldsAt(prev, f), **not** Terminated(time, f) // *EC5*
10 **neg**(HoldsAt(time, f)) :- Step(time, prev), **neg**(HoldsAt(prev, f)), **not** Initiated(time, f) // *EC6*

---

[7] Actually, events can be inserted in retrospect using Fusemate's revision operator, restarting the model computation from there. The paper [11] already has a "supply-chain" example for that.

In the rules above, the variable f stands for fluents and a for actions. The axioms H1 – H3 specify the dependencies between fluents and actions in general. The distinction between Initiates and Initiated was made for being able to distinguish between initiation by actions ("*loading* a box on a truck *initiates* the box being on the truck") and initiation as a matter of circumstances or their consequences ("smoke *initiated* alarm bell ringing").

The core relation is HoldsAt(time,f) which can hold true at time because f is Initiated at time (EC3), or was true at the previous time step but not terminated (EC5, frame axiom). Similarly for the negated case. Notice the difference between Terminated and StronglyTerminated. The former removes HoldsAt(time, f) from the model, the latter inserts **neg**(HoldsAt(time,f)) into it. That is, this is a three-valued logic. With default negation one can distinguish the three cases.

Notice that fluents are initiated or terminated in H1 – H3 with a delay of one time step. This was done so that the Initiates and Terminates predicates can be defined in a stratified way in terms of HoldsAt at the current time. Without the delay SBTP would be violated in such cases. The increase in time will not cause non-termination of model computation because H1 – H3 are conditioned on events happening (as long as there are only finitely many events).

4.1   Linking Description Logic with the Event Calculus

Sect. 3 introduced timed DL-atoms for specifying (timestamped) ABoxes. Typically, ABox assertions should be preserved over time unless there is reason for change. Examples are the initial ABox assertions in Example 1 and role assertions in Example 4 below. This immediately suggests to utilize the event calculus for treating ABox assertions as fluents. The following explains this in more detail.

Domain Independent Axioms. From now on, *untimed* DL-atoms are allowed in fluent positions. Untimed DL-atoms are enough because fluents occur within EC-predicate atoms which by themselves provide the time. The following axioms are added as domain independent axioms to restore the timed DL-atom versions of the fluents:

₁ x : c **@** time :– HoldsAt(time, x : c) // *DL1*
₂ x : Neg(c) **@** time :– **neg**(HoldsAt(time, x : c)) // *DL2*
₃ (x, y): r **@** time :– HoldsAt(time,(x, y) : r) //*DL3*

Notice the use of variables c and r in concept and role positions, which makes it possible to formulate these axioms independent of a concrete DL KB. The DL2 axiom expresses strongly negated concept membership equivalently by membership in the negated concept.

The axioms DL1 – DL3 are obviously reasonable in any domain. Their converse is not, however. Not everything holding true at a point in time should by default extend into the future, e.g., a person's birthday.

Domain Dependent Axioms. Domain dependent axioms comprise fluents that hold initially and specifications of action effects in terms of initiation and termination of fluents. An example for the former is the fact for Box(5) in Example 1, which could be rewritten as HoldsAt(0, Box(5) : Box ⊓ ∃ Temp.TempClass).

Example 3. The following rules specify the effects of Load and Unload actions of boxes in terms of these boxes being OnTruck.

1 Initiates(time, Load(box), OnTruck(box)) :– box : Box @ time
2 StronglyTerminates(time, Unload, OnTruck(box)) :– HoldsAt(time, OnTruck(box))

The first rule makes sure in its body that only boxes that exist at a time can be loaded. The second rule concludes that all boxes loaded will definitely not be not on the truck after unload. All other boxes are untouched. Notice that the OnTruck fluent is not a DL concept (it doesn't have to be).   □

Concrete Actions. What is still missing are concrete actions happening for triggering the model computation in the combined Rules/DL/EC domain model. In the running example we consider the following scenario unfolding:

Time	10	20	30	40	50
Action	Load Box_0 Load Box_1	Load Box_2	Load Box_3 Load Box_4		Unload
Sensor	$Box_0 : -10°$	$Box_2 : 10°$	$Box_0 : 2°$	$Box_0 : 20°$	

These actions are easily represented as facts, e.g., Happens(10, Load(Box(0))). The temperature measurement at time 20 for Box(2) becomes Happens(20, SensorEvent(Box(2), 10)).

Concrete Domains. Real-world applications require reasoning with concrete domains (numeric types, strings, etc.). Extending DLs with concrete domains while preserving satisfiability is possible only under tight expressivity bounds. See [25] for a survey. One way to mitigate this problem is to use rules and built-ins for concrete domains and to pass symbolic abstractions to the DL reasoner.

Example 4. This rule demonstrates abstracting a concrete box temperature sensor reading as a Temp attribute.

1 Initiates(time, SensorEvent(box, temp), (box, High) : Temp) **and**
2   Terminates(time, SensorEvent(box, temp), (box, Low) : Temp)) :–
3   Happens(time, SensorEvent(box, temp)), temp > 0

The given action Happens(20, SensorEvent(Box(2), 10)) with the rule above and rules H1 and H6 will derive HoldsAt(21, (Box(2),High) : Temp). From that, with DL1 and the rules in Example 1, Box(2) will become a TempBox and even a KnownTempBox from time 21 onwards.   □

Fusemate Specific Rules. Fusemate provides the user with a number of non-standard operators, see [12]. One of them is the aggregation operator COLLECT.

Example 5. Consider the rule

```
1 Unloaded(time+1, boxes) :-
2        Happens(time, Unload),
3        COLLECT(boxes, box STH HoldsAt(time, OnTruck(box)))
```

This rule aggregates all unloaded boxes into one set, boxes, one tick after Unload time. It is not formulated as a fluent to make it a time*point* property. In the example, the Unload happens at time 50, which leads to Unloaded(51, Set(Box(0), Box(1), Box(2), Box(3), Box(4))). Notice that these are exactly the boxes loaded over time, at timepoints 10, 20, and 30.   □

4.2 Ramification Problem

The ramification problem is concerned with indirect consequences of an action. Such consequences could be in conflict with facts holding at the time of the action or other consequences. This problem is particularly prominent in the combination with DL, where effects (i.e., fluents) can be entailed implicitly by the DL KB, and possibly in an opaque way. Trying to terminate such a fluent can be futile, as it could be re-instated implicitly or explicitly by materialization.

A good example is the entailment of TempBox(0, Box(0)) as discussed in Example 1. Suppose we wish to re-purpose Box(0) and no longer use it for temperature sensitive transport. In terms of the modelling, Box(0) shall no longer belong to the (entailed) concept ∃Temp.TempClass.

The ramification problem has been extensively researched in the EC literature, see [35]. For instance, one could impose state constraints, if-and-only if conditions, so that terminating an entailed fluent propagates down; or one could use effect constraints that propagate termination of actions to other actions. A first attempt in this direction is a rule that terminates a fluent that entails the property to be removed:

```
1 Terminated(time+1, (box, temp) : Temp)) :-
2        RemoveTemp(time, box), // Some condition for removing box Temp
3        (box, temp) : Temp @ time // Attribute to be removed
```

This rule works as expected for Box$_2$ after explicitly having received a Temp-attribute at time 20, cf. Example 4. It does not work, however, for, e.g., Box$_0$. As a FruitBox, Box$_0$ has a Temp attribute implied by the TBox.

One way to fix this problem *in the running example* is to terminate *all* concept assertions for the box as any of them might entail a Temp attribute, and only retain that it is a Box:

```
1 (Terminated(time, box : concept) and Initiated(time, box : Box)):-
2        RemoveTemp(time, box), // Some condition for removing box Temp
3        box : concept @ time, concept != Box // Concept to be removed
4 // Similar rule for removing role assertions omitted
```

While this measure achieves the desired effect, it may also remove box properties that could be retained, e.g., the size of the box (if it were part of the example, that is).

The KB revision problem has been studied extensively in database and AI settings. For DLs, there are algorithms for *instance level updates* of an ABox, where, in first-order logic terms, the ABox is a set of ground atoms over known individuals, see [19]. Very recently, Baader etal [6,7] devised algorithms for semantically optimally revising ABoxes that may contain quantifiers (e.g. Box_5 in the running example). All these result are for lightweight description logics, though.

5   Putting It All Together

This section completes the running example with rules for diagnostic reasoning. Suppose a given subset of the boxes $\{Box_0, \ldots, Box_5\}$ is unloaded at the destination. We are interested in determining the status of the delivery and computing possible models as explanations under these constraints:

1. If there is no unloaded box with known high temperature then the status is OK.
2. If some unloaded box has a known high temperature then this box has been tampered with or the truck cooling is broken.
3. If some unloaded box has a known low temperature then the truck cooling is not broken (because a broken cooling would affect all boxes).
4. If all unloaded boxes with a temperature sensor can consistently be assumed to have high temperature then box tampering can be excluded (because broken cooling is the more likely explanation).

The following rules determine the status of the delivery as "ok" or "anomalous". There are two cases of anomalies, (a) the truck cooling is broken or (b) some box has been tampered with. The rules feature disjunctive heads, strong negation, DL-calls, Scala builtin calls and the set datatype.

```
1  OK(time) :- Unloaded(time, boxes), not Anomaly(time, _)

3  Anomaly(time, TamperedBox(box)) or Anomaly(time, BrokenCooling) :-
4      Unloaded(time, boxes),
5      (box, High) : Temp @ time,
6      boxes ∋ box

8  neg(Anomaly(time, BrokenCooling)) and neg(Anomaly(time, TamperedBox(box))) :-
9      Unloaded(time, boxes),
10     (box, Low) : Temp @ time,
11     boxes ∋ box

13  fail :-   Anomaly(time, TamperedBox(box)),
14     Unloaded(time, unloadedBoxes),
15     COLLECT(boxes, box STH (TempBox(time, box), unloadedBoxes ∋ box)),
16     LET(assertions, boxes map { (_, High) : Temp }), // unloaded boxes ascribed High Temp
17     DLISSAT(I.aboxAt(time) ++ assertions, tbox)
```

The first rule makes the delivery ok in absence of any anomaly. The second rule observes an anomaly if some unloaded box has a High temperature. The anomaly could be either type, or both, this rule makes a guess. The third and the fourth rule are eliminating guesses. The third rule says that the truck cooling is not broken if evidenced by the existence of a Low temperature box. Moreover, each of these boxes has not been tampered with. The fourth rule is the most interesting one. It eliminates a tampered-box anomaly by considering all unloaded boxes that are known to be equipped with temperature sensors. The rationale is that if *all* these boxes can consistently be assumed to have High temperature then box tampering is unlikely (broken cooling is more likely).

This reasoning is achieved by collecting in line 15 in the boxes variable the mentioned boxes (TempBox was defined is Example 1). Line 16 assigns to a variable assertions the value of the stated Scala expression for constructing High temperature role assertions for boxes. Finally, the DL-call on line 17 checks the satisfiability of the KB consisting of the current abox temporarily extended with assertions and the static TBox. It is important to know that fail rules are always tried last for a fixed current time, after all ordinary rules. This way, the usages of COLLECT and DLISSAT in the last rule *are* stratified.

The correct diagnosis is Anomaly(51, BrokenCooling). In the course of events, the TempBoxes are Box_0, Box_1, Box_2, and Box_5 (Box_2 becomes one only at time 20.) The unloaded boxes at time 50 are Box_0, Box_1, Box_2, and Box_4. In their intersection, Box_0 and Box_2 have High Temp values, which gives rise to an anomaly. Only the box Box_1 has an unknown Temp value, which is consistent with High and, hence, excludes a TamperedBox anomaly. Moreover, for every box, neither a TamperedBox anomaly nor a negated TamperedBox anomaly is derived.

If the Box_0 sensor reading at time 40 is changed from 10 to -10 then the diagnosis is

1 Anomaly(51, TamperedBox(Box(2)))
2 **neg**(Anomaly(51, TamperedBox(Box(0))))
3 **neg**(Anomaly(51, BrokenCooling))

Both diagnosis are the only possible models in each case and nothing is known about Box_1. The Fusemate runtime is approx. 4 s in each case on a modern PC. The main bottleneck is lack of performance of the coupled DL-reasoner, which is a proof-of-concept implementation only.

6   Conclusions

This paper introduced a knowledge representation language that, for the first time, combines the event calculus with description logic in a logic programming framework for model computation. The paper demonstrated the interplay of these three components by means of an elaborated example.

Results are in parts at an abstract level. They include conditions for finite-model soundness and completeness of the rules/DL reasoner coupling that are re-usable in other systems that support stratification in a similar way ([37], e.g.).

The diagnosis rules in Sect. 5, among others, utilized Fusemate's specific set comprehension operator (COLLECT) and might be hard to emulate in other systems. It might be possible to run the example in this paper with an expressive system like DLV [22] without too many changes.

The modelling in the example emphasised the possibility to distinguish between absent, unknown or known attribute values, which was enabled by the description logics/rules integration. One might want to go a step further and add "dynamic existentials" to the picture. These are unknown or implicit actions that must have existed to cause observed effects. Recovered or speculating such actions can be expressed already with the (implemented) belief revision framework of [11]. Experimenting with that within the framework here is future work.

The perhaps most pressing open issue is the EC ramification problem (Sect. 4.2), which is particularly pronounced with the DL integration into the EC. Recent advances on ABox updates might help [6,7].

Acknowledgement. I am grateful to the reviewers for their constructive feedback.

References

1. Artikis, A., Skarlatidis, A., Portet, F., Paliouras, G.: Logic-based event recognition. Knowl. Eng. Rev. **27**(4), 469–506 (2012)
2. Baader, F., et al.: A novel architecture for situation awareness systems. In: Giese, M., Waaler, A. (eds.) TABLEAUX 2009. LNCS (LNAI), vol. 5607, pp. 77–92. Springer, Heidelberg (2009). https://doi.org/10.1007/978-3-642-02716-1_7
3. Baader, F., Borgwardt, S., Lippmann, M.: Temporal conjunctive queries in expressive description logics with transitive roles. In: Pfahringer, B., Renz, J. (eds.) AI 2015. LNCS (LNAI), vol. 9457, pp. 21–33. Springer, Cham (2015). https://doi.org/10.1007/978-3-319-26350-2_3
4. Baader, F., Ghilardi, S., Lutz, C.: LTL over description logic axioms. ACM Trans. Comput. Logic - TOCL **13**, 1–32 (2008)
5. Baader, F., Horrocks, I., Lutz, C., Sattler, U.: An Introduction to Description Logic. Cambridge University Press, Cambridge (2017)
6. Baader, F., Koopmann, P., Kriegel, F., Nuradiansyah, A.: Computing optimal repairs of quantified ABoxes w.r.t. static $\mathcal{EL}$ TBoxes. In: Platzer, A., Sutcliffe, G. (eds.) CADE 2021. LNCS (LNAI), vol. 12699, pp. 309–326. Springer, Cham (2021). https://doi.org/10.1007/978-3-030-79876-5_18
7. Baader, F., Kriegel, F., Nuradiansyah, A., Peñaloza, R.: Computing compliant anonymisations of quantified ABoxes w.r.t. $\mathcal{EL}$ policies. In: Pan, J.Z., et al. (eds.) ISWC 2020. LNCS, vol. 12506, pp. 3–20. Springer, Cham (2020). https://doi.org/10.1007/978-3-030-62419-4_1
8. Baader, F., Lippmann, M., Liu, H.: Using causal relationships to deal with the ramification problem in action formalisms based on description logics. In: Fermüller, C.G., Voronkov, A. (eds.) LPAR 2010. LNCS, vol. 6397, pp. 82–96. Springer, Heidelberg (2010). https://doi.org/10.1007/978-3-642-16242-8_7
9. Baader, F., Lutz, C., Miličic, M., Sattler, U., Wolter, F.: Integrating description logics and action formalisms: first results. In: Proceedings of the 20th National Conference on Artificial Intelligence, AAAI 2005, vol. 2, pp. 572–577. AAAI Press (2005)

10. Bagheri Hariri, B., Calvanese, D., De Giacomo, G., Masellis, R., Felli, P., Montali, M.: Description logic knowledge and action bases. J. Artif. Intell. Res. **46**, 651–686 (2013)
11. Baumgartner, P.: Possible models computation and revision – a practical approach. In: Peltier, N., Sofronie-Stokkermans, V. (eds.) IJCAR 2020. LNCS (LNAI), vol. 12166, pp. 337–355. Springer, Cham (2020). https://doi.org/10.1007/978-3-030-51074-9_19
12. Baumgartner, P.: The Fusemate logic programming system. In: Platzer, A., Sutcliffe, G. (eds.) CADE 2021. LNCS (LNAI), vol. 12699, pp. 589–601. Springer, Cham (2021). https://doi.org/10.1007/978-3-030-79876-5_34
13. Baumgartner, P., Furbach, U., Niemelä, I.: Hyper tableaux. In: Alferes, J.J., Pereira, L.M., Orlowska, E. (eds.) JELIA 1996. LNCS, vol. 1126, pp. 1–17. Springer, Heidelberg (1996). https://doi.org/10.1007/3-540-61630-6_1
14. Beck, H., Dao-Tran, M., Eiter, T.: LARS: a logic-based framework for analytic reasoning over streams. Artif. Intell. **261**, 16–70 (2018)
15. Drescher, C., Thielscher, M.: Integrating action calculi and description logics. In: Hertzberg, J., Beetz, M., Englert, R. (eds.) KI 2007. LNCS (LNAI), vol. 4667, pp. 68–83. Springer, Heidelberg (2007). https://doi.org/10.1007/978-3-540-74565-5_8
16. Eiter, T., Ianni, G., Krennwallner, T., Polleres, A.: Rules and ontologies for the semantic web. In: Baroglio, C., Bonatti, P.A., Małuszyński, J., Marchiori, M., Polleres, A., Schaffert, S. (eds.) Reasoning Web. LNCS, vol. 5224, pp. 1–53. Springer, Heidelberg (2008). https://doi.org/10.1007/978-3-540-85658-0_1
17. Eiter, T., Ianni, G., Lukasiewicz, T., Schindlauer, R., Tompits, H.: Combining answer set programming with description logics for the Semantic Web. Artif. Intell. **172**(12), 1495–1539 (2008)
18. Gelfond, M., Lifschitz, V.: Classical negation in logic programs and disjunctive databases. New Gener. Comput. **9**, 365–385 (1991)
19. Giacomo, G.D., Oriol, X., Rosati, R., Savo, D.F.: Instance-level update in DL-lite ontologies through first-order rewriting. J. Artif. Intell. Res. **70**, 1335–1371 (2021)
20. Kowalski, R.A., Sergot, M.J.: A logic-based calculus of events. New Gener. Comput. **4**(1), 67–95 (1986)
21. Lee, J., Palla, R.: Reformulating the situation calculus and the event calculus in the general theory of stable models and in answer set programming. J. Artif. Intell. Res. **43**, 571–620 (2012)
22. Leone, N., Pfeifer, G., Faber, W., Eiter, T., Gottlob, G., Perri, S., Scarcello, F.: The DLV system for knowledge representation and reasoning. ACM Trans. Comput. Logic **7**(3), 499–562 (2006)
23. Lin, F.: Situation calculus. In: van Harmelen, F., Lifschitz, V., Porter, B.W. (eds.) Handbook of Knowledge Representation, Foundations of Artificial Intelligence, vol. 3, pp. 649–669. Elsevier (2008)
24. Lloyd, J.: Foundations of Logic Programming. Symbolic Computation. Second extended edn. Springer, Heidelberg (1987). https://doi.org/10.1007/978-3-642-83189-8
25. Lutz, C.: Description logics with concrete domains - a survey. In: Balbiani, P., Suzuki, N., Wolter, F., Zakharyaschev, M. (eds.) Advances in Modal Logic 4, Papers from the Fourth Conference on "Advances in Modal Logic", pp. 265–296. King's College Publications (2002)
26. Miller, R., Shanahan, M.: Some alternative formulations of the event calculus. In: Kakas, A.C., Sadri, F. (eds.) Computational Logic: Logic Programming and Beyond. LNCS (LNAI), vol. 2408, pp. 452–490. Springer, Heidelberg (2002). https://doi.org/10.1007/3-540-45632-5_17

27. Motik, B., Sattler, U., Studer, R.: Query answering for OWL-DL with rules. In: McIlraith, S.A., Plexousakis, D., van Harmelen, F. (eds.) ISWC 2004. LNCS, vol. 3298, pp. 549–563. Springer, Heidelberg (2004). https://doi.org/10.1007/978-3-540-30475-3_38

28. Mueller, E.T.: Event calculus reasoning through satisfiability. J. Logic Comput. **14**(5), 703–730 (2004)

29. Özçep, Ö.L., Möller, R., Neuenstadt, C.: A stream-temporal query language for ontology based data access. In: Lutz, C., Thielscher, M. (eds.) KI 2014. LNCS (LNAI), vol. 8736, pp. 183–194. Springer, Cham (2014). https://doi.org/10.1007/978-3-319-11206-0_18

30. Poggi, A., Lembo, D., Calvanese, D., De Giacomo, G., Lenzerini, M., Rosati, R.: Linking data to ontologies. In: Spaccapietra, S. (ed.) Journal on Data Semantics X. LNCS, vol. 4900, pp. 133–173. Springer, Heidelberg (2008). https://doi.org/10.1007/978-3-540-77688-8_5

31. Przymusinski, T.C.: On the declarative and procedural semantics of logic programs. J. Autom. Reasoning **5**(2), 167–205 (1989)

32. Rosati, R.: DL+log: tight integration of description logics and disjunctive datalog. In: Doherty, P., Mylopoulos, J., Welty, C.A. (eds.) Proceedings, Tenth International Conference on Principles of Knowledge Representation and Reasoning, Lake District of the United Kingdom, 2–5 June 2006, pp. 68–78. AAAI Press (2006)

33. Sakama, C.: Possible model semantics for disjunctive databases. In: Kim, W., Nicholas, J.M., Nishio, S. (eds.) Proceedings First International Conference on Deductive and Object-Oriented Databases (DOOD-89), pp. 337–351. Elsevier (1990)

34. Sakama, C., Inoue, K.: An alternative approach to the semantics of disjunctive logic programs and deductive databases. J. Autom. Reasoning **13**, 145–172 (1994)

35. Shanahan, M.: The event calculus explained. In: Wooldridge, M.J., Veloso, M. (eds.) Artificial Intelligence Today. LNCS (LNAI), vol. 1600, pp. 409–430. Springer, Heidelberg (1999). https://doi.org/10.1007/3-540-48317-9_17

36. Tsilionis, E., Artikis, A., Paliouras, G.: Incremental event calculus for run-time reasoning. In: Proceedings of the 13th ACM International Conference on Distributed and Event-Based Systems, DEBS 2019, pp. 79–90. Association for Computing Machinery, New York (2019)

37. Zaniolo, C.: Expressing and supporting efficiently greedy algorithms as locally stratified logic programs. In: Technical Communications of ICLP 2015 1433 (01 2015)

Semantic Forgetting in Expressive Description Logics

Mostafa Sakr$^{(\boxtimes)}$ and Renate A. Schmidt

University of Manchester, Manchester, UK
{Mostafa.Sakr,Renate.Schmidt}@manchester.ac.uk

Abstract. Forgetting is an important ontology extraction technology. We present a semantic forgetting method for $\mathcal{ALC}$ ontologies. The method forgets concept names, and captures the semantic content over the remaining vocabulary of an ontology, possibly, by introducing helper concept symbols. In an evaluation, the method performed well on large-scale ontologies when forgetting 10–50% of the vocabulary and the number of helper symbols occurring in the extracts decreased as the number of forgetting symbols increased. Against the forgetting tool Fame(Q), good performance was achieved while more semantic content was preserved.

1 Introduction

Ontologies are often large-scale, formalizing several related topics of some domain. For example, the SNOMED CT ontology contains more than 340K axioms modelled over 361K concept and role names, and formalizes several topics from medical and biomedical domains such as diseases, symptoms, medicines, procedures, and organisms. Working with large-scale ontologies is a challenge due to their sheer size, while in reality, only small extracts are needed. This presses for ontology extraction methods such as *forgetting* [7–11,17,18,28].

The aim of forgetting is extracting an ontology, hereafter called a *forgetting view*, that is *inseparable* from the original ontology in terms of the captured knowledge relative to some *keep vocabulary* (the unforgotten subset of the vocabulary of the original ontology) [6,18,19,29]. Forgetting uses reasoning to eliminate, or forget, the unwanted vocabulary and capture the knowledge relative to the keep vocabulary, possibly by introducing new axioms.

Two different languages $\mathcal{L}^V$ and $\mathcal{L}^C$ should be differentiated when considering forgetting. These are, respectively, the language of the extracted ontology, and the language of the captured consequences. Different forms of forgetting vary on their choices of $\mathcal{L}^V$ and $\mathcal{L}^C$ [6,19]. A variant of particular interest to this paper is *semantic forgetting* [25,36–38] in which the meaning of the keep vocabulary is preserved in the semantic forgetting view. That is, for every model of the original ontology there is a model of the semantic forgetting view and vice versa, such that both models interpret the keep vocabulary in the same way. It has been shown that in this case, both ontologies agree on all second-order consequences over the keep vocabulary [6,18]. That is, $\mathcal{L}^C$ is the language of all second-order consequences of the original ontology relative to the keep vocabulary.

B. Konev and G. Reger (Eds.): FroCoS 2021, LNAI 12941, pp. 118–136, 2021.
https://doi.org/10.1007/978-3-030-86205-3_7

Despite its high precision, semantic forgetting is not sufficiently studied in the literature. In the context of first-order logic (FOL), predicate symbols can be forgotten by quantifying over them [12,25,26]. Since elimination of second-order quantifiers is not always possible [1,13], the generated semantic forgetting view of a first-order theory is not always representable in FOL but it is always representable in second-order logic. For the $\mathcal{ALC}$ fragment of FOL, examples can be constructed to show that the semantic forgetting view of an $\mathcal{ALC}$ ontology cannot be represented as a set of $\mathcal{ALC}$ axioms formulated over the keep vocabulary [21]. Attempts were made to formulate the semantic forgetting view of $\mathcal{ALC}$ ontologies using the description logic $\mathcal{ALCOQ}^{\neg,\sqcup,\sqcap}$ [42] which extends $\mathcal{ALC}$ with nominals ($\mathcal{O}$), qualified number restrictions ($\mathcal{Q}$), role negation ($\neg$), role disjunction ($\sqcup$), and role conjunction ($\sqcap$). However, even for acyclic ontologies, $\mathcal{ALCOQ}^{\neg,\sqcup,\sqcap}$ is not expressive enough to formulate the complete semantic forgetting view of $\mathcal{ALC}$ ontologies over the keep vocabulary. At present, there are no complete semantic forgetting methods for $\mathcal{ALC}$ ontologies.

Taking ideas from [25], we present a complete semantic forgetting method for the description logic $\mathcal{ALC}$. The method forgets concept names from $\mathcal{ALC}$ ontologies. As in [25], we have the perspective that forgetting symbols are second-order predicate symbols, and use fresh helper symbols to capture the complete semantic forgetting view. However, we use helper symbols differently. Whereas [25] replaces the forgetting symbols with fresh helper symbols, our proposed method uses them to represent the role fillers in which the forgetting symbols occur. The idea of our method is to eliminate the forgetting symbols and as many of the introduced helper symbols as is possible. Eliminating the introduced helper symbols completely is however not possible in some cases. Thus, in general, the language $\mathcal{L}^V$ in which the semantic forgetting view is expressed is the language of all $\mathcal{ALC}$-axioms formulated over the keep vocabulary augmented with a set of fresh helper concept symbols. Using helper symbols in this way gives advantages over [25] in that our method is directly applicable to description logic syntax and is better tailored towards the purpose of ontology extraction. An advantage of our method over other methods in the literature [12,14,20–22,27,39–43] is that the semantic forgetting view preserves the form of the input ontology, thus making it more readable and convenient for ontology development, and debugging.

The use of helper symbols is debatable since they are second-order. However, because they are existentially quantified, and because only $\mathcal{ALC}$ constructs are used to formulate the axioms of the semantic forgetting view, most standard reasoning tasks, such as satisfiability checking, classification, and query answering, can be performed on the semantic forgetting view using the standard $\mathcal{ALC}$ tools. Additionally, reduction in complexity of these reasoning tasks is obtained when the number of the helper symbols is less than the number of symbols being forgotten. Helper symbols are increasingly being used in different applications to increase the expressive power of the used language [16,20].

Complexity of forgetting is studied in [28] where it is shown that the forgetting view of an $\mathcal{ALC}$ ontology is in the worst case triple exponential in the size of the input ontology. We show that using our method the size of the semantic forgetting view is single exponential in the size of the input ontology and double exponential in the number of forgetting symbols. This reduction in the theoretical size complexity can be attributed to the use of helper symbols.[1]

2   Getting Started

The vocabulary of an ontology consists of concept and role names. Assume they belong respectively to two disjoint sets N_c and N_r. $\mathcal{ALC}$ concepts are defined inductively by the grammar: $C, D := \top \mid \bot \mid A \mid \neg C \mid C \sqcap D \mid C \sqcup D \mid \exists r.C \mid \forall r.C$ where $A \in N_c$ and $r \in N_r$. An ontology, or TBox, is a set of axioms of the forms $C \sqsubseteq D$ and $C \equiv D$, where C, D are concepts. An equivalence axiom $C \equiv D$ is short-hand for the two subsumption axioms $C \sqsubseteq D$ and $D \sqsubseteq C$.

Concepts can be referred to using their *position* inside the axiom [32]. A *position* is a word over natural numbers. Let $\alpha = C \odot D$ be an $\mathcal{ALC}$ axiom where $\odot \in \{\sqsubseteq, \equiv\}$, then the positions of C and D relative to α are 1 and 2 respectively, in symbols: $\alpha|1 = C$ and $\alpha|2 = D$. Consider a general $\mathcal{ALC}$ concept ψ. Let $pos(\psi)$ be the set of positions of the sub-concepts occurring in ψ. A sub-concept ϕ of ψ is referred to by $\alpha|i.\pi$ where i is position of ψ relative to the axiom α and $\pi \in pos(\psi)$ is the position of ϕ relative to ψ. The definition of $pos(\psi)$ is given inductively as follows:

1. $i.\pi \in pos(\psi)$ if $\psi = \phi_1 \odot \phi_2 \odot \cdots \odot \phi_n$ where $\odot \in \{\sqcup, \sqcap\}$, $\pi \in pos(\phi_i)$ and $1 \leq i \leq n$.
2. $1.\pi \in pos(\psi)$ if ψ takes any of the forms: $\neg\phi, \exists r.\phi$, or $\forall r.\phi$ and $\pi \in pos(\phi)$.

We write $\alpha[\iota/\psi]$ to denote the axiom generated by replacing the sub-concept ϕ at position ι relative to α with the concept ψ.

The *polarity* of a concept occurring at position ι in a subsumption axiom α is denoted by $pol(\alpha, \iota)$, where $pol(\alpha, 1) = -1$, $pol(\alpha, 2) = 1$, and:

1. $pol(\alpha, i.\pi) = pol(\alpha, i)$ if $\alpha|i$ is a conjunction, disjunction, or a concept of the form $\exists r.C$ or $\forall r.C$.
2. $pol(\alpha, i.\pi) = -pol(\alpha, i)$ if $\alpha|i$ is a concept of the form $\neg C$.

A concept is *positive* in an axiom if it occurs with polarity 1, and *negative* if it occurs with polarity -1.

An interpretation $\mathcal{I}$ in $\mathcal{ALC}$ is a pair $\langle \Delta^{\mathcal{I}}, \cdot^{\mathcal{I}} \rangle$ where the domain $\Delta^{\mathcal{I}}$ is a nonempty set, and $\cdot^{\mathcal{I}}$ is an interpretation function that assigns to each concept symbol $A \in N_c$ a subset of $\Delta^{\mathcal{I}}$, and to each $r \in N_r$ a subset of $\Delta^{\mathcal{I}} \times \Delta^{\mathcal{I}}$. $\mathcal{ALC}$ concepts and axioms can be interpreted by translation to FOL [2,15]. First, we interpret concept and role names respectively as unary and binary predicates in FOL. Then, we define two translation functions π_x and π_y that inductively translate $\mathcal{ALC}$ concepts to FOL formulae with the free variable x and y, respectively:

---

[1] Proofs omitted from this paper are available in the long version at https://github.com/e73898ms/SemanticForgettinginExpressiveDescriptionLogics.

$$\pi_x(\top) = \pi_y(\top) = \text{TRUE} \qquad \pi_x(\bot) = \pi_y(\bot) = \text{FALSE}$$
$$\pi_x(A) = A(x) \qquad\qquad\qquad \pi_y(A) = A(y)$$
$$\pi_x(\neg C) = \neg\pi_x(C) \qquad\qquad \pi_y(\neg C) = \neg\pi_y(C)$$
$$\pi_x(C \sqcap D) = \pi_x(C) \wedge \pi_x(D) \qquad \pi_y(C \sqcap D) = \pi_y(C) \wedge \pi_y(D)$$
$$\pi_x(C \sqcup D) = \pi_x(C) \vee \pi_x(D) \qquad \pi_y(C \sqcup D) = \pi_y(C) \vee \pi_y(D)$$
$$\pi_x(\exists r.C) = \exists y\ (r(x,y) \wedge \pi_y(C)) \qquad \pi_y(\exists r.C) = \exists x\ (r(y,x) \wedge \pi_x(C))$$
$$\pi_x(\forall r.C) = \forall y\ (r(x,y) \rightarrow \pi_y(C)) \qquad \pi_y(\forall r.C) = \forall x\ (r(y,x) \rightarrow \pi_x(C))$$

Let C and D be any $\mathcal{ALC}$ concepts. Define the translation function π which translates axioms to first-order formulae with one free variable.

$$\pi(C \equiv D) = (\pi_x(C) \leftrightarrow \pi_x(D)) \qquad \pi(C \sqsubseteq D) = (\pi_x(C) \rightarrow \pi_x(D))$$

An ontology $\mathcal{O}$, or a set of axioms, is translated as:

$$\pi(\mathcal{O}) = \bigwedge_{C \equiv D \in \mathcal{O}} \forall x\ \pi(C \equiv D) \wedge \bigwedge_{C \sqsubseteq D \in \mathcal{O}} \forall x\ \pi(C \sqsubseteq D) \tag{1}$$

In the presented forgetting method we use FOL formulas on the form (1). To simplify the notation, we allow the conjunction (disjunction) of axioms to mean the conjunction (disjunction) of their FOL translations:

$$(C_1 \sqsubseteq D_1) \wedge (C_2 \sqsubseteq D_2) \qquad \text{means} \qquad \pi(C_1 \sqsubseteq D_1) \wedge \pi(C_2 \sqsubseteq D_2)$$
$$(C_1 \sqsubseteq D_1) \vee (C_2 \sqsubseteq D_2) \qquad \text{means} \qquad \pi(C_1 \sqsubseteq D_1) \vee \pi(C_2 \sqsubseteq D_2)$$

Let $\mathcal{O}$ be an ontology, and α an axiom. We say α is satisfiable with respect to $\mathcal{O}$ if there is a model $\mathcal{I}$ of $\mathcal{O}$ such that $\mathcal{I} \models \alpha$. We say α is a consequence of $\mathcal{O}$, in symbols, $\mathcal{O} \models \alpha$, if for every model $\mathcal{I}$ of $\mathcal{O}$ it holds that $\mathcal{I} \models \alpha$.

Let C be an $\mathcal{ALC}$ concept, we denote by $sig(C)$ the set of concept and role names appearing in C. For an ontology $\mathcal{O}$, $sig(\mathcal{O}) = \bigcup_{C \odot D \in \mathcal{O}} sig(C) \cup sig(D)$, where $\odot \in \{\sqsubseteq, \equiv\}$. The *size* of $\mathcal{O}$, in symbols size $(\mathcal{O})$, is the number of axioms occurring on $\mathcal{O}$.

Definition 1. *Let $\mathcal{F}$ be a set of concept names, and $\mathcal{I}$ and $\mathcal{J}$ two models such that $\Delta^{\mathcal{I}} = \Delta^{\mathcal{J}}$. We write $\mathcal{I} \sim_{\mathcal{F}} \mathcal{J}$ if and only if $p^{\mathcal{I}} = p^{\mathcal{J}}$ for every concept and role name, except possibly for $p \in \mathcal{F}$.*

Definition 2. *Let $\mathcal{O}$ be an $\mathcal{ALC}$ ontology and $\mathcal{F} \subseteq sig(\mathcal{O}) \cap N_c$ be the forgetting signature. We say that the $\mathcal{ALC}$ ontology $\mathcal{V}$ is a semantic forgetting view of $\mathcal{O}$ w.r.t. $\mathcal{F}$ iff the following both hold:*

1. *$sig(\mathcal{V}) \subseteq sig(\mathcal{O}) \backslash \mathcal{F}$;*
2. *for every model $\mathcal{I}$ of $\mathcal{O}$, there is a model $\mathcal{J}$ of $\mathcal{V}$, and vice versa, such that $\mathcal{I} \sim_{\mathcal{F}} \mathcal{J}$.*

The keep vocabulary is the set of concept and role symbols in $sig(\mathcal{O}) \backslash \mathcal{F}$.

The following example suggests that the semantic view of an $\mathcal{ALC}$ ontology is not in general representable in $\mathcal{ALC}$.

Example 1. Let $\mathcal{O} = \{A \sqsubseteq \exists r.B \sqcap \exists r.\neg B\}$ and $\mathcal{F} = \{B\}$. In FOL with *Skolem* functions, the semantic forgetting view $\mathcal{V}$ of $\mathcal{O}$ with respect to $\mathcal{F}$ is:

$$\forall x \forall y ((\neg A(x) \vee r(x, f(x))) \wedge (\neg A(y) \vee r(y, g(y))) \wedge$$
$$(\neg A(x) \vee \neg A(y) \vee f(x) \not\approx g(y))) \quad (2)$$

This was computed with the second-order quantifer elimination method in [12]. f and g are function symbols introduced by *Skolemisation* [3,12] to represent existential quantification. Since (2) cannot be back-translated to FOL without function symbols, representing (2) in the $\mathcal{ALC}$ fragment is not possible [5].

Even the more expressive description logic $\mathcal{ALCOQ}^{\neg,\sqcup,\sqcap}$ is insufficient to capture the semantic view [42]. The following example illustrates this observation.

Example 2. Consider $\mathcal{O}$ and $\mathcal{F}$ from Example 1. The forgetting view generated by the methods [21,42] is $\mathcal{V} = \{A \sqsubseteq \geq 2r.\top\}$, which models the information that every element in A has at least two different successors via r. Let $\mathcal{I}$ be a model with domain of interpretation $\Delta = \{a_1, a_2, a_3, b_1, b_2, b_3\}$,

$$A^{\mathcal{I}} = \{a_1, a_2, a_3\}, \text{ and } r^{\mathcal{I}} = \{(a_1, b_1), (a_1, b_2), (a_2, b_1), (a_2, b_3), (a_3, b_2), (a_3, b_3)\}.$$

$\mathcal{I}$ is a model of $\mathcal{V}$ but there is no extension of $\mathcal{I}$ that is a model of $\mathcal{O}$ because no interpretation of B can separate $\{b_1, b_2, b_3\}$ into two disjoint sets where every element in A is connected to at least one element from each set.

The proposed method captures the semantic view by relaxing the first condition of Definition 2 and allowing fresh helper concept symbols to be used in the semantic forgetting view. Fresh here means that the introduced helper symbols do not occur in the vocabulary of the original ontology.

Example 3. Consider $\mathcal{O}$ and $\mathcal{F}$ from Example 1. The ontology $\mathcal{V} = \{A \sqsubseteq \exists r.D_1 \sqcap \exists r.D_2, D_1 \sqcap D_2 \sqsubseteq \bot\}$ is a semantic forgetting view of $\mathcal{O}$ with respect to $\mathcal{F}$ where D_1 and D_2 are fresh concept symbols.

In the presented method, we use helper symbols to represent role fillers. In Example 3, D_1 and D_2 represent two disjoint subsets of the set $\{y \in \Delta^{\mathcal{I}} | (x, y) \in r^{\mathcal{I}} \wedge x \in A^{\mathcal{I}}\}$, where $\mathcal{I}$ is a model of $\mathcal{V}$. Precise interpretations of D_1 and D_2 cannot be given without knowledge of the forgotten symbol B. So, helper symbols can be seen as second-order existentially quantified symbols.

When ontology extraction is required to replace the original ontology with a smaller one in reasoning applications, these applications are unperturbed if the extracted ontology contains helper symbols in its vocabulary. This is at least correct for standard reasoning applications such as *classification*, *satisfiability checking* and *query answering*. The reasons that the original ontology can be safely replaced by the semantic forgetting view which uses helper symbols are:

1. The introduced helper symbols are implicitly existentially quantified. Thus, existing inference systems that operate on the original ontology are sufficient. That is, inference systems which allow for universally quantified symbols are not needed.
2. Using helper symbols, the semantic forgetting view can be formulated using $\mathcal{ALC}$ syntax. Thus, $\mathcal{ALC}$ reasoning methods can operate directly on the semantic forgetting view.

Let us explain this using a query answering problem. For query answering tasks, forgetting can be used to replace the original ontology with a simpler forgetting view such that the vocabulary of the asked queries is a subset of the vocabulary of the forgetting view [19].

Example 4. Consider the ontology $\mathcal{O} = \{A_1 \sqsubseteq \forall r.B, A_2 \sqsubseteq \forall r.\neg B\}$, and $\mathcal{V} = \{A_1 \sqsubseteq \forall r.D_1, A_2 \sqsubseteq \forall r.D_2, D_1 \sqcap D_2 \sqsubseteq \bot\}$ which is the semantic forgetting view with respect to $\{B\}$ where D_1 and D_2 are helper symbols. Both ontologies model the information that the r-successors of the elements in the interpretation of A_1 are disjoint from the r-successors of the elements in the interpretation of A_2. Suppose $\mathcal{O}$ is used in a Boolean conjunctive query task $(\mathcal{O}, \mathcal{A}) \models r(a_2, b)$ where $\mathcal{A} = \{A_1(a_1), A_2(a_2), r(a_1, b)\}$ is a database, and $(\mathcal{O}, \mathcal{A})$ is the knowledge-base consisting of $\mathcal{O}$ and $\mathcal{A}$. An answer to this query is *yes* if $(\mathcal{O}, \mathcal{A}) \models r(a_2, b)$, and *no* if $(\mathcal{O}, \mathcal{A}) \not\models r(a_2, b)$. Evidently, the answer to this query is *no*, which can be computed by observing that $(\mathcal{O}, \mathcal{A}) \not\models r(a_2, b)$ iff $(\mathcal{O}, \mathcal{A}), \neg r(a_2, b) \not\models \bot$. Replacing $\mathcal{O}$ with $\mathcal{V}$, i.e., answering $(\mathcal{V}, \mathcal{A}) \models r(a_2, b)$, yields the same result, which can also be computed using the satisfiability checking method used above. In this computation, full interpretations of the helper symbols are not required.

3   Forgetting Method

We now present a method to compute the semantic forgetting view of $\mathcal{ALC}$ ontologies. The method uses helper symbols to capture the semantic forgetting view. It proceeds in three stages. The first stage iteratively eliminates *defined* forgetting symbols. A concept symbol B is *defined* if an axiom of the form $B \equiv C$ exists, and $B \notin sig(C)$. Elimination of B is performed by replacing B everywhere in the ontology with C. We call this, *definition expansion*.

Example 5. Let $\mathcal{O} = \{A \sqsubseteq B, B \equiv C\}$ and $\mathcal{F} = \{B\}$. The semantic view of $\mathcal{O}$ with respect to $\mathcal{F}$ is $\mathcal{V} = \{A \sqsubseteq C\}$ obtained by replacing B by C in $\mathcal{O}$.

The second stage of the method eliminates the remaining forgetting symbols. Forgetting is defined by an adaptation of the following formula:

$$Forget(\mathcal{O}, B) = \mathcal{O}_B^\top \vee \mathcal{O}_B^\perp \tag{3}$$

often attributed to [4]. $\mathcal{O}_B^\top(\mathcal{O}_B^\perp)$ denotes the result of replacing B by $\top(\perp)$ everywhere in $\mathcal{O}$. Applied iteratively, (3) provides a method to forget propositional variables from propositional theories [24]. It does not, however, extend to description logics [8–10, 25]. Our method integrates (3) with *structural transformation* [32] to perform forgetting for $\mathcal{ALC}$ ontologies.

Structural transformation extracts forgetting symbols appearing under role restriction and exposes them to resolution. Before applying structural transformation we replace every equivalence axiom $C \equiv D$ that contains a forgetting symbol by the two subsumption axioms $C \sqsubseteq D$ and $D \sqsubseteq C$. Structural transformation is applied as follows:

Definition 3. *Let B be a forgetting symbol and C be a concept such that $B \in sig(C)$. We say C is a B-concept if C is on the form of $B \odot E$ or $\neg B \odot E$, where E is an $\mathcal{ALC}$ concept and $\odot \in \{\sqcup, \sqcap\}$.*

Definition 4. *Let $\mathcal{O}$ be an ontology, B a forgetting symbol, α an axiom in $\mathcal{O}$, and $C = \alpha|_\iota$ a concept of the form $Qr.E$, where E is a B-concept, r is a role name, $Q \in \{\exists, \forall\}$, and C is a concept that occurs in α at position ι. We say α is* structurally transformed *when replacing it with axiom $\alpha[\iota/Qr.D]$, and adding the following axiom to the ontology:*

$$def(\iota, \alpha, D) = \begin{cases} D \sqsubseteq E & if \, pol(\alpha, \iota) = 1; \\ E \sqsubseteq D & if \, pol(\alpha, \iota) = -1, \end{cases}$$

where D is a fresh concept symbol, i.e., $D \notin sig(\mathcal{O})$. We say $\mathcal{O}$ is structurally transformed *if the above transformation is applied exhaustively on all axioms until no forgetting symbol appears under role restriction.*

Example 6. Let $\mathcal{O} = \{A \sqsubseteq \exists r.(B \sqcap C), \exists r.B \sqsubseteq E, E \sqsubseteq \neg \exists r.F\}$, and $\mathcal{F} = \{B, F\}$. Then $\mathcal{O}$ is transformed into $\{A \sqsubseteq \exists r.D_1, D_1 \sqsubseteq B \sqcap C, \exists r.D_2 \sqsubseteq E, B \sqsubseteq D_2, E \sqsubseteq \exists r.D_3, F \sqsubseteq D_3\}$ where D_1, D_2 and D_3 are fresh concept symbols.

The concept symbols introduced by structural transformation are called *helper symbols*. These must be fresh, i.e., they are not in the vocabulary of the ontology when they are introduced. We denote by N_h the set of introduced helper symbol.

Lemma 1. *Let $\mathcal{O}_1$ be an ontology, and $\mathcal{O}_2$ the result of applying the above structural transformation with respect to some forgetting signature $\mathcal{F}$. Let N_h be the set of introduced helper symbols. Then, for every model $\mathcal{I}$ of $\mathcal{O}_1$ there is a model $\mathcal{J}$ of $\mathcal{O}_2$, and vice versa, such that $\mathcal{I} \sim_{N_h} \mathcal{J}$.*

Following structural transformation, the forgetting symbols $\mathcal{F}$ are forgotten iteratively using the rules of the calculus given in Fig. 1. In each iteration, the subset of axioms of the ontology containing the forgetting symbol B is extracted and viewed as a first-order formula ϕ_B. The *Resolution* rule in Fig. 1 is applied to ϕ_B. The rule creates a disjunction of the two first-order formulas $\phi_B^\top$ and $\phi_B^\perp$ where the forgetting symbol is replaced by $\top$ and $\perp$, respectively. The *Normalization* and *Disjunction Elimination* rules eliminate the disjunction between $\phi_B^\top$ and $\phi_B^\perp$; thus prepare the result of the *Resolution* rule to be restored to a set of DL axioms. The *Normalization* rule distributes disjunction between $\phi_B^\top$ and $\phi_B^\perp$

inwards. The *Disjunction Elimination* rule then converts the disjunction of two formulas into a single formula that can be expressed as a DL axiom. In addition to the rules in Fig. 1, we eagerly eliminate tautologous axioms and formulas.

Resolution (Res)

$$\frac{\phi_B}{\phi_B^\top \vee \phi_B^\bot}$$

where ϕ_B is a first-order formula representing the set of axioms of the ontology that contain the symbol B.

Normalization (Norm)

$$\frac{(A_1^1 \wedge \cdots \wedge A_n^1) \vee (A_1^2 \wedge \cdots \wedge A_m^2)}{(A_1^1 \vee A_1^2) \wedge \cdots \wedge (A_n^1 \vee A_m^2)}$$

where $A_1^1, \ldots, A_n^1, A_1^2, \ldots, A_m^2$ are formulas.

Disjunction Elimination (DElim)

$$\frac{(C_1 \sqsubseteq D_1) \vee (C_2 \sqsubseteq D_2)}{(C_1 \sqcap C_2) \sqsubseteq D_1 \sqcup D_2}$$

where $C_1, D_1, C_2,$ and D_2 are concepts.

Fig. 1. Forgetting calculus

Definition 5. *An axiom (formula) is a* tautology *if it takes any of the following forms:* $\bot \sqsubseteq C$ *($\pi(\bot \sqsubseteq C)$), $C \sqsubseteq \top$ ($\pi(C \sqsubseteq \top)$), and $A \sqcap C \sqsubseteq A \sqcup D$, where A, C and D are general concepts.*

A tautologous axiom is eliminated by removing it from the ontology, and a tautologous formula is eliminated by replacing it with $\top$.

Example 7. Consider the ontology $\mathcal{O} = \{A \sqsubseteq \exists r.D_1, D_1 \sqsubseteq B \sqcap C, \exists r.D_2 \sqsubseteq E, B \sqsubseteq D_2\}$ after structural transformation, and suppose we want to forget B.

$$\phi_B = (D_1 \sqsubseteq B \sqcap C) \wedge (B \sqsubseteq D_2)$$
$$\phi_B^\top = (D_1 \sqsubseteq C) \wedge (\top \sqsubseteq D_2), \quad \phi_B^\bot = (D_1 \sqsubseteq \bot) \wedge (\bot \sqsubseteq D_2) \equiv D_1 \sqsubseteq \bot$$
$$\phi_B^\top \vee \phi_B^\bot = ((D_1 \sqsubseteq C) \wedge (\top \sqsubseteq D_2)) \vee (D_1 \sqsubseteq \bot) \qquad \text{Res}$$
$$\equiv ((D_1 \sqsubseteq C) \vee (D_1 \sqsubseteq \bot)) \wedge ((\top \sqsubseteq D_2) \vee (D_1 \sqsubseteq \bot)) \qquad \text{Norm}$$
$$\equiv (D_1 \sqsubseteq C) \wedge (D_1 \sqsubseteq D_2) \qquad \text{DElim}$$

The resulting formula is translated to the set of DL axioms $\{D_1 \sqsubseteq C, D_1 \sqsubseteq D_2\}$ and added to the remaining axioms of $\mathcal{O}$. The semantic forgetting view is therefore $\mathcal{V} = \{A \sqsubseteq \exists r.D_1, \exists r.D_2 \sqsubseteq E, D_1 \sqsubseteq C, D_1 \sqsubseteq D_2\}$.

Definition 6. *Suppose B is the forgetting symbol. Consider the forgetting rules in Fig. 1. We say that a rule is* sound *if and only if for every model $\mathcal{I}$ of the premise there is a model $\mathcal{J}$ of the conclusion, and vice versa, such that $\mathcal{I} \sim_B \mathcal{J}$.*

Theorem 1. *The rules in Fig. 1 are sound.*

Theorem 2. *The size of the semantic forgetting view is, in the worst case, exponential in the size of the original ontology and double exponential in the size of the forgetting signature.*

4   Eliminating Helper Symbols

In the third stage of the method, the goal is to attempt to eliminate the helper symbols introduced in the vocabulary of the semantic forgetting view. Since it is not always possible to represent the semantic forgetting view in $\mathcal{ALC}$, complete elimination of helper symbols is not guaranteed. The elimination of helper symbols is done by reversing the structural transformation process.

Definition 7. *Let D be a helper symbol. We denote by $\operatorname{def}(D)$ the set of all axioms that can be put in the forms $D \sqsubseteq C$ or $C \sqsubseteq D$.*

Definition 8. *Let D be a helper symbol and consider any $\alpha \in \operatorname{def}(D)$. Then, α is* improper *if:*

1. *α can be put equivalently in the forms $D \sqcap \bar{D} \sqsubseteq C$ or $C \sqsubseteq D \sqcup \bar{D}$ for any $\bar{D} \in N_h$ where $\bar{D} \neq D$ and C is a general $\mathcal{ALC}$ concept; or*
2. *α can be put equivalently in the forms $D \sqsubseteq C$ or $C \sqsubseteq D$ and $\mathcal{Q}r.D$ occurs in C where $\mathcal{Q} \in \{\exists, \forall\}$, and r is any role name.*

Otherwise, the definition axiom is proper. *$\operatorname{def}(D)$ is* proper *if all axioms $\alpha \in \operatorname{def}(D)$ are proper, otherwise, $\operatorname{def}(D)$ is* improper.

Example 8. Let D_1 and D_2 be two helper symbols. Consider the axioms $\alpha_1 = D_1 \sqsubseteq C, \alpha_2 = D_1 \sqcap D_2 \sqsubseteq C, \alpha_3 = D_1 \sqsubseteq D_2, \alpha_4 = \forall r.D_1 \sqsubseteq D_1$. The axioms α_1 is a proper axiom of $\operatorname{def}(D_1)$, and α_3 is a proper axiom of $\operatorname{def}(D_1)$ and $\operatorname{def}(D_2)$. The axiom α_2 is improper because it satisfies the first condition of Definition 8. The axiom α_4 is also improper because it satisfies the second condition of Definition 8.

A helper symbol D for which $\operatorname{def}(D)$ is improper cannot be eliminated. Improper axioms satisfying Definition 8.8 have been investigated in [33] where it was shown that eliminating these helper symbols leads to loss of semantic information that we want to preserve. Definition 8.8 is the case when the ontology contains a cycle over a subset of the forgetting vocabulary. The helper symbol in this case functions as a witness to the cycle. Eliminating this helper symbol requires extending the language of the semantic view with fixpoints [20,31,35].

A helper symbol D for which $\operatorname{def}(D)$ is proper can be eliminated. The elimination rules of D are presented in Fig. 2. The *NDef* and the *PDef* rules replace the set $\operatorname{def}(D)$ in the ontology with the semantically equivalent conclusion axioms.

The *Negative Ackermann Substitution* and the *Positive Ackermann Substitution* rules eliminate D using the Ackermann approach [1,34]. The premise $C \sqsubseteq D$ ($D \sqsubseteq C$) of the Positive (Negative) Ackermann Substitution rule is usually the result generated by the PDef (NDef) rule.

NDef

$$\frac{(D \sqcap C_1 \sqsubseteq E_1) \wedge \cdots \wedge (D \sqcap C_n \sqsubseteq E_n)}{D \sqsubseteq ((\neg C_1 \sqcup E_1) \sqcap \cdots \sqcap (\neg C_n \sqcup E_n))}$$

where D is a helper symbol, and the axioms $D \sqcap C_i \sqsubseteq E_i$ are proper axioms in def(D) with $1 \leq i \leq n$.

PDef

$$\frac{(C_1 \sqsubseteq D \sqcup E_1) \wedge \cdots \wedge (C_n \sqsubseteq D \sqcup E_n)}{((C_1 \sqcap \neg E_1) \sqcup \cdots \sqcup (C_n \sqcap \neg E_n)) \sqsubseteq D}$$

where D is a helper symbol, and the axioms $C_i \sqsubseteq D \sqcup E_i$ are proper axioms in def(D) with $1 \leq i \leq n$.

Negative Ackermann Substitution (NAck)

$$\frac{\mathcal{O} \cup (D \sqsubseteq C)}{\mathcal{O}[D/C]}$$

where D is a helper symbol and may occur in $\mathcal{O}$ only positively.

Positive Ackermann Substitution (PAck)

$$\frac{\mathcal{O} \cup (C \sqsubseteq D)}{\mathcal{O}[D/C]}$$

where D is a helper symbol and may occur in $\mathcal{O}$ only negatively.

Fig. 2. Helper symbol elimination rules

Lemma 2. *Let $\mathcal{O}_1$ be an ontology and let $\mathcal{O}_2$ be the ontology after eliminating a helper symbol D using the rules in Fig. 2. Then, for every model $\mathcal{I}$ of $\mathcal{O}_1$ there is a model $\mathcal{J}$ of $\mathcal{O}_2$, and vice versa, such that $\mathcal{I} \sim_D \mathcal{J}$.*

Theorem 3. *Let $\mathcal{O}$ be an ontology, $\mathcal{F}$ a forgetting signature, and $\mathcal{V}$ be the semantic forgetting view generated as described in Sects. 3 and 4. For every model $\mathcal{I}$ of $\mathcal{O}$ there is a model $\mathcal{J}$ of $\mathcal{V}$, and vice versa, such that $\mathcal{I} \sim_{\mathcal{F} \cup N_h} \mathcal{J}$, where N_h is the set of helper symbols in $\mathcal{V}$.*

5 Discussion of the Forgetting Method

The presented forgetting method implicitly views the forgetting symbols as existentially quantified second-order symbols. In order to completely eliminate the forgetting symbols, the method introduces helper symbols which can also be seen as existentially quantified second-order symbols. Therefore, the language of the generated semantic view can be viewed as a fragment of second-order logic (SOL). An alternative method [25] which also generates a semantic forgetting view in SOL is to quantify over the forgetting symbols. Using this approach, the semantic forgetting view of the ontology $\mathcal{O}$ with respect to $\{B\}$ is $\exists \bar{B}\ \mathcal{O}[B/\bar{B}]$, where $\mathcal{O}[B/\bar{B}]$ is the result of replacing B by the helper symbol $\bar{B}$ everywhere in $\mathcal{O}$. Since $\bar{B}$ can be renamed to B, this is equivalent to $\exists B\ \mathcal{O}$. Therefore, a simpler form of the semantic forgetting view generated by [25] is $\exists B_1 \exists B_2 \ldots \exists B_n\ \mathcal{O}$ where $B_1, B_2, \ldots, B_n$ are the forgetting symbols.

Our presented method can be seen as a non-trivial extension of the method in [25], because it introduces further existentially quantified symbols. Extending the forgetting method in this way is necessary to make the method suitable for ontology extraction and applicable to DL syntax.

Example 9. Let $\mathcal{O} = \{A \sqsubseteq \exists r.(B \sqcup C) \sqcap \exists r.(\neg B \sqcup \neg C)\}$, and $\mathcal{F} = \{B\}$. The semantic forgetting view $\mathcal{V}_1$ obtained by quantifying over B is $\exists B\ (A \sqsubseteq \exists r.(B \sqcup C) \sqcap \exists r.(\neg B \sqcup \neg C))$. The equivalent semantic forgetting view is $\mathcal{V}_2 = \{A \sqsubseteq \exists r.\top\}$ which is generated by our method. In essence, $\mathcal{V}_1$ is syntactically the same as $\mathcal{O}$. So, only quantifying over the forgetting symbol returns the original ontology and fails to extract the expected ontology. With our method, we can obtain the expected semantic forgetting view.

The above example shows that the method in [25] is not suitable for ontology extraction. To make it suitable to this purpose, augmenting the method in [25] with a second-order quantifier elimination method such as formula (3) is required. While second-order quantifier elimination is sufficient in the syntax of FOL [12,13], it is not directly applicable to DL ontologies.

Example 10. Let $\mathcal{O} = \{A \sqsubseteq \exists r.B \sqcap \exists r.\neg B\}$ and $\mathcal{F} = \{B\}$. By quantifying over B, we get the semantic forgetting view $\mathcal{V}_1 = \exists B\ (A \sqsubseteq \exists r.B \sqcap \exists r.\neg B)$ Applying the calculus in Fig. 1 directly to $\mathcal{V}_1$ gives: $\mathcal{V}_2 = \{A \sqsubseteq \exists r.\top\}$ which is not the correct semantic forgetting view of $\mathcal{O}$ with respect to $\mathcal{F}$. Our method solves this problem by applying structural transformation prior to the calculus in Fig. 1. The correct semantic forgetting view generated by our method is $\{A \sqsubseteq \exists r.D_1 \sqcap \exists r.D_2, D_1 \sqcap D_2 \sqsubseteq \bot\}$.

6   Preserving Ontology Structure

A common criticism of existing forgetting methods, e.g. [12,20–22,27,39–42], is that they do not preserve the *form* of the original ontology. This reduces the readability of the extracted ontology, and makes it harder for human inspection and debugging.

Example 11. Let $\mathcal{O}_1 = \{A \sqsubseteq B \sqcap C \sqcap D\}$, $\mathcal{O}_2 = \{A \equiv B, B \equiv C \sqcap D\}$, and $\mathcal{O}_3 = \{\forall r.B \sqsubseteq C, A \sqsubseteq B\}$. Consider the forgetting signature $\mathcal{F} = \{B\}$. The forgetting views with respect to $\mathcal{F}$ generated by the methods [20–22,39–42] of $\mathcal{O}_1, \mathcal{O}_2$, and

$\mathcal{O}_3$ respectively are: $\mathcal{V}_1 = \{\top \sqsubseteq \neg A \sqcup C, \top \sqsubseteq \neg A \sqcup D\}$, $\mathcal{V}_2 = \{\top \sqsubseteq \neg A \sqcup C, \top \sqsubseteq \neg A \sqcup D, \top \sqsubseteq \neg C \sqcup \neg D \sqcup A\}$, and $\mathcal{V}_3 = \{\top \sqsubseteq C \sqcup \exists r.\neg A\}$. Our forgetting method produces: $\mathcal{V}'_1 = \{A \sqsubseteq C \sqcap D\}$ (instead of $\mathcal{V}_1$), $\mathcal{V}'_2 = \{A \equiv C \sqcap D\}$ (instead of $\mathcal{V}_2$), and $\mathcal{V}'_3 = \{\forall r.A \sqsubseteq C\}$ (instead of $\mathcal{V}_3$).

It may be observed that the forgetting views generated by our method are more readable and preserve the forms of the original ontologies. They:

1. *Reuse concepts of the original ontology*: $\mathcal{V}'_1$ consists of one subsumption axiom which reuses the concept $C \sqcap D$ whereas the concept $C \sqcap D$ does not occur in $\mathcal{V}_1$.
2. *Preserve equivalence axioms*: $\mathcal{V}'_2$ consists of one equivalence axiom whereas $\mathcal{V}_2$ consists of three subsumption axioms.
3. *Preserve position and polarity of concepts*: Similar to $\mathcal{O}_3$, $\mathcal{V}'_3$ has the universal quantifier on the left hand side of the output axiom, whereas $\mathcal{V}_3$ contains an existential quantifier on the right hand side of the axiom. In general, axioms of $\mathcal{V}_1, \mathcal{V}_2$, and $\mathcal{V}_3$ appear on the form $\top \sqsubseteq E$ which is not the case for $\mathcal{V}'_1, \mathcal{V}'_2$, and $\mathcal{V}'_3$.

These properties are achieved in the following ways: (1) The initial definition expansion step avoids unnecessary conversion of equivalence axioms into subsumption axioms. (2) The forgetting calculus does not require the input axioms to be transformed to a special normal or clausal form (like other methods [12,20–22,27,39–42]). For example, while traditional resolution requires the premises in disjunctive clausal form, we use a non-traditional form of resolution which only replaces a forgetting symbol with $\top$ and $\bot$. (3) The *Disjunction Elimination* rule reuses the concept expressions of the premise axioms in the generated axiom, and preserves their position relative to the subsumption operator. (4) Although effort has been put into eliminating the helper symbols, some helper symbols may be present in the returned semantic forgetting view only to preserve the form of the original ontology.

Example 12. Consider the ontology $\mathcal{O}_1 = \{\forall r.B \sqsubseteq \exists r.B\}$ and the forgetting signature $\mathcal{F} = \{B\}$. The semantic forgetting view of $\mathcal{O}_1$ with respect to $\mathcal{F}$ computed by e.g. the method of [42] is $\mathcal{V}_1 = \{\top \sqsubseteq \exists r.\top\}$. However, the result generated by our method is $\{\forall r.D \sqsubseteq \exists r.D\}$ where D is a helper symbol. The helper symbol D allows the form of the original ontology to be preserved.

In the next example, we show that even for semantically equivalent ontologies, the number of helper symbols in the language of the semantic view may differ.

Example 13. Consider the ontology $\mathcal{O}_2 = \{\top \sqsubseteq \exists r.B \sqcup \exists r.\neg B\}$ which is a syntactic variant of $\mathcal{O}_1$ in Example 12. Let $\mathcal{F} = \{B\}$. The semantic forgetting view of $\mathcal{O}_2$ with respect to $\mathcal{F}$ generated by the proposed method is: $\mathcal{V}_2 = \{\top \sqsubseteq \exists r.D_1 \sqcup \exists r.D_2, D_1 \sqcap D_2 \sqsubseteq \bot\}$ where D_1 and D_2 are helper symbols. Thus, the method uses two helper symbols to represent the semantic forgetting view instead of one helper symbol as in Example 12. Note that the semantic forgetting view of $\mathcal{O}_2$ generated by [42] is $\mathcal{V}_1$ as in Example 12.

The above examples show that the preservation of the original ontology form is valued by the proposed method over the elimination of the helper symbols. This is an advantage of our method over the other methods [12, 20–22, 39–42] as it preserves the syntactic modeling choices made in the original ontology. This is beneficial for domains such as medical ontologies where often strict modelling guidelines must be followed.

Table 1. Statistics of the used BioPortal ontologies and forgetting signatures.

	Maximum	Minimum	Average	Median
Ontology size (axioms)	133290	40	24760	4653
Forgetting signature size (concepts)	36697	1	3526	771

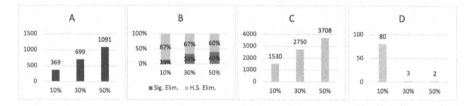

Fig. 3. Chart A: Average execution times (seconds) of the proposed method. Chart B: Breakdown of the execution time into the time consumed eliminating forgetting symbols and the time consumed eliminating helper symbols. Chart C: Average number of helper symbols introduced by *structural transformation*. Chart D: Average number of helper symbols remaining in the semantic forgetting view.

7   Empirical Evaluation

We conducted experiments on popular ontologies from the NCBO BioPortal repository [30]. Starting with 40 ontologies, three experiments were run on each ontology in a total of 120 experiments. The forgetting signatures $\mathcal{F}_1, \mathcal{F}_2$, and $\mathcal{F}_3$ of these three experiments respectively were selected such that $\mathcal{F}_1 \subset \mathcal{F}_2 \subset \mathcal{F}_3$. Statistics about the sizes of the ontologies and forgetting signatures are presented in Table 1. Each experiment was assigned 2 GB memory and ran on a x64-based processor Intel(R) Core(TM) i5 CPU @ 2.7 GHz with a 64-bit operating system (macOS Catalina 10.15.7). Results gathered from the experiments are shown in Fig. 3. Chart A of Fig. 3 shows the average running time of the experiments across the three settings of forgetting 10%, 30%, and 50% of the signature. The chart shows a polynomial increase in the average running times (369, 699, and 1091 s in the 10%, 30%, and 50% settings respectively).

A breakdown of the average running times is shown in Chart B of Fig. 3. The chart shows the average time consumed for eliminating the forgetting symbols using the rules in Fig. 1, and the average time consumed for eliminating the helper symbol using the rules in Fig. 2, relative to the average execution time of the whole forgetting process. We found that the time consumed for eliminating the helper symbols occupied the majority of the time of the whole forgetting process. However, we noticed a decreasing trend in the time consumed for eliminating the helper symbols. Execution of the rules in Fig. 1 consumed on average 13%, 33%, and 40% of the time of the whole forgetting process in the 10%, 30%, and 50% settings respectively, whereas execution of the rules in Fig. 2 consumed on average 87%, 67%, and 60% of the time. This suggests that helper symbols not only simplify the forgetting method, but also the cost of eliminating them becomes less significant when forgetting large subsets of the vocabulary.

In Chart C of Fig. 3 we measured the trend of introducing helper symbols by structural transformation. We observed a linear increase in the average number of introduced helper symbols. On average there were 1530, 2750, and 3708 introduced helper symbols in the 10%, 30%, and 50% settings respectively. This increase was expected given the increase in the number of forgetting symbols. We also measured the number of introduced helper symbols as a ratio to the forgetting signature. On average, the helper symbols introduced by the structural transformation process were 107%, 56%, and 47% of the forgetting signature in the 10%, 30%, and 50% settings respectively. We may conclude that a factor of the downward trend in the time consumed by the elimination of helper symbols was the relative decrease in the number forgetting symbols which caused new helper symbols to be introduced.

We observed that in some cases the above factor also reduced the number of helper symbols that remained in the semantic forgetting view. The following example shows the idea.

Example 14. Let $\mathcal{O} = \{A_1 \sqsubseteq C \sqcup \exists r.B, A_2 \sqsubseteq \exists r.\neg B\}$, $\mathcal{F}_1 = \{B\}$, and $\mathcal{F}_2 = \{B, C\}$. The semantic forgetting view of $\mathcal{O}$ with respect to $\mathcal{F}_1$ is $\mathcal{V}_1 = \{A_1 \sqsubseteq C \sqcup \exists r.D_1, A_2 \sqsubseteq \exists r.D_2, D_1 \sqcap D_2 \sqsubseteq \bot\}$. The semantic forgetting view of $\mathcal{O}$ with respect to $\mathcal{F}_2$ is $\mathcal{V}_2 = \{A_2 \sqsubseteq \exists r.\top\}$. The concept name C does not appear under role restriction in $\mathcal{O}$, and does not lead to introducing a helper symbol. If only B is forgotten from $\mathcal{O}$, then the helper symbols D_1 and D_2 appear in the semantic forgetting view. Forgetting additionally the concept name C prevents D_1 and D_2 from occurring in the semantic forgetting view.

The observation illustrated by the example explains Chart D in Fig. 3. Chart D shows the average number of helper symbols that appeared in the vocabulary of the final forgetting view. While on average 80 helper symbols appeared in the forgetting views of the 10% setting, on average only 3 and 2 helper symbols appeared respectively in the forgetting views of the 30% and 50% settings.

Next we compared the performance of our method with the Fame(Q) tool [43], a Java implementation of the method of [42]. While Fame(Q) does not produce the complete semantic view (see Example 2), it captures the semantic information that is representable in $\mathcal{ALCOQ}^{\neg,\sqcup,\sqcap}$. We tried executing the above experiments using Fame(Q). However, we observed memory issues in 52 experiments. This happened more often in experiments with large forgetting signatures and ontologies. Instead we constructed our own ontologies and experiments. The ontologies are constructed such that: (1) They are extracted from real life ontologies; and (2) they model one or several related topics. Construction was done in the following way: (1) Collect a set of random concept names Σ from the *Interlinking Ontology for Biological Concepts (IOBC)* ontology [23]. (2) Retrieve from the *NCBO Bioportal* the related ontologies where the symbols in Σ appeared more frequently. (3) From the retrieved ontologies, extract and combine into a single ontology, the subsets of the axioms containing symbols in Σ.

Table 2. Statistics of the constructed ontologies and forgetting signatures.

	Maximum	Minimum	Average	Median
Ontology size (axioms)	1422	78	302	201
Forgetting signature size (concepts)	324	1	27	10

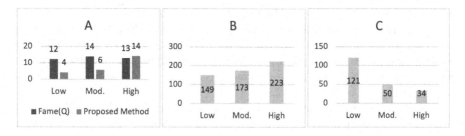

Fig. 4. Chart A: Execution time(seconds) comparison with Fame. Chart B: Average number of helper symbols introduced by *structural transformation*. Chart C: Average number of the introduced helper symbols as a ratio to the number of forgetting symbols.

The construction guaranteed that each generated ontology contained information that described the concept names (topics) extracted from the IOBC ontology. Since these concepts were extracted from the same ontology, i.e., the IOBC ontology, they were semantically related. In total, 28 ontologies were constructed using the method described above. In each construction, at least 25% of the input ontologies were expressed in $\mathcal{ALC}$ or a more expressive logic. Next, we used the constructed ontologies in three different experimental settings: *Low*, *Moderate*, and *High* with a total of 84 experiments. Each setting corresponded to a different choice of the forgetting signature. The *Low* setting meant that at least half of the axioms of the ontology contained a forgetting symbol, and the probability of two forgetting symbols appearing in the same axiom was low. The *Moderate* setting meant that all axioms of the ontology contained a forgetting symbol, and at least one axiom contained two or more forgetting symbols. The *High* setting meant that all axioms of the ontology contained a forgetting symbol, and at least half of the axioms contained two or more forgetting symbols.

The occurrence of several forgetting symbols in the same axiom means axioms generated from one forgetting round are processed in subsequent rounds, because each round in the proposed method and Fame(Q) eliminates only one forgetting symbol. This made the experiments computationally more challenging for both methods, and avoided the drawbacks of reducing the size of the input ontologies.

Statistics about the ontologies and the forgetting signatures are presented in Table 2. Statistics gathered from the experiments are shown in Fig. 4. Chart A in Fig. 4 compares the average execution times of Fame(Q) and our proposed method. In general we found the execution time of Fame(Q) stable across the *Low*, *Moderate*, and *High* settings. The average execution times of Fame(Q) were 12, 14, 13 s respectively in the three settings. In contrast, the time consumed by our method grew polynomially over the different settings. This growth was expected since more more semantic information was captured by our method as the forgetting problem becomes harder. Since Fame(Q) is not complete, we do not see the same increase in the time consumed by Fame(Q). We notice in the *Low* and *Moderate* settings that our method consumed less time than Fame(Q), which is not expected since it should still preserve more information than Fame(Q). We found that Fame(Q) used a reasoner to perform some optimizations the output, which resulted in consuming more time than our method.

We measured the number of introduced helper symbols across the three settings in the same way as before. Chart B in Fig. 4 shows an increase in the number introduced helper symbols as we moved to harder settings. On average, 149, 173, and 223 helper symbols were introduced by *structural transformation* in the *Low, Moderate,* and *High* settings respectively. This increase was expected since the number of forgetting symbols increased. However, as shown in Chart C of Fig. 4, the average number of introduced helper symbols as a ratio to the number of forgetting symbols decreased as we went to harder settings. This agreed with the ratios of 107%, 56%, and 47% that were found before when forgetting was applied directly on the original BioPortal ontologies.

8   Conclusions

We developed a semantic forgetting method for ontologies in the context of the description logic $\mathcal{ALC}$. Our method captures the semantic forgetting view by possibly allowing helper symbols in the vocabulary of the generated semantic view. Although helper symbols can be seen as second-order predicate symbols, because they are only existentially quantified, and because only $\mathcal{ALC}$ constructs are used to formulate the axioms of the semantic forgetting view, most standard reasoning tasks, such as satisfiability checking, classification, and query answering, can be performed on the semantic forgetting view using the standard $\mathcal{ALC}$ tools. An important feature of our method is that it preserves the syntactic form of the original ontology, which increases the readability of the semantic view.

Experimental evaluation validated that our method performed well on large-scale ontologies. The method consumed 6, 11, and 18 min on average to forget respectively 10%, 30%, and 50% of the vocabulary of a dataset of large-scale ontologies with on average 25K axioms. The evaluation also showed that the number of helper symbols that are used in the extracted semantic forgetting view decreases as the number of forgetting symbols increases. We additionally compared our method with Fame(Q), a tool that forgets concept and role names in $\mathcal{ALCOQ}^{\neg,\sqcup,\sqcap}$, in three settings of hardness: *Low*, *Moderate*, and *High*. While Fame(Q) does not capture the complete semantic forgetting view, experiments showed that our method performed faster in the *Low* and *Moderate* settings. In the *High* setting, Fame(Q) performed marginally faster than our method.

References

1. Ackermann, W.: Untersuchungen über das Eliminationsproblem der mathematischen Logik. Math. Ann. **110**, 390–413 (1935)
2. Baader, F., Horrocks, I., Sattler, U.: Description logics. In: Handbook of Knowledge Representation, pp. 135–179. Elsevier, San Diego (2007)
3. Baaz, M., Egly, U., Leitsch, A.: Normal form transformations. In: Handbook of Automated Reasoning, pp. 275–332. North-Holland (12 2001)
4. Boole, G.: An Investigation of the Laws of Thought: On Which Are Founded the Mathematical Theories of Logic and Probabilities. Cambridge University Press, Cambridge (1854)
5. Borgida, A.: On the relative expressiveness of description logics and predicate logics. Artif. Intell. **82**(1–2), 353–367 (1996)
6. Botoeva, E., Konev, B., Lutz, C., Ryzhikov, V., Wolter, F., Zakharyaschev, M.: Inseparability and conservative extensions of description logic ontologies: A survey. In: Reasoning Web: Logical Foundation of Knowledge Graph Construction and Query Answering: 12th International Summer School. pp. 27–89. Springer (2017)
7. Chen, J., Alghamdi, G., Schmidt, R.A., Walther, D., Gao, Y.: Ontology extraction for large ontologies via modularity and forgetting. In: Proceedings of the 10th International Conference on Knowledge Capture (K-CAP 2019), pp. 45–52. ACM (2019)
8. Delgrande, J.: A knowledge level account of forgetting. J. Artif. Intell. Res. **60**, 1165–1213 (2017)
9. Delgrande, J.P.: Towards a knowledge level analysis of forgetting. In: Proceedings of the 14th International Conference on Principles of Knowledge Representation and Reasoning, pp. 606–609. AAAI Press, Palo Alto (2014)
10. Ditmarsch, H., Herzig, A., Lang, J., Marquis, P.: Introspective forgetting. In: Proceedings of the 21st Australasian Joint Conference on Artificial Intelligence. pp. 18–29. Springer (2008). https://doi.org/10.1007/s11229-009-9554-4
11. Eiter, T., Kern-Isberner, G.: A brief survey on forgetting from a knowledge representation and reasoning perspective. KI - Künstliche Intelligenz **33**(1), 9–33 (2019)
12. Gabbay, D.M., Ohlbach, H.J.: Quantifier elimination in second-order predicate logic. In: Proceedings of the Third International Conference on Principles of Knowledge Representation and Reasoning, pp. 425–435. Morgan Kaufmann, San Mateo (1992)
13. Gabbay, D.M., Schmidt, R.A., Szałas, A.: Second-Order Quantifier Elimination: Foundations. College Publications, Computational Aspects and Applications (2008)
14. Herzig, A., Mengin, J.: Uniform interpolation by resolution in modal logic. In: Hölldobler, S., Lutz, C., Wansing, H. (eds.) JELIA 2008. LNCS (LNAI), vol. 5293, pp. 219–231. Springer, Heidelberg (2008). https://doi.org/10.1007/978-3-540-87803-2_19

15. Hustadt, U., Schmidt, R.A., Georgieva, L.: A survey of decidable first-order fragments and description logics. J. Relat. Methods Comput. Sci. **1**, 251–276 (2004)
16. Jung, J., Lutz, C., Pulcini, H., Wolter, F.: Logical separability of incomplete data under ontologies. In: 17th International Conference on Principles of Knowledge Representation and Reasoning, pp. 517–528 (2020)
17. Konev, B., Lutz, C., Walther, D., Wolter, F.: Formal properties of modularisation. In: Stuckenschmidt, H., Parent, C., Spaccapietra, S. (eds.) Modular Ontologies. LNCS, vol. 5445, pp. 25–66. Springer, Heidelberg (2009). https://doi.org/10.1007/978-3-642-01907-4_3
18. Konev, B., Lutz, C., Walther, D., Wolter, F.: Model-theoretic inseparability and modularity of description logic ontologies. Artif. Intell. **203**, 66–103 (2013)
19. Konev, B., Walther, D., Wolter, F.: Forgetting and uniform interpolation in large-scale description logic terminologies. In: Proceedings of the 21st International Joint Conference on Artificial Intelligence, pp. 830–835. Morgan Kaufmann (2009)
20. Koopmann, P., Schmidt, R.A.: Uniform interpolation of $\mathcal{ALC}$-ontologies using fixpoints. In: Fontaine, P., Ringeissen, C., Schmidt, R.A. (eds.) FroCoS 2013. LNCS (LNAI), vol. 8152, pp. 87–102. Springer, Heidelberg (2013). https://doi.org/10.1007/978-3-642-40885-4_7
21. Koopmann, P., Schmidt, R.A.: Count and forget: uniform interpolation of $\mathcal{SHQ}$-ontologies. In: Automated Reasoning. Lecture Notes in Artificial Intelligence, vol. 8562, pp. 434–448. Springer, Berlin (2014). https://doi.org/10.1007/3-540-45470-5
22. Koopmann, P., Schmidt, R.A.: Saturation-based forgetting in the description logic $\mathcal{SIF}$. In: Proceedings of the 28th International Workshop on Description Logics, vol. 1350. CEUR-WS.org (2015)
23. Kushida, T., Kozaki, K., Kawamura, T., Tateisi, Y., Yamamoto, Y., Takagi, T.: Interconnection of biological knowledge using NikkajiRDF and interlinking ontology for biological concepts. New Gen. Compu. **37**, 1–25 (2019)
24. Lang, J., Liberatore, P., Marquis, P.: Propositional independence: formula-variable independence and forgetting. J. Artif. Intell. Res. **18**, 391–443 (2003)
25. Lin, F., Reiter, R.: Forget it!. Proc. AAAI **1994**, 154–159 (1994)
26. Lin, F., Reiter, R.: How to progress a database (and why) I. logical foundations. In: Principles of Knowledge Representation and Reasoning, pp. 425–436. Morgan Kaufmann, Cambridge (1994)
27. Ludwig, M., Konev, B.: Towards practical uniform interpolation and forgetting for $\mathcal{ALC}$ tboxes. In: Proceedings of the 26th International Workshop on Description Logics. CEUR-WS (2013)
28. Lutz, C., Wolter, F.: Foundations for uniform interpolation and forgetting in expressive description logics. In: IJCAI International Joint Conference on Artificial Intelligence. AAAI Press (2011)
29. Lutz, C., Wolter, F.: Deciding inseparability and conservative extensions in the description logic $\mathcal{EL}$. J. Symbol. Comput. **45**, 194–228 (2010)
30. Matentzoglu, N., Bail, S., Parsia, B.: A snapshot of the OWL web. In: The Semantic Web - ISWC 2013, pp. 331–346. Springer (2013)
31. Nonnengart, A., Szalas, A.: A fixpoint approach to second-order quantifier elimination with applications to correspondence theory. In: Orlowska, E. (ed.) Logic at Work: Essays Dedicated to the Memory of Helena Rasiowa (1999) vol. 24, January 1998
32. Nonnengart, A., Weidenbach, C.: Computing small clause normal forms. In: Handbook of Automated Reasoning, pp. 335–367. North-Holland, Amsterdam (2001)

33. Sakr, M., Schmidt, R.A.: Fine-grained forgetting for the description logic $\mathcal{ALC}$ (2021). http://www.cs.man.ac.uk/~schmidt/publications/SakrSchmidt21a.pdf.
34. Schmidt, R.A.: The Ackermann approach for modal logic, correspondence theory and second-order reduction. J. Appl. Logic **10**(1), 52–74 (2012)
35. Tarski, A.: A lattice-theoretical fixpoint theorem and its applications. Pacif. J. Math. **5**(2), 285–309 (1955)
36. Wernhard, C.: Projection and scope-determined circumscription. J. Symbol. Comput. **47**, 1089–1108 (2012)
37. Wernhard, C.: Application patterns of projection/forgetting. In: Workshop on Interpolation: From Proofs to Applications (iPRA 2014) (2014)
38. Zhang, Y., Zhou, Y.: Forgetting revisited. In: Twelfth International Conference on the Principles of Knowledge Representation and Reasoning (2010)
39. Zhao, Y., Schmidt, R.A.: Concept forgetting in $\mathcal{ALCOI}$-ontologies using an Ackermann approach. In: The Semantic Web, 14th International Semantic Web Conference. Lecture Notes in Computer Science, vol. 9366, pp. 587–602. Springer (2015). https://doi.org/10.1007/b102467
40. Zhao, Y., Schmidt, R.A.: Forgetting concept and role symbols in $\mathcal{ALCOIH}\mu^+(\nabla, \sqcap)$-ontologies. In: Proceedings of the Twenty-Fifth International Joint Conference on Artificial Intelligence, pp. 1345–1352. AAAI Press/IJCAI (2016)
41. Zhao, Y., Schmidt, R.A.: Role forgetting for $\mathcal{ALCOQH}(\nabla)$-ontologies using an Ackermann approach. In: Proceedings of the Twenty-Sixth International Joint Conference on Artificial Intelligence, pp. 1354–1361. AAAI Press/IJCAI (2017)
42. Zhao, Y., Schmidt, R.A.: On concept forgetting in description logics with qualified number restrictions. In: Proceedings of the Twenty-Seventh International Joint Conference on Artificial Intelligence, pp. 1984–1990. AAAI Press/IJCAI (2018)
43. Zhao, Y., Schmidt, R.A.: FAME(Q): an automated tool for forgetting in description logics with qualified number restrictions. In: Fontaine, P. (ed.) CADE 2019. LNCS (LNAI), vol. 11716, pp. 568–579. Springer, Cham (2019). https://doi.org/10.1007/978-3-030-29436-6_34

Interactive Theorem Proving

Improving Automation for Higher-Order Proof Steps

Antoine Defourné[(✉)]

Université de Lorraine, CNRS, Inria, LORIA, Nancy, France
antoine.defourne@inria.fr

Abstract. We have extended the TLA$^+$ proof system TLAPS with a new backend to improve the automation of proof steps that involve higher-order reasoning. The current support for such steps is poor, requiring the user to break down proofs into unnecessarily small steps. We defined a translation from TLA$^+$ to THF, the TPTP dialect for higher-order logic, and evaluated several higher-order solvers on proof obligations generated from the standard library of TLA$^+$. Our results demonstrate that the solvers are able to handle much coarser proof steps than the other strategies provided by TLAPS, reducing the amount of necessary user interactions by a significant margin.

Keywords: Automated deduction · Higher-order theorem proving · TLA$^+$ · TLAPS

1 Introduction

TLA$^+$ is a specification language for modelling and expressing properties of distributed systems [10]. Its core logic is the Temporal Logic of Actions (TLA) with the operators and axioms of ZF set theory. The language admits a syntax for expressing theorems and proofs in the hierarchical style of Leslie Lamport [9]. These proofs are treated by the TLA$^+$ Proof System (TLAPS) tool, which dispatches the proof obligations it generates to an array of external solvers, among which there are Isabelle, Zenon, and SMT solvers such as Z3 and CVC4 [6].

This article is about a particular problem that impacts the experience of TLAPS users when writing proofs for TLA$^+$. The language is often categorized as a first-order logic, but in the context of TLAPS, there are situations in which a proof obligation cannot be directly expressed without second-order features. More precisely, a lemma can be parameterized by a first-order operator; when such a lemma is invoked as part of a proof, a second-order unification is necessary. To dispatch obligations to the available backends, TLAPS uses encodings which were almost all designed with first-order logic as a target language. The exception is Isabelle, which means only this solver is currently invoked on the higher-order obligations of TLA$^+$.

Although such higher-order obligations are not the primary kind of obligations one encounters in TLAPS, they are mandatory in some contexts, notably

© Springer Nature Switzerland AG 2021
B. Konev and G. Reger (Eds.): FroCoS 2021, LNAI 12941, pp. 139–153, 2021.
https://doi.org/10.1007/978-3-030-86205-3_8

when any form of reasoning by induction is involved. The current support of these obligations by TLAPS is poor: the generic tactics of Isabelle are often unable to handle mildly complex obligations, which forces the user to break down its proofs into smaller steps until they are simple enough for Isabelle. This is a time-consuming process that we want to avoid.

We saw this issue as an opportunity to experiment with a higher-order solver on some TLA$^+$ proofs. Zipperposition was our initial choice for this experiment. It is a superposition theorem prover for first-order logic with equality and theories, recently extended with support for higher-order logic [3,16,17], and the winner of the 10th CASC competition (2020) in the THF category [14]. Our main contribution is the implementation of a translation from TLA$^+$ to THF, and the integration of Zipperposition as a new backend for TLAPS. In this article, we also consider other solvers that performed well in the THF division of CASC: Satallax [5], Leo-III [13], Vampire [4] and CVC4 [2]. We evaluate these solvers along with Zipperposition on the same THF problems that TLAPS generates.

The rest of this paper is outlined as follows: in Sect. 2, we present a TLA$^+$ proof that illustrates the problem in more details; in Sect. 3, we present the relevant aspects of the encoding into THF that was implemented; in Sect. 4, we evaluate the solvers and measure how much proof steps we can remove from the original proofs, compared to what is possible with only Isabelle.

2   The Difficulty of Second-Order Proofs in TLA$^+$

The difficulties we are interested in arise mostly when dealing with induction in some way. Our example is about defining an operator by recursion in TLA$^+$. We define the operator Sum to represent finite sums over series. The term $\text{Sum}(n, S)$ represents $\sum_{i=1}^{n} S(i)$, where S is any TLA$^+$ first-order operator. The standard library provides a module NaturalsInduction with facilities to deal with such definitions, and a guideline example. Following these guidelines, this is the definition we obtain:

```
sumF(S(_)) ==
    LET sumRec[ m ∈ Nat ] ==
        IF m = 0 THEN 0 ELSE S(m) + sumRec[m - 1]
    IN
    sumRec

Sum(n, S(_)) == sumF(S)[n]
```

Before this definition can be used, a few lemmas need to be proven. The first lemma expresses the fact that a recursive function that matches the definition does exist:

```
THEOREM SumDefConclusion ==
    ASSUME NEW S(_)
    PROVE NatInductiveDefConclusion(sumF(S), 0, LAMBDA v,n : S(n) + v)
```

TLA$^+$ theorems are typically expressed in this manner. The keyword "ASSUME" precedes a list of declarations and hypotheses, separated by commas. Declarations are introduced by "NEW", here the only declaration is of an operator S. The keyword "PROVE" precedes the actual goal. The content of NatInductiveDefConclusion and the proof of this lemma (omitted here) are not relevant to us. The next lemma reads:

```
THEOREM SumDef ==
    ASSUME NEW S(_), NEW n ∈ Nat
    PROVE Sum(n, S) = IF n = 0 THEN 0 ELSE S(n) + Sum(n - 1, S)
    BY SumDefConclusion DEF NatInductiveDefConclusion, Sum
```

This time we have included the proof, which consists of a single line. The keyword "BY" is followed by a list of proven facts to be invoked as hypotheses. "DEF" is followed by a list of defined identifiers to expand (by default, operators declared at the top level are not expanded). Here it suffices to invoke the previous lemma, SumDefConclusion, and expand two definitions. As SumDefConclusion is parameterized by an operator S, the resulting obligation for SumDef is higher-order. Unfortunately, Isabelle is unable to solve it.

Inspecting the obligation, we notice that two higher-order instantiations are in fact needed: one for the lemma, the other to instantiate an axiom schema regarding functional application. The usual way to go around such issues is to make an intermediate step to isolate each difficult instantiation:

```
THEOREM SumDef ==
    ASSUME NEW S(_),
           NEW n ∈ Nat
    PROVE Sum(n, S) = IF n = 0 THEN 0 ELSE S(n) + Sum(n - 1, S)
<1>1 NatInductiveDefConclusion(sumF(S), 0, LAMBDA v,m : S(m) + v)
    BY SumDefConclusion
<1> QED
    BY <1>1 DEF NatInductiveDefConclusion, Sum
```

We have replaced the single-line proof by a two-steps proof. The intermediary step is labelled "<1>1", the last step's goal is necessarily "QED" to refer to the main goal. Each step must be justified by its own proof. Note that step <1>1 is invoked as a proved fact for the last step. This time, Isabelle manages to solve <1>1, but the final step is still too difficult. A potential reason for this is that the required instance, sum(S), is too complex a term. We rearrange the proof so that this term is a constant instead, inserting yet another step plus a local definition. This time, Isabelle finishes the proof:

```
THEOREM SumDef ==
    ASSUME NEW S(_),
           NEW n ∈ Nat
    PROVE Sum(n, S) = IF n = 0 THEN 0 ELSE S(n) + Sum(n - 1, S)
<1> DEFINE f == sumF(S)
<1>1 SUFFICES f[n] = IF n = 0 THEN 0 ELSE S(n) + f[n - 1]
    BY DEF Sum
<1>2 NatInductiveDefConclusion(f, 0, LAMBDA v,m : S(m) + v)
```

      BY SumDefConclusion
<1> **HIDE DEF** f
<1> **QED**
      BY <1>2 **DEF** NatInductiveDefConclusion

The line starting with "DEFINE" is not an intermediary step, but a local definition. Operators declared locally are expanded by default. This is why we also insert the other special line starting with "HIDE DEF": this command makes the operator opaque for the rest of the proof. The new step <1>1 is an intermediary step that starts with the keyword "SUFFICES". Such steps are used for backward reasoning: instead of proving a new fact, they prove that the current goal can be reformulated.

Not only have we gone from a single-line proof to an over-detailed script, we have also lost time figuring out what made the obligations too complex for Isabelle, and trying different ways to formulate the proof.

Proofs such as this one are typical of the difficult higher-order obligations of TLAPS. Working on these, the user is essentially wasting time trying to find a formulation that accommodates the solvers. This very case is especially problematic, since it was written in accordance with the guidelines provided at the bottom of the module NaturalsInduction—thus it is representative of TLAPS proofs. It would be desirable that the first version, a single-line proof, be handled by TLAPS, and after adding support for Zipperposition we found that the new backend could solve it. Before we develop on the performances of Zipperposition and other higher-order solvers, let us detail how the encoding to THF was implemented.

3   The Encoding of TLA$^+$ into THF

3.1   Overview

Each TLA$^+$ obligation must be encoded into the input language of the relevant backends. We encode the obligations into THF, the component of the TPTP standard for representing problems of higher-order logic.

We ignore the temporal aspects of the logic and view TLA$^+$ as an untyped second-order logic with a standard theory on top (of sets, arithmetic, etc.) [10]. The only logical aspect of TLA$^+$ that sets it apart from traditional logic is the absence of the term/formula distinction. This will be discussed in the next subsection. Although the implementation is new, it is largely inspired by the SMT encoding of TLAPS [15].

The encoding of TLA$^+$ consists in the following sequence of steps:

1. *Disambiguate expressions.* This is where the usual distinction between terms and formulas is recovered.
2. *Apply some elementary simplifications.* Syntactic sugar is removed. Some rewritings are applied to accommodate solvers.

3. *Standardize expressions.* This step only serves a technical purpose. It consists in changing the internal representation of TLA$^+$ primitives. These primitive constructs are rewritten as first- or second-order applications. For instance, the expression $\{x \in S : P(x)\}$ is rewritten as $\mathsf{SetSt}(S, \lambda x. P(x))$, where SetSt is a new operator.

4. *Complement the problem with the necessary axioms.* This effectively makes the operators added during the previous step behave like the original constructs. For instance, the axiom of set comprehension will be added to specify SetSt. Only the axioms that specify the operators that occur in the obligation are included.

5. *Translate the problem into THF.* At this point the obligation has been processed enough so that the translation can be direct.

In the next subsections, we give relevant details about the encoding, covering mostly the steps 1 and 2 of this overview.

3.2   Recovering Formulas

First-order logic, even monosorted, still makes a distinction between terms and formulas—we can characterize them with the respective sorts ι and o. The logic of TLA$^+$ can be largely derived from traditional logic, but the distinction between term and formula is absent. All TLA$^+$ expressions belong to the same sort ι, even those that look like formulas.

An important consequence is that any expression can occur in a context where a formula would normally be expected. The expression "$2 \Rightarrow \neg 5$" is legitimate in TLA$^+$. As a particular case, any expression can be treated as a statement; it is allowed to ask if "$1 + 1$" is true or false, for example. The problem arises more commonly with statements of this kind:

ASSUME NEW P(_),
        NEW a
PROVE P(a) => P(a)

In the absence of any syntactic indication, P cannot be assumed to denote a predicate, even though it can be treated like one in the goal.

In the very first phase of the encoding, expressions are transformed so that the usual distinction between ι and o is recovered. To define this mapping we need some understanding of the semantics of TLA$^+$, which are described in [10, sec. 16.1.3]. TLAPS follows the so-called liberal interpretation of TLA$^+$, which can be summarized as follows: if some e occurs in a boolean context (*i.e.* it must be evaluated as a formula), then it is treated as $e = \top$. For instance, the expression "$2 \Rightarrow \neg 5$" is interpreted like "$(2 = \top) \Rightarrow \neg(5 = \top)$", which happens to be provable by $2 \neq 5$. The last example becomes:

ASSUME NEW P(_),
        NEW a
PROVE (P(a) = **TRUE**) => (P(a) = **TRUE**)

This principle is implemented by the mappings $[\cdot]^f$ and $[\cdot]^t$, defined below. The target language is first-order logic with the sorts ι and o. Two operators are introduced by this mapping: from_bool and tt. The former is an injector of o into ι. The latter is the counterpart of $\top$ in the domain of ι—it is needed because $\top$ is treated as a o in the target language, so rewriting e as "$e = \top$" would result in an equality between a ι and a o.

The functions $[\cdot]^f$ and $[\cdot]^t$ map expressions of TLA$^+$ to formulas and terms (respectively) of first-order logic. Variables are denoted by x, operators are denoted by k.

$$[\bot]^f \triangleq \bot \qquad\qquad\qquad [x]^t \triangleq x$$

$$[e_1 \Rightarrow e_2]^f \triangleq [e_1]^f \Rightarrow [e_2]^f \quad [k(e_1,\ldots,e_n)]^t \triangleq k([e_1]^t,\ldots,[e_n]^t)$$

$$[\forall x.\, e]^f \triangleq \forall x.\, [e]^f \qquad\qquad [e]^t \triangleq \mathsf{from\_bool}([e]^f)$$

$$[e_1 = e_2]^f \triangleq [e_1]^t = [e_2]^t$$

$$[e]^f \triangleq [e]^t = \mathsf{tt}$$

The rules that introduce from_bool and tt are the ones that convert terms and formulas into each other. These conversions rules are applied with lowest priority. The actual implementation also accounts for second-order applications; operator arguments are expected to take inputs from ι and return values from ι. Some optimizations are applied: set membership is specified to be a predicate in TLA$^+$, so $\in$ is given a predicate type and no conversion is applied on membership statements; some constructs expect a predicate argument, for example in "$\{x \in S : P(x)\}$", the function $[\cdot]^f$ is called on "$P(x)$".

The mapping $[\cdot]^f$ is sound in the sense that if $[e]^f$ is valid in FOL, then e is valid in TLA$^+$. The mapping is made complete by enforcing the interpretations of the new operators in the target language. This is done by adding a single axiom to the problem:

$$\mathsf{from\_bool}(\top) = \mathsf{tt} \wedge \mathsf{from\_bool}(\bot) \neq \mathsf{tt} \qquad\qquad (B)$$

To summarize: for all TLA$^+$ expression e, e is valid iff $[e]^f$ is satisfied by all models of (B) in FOL. The encoding applies $[\cdot]^f$ to all top expressions and adds the axiom (B) to the problem.

3.3   Arithmetic

TLA$^+$ admits a number of primitive operators and axioms, which constitute its standard theory. The main components of this theory are: set theory, functions, and arithmetic. Our encoding simply makes the necessary standard declarations and axioms explicit in the final THF problem, but arithmetic is treated differently.

The SMT encoding uses special axioms that make use of the sort Int of SMT-LIB. That way, specialized reasoning implemented by the solvers for arithmetic can be leveraged. But the version of Zipperposition that supports higher-order reasoning does not also support arithmetic, so it is not possible to replicate the method of the SMT encoding.

However, the purpose of using a higher-order solver for TLA$^+$ is not to solve arithmetical goals. The encoding must only be complete enough for goals that involve higher-order reasoning. Therefore, the theory of arithmetic is discarded for our needs; the encoding merely declares the operators it needs, giving them a generic type according to their arities. That includes declaring constants for each literal number that occurs in the obligation.

We don't expect users to invoke the new backend for obligations that require arithmetical reasoning. However, we inspected goals that Zipperposition would not solve and found that simple arithmetical checks were often mandatory. Checking that some value is a member of Int or Nat is a common case. We chose a few axioms to include in the problem so that these checks can be made and more goals can be proven. Here are the axioms we include in the THF file:

Typing axioms. Each literal number (constant that identifies a number) is specified to be a member of the set of integers:

$$0 \in \text{Int} \qquad 1 \in \text{Int} \qquad 2 \in \text{Int} \qquad \cdots$$

There is a typing axiom for almost all arithmetical operators, for instance:

$$\forall z_1, z_2 \in \text{Int}. (z_1 + z_2) \in \text{Int}$$

Comparisons to 0. In complement to the typing axioms, we add an axiom for each literal number:

$$z \leq 0 \quad \text{if } z \text{ is negative}$$
$$0 \leq z \quad \text{if } z \text{ is positive}$$

Only the operator for $\leq$ is declared in the THF file. The other comparisons $\geq$, $<$ and $>$ are rewritten so that only $\leq$ occurs during the simplification phase. This is sound with respects to TLA$^+$ semantics, as these operators are defined from each other this way, even for non-integer values.

Distinct literals. For every two distinct literals z_1 and z_2 that we declare, we add the axiom:

$$z_1 \neq z_2$$

3.4   Set Extensionality

Past experiences with the SMT encoding of TLA$^+$ showed that encoding set extensionality by including the axiom hardly ever worked, as it is difficult to determine how this axiom should be instantiated in practice. We followed the example of SMT and omitted the axiom of set extensionality. However, while experimenting with our encoding we found that some obligations required set extensionality to be solved. In order to solve more goals, we decided to partially support the axiom by applying simple rewritings.

The axiom states

$$\forall x, y. (\forall z. z \in x \Leftrightarrow z \in y) \Rightarrow x = y$$

The converse implication is trivially true, so we may apply the axiom as the following rewriting rule:

$$x = y \longrightarrow \forall z. z \in x \Leftrightarrow z \in y$$

We determine which equalities are rewritten using polarities. A polarity can be attributed to every subexpression of an expression: the top expression is positive; the polarity is reversed by negation, or by implication for the left member. It is only necessary to rewrite the positive equalities in a goal. These are the equalities that need to be justified, while the negative ones serve as hypotheses and lead to substitutions. For instance, in the goal

$$\forall x, y. \{x, y\} = \{y, x\}$$

the equality occurs neither under a negation nor on the left of an implication, so the rewrite rule is applied. However, in the goal

$$\forall x, y. x = \emptyset \Rightarrow y \notin x$$

the equality occurs on the left of an implication. No rewriting is applied: the goal is proven by substituting $\emptyset$ for x on the right.

TLA$^+$ is untyped and considers any object to be a set. That means set extensionality is always applicable, and the rewriting rule is sound in every context. But we would not want to rewrite an equality like "$0 = 1$", for instance. The rule is restricted to cases where one of the members of the equality is built from a set-theoretical primitive (set enumeration, set comprehension, etc.)

This approach is obviously incomplete. Set extensionality may be needed while there is not an equality to rewrite in the goal. For example, this goal cannot be proven with our method:

ASSUME NEW F(_), **NEW** S
PROVE F(S \cup {}) = F(S)

Our treatments of set extensionality and arithmetic are the prime sources of incompleteness in the encoding. We do not see this as a problem in the case of arithmetic, as this backend is not intended to be called on arithmetical goals. The lack of a complete support for set extensionality is more often a problem, as it can be natural to write goals that require it when reasoning in terms of set.

4   Evaluation

4.1   Proof Simplification

Having defined and implemented an encoding of TLA$^+$ into THF, we now turn to the evaluation of the higher-order solvers. The purpose of this evaluation is to show that proofs can be written with less details using a higher-order solver, compared to what is currently possible with only Isabelle. Our method consists in evaluating the solvers on simpler versions of existing proofs. Here by "simpler" we mean: proofs carried out in fewer steps. As the proofs get simpler, the resulting obligations must get more complex for the backends.

The general method we applied to evaluate a given solver can be outlined as follows:

1. Select specifications that feature higher-order obligations and identify said obligations;
2. Test the higher-order solver on those obligations, and the surrounding obligations as well;
3. Simplify proofs by merging proof steps around the relevant obligations;
4. Evaluate the solver and Isabelle on the new obligations—we are mostly interested in the number of goals that are uniquely handled by the higher-order solver.

The specifications were selected from the standard library of TLA$^+$. An obligation was considered higher-order if it featured one fact that is parameterized by an operator (proving it requires higher-order unification). Before we show the results, let us briefly explain how step 4.1 was carried out.

Consider the following proof:

```
THEOREM TailInductiveDef ==
  ASSUME NEW S, NEW Def(_,_), NEW f, NEW f0,
      TailInductiveDefHypothesis(f, S, f0, Def)
  PROVE TailInductiveDefConclusion(f, S, f0, Def)
<1>. DEFINE Op(h,s) == IF s = <<>> THEN f0 ELSE Def(h[Tail(s)], s)
<1>1. StrictSuffixesDetermineDef(S, Op)
  (* ... *)
<1>2. OpDefinesFcn(f, Seq(S), Op)
  BY DEF OpDefinesFcn, TailInductiveDefHypothesis
<1>3. WFInductiveDefines(f, Seq(S), Op)
  BY <1>1, <1>2, SuffixRecursiveSequenceFunctionDef
<1>. QED
  BY <1>3 DEF WFInductiveDefines, TailInductiveDefConclusion
```

The higher-order step here is <1>3. Indeed, the statement of SuffixRecursiveSequenceFunctionDef is:

```
THEOREM SuffixRecursiveSequenceFunctionDef ==
  ASSUME NEW S, NEW Def(_,_), NEW f,
      StrictSuffixesDetermineDef(S, Def),
      OpDefinesFcn(f, Seq(S), Def)
  PROVE WFInductiveDefines(f, Seq(S), Def)
```

The lemma is parameterized by an operator Def(_, _), which makes the obligation associated to <1>3 higher-order. Zipperposition was able to solve that obligation. To find potential simplifications, we test the solver on the surrounding obligations.

Let us assume Zipperposition was able to solve step <1>2 and the QED step, but not <1>1. We can merge <1>3 with <1>2 because the latter is referenced in the proof of the former. We can also merge <1>3 with the QED step, for the same reason. Merging proofs amounts to merging their lists of invoked facts and definitions. After simplification, the result is:

THEOREM TailInductiveDef ==
  ASSUME NEW S, **NEW** Def(_ , _), **NEW** f, **NEW** f0,
        TailInductiveDefHypothesis(f, S, f0, Def)
  PROVE TailInductiveDefConclusion(f, S, f0, Def)
<1>. **DEFINE** Op(h,s) == **IF** s = <<>> **THEN** f0 **ELSE** Def(h[Tail(s)], s)
<1>1. StrictSuffixesDetermineDef(S, Op)
  (* ... *)
<1>. **QED**
  BY <1>1, SuffixRecursiveSequenceFunctionDef
  DEF OpDefinesFcn, TailInductiveDefHypothesis,
    WFInductiveDefines, TailInductiveDefConclusion

The new step still contains a reference to <1>1. As Zipperposition was not able to solve this step, it would necessary fail if we merged QED with <1>1, so we stop here. The new proof is 2 steps shorter than the original one, so we measure that simplification by "2 steps". We took Zipperposition as an example, but the same process must be carried out for every solver, resulting in several simplified versions of each specification.

Other simplifications may be applied in particular cases. Some proofs may include inline facts to prove instead of a reference to a lemma or proof step. The proof

<1> Cardinality(x \cup {}) = Cardinality(x)
  BY x \cup {} = x, SomeLemma **DEF** SomeDef

is equivalent to

<1>1 x \cup {} = x
  OBVIOUS
<1> Cardinality(x \cup {}) = Cardinality(x)
  BY <1>1, SomeLemma **DEF** SomeDef

So the removal of " " counts as simplification by one step.

It is also common to find local definitions made opaque for a proof step in order to facilitate unification:

<1> **DEFINE** P(n) == (* ... *)
(* ... *)
<1> **HIDE DEF** P
<1> ∀ n ∈ Nat : P(n)
  BY <1>1, <1>2, NatInduction

We counted as simplification by one step the removal of the HIDE command. Removing this line equates to removing the local definition itself, since such a definition is expanded by default.

Table 1. Proof obligations solved by each solver in original specifications

Specification	# Solved higher-order obligations					
	Out of	CVC4	Leo-III	Satallax	Vampire	Zip.
SequenceOpTheorems	18	10	8	10	10	12
FiniteSetTheorems	9	7	0	8	8	8
FunctionTheorems	4	2	1	2	2	3
WellFoundedInduction	8	3	2	4	3	3
Total	**39**	**22**	**11**	**24**	**23**	**26**

4.2 Results

We used TLAPS to generate the necessary Isabelle and THF files from the TLA$^+$ specifications, and then evaluated the backends on these problem files. Isabelle was always tested with the three tactics available in TLAPS: auto, blast and force. The higher-order solvers were evaluated on the same TPTP files. All solvers were run with a timeout of 30 s, the default configuration for the Isabelle backend. The experiment was carried out with an Intel Core i7-8650U with 4 cores at 1.90 GHz and 16 GB of RAM. All modules and problem files used for the experiment are publicly available.[1]

The experiment was carried out in two phases, the results of which are summarized in Tables 1 and 2. In the first table, we report how many of the original obligations were identified as higher-order and handled by each solver. These obligations come from the standard library of TLA$^+$, so Isabelle necessarily solves all of them.

For each solver, based on the results of that first phase, we edited the specifications by removing a number of proof steps, following the process we described in the previous section. Then, Isabelle and the considered solver were tested on the new specification. In the second table, we report how many proof steps were removed (first column), how many were handled by Isabelle (second column), and how many of the remaining ones were handled by the solver (third column). To compute the results for the last two columns, we searched how many proof steps were removed to obtain each individual obligation. For instance, if one obligation resulted from merging three steps together, it was counted as a reduction by 2 steps. If that obligation was handled by Isabelle or another solved, that would add 2 to its score. An empty cell indicates that the evaluation was not run, because the result could not be other than 0.

4.3 Discussion

On the original specifications (Table 1), the performances of all higher-order solvers compare, with only slight variations. Zipperposition solves a bit more obligations, and Leo-III a bit less in general, except for the specification FiniteSetTheorems, on which it did not solve any goal.

---

[1] https://github.com/adef-inr/Improving-TLAPS-Automation-Frocos-2021.git.

Table 2. Proof steps that could be uniquely removed by each HO solver

Solver	Specification	# Proof steps removed		
		Out of	Removed by Isa.	Uniq. removed by solver
CVC4	SequenceOpTheorems	6	0	6
	FiniteSetTheorems	9	2	3
	FunctionTheorems	1	1	–
	WellFoundedInduction	5	1	4
	Total	**21**	**4**	**13**
Leo-III	SequenceOpTheorems	2	0	0
	FiniteSetTheorems	–	–	–
	FunctionTheorems	2	0	0
	WellFoundedInduction	2	0	2
	Total	**6**	**0**	**2**
Satallax	SequenceOpTheorems	4	0	4
	FiniteSetTheorems	10	3	3
	FunctionTheorems	1	1	–
	WellFoundedInduction	4	1	2
	Total	**19**	**5**	**9**
Vampire	SequenceOpTheorems	6	0	4
	FiniteSetTheorems	10	3	3
	FunctionTheorems	1	1	–
	WellFoundedInduction	4	1	3
	Total	**21**	**5**	**10**
Zipperposition	SequenceOpTheorems	19	0	17
	FiniteSetTheorems	10	3	4
	FunctionTheorems	4	1	0
	WellFoundedInduction	4	1	3
	Total	**37**	**5**	**24**

The differences between solvers are more pronounced when we look at the number of proof steps they allowed us to remove (Table 2). We could not make much progress with Leo-III, with only 2 steps removed. CVC4, Vampire and Satallax have similar results, with 9–13 proof steps removed. Zipperposition let us remove 24 steps in total, which is significantly higher than any other solver. Out of these 24 steps, 17 come from SequenceOpTheorems, the biggest specification. These 17 steps are shared among only 4 different obligations: two that resulted from the removal of 2 steps each, one from 6 steps, and the last from 7. These are the only cases of obligations resulting from the removal of more than 4 steps. It should also be pointed that we attempted to remove 37 steps with Zipperposition in total. This is higher than for the other solvers, which indicates that Zipperposition could also solve the steps around a higher-order step more often.

Overall, higher-order solvers prove to be helpful for proofs with a few intermediary easy steps. It is often possible to remove a few steps with Zipperposition, CVC4, Satallax or Vampire, and in some cases reduce the whole proof to a single line, as is the case for the following proof:

THEOREM SuffixRecursiveSequenceFunctionType ==
  ASSUME NEW S, **NEW** T, **NEW** Def(_,_), **NEW** f,
      T # {},
      StrictSuffixesDetermineDef(S, Def),
      WFInductiveDefines(f, Seq(S), Def),
      $\forall$ g $\in$ [Seq(S) -> T], s $\in$ Seq(S) : Def(g,s) $\in$ T
  PROVE f $\in$ [Seq(S) -> T]
<1>1. IsWellFoundedOn(OpToRel(IsStrictSuffix, Seq(S)), Seq(S))
  BY IsStrictSuffixWellFounded
<1>2. WFDefOn(OpToRel(IsStrictSuffix, Seq(S)), Seq(S), Def)
  BY StrictSuffixesDetermineDef_WFDefOn
<1>. **QED**
  BY <1>1, <1>2, WFInductiveDefType

An important portion of the original obligations are the application of some induction principle. They are variations of this pattern:

<1> **DEFINE** P(n) == (* ... *)
<1>1 P(0)
<1>2 $\forall$ n $\in$ Nat : P(n) => P(n + 1)
<1> **HIDE DEF** P
<1>3 $\forall$ n $\in$ Nat : P(n) **BY** <1>1, <1>2, NatInduction (* The HO obligation *)

The induction can be on a different structure, but the pattern is the same. All solvers tended to fail on these obligations. When they did succeed, we only removed the HIDE line, but after doing so the solver would fail on the new obligation. This is most likely due to the fact that NatInduction must be instantiated with an arbitrary expression instead of the constant P, as P is expanded in the goal when HIDE is removed. In some cases, however, Isabelle was able to handle the new obligation—these cases constitute the majority of removed steps that are reported in the second column of table 2. They are especially prevalent in FiniteSetTheorems, as they represent 8 out of the 9 original obligations. This may be the main reason for Leo-III's poor performances on that particular specification.

5   Conclusion

Motivated by the most recent advances in higher-order theorem proving, and the poor support for higher-order proof steps in TLAPS, we implemented an encoding of TLA$^+$ into THF and evaluated several higher-order solvers on a range of proof obligations. Our experiment demonstrated that higher-order solvers are indeed able to handle obligations more complex than TLAPS currently does. Zipperposition in particular outperformed the others by a significant margin, and was integrated in TLAPS as a new backend.

This new backend was not intended to be general-purpose for TLA$^+$, but rather specialized in those obligations that involve a bit of higher-order reasoning. Thus the encoding of TLA$^+$ we implemented is very simple and unoptimized. It appears however that we are unable to solve many obligations precisely because the encoding is lacking on some aspects. Our treatment of set extensionality is insufficient for solving goals such as $\text{Card}(S \cup \emptyset) = \text{Card}(S)$. Our support of arithmetic is very limited, as we provide only a few theory axioms to the solvers, and never consider the full theory. It should also be noted that the encoding was primarily designed with Zipperposition in mind, and that we did not fully explore the options that other solvers offer. For instance, we are aware that Vampire features a special rule for instantiating extensionality axioms, and a set of support strategy for dealing with explicit theory axioms [7,12]. CVC4 features a decision procedure for reasoning about finite sets and cardinalities [1]. These are all potential leads for future improvements of TLA$^+$ encodings, including the general-purpose ones.

Acknowledgment. I thank Jasmin Blanchette, Pascal Fontaine and Stephan Merz for their support and guidance through the development of this work. Peter Vukmirović helped with the integration of Zipperposition in TLAPS and its configuration. Simon Cruanes provided additional insights on Zipperposition. Martin Riener tested and helped debugging the new backend. Damien Doligez and Ioannis Filippidis explained to me the inner working of TLAPS, which helped in implementing the extension. This research is funded by the European Research Council (ERC) under the European's Union Horizon 2020 research and innovation program (grant agreement No. 713999, Matryoshka), and from the Région Grand Est.

References

1. Bansal, K., Reynolds, A., Barrett, C.W., Tinelli, C.: A new decision procedure for finite sets and cardinality constraints in SMT. In: Proceedings of the Automated Reasoning - 8th International Joint Conference (IJCAR 2016), Coimbra, Portugal, June 27–July 2, 2016, pp. 82–98 (2016)
2. Barbosa, H., Reynolds, A., Ouraoui, D.E., Tinelli, C., Barrett, C.W.: Extending SMT solvers to higher-order logic. In: Proceedings of the Automated Deduction - CADE 27–27th International Conference on Automated Deduction, Natal, Brazil, 27–30 August 2019, pp. 35–54 (2019)
3. Bentkamp, A., Blanchette, J., Tourret, S., Vukmirovic, P., Waldmann, U.: Superposition with lambdas. In: Proceedings of the Automated Deduction - CADE 27–27th International Conference on Automated Deduction, Natal, Brazil, August 27–30, 2019, pp. 55–73 (2019)
4. Bhayat, A., Reger, G.: A combinator-based superposition calculus for higher-order logic. In: Proceedings of the Automated Reasoning - 10th International Joint Conference, IJCAR 2020, Paris, France, July 1–4, 2020, Part I, pp. 278–296 (2020)
5. Brown, C.E.: Satallax: an automatic higher-order prover. In: Proceedings of the Automated Reasoning - 6th International Joint Conference, IJCAR 2012, Manchester, UK, June 26–29, 2012, pp. 111–117 (2012)
6. Cousineau, D., Doligez, D., Lamport, L., Merz, S., Ricketts, D., Vanzetto, H.: TLA+ Proofs. In: Giannakopoulou, D., Méry, D. (eds.) 18th International Symposium On Formal Methods - FM 2012. Lecture Notes in Computer Science, vol. 7436, pp. 147–154. Springer, Paris, France, August 2012. http://www.springerlink.com

7. Gupta, A., Kovács, L., Kragl, B., Voronkov, A.: Extensional crisis and proving identity. In: Proceedings of the Automated Technology for Verification and Analysis - 12th International Symposium, ATVA 2014, Sydney, NSW, Australia, November 3–7, 2014, pp. 185–200 (2014)

8. Kotelnikov, E., Kovács, L., Voronkov, A.: A first class boolean sort in first-order theorem proving and TPTP. In: Proceedings of the Intelligent Computer Mathematics - International Conference (CICM 2015), Washington, DC, USA, July 13–17, 2015, pp. 71–86 (2015)

9. Lamport, L.: How to write a proof. Am. Math. Monthly **102**, 600–608 (1995)

10. Lamport, L.: Specifying Systems. Addison-Wesley, The TLA+ Language and Tools for Hardware and Software Engineers (2002)

11. Mentré, D., Marché, C., Filliâtre, J., Asuka, M.: Discharging proof obligations from atelier B using multiple automated provers. In: Proceedings of the Abstract State Machines, Alloy, B, VDM, and Z - Third International Conference, ABZ 2012, Pisa, Italy, June 18–21, 2012, pp. 238–251 (2012)

12. Reger, G., Suda, M.: Set of support for theory reasoning. In: IWIL@LPAR 2017 Workshop and LPAR-21 Short Presentations, Maun, Botswana, 7–12 May 2017 (2017)

13. Steen, A., Benzmüller, C.: The higher-order prover leo-iii. In: Proceedings of the Automated Reasoning - 9th International Joint Conference, IJCAR 2018, Held as Part of the Federated Logic Conference (FloC 2018), Oxford, UK, July 14–17, 2018, pp. 108–116 (2018)

14. Sutcliffe, G. (ed.): Proceedings of the 10th IJCAR ATP System Competition (CASC-J10), July 2020

15. Vanzetto, H.: Proof automation and type synthesis for set theory in the context of TLA+. (Automatisation de preuves et synthèse de types pour la théorie des ensembles dans le contexte de TLA+). Ph.D. thesis, University of Lorraine, Nancy, France (2014), https://tel.archives-ouvertes.fr/tel-01096518

16. Vukmirovic, P., Bentkamp, A., Nummelin, V.: Efficient full higher-order unification. In: 5th International Conference on Formal Structures for Computation and Deduction (FSCD 2020), June 29-July 6, 2020, Paris, France (Virtual Conference). pp. 5:1–5:17 (2020)

17. Vukmirovic, P., Nummelin, V.: Boolean reasoning in a higher-order superposition prover. In: Joint Proceedings of the 7th Workshop on Practical Aspects of Automated Reasoning (PAAR) and the 5th Satisfiability Checking and Symbolic Computation Workshop (SC-Square) Workshop, 2020 Co-located with the 10th International Joint Conference on Automated Reasoning (IJCAR 2020), Paris, France, June-July, 2020 (Virtual). pp. 148–166 (2020)

JEFL: Joint Embedding of Formal Proof Libraries

Qingxiang Wang[1] and Cezary Kaliszyk[1,2]($\boxtimes$)

[1] University of Innsbruck, Innsbruck, Austria
`cezary.kaliszyk@uibk.ac.at`
[2] University of Warsaw, Warsaw, Poland

Abstract. The heterogeneous nature of the logical foundations used in different interactive proof assistant libraries has rendered discovery of similar mathematical concepts among them difficult. In this paper, we compare a previously proposed algorithm for matching concepts across libraries with our unsupervised embedding approach that can help us retrieve similar concepts. Our approach is based on the `fasttext` implementation of Word2Vec, on top of which a tree traversal module is added to adapt its algorithm to the representation format of our data export pipeline. We compare the explainability, customizability, and online-servability of the approaches and argue that the neural embedding approach has more potential to be integrated into an interactive proof assistant.

Keywords: Unsupervised embedding · Concept alignments · Proof formalization · System integration

1 Introduction

One of the challenges hindering massive formalization of mathematics is the heterogeneous nature of the logical frameworks used in various interactive proof assistants [8,11,13,27]. When formalizing proofs against one formal library, it is informative to explore whether and how similar things are done in other libraries. Such exploration has to be done manually and would usually require expertise in the other proof assistants. It would be nice if a tool could let users more systematically explore and discover commonality among formal libraries.

Not only can such a tool be an informative recommender when integrated into an interactive proof assistant, but exploring commonalities among formal libraries is also an interesting problem per se. Through time, multiple versions of the same or similar mathematical concepts have been formalized separately, resulting in repetitive work [21]. To the mathematically oriented, it is quite irksome that identical mathematical concepts must require idiosyncratic formalizations in order to achieve assurance. We believe that by investigating their commonalities, insights on improving interoperability among proof assistants can be obtained, thereby advancing the frontiers of combining systems.

B. Konev and G. Reger (Eds.): FroCoS 2021, LNAI 12941, pp. 154–170, 2021.
https://doi.org/10.1007/978-3-030-86205-3_9

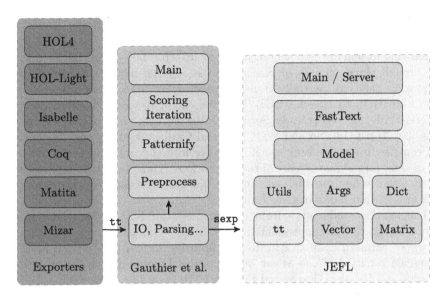

Fig. 1. The architectural relationship between Gauthier's approach and JEFL. At the current stage, the exporters dump text in the tt format (Sect. 2). JEFL reuses the IO/parsing module of Gauthier and passes s-expressions to the fasttext implementation.

Previous works [4,6] on this problem let us obtain a data export pipeline that could transform data from six proof assistants into a common term representation format (Fig. 1), on top of which an iterative pattern-matching algorithm that could output constant/theorem pairs with high similarity scores was invented by Gauthier. The alignments between the concepts across multiple proof libraries or within one library have been useful for tasks including conjecturing [7], browsing multiple libraries simultaneously [25], and proof automation using learned alignments [5].

The Gauthier approach, while being remarkably effective and useful, lacks *explainability, customizability* and *online-servability* that hamper its integration into proof assistants. By these three notions we mean the lack of *mathematical intuitiveness*, lack of *room for customization*, and lack of *possibility for system integration*, respectively. We introduce an alternative embedding approach based on the superb engineering of the fasttext implementation [1]. This new approach could potentially overcome these drawbacks while providing competitive performance. It could also serve as a highly configurable experiment platform for studying the alignment of multiple proof assistant libraries. We coin this research *JEFL*, as an acronym for *Joint Embedding of Formal Libraries*.

2   Previous Works and the tt Format

Exchanging formal developments within or across formal systems has been studied through three strands of research. First, on the library translation side, many tools that can partially translate proofs have been developed, including those from HOL to Isabelle/HOL [26], HOL Light to Coq [20], HOL Light to Isabelle/HOL [16], respectively. Second, on the ontology sharing side, Bortin [2], Rabe [30], Hurd [14], So and Watt [32], and Carlisle et al. [3] each made their own contribution translating specifications or formal proof objects between formal or semi-formal mathematical representations. These two strands of research mostly either solely provide guidelines on manual processing or require manual work at a certain phase of their framework.

The third strand comes from enhancements of ITP systems. Heras and Komendantskaya [12] implemented a recurrent term clustering algorithm to find proof similarities in Coq/SSReflect libraries. Urban [34] created tools for large-scale retrieval of the Mizar Mathematical Library into a clausal format. Kaliszyk and Urban [17] exported the core HOL Light library as well as the Flyspeck [10] library to evaluate the relevance of lemmas by combining the power of automated theorem provers. This work was later extended to a web service [19] and experimented with using multiple representation formats and different automated theorem provers in [18].

A byproduct along [17–19] was a collection of exporting and post-processing techniques specific to HOL Light, including a TPTP-style [33] data representation format which we internally called "the tt format". The formalism of tt is based on a simple term structure that is flexible enough to represent the kernel representations of formal data on diverse logical foundations, so there is a potential to export data from multiple proof assistants into this common format. Based on the export of three HOL libraries (HOL Light, HOL4, and Isabelle/HOL), Gauthier and Kaliszyk proposed the first version of their scoring algorithm [4] and used for various conjecturing and transfer learning tasks. A more comprehensive set of alignment experiments refined the scoring algorithm, provided a more uniform pattern-matching and guaranteed convergence, and was used on six proof assistant libraries (adding Coq, Matita, and Mizar) [6].

Listing 2.1 and 2.2 illustrate the definition of the predecessor of the naturals (PRE) of HOL Light being translated into a list of three tt items. The last arguments of them can be parsed into term structures (Fig. 2) using the type definition in Listing 2.3.

Listing 2.1. Definition of the predecessor of the naturals PRE in HOL Light.

```
let PRE = new_recursive_definition num_RECURSION
 '(PRE 0 = 0) /\
  (!n. PRE (SUC n) = n)';;
```

Listing 2.2. PRE transformed to three **tt** items.

```
01. tt('const/arith/PRE', ty, ('type/nums/num' > 'type/nums/num')).
02. tt('thm/arith/PRE_0', ax,
     (('const/arith/PRE' ('const/nums/NUMERAL' 'const/nums/_0')) =
      ('const/nums/NUMERAL' 'const/nums/_0'))).
03. tt('thm/arith/PRE_1', ax,
     (![n : 'type/nums/num']:
      (('const/arith/PRE' ('const/nums/SUC' n)) = n))).
```

Listing 2.3. Type definition of **tt** term in OCaml for parsing.

```
type ttterm =
| Id of string (* may be a constant or variable *)
| Comb of ttterm * ttterm
| Abs of string * ttterm * ttterm;;
```

The HOL Light and HOL4 exports directly use HOLyHammer's export [18]. For Isabelle, an ML component was implemented that extracts all theorems of the theory and writes them together with the declared constants and types in a text file. The Coq export to the **tt** format was implemented by Gauthier as part of his work [6]. For Mizar, we rely on Urban's MPTP pipeline [35] and transform the intermediate XML2 representation.

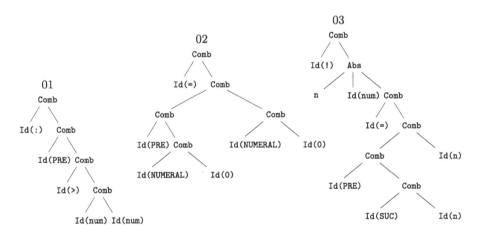

Fig. 2. Term structures of the definition of PRE. The tokens PRE, num, NUMERAL and SUC are short for `const/arith/PRE`, `type/nums/num`, `const/nums/NUMERAL` and `const/nums/SUC`, respectively. Note that the constant `const/arith/PRE` is included into the term *01* with a type assignment operator ':'. This allows embedding vectors to be assigned to the definition constants.

3   The Architecture of JEFL

In this paper, we focus on the core similarity discovery algorithm. Our claim on advantages in JEFL is with respect to the algorithmic part of the system.

We leave the eventual integration of the whole framework into proof assistants, with issues such as handling constants that have not been encountered during training, as future work.

3.1 Similarity Through Embedding

A natural way to find similarities among concepts is to treat our problem as a distributed representation learning task. Generally speaking, given a structure composed of atomic units, distributed representation learning seeks to represent each of the atomic units with a low-dimensional vector. In effect, all the units are embedded into a Euclidean space, with their coordinates respecting the overall structure. The notion *distributedness* comes from the fact that the vocabulary size of a corpus is much larger than the dimension of a vector, and the information of an atomic unit is distributed in the coordinates of a vector.

The vectors are learned by analyzing the *context* of each unit, i.e. the information of units adjacent to or surrounding a target unit. Once vector representations for units are learned, similarity between units can then be computed by cosine similarity with a range from $[-1, 1]$. For a set of units, vector representation can be computed by taking average of the vectors, and then similarity between different sets of units can also be computed using cosine similarity.

Notable unsupervised distributed representation learning algorithms include Pennington et al.'s GloVe algorithm [28] and Mikolov et al.'s Word2Vec algorithm [23,24]. In this paper, we use Mikolov's Word2Vec algorithm. Word2Vec works on texts or lists of word tokens. For each word in the training corpus, a randomized span of words surrounding that word is picked to form the context of that word. The context is then consumed by the Word2Vec model to conduct one step of the stochastic gradient descent updates.

3.2 Adaptation of the tt Format in Word2Vec

To illuminate our technique, it is interesting to note that DeepWalk [29] and Node2Vec [9], two methods on embedding large networks, also use Word2Vec as their underlying algorithm. The data used by DeepWalk and Node2Vec are single-graph datasets with nodes that contain heterogenous information such as social profile details. To fit Word2Vec, first the node information of the graph has to be transformed into a dictionary through data processing. Then we perform random walks along the paths of the graph to generate node sequences that resemble text corpus. For each node in a node sequence, the corresponding context is generated as a span of nodes surrounding that node.

In our case, different from DeepWalk and Node2Vec, the formal library data in the tt format are not a single graph but a collection of trees. More precisely, in order to compare two libraries, we need two lists of tt items from the two libraries to provide as training data. The tt items are parsed as trees and then traversed in different ways to create sequences of node constants. Examples of traversals include preorder, inorder, postorder traversals and their reverses, random walks from the root to a leaf, or just dump the leaves of a tree in some order. With clever design, these traversals can also be combined to create hybrid orders. At the current phase we implemented a simple weighted mechanism combining preorder, inorder and postorder traversals. The weights of traversals are used to control the learning rate for SGD updates and are hyperparameters determined before training (Fig. 3). We anticipate further experimental insights when other forms of traversals are implemented in the future.

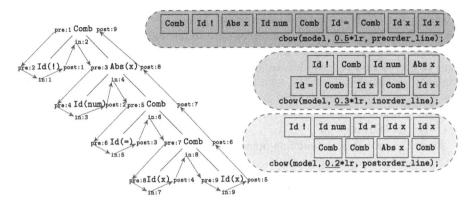

Fig. 3. Preorder, inorder, and postorder traversals of a simple theorem $\forall x$: num. $(x = x)$, with weights 0.5, 0.3, 0.2, respectively. Example illustrated by calling the CBOW method of `fasttext`, where `lr` is the learning rate and the third argument contains the token sequence above it. Inside the CBOW method, for each token, a randomized span of words surrounding that token is obtained to compute the hidden vector.

Both DeepWalk and Node2Vec directly use the Word2Vec implementation of the Gensim [31] topic modeling library. For ease of future integration into proof assistants we pick a dedicated Word2Vec implementation `fasttext` [15] as our base platform. To make our customization less intrusive we add a custom tree traversal module to the codebase of `fasttext`, also called the `tt` module (Fig. 1). The `tt` module parses the terms in the `tt` format and builds corresponding trees in the memory of JEFL.

3.3   The SGD Updates of Word2Vec

It remains to discuss the core Word2Vec algorithm, which is divided into two aspects: 1. what is the probability model for Word2Vec training and 2. how the loss function is computed. In the former, there are the *continuous bag-of-words* model (CBOW) and the *skip-gram* model. They appear at the step of the training loop outside stochastic gradient descent (SGD) updates and determine how data samples are used. In the latter, there are the *softmax* loss, the *hierarchical softmax* loss, and the *negative sampling* loss. They compute the loss function, at the same time determine the gradients and update the input and output matrices. The two training models are compatible with the three loss functions, so there are in total six variations of the Word2Vec algorithm[1].

As the full Word2Vec algorithm is extensive, we briefly describe the difference between skip-gram and CBOW using the simplest softmax case. We skip detailed derivations and remind the reader of the abundance of study materials of Word2Vec on the internet[2].

Let $\mathcal{C}$ be the training corpus, V be the size of the dictionary of $\mathcal{C}$, and D be the dimension of a word vector. Denote $M \in \mathbb{R}^{V \times D}$ as the *input matrix* which we use to store all the word vectors. Denote $N \in \mathbb{R}^{V \times D}$ as the *output matrix* which we use to store customized data items depending on the loss function. Let $w \in \{1, 2, \ldots, V\}$ be a word, or more precisely, the index of an actual word in the dictionary. We denote M_w as the w-th row of the input matrix M. Similarly we denote N_u as the u-th row of the output matrix N, given a word $u \in \{1, 2, \ldots, V\}$. Both M_w and N_u are D-dimensional row vectors. For each word w, denote context(w) as a randomized span of words surrounding w. Let $\eta > 0$ be the learning rate.

From the probability modeling point of view, CBOW amounts to maximizing the log-likelihood of the form

$$\mathcal{L} = \log \prod_{w \in \mathcal{C}} P\left(w|\text{context}(w)\right) = \sum_{w \in \mathcal{C}} \log \text{softmax}(Nh^T)_w,$$

where

$$h = \frac{1}{|\text{context}(w)|} \sum_{u \in \text{context}(w)} M_u$$

is the hidden vector. The SGD updates are computed by taking *increments* of the gradients of the objective (as we want to *maximize* the log-likelihood)[3]

$$N_u := N_u + \eta \left(\delta_{uw} - \text{softmax}(Nh^T)_u\right) h \qquad \text{for } u \in \{1, \ldots, V\}$$

$$M_u := M_u + \frac{\eta}{|\text{context}(w)|} \sum_{v=1}^{V} \left(\delta_{vw} - \text{softmax}(Nh^T)_v\right) N_v \quad \text{for } u \in \text{context}(w)$$

The skip-gram model amounts to maximizing the log-likelihood of the following form

$$\mathcal{L} = \log \prod_{w \in \mathcal{C}} P\left(\text{context}(w)|w\right) = \log \prod_{w \in \mathcal{C}} \prod_{u \in \text{context}(w)} p(u|v)$$

$$= \sum_{w \in \mathcal{C}} \sum_{u \in \text{context}(w)} \log \text{softmax}(Nh^T)_u$$

---

[1] As to writing of this paper, one more loss function (the **one-vs-all**, or the **ova** loss) has been added to the latest version of **fasttext**, making in total eight variations.

[2] The first author finds this note https://github.com/renpengcheng-github/nlp/tree/master/3.word2vec (in Chinese) particularly helpful in understanding Word2Vec.

[3] We use the term stochastic gradient *descent* here for convention though we are in fact doing stochastic gradient *ascent*.

where
$$h = M_w$$

is a D-dimensional row vector. For each $u \in \text{context}(w)$, the SGD updates are

$$N_{\widetilde{w}} := N_{\widetilde{w}} + \eta \left(\delta_{\widetilde{w}u} - \text{softmax}(Nh^T)_{\widetilde{w}} \right) M_w \qquad \text{for } \widetilde{w} \in \{1, \ldots, V\}$$

$$M_w := M_w + \eta \sum_{v=1}^{V} \left(\delta_{vu} - \text{softmax}(Nh^T)_v \right) N_v.$$

Algorithm 1. Full algorithm for CBOW and skip-gram with softmax loss

1: **for** $w \in \mathcal{C}$ **do**
2:      Get sample $(w, \text{context}(w))$.   ▷ See Section 3.2
3:      **if** CBOW **then**
4:          $h := \mathbf{0}$
5:          **for** $v \in \text{context}(w)$ **do**
6:              $h := h + M_v$
7:          **end for**
8:          $h := h/|\text{context}(w)|$ ▷ 1. Get hidden vector (cbow)
9:          $g := \mathbf{0}$
10:         **for** $u \in \{1, \ldots, V\}$ **do**   ▷ Room for speedup
11:             $s := \text{softmax}\left(Nh^T\right)_u$
12:             $\alpha := \eta \left(\delta_{uw} - s \right)$
13:             $g := g + \alpha N_u$ ▷ 2. Accumulate gradient (cbow)
14:             $N_u := N_u + \alpha h$ ▷ 3. Update output matrix (cbow)
15:         **end for**
16:         $g := g/|\text{context}(w)|$
17:         **for** $u \in \text{context}(w)$ **do**
18:             $M_u := M_u + g$ ▷ 4. Update input rows (cbow)
19:         **end for**
20:     **else**   ▷ Skip-gram
21:         $h := M_w$ ▷ 1. Get hidden vector (skipgram)
22:         **for** $u \in \text{context}(w)$ **do**
23:             $g := \mathbf{0}$
24:             **for** $\widetilde{w} \in \{1, \ldots, V\}$ **do**   ▷ Room for speedup
25:                 $s := \text{softmax}\left(Nh^T\right)_{\widetilde{w}}$
26:                 $\alpha := \eta \left(\delta_{\widetilde{w}u} - s \right)$
27:                 $g := g + \alpha N_{\widetilde{w}}$ ▷ 2. Accumulate gradient (skipgram)
28:                 $N_{\widetilde{w}} := N_{\widetilde{w}} + \alpha h$ ▷ 3. Update output matrix (skipgram)
29:             **end for**
30:             $M_w := M_w + g$ ▷ 4. Update input rows (skipgram)
31:         **end for**
32:     **end if**
33: **end for**

3.4   The `fasttext` Implementation of Word2Vec

The full SGD update algorithm is shown in Algorithm 1. Notice that, for both CBOW and skip-gram, in each round of model updates there are essentially four identical steps: 1. obtain hidden vector, 2. accumulate gradient, 3. update rows of the output matrix, and 4. update rows of the input matrix. This four-step abstraction is general not only for softmax but also for hierarchical softmax and negative sampling, which are specifically designed to speed up the calculation of the inner loop in line 10, 24 of Algorithm 1.

The architecture of `fasttext` was inspired by this four-step abstraction. Since its initial development in 2016, lots of advanced functionalities have been added on top of the Word2Vec algorithm, including model quantization, auto-tuning, python binding, etc. This makes the codebase large and many of those functionalities are irrelevant to our research. Therefore we use an earlier commit in late 2016 as our base[4]. In this commit, all six variations of Word2Vec have been implemented and very few advanced functionalities are added. Two of them worth mentioning are: 1. subsampling of most frequent words, and 2. subword information enrichment trick. The first is an extension of the Word2Vec algorithm in [24] to filter out disproportionally frequent words in the training corpus. This function is disabled since it is obvious in our dataset that the most frequent tokens are always `Comb`, `Id`, and `Abs`, respectively, and they have to be included to allow for correct parsing of `tt` items. The second is a feature in the `fasttext` implementation [15] which breaks a word token into segments of character-level n-gram tokens. This is also disabled since constants in our embedding task (e.g. `'const/arith/PRE'`) constitute a unique and separate entity, and enabling this feature would normally increase the size of a training model by more than a hundred times. The original `src` directory of this commit contains 2054 lines of C++ code written in C++11.

4   Experimenting with JEFL

The core algorithm part of JEFL consists of 8 modules of the original `fasttext` plus a custom module for term parsing and traversal (Fig. 1 right). We find that the best way for customization is to add to the `args` module a new flag (`isTT`) to denote whether our training corpus is a list of `tt` items or plain texts. The normal process flow is not interrupted if this flag is `false`, so JEFL can also train on plain text. If `isTT` is `true`, then subsampling is suppressed when reading in the input files. This allows all tokens of `tt` terms to be read so that term parsing can be done correctly. The `tt` items are read, parsed and the parsed terms can be reconstructed as trees in the C++ side. Helper functions are then called to traverse a tree in different orders, look up the index values of its constants from a dictionary, and call `fasttext`'s original CBOW or skip-gram method for SGD updates (Fig. 3).

---

[4] c62abb89396a94520f009f9095874953735e0d75.

We report our initial round of experiments with this platform and two formal proof libraries, HOL4 and HOL Light, testing the performance of different hyper-parameter combinations. There are in total 18723 and 16874 lines of `tt` items in HOL4 and HOL Light, respectively. We concatenate and shuffle the exported theorems from the two libraries, and then write them out as s-expressions [22].[5] We evaluate the performance by comparing against the 1000 highest-scoring constant pairs, that have been manually checked by Gauthier in his work, and considered here as a baseline.

Table 1. Comparison of theorem export formats. Tree-dump exports the whole tree representation in the given order, while leaf-dump exports only the sequence of data present in the leafs.

	Top-1 Hit	Top-3 Hit	Top-10 Hit	Top-20 Hit
Tree-Dump	51	101	188	261
Leaf-Dump	21	61	96	144

Table 2. Comparison of models skip-gram and continuous bag of words.

	Top-1 Hit	Top-3 Hit	Top-10 Hit	Top-20 Hit
Skip-Gram	54	108	264	283
CBOW	51	101	188	261

Table 3. Comparison of sampling hierarchical softmax vs. negative sampling

	Top-1 Hit	Top-3 Hit	Top-10 Hit	Top-20 Hit
Hierarchical Softmax	78	161	304	419
Negative Sampling	51	101	188	261

We present four sets of experiments for the initial comparison. We measure JEFL's performance against the Gauthier baseline by using the "Top-N Hit" metric, which means the inclusion of the correct answer from the closest N neighbors of the target constant. By default, we use leaf-dump (sequences of data present in the leafs), CBOW, negative sampling, and equal (0.33, 0.33, 0.33) weights. For other key parameters of `fasttext`, we set vector dimension as 100, learning rate 0.05, random uniform context window size 1 to 10, training epoch 5 (for most experiments we see little training progress after epoch 5, so for a fair evaluation we stick with 5 epochs for all evaluations), 5 negative samples for negative sampling loss, and 4 training threads.

Experiment 1 (Table 1) tests the difference between tree-dump (dumping s-expression) vs. leaf-dump (dumping leaves as token sequences). This experiment is the first one to test that our customization blends with the normal process

---

[5] This gives a total of 35597 s-expressions for Word2Vec training.

Table 4. Combination of the effect of weights given to the different traversals. The table shows the weights given to pre-order, in-order, and post-order respectively, together with their effects on finding same constants across libraries.

(pre-, in-, post-order)	Top-1 Hit	Top-3 Hit	Top-10 Hit	Top-20 Hit
(0.33, 0.33, 0.33)	51	101	188	261
(0.5, 0.3, 0.2)	58	103	205	267
(1, 0, 0)	53	110	204	256
(0.5, 0.5, 0)	49	113	207	276
(0, 0.5, 0.5)	57	106	203	268

flow of `fasttext`. We see that tree traversal gives better hit rates than just use the leaves as the former uses more information in training.

Experiment 2 (Table 2) tests the difference between skip-gram and CBOW. We see that skip-gram performs better than CBOW in all hit rates. However, as noted in Sect. 3.3, skip-gram takes longer time to train (this depends on the size of the contexts, and in our experiments skip-gram takes about five times longer). For ease of experiment, we fall back to use CBOW as our default.

Experiment 3 (Table 3) shows a clear advantage of hierarchical softmax over negative sampling. We see a 60% increase in all the hit rates. We speculate that this improvement is due to the fact, that the Huffman tree computation in hierarchical softmax might put an advantage in mining patterns in tree-like data structures.

Experiment 4 (Table 4) explores different combinations of weights in tree-traversal. They all outperform leaf-dump, however, none of the combinations performs significantly better than others. We plan to explore other forms of traversal such as random walks to see further results.

5   Comparison with Iterative Pattern-Matching

In this section, we shortly recall the iterative pattern-matching algorithm developed by Gauthier and Kaliszyk [6], and compare it with the work presented here. The iterative pattern matching algorithm is based on the observation that once mathematical information in different formal libraries is represented in the same `tt` format, similar theorems or typing judgements (as terms of `tt`) tend to have identical term structures. Accordingly, similar constants (as leaves of terms) tend to locate in corresponding slots of a term (Fig. 4). To abstract out common term structure, Gauthier invented the notion *pattern of a term*. The pattern of a term T is created by abstracting out, in a canonical order, all the T's non-logical constants. Two terms T_1 and T_2 sharing the same pattern form a *matching pair of terms*. Corresponding slots of a matching pair of terms *induce* a collection of *matching pairs of constants*.

T_1 $\forall x : \text{num.} \ (\ x + 0 = x\ )$ T_2 $\forall x : \text{real.} \ (\ x \times 1 = x\ )$

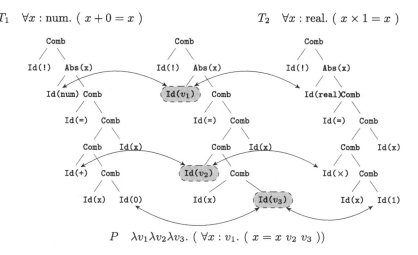

P $\lambda v_1 \lambda v_2 \lambda v_3. \ (\ \forall x : v_1. \ (\ x = x \ v_2 \ v_3\ ))$

Fig. 4. T_1 and T_2 form a matching pair of terms with pattern P. Three matching pairs of constants can be induced from this pattern. We treat equality = and universal quantification ! as logical constants. Bound variables are assumed to be normalized.

Given two formal libraries L_1 and L_2. Let $\{t_i\}_{1 \le i \le m}$ be the collection of all matching pairs of terms, with $t_i = (t_{i1}, t_{i2})$, $t_{i1} \in L_1$, and $t_{i2} \in L_2$. Let $\{c_j\}_{1 \le j \le n}$ be the collection of all matching pairs of constants, with $c_j = (c_{j1}, c_{j2})$. Let $g(x) = x/(x+1) : \mathbb{R}^+ \to [0,1)$ be a strictly increasing *normalization function*. Define an *indicator function* $\delta(c_j, t_i)$ and set $\delta(c_j, t_i) = 1$ if constant pair c_j can be induced by term pair t_i and 0 otherwise. Similarity scores between pairs of terms and pairs of constants can be calculated using the following recurrence relations

$$\begin{cases} \text{score}_c^0(c_j) = 1, & j = 1, \dots, n. \\ \text{score}_t^T(t_i) = w_t(t_i) \sum_{l=1}^n \delta(c_l, t_i) \text{score}_c^{T-1}(c_l), & i = 1, \dots, m. \\ \text{score}_t^T(c_j) = g\left(w_c(c_j) \sum_{k=1}^m \delta(c_j, t_k) \text{score}_t^T(t_k)\right), & j = 1, \dots, n. \end{cases} \quad (1)$$

where $T = 0, 1, 2, \dots$ is the iteration step and the weighting functions for terms $w_t(t_i)$ and constants $w_c(c_j)$ are determined using heuristics

$$\begin{cases} w_t(t_i) = \frac{1}{\ln(2+p(t_i))} \frac{1}{\ln(2+q(t_i))}, & i = 1, \dots, m. \\ w_c(c_j) = \frac{1}{\ln(2+r(c_{j1}) \times r(c_{j2}))}, & j = 1, \dots, n. \\ p(t_i) = \#\{\text{term pairs sharing the same pattern as } t_i\}, & i = 1, \dots, m. \\ q(t_i) = \#\{\text{constant pairs induced by } t_i\}, & i = 1, \dots, m. \\ r(c_{jd}) = \#\{\text{terms containing } c_{jd}\}, & d = 1 \text{ or } 2, \ j = 1, \dots, n. \end{cases}$$
$$(2)$$

By rewriting Eq. (1) with respect to $\text{score}_t^T(c_j)$ and using properties of g, δ, w_t, and w_c, Gauthier proved the convergence of this scoring algorithm (using monotone convergence theorem coordinate-wise in $[0,1]^n$) [6].

5.1   Advantages and Drawbacks of Iterative Pattern Matching

Gauthier's iterative pattern-matching algorithm is cleverly designed. Intuitively, the existence of a pattern already indicates a strong correlation among term pairs, and the existence of constant pairs at corresponding slots of a pattern already indicates a strong correlation among those constant pairs; The indicator function δ transports "similarity awards" among those pairs, while the weighting functions w_t and w_c penalize frequently occurring patterns. Above all, the normalization function g ensures the validity of the scores and is crucial for convergence of the algorithm. All these components are intricately combined to make the whole algorithm effective in discovering identical or similar mathematical concepts.

Nevertheless, Gauthier's algorithm possesses some inherent drawbacks. From the *explainability* angle, the balance between the heuristics (w_t, w_c and their components p, q, and r) in Eq. (2) and the score accumulation terms ($\sum$ and δ) in Eq. (1) is, to our mind, hard to explain clearly and difficult to readjust. The convergence of the algorithm is mostly due to the property of the normalization function g but the link between this convergence and how similarity scores are sorted is weak. The algorithm works on spaces of similarity scores between matching pairs of terms and constants, so from its beginning, the information on non-matching terms and constants is thrown away, losing the possibility to look at the alignment of different proof assistant libraries holistically.

Comparatively, our approach provides much more flexibility and intuitiveness. Using distributed representation learning, all the constants are movable points in Euclidean space and similarity between constants are naturally described as cosine similarity between their coordinates. By using an embedding approach, not only the "matching" pairs, but also similarity between all pairs of constants can be retrieved and their computation is cheap.

From the *customizability* angle, the components of Gauthier's algorithm are so intricately combined that there seems little opportunity to adjust the algorithm further. In the implementations of both [4] and [6], most of the extra work is on preprocessing terms using combinations of rewriting rules to create a varying set of patterns. These rewriting rules include, *e.g.* rewriting to conjunctive normal forms, reordering commutative/associative connectives, substituting subterms with definitions, as well as exposing various levels of typing information. All these customizations are only allowed in the preprocessing phase and limited to only employing rewriting rules. Some of the typing exposure rules require specific knowledge of representing a library in the tt format. As these rewriting-based customizations have already been thoroughly investigated in [6], it seems to us that further investigation along this line is destined to a diminishing return.

Comparatively, customization of JEFL can be done at different phases of the full training algorithm, such as the data generation phase, term traversal phase, model update phase, etc. This multi-level customization can create combinatorially much more room for parameter-tuning and experimentation. Moreover, except data generation, all other customizations that are within the algorithm can be more uniformly done. Specifically, data fields and command parsing can be added to the `args` module, and then used at desired places of the data flow.

From the *online-servability* angle, despite the fact that Gauthier's algorithm is overall fast and effective on small data, it is still quadratic on the size of the input libraries, since it needs to enumerate all pairs of terms to find patterns. Being a batch program without a separated and instantaneous evaluation phase, it is not tempting to integrate the whole algorithm into an actual interactive proof assistant. Moreover, even if it were to be used as an online recommender, the only information we can retrieve would be limited to only the matching pairs.

In JEFL, despite more computations are involved, training is linear with respect to the size of the corpus. This makes JEFL more suitable for obtaining similarity measurements on a large training corpus. JEFL provides a clear separation between a training phase and an evaluation phase. The evaluation phase is instant once the model is loaded. This allows JEFL to have more potential to be integrated as a service. In the version of the `fasttext` commit used in JEFL, if subword information is disabled, the size of most of the models dumped after training are less than 5 MB. This is a negligible size comparing to the size of a modern proof assistant.

6   Conclusion

In this paper, we identify the need for commonality discovery among formal libraries. We introduce our data pipeline, especially its preceding works, and elaborate our internal `tt` formalism. Methodologically, we describe the architecture of JEFL and make a series of first experiments to test the efficacy of our experiment platform and provide a high-level comparative analysis with the iterative pattern matching algorithm.

6.1   Limitations and Future Work

There are a lot of future possibilities in our JEFL platform. Continuing in the current line of development, we still need to experiment on the other four libraries and additionally explore similarity discovery of not only constants but also terms. We could also explore the effect of vector initialization in our discovery algorithm. To go deeper we could implement custom "dragging" and "repelling" steps using geometric manipulation and intersperse these custom steps with SGD updates. We have focused on one pair of libraries, which could be extended to an embedding of multiple libraries combined. This would provide further experiment opportunities. We also plan to use the newly discovered samples from JEFL to do tasks such as conjecturing [7], cross-browsing [25], and stronger learning for hammers [5]. Last but not least, we hope there could be use cases to integrate our pipeline into an actual proof assistant and see improved formalization productivity.

Acknowledgements. We are largely indebted to Thibault Gauthier for his work on alignments and the various data exports that we re-use. We thank Josef Urban for the Mizar export and his invitation to Prague to discuss research. We also thank Tomáš Mikolov for valuable insights for the current work. This work was supported by the ERC grant no. 714034 *SMART* and by the *University of Innsbruck PhD scholarship*.

References

1. Bojanowski, P., Grave, E., Joulin, A., Mikolov, T.: Enriching word vectors with subword information. Trans. Assoc. Comput. Linguist. **5**, 135–146 (2017). https://aclanthology.org/Q17-1010
2. Bortin, M., Lüth, C.: Structured formal development with quotient types in Isabelle/HOL. In: Autexier, S., et al. (eds.) CICM 2010. LNCS (LNAI), vol. 6167, pp. 34–48. Springer, Heidelberg (2010). https://doi.org/10.1007/978-3-642-14128-7_5
3. Carlisle, D., Davenport, J., Dewar, M., Hur, N., Naylor, W.: Conversion between MathMl and OpenMath. Technical Report 24.969, The OpenMath Society (2001)
4. Gauthier, T., Kaliszyk, C.: Matching concepts across HOL libraries. In: Watt, S.M., Davenport, J.H., Sexton, A.P., Sojka, P., Urban, J. (eds.) CICM 2014. LNCS (LNAI), vol. 8543, pp. 267–281. Springer, Cham (2014). https://doi.org/10.1007/978-3-319-08434-3_20
5. Gauthier, T., Kaliszyk, C.: Sharing HOL4 and HOL light proof knowledge. In: Davis, M., Fehnker, A., McIver, A., Voronkov, A. (eds.) LPAR 2015. LNCS, vol. 9450, pp. 372–386. Springer, Heidelberg (2015). https://doi.org/10.1007/978-3-662-48899-7_26
6. Gauthier, T., Kaliszyk, C.: Aligning concepts across proof assistant libraries. J. Symbol. Comput. **90**, 89–123 (2019). https://doi.org/10.1016/j.jsc.2018.04.005
7. Gauthier, T., Kaliszyk, C., Urban, J.: Initial experiments with statistical conjecturing over large formal corpora. In: Kohlhase, A. (ed.) Work in Progress at the Conference on Intelligent Computer Mathematics 2016 (CICM-WiP 2016), CEUR, vol. 1785, pp. 219–228. CEUR-WS.org (2016)
8. Grabowski, A., Korniłowicz, A., Naumowicz, A.: Mizar in a nutshell. J. Formalized Reasoning **3**(2), 153–245 (2010). https://doi.org/10.6092/issn.1972-5787/1980
9. Grover, A., Leskovec, J.: node2vec: scalable feature learning for networks (2016)
10. Hales, T.C.: Introduction to the Flyspeck project. In: Coquand, T., Lombardi, H., Roy, M.F. (eds.) Mathematics, Algorithms, Proofs, No. 05021 in Dagstuhl Seminar Proceedings, Internationales Begegnungs- und Forschungszentrum für Informatik (IBFI), Schloss Dagstuhl, Germany, Dagstuhl, Germany, pp. 1–11 (2006). http://drops.dagstuhl.de/opus/volltexte/2006/432
11. Harrison, J.: HOL light: an overview. In: Berghofer, S., Nipkow, T., Urban, C., Wenzel, M. (eds.) TPHOLs 2009. LNCS, vol. 5674, pp. 60–66. Springer, Heidelberg (2009). https://doi.org/10.1007/978-3-642-03359-9_4
12. Heras, J., Komendantskaya, E.: Proof pattern search in Coq/SSReflect. CoRR abs/1402.0081 (2014). http://arxiv.org/abs/1402.0081

13. Huet, G.P., Herbelin, H.: 30 years of research and development around Coq. In: Jagannathan, S., Sewell, P. (eds.) ACM Symposium on Principles of Programming Languages, POPL 2014, pp. 249–250. ACM (2014). https://doi.org/10.1145/2535838.2537848

14. Hurd, J.: The OpenTheory standard theory library. In: Bobaru, M., Havelund, K., Holzmann, G.J., Joshi, R. (eds.) NFM 2011. LNCS, vol. 6617, pp. 177–191. Springer, Heidelberg (2011). https://doi.org/10.1007/978-3-642-20398-5_14

15. Joulin, A., Grave, E., Bojanowski, P., Mikolov, T.: Bag of tricks for efficient text classification. In: Proceedings of the 15th Conference of the European Chapter of the Association for Computational Linguistics: Volume 2, Short Papers, Valencia, Spain, pp. 427–431. Association for Computational Linguistics, April 2017. https://www.aclweb.org/anthology/E17-2068

16. Kaliszyk, C., Krauss, A.: Scalable LCF-style proof translation. In: Blazy, S., Paulin-Mohring, C., Pichardie, D. (eds.) ITP 2013. LNCS, vol. 7998, pp. 51–66. Springer, Heidelberg (2013). https://doi.org/10.1007/978-3-642-39634-2_7

17. Kaliszyk, C., Urban, J.: Lemma mining over HOL Light. In: LPAR, pp. 503–517 (2013)

18. Kaliszyk, C., Urban, J.: Learning-assisted automated reasoning with Flyspeck. J. Autom. Reasoning **53**(2), 173–213 (2014). https://doi.org/10.1007/s10817-014-9303-3

19. Kaliszyk, C., Urban, J.: HOL(y)Hammer: online ATP service for HOL Light. Math. Comput. Sci. **9**(1), 5–22 (2014). https://doi.org/10.1007/s11786-014-0182-0

20. Keller, C., Werner, B.: Importing HOL light into Coq. In: Kaufmann, M., Paulson, L.C. (eds.) ITP 2010. LNCS, vol. 6172, pp. 307–322. Springer, Heidelberg (2010). https://doi.org/10.1007/978-3-642-14052-5_22

21. Klein, G.: Proof engineering considered essential. In: Jones, C., Pihlajasaari, P., Sun, J. (eds.) FM 2014. LNCS, vol. 8442, pp. 16–21. Springer, Cham (2014). https://doi.org/10.1007/978-3-319-06410-9_2

22. McCarthy, J.: Recursive functions symbolic expressions and their computation by machine, Part I. Commun. ACM **3**(4), 184–195 (1960). https://doi.org/10/fvx5pv. http://dl.acm.org/citation.cfm?id=367177.367199. zSCC: NoCitationData[s0]. ISBN 0001-0782

23. Mikolov, T., Chen, K., Corrado, G., Dean, J.: Efficient estimation of word representations in vector space. In: Bengio, Y., LeCun, Y. (eds.) 1st International Conference on Learning Representations, ICLR 2013, Scottsdale, Arizona, USA, 2–4 May 2013, Workshop Track Proceedings (2013). http://arxiv.org/abs/1301.3781

24. Mikolov, T., Sutskever, I., Chen, K., Corrado, G.S., Dean, J.: Distributed representations of words and phrases and their compositionality. In: Burges, C.J.C., Bottou, L., Welling, M., Ghahramani, Z., Weinberger, K.Q. (eds.) Advances in Neural Information Processing Systems. vol. 26. Curran Associates, Inc. (2013). https://proceedings.neurips.cc/paper/2013/file/9aa42b31882ec039965f3c4923ce901b-Paper.pdf

25. Müller, D., Gauthier, T., Kaliszyk, C., Kohlhase, M., Rabe, F.: Classification of alignments between concepts of formal mathematical systems. In: Geuvers, H., England, M., Hasan, O., Rabe, F., Teschke, O. (eds.) CICM 2017. LNCS (LNAI), vol. 10383, pp. 83–98. Springer, Cham (2017). https://doi.org/10.1007/978-3-319-62075-6_7

26. Obua, S., Skalberg, S.: Importing HOL into Isabelle/HOL. In: Furbach, U., Shankar, N. (eds.) IJCAR 2006. LNCS (LNAI), vol. 4130, pp. 298–302. Springer, Heidelberg (2006). https://doi.org/10.1007/11814771_27

27. Paulson, L.C.: Isabelle: the next seven hundred theorem provers. In: Lusk, E., Overbeek, R. (eds.) CADE 1988. LNCS, vol. 310, pp. 772–773. Springer, Heidelberg (1988). https://doi.org/10.1007/BFb0012891

28. Pennington, J., Socher, R., Manning, C.D.: GloVe: global vectors for word representation. In: EMNLP, vol. 14, pp. 1532–1543 (2014)

29. Perozzi, B., Al-Rfou, R., Skiena, S.: DeepWalk: online learning of social representations. In: Proceedings of the 20th ACM SIGKDD International Conference on Knowledge Discovery and Data Mining, August 2014. https://doi.org/10.1145/2623330.2623732

30. Rabe, F.: The MMT API: a generic MKM system. In: Carette, J., Aspinall, D., Lange, C., Sojka, P., Windsteiger, W. (eds.) CICM 2013. LNCS (LNAI), vol. 7961, pp. 339–343. Springer, Heidelberg (2013). https://doi.org/10.1007/978-3-642-39320-4_25

31. Řehůřek, R., Sojka, P.: Software framework for topic modelling with large corpora. In: Proceedings of the LREC 2010 Workshop on New Challenges for NLP Frameworks, ELRA, Valletta, Malta, pp. 45–50, May 2010. http://is.muni.cz/publication/884893/en

32. So, C.M., Watt, S.M.: On the conversion between content MathMl and OpenMath. In: Proceedings of the Conference on the Communicating Mathematics in the Digital Era (CMDE 2006), pp. 169–182 (2006)

33. Sutcliffe, G.: The TPTP world - infrastructure for automated reasoning. In: LPAR (Dakar), pp. 1–12 (2010)

34. Urban, J.: MoMM - fast interreduction and retrieval in large libraries of formalized mathematics. Int. J. Artif. Intell. Tools **15**(1), 109–130 (2006). http://ktiml.mff.cuni.cz/~urban/MoMM/momm.ps

35. Urban, J.: MPTP 0.2: design, implementation, and initial experiments. J. Autom. Reasoning **37**(1–2), 21–43 (2006). https://doi.org/10.1007/s10817-006-9032-3

Machine Learning

Fast and Slow Enigmas and Parental Guidance

Zarathustra A. Goertzel[1(✉)], Karel Chvalovský[1], Jan Jakubův[1,2],
Miroslav Olšák[2], and Josef Urban[1]

[1] Czech Technical University in Prague, Prague, Czech Republic
[2] University of Innsbruck, Innsbruck, Austria

Abstract. We describe several additions to the ENIGMA system that guides clause selection in the E automated theorem prover. First, we significantly speed up its neural guidance by adding server-based GPU evaluation. The second addition is motivated by fast weight-based rejection filters that are currently used in systems like E and Prover9. Such systems can be made more intelligent by instead training fast versions of ENIGMA that implement more intelligent pre-filtering. This results in combinations of trainable fast and slow thinking that improves over both the fast-only and slow-only methods. The third addition is based on "judging the children by their parents", i.e., possibly rejecting an inference before it produces a clause. This is motivated by standard evolutionary mechanisms, where there is always a cost to producing all possible offsprings in the current population. This saves time by not evaluating all clauses by more expensive methods and provides a complementary view of the generated clauses. The methods are evaluated on a large benchmark coming from the Mizar Mathematical Library, showing good improvements over the state of the art.

1 Introduction: The Fast and The Smart

Throughout the history of automated theorem proving, there have been two very different approaches to strengthening automated theorem provers (ATPs). The first one (*the fast*) relies on better engineering, such as improving the indexing for inference and reduction rules and on optimized low-level implementations. The gains achieved in this way can be quite high [9,15,22,28,31,38].

The second approach (*the smart*) relies on advanced strategies and heuristics for guiding the proof search. This includes methods using extensive previous knowledge, e.g., various kinds of *symbolic* machine learning, such as the *hints* method in Otter [37] and Prover9 [19], and its *watchlist* [26] and *proofwatch* [6] variants implemented in E [29,30]. With the recent advent of *statistical* machine learning (ML), a number of knowledge-based ATP-guiding methods have been created [3,10,11,17]. This is done by compiling (extracting, compressing, generalizing) the previous knowledge into statistical ML *predictors* (models) that are then used to predict the usefulness of inference steps in the proof search.

© Springer Nature Switzerland AG 2021
B. Konev and G. Reger (Eds.): FroCoS 2021, LNAI 12941, pp. 173–191, 2021.
https://doi.org/10.1007/978-3-030-86205-3_10

The *smart* approaches, while potentially sophisticated and AI-motivated, may incur prohibitively high costs in their prediction modules, in particular when naively implemented [21,36]. This can make them inferior in practice to faster alternative approaches, such as various kinds of randomization [25] and building of portfolios of complementary fast strategies [13,27,35]. This issue is getting increasingly important as deep learning (DL) is used for ATP guidance, sometimes with large cloud-based DL-predictors running on specialized hardware that hides the amount of resources used. It also complicates rigorous comparisons in established ATP competitions such as CASC/LTB [32,33].

Another issue related to the use of expensive predictors can be summarized as the *explore-exploit tradeoff* introduced in reinforcement learning research [5]. In short, running an ATP guided by a 100-times slower predictor that is only slightly better (possibly due to insufficient previous data for learning) will not only typically solve fewer problems due to much more expensive backtracking but also generate much less data for training the predictor in the next iteration. Hence, given a global time limit allowing many proving/learning iterations over a large set of related problems in a realistic problem-solving setup such as CASC LTB, a faster predictor will in the same time generate much more data to learn from. This in turn often leads to better performance: a slightly weaker ML system trained on much more data will often ultimately outperform a slightly stronger ML system trained on much less data.

1.1   Contributions

In this work we develop combinations of the fast(er) and smart(er) approaches in the context of the learning-guided ENIGMA framework. After giving a summary of ENIGMA in Sect. 2, Sect. 3 introduces our new methods.[1]

First, Sect. 3.1 describes a large increase in the speed of neural guidance in ENIGMA. We add an efficient server-based evaluation that uses dedicated GPUs instead of a CPU. When using four commodity GPU cards, this speeds up the neural evaluation of the clauses about four times in real time.

Section 3.2 describes the second addition, motivated by fast weight-based rejection filters used in systems such as E and Prover9. Such methods can be replaced by training fast predictors that implement more intelligent pre-filtering. In the context of ENIGMA, fast(er) is easy to implement by variously parameterized predictors based on gradient-boosted decision trees (GBDTs). Slow(er) models are in those based on graph neural networks (GNNs).

Section 3.3 describes the third addition based on "judging the children by their parents", i.e., possibly rejecting an inference before it even produces a clause. This grants the machine learning methods greater control of the proof search and saves time by not evaluating all clauses by more expensive methods, also providing a complementary view of the generated clauses.

---

[1] The E and ENIGMA versions used in this paper can be found at https://github. com/ai4reason/enigma-gpu-server.

In Sect. 4 we describe the experimental setting and a large evaluation corpus based on the Mizar Mathematical Library and its MPTP translation. We also present our baseline methods there. Section 5 evaluates the new methods and shows that even in relatively low time limits the methods provide good performance improvements over the previous versions of ENIGMA.

2 Saturation Proving and Its Guidance by ENIGMA

State-of-the-art automated theorem provers (ATP), such as E, Prover9, and Vampire [20], are based on the saturation loop paradigm and the *given clause algorithm* [24]. The input problem, in first-order logic (FOF), is translated into a refutationally equivalent set of clauses, and a search for contradiction is initiated. The ATP maintains two sets of clauses: *processed* (initially empty) and *unprocessed* (initially the input clauses). At each iteration, one unprocessed clause is selected (*given*), and all of the possible inferences with all the processed clauses are generated (typically using resolution, paramodulation, etc.), extending the unprocessed clause set. The selected clause is then moved to the processed clause set. Hence the invariant holds that all the mutual inferences among the processed clauses have been computed.

The selection of the "right" given clause is known to be vital for the success of the proof search. The ENIGMA system [3,7,10–12,14] applies various machine learning methods for given clause selection, learning from a large number of previous successful proof searches. The training data consists of clauses processed during a proof search, labeling the clauses that appear in the discovered proof as *positive*, and the other (thus unnecessary) processed clauses as *negative*.

The first ENIGMA [11] used fast linear classification [4] with hand-crafted clause *features* based on symbol names, representing clauses by fixed-length numeric vectors. Follow-up versions [3,7,12,14] introduced context-based clause evaluation and fast dimensionality reduction by feature hashing, and employed Gradient Boosting Decision Trees (GBDTs), implemented by the XGBoost and LightGBM systems [2,18]), and Recursive Neural Networks (implemented in PyTorch) as the underlying machine learning methods.

The latest version, ENIGMA Anonymous [10], abstracts from name-based clause representations and provides the best results so far both with GBDTs and Graph Neural Networks (GNNs) [1]. For GBDTs, clauses are again represented by fixed-length vectors based on syntax trees and anonymization is achieved by replacing symbol names by their arities. Our GNN [23] represents clauses by variable-length numeric tensors encapsulating syntax trees as graph structures with symbol names omitted. ENIGMA-GNN evaluates new clauses jointly in larger batches (*queries*) and with respect to a large number of already selected clauses (*context*). The GNN predicts the collectively most useful subset of the clauses in several rounds (*layers*) of message passing. This means that approximative inference rounds done by the GNN are efficiently interleaved with precise symbolic inference rounds done inside E. The GBDT and GNN versions have so far been used separately and only with CPU-based evaluation. In this work, we add efficiently implemented GPU-based evaluation for the GNN and start to use the two methods cooperatively.

3   Cooperative Filtering: Faster and Smarter

The set of generated clauses in saturation-style ATPs typically grows quadratically with the number of processed clauses. Each new given clause is combined with all compatible previously processed clauses, followed by (possibly expensive) evaluation of all newly generated clauses. In particular, the GNN predictors typically incur a significant evaluation cost per clause. The quadratic growth means that longer ENIGMA-GNN runs may get very slow.

To avoid large memory consumption and similar expensive evaluations in long hint-based Prover9 runs (often taking several days) on the AIM problems [19], Veroff has used weight-based filtering, discarding immediately clauses that reach a certain weight limit. This often helps, but counterexamples are common, and in practice, such schemes often need to be made more complicated.[2] The three methods that we introduce below are instead targeting this issue by using faster learning-based filtering.

3.1   Fast GNN Evaluation Using a GPU Server

The main weakness of the GNN version of ENIGMA is its slow clause evaluation. In our previous ENIGMA Anonymous experiments [10], we used GPUs for model training, but during the proof search we evaluated the clauses on a single CPU (per each E prover's instance). This was partly to provide a fair comparison with GBDTs which we also evaluate on a single CPU, but also to avoid large start-up overheads when loading the neural models to a GPU and running with low time limits. Here we instead develop a persistent multi-threaded GPU server that evaluates clauses from multiple E prover runs using multiple GPUs.

The modification is as follows. During the proof search, after computing the tensor representation of the newly generated clauses, an E Prover client sends the tensors (in a JSON text format) over a network socket to a remote server. The client then waits for the server response which provides the scores (GNN evaluations) of the new clauses. This means that the clients are inactive for some time and more of them are needed to saturate the CPUs on the machines (see the detailed experimental discussion in Sect. 5.1). This is typically not a problem due to many instances of E running with different premises and parameters in hammering and CASC LTB scenarios, as well as in many iterations of the learning/proving loop that attempt to solve harder and harder problems over a large problem set.

The remote server, written in Python, is launched before the E clients, loading the GNN model to the (multiple) GPUs in advance. Once the model is loaded

---

[2] We thank Bob Veroff for explaining that this is done by gradually lowering the weight limit inside a single longer Prover9 run, and by raising the initial weight limit and slowing down the weight reduction scheme across multiple Prover9 runs.

to the GPUs, the server accepts tensor queries on a designated port, evaluates them on the GPUs, and sends the clause evaluations back to the clients. In more detail, the server is parameterized by the number N (our default is 28) of independent worker threads, the batch size b (our default is 8) and the waiting time T (our default is 0.01 s). The client queries are accumulated in a shared queue that the N worker threads process. Each worker operates in two steps. First, it checks the queue, and if it contains less than b queries, it waits for T seconds. Then it evaluates the first b queries on the queue, or less if there are not enough of them available. Note that when the worker waits or evaluates queries, other workers can process the queue.

The advantage is that the single GNN server amortizes the startup costs and handles queries of many E prover clients and distributes them across multiple GPUs. This means that much larger batches (containing clauses coming from multiple clients) are typically loaded onto the GPUs, amortizing also the relatively high cost of communication with the GPUs. This results in large real time speed-ups over the CPU version, see Sect. 5.1. In our experiments, we run the GPU server and the E clients on the same machine. Hence the network overhead is low because the communication is done over a local loopback interface. In the case of a remote connection, the architecture would benefit from data compression and/or binary data formats to decrease the network overhead. See Sect. 5.1 for the current average sizes of the data exchanged.

3.2   Best of Both Worlds: GNN with GBDT Filtering

While the GPU server evaluation provides a considerable speed up, the evaluation of clauses on a GPU is still relatively costly compared to the GBDT clause evaluation. Hence we develop the following combination of the two methods, where the GBDT is used to pre-filter the clauses for the GNN.

In more detail, the set of clauses to be evaluated by the GNN is first evaluated by a fast GBDT model.[3] The GBDT model assigns a score between 0 and 1 to each clause, and only the clauses with scores higher than a selected threshold are sent to the GPU server for evaluation by the GNN. The clauses which are filtered out by the GBDT model are assigned a very high weight inside E Prover, which makes them unlikely to ever be selected for processing. This way we prevent E from incorrectly reporting satisfiability when the good clauses run out.

Several requirements must be met for this filtering to be effective. First, the GBDT filtering model must be small enough so that the evaluation is fast, yet precise enough so that the more important clauses are not mistakenly filtered out too often. Second, the score threshold must be properly fine-tuned, which typically requires experimental grid search on smaller samples. Experiments with a GBDT pre-filtering for a GNN are presented in Sect. 5.2.

---

[3] This feature is implemented for the LightGBM models, which seem more easily tunable for such tasks.

3.3   Parental Guidance: Pruning the Given Clause Loop

We define *(clausal) parental guidance* as clause evaluation based on the features of the parents of a clause rather than on the clause itself. Such fast rejection filters often help: in nature, mating is typically highly restricted by various features of parents (e.g., their age, appearance, finances, etc.). Similarly, it does not often happen that clauses from very different parts of mathematics (e.g., differential geometry and graph theory) need to be resolved.

Parental guidance can be seen as "just another filter" of the generated clauses, but its motivation is more radical: The "good old"[4] given clause loop [24] insists, for completeness reasons, on performing all possible inferences between the processed clauses and the given clause, typically leading to a quadratic growth of the set of generated clauses. However, if we had perfect information about the proof, this would be wasteful and could be replaced by just performing the inferences needed for the proof in each given clause loop. With parental guidance, we instead propose to prune the given clause loop in a soft way: a trained predictor judges the likelihood of the particular inference being needed for the proof. When an inference is deemed useless, the clause is still generated but immediately *frozen* so that it does not have to be evaluated by additional heuristics.

The parental guidance is implemented using GBDTs (our *parental model*), and the filter is directly put inside E's given clause loop as follows. When E selects a given clause g, E uses term indexes to efficiently determine which clauses can be combined with g to generate new clauses. After generating the clauses, E performs simplifications, removes trivial clauses, evaluates the remaining clauses with the clause evaluation functions, and inserts them into the unprocessed set. The call to the parental model is executed after the clause generation and prior to the simplifications. Clauses generated by paramodulation, which also implements resolution in E, have two parents, and these are judged by the parental model. Clauses whose parents are jointly scored below a chosen threshold are put into the *freezer* set to avoid impairing the completeness of the proof search. Clauses with good parents continue on to the unprocessed set. In case the unprocessed set becomes empty, the frozen clauses are revived and treated as usual.

Note that a naive alternative way to implement parental guidance would be to evaluate each given clause's compatibility with all previously processed clauses. This would, however, result in many unnecessary GBDT queries and evaluations. Instead, our approach allows E's indexing to find the typically much smaller set of potential inferences and to limit the parental evaluation to them.[5]

There are various ways to represent the pair of parent clauses for the learning of the parental model. In this work, we evaluate two methods:

---

[4] The given clause loop is almost 50 years old as of 2021.

[5] The efficiency boost obtained by using intelligent indexing is analogous to the boost obtained by using our structure-aware GNN for context-based neural clause selection (Sect. 2) rather than off-the-shelf Transformer models. The latter would quadratically consider interactions of all symbols in the context and query clauses, decreasing the evaluation speed by orders of magnitude, resulting in a very inefficient prover.

1. $\mathcal{P}_{\text{fuse}}$ merges the feature vectors of the parent clauses into one vector, typically by simply adding the feature counts[6]
2. $\mathcal{P}_{\text{cat}}$ concatenates the feature vectors of the parent clauses to preserve their information in full.

An interesting future alternative is to include the difference of the parents' feature vectors in addition to their union and concatenation, which allows the GBDT to choose the most informative features.

4 Experimental Setting and Baselines

4.1 Evaluation Problems and Training Data

All our experiments are performed[7] on a large benchmark of 57 880 problems[8] originating from the Mizar Mathematical Library (MML) [16] exported to first-order logic by MPTP [34]. We make use of our ongoing extensive evaluation of many AI/TP methods over this corpus[9] that measures the overall improvement on this large dataset over the last similar evaluation done in [16]. In these experiments we have significantly extended our previously published results [10].[10] Proofs of 73.5% (more than 40k) Mizar problems have been so far found by learning-guided ATPs, and numerous GBDT and GNN models for ATP guidance have been trained.

In that experiment, all Mizar problems[11] are split (in a 90-5-5% ratio) into 3 subsets: (1) 52k problems for *training*, (2) 2896 problems for *development*, and (3) 2896 problems for final evaluation (*holdout*). We use this split here, and additionally we use a random subset of 5792 of the training problems to speed up the training of various experimental methods.

4.2 Baseline ENIGMA Models

Out of the 52k training problems, we were previously able to prove more than 36k problems, obtaining varied numbers of proofs for each problem (ranging from 1 to hundreds). On these 36k problems we train our baseline GBDT and GNN predictors. To balance the contribution of different problems during the training of the predictors, we randomly choose at most 3 proofs for every proved training problem. This yields a set of about 100k proofs, denoted further as the *large* (training) set. When limited to the 5792 random subset of the training problems, this yields 11 748 proofs, denoted further as the *small* training set.

---

[6] In some special cases of features, we instead take their maximum/minimum.

[7] On a server with 36 hyperthreading Intel(R) Xeon(R) Gold 6140 CPU @ 2.30 GHz cores, 755 GB of memory, and 4 NVIDIA GeForce GTX 1080 Ti GPUs.

[8] http://grid01.ciirc.cvut.cz/~mptp/1147/MPTP2/problems_small_consist.tar.gz.

[9] https://github.com/ai4reason/ATP_Proofs.

[10] The publication of this large evaluation is in preparation.

[11] http://grid01.ciirc.cvut.cz/~mptp/Mizar_eval_final_split.

On the *large* set we train the first baseline predictor denoted by $\mathcal{D}_{\text{large}}$. This is a GBDT model (implemented by the LightGBM framework) trained using the ENIGMA Anonymous clause representation (Sect. 2). The model consists of 150 decision trees of depth 40 with 2048 leaves. This model was selected as it performed best in our previous experiments with standard GBDTs, being able to prove 1377 of the *holdout* problems using a 5 s limit per problem. Additionally, we train another model $\mathcal{D}_{\text{small}}$ only on the *small* set of training problems. The model $\mathcal{D}_{\text{small}}$ is a LightGBM model with 150 trees of depth 30 and with 9728 leaves. The training of $\mathcal{D}_{\text{large}}$ took around 27 min and the training of $\mathcal{D}_{\text{small}}$ around 10 min, both on 30 CPUs. These are relatively low and practical times compared to the training of neural networks.

We also train baseline GNN models on the same data, denoted $\mathcal{G}_{\text{large}}$ and $\mathcal{G}_{\text{small}}$ respectively. The training of $\mathcal{G}_{\text{large}}$ for 45 epochs takes about 15 h on the full set of 100k proofs on a high-end NVIDIA V100 GPU card.[12] It would likely take days when training with CPUs only. We choose for the ATP evaluation the (39th) snapshot that achieves both the best loss (0.2063) and the best weighted accuracy (0.9147) on 5% of the data that we do not use for training. The training of $\mathcal{G}_{\text{small}}$ for 100 epochs takes about 4 h on the *small* set using the same GPU card. We choose for the ATP evaluation the (56th) snapshot that achieves the best loss (0.2988) on 5% of the data that we do not use for training. The weighted accuracy on this set is 0.8685, which is also among the highest values.

In the evaluation we run all our baseline ENIGMA predictors in an equal combination with a strong non-learning E strategy $\mathcal{S}$. This means that the processed clauses are selected in (equal) turns by ENIGMA and by $\mathcal{S}$. This *coop* mode has typically worked better than the *solo* mode, where only the ENIGMA predictor is doing the clause selection.

4.3   Training of the Parental GBDT Models

The training data for the parental guidance models are generated by running E using either $\mathcal{D}_{\text{large}}$ or $\mathcal{G}_{\text{large}}$ on the 52k *training* problems with a 30 s time limit and by printing the derivation of all clauses generated during the proof search.[13] We considered the following two schemes to classify the good pairs of parents and to generate the training data:

1. $\mathcal{P}^{\text{proof}}$ classifies parents of only the proof clauses as *positive* and all other generated clauses as *negative*.
2. $\mathcal{P}^{\text{given}}$ classifies parents of all processed (selected) clauses as *positive* and the unprocessed generated clauses as *negative*.

The rationale behind $\mathcal{P}^{\text{proof}}$ is that every non-proof clause should be pruned if possible. The rationale behind $\mathcal{P}^{\text{given}}$ is that if an effective clause selection strategy, such as $\mathcal{D}_{\text{large}}$, predicted a clause to be useful, then it is probably worth

---

[12] We use the same GNN hyper-parameters as in [10,23] with the exception of the number of *layers* that we increase here to 10.

[13] Using E's option "`--full-deriv`".

generating. However, such data may be confusing as it includes clauses that did not contribute to the proof.

If a pair of parents produces both positive and negative clauses, we consider the pair positive in our implementation. However, this does not happen very often. Based on a survey on the *small* set labeled according to $\mathcal{P}_{\mathsf{fuse}}^{\mathsf{proof}}$, 73% of the problems have no conflict. There are 1519 parents of both positive and negative clauses, 53 359 are positive, and 6086 414 are negative. Under $\mathcal{P}_{\mathsf{fuse}}^{\mathsf{given}}$, 9798 of the parents are mixed, 854 778 are positive, and 5178 592 are negative. In either case, the primary learning task is to identify and prune as many negative clauses as possible without filtering a necessary proof clause by mistake.

One parameter to experimentally tune is the *pos-neg ratio* used in the GBDT training: the ratio of positive and negative examples. The pos-neg ratio is 1:192 over the *large* $\mathcal{P}_{\mathsf{fuse}}^{\mathsf{proof}}$ data, which is more than ten times more than the ratio of the training data for $\mathcal{D}_{\mathsf{large}}$ and $\mathcal{G}_{\mathsf{large}}$. Hence, reducing the pos-neg ratio by randomly sampling negative examples could further boost the training performance.

The parental guidance models are trained using GBDTs. Trained models are evaluated in combination with the GBDT or GNN clause evaluation heuristic using either the $\mathcal{D}_{\mathsf{large}}$ or $\mathcal{G}_{\mathsf{large}}$ model, see Sect. 5.3.

5   Evaluation of the New Methods

5.1   Speedup by Using a GPU Server

First we measure the speedup obtained by evaluating the ENIGMA GNN calls on a separate GPU server. To avoid network latency and for a cleaner comparison, we run both the clients (E/ENIGMA) and the GPU server on the same machine equipped with four NVIDIA GeForce GTX 1080 GPU cards and 36 hyperthreading CPU cores. We configure the server to use all four GPU cards. Its other important parameters are the number of worker threads and the batch size. We experimentally set them to 28 and 8, and we use $\mathcal{G}_{\mathsf{large}}$ for all proof runs.

Comparison of the CPU-only and GPU-server versions is complicated by the fact that the server-based GNN evaluations do not count towards the CPU time taken by E, as reported by the operating system. Still, a comparison using the CPU time is interesting and we include it, using 30 and 60 s CPU limits for the CPU-only version, and a 30 s CPU limit for the client-server version.

Another way to compare the two is by using parallelization, i.e., running many instances of E in parallel. In the client-server version the instances talk to the GPU server simultaneously. We saturate the machine's CPUs fully for both versions, and run for approximately equal overall real time over the development and holdout sets. This is roughly achieved by using 60 s time limit with 70-fold parallelization for the CPU version, and 30 s time limit with 160-fold parallelization for the client/server version. The CPU version then takes about 27.5 min to finish on the 2896 problems, while the client-server takes about 34 min to finish. Table 1 compares the number of solved problems on the development and holdout sets. The GPU server improves the performance on the development resp. holdout sets by 9.5% resp. 11.5%.

We also compare the average number of generated clauses on the problems that timed out in both versions. In the 60 s CPU version it is 16 835, while in the 30 s client-server it is 63 305. This is a considerable speedup, achieved by employing the additional custom hardware—our four GPU cards. The average number of GNN queries in the 1358 problems that timed out in the 30 s GPU server runs is 243.8, and on average the communication with the GPU server took 155 MB in a timed-out problem. A single GNN query took on average 637 kB.

Table 1. Comparison of the CPU-only GNN ENIGMA with the client-server version using GPUs. All runs are evaluating $\mathcal{G}_{\text{large}}$ on the whole development (D) and holdout (H) datasets. The percentage improvement is computed over the 60 s CPU version that corresponds more closely in real time to the client-server version. All runs use queries of size 256 and contexts of size 768.

Set	Model	Method	Time	Solved	Set	Model	Method	Time	Solved
D	$\mathcal{G}_{\text{large}}$	CPU	30	1311	H	$\mathcal{G}_{\text{large}}$	CPU	30	1301
D	$\mathcal{G}_{\text{large}}$	CPU	60	1380	H	$\mathcal{G}_{\text{large}}$	CPU	60	1371
D	$\mathcal{G}_{\text{large}}$	GPU	30	1511 (+9.5%)	H	$\mathcal{G}_{\text{large}}$	GPU	30	1529 (+11.5%)

5.2 Evaluation of 2-Phase ENIGMA

Small GBDT and Small GNN: In the first experiment we use the GBDT and GNN predictors $\mathcal{D}_{\text{small}}$ and $\mathcal{G}_{\text{small}}$ trained on the *small* subset of the training dataset. We first do a grid search over the parameters on a smaller dataset of 300 development problems. Then we evaluate the best parameters on the development and holdout sets and compare them with the standalone performance of $\mathcal{G}_{\text{small}}$, which is the stronger of the two baselines (Table 2). The best combined methods are then evaluated also in 60 s. This gives a relatively fair real-time comparison to the standalone GNN, because the reported CPU times do not include the time taken by the GPU server.[14]

Our best combined method solves (in real time) 10.4%, resp. 9.0%, more problems on the development, resp. holdout, set than the standalone GNN. This is a significant improvement, which will likely get even more visible with higher time limits, because of the quadratic growth of the set of generated clauses. The performance improvement over the standalone GBDT model is even larger.

---

[14] We have made this estimate based on a comparison of real and CPU times done on a set of problems that time out in both methods.

Table 2. Final evaluation of the best combination of $\mathcal{D}_{small}$ with $\mathcal{G}_{small}$ on the whole development (D) and holdout (H) datasets.

Set	Model	Thresh.	Time	Query	Context	Solved
D	$\mathcal{G}_{small}$	–	30	256	768	1251
D	$\mathcal{D}_{small}$	–	30	–	–	1011
D	$\mathcal{D}_{small}+\mathcal{G}_{small}$	0.01	60	512	1024	1381 (+10.4%)
D	$\mathcal{D}_{small}+\mathcal{G}_{small}$	0.03	60	512	1024	1371 (+9.6%)
D	$\mathcal{D}_{small}+\mathcal{G}_{small}$	0.03	30	512	1024	1341 (+7.2%)
D	$\mathcal{D}_{small}+\mathcal{G}_{small}$	0.01	30	512	1024	1339 (+7.0%)
H	$\mathcal{G}_{small}$	–	30	256	768	1277
H	$\mathcal{D}_{small}$	–	30	–	–	1002
H	$\mathcal{D}_{small}+\mathcal{G}_{small}$	0.01	60	512	1024	1392 (+9.0%)
H	$\mathcal{D}_{small}+\mathcal{G}_{small}$	0.03	60	512	1024	1387 (+8.6%)
H	$\mathcal{D}_{small}+\mathcal{G}_{small}$	0.01	30	512	1024	1361 (+6.6%)
H	$\mathcal{D}_{small}+\mathcal{G}_{small}$	0.03	30	512	1024	1353 (+6.0%)

Large GBDT and Small GNN: In the next experiment, we want to see how much the training of the less expensive model (GBDT) on more data helps. I.e., we replace $\mathcal{D}_{small}$ with $\mathcal{D}_{large}$ and keep $\mathcal{G}_{small}$. This has practical applications in real time, because cheaper ML predictors such as GBDTs are faster to train than more expensive ones such as the GNN. We again first do a grid search over the parameters on a small dataset of 300 development problems. Then we evaluate the best models on the development and holdout sets and compare them with the standalone performance of $\mathcal{D}_{large}$ and $\mathcal{G}_{small}$ (Table 3). The best combined methods are then again evaluated also in 60 s, which makes it comparable in real time to the standalone GNN model.

Table 3. Final evaluation of the best combination of $\mathcal{D}_{large}$ and $\mathcal{G}_{small}$ on the whole development (D) and holdout (H) datasets.

Set	Model	Thresh.	Time	Query	Context	Solved
D	$\mathcal{G}_{small}$	–	30	256	768	1251
D	$\mathcal{D}_{large}$	–	30	–	–	1397
D	$\mathcal{D}_{large}+\mathcal{G}_{small}$	0.3	60	2048	768	1527 (+9.3%)
D	$\mathcal{D}_{large}+\mathcal{G}_{small}$	0.3	30	2048	768	1496 (+7.1%)
H	$\mathcal{G}_{small}$	–	30	256	768	1277
H	$\mathcal{D}_{large}$	–	30	–	–	1390
H	$\mathcal{D}_{large}+\mathcal{G}_{small}$	0.3	60	2048	768	1494 (+7.5%)
H	$\mathcal{D}_{large}+\mathcal{G}_{small}$	0.3	30	2048	768	1467 (+5.5%)

Our best combined method solves (in CPU time) 7.1%, resp. 5.5%, more problems on the development, resp. holdout, set than the standalone GBDT. For the GNN, this is (in real time) 9.3% resp. 7.5%. These are smaller gains than in the previous $\mathcal{D}_{small} + \mathcal{G}_{small}$ scenario, most likely because the stronger predictor dominates here. Also note that the large query (2048) used in our strongest model is typically diminished a lot by the GBDT pre-filter, resulting in average query sizes after the GBDT pre-filtering of 256–512.

Large GBDT and Large GNN: Finally, we evaluate the large setting, using the GBDT and GNN predictors $\mathcal{D}_{large}$ and $\mathcal{G}_{large}$ trained on the full training dataset. Again, we first do a grid search over the parameters on the small set of 300 development problems. Then we evaluate the best parameters on the development and holdout sets, and we compare them with the standalone performance of $\mathcal{D}_{large}$ and $\mathcal{G}_{large}$ (Table 4). The improvements on the development, resp. holdout, set is 9.1%, resp. 7.3%, in real time, and 6.9%, resp. 4.8%, when using CPU time. The E auto-schedule solves in 30 s (CPU time) 1020 of the holdout problems. Our strongest 2-phase method solves 1602 of these problems in the same CPU time, i.e., 57.1% more problems.

Table 4. Final evaluation of the best combination of $\mathcal{D}_{large}$ and $\mathcal{G}_{large}$ on the whole development (D) and holdout (H) datasets.

Set	Model	Thresh.	Time	Query	Context	Solved
D	$\mathcal{G}_{large}$	–	30	256	768	1511
D	$\mathcal{D}_{large}$	–	30	–	–	1397
D	$\mathcal{D}_{large}+\mathcal{G}_{large}$	0.1	60	1024	768	1648 (+9.1%)
D	$\mathcal{D}_{large}+\mathcal{G}_{large}$	0.1	30	1024	768	1615 (+6.9%)
H	$\mathcal{G}_{large}$	–	30	256	768	1529
H	$\mathcal{D}_{large}$	–	30	–	–	1390
H	$\mathcal{D}_{large}+\mathcal{G}_{large}$	0.1	60	1024	768	1640 (+7.3%)
H	$\mathcal{D}_{large}+\mathcal{G}_{large}$	0.1	30	1024	768	1602 (+4.8%)

5.3   Evaluation of the Parental Guidance Combined with $\mathcal{D}_{large}$

The parameters for parental guidance models are explored via a series of grid searches to reduce the number of combinations. Initially, we only use $\mathcal{D}_{large}$ in conjunction with the parental models. First, the training data classification schemes, $\mathcal{P}_{fuse}^{proof}$ and $\mathcal{P}_{fuse}^{given}$, are compared with a grid search over the pos-neg reduction ratio. The best combination of reduction ratio and classification scheme is used to perform a grid search over LightGBM parameters for $\mathcal{P}_{fuse}$. Next, reduction ratio and LightGBM parameter grid searches are done with the $\mathcal{P}_{cat}$ featurization method data, starting with the best $\mathcal{P}_{fuse}$ parameters from the previous experiments. Every model is evaluated with the same set of nine parental filtering thresholds $\{0.005, 0.01, 0.03, 0.05, 0.1, 0.2, 0.3, 0.4, 0.5\}$. The grid searches are done over the 300 problem development set and run for 30 s. On this dataset, $\mathcal{D}_{\text{large}}$ solves 159 problems.

Pos-Neg Reduction Ratio Tuning (Merge): The first grid search examines the pos-neg reduction ratio denoted as ρ. Before the reduction, the average pos-neg ratio for $\mathcal{P}_{\text{fuse}}^{\text{given}}$ is 1:9.2 and the average for $\mathcal{P}_{\text{fuse}}^{\text{proof}}$ is 1:191.8. We reduce the pos-neg ratio to a given ρ by randomly sampling the negative examples on a problem-specific basis. This means that the average pos-neg ratio over the whole dataset is typically a bit smaller than ρ. For example, using $\rho = 4$ on the $\mathcal{P}_{\text{fuse}}^{\text{proof}}$ results in an average of 3.95 times more negative than positive examples. Both $\mathcal{P}_{\text{fuse}}^{\text{given}}$ and $\mathcal{P}_{\text{fuse}}^{\text{proof}}$ are tested using $\rho \in \{-, 1, 2, 4, 8, 16\}$ where "$-$" denotes using the full training dataset. We use the best LightGBM model parameters discovered during prototyping of the parental guidance features: the parameters are 50 trees of depth 13 with 1024 leaves.

Table 5 shows that the reduction ratio makes significant difference for the $\mathcal{P}_{\text{fuse}}^{\text{proof}}$ data and almost none for $\mathcal{P}_{\text{fuse}}^{\text{given}}$ data, which is probably because the $\mathcal{P}_{\text{fuse}}^{\text{given}}$ data are already reasonably balanced. Moreover, parental guidance seems to perform better with $\mathcal{P}_{\text{fuse}}^{\text{proof}}$ data than $\mathcal{P}_{\text{fuse}}^{\text{given}}$ data, probably because mistakes of $\mathcal{D}_{\text{large}}$ are included in the training data. In the following experiments, only the $\mathcal{P}^{\text{proof}}$ classification scheme is used (so the prefix is dropped).

Table 5. The best threshold for each tested reduction ratio. The threshold of 0.03 was identical to 0.05 for all tested ratios with $\mathcal{P}_{\text{fuse}}^{\text{given}}$, whereas there are no ties among thresholds for $\mathcal{P}_{\text{fuse}}^{\text{proof}}$.

$\rho_{\text{fuse}}^{\text{given}}$	$-$	1	2	4	8	16	$\rho_{\text{fuse}}^{\text{proof}}$	$-$	1	2	4	8	16
Threshold	0.05	0.05	0.05	0.05	0.05	0.05	Threshold	0.005	0.2	0.2	0.2	0.2	0.2
Solved	161	161	161	161	161	160	Solved	111	164	163	165	162	164

Table 6. The best threshold for each tested reduction ratio of $\mathcal{P}_{\text{cat}}$.

ρ_{cat}	$-$	1	2	4	8	16
Threshold	0.5	0.1	0.05	0.3	0.1	0.05
Solved	117	168	170	168	173	169

LightGBM Parameter Tuning (Merge): Next we perform the second grid search over the LightGBM training hyper-parameters for $\mathcal{P}_{\text{fuse}}$, fixing $\rho = 4$ as it performed best. We try the following values for the three main hyper-parameters, namely, for the number of trees in a model, the maximum number of tree leaves, and the maximum tree depth:

$$\text{trees} \in \{50, 100, 150\}$$
$$\text{leaves} \in \{1024, 2048, 4096, 8192, 16384\}$$
$$\text{depth} \in \{13, 40, 60, 256\}$$

The best model for $\mathcal{P}_{\text{fuse}}$ solves 171 problems and consists of 100 trees, with the depth 40, and 8192 leaves, and a threshold of 0.05. Another eight models solve 169 problems. We also tested these parameters to find a better model for $\mathcal{P}_{\text{fuse}}^{\text{given}}$, which solves 163 problems with $\rho = 8$ and a threshold of 0.1.

Pos-Neg Reduction Ratio Tuning (Concat): This grid search uses the best LightGBM hyper-parameters for $\mathcal{P}_{\text{fuse}}$ to test the same reduction ratios and thresholds for $\mathcal{P}_{\text{cat}}$. Table 6 shows that $\mathcal{P}_{\text{cat}}$ outperforms $\mathcal{P}_{\text{fuse}}$ and $\rho = 8$ is the best. Reducing the negatives is even more important here.

LightGBM Parameter Tuning (Concat): The grid search for the $\mathcal{P}_{\text{cat}}$ data is done over the following hyper-parameters:

$$\text{trees} \in \{50, 100, 150, 200\}$$
$$\text{leaves} \in \{1024, 2048, 4096, 8192, 16384, 32768\}$$
$$\text{depth} \in \{13, 40, 60, 256, 512\}$$

The upper limits have increased compared to the $\mathcal{P}_{\text{fuse}}$ grid-search because one of the best models had 150 trees of depth 256, placing it at the edge of the grid. The best models solve 174–175 problems. These are evaluated on the full development set (Table 7). The larger models seem to work best with a threshold of 0.05 and the smaller models with a threshold of 0.2, which is likely because they can be less precise. The full distribution of the results can be seen in Fig. 1. The number of parameter configurations that outperform the baseline suggests that parental guidance is an effective method.

Table 7. The best $\mathcal{P}_{\text{cat}}$ models with $\rho = 8$.

Trees	Depth	Leaves	Threshold	Solved (300)	Solved (D)
200	60	4096	0.05	175	1557
200	512	4096	0.05	175	1561
200	256	4096	0.05	174	1558
150	512	1024	0.2	174	1568
150	256	1024	0.2	174	1556
100	60	8192	0.05	174	**1571**
100	40	2048	0.2	174	1544
100	40	2048	0.1	174	1544

Table 8. Final 30 s evaluation on small trains (T), development (D), and holdout (H) compared with $\mathcal{D}_{large}$.

Model	Threshold	Solved (T)	Solved (D)	Solved (H)
$\mathcal{D}_{large}$	–	3269	1397	1390
$\mathcal{P}_{fuse}^{given}+\mathcal{D}_{large}$	0.05	3302 (+1.0%)	1411 (+1.0%)	1417 (+1.9%)
$\mathcal{P}_{fuse}^{proof}+\mathcal{D}_{large}$	0.1	3389 (+3.7%)	1489 (+6.6%)	1486 (+6.9%)
$\mathcal{P}_{cat}+\mathcal{D}_{large}$	0.05	3452 (+5.6%)	1571 (+12.4%)	1553 (+11.7%)

Finally we evaluate the best models on the small training, development, and holdout sets, and we compare them with the standalone performance of $\mathcal{D}_{large}$ (Table 8). Parental guidance achieves a significant improvement in performance on all datasets, solving 11.7% more on the holdout set. It is interesting to note that the improvement is greater on the development and holdout sets than on the training set. For parental guidance it seems superior to classify only *proof clauses* as positive examples. This is most likely due to LightGBM being confused by processed clauses that did not contribute to any proof. The method of concatenating the parent clause feature vectors ($\mathcal{P}_{cat}$) seems far superior to merging them ($\mathcal{P}_{fuse}$). This is likely because merging the features is lossy and the order of the parents matters when performing inferences.

The results indicate that pruning clauses prior to clause evaluation is helpful. ENIGMA models tend to run best in equal combination with a strong E strategy, but this means they have no control over 50% of the clauses selected for processing. The ability to filter which clauses the strong E strategy can evaluate and select may be part of the strength behind parental guidance.

5.4   Parental Guidance with $\mathcal{G}_{large}$ and 3-Phase ENIGMAs

We also explore a limited number of the most useful hyper-parameters from Sects. 5.3 and 5.2 to combine the parental filtering with ENIGMA-GNN using $\mathcal{G}_{large}$ and to create a 3-phase ENIGMA. We train a new LightGBM parental filtering model on the $\mathcal{P}_{cat}$ data generated by running $\mathcal{G}_{large}$, using $\rho = 8$, trees $= 100$, leaves $= 8192$, and depth $= 60$. The grid search on the 300 development problems leads to the best threshold values of 0.005 and 0.01 when using context $= 768$ and query $= 256$ for ENIGMA-GNN with $\mathcal{G}_{large}$.

The version with the 0.01 threshold then reaches so far the highest value of 1621 development problems in 30 s CPU time. This is 50 more than the best parental result using $\mathcal{D}_{large}$ and 6 more than the best 2-phase result. On the holdout set this setting yields 1623 problems, i.e., 70 more than the best $\mathcal{D}_{large}$ parental result and 21 more than the best 2-phase result.

Finally, we explore 3-phase ENIGMAs, i.e., combinations of all the methods developed in this work. This means that we first use the parental guidance filtering, followed by the 2-phase evaluation which in turn uses the GPU server. This implies a higher evaluation cost, since both the parental and the first-stage LightGBM models are loaded on startup and are used to filter the clauses.

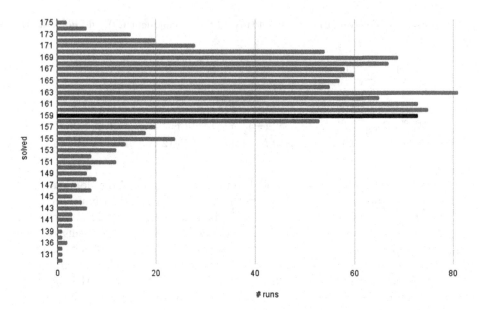

Fig. 1. The number of settings (and runs) corresponding to each number of solutions for the $\mathcal{P}_{\text{cat}}$ grid search. The black bar is 159, the number of problems solved by $\mathcal{D}_{\text{large}}$. Only 154 (20%) of the runs interfere with $\mathcal{D}_{\text{large}}$'s performance and solve fewer problems. These runs largely consist of the thresholds, $\{0.3, 0.4, 0.5\}$, but the only parameter whose majority of runs score below $\mathcal{D}_{\text{large}}$ is a threshold of 0.5. The outliers tend to be larger models.

We only tune the parental threshold and context and query values, keeping the 2-phase threshold fixed at 0.1. The best result is again obtained by setting the parental threshold to 0.01, context = 768 and query = 256. This solves 1631 resp. **1632** of the development resp. holdout problems in 30 s CPU time. This is our ultimate result, which is exactly 60% higher than the 1020 problems solved by E's auto-schedule in 30 s CPU time. It is also 17.4% higher than the best ENIGMA result prior to this work (1390 by standalone $\mathcal{D}_{\text{large}}$).

6   Conclusion and Examples

We have described several additions to the ENIGMA system. The new methods combine fast(er) and smart(er) clause evaluation using ENIGMA's parameterizable learning-based setting. The GPU server allows much faster runs of the neurally-guided ENIGMA, improving its real-time performance by about 10%. The parental guidance allows one to train clause evaluation differently from standard ENIGMA, providing an improvement of 11.7% on the holdout set. Both when training on small and on large datasets, the 2-phase methods provide good improvements on the holdout sets (9% and 7.3%) over the strongest standalone methods. The methods are adjustable and they will likely lead to even higher improvements in longer runtimes, due to the typically quadratic growth of the set of generated clauses in saturation-style ATPs. Our strongest 3-phase method improves E's auto-schedule on the holdout set by 60% in 30 s and our best prior ENIGMA result by 17.4%.

Several examples of the new proofs produced only by the methods developed here are available on our project's web page. Theorem `INTEGR13:27`[15] about the differentiation of $-cot(ln(x))$ needed 3904 nontrivial given clause loops and 38826 nontrivial generated clauses, taking only 18 s with the 2-phase ENIGMA. This can be compared to the previous related theorem `FDIFF_7:36`[16] (differentiation of $exp(cos(x))$) done in the old setting, taking 28.4 s to do only 1284 nontrivial given clause loops and 13287 nontrivial generated clauses. Other examples include a 486-long proof[17] of a theorem about integrals done only in 41 s with the 2-phase ENIGMA evaluating 100k clauses, or a 259-long computational proof[18] about Fermat primes found in 11 s while evaluating 52k clauses. Such proofs are found despite hundreds of redundant axioms, by using new combinations of faster and smarter trained ENIGMAs that efficiently guide the search.

Acknowledgments. This work was partially supported by the ERC Consolidator grant *AI4REASON* no. 649043 (ZG, JJ, and JU), the European Regional Development Fund under the Czech project AI&Reasoning no. CZ.02.1.01/0.0/0.0/15_003/0000466 (ZG, JU, KC), the ERC Starting Grant *SMART* no. 714034 (JJ, MO), and by the Czech MEYS under the ERC CZ project *POSTMAN* no. LL1902 (JJ).

References

1. Abadi, M., et al.: TensorFlow: large-scale machine learning on heterogeneous distributed systems. arXiv preprint arXiv:1603.04467 (2016)
2. Chen, T., Guestrin, C.: XGBoost: a scalable tree boosting system. In: Proceedings of the 22nd ACM SIGKDD International Conference on Knowledge Discovery and Data Mining, KDD 2016, pp. 785–794. ACM, New York (2016)
3. Chvalovský, K., Jakubův, J., Suda, M., Urban, J.: ENIGMA-NG: efficient neural and gradient-boosted inference guidance for E. In: Fontaine, P. (ed.) CADE 2019. LNCS (LNAI), vol. 11716, pp. 197–215. Springer, Cham (2019). https://doi.org/10.1007/978-3-030-29436-6_12
4. Fan, R.-E., Chang, K.-W., Hsieh, C.-J., Wang, X.-R., Lin, C.-J.: LIBLINEAR: a library for large linear classification. J. Mach. Learn. Res. **9**, 1871–1874 (2008)
5. Gittins, J.C.: Bandit processes and dynamic allocation indices. J. Roy. Stat. Soc. Ser. B (Methodol.) **41**, 148–177 (1979)
6. Goertzel, Z., Jakubův, J., Schulz, S., Urban, J.: ProofWatch: watchlist guidance for large theories in E. In: Avigad, J., Mahboubi, A. (eds.) ITP 2018. LNCS, vol. 10895, pp. 270–288. Springer, Cham (2018). https://doi.org/10.1007/978-3-319-94821-8_16

---

[15] https://github.com/ai4reason/ATP_Proofs/#differentiation---cot--ln-x--1--x--sin-ln-x2-.

[16] https://github.com/ai4reason/ATP_Proofs/#differentiation-exp_r--cos--x----exp_r--cos--x--sin-x.

[17] https://github.com/ai4reason/ATP_Proofs/#integral-chi-aa-is-integrable--integral-chi-aa--vol-a-486-long-atp-proof-from-63-premises.

[18] https://github.com/ai4reason/ATP_Proofs/#17-is-prime.

7. Goertzel, Z., Jakubův, J., Urban, J.: ENIGMAWatch: ProofWatch meets ENIGMA. In: Cerrito, S., Popescu, A. (eds.) TABLEAUX 2019. LNCS (LNAI), vol. 11714, pp. 374–388. Springer, Cham (2019). https://doi.org/10.1007/978-3-030-29026-9_21

8. Gottlob, G., Sutcliffe, G., Voronkov, A. (eds.): Global Conference on Artificial Intelligence, GCAI 2015, Tbilisi, Georgia, 16–19 October 2015, Volume 36 of EPiC Series in Computing. EasyChair (2015)

9. Hillenbrand, T.: Citius altius fortius: lessons learned from the theorem prover WALDMEISTER. ENTCS **86**(1), 9–21 (2003)

10. Jakubův, J., Chvalovský, K., Olšák, M., Piotrowski, B., Suda, M., Urban, J.: ENIGMA anonymous: symbol-independent inference guiding machine (system description). In: Peltier, N., Sofronie-Stokkermans, V. (eds.) IJCAR 2020. LNCS (LNAI), vol. 12167, pp. 448–463. Springer, Cham (2020). https://doi.org/10.1007/978-3-030-51054-1_29

11. Jakubův, J., Urban, J.: ENIGMA: efficient learning-based inference guiding machine. In: Geuvers, H., England, M., Hasan, O., Rabe, F., Teschke, O. (eds.) CICM 2017. LNCS (LNAI), vol. 10383, pp. 292–302. Springer, Cham (2017). https://doi.org/10.1007/978-3-319-62075-6_20

12. Jakubův, J., Urban, J.: Enhancing ENIGMA given clause guidance. In: Rabe, F., Farmer, W.M., Passmore, G.O., Youssef, A. (eds.) CICM 2018. LNCS (LNAI), vol. 11006, pp. 118–124. Springer, Cham (2018). https://doi.org/10.1007/978-3-319-96812-4_11

13. Jakubův, J., Urban, J.: Hierarchical invention of theorem proving strategies. AI Commun. **31**(3), 237–250 (2018)

14. Jakubův, J., Urban, J.: Hammering Mizar by learning clause guidance. In: Harrison, J., O'Leary, J., Tolmach, A. (eds.) 10th International Conference on Interactive Theorem Proving, ITP 2019, Portland, OR, USA, 9–12 September 2019, LIPIcs, vol. 141, pp. 34:1–34:8. Schloss Dagstuhl - Leibniz-Zentrum für Informatik (2019)

15. Kaliszyk, C.: Efficient low-level connection tableaux. In: De Nivelle, H. (ed.) TABLEAUX 2015. LNCS (LNAI), vol. 9323, pp. 102–111. Springer, Cham (2015). https://doi.org/10.1007/978-3-319-24312-2_8

16. Kaliszyk, C., Urban, J.: MizAR 40 for Mizar 40. J. Autom. Reasoning **55**(3), 245–256 (2015)

17. Kaliszyk, C., Urban, J., Michalewski, H., Olšák, M.: Reinforcement learning of theorem proving. In: Advances in Neural Information Processing Systems 31: Annual Conference on Neural Information Processing Systems 2018, NeurIPS 2018, Montréal, Canada, 3–8 December 2018, pp. 8836–8847 (2018)

18. Ke, G., et al.: LightGBM: a highly efficient gradient boosting decision tree. In: NIPS, pp. 3146–3154 (2017)

19. Kinyon, M., Veroff, R., Vojtěchovský, P.: Loops with abelian inner mapping groups: an application of automated deduction. In: Bonacina, M.P., Stickel, M.E. (eds.) Automated Reasoning and Mathematics. LNCS (LNAI), vol. 7788, pp. 151–164. Springer, Heidelberg (2013). https://doi.org/10.1007/978-3-642-36675-8_8

20. Kovács, L., Voronkov, A.: First-order theorem proving and VAMPIRE. In: Sharygina, N., Veith, H. (eds.) CAV 2013. LNCS, vol. 8044, pp. 1–35. Springer, Heidelberg (2013). https://doi.org/10.1007/978-3-642-39799-8_1

21. Loos, S.M., Irving, G., Szegedy, C., Kaliszyk, C.: Deep network guided proof search. In: Eiter, T., Sands, D. (eds.) LPAR-21, 21st International Conference on Logic for Programming, Artificial Intelligence and Reasoning, Maun, Botswana, 7–12 May 2017, EPiC Series in Computing, vol. 46, pp. 85–105. EasyChair (2017)

22. McCune, W.: Experiments with discrimination-tree indexing and path indexing for term retrieval. J. Autom. Reasoning **9**(2), 147–167 (1992)
23. Olšák, M., Kaliszyk, C., Urban, J.: Property invariant embedding for automated reasoning. In: De Giacomo, G., et al. (eds.) ECAI 2020–24th European Conference on Artificial Intelligence, 29 August-8 September 2020, Santiago de Compostela, Spain, 29 August–8 September 2020 - Including 10th Conference on Prestigious Applications of Artificial Intelligence (PAIS 2020), Frontiers in Artificial Intelligence and Applications, vol. 325, pp. 1395–1402. IOS Press (2020)
24. Overbeek, R.A.: A new class of automated theorem-proving algorithms. J. ACM **21**(2), 191–200 (1974)
25. Raths, T., Otten, J.: randoCoP: randomizing the proof search order in the connection calculus. In: Konev, B., Schmidt, R.A., Schulz, S. (eds.) Proceedings of the First International Workshop on Practical Aspects of Automated Reasoning, Sydney, Australia, 10–11 August 2008, CEUR Workshop Proceedings, vol. 373. CEUR-WS.org (2008)
26. Ruhdorfer, C., Schulz, S.: Efficient implementation of large-scale watchlists. In: Fontaine, P., Korovin, K., Kotsireas, I.S., Rümmer, P., Tourret, S. (eds.) Joint Proceedings of the 7th Workshop on Practical Aspects of Automated Reasoning (PAAR) and the 5th Satisfiability Checking and Symbolic Computation Workshop (SC-Square) Workshop, 2020 Co-Located with the 10th International Joint Conference on Automated Reasoning (IJCAR 2020), Paris, France, June–July 2020 (Virtual), CEUR Workshop Proceedings, vol. 2752, pp. 120–133. CEUR-WS.org (2020)
27. Schäfer, S., Schulz, S.: Breeding theorem proving heuristics with genetic algorithms. In: Gottlob et al. [8], pp. 263–274
28. Schulz, S.: Fingerprint indexing for paramodulation and rewriting. In: Gramlich, B., Miller, D., Sattler, U. (eds.) IJCAR 2012. LNCS (LNAI), vol. 7364, pp. 477–483. Springer, Heidelberg (2012). https://doi.org/10.1007/978-3-642-31365-3_37
29. Schulz, S.: System description: E 1.8. In: McMillan, K., Middeldorp, A., Voronkov, A. (eds.) LPAR 2013. LNCS, vol. 8312, pp. 735–743. Springer, Heidelberg (2013). https://doi.org/10.1007/978-3-642-45221-5_49
30. Schulz, S., Cruanes, S., Vukmirović, P.: Faster, higher, stronger: E 2.3. In: Fontaine, P. (ed.) CADE 2019. LNCS (LNAI), vol. 11716, pp. 495–507. Springer, Cham (2019). https://doi.org/10.1007/978-3-030-29436-6_29
31. Stickel, M.E.: The path-indexing method for indexing terms. Technical report, SRI International Menlo Park CA Artificial Intelligence Center (1989)
32. Sutcliffe, G., Suttner, C.B.: The state of CASC. AI Commun. **19**(1), 35–48 (2006)
33. Sutcliffe, G., Urban, J.: The CADE-25 automated theorem proving system competition - CASC-25. AI Commun. **29**(3), 423–433 (2016)
34. Urban, J.: MPTP 0.2: design, implementation, and initial experiments. J. Autom. Reasoning **37**(1–2), 21–43 (2006)
35. Urban, J.: BliStr: the blind strategymaker. In: Gottlob et al. [8], pp. 312–319
36. Urban, J., Vyskočil, J., Štěpánek, P.: MaLeCoP machine learning connection prover. In: Brünnler, K., Metcalfe, G. (eds.) TABLEAUX 2011. LNCS (LNAI), vol. 6793, pp. 263–277. Springer, Heidelberg (2011). https://doi.org/10.1007/978-3-642-22119-4_21
37. Veroff, R.: Using hints to increase the effectiveness of an automated reasoning program: case studies. J. Autom. Reasoning **16**(3), 223–239 (1996)
38. Voronkov, A.: The anatomy of Vampire implementing bottom-up procedures with code trees. J. Autom. Reasoning **15**(2), 237–265 (1995)

Vampire with a Brain Is a Good ITP Hammer

Martin Suda[✉][ID]

Czech Technical University in Prague, Prague, Czech Republic
martin.suda@cvut.cz

Abstract. Vampire has been for a long time the strongest first-order automatic theorem prover, widely used for hammer-style proof automation in ITPs such as Mizar, Isabelle, HOL, and Coq. In this work, we considerably improve the performance of Vampire in hammering over the full Mizar library by enhancing its saturation procedure with efficient neural guidance. In particular, we employ a recently proposed recursive neural network classifying the generated clauses based only on their derivation history. Compared to previous neural methods based on considering the logical content of the clauses, our architecture makes evaluating a single clause much less time consuming. The resulting system shows good learning capability and improves on the state-of-the-art performance on the Mizar library, while proving many theorems that the related ENIGMA system could not prove in a similar hammering evaluation.

1 Introduction

The usability of interactive theorem provers (ITPs) is significantly enhanced by proof automation. In particular, employing so-called *hammers* [6], systems that connect the ITP to an automatic theorem prover (ATP), may greatly speed up the formalisation process.

There are two ingredients of the hammer technology that appear to be best implemented using machine learning, especially while taking advantage of the corresponding large ambient ITP libraries, which can be used for training. One is the *premise selection* task, in which the system decides on a manageable subset of the most relevant facts from the ITP library to be passed to the ATP as axioms along with the current conjecture [1,2,10,29,44]. The other is the *internal guidance* of the ATP's proof search [11,42], where a machine-learned component helps to resolve some form of don't-care non-determinism in the prover algorithm with the aim of speeding up the proof search. In the predominant saturation-based proving paradigm, employed by the leading ATPs such as E [35], SPASS [45], or Vampire [24], internal guidance typically focuses on the *clause selection* choice point [20,26].

ENIGMA [7,19–21] is a system delivering internal proof search guidance driven by state-of-the-art machine learning methods to the automatic theorem prover E [35]. In 2019, the authors of ENIGMA announced [22] a 70% improvement (in terms of the number of problems solved under a certain wall clock time

© Springer Nature Switzerland AG 2021
B. Konev and G. Reger (Eds.): FroCoS 2021, LNAI 12941, pp. 192–209, 2021.
https://doi.org/10.1007/978-3-030-86205-3_11

limit) of E on the Mizar mathematical library (MML) [17]. This was achieved using gradient boosted trees coupled with a clause representation by efficiently extracted manually designed features.

In our recent work [39], we presented an enhancement of the automatic theorem prover Vampire [24] by a new form of clause selection guidance. The idea is to employ a recursive neural network [15] and to train it to classify clauses based solely on their derivation history. This means we deliberately abstract away the logical content of a clause, i.e. "what the clause says", and only focus on "where the clause is coming from (and how)". There is a pragmatic appeal in this design decision: evaluating a clause becomes relatively fast compared to other approaches based on neural networks (cf., e.g., [7,26]). It is also very interesting that such a simple approach works at all, let alone being able to match or even improve on the existing "better informed" methods.

We originally developed and evaluated [39] the architecture in the experimental setting of theory reasoning over the SMT-LIB library. In this paper, we instead explore its utility for improving the performance of Vampire in the role of an ITP hammer, focusing on the well-established Mizar benchmark [23]. Mizar requires the architecture to be adapted to a different set of features, notably a much larger set of background axioms (used instead of theory axioms) and a conjecture. While we previously [39] evaluated various modes of integrating the learned guidance and some supporting techniques, here we conduct new experiments that shed light on how the behaviour of the prover changes with varying parameters of the network itself. Finally, our evaluation allows for a direct comparison with the ENIGMA work of Jakubův and Urban [22].

In the rest of this paper, we first recall (in Sect. 2) how the saturation-based ATP technology can be enhanced by internal guidance learnt from previous proofs. We then explain (in Sect. 3) how to construct and train recursive neural networks as successful classifiers of clause derivations. While there is a certain overlap with our previous work [39], the new benchmark allows for the incorporation of conjecture-related features (Sect. 3.2) and we also find room to explain how to efficiently train our networks using parallelisation (Sect. 3.4). Finally, we report (in Sect. 4) on an experimental evaluation of our extension of Vampire with the described techniques over the Mizar mathematical library.

2   Internal Guidance of an ATP Using Machine Learning

Modern automatic theorem provers (ATPs) for first-order logic such as E [35], SPASS [45], or Vampire [24] are one of the most mature tools for general reasoning in a variety of domains. In a nutshell, they work in the following way.

Given a list of *axioms* $A_1, \ldots, A_l$ and a *conjecture* G to prove, an ATP translates $\{A_1, \ldots, A_l, \neg G\}$ into an equisatisfiable set of *initial clauses* $\mathcal{C}$. It then tries to derive a contradiction $\bot$ from $\mathcal{C}$ (thus showing that $A_1, \ldots, A_l \models G$) using a logical calculus, such as resolution or superposition [4,27]. The employed process of iteratively deriving (according to the inference rules of the calculus) new clauses, logical consequences of $\mathcal{C}$, is referred to as *saturation* and is typically implemented using some variant of a *given-clause algorithm* [32]: in each iteration, a single clause C is *selected* and inferences are performed between C and all previously selected clauses. Deciding which clause to select next is known to be a key heuristical choice point, hugely affecting the performance of an ATP [36].

The idea to improve clause selection by learning from past prover experience goes (to the best of our knowledge) back to Schulz [9,34] and has more recently been successfully employed by the ENIGMA system [7,19–21] and variations [3,8,26]. Experience is collected from successful prover runs, where each selected clause constitutes a training example and the example is marked as *positive* if the clause ended up in the discovered proof, and *negative* otherwise. A machine learning (ML) algorithm is then used to *fit* this data and produce a *model* $\mathcal{M}$ for *classifying* clauses into positive and negative, accordingly. A good learning algorithm produces a model $\mathcal{M}$ which accurately classifies the training data but also *generalizes* well to unseen examples; ideally, of course, with a low computational cost of both (1) training and (2) evaluation.

When a model is prepared, we need to *integrate* its advice back to the prover's clause selection process. An ATP typically organizes this process by maintaining a set of priority queues, each ordering the yet-to-be-processed clauses by a certain *criterion*, and alternates—under a certain configurable *ratio*—between selecting the best clause from each queue. One way of integrating the learnt advice, adopted by ENIGMA, is to add another queue $Q_{\mathcal{M}}$ in which clauses are ordered such that those positively classified by $\mathcal{M}$ precede the negatively classified ones, and extend the mentioned ratio such that $Q_{\mathcal{M}}$ is used for, e.g., half of the selections (while the remaining ones fall back to the original strategy).

In this work, we rely instead on the *layered clause selection* paradigm [13,14, 40], in which a clause selection mechanism inherited from an underlying strategy is applied separately to the set A of clauses classified as *positive* by $\mathcal{M}$ and to the set B of *all* yet-to-be-processed clauses (i.e., $A \subseteq B$). A "second level" ratio then dictates how often will the prover relay to select from either of these two sets. For example, with a *second-level ratio* 2:1, the prover will select twice from A (unless A is currently empty and a fallback to B happens) before selecting once from B. An advantage of this approach is that the original, typically well-tuned, selection mechanism is still applied within both A and B.[1]

3   Neural Classification of Clause Derivations

In our previous work [39], we introduced a method for classifying clauses for clause selection based on their derivation history, i.e., ignoring the logical content of the clauses. Each clause is characterised by the initial clauses from which it was derived, the inference rules by which it was derived, and the exact way in which the rules were used to derive it. The method relies on a recursive neural network (RvNN) as the machine learning architecture, with the recursion running "along" the clause derivations, starting off from the initial clauses.

---

[1] We compared and empirically evaluated various modes of integrating the model advice into the clause selection process in our previous work [39].

The previous work [39] focused on the SMT-LIB benchmark [5] and on the aspect of theory reasoning in Vampire implemented by adding theory axioms to formalise various theories of interest (arithmetic, arrays, data structures, ...). Together with the actual problem formulation, i.e., the user-supplied axioms, the theory axioms become the initial clauses to start off the recursion for a RvNN. Because these theory axioms are added by Vampire itself, their use in derivations can be traced and meaningfully compared across problems from different sources such as those comprising SMT-LIB.

In this paper, we adapt the method to work with a different benchmark, namely, the Mizar40 [23] problem set (see Sect. 4 for more details). There is no explicit theory reasoning (in the sense of "satisfiability modulo theories") needed to solve problems in this benchmark. On the other hand, many axioms appear in many problems across the Mizar40 benchmark and they are consistently named. We rely on these consistently named axioms to seed the recursion here.

In this section, we first recall the general RvNN architecture for learning from clause derivations. We then explain how this can be enhanced by incorporating information about the conjecture (which is missing in SMT-LIB). We avoid repeating the technical details mentioned previously [39], but include a subsection on our parallel training setup that we believe is of independent interest.

3.1 A Recursive Neural Network Clause Derivation Classifier

A recursive neural network (RvNN) is a network created by composing a finite set of neural building blocks *recursively* over a structured input [15].

In our case, the structured input is a clause derivation: a directed acyclic (hyper-)graph (DAG) with the initial clauses $C \in \mathcal{C}$ as leaves and the derived clauses as internal nodes, connected by (hyper-)edges labeled by the corresponding applied inference rules. To enable the recursion, an RvNN represents each node C by a real vector v_C (of fixed dimension n) called a (learnable) *embedding*. During training, our network learns to embed the space of derivable clauses into $\mathbb{R}^n$ in a priori unknown, but hopefully reasonable way.

We assume that each initial clause C can be identified with an axiom A_C from which it was obtained through clausification (unless it comes from the conjecture) and that these axioms form a finite set $\mathcal{A}$, fixed for the domain of interest. Now, the specific building blocks of our architecture are (mainly; see below) the following three (indexed families of) functions:

- for every axiom $A_i \in \mathcal{A}$, a nullary *init* function $I_i \in \mathbb{R}^n$ which to an initial clause $C \in \mathcal{C}$ obtained through clausification from the axiom A_i assigns its embedding $v_C := I_i$,
- for every inference rule r, a *deriv* function, $D_r : \mathbb{R}^n \times \cdots \times \mathbb{R}^n \to \mathbb{R}^n$ which to a conclusion clause C_c derived by r from premises $(C_1, \ldots, C_k)$ with embeddings $v_{C_1}, \ldots, v_{C_k}$ assigns the embedding $v_{C_c} := D_r(v_{C_1}, \ldots, v_{C_k})$,
- and, finally, a single *eval* function $E : \mathbb{R}^n \to \mathbb{R}$ which evaluates an embedding v_C such that the corresponding clause C is classified as *positive* whenever $E(v_C) \geq 0$ and negative otherwise.

By recursively composing these functions, any derived clause C can be assigned an embedding v_C and can be evaluated to see whether the network recommends it as positive, that should be preferred in the proof search, or negative, which will (according to the network) not likely contribute to a proof. Notice that the amortised cost of evaluating a single clause by the network is low, as it amounts to a *constant number* of function compositions.

3.2   Information Sources, the Conjecture, and SInE Levels

Let us first spend some time here to consider what kind of information about a clause can the network take into account to perform its classification.

The assumption about a fixed axiom set enables meaningfully carrying between problems observations about which axioms and their combinations quickly lead to good lemmas and which are, on the other hand, rarely useful. We believe this is the main source of information for the network to classify well. However, it may not be feasible to represent in the network all the axioms available in the benchmark. It is then possible to only *reveal* a specific subset to the network and represent the remaining ones using a single special embedding $I_{unknown}$.

Another, less obvious, source of information are the inference rules. Since there are distinct *deriv* functions D_r for every rule r, the network can also take into account that different inference rules give rise to conclusions of different degrees of usefulness. In Sect. 4.4, we dedicate an experiment to establishing how much this aspect of the architecture helps clause classification.

Finally, we always "tell the network" what the current conjecture G is by marking the conjecture clauses using a special initial embedding I_{goal}.[2] Focusing search on the conjecture is a well-known theorem proving heuristic and we give the network the opportunity to establish how strongly this heuristic should be taken into account.

We actually implemented a stronger version of the conjecture-focus idea by precomputing (and incorporating into the network) for every initial clause its SInE level [13,18,38]. A SInE level is a heuristical distance of a formula from the conjecture along a relation defined by sharing signature symbols [38]. Roughly, the SInE levels are computed as a byproduct of the iterative SInE premise selection algorithm [18], where we assign the level l to axiom A if the SInE algorithm first considers adding axiom A among the premises in its l-th iteration. Thus, the conjecture itself is assigned level 0, and a typical configuration of the algorithm on a typical formula (as witnessed by our experiments) assigns levels between 1 to around 10 to the given axioms.

To incorporate SInE levels into our network, we pass the embedding $I \in \mathbb{R}^n$ produced by an init function through an additional (learnable) *SInE embedder* function $S : \mathbb{R}^n \times \mathbb{R} \to \mathbb{R}^n$. Thus, an initial clause $C \in \mathcal{C}$ obtained through clausification from the axiom A_i and with a SInE level l receives an embedding

---

[2] By special we mean "in principle distinct". Since all the embeddings are learnable, the network itself "decides" during training how exactly to distinguish I_{goal} and all the other axioms embeddings I_i (and also the "generic" $I_{unknown}$).

$S(I_i, l) \in \mathbb{R}^n$. Also the effect of enabling or disabling this extension is demonstrated in the experiments in Sect. 4.4.

3.3 Training the Network

Our RvNN is parametrized by a tuple of *learnable parameters* $\Theta = (\theta^I, \theta^D, \theta^E, \theta^S)$ which determine the corresponding init, deriv, eval, and SInE embedder functions (please consult our previous work [39], Sect. 4.2, for additional details). To train the network means to find suitable values for these parameters such that it successfully classifies positive and negative clauses from the training data and ideally also generalises to unseen future cases.

We follow a standard methodology for training our networks. In particular, we use the gradient descent (GD) optimization algorithm minimising a binary cross-entropy *loss* [16]. Every clause in a derivation DAG selected by the saturation algorithm constitutes a contribution to the loss, with the clauses that participated in the found proof receiving the target label 1.0 (positive example) and the remaining ones the label 0.0 (negative example). We *weight* these contributions such that each derivation DAG (corresponding to a prover run on a single problem) receives equal weight, and, moreover, within each DAG we scale the importance of positive and negative examples such that these two categories contribute evenly.

We split the available successful derivations into 90% *training* set and 10% *validation* set, and only train on the first set using the second to observe generalisation to unseen examples. As the GD algorithm progresses, iterating over the training data in rounds called *epochs*, typically, the loss on the training examples steadily decreases while the loss on the validation set at some point stops improving or even starts getting worse. In our experiments, we always pick the model with the smallest validation loss for evaluation with the prover, as these models were shown to lead to the best performance in our previous work [39].

3.4 Implementation and the Parallel Training Setup

We implemented an infrastructure for training an RvNN clause derivation classifier in Python, using the PyTorch (version 1.7) library [28] and its TorchScript extension for later interfacing the trained model from C++.[3]

PyTorch is built around the concept of dynamic computational graphs for the calculation of gradient values required by the GD algorithm. This is an extremely flexible approach in which the computational graph is automatically constructed while executing code that looks like simply performing the vector operations pertaining to evaluating the network's concrete instance on a concrete set of training examples (corresponding, in our case, to a concrete clause derivation). A downside of this approach is that the computational graph cannot be stored and reused when the same example is to be evaluated and used for training in the next epoch. As a consequence, most of the time of training an RvNN like ours is spent on constructing computational graphs over and over again.

---

[3] The implementation is available as a public repo at https://git.io/JOh6S.

Batching: One general way of speeding up the training of a neural network amounts to grouping training examples into reasonably sized sets called *batches* and processing them in parallel—in the sense of single instruction multiple data (SIMD)—typically on a specialized hardware such as a GPU. However, this is most easily done only when the training examples have the same shape and can be easily aligned, such as, e.g., with images, and is not immediately available with RvNNs.[4]

Because each clause derivation that we want to process in training is in general of a unique shape, we do not attempt to align multiple derivations to benefit from SIMD processing. Instead, we create batches by merging multiple derivations to simply create DAGs of comparable size (some derivations are relatively small, while the largest we encountered were of the order of hundred thousand nodes). By merging we mean: (1) putting several derivations next to each other, and (2) identifying and collapsing nodes that are indistinguishable from the point of view of the computation our RvNN performs.[5] This means that a batch contains at most one node for all initial clauses corresponding to the conjecture or at most one node for all clauses derived from two such initial clauses in a single step by resolution, etc. When collapsing nodes from different derivations, we make sure to compute the correct target labels and their weights to preserve the semantics the network had before the merge.[6]

A Multi-process Training Architecture: To utilise parallelism and speed up the training in our case (i.e., with similarly sized but internally heterogenous batches), we implemented a master-worker multiprocess architecture to be run on a computer with multiple CPUs (or CPU cores).

The idea is that a master process maintains a single official version of the network (in terms of the learnable parameters Θ) and dispatches training tasks to a set of worker processes. A training task is a pair (Θ_t, B) where Θ_t is the current version of the network at time t (the moment when the task is issued by the master process) and B is a selected batch. A worker process constructs the computation graph corresponding to B, performs a back-propagation step, and sends the obtained gradient $\nabla\Theta_t(B)$ back to the master. The master dispatches tasks and receives gradients from finished workers using two synchronization queues. The master updates the official network after receiving a gradient from a worker via

$$\Theta_{T+1} \leftarrow \Theta_T - \alpha\nabla\Theta_t(B),$$

where α is the learning rate.

A curious aspect of our architecture is that Θ_T, the network the master updates at moment T using $\nabla\Theta_t(B)$, is typically a later version than Θ_t from which the corresponding task has been derived. In other words, there is a certain

---

[4] There exist non-trivial preprocessing techniques for achieving graph batching [25].

[5] The latter is already relevant within a single derivation (c.f. [39], Sect. 4.4).

[6] E.g., a node can be designated a positive example (label 1.0, weight w_1) in one derivation and a negative one (label 0.0, weight w_2) in another. The corresponding collapsed node receives the label $w_1/(w_1 + w_2)$ and weight $(w_1 + w_2)$.

drift between the version of the network an update has been computed for and the version the update is eventually applied to. This drift arises because the master issues a task as soon as there is a free worker and receives an update as soon as there is a finished worker. In a sense, such drift is necessary if we want to keep the workers busy and capitalise on parallelisation at all.

Surprisingly, the drift seems to have a beneficial effect on learning in the sense that it helps to prevent overfitting. Indeed, we were able to train models with slightly smaller validation loss using parallelisation than without it.[7]

4   Experiments

We implemented clause selection guidance (Sect. 2) by a recursive neural network classifier for clause derivations (Sect. 3) in the automatic theorem prover Vampire (version 4.5.1).[8] In our previous work [39], we used the SMT-LIB benchmark [5] and empirically compared several modes of integration of the learned advice into the prover as well as several supporting techniques. In this paper, we set out with the best configuration identified therein[9] and focus on evaluating various aspects of the neural architecture itself and do that using the problems from the Mizar mathematical library.

Following Jakubův and Urban [22], we use the Mizar40 [23] benchmark consisting of 57 880 problems from the MPTP [41] and, in particular, the small (*bushy*, re-proving) version. This version emulates the scenario where some form of premise selection has already occurred and allows us to directly focus on evaluating internal guidance in an ATP. To enable a direct comparison with Jakubův and Urban's remarkable results [22], we adopt the base time limit of 10 s per problem and use comparable hardware for the evaluation.[10]

This section has several parts. First, we explain the details concerning the initial run from which the training derivations got collected, describe the various ways of setting up the training procedure we experimented with, and evaluate the performance of the obtained models (Sects. 4.1–4.3). We then set out to establish how the individual aspects of our architecture (as discussed in Sect. 3.2) contribute to the overall performance (Sect. 4.4). Finally, we follow Jakubův and Urban [22] in training better and better models using the growing set of solved problems for more training and compare with their results (Sect. 4.5).

4.1   Data Preparation

We first identified a Vampire strategy (from among Vampire's standard CASC schedule) which performed well on the Mizar40 benchmark. We denote the strategy here as $\mathcal{V}$ and use it as a baseline. This strategy solved a total of 20 197 problems under the base 10 s time limit.

---

[7] This effect has already been observed by researches in a related context [30].

[8] Supplementary materials for the experiments can be found at https://git.io/JOY71.

[9] This means layered clause selection with second-level ratio 2:1 (as explained in Sect. 2) and lazy model evaluation and abstraction caching (see [39]).

[10] A server with Intel(R) Xeon(R) Gold 6140 CPUs @ 2.3 GHz with 500 GB RAM.

Table 1. Training statistics of models in the first experiment.

Model shorthand	$\mathcal{H}^{n128}$	$\mathcal{M}^{n64}$	$\mathcal{M}^{n128}$	$\mathcal{M}^{n256}$	$\mathcal{D}^{n128}$
Revealed axioms m	500	1000	1000	1000	2000
Embedding size n	128	64	128	256	128
Wall training time per epoch (min)	42	32	48	74	58
Model size (MB)	4.6	1.6	5.0	17.9	5.8
Overall best epoch	69	52	60	60	46
Validation loss	0.475	0.455	0.455	0.452	0.467
True positive rate	0.947	0.952	0.954	0.949	0.948
True negative rate	0.872	0.870	0.868	0.874	0.858

The corresponding successful derivations amount to roughly 800 MB of disk space when zipped. There are 43 080 named Mizar axioms occurring in them (and in each also some conjecture clauses), and 12 inference rules including resolution, factoring, superposition, forward and backward demodulation, subsumption resolution, unit resulting resolution and AVATAR (which represents the connection between a clause getting split and its components) [31,43].

As the total number of axioms seemed too large, we only took a subset of size m of the most often occurring ones to be represented by distinct labels for the network to distinguish and replaced the remaining ones in the dataset by the single generic label *unknown* (c.f. $I_{unknown}$ in Sect. 3.2). To evaluate the effect of this hyper-parameter on performance, we initially experimented with three values of m, namely, 500, 1000, and 2000.

To finalize the preparation of the training dataset(s), we constructed merged batches of approximately 20 thousand nodes each. 71 derivations were larger than this threshold (the largest had 242 023 merged nodes), but a typical batch merged 5–20 derivations. In the particular case of $m = 1000$, which we consider the default, we constructed 2167 batches in total. We then randomly split these, as mentioned, into 90% of training and 10% of validation examples.

4.2   Training

We trained our models using the parallel setup with 20 cores, for up to 100 epochs, in the end choosing the model with the best validation loss as the result. Similarly to our previous work [39], we used a variable learning rate.[11]

In total, we ran five independent training attempts. In addition to the number of revealed axioms m, we also set out to evaluate how the behaviour of the network changes with the size of the embedding n. For the default number of revealed axioms $m = 1000$, we tried the embedding sizes $n = 64, 128$, and 256.

---

[11] The learning rate was set to grow linearly from 0 to a maximum value $\alpha_m = 2.0 \times 10^{-4}$ in epoch 40: $\alpha(t) = t \cdot \alpha_m/40$ for $t \in (0, 40]$; and then to decrease from that value as the reciprocal function of time: $\alpha(t) = 40 \cdot \alpha_m/t$ for $t \in (40, 100)$.

Table 2. Performance statistics of the base strategy $\mathcal{V}$ and five strategies enhancing $\mathcal{V}$ with a clause selection guidance by the respective neural models from Table 1.

Strategy	$\mathcal{V}$	$\mathcal{H}^{n128}$	$\mathcal{M}^{n64}$	$\mathcal{M}^{n128}$	$\mathcal{M}^{n256}$	$\mathcal{D}^{n128}$
Solved	20 197	24 581	25 484	25 805	25 287	**26 014**
$\mathcal{V}\%$	+0%	+21.7%	+26.1%	+27.7%	+25.2%	**+28.8%**
$\mathcal{V}+$	+0	+5022	+5879	+6129	+5707	**+6277**
$\mathcal{V}-$	−0	−638	−592	−521	−617	**−460**
Model eval. time	0%	37.1%	**32.9%**	37.7%	48.6%	36.7%

The training statistics of the corresponding five models are summarized in Table 1. For each of the tried combination of m and n, the table starts by giving a shorthand to the best obtained model for later reference.

The next block documents the speed of training and the size of the obtained models. We can see that the model sizes are dictated mainly by the embedding size n and not so much by the number of revealed axioms m. (Roughly, $\Theta(n^2)$ of space is needed for storing the matrices representing the deriv and eval functions, while $\Theta(n \cdot m)$ space is required for storing the axiom embeddings.) We note that the sizes are comparable to those of the gradient boosted trees used by Jakubův and Urban [22] (5.0 MB for a tree of size 9 in their main experiment). Concerning the training times, the 48 min per epoch recorded for $\mathcal{M}^{n128}$ corresponds in 100 epochs to approximately 3 days of 20 core computation and almost 70 single-core days. Jakubův and Urban [22] trained a similarly sized model in under 5 single-core days, which indicates that training neural networks is much more computation intensive.

Finally, Table 1 also reports for each training process the epoch in which the validation loss was in the end the lowest, the achieved validation loss and the (weighted) true positive and negative rates (on the validation examples).[12] The true positive rate (TPR) is the fraction of positive examples that the network identifies as such. The true negative rate (TNR) is defined analogously. In our case, we use the same weighting formula as for computing the contributions of each example to the loss (recall Sect. 3.3). It is interesting to observe that on the Mizar benchmark here the training process automatically produces models biased towards better TPR (c.f. [39], Sect. 5.5), while the weighting actually strives for an equal focus on the positive and the negative examples.

4.3   Evaluation with the Prover

Next, we reran Vampire's strategy $\mathcal{V}$, now equipped with the obtained models for guidance, again using the time limit of 10 s. The results are shown in Table 2.

---

[12] Please note that the batches of training and validation examples for different numbers of revealed axioms were constructed and split independently, so meaningful comparisons are mainly possible between the values of the middle column (for $m = 1000$).

We can see that the highest number of problems is solved with the help of $\mathcal{D}^{n128}$, the model with the intermediate embedding size $n = 128$ but with the largest tried number of revealed axioms $m = 2000$. The strategy equipped with $\mathcal{D}^{n128}$ solves 26 014 problems, which is 28.8% of the baseline $\mathcal{V}$.

In addition to the solved counts and the percentages, Table 2 also shows the number of gained ($\mathcal{V}+$) and lost ($\mathcal{V}-$) problems with respect to the base strategy $\mathcal{V}$. Note that the problems from $\mathcal{V}+$ were not present in the training set, so solving those is a sign of successful generalization. On the other hand, the non-negligible number of no-longer-solved problems under $\mathcal{V}-$ reminds us of the overhead connected with interfacing the network.

The last row of the table elaborates on this, presenting the average time spent by the strategies on evaluating their respective models. The numbers indicate that the evaluation time is mainly determined by the embedding size n, as the models with $n = 128$ all spend approximately 37% on evaluating, while notable differences appear with n getting varied.

It is now interesting to compare the evaluation time (i.e., how fast the advice is) and the validation loss from Table 1 (i.e., how good the advice is) with the observed ATP performance. It appears that $\mathcal{M}^{n256}$ is too slow to capitalize on its superior advice quality over $\mathcal{M}^{n64}$ and $\mathcal{M}^{n128}$. However, there must be limits to how indicative the validation loss is for the final performance, because this metric does not help distinguish between $\mathcal{M}^{n64}$ and $\mathcal{M}^{n128}$ and yet the slower to evaluate $\mathcal{M}^{n128}$ eventually helps Vampire solve substantially more problems.

4.4   Information Source Performance Breakdown

So far, we observed how the performance of the guided prover changes when we vary the two numerical parameters of our architecture, namely, the size of the embedding n and the number of revealed axioms m. Here we want to shed more light on how the performance arises from the contributions of our architecture's main information sources: the ability to distinguish the input axioms at all (i.e., the information channelled through the init functions), the ability to distinguish individual inference rules (corresponding to the deriv functions), and the ability to track relatedness to the conjecture via the SInE levels. We do this by disabling these sources in turn and rerunning the prover.

No Distinguished Input Axioms. With each information source, we have in principle two options. One option is to train a new network from scratch, but on a dataset which does not contain the extra information corresponding to the disabled source (e.g., with $m = 0$ revealed axioms). The other option is to use an already trained model (we will use $\mathcal{M}^{n128}$ for this), but to withhold the extra information while evaluating the model in the prover. For this, we need to provide a default value for "masking out" the extra information. (When disabling input axioms, we simply use $I_{unknown}$ as the default to embed any input clause

Table 3. Performance decrease when no axiom information is a available ($\mathcal{A}^0$ and $\mathcal{M}_{noAx}$) and when inference rules are not distinguished ($\mathcal{R}_{defR}$). All models used $n = 128$ and $\mathcal{M}$ stands for $\mathcal{M}^{n128}$ from Tables 1 and 2. Further details in the main text.

Strategy	$\mathcal{M}$	$\mathcal{A}^0$	$\mathcal{M}_{noAx}$	$\mathcal{R}$	$\mathcal{R}_{defR}$
Solved	25 805	21 400	21 011	25 686	24 544
$\mathcal{M}\%$	+0.0%	−17.0%	−18.5%	−0.4%	−4.8%
$\mathcal{V}\%$	+27.7%	+5.9%	+4.0%	+27.1%	+21.5%

except the conjecture ones.) Note that the two options are not equivalent and, intuitively, the first one should not perform worse than the second.[13]

We can observe the effect of disabling access to the input axioms in Table 3. Model $\mathcal{A}^0$ represents the just described option one, where the axiom information was already witheld during training. The column $\mathcal{M}_{noAx}$, on the other hand, used the original model $\mathcal{M}^{n128}$ (here dubbed simply $\mathcal{M}$), but during evaluation in the prover all axioms were deliberately presented as *unknown*.

Most important to notice is that both options perform much worse than the original model $\mathcal{M}$, which shows that the ability to distinguish the input axioms is crucial for the good performance of our architecture. Nevertheless, when compared to the baseline strategy $\mathcal{V}$, the guided prover still solves around 5% more problems. This means the guidance is still reasonably good (given that almost 40% of the proving time is spent evaluating the network). Finally, $\mathcal{A}^0$ performs slightly better than $\mathcal{M}_{noAx}$, which conforms with our intuition.

No Distinguished Derivation Rules. There seems to be no obvious way to pick a default inference rule for masking out the functionality of this information source. The situation is further complicated by the fact that we need at least two defaults based on the inference rule arity.[14] To prepare such defaults,[15] we came up with a modification of the training regime that we call *swapout*.[16]

Training with swapout means there is a nonzero probability p (we used $p = 0.1$ in the experiment) that an application of a particular inference rule r in a derivation—i.e. applying the deriv function D_r to produce the next clause embedding—will instead use a generic function $D_{arity(r)}$ shared by all rules of the same arity as r. This is analogous to using $I_{unknown}$ for axioms not important enough to deserve their own init function, but decided probabilistically.

The right part of Table 3 presents the performance of a model obtained using swapout. First, under $\mathcal{R}$, the additionally trained generic deriv functions were

---

[13] The first option is like being born blind, learning during life how to live without the missing sense, the second option is like losing a sense "just before the final exam".

[14] Our architecture separately models arity one rules, binary rules, and rules with arity of 3 and more for which a binary building block is iteratively composed with itself.

[15] These could also be used whenever a trained model is combined with a strategy not used to produce the training data, possibly invoking rules not present in training.

[16] In honor of *dropout* [37], a well-know regularization technique that inspired this.

Table 4. The effect of training without SInE levels information ($\mathcal{S}^0$) and of imposing various fixed SInE levels on $\mathcal{M} = \mathcal{M}^{n128}$.

Strategy	$\mathcal{M}$	$\mathcal{S}^0$	$\mathcal{M}_{l=0}$	$\mathcal{M}_{l=1}$	$\mathcal{M}_{l=2}$	$\mathcal{M}_{l=3}$	$\mathcal{M}_{l=4}$	$\mathcal{M}_{l=5}$
Solved	25 805	25 440	25 724	25 823	25 882	**25 884**	25 866	25 802
$\mathcal{M}\%$	+0.0%	−1.4%	−0.3%	+0.0%	+0.2%	**+0.3%**	+0.2%	−0.0%
$\mathcal{V}+$	**+6129**	+5783	+5878	+6002	+6092	+6101	+6114	+6108
$\mathcal{V}-$	−521	−540	**−351**	−376	−407	−414	−445	−503

ignored. This means that $\mathcal{R}$ uses the same full set of information sources as $\mathcal{M}$. We should remark that training with swapout took longer to reach the minimal validation loss and the final loss was lower than that of $\mathcal{M}$ (0.454 in epoch 95). Nevertheless, $\mathcal{R}$ performs slightly worse than $\mathcal{M}$.

Under $\mathcal{R}_{defR}$, we see the performance of $\mathcal{R}$ where the trained generic deriv functions are exclusively used to replace (based on arity) the specific ones. The performance drops by approximately 5% compared to $\mathcal{M}$, which shows that there is value in the architecture being able to distinguish the derivation rules.

No SInE Levels. Let us finally move to the information source provided by the SInE levels and a corresponding experiment documented in Table 4. In that table, $\mathcal{S}^0$ is a model trained without access to this source, while the remaining columns represent $\mathcal{M}$ with increasingly large values of the SInE level l uniformly hardwired for evaluation in the prover.

Confusingly, all $\mathcal{M}$-derived models fare better than $\mathcal{S}^0$ and some of them are even better than $\mathcal{M}$ itself. We currently do not have a good general explanation for this phenomenon, although an analogy with the success of "positive bias" observed in our previous work on SMT-LIB can be drawn (c.f. [39], Sect. 5.5). Hardwiring a low SInE level l means the network will consider many clauses to be more related to the conjecture than they actually are, which will likely lead to more clauses classified as positive. Then the general intuition would be that it is more important for performance not to dismiss a clause needed for the proof than to dismiss clauses that will not be needed.

It is worth pointing out that $\mathcal{M}_{l=0}$ is the most "careful" configuration of these, scoring the lowest in terms of $\mathcal{V}-$, the number of problems lost with respect to the baseline strategy $\mathcal{V}$. Additionally, $\mathcal{M}$ still scores the highest on $\mathcal{V}+$, the number of newly solved problems, not present in the training data, although $\mathcal{M}_{l=4}$ comes quite close. More analysis seems to be needed to fully understand the effect of the SInE levels on the architecture's performance.

4.5 Looping to Get Even Better

When evaluating a strategy guided by a model leads to solving previously unsolved problems, the larger set of proofs may be used for training a potentially even better model to help solve even more problems. Jakubův and Urban [22] call this method *looping* and successfully apply it on Mizar for several iterations.

Table 5. Summary of the looping procedure. *Collected* stands for the number of derivations available for training. *Performance* refers to the best strategy of the loop (in 10 s).

Loop index	Training		Evaluation		
	Collected	m	Performance	$\mathcal{V}$%	%collected
0	–	–	20 197	+0.0%	–
1	20 197	500/1000/2000	26 014	+28.8%	128.8%
2	29 065	3000	27 348	+35.4%	94.0%
3	32 020	5000	28 947	+43.3%	90.4%

Here we report on applying looping to our neural architecture. We follow our previous work and adhere to the following two rules when using the method: First, we use exactly one successful derivation to train on for every previously solved problem. Second, if a derivation was obtained with the help of previously trained guidance, we augment the derivation with the unsuccessful run of plain $\mathcal{V}$ on that problem. The first rule ensures the dataset does not grow too large too quickly. The second rule helps to create a sufficient pool of negative examples, "typical bad decisions", that might otherwise not be present in a derivation obtained with some form of guidance already in place (c.f. [39], Sect. 5.6).

The results of looping are summarized in Table 5. We can already recognize the values of the first two rows: "Loop 0" means the run of the baseline strategy $\mathcal{V}$. Then, in loop 1, the obtained 20 197 successful derivations become available for training (some actually get used for training, others for validation), and, as we know from Table 2, the best model of this first round of training was $\mathcal{D}^{n128}$, solving 26 014 Mizar40 problems under the 10 s time limit.

For the next loop—observing the two rules mentioned above—we collected a total of 29 065 successful derivations and trained the next model using an increased number of revealed axioms $m = 3000$. To create additional variability in the runs and thus to increase the chances of collecting even more derivations for the next loop, we varied the modes of interfacing a model, studied in more detail in our previous work [39]. The best configuration of loop 2 solved 27 348 problems and the union of solved problems grew to 32 020. Finally, training using the corresponding successful derivations in loop 3, we were able to produce a model $\mathcal{B}$ with $n = 128$, $m = 5000$ that can guide Vampire[17] to solve 28 947 problems and thus improves over the baseline $\mathcal{V}$ by more than 43%.

As can be seen from Table 5, while the best strategy's performance improves with every loop, there is clearly an effect of diminishing returns at play. In particular, after loop 1 the best strategy is no longer able to solve more problems than was the number of solutions used for training the corresponding model and in loop 3 their percentage comparison (i.e., %collected) only reaches 90%. Another observation is that our initial estimate $m = 1000$ for a reasonable number of revealed axioms was too low. The additional capacity is paying off

---

[17] Using again the here prevalent layered clause selection with second-level ratio 2:1.

even for $\mathcal{B}$, which with its $m = 5000$ reaches a size of 8.8 MB (c.f. Table 1) and 40.1% running time spent on model evaluation (c.f. Table 2).

Let us conclude here by a comparison with the results of Jakubův and Urban [22]. They start off with a strategy of E [35] solving 14 933 Mizar40 problems under a 10 s time limit and their best loop 4 model guides ENIGMA to solve 25 397 problems (i.e., +70%) under that time limit. The authors kindly provided us with the precise set of problems solved by their runs. Their runs cover 27 425 problems. Our collection, that could be used for training in our next loop, counts 32 531 solved problems. Our architecture solved 6356 problems that ENIGMA could not (and did not solve 1250 problems that ENIGMA could).

5   Conclusion

There is a new neural architecture for guiding clause selection in saturation-based ATPs based solely on clause derivation history [39]. We adapted this architecture to work in the context of a large library of formalized mathematics, in particular the Mizar mathematical library (MML) [17], and conducted a series of experiments on the Mizar40 export of the library [23] with the new architecture interfaced from the ATP Vampire. We established how the performance of the obtained system depends on parameters of the network and on its architectural building blocks. We also compared its performance to that of ENIGMA and saw our architecture further improve on ENIGMA's remarkable results [22].

It is perhaps surprising that so much can be gained by simply paying attention to the clause's pedigree while ignoring what it says as a logical formula. In future work, we would like to have a closer look at the trained models (and thus, implicitly, at the successful derivations) and employ the techniques of explainable AI to get a better understanding of the architecture's success. We hope to distill new general purpose theorem proving heuristics or, at least, contribute to knowledge transfer from Mizar to other libraries of formalized mathematics.

Acknowledgement. This work was supported by the Czech Science Foundation project 20-06390Y and the project RICAIP no. 857306 under the EU-H2020 programme.

References

1. Alama, J., Heskes, T., Kühlwein, D., Tsivtsivadze, E., Urban, J.: Premise selection for mathematics by corpus analysis and kernel methods. J. Autom. Reason. **52**(2), 191–213 (2014). https://doi.org/10.1007/s10817-013-9286-5
2. Alemi, A.A., Chollet, F., Irving, G., Szegedy, C., Urban, J.: DeepMath - deep sequence models for premise selection. CoRR abs/1606.04442 (2016)
3. Aygün, E., et al.: Learning to prove from synthetic theorems. CoRR abs/2006.11259 (2020)
4. Bachmair, L., Ganzinger, H.: Resolution theorem proving. In: Robinson and Voronkov [33], pp. 19–99. https://doi.org/10.1016/b978-044450813-3/50004-7

5. Barrett, C., Fontaine, P., Tinelli, C.: The Satisfiability Modulo Theories Library (SMT-LIB) (2016). www.SMT-LIB.org
6. Blanchette, J.C., Kaliszyk, C., Paulson, L.C., Urban, J.: Hammering towards QED. J. Formaliz. Reason. **9**(1), 101–148 (2016). https://doi.org/10.6092/issn.1972-5787/4593
7. Chvalovský, K., Jakubův, J., Suda, M., Urban, J.: ENIGMA-NG: efficient neural and gradient-boosted inference guidance for E. In: Fontaine [12], pp. 197–215. https://doi.org/10.1007/978-3-030-29436-6_12
8. Crouse, M., et al.: A deep reinforcement learning based approach to learning transferable proof guidance strategies. CoRR abs/1911.02065 (2019)
9. Denzinger, J., Schulz, S.: Learning domain knowledge to improve theorem proving. In: McRobbie, M.A., Slaney, J.K. (eds.) CADE 1996. LNCS, vol. 1104, pp. 62–76. Springer, Heidelberg (1996). https://doi.org/10.1007/3-540-61511-3_69
10. Färber, M., Kaliszyk, C.: Random forests for premise selection. In: Lutz, C., Ranise, S. (eds.) FroCoS 2015. LNCS (LNAI), vol. 9322, pp. 325–340. Springer, Cham (2015). https://doi.org/10.1007/978-3-319-24246-0_20
11. Färber, M., Kaliszyk, C., Urban, J.: Monte Carlo tableau proof search. In: de Moura, L. (ed.) CADE 2017. LNCS (LNAI), vol. 10395, pp. 563–579. Springer, Cham (2017). https://doi.org/10.1007/978-3-319-63046-5_34
12. Fontaine, P. (ed.): CADE 2019. LNCS (LNAI), vol. 11716. Springer, Cham (2019). https://doi.org/10.1007/978-3-030-29436-6
13. Gleiss, B., Suda, M.: Layered clause selection for saturation-based theorem proving. In: Fontaine, P., Korovin, K., Kotsireas, I.S., Rümmer, P., Tourret, S. (eds.) Joint Proceedings of the 7th Workshop on Practical Aspects of Automated Reasoning (PAAR) and the 5th Satisfiability Checking and Symbolic Computation Workshop (SC-Square), co-located with the 10th International Joint Conference on Automated Reasoning (IJCAR 2020), Paris, France, June–July, 2020 (Virtual). CEUR Workshop Proceedings, vol. 2752, pp. 34–52. CEUR-WS.org (2020)
14. Gleiss, B., Suda, M.: Layered clause selection for theory reasoning. In: Peltier, N., Sofronie-Stokkermans, V. (eds.) IJCAR 2020, Part I. LNCS (LNAI), vol. 12166, pp. 402–409. Springer, Cham (2020). https://doi.org/10.1007/978-3-030-51074-9_23
15. Goller, C., Küchler, A.: Learning task-dependent distributed representations by backpropagation through structure. In: Proceedings of International Conference on Neural Networks (ICNN 1996), Washington, DC, USA, 3–6 June 1996, pp. 347–352. IEEE (1996). https://doi.org/10.1109/ICNN.1996.548916
16. Goodfellow, I.J., Bengio, Y., Courville, A.C.: Deep Learning. Adaptive Computation and Machine Learning. MIT Press, Cambridge (2016)
17. Grabowski, A., Kornilowicz, A., Naumowicz, A.: Mizar in a nutshell. J. Formaliz. Reason. **3**(2), 153–245 (2010). https://doi.org/10.6092/issn.1972-5787/1980
18. Hoder, K., Voronkov, A.: Sine Qua non for large theory reasoning. In: Bjørner, N., Sofronie-Stokkermans, V. (eds.) CADE 2011. LNCS (LNAI), vol. 6803, pp. 299–314. Springer, Heidelberg (2011). https://doi.org/10.1007/978-3-642-22438-6_23
19. Jakubův, J., Chvalovský, K., Olšák, M., Piotrowski, B., Suda, M., Urban, J.: ENIGMA anonymous: symbol-independent inference guiding machine (system description). In: Peltier, N., Sofronie-Stokkermans, V. (eds.) IJCAR 2020, Part II. LNCS (LNAI), vol. 12167, pp. 448–463. Springer, Cham (2020). https://doi.org/10.1007/978-3-030-51054-1_29
20. Jakubův, J., Urban, J.: ENIGMA: efficient learning-based inference guiding machine. In: Geuvers, H., England, M., Hasan, O., Rabe, F., Teschke, O. (eds.) CICM 2017. LNCS (LNAI), vol. 10383, pp. 292–302. Springer, Cham (2017). https://doi.org/10.1007/978-3-319-62075-6_20

21. Jakubův, J., Urban, J.: Enhancing ENIGMA given clause guidance. In: Rabe, F., Farmer, W.M., Passmore, G.O., Youssef, A. (eds.) CICM 2018. LNCS (LNAI), vol. 11006, pp. 118–124. Springer, Cham (2018). https://doi.org/10.1007/978-3-319-96812-4_11

22. Jakubuv, J., Urban, J.: Hammering Mizar by learning clause guidance (short paper). In: Harrison, J., O'Leary, J., Tolmach, A. (eds.) 10th International Conference on Interactive Theorem Proving, ITP 2019, Portland, OR, USA, 9–12 September 2019. LIPIcs, vol. 141, pp. 34:1–34:8. Schloss Dagstuhl - Leibniz-Zentrum für Informatik (2019). https://doi.org/10.4230/LIPIcs.ITP.2019.34

23. Kaliszyk, C., Urban, J.: Mizar 40 for mizar 40. J. Autom. Reason. **55**(3), 245–256 (2015). https://doi.org/10.1007/s10817-015-9330-8

24. Kovács, L., Voronkov, A.: First-order theorem proving and VAMPIRE. In: Sharygina, N., Veith, H. (eds.) CAV 2013. LNCS, vol. 8044, pp. 1–35. Springer, Heidelberg (2013). https://doi.org/10.1007/978-3-642-39799-8_1

25. Looks, M., Herreshoff, M., Hutchins, D., Norvig, P.: Deep learning with dynamic computation graphs. In: 5th International Conference on Learning Representations, ICLR 2017, Toulon, France, 24–26 April 2017, Conference Track Proceedings. OpenReview.net (2017)

26. Loos, S.M., Irving, G., Szegedy, C., Kaliszyk, C.: Deep network guided proof search. In: Eiter, T., Sands, D. (eds.) LPAR-21, 21st International Conference on Logic for Programming, Artificial Intelligence and Reasoning, Maun, Botswana, 7–12 May 2017. EPiC Series in Computing, vol. 46, pp. 85–105. EasyChair (2017)

27. Nieuwenhuis, R., Rubio, A.: Paramodulation-based theorem proving. In: Robinson and Voronkov [33], pp. 371–443. https://doi.org/10.1016/b978-044450813-3/50009-6

28. Paszke, A., et al.: PyTorch: an imperative style, high-performance deep learning library. In: Wallach, H., Larochelle, H., Beygelzimer, A., d'Alché-Buc, F., Fox, E., Garnett, R. (eds.) Advances in Neural Information Processing Systems, vol. 32, pp. 8024–8035. Curran Associates, Inc. (2019). http://papers.neurips.cc/paper/9015-pytorch-an-imperative-style-high-performance-deep-learning-library.pdf

29. Piotrowski, B., Urban, J.: Stateful premise selection by recurrent neural networks. In: Albert, E., Kovács, L. (eds.) LPAR 2020: 23rd International Conference on Logic for Programming, Artificial Intelligence and Reasoning, Alicante, Spain, 22–27 May 2020. EPiC Series in Computing, vol. 73, pp. 409–422. EasyChair (2020). https://easychair.org/publications/paper/g38n

30. Recht, B., Re, C., Wright, S., Niu, F.: HOGWILD!: a lock-free approach to parallelizing stochastic gradient descent. In: Shawe-Taylor, J., Zemel, R., Bartlett, P., Pereira, F., Weinberger, K.Q. (eds.) Advances in Neural Information Processing Systems, vol. 24. Curran Associates, Inc. (2011). https://proceedings.neurips.cc/paper/2011/file/218a0aefd1d1a4be65601cc6ddc1520e-Paper.pdf

31. Reger, G., Suda, M., Voronkov, A.: Playing with AVATAR. In: Felty, A.P., Middeldorp, A. (eds.) CADE 2015. LNCS (LNAI), vol. 9195, pp. 399–415. Springer, Cham (2015). https://doi.org/10.1007/978-3-319-21401-6_28

32. Riazanov, A., Voronkov, A.: Limited resource strategy in resolution theorem proving. J. Symb. Comput. **36**(1–2), 101–115 (2003). https://doi.org/10.1016/S0747-7171(03)00040-3

33. Robinson, J.A., Voronkov, A. (eds.): Handbook of Automated Reasoning (in 2 volumes). Elsevier and MIT Press (2001)

34. Schulz, S.: Learning Search Control Knowledge for Equational Deduction. No. 230 in DISKI, Akademische Verlagsgesellschaft Aka GmbH Berlin (2000)

35. Schulz, S., Cruanes, S., Vukmirovic, P.: Faster, higher, stronger: E 2.3. In: Fontaine [12], pp. 495–507. https://doi.org/10.1007/978-3-030-29436-6_29
36. Schulz, S., Möhrmann, M.: Performance of clause selection heuristics for saturation-based theorem proving. In: Olivetti, N., Tiwari, A. (eds.) IJCAR 2016. LNCS (LNAI), vol. 9706, pp. 330–345. Springer, Cham (2016). https://doi.org/10.1007/978-3-319-40229-1_23
37. Srivastava, N., Hinton, G.E., Krizhevsky, A., Sutskever, I., Salakhutdinov, R.: Dropout: a simple way to prevent neural networks from overfitting. J. Mach. Learn. Res. **15**(1), 1929–1958 (2014). http://dl.acm.org/citation.cfm?id=2670313
38. Suda, M.: Aiming for the goal with SInE. In: Kovács, L., Voronkov, A. (eds.) Vampire 2018 and Vampire 2019. The 5th and 6th Vampire Workshops. EPiC Series in Computing, vol. 71, pp. 38–44. EasyChair (2020). https://doi.org/10.29007/q4pt
39. Suda, M.: Improving ENIGMA-style clause selection while learning from history. In: Platzer, A., Sutcliffe, G. (eds.) Proceedings of the 28th CADE (2021, to appear). https://arxiv.org/abs/2102.13564
40. Tammet, T.: GKC: a reasoning system for large knowledge bases. In: Fontaine [12], pp. 538–549. https://doi.org/10.1007/978-3-030-29436-6_32
41. Urban, J.: MPTP 0.2: Design, implementation, and initial experiments. J. Autom. Reason. **37**(1–2), 21–43 (2006). https://doi.org/10.1007/s10817-006-9032-3
42. Urban, J., Vyskočil, J., Štěpánek, P.: MaLeCoP machine learning connection prover. In: Brünnler, K., Metcalfe, G. (eds.) TABLEAUX 2011. LNCS (LNAI), vol. 6793, pp. 263–277. Springer, Heidelberg (2011). https://doi.org/10.1007/978-3-642-22119-4_21
43. Voronkov, A.: AVATAR: the architecture for first-order theorem provers. In: Biere, A., Bloem, R. (eds.) CAV 2014. LNCS, vol. 8559, pp. 696–710. Springer, Cham (2014). https://doi.org/10.1007/978-3-319-08867-9_46
44. Wang, M., Tang, Y., Wang, J., Deng, J.: Premise selection for theorem proving by deep graph embedding. In: Guyon, I., et al. (eds.) Advances in Neural Information Processing Systems 30: Annual Conference on Neural Information Processing Systems 2017, Long Beach, CA, USA, 4–9 December 2017, pp. 2786–2796 (2017). https://proceedings.neurips.cc/paper/2017/hash/18d10dc6e666eab6de9215ae5b3d54df-Abstract.html
45. Weidenbach, C., Dimova, D., Fietzke, A., Kumar, R., Suda, M., Wischnewski, P.: SPASS version 3.5. In: Schmidt, R.A. (ed.) CADE 2009. LNCS (LNAI), vol. 5663, pp. 140–145. Springer, Heidelberg (2009). https://doi.org/10.1007/978-3-642-02959-2_10

Satisfiability Modulo Theories

Optimization Modulo Non-linear Arithmetic via Incremental Linearization

Filippo Bigarella[1], Alessandro Cimatti[2], Alberto Griggio[2], Ahmed Irfan[1,2], Martin Jonáš[2], Marco Roveri[1], Roberto Sebastiani[1(✉)], and Patrick Trentin[1]

[1] DISI, University of Trento, Trento, Italy
roberto.sebastiani@unitn.it
[2] Fondazione Bruno Kessler - FBK, Trento, Italy

Abstract. Incremental linearization is a conceptually simple, yet effective, technique that we have recently proposed for solving SMT problems on the theories of non-linear arithmetic over the reals and the integers. Optimization Modulo Theories (OMT) is an important extension of SMT which allows for finding models that optimize given objective functions. In this paper, we show how incremental linearization can be extended to OMT in a simple way, producing an incomplete though effective OMT procedure. We describe the main ideas and algorithms, we provide an implementation within the OptiMathSAT OMT solver, and perform an empirical evaluation. The results support the effectiveness of the approach.

1 Introduction

Context. Satisfiability Modulo Theories (SMT) is the problem of deciding the satisfiability of a first-order formula with respect to some theories of interest (e.g. theory of linear arithmetic, of arrays, of bit-vectors, ...) and combination thereof [5]. Powerful and effective SMT techniques and tools are available for a large variety of theories, including the quantifier-free theories[1] of Uninterpreted Functions (UF) and Linear Arithmetic (LA), either over the reals (LRA) or the integers (LIA), as well as their combinations (UFLRA, UFLIA), of bit-vector (BV) and floating-point arithmetic (FP).

When dealing with arithmetic, a fundamental challenge is to go beyond the linear case, by introducing multiplications between variables, and hence between complex terms – over the reals (NRA) or over theIn the following, we only consider quantifier-free theories, and we abuse the accepted notation and omit the "QF_" prefix in the names of the theories. integers (NIA). (We also use the term "NIRA" [resp. "LIRA"] when we do not distinguish between NRA and NIA [resp. LRA and LIA].) Unfortunately, dealing with non-linearity is a very hard

---

[1] In the following, we only consider quantifier-free theories, and we abuse the accepted notation and omit the "QF_" prefix in the names of the theories.

A. Irfan—The author's contribution dates when he was still at FBK, Trento.

© Springer Nature Switzerland AG 2021
B. Konev and G. Reger (Eds.): FroCoS 2021, LNAI 12941, pp. 213–231, 2021.
https://doi.org/10.1007/978-3-030-86205-3_12

challenge. Going from SMT(LRA) to SMT(NRA) yields a complexity gap that results in a computational barrier in practice – most available complete solvers rely on Cylindrical algebraic decomposition (CAD) techniques [15], which require double exponential time in worst case. Reasoning in NIA is even undecidable [30].

Incremental Linearization. Recently, we have proposed a conceptually-simple, incomplete yet effective practical approach for SMT dealing with the quantifier-free theory of non-linear arithmetic over the reals, over the reals extended with transcendental functions, and over integers, called *Incremental Linearization* [13]. Its underlying idea is that of trading the use of expensive, exact solvers for non-linear arithmetic for an abstraction-refinement loop on top of much cheaper solvers for linear arithmetic and uninterpreted functions.

Optimization Modulo Theories. Many SMT problems of interest, however, require the capability of finding models that are optimum wrt. some objective functions. These problems are grouped under the umbrella term of Optimization Modulo Theories – OMT [8,32,34]. OMT techniques have been conceived for a variety of theories, including LRA [8,34], LIA [8,36], BV [31], FP [39]. In general, they work by performing sequences of incremental SMT calls, possibly combined with theory-specific optimization techniques for the conjunctive fragment of the given theory, which progressively tighten the range of values of the objective function.

OMT by Incremental Linearization. In this paper, we show how incremental linearization can be extended from SMT to OMT in a very simple way, producing an incomplete though effective OMT procedure. As with the SMT case in [13], the goal is to build an OMT(NIRA) solver on top of "cheap" ingredients: SMT(UFLIRA) and OMT(UFLIRA) incremental calls driven by an abstraction-refinement loop, with no expensive solver or optimizer for non-linear arithmetic, so that the task of progressing towards the optimum is performed by a combination of Boolean search and optimization in the abstract UFLIRA space. We describe the main ideas and algorithms.

We have implemented the novel OMT(NIRA) algorithms within the OMT solver OptiMathSAT [37], which is built on top of the MathSAT5 SMT solver [14], where the incremental linearization for SMT(NIRA) procedures have been implemented [13]. We have experimentally validated our algorithm with an analysis of the performance of OptiMathSAT in dealing with OMT(NRA) and OMT(NIA) problems, and compared these results with those of another state-of-the-art OMT solver, Z3 [8], which offers a limited support for OMT(NRA) and OMT(NIA). Although quite preliminary to some extent, the results show that, despite the simplicity of the implemented procedures, OptiMathSAT solves the largest number of benchmarks overall, thus supporting the effectiveness of the approach.

Related Work. Efficient SMT solving for non-linear arithmetic is an open research problem for which a variety of approaches have been proposed; these are often complementary with one another [13]. Methods for dealing with SMT(NRA) are typically based on: *cylindrical algebraic decomposition* (CAD) [3,15,23,25], *virtual substitution* (VS) [40], *interval constraint propagation* (ICP) [6,21], *bit-blasting* [20,41], *linearization* [9–11,19,28,33] and *incremental linearization* [13]. Methods for dealing with SMT(NIA) are based on the combination of branch-and-bound search with some SMT(NRA) solving technique. See, for example, [22] and [26] based on CAD and CAD+VS respectively, and [12] based on *incremental linearization*.

OMT for non-linear arithmetic, instead, is a largely unexplored territory: the Z3 [8] OMT solver does not officially support optimization with NIRA constraints or objective functions.[2] However, in practice, it can compute optimal solutions for some of these problems, albeit without providing any guarantees.

DREAL is a SMT(NRA) solver based on the notion of δ-satisfiability [21], that basically guarantees that there exists a variant (within a user-specified δ "radius") of the original problem such that it is satisfiable. Importantly, we notice that the approach cannot guarantee that the original problem is satisfiable, since it relies on numerical approximation techniques that only compute safe over-approximations of the solution space. DREAL supports optimization with NRA objective functions and/or in the presence of NRA constraints [24].

Content. The paper is organized as follows. In Sect. 2 we provide some background knowledge on OMT and incremental linearization; in Sect. 3 we present our main ideas and new OMT(NIRA) procedures; in Sect. 4 we perform the empirical evaluation, discussing the results; in Sect. 5 we draw some conclusions, and illustrate possible future research directions.

2   Background

2.1   Optimization Modulo Theories

We assume the reader is familiar with the main theoretical and algorithmic concepts in SAT and SMT solving (see e.g. [5,29]). Optimization Modulo Theories (OMT) is an extension of SMT which addresses the problem of finding a model for an input formula φ which is optimal wrt. some objective function obj [32,34]. (In this paper we consider optimization as minimization; the narration for maximization is dual.) A little more formally, given some theory $\mathcal{T}$ admitting some total order "$\leq$" over its domain, an OMT($\mathcal{T}$) problem is given by a pair $\langle \varphi, \text{obj} \rangle$ where φ, obj are a formula and a term over $\mathcal{T}$, and consists in finding a model for φ (if any) which makes the value of obj minimum according to the order given by $\leq$.[3]

The basic minimization strategy implemented in all state-of-the-art OMT solvers, is known as *linear-search* strategy [32,34,35]. It requires solving an SMT problem with a feasible space that is progressively tightened by learning a

---

[2] https://github.com/Z3Prover/z3/issues/2247
  https://github.com/Z3Prover/z3/issues/5339.

[3] More generally the formula can be built on a combination of $\mathcal{T}$ with other theories, see e.g. [35]. However, to simplify the narration and the notation, here we refer to one single theory.

sequence of unit clauses of the form (obj < ub), where ub is the current upper bound of the optimization search. At each iteration, the SMT solver can either find a model $\mathcal{M}$ of φ whose value of obj, denoted with $\mathcal{M}[\text{obj}]$, is smaller than the current upper bound ub, or discover that the stack of formulas has become unsatisfiable. In the first case, the OMT solver invokes a $\mathcal{T}$-specific minimization procedure over the propositional truth assignment ψ induced by $\mathcal{M}$ on the atoms of the formula, so as to generate a model $\mathcal{M}'$ of φ such that the value of $\mathcal{M}'[\text{obj}]$ is minimum for the given propositional assignment ψ. Then, the $\mathcal{M}'[\text{obj}]$ becomes the new upper bound ub of the optimization search. The OMT search terminates when such procedure finds that obj is unbounded or when the SMT search is UNSAT, in which case the last model $\mathcal{M}_i$ of φ (if any) is the optimal solution.

If, for some theory $\mathcal{T}$, $\mathcal{T}$-specific minimization is hard to implement (e.g. for floating-point arithmetic [39]) or computationally too expensive (e.g., for linear integer arithmetic [36]), then we can rely on other strategies.

One possible approach for the latter case is to implement a cheaper though incomplete $\mathcal{T}$-specific minimization procedure, which may only improve the value of $\mathcal{M}[\text{obj}]$ with no guarantee to find a minimum one for the given truth assignment. This comes at the risk of generating and exploring the same truth assignment more than once, overall trading arithmetic minimization search for extra Boolean search [36].

An alternative minimization approach is the *binary-search* strategy described in [34]. At the beginning of each binary search step, the OMT solver calls a function ComputePivot() to compute a pivoting value contained in the current search interval. (In its simplest implementation, ComputePivot() returns the value of $\frac{(\text{ub}-\text{lb})}{2}$, where lb and ub are the lower and the upper bound currently delimiting the optimization search respectively). Then, the OMT solver temporarily assumes a unit-clause of the form (obj < pivot). This effectively restricts the search space so that it includes only satisfiable truth assignments (if any) for which obj has a value included in the interval [lb, pivot). If any such solution is found by the OMT solver, the algorithm proceeds like in *linear-search* mode, and updates the current upper bound ub. Otherwise, if no such solution exists, then the pivoting unit-clause (obj < pivot) is replaced by its negation ¬(obj < pivot) and pivot becomes the new lower bound. Notice that, in case of continuous domains (e.g., LRA, NRA) the binary search alone may not terminate, so that it is necessary to interleave binary-search steps with linear-search ones [35].

2.2 SMT(NIRA) via Incremental Linearization

The main idea of incremental linearization [13] is to trade the use of expensive, exact solvers for non-linear arithmetic for an abstraction-refinement loop on top of much cheaper solvers for linear arithmetic and uninterpreted functions, UFLIRA. The pseudo-code of the baseline procedure is shown in Fig. 1.

First, the input SMT(NIRA) formula φ is abstracted to the SMT(UFLIRA) formula $\hat{\varphi}$ (called its UFLIRA-abstraction) by substituting every non-linear

function SMT-INCREMENTAL-LINEARIZATION(φ)

1: $\hat{\varphi} := $ SMT-INITIAL-ABSTRACTION(φ) ;   // $\hat{\varphi}$ over-approximates φ
2: $\Gamma := \emptyset$;   // linearization lemmas
3: **while** *true* **do**
4:      $\langle sat, \hat{\mu} \rangle := $ SMT-UFLIRA-CHECK($\hat{\varphi} \wedge \bigwedge \Gamma$)
         // $\hat{\varphi} \wedge \bigwedge \Gamma$ over-approximates φ
5:      **if not** *sat* **then**
6:          **return** $\langle false, \emptyset \rangle$
7:      $\langle sat, \mu, \Gamma' \rangle := $ SMT-CHECK-REFINE($\hat{\varphi}, \hat{\mu}$)
8:      **if** *sat* **then**
9:          **return** $\langle true, \mu \rangle$
10:     **else**
11:         $\Gamma := \Gamma \cup \Gamma'$

Fig. 1. Solving SMT(NIRA) via incremental linearization.

function SMT-CHECK-REFINE($\hat{\varphi}, \hat{\mu}$)

1: $\hat{\psi} := $ EXTRACTASSIGNMENT($\hat{\varphi}, \hat{\mu}$) ;   // Eq. (1)
2: $\hat{\psi}^* := \hat{\psi} \wedge $ LINEARIZATION-CONSTRAINTS($\hat{\psi}$) ;   // Eq. (2)
3: $\langle sat, \hat{\mu}' \rangle := $ SMT-UFLIRA-CHECK($\hat{\psi}^*$)
4: **if** *sat* **then**
5:      **return** $\langle true, \hat{\mu}', \emptyset \rangle$;   // $\hat{\mu}'$ is a model of φ
6: **else**
7:      $\Gamma := $ BLOCK-SPURIOUS-PRODUCT-TERMS($\hat{\varphi}, \hat{\mu}$)
8:      **return** $\langle false, \emptyset, \Gamma \rangle$

Fig. 2. The procedure checking whether $\hat{\mu}$ can be refined into a model of φ.

multiplication term $x * y$ with $f_*(x, y)$, where both x and y are variables[4] and f_* is an uninterpreted function symbol (function SMT-INITIAL-ABSTRACTION in line 1). Then, the set of linearization lemmas Γ (i.e. UFLIRA-abstraction of NIRA-valid multiplication lemmas in Fig. 3) is initialized to the empty set, and the loop begins.[5]

First, the UFLIRA-satisfiability of $\hat{\varphi}$ augmented with the linearization lemmas in Γ is checked. If the SMT(UFLIRA) check returns false, then the input formula is NIRA-unsatisfiable, because $\hat{\varphi} \wedge \bigwedge \Gamma$ is an over-approximation of φ by construction (lines 4–6).

---

[4] As in [13] and with no loss of generality, hereafter we assume that all multiplications in φ are either between two variables or between one constant and one variable, because more complex terms occurring in a multiplication can be renamed by fresh variables. Notice that this assumption is not necessary in practice, but it simplifies the explanation.

[5] In order to keep the narration simple, in Fig. 1 we have omitted some details. First, the input formula can be simplified by some preprocessing steps. Furthermore, for each fresh $f_*(x, y)$ term, $\hat{\varphi}$ can be extended from the beginning with simple multiplication lemmas. We refer the reader to [13] for details.

Otherwise, the abstract model $\hat{\mu}$ for $\widehat{\varphi}$ is used to build an UFLIRA under-approximation $\widehat{\psi}^*$ of φ, with the aim of finding a model μ for $\widehat{\psi}^*$, and thus for the original NIRA formula φ (function SMT-CHECK-REFINE in line 7). If this succeeds, then φ is also satisfiable. Otherwise, SMT-CHECK-REFINE returns a set Γ' of linear *lemmas* which are sufficient to rule out the spurious model $\hat{\mu}$. Γ' is then added to Γ, thus improving the precision of the abstraction, and another iteration of the loop is performed.

The lemmas added are instances of the axioms of Fig. 3, obtained by replacing the free variables with terms occurring in φ, selected among those that evaluate to false under the current spurious model μ.

The pseudo-code of the model search procedure (SMT-CHECK-REFINE) is reported in Fig. 2. In particular, $\widehat{\psi}^*$ is built by first generating the truth assignment $\widehat{\psi}$ for the atoms in $\widehat{\varphi}$ which is entailed by the current abstract model $\widehat{\mu}$, and then by adding *multiplication line constraints* that force all multiplications in ψ to be linear (lines 1–2):

$$\widehat{\psi} = \bigwedge_{[\hat{A}\in\, atoms(\hat{\varphi})\; s.t.\; \hat{\mu}\models\hat{A}]} \hat{A} \;\wedge\; \bigwedge_{[\hat{A}\in\, atoms(\hat{\varphi})\; s.t.\; \hat{\mu}\not\models\hat{A}]} \neg\hat{A} \qquad (1)$$

$$\widehat{\psi}^* = \widehat{\psi}\wedge \bigwedge_{f_*(x,y)\in\hat{\psi}} (x = \hat{\mu}[x]\wedge f_*(x,y) = \hat{\mu}[x]*y))\vee(y = \hat{\mu}[y]\wedge f_*(x,y) = \hat{\mu}[y]*x)) \qquad (2)$$

Then the UFLIRA-satisfiability of $\widehat{\psi}^*$ is checked: if satisfiable, then φ is NIRA-satisfiable and its model $\hat{\mu}'$ is also a model for φ (lines 3–5). Otherwise, a set Γ of lemmas ruling out the spurious model $\hat{\mu}'$ is produced and returned (lines 6–8).

3   Optimization Modulo Non-linear Arithmetic

In this section, we present our novel Optimization Modulo Non-Linear Arithmetic procedure based on the combination of the optimization schema described in Sect. 2.1 and the incremental linearization approach described in Sect. 2.2. In Sect. 3.1, we describe the basic version of this new algorithm, based on the linear optimization search schema, and discuss the termination of the algorithm. Then, in Sect. 3.2, we describe some simple improvements over the basic approach that can significantly improve the effectiveness of the procedure, despite remaining incomplete.

3.1   Linear Optimization Search

The pseudo-code of the basic approach to Optimization Modulo Non-Linear Arithmetic, based on the linear optimization search schema, is shown in Fig. 4.

Basic:	*Sign:*	$v_1 * v_2 = (-v_1 * -v_2)$
		$v_1 * v_2 = -(-v_1 * v_2)$
		$v_1 * v_2 = -(v_1 * -v_2)$
	Zero:	$(v_1 = 0 \lor v_2 = 0) \leftrightarrow v_1 * v_2 = 0$
		$((v_1 > 0 \land v_2 > 0) \lor (v_1 < 0 \land v_2 < 0)) \leftrightarrow v_1 * v_2 > 0$
		$((v_1 < 0 \land v_2 > 0) \lor (v_1 > 0 \land v_2 < 0)) \leftrightarrow v_1 * v_2 < 0$
	Neutral:	$(v_1 = 1 \lor v_2 = 0) \leftrightarrow v_1 * v_2 = v_2$
		$(v_2 = 1 \lor v_1 = 0) \leftrightarrow v_1 * v_2 = v_1$
	Proportionality:	$|v_1 * v_2| \geq |v_2| \leftrightarrow (|v_1| \geq 1 \lor v_2 = 0)$
		$|v_1 * v_2| \leq |v_2| \leftrightarrow (|v_1| \leq 1 \lor v_2 = 0)$
		$|v_1 * v_2| \geq |v_1| \leftrightarrow (|v_2| \geq 1 \lor v_1 = 0)$
		$|v_1 * v_2| \leq |v_1| \leftrightarrow (|v_2| \leq 1 \lor v_1 = 0)$
Order:		$(v_1 * v_2 \bowtie v_3 \land v_4 > 0) \rightarrow v_1 * v_2 * v_4 \bowtie v_3 * v_4$
		$(v_1 * v_2 \bowtie v_3 \land v_4 < 0) \rightarrow v_3 * v_4 \bowtie v_1 * v_2 * v_4$
Monotonicity:		$(|v_1| \leq |v_2| \land |v_3| \leq |v_4|) \rightarrow |v_1 * v_3| \leq |v_2 * v_4|$
		$(|v_1| < |v_2| \land |v_3| \leq |v_4| \land v_4 \neq 0) \rightarrow |v_1 * v_3| < |v_2 * v_4|$
		$(|v_1| \leq |v_2| \land |v_3| < |v_4| \land v_2 \neq 0) \rightarrow |v_1 * v_3| < |v_2 * v_4|$
Tangent plane:		$v_1 = a \rightarrow v_1 * v_2 = a * v_2$
		$v_2 = b \rightarrow v_1 * v_2 = b * v_1$
		$(v_1 > a \land v_2 < b) \rightarrow v_1 * v_2 < b * v_1 + a * v_2 - a * b$
		$(v_1 < a \land v_2 > b) \rightarrow v_1 * v_2 < b * v_1 + a * v_2 - a * b$
		$(v_1 < a \land v_2 < b) \rightarrow v_1 * v_2 > b * v_1 + a * v_2 - a * b$
		$(v_1 > a \land v_2 > b) \rightarrow v_1 * v_2 > b * v_1 + a * v_2 - a * b$

Fig. 3. Axioms of the multiplication function.

Input and Initialization. The algorithm takes as input an SMT(NIRA) formula φ, a LIRA objective obj and a threshold precision value ϵ. (We can assume wlog. that obj is a LIRA term because, if not so, we can rewrite $\langle \varphi, \text{obj} \rangle$ into $\langle \varphi \land (v = \text{obj}), v \rangle$, v being a fresh variable.) Lines 1–4 are part of the startup phase of the OMT(NIRA) algorithm. First, the UFLIRA abstraction $\hat{\varphi}$ over-approximating φ is computed at line 1. Next, the current best model $\mathcal{M}$, the set of optimization constraints Θ and the set of linearization lemmas Γ are initialized to the empty set (lines 2–4).[6]

Main Loop. Given the current best model $\mathcal{M}$, optimization constraints Θ and linearization constraints Γ, the algorithm enters into its main loop (lines 5–19), which can be virtually divided into two distinct blocks.

The first block, lines 6–9, corresponds to a single application of the incremental linearization schema presented in Fig. 1, lines 4–7. The goal of this phase is to find an initial abstract UFLIRA model $\hat{\mu}$ of $\hat{\varphi} \land \bigwedge \Gamma \land \bigwedge \Theta$ that is refined into a NIRA model μ of $\varphi \land \bigwedge \Theta$. This step can have three possible outcomes.

(i) SMT-UFLIRA-CHECK fails to find such $\hat{\mu}$ because $\hat{\varphi} \land \bigwedge \Gamma \land \bigwedge \Theta$ is UFLIRA-unsatisfiable. This implies that $\varphi \land \bigwedge \Theta$ is also NIRA-unsatisfiable,

---

[6] The same considerations as in Footnote 5 apply here as well.

function OMT-NIRA-LINEAR-SEARCH(φ, obj, ϵ)

1: $\hat{\varphi} :=$ SMT-INITIAL-ABSTRACTION(φ)   // $\hat{\varphi}$ over-approximates φ

2: $\mathcal{M} := \emptyset$ // current best model

3: $\Theta := \emptyset$ // optimization constraints as (obj < ub)

4: $\Gamma := \emptyset$ // linearization lemmas

5: **while** *true* **do**

6:     $\langle sat, \hat{\mu} \rangle :=$ SMT-UFLIRA-CHECK($\hat{\varphi} \wedge \bigwedge \Gamma \wedge \bigwedge \Theta$) // $\hat{\mu}$ abstract model
       // $\hat{\varphi} \wedge \bigwedge \Gamma$ over-approximates φ

7:     **if not** *sat* **then**

8:        **break**

9:     $\langle sat, \mu, \Gamma' \rangle :=$ SMT-CHECK-REFINE($\hat{\varphi} \wedge \bigwedge \Theta, \hat{\mu}$)

10:    **if** *sat* **then**

11:      $\mathcal{M} := \mu$

12:      $\hat{\psi} :=$ EXTRACTASSIGNMENT($\hat{\varphi}, \mu$)   // Eq. (1)

13:      $\hat{\mu}' :=$ UFLIRA-MINIMIZE($\hat{\psi}$, obj)

14:      $\langle sat, \mu', \Gamma' \rangle :=$ OMT-CHECK-REFINE($\hat{\varphi} \wedge \bigwedge \Theta, \hat{\mu}'$, obj)

15:      **if** *sat* **then**

16:        $\mathcal{M} := \mu'$ // $\hat{\mu}'[\text{obj}] \leq \mu'[\text{obj}] \leq \mu[\text{obj}]$

17:      ub $:=$ GET-UPPER-BOUND($\hat{\mu}'[\text{obj}], \mathcal{M}[\text{obj}], \epsilon$)

18:      $\Theta := \Theta \cup \{(\text{obj} < \text{ub})\}$ // linear-search step

19:     $\Gamma := \Gamma \cup \Gamma'$

20: **if** $\mathcal{M} \neq \emptyset$ **then**

21:    **return** $\langle$ SAT, $\mathcal{M} \rangle$

22: **else**

23:    **return** $\langle$ UNSAT, $\emptyset \rangle$

Fig. 4. A baseline schema of our OMT(NIRA) procedure, with linear search.

function OMT-CHECK-REFINE($\hat{\varphi}$, $\hat{\mu}$, obj)

1: $\hat{\psi} :=$ EXTRACTASSIGNMENT($\hat{\varphi}, \hat{\mu}$)   // Eq. (1)

2: $\hat{\psi}^* := \hat{\psi} \wedge$ LINEARIZATION-CONSTRAINTS($\hat{\psi}$)   // Eq. (2)

3: $\langle sat, \hat{\mu}' \rangle :=$ OMT-UFLIRA-CHECK-MINIMIZE($\hat{\psi}^*$, obj)

4: **if** *sat* **then**

5:    **return** $\langle true, \hat{\mu}', \emptyset \rangle$ // $\hat{\mu}'$ is a model of φ

6: **else**

7:    $\Gamma :=$ BLOCK-SPURIOUS-PRODUCT-TERMS($\hat{\varphi}, \hat{\mu}$)

8:    **return** $\langle false, \emptyset, \Gamma \rangle$

Fig. 5. The OMT counterpart of the SMT-CHECK-REFINE in Fig. 5.

because the former is an over-approximation of the latter. Thus, there is no better model than the current one (if any), so that the execution breaks out of the loop (lines 6–8);

(ii) SMT-UFLIRA-CHECK succeeds in finding an UFLIRA model $\hat{\mu}$, but SMT-CHECK-REFINE fails to refine $\hat{\mu}$ into a NIRA model μ for $\varphi \wedge \bigwedge \Theta$ (lines 6,

9).[7] If so, SMT-CHECK-REFINE returns a set of UFLIRA constraints Γ' ruling out $\hat{\mu}$ (and other spurious solutions) from the feasible search space, and the procedure skips the second block of lines 10–18, jumping directly to line 19;

(iii) $\hat{\mu}$ is successfully refined and rewritten into a NIRA model μ for $\varphi \wedge \bigwedge \Theta$, allowing for entering into the second block of lines 10–18.

The second block, lines 10–18, is responsible for advancing the optimization search. First, the new current best NIRA model μ for $\varphi \wedge \bigwedge \Theta$ is stored into $\mathcal{M}$ (line 11). Then the algorithm finds a new UFLIRA model $\hat{\mu}'$ for $\hat{\varphi} \wedge \bigwedge \Gamma \wedge \bigwedge \Theta$ with the best possible value of obj s.t. $\hat{\mu}'$ assigns the same truth values as μ to the atoms in $\hat{\varphi} \wedge \bigwedge \Gamma \wedge \bigwedge \Theta$ (lines 12–13). (The latter restriction forces the minimization procedure to search for an improving solution in the same region as the non-linear model μ.) To do this, the truth assignment $\hat{\psi}$ induced by μ on the atoms in $\hat{\varphi} \wedge \bigwedge \Gamma \wedge \bigwedge \Theta$ is extracted (line 12), and a standard minimization algorithm for linear arithmetic is invoked on $\hat{\psi}$ to find an UFLIRA model $\hat{\mu}'$ for $\hat{\psi}$ which minimizes obj (line 13).

Notice that, $\hat{\mu}'$ is a model for $\hat{\varphi} \wedge \bigwedge \Gamma \wedge \bigwedge \Theta$, but not necessarily so for $\varphi \wedge \Theta$. Therefore $\hat{\mu}'$ is checked for spuriousness with a call to a function OMT-CHECK-REFINE (see Fig. 5), the OMT counterpart of SMT-CHECK-REFINE (line 14). If the refinement process succeeds, then $\mathcal{M}$ is updated with the new current best NIRA model μ' (lines 15–16). Notice that $\hat{\mu}'[\text{obj}] \leq \mu'[\text{obj}] \leq \mu[\text{obj}]$, because $\hat{\mu}'[\text{obj}]$ is the lower bound for the value of obj in models sharing the same truth assignment $\hat{\psi}$. Otherwise, OMT-CHECK-REFINE returns a set of UFLIRA constraints Γ' ruling out $\hat{\mu}'$ (and other spurious solutions) from the feasible search space.

In either case, the optimization search is advanced by extending the set of optimization constraints Θ with a fresh linear constraint of the form $(\text{obj} < \text{ub})$, where ub is computed by an external call to GET-UPPER-BOUND (lines 17–18). In its simplest form, GET-UPPER-BOUND simply returns the value of obj in the current non-linear optimal model $\mathcal{M}$. (A more sophisticate version will be discussed later.)

At the end of each iteration of the loop (line 19), the set of linearization constraints Γ is extended with the set of UFLIRA constraints Γ', generated by either SMT-CHECK-REFINE (line 9) or OMT-CHECK-REFINE (line 14), so as to permanently rule out spurious solutions that have already been encountered.

The control-flow reaches lines 20–23 only after breaking the loop at line 8. At this point the algorithm returns SAT and the latest non-linear optimal model $\mathcal{M}$ if available, and UNSAT plus an empty model otherwise.

OMT-CHECK-REFINE in Fig. 5 is the OMT counterpart of SMT-CHECK-REFINE in Fig. 2. The only difference between these two functions is that OMT-CHECK-REFINE tries also to improve as much as possible the value of obj while refining the input model. This happens in line 3, where an UFLIRA OMT call

---

[7] We stress the fact that SMT-CHECK-REFINE returning false does not mean that $\hat{\varphi} \wedge \bigwedge \Theta$ is NIRA-unsatisfiable, rather that it failed to prove it satisfiable.

is performed instead of an SMT one, so that the resulting model (if any) is the best possible among those allowed by the multiplication line constraint in (2).

Notice that OMT-UFLIRA-CHECK-MINIMIZE can even find that obj is unbounded, i.e., that $\hat{\psi}^*$ has models with arbitrarily big negative $\mathcal{M}[\mathrm{obj}]$. If so, then the main procedure can return that obj is unbounded, because $\hat{\psi}^*$ is an underapproximation of the original formula, s.t. the latter has models with arbitrarily big negative $\mathcal{M}[\mathrm{obj}]$ as well.

Progress. The progress towards an optimum solution within the same truth assignment $\hat{\psi}$ is achieved in two distinct steps.

First, in Fig. 4 line 13, UFLIRA-MINIMIZE searches for the best abstract model $\hat{\mu}'$ which is compatible with the current truth assignment $\hat{\psi}$, so that to search for a refined model μ' starting from a point $\hat{\mu}'$ which is positioned in the direction indicated by obj.

Second, in Fig. 5 line 3, OMT-UFLIRA-CHECK-MINIMIZE finds the best possible among the possible refinements of $\hat{\psi}$ allowed by the multiplication line constraint in (2).

Termination. We notice that the algorithm in Fig. 4 is not guaranteed to terminate, even when the objective function is lower-bounded.

First, the SMT(NIRA) decision procedure based on incremental linearization is incomplete, as described in [13]. Therefore, it is possible for the algorithm to get indefinitely stuck in the main loop enumerating one spurious solution after another.[8]

Second, whereas an OMT(NIRA) problem may admit irrational minimum values for obj, the algorithm in Fig. 4 can return only rational values because it is based only on UFLIRA SMT/OMT calls, so that it may produce an infinite sequence of rational solutions progressively approaching the irrational minimum one.

Third, the linear search strategy in the algorithm of Fig. 4 is not guaranteed to converge towards the optimum value of obj in φ. In fact, each linear step may improve the value of the objective function by a negligible amount only (in particular when working on a continuous domain), even maintaining the same truth assignment $\hat{\psi}$, i.e., without toggling the truth values of the atoms of $\hat{\varphi}$ (and hence of φ) induced by the current models. As a result, the algorithm may end up enumerating an infinite sequence of improving solutions within the same propositional branch of the search.

The latter fact deserves some more explanation. Let $\Delta \stackrel{\mathrm{def}}{=} \mathcal{M}[\mathrm{obj}] - \hat{\mu}'[\mathrm{obj}]$ be the difference between the optimization search upper bound ub computed at line 17 by the basic implementation of GET-UPPER-BOUND ($\mathcal{M}[\mathrm{obj}]$, i.e. either $\mu'[\mathrm{obj}]$ or $\mu[\mathrm{obj}]$), and the UFLIRA-optimum $\hat{\mu}'[\mathrm{obj}]$ computed by OMT-UFLIRA-MINIMIZE at line 13. Then $\Delta \geq 0$ because $\hat{\mu}'[\mathrm{obj}] \leq \mu'[\mathrm{obj}] \leq \mu[\mathrm{obj}]$. When $\Delta = 0$, the unit clause (obj $<$ ub) learned at line 18 forces the change

---

[8] For the sake of simplicity, here we do not take into consideration the special termination condition based on a finite budget described in [13].

to a new propositional branch $\hat{\psi}$ of the search because $\hat{\psi} \wedge (\text{obj} < \text{ub})$ is LIRA-inconsistent, and moves the optimization search to explore a new region of the search space. Instead, when $\Delta > 0$ this is not the case, so that the OMT solver may keep looking for an improving NIRA solution in the same region.

Early Termination. We remark that, when forced to terminate by external events (e.g., a timeout), our procedure can return the current best result as a partial-optimum solution.

3.2   Algorithm Improvements

Incrementality of SMT(UFLIRA) and OMT(UFLIRA) Calls. In the algorithms of Fig. 4 and Fig. 5, all the calls to SMT(UFLIRA) and OMT(UFLIRA) (functions SMT-UFLIRA-CHECK and OMT-UFLIRA-CHECK-MINIMIZE) can be performed incrementally (in our implementation, by exploiting the incremental interface of OPTIMATHSAT), so that to avoid exploring the same portions of the search space multiple times.

Linear-Search Strengthening. In order to increase the pruning power of the linear search constraints learned during the optimization search, we modify the behavior of the function GET-UPPER-BOUND called at line 17 in Fig. 4 as follows. First, we compute

$$\gamma \stackrel{\text{def}}{=} \frac{|\hat{\mu}'[\text{obj}] - \mathcal{M}[\text{obj}]|}{\max\{|\hat{\mu}'[\text{obj}]|, |\mathcal{M}[\text{obj}]|\}}, \tag{3}$$

where $\mathcal{M}$ is the current best NIRA model for $\varphi \wedge \bigwedge \Theta$ and $\hat{\mu}'$ is the UFLIRA-optimal model for $\hat{\varphi} \wedge \bigwedge \Gamma \wedge \bigwedge \Theta$. (We recall that $\hat{\mu}'[\text{obj}]$ is the lower bound for the value of obj in models sharing the same truth assignment $\hat{\psi}$.)

If the value of γ is greater than the input threshold precision value ϵ, then GET-UPPER-BOUND returns $\mathcal{M}[\text{obj}]$ as above. Otherwise, we are not interested in further improving the current best solution in the interval $[\hat{\mu}'[\text{obj}], \mathcal{M}[\text{obj}])$. Therefore, GET-UPPER-BOUND returns $\hat{\mu}'[\text{obj}]$ instead of $\mathcal{M}[\text{obj}]$ as the new upper bound ub, which is such that $\hat{\psi} \wedge (\text{obj} < \text{ub})$ is UFLIRA-inconsistent. Thus in the next loop the procedure is forced to search for models in a new propositional branch.

Henceforth, $\mathcal{M}$ is considered the current best model unless/until some new model $\mathcal{M}'$ is found s.t. $\mathcal{M}'[\text{obj}] < \hat{\mu}'[\text{obj}]$. If this is the case, then the search proceeds. Otherwise, if the procedure concludes that no such model exists (line 8) then $\mathcal{M}$ is returned as best model, within the relative error margin of γ (3).

Notice that, in this case, it is also possible to further refine the search by setting $\Theta := \Theta \setminus \{(\text{obj} < \hat{\mu}'[\text{obj}])\} \cup \{\neg(\text{obj} < \hat{\mu}'[\text{obj}]), (\text{obj} < \mathcal{M}[\text{obj}])\}$, and then proceed the search for a better solution within the interval $[\hat{\mu}'[\text{obj}], \mathcal{M}[\text{obj}])$, either by linear or binary search.

function COMPUTEPIVOT(obj, lb, ub, $\hat{\mu}'$, $\mathcal{M}$)
1: **if** lb $\neq$ $-\infty$ **then**
2:     **return** $(lb+ub)/2$
3: **else if** $\hat{\mu}'[obj] \neq -\infty$ **then**
4:     **return** $\hat{\mu}'[obj]$
5: **else if** $0 < \mathcal{M}[obj]$ **then**
6:     **return** 0
7: **else**
8:     **return** $2 \cdot \mathcal{M}[obj]$

Fig. 6. The COMPUTEPIVOT function for OMT(NIRA) in OPTIMATHSAT.

Binary Search. We use the binary search strategy to gain some control on the amount of progress that is made at each step of the optimization search. The ComputePivot() procedure is displayed in Fig. 6.

If a lower bound lb $\neq -\infty$ is available, then $(lb+ub)/2$ is returned (lines 1–2). The main difference with the binary search strategy described in Sect. 2.1 is in how an initial pivot is computed when no lower bound lb is available (lines 3–8). In this case, the procedure determines the best pivoting value heuristically:

- if $\hat{\mu}'[obj] \neq -\infty$, then its value is returned as the new pivot (lines 3–4). Intuitively, this results in a pivoting constraint that is just strong enough to force the OMT solver to look for a model of $\hat{\varphi} \wedge \bigwedge \Gamma \wedge \bigwedge \Theta$ on a different propositional branch;
- otherwise, if the current interval contains 0, then a pivoting step on 0 is forced (lines 5–6). The idea is to discover as quickly as possible the sign of the optimum solution;
- if none of the above apply, so that the actual optimal value of obj can be anywhere within the negative interval $(-\infty, \mathcal{M}[obj]]$, then the double of the (negative) value of $\mathcal{M}[obj]$ is returned (lines 7–8). Doubling the negative value at each iteration ensures that the search proceeds as quickly as possible to the discovery of an initial lower bound, or to a concrete solution as close as possible to $-\infty$ if no such lower bound exists.

4   Experimental Evaluation

Tools Under Test. We have implemented the novel OMT(NIRA) algorithm described in Sect. 3 within the OMT solver OPTIMATHSAT [37]. We have experimentally validated our algorithm with an analysis of the performance of OPTI-MATHSAT in dealing with OMT(NRA) and OMT(NIA) problems, and compared these results with the other available OMT solver, Z3 4.8.10 [8]. Although Z3 does not officially support optimization with non-linear constraints, we use it as a baseline for the evaluation of the presented approach as no other tools can handle our benchmarks. We did not compare against DREAL [21] because it supports neither OMT(NIA) problems, nor our generated OMT(NRA) problems coming from planning applications. We did not modify default options of any of the tools, besides using the option smt.arith.solver=2 for Z3.[9] We have tested OPTIMATHSAT with two configurations: OPTIMATHSAT(LIN), using linear search for optimization, and OPTIMATHSAT(BIN), using binary search. For OPTIMATHSAT we have set the relative-error value ϵ (see Sect. 3) to its default value $\epsilon \stackrel{\text{def}}{=} 10^{-6}$.

We have run the experimental evaluation on a cluster consisting of 20 identical machines. Each of the machines is equipped with Intel Xeon CPU E5-2440 0 2.40 GHz CPU and 96 GB of RAM. The time limit for finding the optimal solution was set to 300 s for each job pair. Memory limit per job pair was set to 8 GiB.

The benchmark-sets, the results and the scripts necessary to reproduce the experiment are made publicly available and can be downloaded from [1].

Benchmark Sets. We have automatically generated OMT(NRA) benchmark set using the tool OMTPLAN [27] extended to dump OMT(NRA) problems in files to enable experimenting with different solvers.[10] OMTPLAN is an AI Planner, which uses Z3 as backend OMT engine, that searches for a sequence of actions of increasing length from one initial completely-specified condition to a goal state, so that a given cost function is minimized. The tool encodes the search for a given plan length leveraging on the Z3 Python API to build and solve the OMT problem. To generate the OMT(NRA) problems, we took existing planning problems from the AI planning literature, and we adapted them to include non-linear constraints in action preconditions, effects and cost functions. We then ran the tool to generate OMT problem files corresponding to problem encodings of increasing length (namely 10, 15, 20, 25, 35, 50, 75, 100). This yielded 752 OMT(NRA) benchmarks that were used for the evaluation.

To evaluate the proposed approach also on OMT(NIA), we have automatically generated OMT(NIA) benchmark sets by starting from the SMT problems contained in the SMT-LIBv2 repository [4]. First, we selected 6680 SMT(NIA) instances that are marked as satisfiable in the repository. In order to transform a SMT instance into an OMT problem, we randomly select an arithmetic variable and use it as the objective of the optimization search. We have repeated this step up to 5 times for each instance, depending on the available number of variables, and generated 33397 OMT(NIA) problems. The vast majority – 92.3% – of the generated OMT(NIA) benchmarks comes from the benchmark family *VeryMax*. Therefore, to keep the evaluation time reasonable, we randomly selected 10% of the benchmarks from this family and evaluated the tools only on this subset. We used all the benchmarks from the other families. In total, we thus evaluated the tools on 5744 OMT(NIA) benchmarks.

---

[9] This option has the effect of enabling the legacy arithmetic solver. Without this option, Z3 produced a significant number of incorrect results.

[10] The modified version of OMTPLAN, together with the planning domain and problems used to generate this benchmark set, is available at [2].

tool & configuration	total	t/o	partial	terminated				time (s.)	unique s.
				unsat	unver.	incor.	correct		
OptiMathSAT(lin)	752	360	231	144	1	0	16	887	0
OptiMathSAT(bin)	752	360	236	140	0	0	16	827	0
Z3	752	266	312	161	6	0	7	315	1
v. best(OptiMathSAT)	752	356	235	144	1	0	16	810	10
v. best(all)	752	260	318	161	6	0	17	899	-

Fig. 7. Experimental results over the OMTPlan benchmark-set.

Verification of Results. We have independently verified the correctness of the optimal results found in this experiment using a portfolio of three SMT solvers: CVC4 [38], MathSAT5 [14] and Z3 [17]. OptiMathSAT and Z3 produce in output a minimum-cost value min.[11] Thus, in order to verify the correctness of such solution, we act as follows. For every OMT problem $\langle \varphi, \mathsf{obj} \rangle$ s.t. the solver terminated and returned a model $\mathcal{M}$ with minimum value min $\overset{\text{def}}{=} \mathcal{M}[\mathsf{obj}]$, we verify (i) that there exists indeed a solution of $\mathsf{obj} = \mathsf{min}$ by checking if $\varphi \wedge (\mathsf{obj} = \mathsf{min})$ is NIRA-satisfiable and (ii) that min is a minimum solution by checking that $\varphi \wedge (\mathsf{obj} < \mathsf{min})$ is NIRA-unsatisfiable. In some cases, OptiMathSAT and Z3 can also decide that the optimization problem is unbounded. In these cases, we checked whether the formula $\varphi \wedge (\mathsf{obj} < -10^6)$ is NIRA-satisfiable. Note that this is not sufficient to prove that the problem indeed is unbounded; this would require quantified reasoning. On the OMT(NRA) formulas, the solvers can also decide that the optimum is infinitesimally close to a given real number, i.e., return an optimum $k + \varepsilon$. For these cases, we checked that (i) the formula $\varphi \wedge (\mathsf{obj} > k) \wedge (\mathsf{obj} < k + 10^{-6})$ is NIRA-satisfiable and that (ii) the formula $\varphi \wedge (\mathsf{obj} \leq k)$ is NIRA-unsatisfiable. Note that this would also require quantified reasoning to confirm the real optimum. If the result passes these checks, we consider it as *verified*.

During the verification, we imposed a timeout of 1200 s on the portfolio's execution for each problem, i.e., 600 s for checking (i) and 600 s for checking (ii). To get more independent verification results, we did not stop the portfolio after the first obtained result and let all the solvers finish. We did not observe any incorrect results; unverified results are discussed in the presentation of the results.

Result Tables and Scatter-Plots. The results of the experimental evaluation are summarized in the two tables in Figs. 7 and 8. The columns list the total number of instances (col. *total*), the number of timeouts (col. *t/o*), the number of timeouts after which the solver was able to provide a partial minimum (col. *partial*), the number of formulas decided as unsatisfiable, if any (col. *unsat.*), the number of formulas with an unverified optimal result (col. *unver.*), the number of formulas with a verified incorrect optimal result (col. *incor.*), the number of formulas with a verified correct optimal result (col. *correct*), the total solving time including all formulas solved correctly (col. *time (s.)*) and the number of formulas

---

[11] Here we describe the case for minimization; the case for maximization is dual.

tool & configuration	total	t/o	partial	terminated			time (s.)	unique s.
				unver.	incor.	correct		
OPTIMATHSAT(LIN)	5744	1449	1019	14	0	3262	97011	85
OPTIMATHSAT(BIN)	5744	1433	1047	11	0	3247	96329	72
Z3	5744	2664	1105	18	0	1957	55319	127
V. BEST(OPTIMATHSAT)	5744	1415	972	15	0	3342	104454	1512
V. BEST(ALL)	5744	1130	1122	23	0	3469	95367	-

Fig. 8. Experimental results over the OMT(NIA) benchmark-set.

that were uniquely solved by the given solver configuration (col *unique s.*). (The *unique s.* column for the V. BEST(OPTIMATHSAT) configuration reports the number of formulas that were solved only by one or both of OPTIMATHSAT versions.)

In the scatter-plots (Fig. 9), we compare the size of the partial minima found by OPTIMATHSAT(LIN) and OPTIMATHSAT(BIN) vs. those of Z3, when the solvers were able to provide at least a partial minimum after the timeout, on OMTPlan problems (1st row) and OMT(NIA) problems (2nd row) respectively. The plots also include results where one of the solvers reported the minimum but the other only finished with a partial minimum. As OMT(NIA) problems are not bounded from below, their partial minima can happen to be arbitrarily big negative numbers. We thus show partial minima smaller than -10^4 on the very left and very bottom lines marked as < -10000. Because OMT(NIA) problems are also discrete, we apply a small random jitter to their results, to better show the number of benchmarks with identical results, which would otherwise overlap.

OMTPlan Results. Figure 7 presents the results for the OMTPlan benchmark set. We note that the generated problems are very difficult for all the solvers; only 17 benchmarks were solved by any of the solvers. On the whole, OPTIMATHSAT solved the largest number of benchmarks within the timeout. On the other hand, there is one benchmark[12] that was correctly solved by Z3 but not by any of the OPTIMATHSAT configurations.

While OPTIMATHSAT with linear search solves one more instance than with binary search, our verification portfolio solver was not able to verify the correctness of this result. More generally, 16 out of 17 results of OPTIMATHSAT(LIN) were verified (7 by one solver, 2 by two solvers, and 7 by all three solvers); all 16 results of OPTIMATHSAT(BIN) were verified (7 by one solver, 2 by two solvers, and 7 by all three solvers); and 7 out of 13 results of Z3 were verified (all by all three solvers). The remaining 6 results of Z3 on which the verification did not finish were of form $k + \varepsilon$.

Note that by the nature of how the benchmarks were generated, some of them are not satisfiable. Although the numbers of unsatisfiable benchmarks are reported in the table, they are not relevant to the evaluation, as they depend only on the performance of the base SMT(NRA) solver and do not compare capabilities of its OMT(NRA) extension.

---

[12] nl_counters_simple/fn-counters-simp__instance_2_75.smt2.

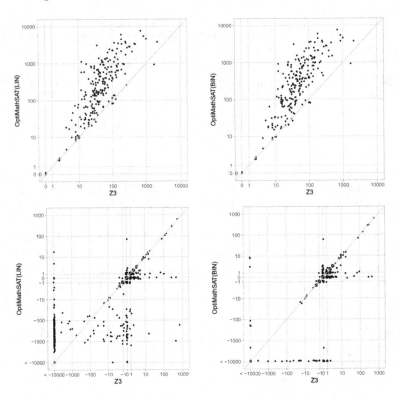

Fig. 9. Size of the partial minima found by OPTIMATHSAT(LIN) (left) and OPTI-MATHSAT(BIN) (right) on Y axis vs. those of Z3 on X axis.
First row shows OMTPlan problems, second row shows OMT(NIA) problems.

Looking at the scatterplots (Fig. 9) we notice that, whereas OPTIMATHSAT finds more minima, Z3 partial minima within the timeout are generally much better than those of OPTIMATHSAT. We do not have a clear-cut explanation of this apparently-contradictory fact.

OMT(NIA) Results. Figure 8 presents the results for the OMT(NIA) benchmark set. In general, almost all the results produced by the solvers were verified to be correct. For OPTIMATHSAT(LIN), 3262 of total 3276 results were verified (128 by one of the solvers, 1076 by two of the solvers, and 2058 by all three); for OPTIMATHSAT(BIN), 3247 of total 3258 results were verified (124 by one of the solvers, 1078 by two of the solvers, and 2045 by all three); for Z3, 1957 of total 1975 results were verified (28 by one of the solvers, 518 by two of the solvers, and 1411 by all three).

On the whole, OPTIMATHSAT solved the largest number of benchmarks within the timeout. We note that there is not a significant difference between the performance of OPTIMATHSAT(LIN) and OPTIMATHSAT(BIN).

Looking at the scatterplots (Fig. 9) we notice that, unlike with the OMTPlan, there is no tool whose partial minima are definitely better than the others.

5   Conclusions and Future Work

In this paper, we have shown how incremental linearization can be extended from SMT(NIRA) to OMT(NIRA) in a very simple way, producing an incomplete though effective OMT procedure. We believe that this procedure, in its simplicity, can also be used as a baseline for more elaborated procedures.

To this extent, we believe that many possible extension are possible. In a short term, we plan to extend it to work also with transcendental functions, exploiting the full expressive power of incremental-linearization approach in SMT presented in [13], and then to test the effectiveness of the procedures on real word verification problems, in particular of cyber-physical systems. In the middle term, we plan to extend our encoders from MiniZinc to OMT and vice-versa [16] to work with non-linear constraints, so that to be able to compare with tools and problems coming from the Constraint Solving & Optimization community. In a longer term, we plan to integrate our approach with more elaborated –though possibly expensive– procedures.

References

1. https://es-static.fbk.eu/people/mjonas/papers/frocos21_oms/
2. https://github.com/roveri-marco/OMTNPlan
3. Ábrahám, E., Davenport, J.H., England, M., Kremer, G.: Deciding the consistency of non-linear real arithmetic constraints with a conflict driven search using cylindrical algebraic coverings. J. Log. Algebraic Methods Program. **119**, 100633 (2021)
4. Barrett, C., Ranise, S., Stump, A., Tinelli, C.: The satisfiability modulo theories library (SMT-LIB) (2010). http://www.smtlib.org
5. Barrett, C., Sebastiani, R., Seshia, S.A., Tinelli, C.: Satisfiability modulo theories, chapter 26, pp. 825–885. Volume 185 of Biere et al. [7], February 2009
6. Benhamou, F., Granvilliers, L.: Continuous and interval constraints. In: Rossi, F., van Beek, P., Walsh, T. (eds.) Handbook of Constraint Programming, Volume 2 of Foundations of Artificial Intelligence, pp. 571–603. Elsevier (2006)
7. Biere, A., Heule, M.J.H., van Maaren, H., Walsh, T. (eds.): Handbook of Satisfiability. IOS Press, February 2009
8. Bjørner, N., Phan, A.-D., Fleckenstein, L.: νZ - an optimizing SMT solver. In: Baier, C., Tinelli, C. (eds.) TACAS 2015. LNCS, vol. 9035, pp. 194–199. Springer, Heidelberg (2015). https://doi.org/10.1007/978-3-662-46681-0_14
9. Borralleras, C., Larraz, D., Rodríguez-Carbonell, E., Oliveras, A., Rubio, A.: Incomplete SMT techniques for solving non-linear formulas over the integers. ACM Trans. Comput. Log. **20**(4), 25:1–25:36 (2019)
10. Borralleras, C., Lucas, S., Oliveras, A., Rodríguez-Carbonell, E., Rubio, A.: SAT modulo linear arithmetic for solving polynomial constraints. J. Autom. Reason. **48**(1), 107–131 (2012). https://doi.org/10.1007/s10817-010-9196-8

11. Brauße, F., Korovin, K., Korovina, M., Müller, N.: A CDCL-style calculus for solving non-linear constraints. In: Herzig, A., Popescu, A. (eds.) FroCoS 2019. LNCS (LNAI), vol. 11715, pp. 131–148. Springer, Cham (2019). https://doi.org/10.1007/978-3-030-29007-8_8

12. Cimatti, A., Griggio, A., Irfan, A., Roveri, M., Sebastiani, R.: Experimenting on solving nonlinear integer arithmetic with incremental linearization. In: Beyersdorff, O., Wintersteiger, C.M. (eds.) SAT 2018. LNCS, vol. 10929, pp. 383–398. Springer, Cham (2018). https://doi.org/10.1007/978-3-319-94144-8_23

13. Cimatti, A., Griggio, A., Irfan, A., Roveri, M., Sebastiani, R.: Incremental linearization for satisfiability and verification modulo nonlinear arithmetic and transcendental functions. ACM Trans. Comput. Log. **19**(3), 19:1–19:52 (2018)

14. Cimatti, A., Griggio, A., Schaafsma, B.J., Sebastiani, R.: The MathSAT5 SMT solver. In: Piterman, N., Smolka, S.A. (eds.) TACAS 2013. LNCS, vol. 7795, pp. 93–107. Springer, Heidelberg (2013). https://doi.org/10.1007/978-3-642-36742-7_7

15. Collins, G.E.: Quantifier elimination for real closed fields by cylindrical algebraic decomposition-preliminary report. ACM SIGSAM Bull. **8**(3), 80–90 (1974)

16. Contaldo, F., Trentin, P., Sebastiani, R.: From MiniZinc to optimization modulo theories, and back. In: Hebrard, E., Musliu, N. (eds.) CPAIOR 2020. LNCS, vol. 12296, pp. 148–166. Springer, Cham (2020). https://doi.org/10.1007/978-3-030-58942-4_10

17. de Moura, L., Bjørner, N.: Z3: an efficient SMT solver. In: Ramakrishnan, C.R., Rehof, J. (eds.) TACAS 2008. LNCS, vol. 4963, pp. 337–340. Springer, Heidelberg (2008). https://doi.org/10.1007/978-3-540-78800-3_24

18. Dixon, C., Finger, M. (eds.): FroCoS 2017. LNCS (LNAI), vol. 10483. Springer, Cham (2017). https://doi.org/10.1007/978-3-319-66167-4

19. Fontaine, P., Ogawa, M., Sturm, T., Vu, X.: Subtropical satisfiability. In: Dixon and Finger [18], pp. 189–206

20. Fuhs, C., Giesl, J., Middeldorp, A., Schneider-Kamp, P., Thiemann, R., Zankl, H.: SAT solving for termination analysis with polynomial interpretations. In: Marques-Silva, J., Sakallah, K.A. (eds.) SAT 2007. LNCS, vol. 4501, pp. 340–354. Springer, Heidelberg (2007). https://doi.org/10.1007/978-3-540-72788-0_33

21. Gao, S., Kong, S., Clarke, E.M.: dReal: an SMT solver for nonlinear theories over the reals. In: Bonacina, M.P. (ed.) CADE 2013. LNCS (LNAI), vol. 7898, pp. 208–214. Springer, Heidelberg (2013). https://doi.org/10.1007/978-3-642-38574-2_14

22. Jovanović, D.: Solving nonlinear integer arithmetic with MCSAT. In: Bouajjani, A., Monniaux, D. (eds.) VMCAI 2017. LNCS, vol. 10145, pp. 330–346. Springer, Cham (2017). https://doi.org/10.1007/978-3-319-52234-0_18

23. Jovanovic, D., de Moura, L.: Solving non-linear arithmetic. ACM Commun. Comput. Algebra **46**(3/4), 104–105 (2012)

24. Kong, S., Solar-Lezama, A., Gao, S.: Delta-decision procedures for exists-forall problems over the reals. In: Chockler, H., Weissenbacher, G. (eds.) CAV 2018. LNCS, vol. 10982, pp. 219–235. Springer, Cham (2018). https://doi.org/10.1007/978-3-319-96142-2_15

25. Kremer, G., Ábrahám, E.: Fully incremental cylindrical algebraic decomposition. J. Symb. Comput. **100**, 11–37 (2020)

26. Kremer, G., Corzilius, F., Ábrahám, E.: A generalised branch-and-bound approach and its application in SAT modulo nonlinear integer arithmetic. In: Gerdt, V.P., Koepf, W., Seiler, W.M., Vorozhtsov, E.V. (eds.) CASC 2016. LNCS, vol. 9890, pp. 315–335. Springer, Cham (2016). https://doi.org/10.1007/978-3-319-45641-6_21

27. Leofante, F., Giunchiglia, E., Ábrahám, E., Tacchella, A.: Optimal planning modulo theories. In: Bessiere, C. (ed.) Proceedings of the Twenty-Ninth International Joint Conference on Artificial Intelligence, IJCAI 2020, pp. 4128–4134. ijcai.org (2020)

28. Maréchal, A., Fouilhé, A., King, T., Monniaux, D., Périn, M.: Polyhedral approximation of multivariate polynomials using Handelman's theorem. In: Jobstmann, B., Leino, K.R.M. (eds.) VMCAI 2016. LNCS, vol. 9583, pp. 166–184. Springer, Heidelberg (2016). https://doi.org/10.1007/978-3-662-49122-5_8

29. Marques-Silva, J.P., Lynce, I., Malik, S.: Conflict-driven clause learning SAT solvers, chapter 4, pp. 131–153. Volume 185 of Biere et al. [7], February 2009

30. Matiyasevich, Y.V.: Hilbert's Tenth Problem. Foundations of Computing, MIT Press, Cambridge (1993)

31. Nadel, A., Ryvchin, V.: Bit-vector optimization. In: Chechik, M., Raskin, J.-F. (eds.) TACAS 2016. LNCS, vol. 9636, pp. 851–867. Springer, Heidelberg (2016). https://doi.org/10.1007/978-3-662-49674-9_53

32. Nieuwenhuis, R., Oliveras, A.: On SAT modulo theories and optimization problems. In: Biere, A., Gomes, C.P. (eds.) SAT 2006. LNCS, vol. 4121, pp. 156–169. Springer, Heidelberg (2006). https://doi.org/10.1007/11814948_18

33. Reynolds, A., Tinelli, C., Jovanovic, D., Barrett, C.W.: Designing theory solvers with extensions. In: Dixon and Finger [33], pp. 22–40

34. Sebastiani, R., Tomasi, S.: Optimization in SMT with $\mathcal{LA}(\mathbb{Q})$ cost functions. In: Gramlich, B., Miller, D., Sattler, U. (eds.) IJCAR 2012. LNCS (LNAI), vol. 7364, pp. 484–498. Springer, Heidelberg (2012). https://doi.org/10.1007/978-3-642-31365-3_38

35. Sebastiani, R., Tomasi, S.: Optimization modulo theories with linear rational costs. ACM Trans. Comput. Log. **16**(2), 1–46 (2015)

36. Sebastiani, R., Trentin, P.: Pushing the envelope of optimization modulo theories with linear-arithmetic cost functions. In: Baier, C., Tinelli, C. (eds.) TACAS 2015. LNCS, vol. 9035, pp. 335–349. Springer, Heidelberg (2015). https://doi.org/10.1007/978-3-662-46681-0_27

37. Sebastiani, R., Trentin, P.: OptiMathSAT: a tool for optimization modulo theories. J. Autom. Reason. **64**, 423–460 (2020). https://doi.org/10.1007/s10817-018-09508-6

38. Stump, A., Barrett, C.W., Dill, D.L.: CVC: a cooperating validity checker. In: Brinksma, E., Larsen, K.G. (eds.) CAV 2002. LNCS, vol. 2404, pp. 500–504. Springer, Heidelberg (2002). https://doi.org/10.1007/3-540-45657-0_40

39. Trentin, P., Sebastiani, R.: Optimization modulo the theory of floating-point numbers. In: Fontaine, P. (ed.) CADE 2019. LNCS (LNAI), vol. 11716, pp. 550–567. Springer, Cham (2019). https://doi.org/10.1007/978-3-030-29436-6_33

40. Weispfenning, V.: Quantifier elimination for real algebra - the quadratic case and beyond. Appl. Algebra Eng. Commun. Comput. **8**(2), 85–101 (1997). https://doi.org/10.1007/s002000050055

41. Zankl, H., Middeldorp, A.: Satisfiability of non-linear (Ir)rational arithmetic. In: Clarke, E.M., Voronkov, A. (eds.) LPAR 2010. LNCS (LNAI), vol. 6355, pp. 481–500. Springer, Heidelberg (2010). https://doi.org/10.1007/978-3-642-17511-4_27

Quantifier Simplification by Unification in SMT

Pascal Fontaine[1,2] and Hans-Jörg Schurr[1]

[1] University of Lorraine, CNRS, Inria, and LORIA, Nancy, France
hans-jorg.schurr@inria.fr
[2] Université de Liège, Liège, Belgium
pascal.fontaine@uliege.be

Abstract. Quantifier reasoning in SMT solvers relies on instantiation: ground instances are generated heuristically from the quantified formulas until a contradiction is reached at the ground level. Current instantiation heuristics, however, often fail in presence of nested quantifiers. To address this issue we introduce a unification-based method that augments the problem with shallow quantified formulas obtained from assertions with nested quantifiers. These new formulas help unlocking the regular instantiation techniques, but parsimony is necessary since they might also be misguiding. To mitigate this, we identify some effective restricting conditions. The method is implemented in the veriT solver, and tested on benchmarks from the SMT-LIB. It allows the solver to prove more formulas, faster.

Keywords: SMT · Quantifier instantiation · Theorem proving

1 Introduction

Satisfiability modulo theories (SMT) solvers are successfully used as back-ends for formal method applications, within interactive proof assistants or verification platforms. SMT solvers based on the CDCL($\mathcal{T}$) calculus [6] excel at handling quantifier-free problems with theories—SMT problems with thousands of assertions are frequent. While originally SMT solvers were mostly applied on such problems, an increasing number of applications require some support for quantifier reasoning. Their main approach to handle quantifiers is *quantifier instantiation*. This approach separates the quantified assertions from the ground part of the problem. Whenever the solver finds a model for the ground part, it generates new ground instances of the quantified formulas. This is repeated until the ground solver determines that the ground problem is unsatisfiable. When done fairly, this approach is refutationally complete for many theories and due to the strength of ground solving it is also very powerful in practice. SMT solvers use multiple instantiation strategies to find these instances. The main challenge is to find the right instances without misguiding or overwhelming the solver. Often one can observe some kind of *butterfly effect*: if the instantiation methods

© Springer Nature Switzerland AG 2021
B. Konev and G. Reger (Eds.): FroCoS 2021, LNAI 12941, pp. 232–249, 2021.
https://doi.org/10.1007/978-3-030-86205-3_13

are unlucky, the solver might be misguided to explore a large set of irrelevant instances and reach the solving timeout. In this regard, every strategy has its own strengths and weaknesses (Sect. 2).

If the problem contains a quantified lemma that also occurs, for example, as an antecedent for another formula, the common instantiation methods often fail to quickly produce the right instances. This structure is quite typical of problems generated by interactive theorem provers—a domain to which the SMT solver veriT has been successfully applied [10, 20]. The following toy example illustrates this issue. We will use it to illustrate various ideas.

Example 1.

$$\forall x. \, P(x) \rightarrow P(f(x, c)) \tag{1}$$
$$\forall y. \, ((\forall z. \, P(z) \rightarrow P(f(z, y))) \rightarrow \neg P(y)) \tag{2}$$
$$P(c) \tag{3}$$

This problem is trivially unsatisfiable: when y is set to c, Assertion 1 occurs as the antecedent of the implication in Assertion 2, so $\neg P(c)$ is a direct consequence of the first two assertions, in contradiction with the third. As described in Sect. 2.3, all major instantiation techniques fail to directly produce the correct instances for this problem. Because SMT solvers typically only perform very limited preprocessing on quantified formulas and especially do not calculate a full clause normal form, the instantiation methods fail to recognize and exploit the fact that Assertion 1 and the antecedent in Assertion 2 are so similar. Since the instantiation methods do not produce the correct instances early, the SMT solver will need multiple instantiation rounds to solve the problem. This can lead to the butterfly effect mentioned above. Real world examples are usually more complex. For example, there are often many ground terms which mislead the instantiation heuristics. Furthermore, the assertions in this example are Horn clauses and could be handled by specialized reasoning. Practical problems, however, are not restricted to Horn clauses.

In CDCL(T) quantified formulas are considered black boxes, and are abstracted as propositional variables in the propositional abstraction of the input formula. These propositional literals are generally of no value to the ground solver. We here make use of them to simplify larger formulas. To solve the example above we identify the occurrence of the unit Assertion 1 within Assertion 2. By using unification we can eliminate this quantified subformula. The result after simplification is the ground formula $\neg P(c)$. After this formula is conjoined to the problem, it is trivially contradictory. In the general case, we use asserted quantified formulas to soundly simplify nested formulas and augment the problem with the result. We propose multiple variants of the core procedure (Sect. 3).

So far, techniques inspired by resolution-based theorem provers are underrepresented in SMT solvers. Systems such as DPLL(Γ) [15], DPLL($\Gamma + T$) [7], and AVATAR [22] combine the inference system of theorem provers with the CDCL(T) transition system on a fundamental level, but the combination is coarse—in those systems the two worlds work side-by-side in tandem. Instead,

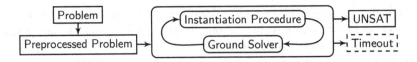

Fig. 1. The instantiation loop of an SMT solver refuting a problem.

our unification-based method is a lightweight and easily implemented preprocessing technique that solves some concrete shortcoming of current instantiation
techniques.

We implemented our method in the SMT solver veriT [8]. To ensure the
process is fast, we use a standard term index and unification algorithm which
we extended to handle the presence of strongly quantified variables (Sect. 4).

The evaluation shows that our technique enables veriT to solve benchmarks
not solved by any strategy before. When applicable, the method often allows
veriT to solve problems within a short timeout. The different variants of the
simplification process are useful within a strategy schedule (Sect. 5).

2   CDCL($\mathcal{T}$) and Quantifier Instantiation

Figure 1 shows the operation of a typical SMT solver when refuting a problem.
It first preprocesses the input problem (Sect. 2.2). Then two procedures together
refute the problem: the ground solver either refutes the problem on the ground
level, or finds a ground model. If a model is found the instantiation procedure
creates new ground lemmas (Sect. 2.3).

2.1   Preliminaries

We use the many-sorted first-order logic with equality as defined in the SMT-LIB
standard [5] and assume the reader is familiar with the notions of signature, term,
free and bound variable, quantified and ground formula, literal, and substitution.
We use x, y, z to denote variables; s, t to denote terms; φ, ψ to denote formulas
(i.e., terms of sort Bool); P to denote a predicate (i.e., a function with codomain
sort Bool); and c to denote constants. To denote the substitution which replaces
a variable x with a term t we write $[t/x]$. As usual, σ stands for a substitution.
We write $\bar{t}$ for the sequence of terms $t_1, \ldots, t_n$ for an unspecified $n \in \mathbb{N}^+$ that is
either irrelevant or clear from the context. Hence, $\forall \bar{x}.\varphi$ corresponds to a term
$\forall x_1, \ldots, x_n.\varphi$. We write **free**$(t)$ to denote the free variables of a term t. The set
$\mathcal{T}(S)$ is the set of all subterms of the terms in S. We omit sorts when they are
clear from the context and assume that sort constraints are always respected,
e.g., substitutions only use terms of the same sort as the substituted variable.

Like in the SMT-LIB standard, the signature Σ always contains a sort Bool,
two constants $\top$ and $\bot$, the usual Boolean connectives, and a family of predicate
symbols ($\approx: \tau \times \tau \to$ Bool) interpreted as equality for each sort τ.

A trimmed formula is the generalization of the notion of atom to arbi-
trary formulas: **trim**(φ) is the formula φ after removing all leading negations.

For example, $\mathbf{trim}(\neg\neg(\varphi_1 \vee \neg\varphi_2))$ is $\varphi_1 \vee \neg\varphi_2$. The *polarity* $\mathbf{pol}(\varphi) \in \{+, -\}$ of a formula φ is $-$ (*negative*) if $\mathbf{trim}(\varphi)$ removes an odd number of negations and $+$ (*positive*) otherwise.

We write $t[\,]$ for a term with a hole and $t[u]$ for the term where the hole has been replaced by u. Any term has at most one hole. We borrow the notions of weak and strong quantifiers [2]: since we are working in a refutation context, a positive occurrence of a quantifier $\exists \bar{x}.\,\varphi$ or a negative occurrence of a quantifier $\forall \bar{x}.\,\varphi$ is strong and a negative occurrence of a quantifier $\exists \bar{x}.\,\varphi$ or a positive occurrence of a quantifier $\forall \bar{x}.\,\varphi$ is weak. We will call the subformula ψ of $Q\bar{x}.\psi$, where $Q \in \{\forall, \exists\}$, the *matrix*, even though ψ might not be in clausal normal form. Without loss of generality, we assume that all quantified variables have been renamed to be distinct.

To handle strong quantifiers we use the Skolemization operator $\mathbf{sk}$. For a formula $Q\bar{x}.\psi$ it is defined as $\mathbf{sk}(Q\bar{x}.\psi, \bar{y}) := \psi[s_1(\bar{y})/x_1] \ldots [s_n(\bar{y})/x_n]$ and each s_i is a fresh function symbol of correct arity. The strong quantifier Q might not be below a weak quantifier. In this case, we write $\mathbf{sk}(Q\bar{x}.\psi, \emptyset)$ and the fresh symbols are constants.

2.2 Preprocessing

Given an input formula $\mathcal{P}$ (i.e., a term of sort Bool) a CDCL($\mathcal{T}$) solver performs multiple preprocessing steps before the solving phase is started. This produces an equisatisfiable problem $\mathcal{P}'$ which is a conjunction of clauses.

To make efficient use of the ground solver, ground formulas are classified. Quantified formulas, however, are treated differently. Their are usually not put in prenex form or clausified. Furthermore, strong quantifiers are usually not fully Skolemized. This has the benefit that the original structure of quantified formulas is preserved, which is crucial for some instantiation techniques.

Preprocessing applies some light form of rewriting on quantified formulas. In veriT, most rewriting steps apply to constants below arithmetic operators and Boolean connectives. For example, the term $f(5+c_1+3, c_2*(3-3))$ is simplified to $f(8 + c_1, 0)$ and $(\bot \rightarrow \varphi_1) \rightarrow \varphi_2$ is replaced by φ_2. Rewriting also ensures that certain global invariants of veriT are met: for instance, all occurrences of bound variables are renamed to distinct variables, and quantifiers over Boolean variables are removed by Shannon expansion.

Skolemization is another preprocessing step applied to quantified formulas. How Skolemization is applied is implementation dependent. The common CDCL($\mathcal{T}$) calculus [6] is only concerned with ground reasoning. While the SMT solver Z3 [16] has a builtin tactic called *nnf* that fully applies Skolemization, CVC4 [4] and veriT only Skolemize outermost strong quantifiers in their default configuration. The rewriter of veriT Skolemizes outermost strong quantifiers by replacing the subformula $\mathbf{trim}(\ell)$ of a formula ℓ by $\mathbf{sk}(\mathbf{trim}(\ell), \emptyset)$ if $\mathbf{trim}(\ell)$ has the form $Q\bar{x}.\,\varphi$, the quantifier Q is strong, and ℓ does not occur below any quantifier.

Due to the limited preprocessing of quantified formulas, some disjuncts of P' start with a weak quantifier and contain complicated formulas. To clarify the distinction, we call the disjuncts which start with a quantifier, and are hence black boxes to the ground solver, *boxes*. Without loss of generality, we assume all boxes are universally quantified. Disjuncts which are not boxes are ground literals. A *unit-box* is a clause with only one disjunct that is a box.

Example 2. The preprocessor will not perform any operations on Example 1. We can illustrate the perspective of the ground solver by replacing quantified formulas by frames. The resulting clause are: $\boxed{1}$, $\boxed{2}$, and $P(c)$. The first two clause are unit-boxes and both boxes will be abstracted to different propositional variables for the SAT solver.

2.3 Instantiation Techniques

The instantiation loop (Fig. 1) starts with the *ground solver*. It either determines that the ground literals of the preprocessed problem $\mathcal{P}'$ are unsatisfiable or produces a *ground model* $\mathcal{M}$. If the ground problem is unsatisfiable, then $\mathcal{P}$ is unsatisfiable. $\mathcal{M}$ is a set of formulas $\mathcal{G} \cup \mathcal{Q}$ where $\mathcal{G}$ are ground literals, and $\mathcal{Q}$ are boxes. $\mathcal{M}$ propositionally satisfies $\mathcal{P}'$, and $\mathcal{G}$ is consistent with respect to the used theories. The instantiation procedure will then generate lemmas $(\forall \bar{x}. \varphi) \rightarrow \varphi\sigma$ where $(\forall \bar{x}. \varphi) \in \mathcal{Q}$ and σ is a substitution of $\bar{x}$ with ground terms. The generated lemmas are added conjunctively to $\mathcal{P}'$ and the ground solver is called again.

We now give an overview of common instantiation techniques and illustrate why they cannot tackle Example 1 quickly. These techniques are presented in the order they are used by veriT: it first tries conflict-driven instantiation. If this fails, it will try trigger-based instantiation. Should this produce no instances, it will fall back to enumerative instantiation. Model-based quantifier instantiation is not implemented by veriT: it is crucial for satisfiability, but veriT focuses on proving unsatisfiability.

Conflict-Driven Instantiation. This method tries to find an instance that contradicts the ground model $\mathcal{M}$ in the theory of equality and uninterpreted functions (EUF) [3,18]. Hence, it searches for a box $\forall \bar{x}. \varphi \in Q$ and a substitution σ such that $\mathcal{G} \wedge \varphi\sigma \vDash_{\text{EUF}} \bot$. It returns the instance $\varphi\sigma$ or fails. It can also search for substitutions which solve multiple constraints simultaneously. Hence, this method can find a contradicting instance of a clause $\psi_1 \vee \cdots \vee \psi_n$ by solving $\mathcal{G} \wedge \psi_1\sigma \vDash_{\text{EUF}} \bot, \ldots, \mathcal{G} \wedge \psi_n\sigma \vDash_{\text{EUF}} \bot$, but all ψ_is must be quantifier-free.

Conflict-driven instantiation is very helpful, since it only generates instances that are immediately useful. It forces the ground solver to find new models and eliminates spurious models from the search space.

Since Assertion 2 of Example 1 contains a quantifier, it cannot be instantiated by conflict driven instantiation. Conflict driven instantiation also fails for Assertion 1, because initially there is no ground formula that would be in conflict with an instance of $P(f(x,c))$. Even if the second assertion was Skolemized, conflict-driven instantiation would fail: since there is no ground instance of the Skolem term, no conflicting instance can be found.

Trigger-Based Instantiation. This instantiation scheme works by matching *triggers* with the current ground model. Triggers associate with every box $\forall \bar{x}. \varphi \in \mathcal{Q}$ one or more lists of quantifier-free terms $t_1, \ldots, t_n$ such that $\mathbf{free}(t_1) \cup \cdots \cup \mathbf{free}(t_n) = \{\bar{x}\}$. The triggers are either provided by the user or are heuristically generated. Trigger inference uses the structure of the quantified formulas which is preserved by preprocessing. To construct instances of φ, trigger-based instantiation searches for substitutions σ and terms $g_1, \ldots, g_n \in \mathcal{T}(\mathcal{G})$ such that $\mathcal{G} \models_{\mathrm{EUF}} t_i\sigma \approx g_i$. If the search is successful, it returns the instance $\varphi\sigma$.

The process of matching terms within the theory of equality and uninterpreted functions is called *E-matching* [9,11,14]. Due to the heuristic nature of trigger-based instantiation, the generated instances might not be useful to solve the problem. Instead they can slow down or mislead the solver.

In the case of Example 1, a trigger $P(x)$ on Assertion 1 would produce the useless instance $P(c) \to P(f(c,c))$ and a trigger $P(f(x,c))$ initially cannot match anything. The trigger $P(y)$ on Assertion 2 would produce the instance $(\forall z. P(z) \to P(f(z,c))) \to \neg P(c)$. This instance is a step towards solving the problem: the strong variable z is no longer below a quantifier and will be Skolemized to create the formula $P(s_1) \to P(f(s_1,c)) \to \neg P(c)$ where s_1 is a fresh constant. During the next instantiation round the trigger $P(x)$ on Assertion 1 generates the instance $P(s_1) \to P(f(s_1,c))$ which leads to the contradiction.

This technique is very sensitive to the availability of the right ground terms in the ground model. In the above example, if the formula contained $\forall x. P(x)$ instead of $P(c)$, trigger-based instantiation would have been helpless.

Enumerative Instantiation. While conflict driven instantiation is guided by the ground model it tries to contradict, and trigger-based instantiation is guided by the triggers, enumerative instantiation [17] is unguided. For a box with the form $\forall \bar{x}. \varphi \in \mathcal{Q}$ it creates all substitutions $[\bar{t}/\bar{x}]$ where the terms $\bar{t}$ are ground terms from $\mathcal{T}(\mathcal{M})$. To limit the number of generated instances the procedure only uses the ground terms minimal with respect to some term order and does not return instances already implied by the ground model (i.e., it only returns $\varphi\sigma$ if $\mathcal{G} \not\models_{\mathrm{EUF}} \varphi\sigma$). Enumerative instantiation ensures the theoretical completeness of the SMT solver for the theory of uninterpreted functions. It can also find the small ground terms that are sometimes necessary to enable the two previous techniques to work, and is thus a useful fallback strategy.

For Example 1, enumerative instantiation also needs at least two rounds. First, the variable y of Assertion 2 is instantiated with c. Then, after Skolemization, Assertion 1 can be instantiated with the new Skolem constant. Eventually, the cooperation of enumerative instantiation and the above techniques would succeed. However, in presence of many ground terms of the same sort as c, enumerative instantiation might have needed a lot of time to find the right instance.

Model-Based Quantifier Instantiation. Finally, model-based quantifier instantiation [12] extends heuristically the ground model $\mathcal{M}$ to a first-order interpretation $\mathfrak{I}$ and tests if this interpretation is a model: if there exists a box of the form $\forall \bar{x}. \varphi \in \mathcal{Q}$ and a substitution σ of $\bar{x}$ with terms from $\mathcal{T}(\mathcal{G})$ such that $\mathfrak{I} \models \neg\varphi\sigma$, then $\mathcal{M}$ is not a true model of $\mathcal{P}'$ and the ground instance $\varphi\sigma$ is produced. If this is not the case, then $\mathfrak{I}$ is a model of $\mathcal{P}'$ and the input problem is satisfiable. This methods works for every fragment that has the finite model property.

For Example 1, model-based quantifier instantiation fails to generate the right instances in one round for the same reason that trigger-based and enumerative instantiation fail: it might instantiate Assertion 2 with c for y, but other rounds of instantiations will still be required to reach a contradiction.

3   Quantifier Simplification by Unification

The essence of our technique is to simplify boxes by replacing a quantified sub-formula of the box with the Boolean constant $\top$ or $\bot$. This can be done if the matrix of this quantified subformula can be unified with the matrix of a unit-box.

Example 3. On our running Example 1, the first assertion serves as unit-box, whose matrix is unifiable with the matrix of the box in the second assertion. As a result, the quantified subformula can be reduced to the Boolean constant $\top$, for some instance of the second formula.

$$\frac{\forall x.\, P(x) \to P(f(x,c)) \quad \forall y.\, ((\forall z.\, P(z) \to P(f(z,y))) \to \neg P(y))}{\top \to \neg P(c)}$$

The rewriter simplifies the formula $\top \to \neg P(c)$ to $\neg P(c)$. Notice that, in this example, the variable z must be Skolemized because its quantifier is strong.

The SUB rule (Sect. 3.1) formalizes this derivation. An SMT solver can use this rule to augment the problem with simplified formulas. It is carefully restricted to generate formulas which help the instantiation procedures (Sect. 3.2). In Sect. 3.3 we propose several variants of the rule with different tradeoffs.

3.1   The Core Rule

The simplification by unification of subformulas (SUB) rule simplifies a box by replacing a quantified subformula with a Boolean constant. To be able to do so, the rule unifies the matrix of the subformula with a unit-box using a substitution. The Boolean constant depends on the polarities of the matrices: if they have the same polarity the subformula is replaced by $\top$, if they have different polarity it is replaced by $\bot$. The conclusion of the rule is the *pre-simplified* formula and will be fully simplified by the rewriter.

Definition 1 (SUB Rule).

$$\frac{\forall x_1, \ldots, x_n.\, \psi_1 \quad \forall x_{n+1}, \ldots, x_m.\, \varphi[Q\bar{y}.\, \psi_2]}{\forall x_{k_1}, \ldots, x_{k_j}.\, \varphi[b]\sigma} \text{ SUB}$$

where $Q \in \{\exists, \forall\}$, the subformula $Q\bar{y}.\, \psi_2$ appears only below the outermost universal quantifier of φ, and σ is a substitution. The rule is subject to the conditions:

1. $\mathbf{trim}(\psi_1)\sigma = \mathbf{trim}(\psi_2)\sigma$, if $Q\bar{y}.\,\psi_2$ is weak;
2. $\mathbf{trim}(\psi_1)\sigma = \mathbf{trim}(\mathbf{sk}(Q\bar{y}.\,\psi_2, x_{n+1}\dots x_m))\sigma$, if $Q\bar{y}.\,\psi_2$ is strong;
3. The bound variables of the conclusion $\{x_{k_1},\dots,x_{k_j}\}$ are exactly $\mathbf{free}(\varphi[b]\sigma)$;
4. $b = \top$ if $\mathbf{pol}(\psi_1) = \mathbf{pol}(\psi_2)$ or $b = \bot$ if $\mathbf{pol}(\psi_1) \neq \mathbf{pol}(\psi_2)$.

Example 4. In the running example the subformula $\forall z.\,P(z) \;\rightarrow\; P(f(z,y))$ occurs negatively. Since $Q = \forall$, the formula must be Skolemized (Condition 2):

$$\mathbf{sk}(\forall z.\,P(z) \rightarrow P(f(z,y)), y) = P(s_1(y)) \rightarrow P(f(s_1(y),y))$$

Hence, the unifier used in Example 3 is $\sigma = [s_1(c)/x][c/y]$.

Example 5. Ignoring Skolemization (Condition 2) leads to unsoundness:

$$\frac{\forall x.\,P(x,x) \quad \forall y.\,\neg(\forall z.\,P(y,G(z)))}{\neg\top}$$

The result of Skolemization $\mathbf{sk}(\forall z.\,P(y,G(z)), y)) = P(y,G(s_1(y)))$ is not unifiable with $P(x,x)$. The rule is not applicable.

Example 6. The conclusion can contain variables from both premises. Here the unifier is $\sigma = [G(x)/y_1][c/z]$.

$$\frac{\forall x.\,P(G(x),c) \quad \forall y_1, y_2.\,(\forall z.\,P(y_1,z)) \wedge P(y_1, y_2)}{\forall x, y_2.\,\top \wedge P(G(x), y_2)} \ \text{SUB}$$

Example 7. The above examples were cases where $\mathbf{pol}(\psi_1) = \mathbf{pol}(\psi_2)$. This example illustrates the other case:

$$\frac{\forall x.\,\neg P(x,x) \quad \forall y.\,G(c) \wedge (\forall z.\,P(y,z))}{G(c) \wedge \bot} \ \text{SUB}$$

In this case, the rewriter will simplify the pre-simplified formula $G(c) \wedge \bot$ to $\bot$ and the SMT solver can directly deduce unsatisfiability.

The SUB rule allows us to simply combine and restrict Skolemization, unification, and the replacement of subformulas with the appropriate constant. In the next section we will see the role it has within an SMT solver. The rule soundly combines these sound steps. First, it Skolemizes the variables $\bar{y}$. Second, it applies the unifier σ. Now the subformula of ψ_1 corresponding to $Q\bar{y}.\,\psi_2$ in the SUB rule is equivalent to $\mathbf{trim}(\psi_1)\sigma$ and is replaced with a Boolean constant. The constant is chosen appropriately according to the polarity of the formulas. This replacement is sound since $\psi_1\sigma$ always holds. Overall, the SUB rule, together with applying the rewriter, somewhat resembles unit resolution where $\forall x_1,\dots,x_n.\,\psi_1$ is the unit clause. In the case of SMT solvers, however, φ might not be a clause. Furthermore, ψ_1 and ψ_2 will have the complex structure that is preserved from the input, since most currently used instantiation techniques have no advantage from applying full clausification.

3.2   The Simplification Within the SMT Solver

Since the SUB rule eliminates a quantified subformula, the conclusion is easier
to handle for the SMT solvers. In general, however, the conclusion does not
subsume the box serving as the second premise. Hence, this box cannot simply
be replaced by the conclusion. Instead, the problem must be augmented with
the derived box. As the evaluations show, augmenting the problem still helps
the SMT instantiation procedures to find the appropriate ground instances.

$I \leftarrow \emptyset$
Q is an empty queue.
for each clause C in $\mathcal{P}'$ **do**
4   **if** C is unit-box with the box ℓ **then** $I \leftarrow I \cup \{\ell\}$
5   **if** C contains a box **then** $\text{push}(Q, C)$
     while Q is not empty **do**
        $\ell_1 \vee \cdots \vee \ell_n \leftarrow \text{pop}(Q)$
8   **if** there is $\psi \in I$ and a box ℓ_i such that $\dfrac{\psi \quad \ell_i}{\ell'}$ SUB **then**
9         $\ell' \leftarrow \text{rewrite}(\ell')$
10     $C' \leftarrow \ell_1 \vee \cdots \vee \ell_{i-1} \vee \ell' \vee \ell_{i+1} \vee \cdots \vee \ell_n$
11   append C' to $\mathcal{P}'$
       if C' contains a box and is not an unit-box **then**
13        $\text{push}(Q, C')$

Fig. 2. The augmentation procedure.

The pseudocode in Fig. 2 shows the loop which augments the problem. It is
executed after preprocessing finishes and before the ground solver starts. The
procedure first iterates over the clauses in the preprocessed problem $\mathcal{P}'$ to build a
set I of unit-boxes (Line 4) which can be used to simplify quantified subformulas.
At the same time, this loop collects in a queue Q all clauses containing boxes
(Line 5). Then the procedure takes a clause from the queue and tries to simplify
one of its boxes. To do so, it uses the SUB rule. If this succeeds, the conclusion
is the pre-simplified formula. The procedure then uses the rewriter to finish
the simplification and the problem is augmented with the simplified formula by
adding it conjunctively to the problem (Lines 8 to 11). If the simplified clause
still contains a box, it is pushed back onto the queue (Line 13).

The procedure terminates since the queue Q will eventually be empty. Every
iteration removes a clause from the queue and adds at most one new clause.
When the test in line 8 fails, i.e., the SUB rule can not be applied, no new clause
is added. Otherwise, it adds a clause with fewer nested formulas that can serve
as $Q\bar{y}.\psi_2$ in the SUB rule. Hence, the SUB rule will eventually no longer apply
to any box left in the clauses in Q.

The approach of augmenting the problem with derived, but new, formulas bears the risk that the instantiation procedures create more useless ground
instances from the new formulas. To minimize this risk, the SUB rule is restricted

to only apply when the result is likely to be helpful. First, the detection of sub-formulas which can be eliminated only uses unification instead of a more general approach. Since preprocessing preserves the structure of quantified formulas, unifiability can indicate the intention of the user. For example, the unit-box might be a lemma that is used within the box that is simplified. Second, the first premise must be a box. In principle it could also be a ground literal, but ground literals are already directly usable by the ground solver. Third, the simplified subformula must start with a quantifier because the instantiation procedures struggle to instantiate the quantified subformula. One of the variants described in the next section drops this restriction, but it is not as useful as the restricted rule.

3.3 Variants

As the experimental evaluation (Sect. 5) shows, the above version of quantifier simplification by unification solves more instances at little cost. Nevertheless, we also developed several variants with different tradeoffs. We will call quantifier simplification by unification as presented so far the *normal variant* and will often drop the phrase *by unification* to avoid repetition.

Eager Simplification. Since quantified subformulas block the instantiation procedures from creating the right instances quickly, the SUB rule is restricted to only simplify quantified subformulas. This restriction, however, can be removed to generate more simplified formulas. The eager SUB rule is the rule

$$\frac{\forall x_1, \ldots, x_n.\, \psi_1 \quad \forall x_{n+1}, \ldots, x_m.\, \varphi[\psi_2]}{\forall x_{k_1}, \ldots, x_{k_j}.\, \varphi[b]\sigma} \text{ eager-SUB}$$

and all side conditions of SUB are changed to read ψ_2 in-place of $Q\bar{x}.\,\psi_2$.

The eager SUB rule can be applied on any subformula not below an extra quantifier. On the one hand, this corresponds to deriving general consequences of unit-boxes in full first-order logic, but on the other hand, it will generate many more new formulas which potentially slow down or misguide the solver.

Solitary Variable Heuristic. To limit the potential downsides of eager simplification, we can limit the cases when the rule is applied: we apply the rule when it potentially removes a variable from the outermost quantifier of the second premise. The resulting formula will produce fewer misleading instances.

A variable is removed from the pre-simplified formula if it is *solitary*: it appears in the subformula ψ_2, but not in any other subformula of φ. Hence, for example, in the case $\varphi = t_1 \vee \cdots \vee t_i \vee \cdots \vee t_n$ we apply the rule with $\psi_2 = t_i$ if there is a variable $x \in \mathbf{free}(t_i)$ such that $x \notin \mathbf{free}(t_1 \vee \cdots \vee t_{i-1} \vee t_{i+1} \vee \cdots \vee t_n)$.

Deletion of Simplified Clauses. Another way to restrict the number of newly created instances is to delete the clause that contains the box used as the second premise of the SUB rule after it has been simplified. While this is no longer complete, it can guide the solver towards solving the refutation problem. Especially, within a strategy schedule this can be a valuable strategy.

This variant can be combined with the three other variants. Overall, this results in six variants of quantifier simplification. The amount of clauses deleted depends on the activity of the simplification variant used. Especially in the case of eager simplification with deletion many input assertions will be deleted.

4   Implementation

Our implementation of quantifier simplification by unification in veriT uses a non-perfect discrimination tree as term index and a subsequent unifiability check (Sect. 4.1). Both steps are amended to take strong variables into account without explicit Skolemization and avoid the creation of unnecessary Skolem symbols.

The implementation also does not apply the simplification of clauses everywhere, but focuses on unit-boxes only: the queue Q will only be populated by unit-boxes. This simplifies the implementation, since we do not have to track which boxes of a clause have already been simplified. It indeed appears that in SMT-LIB benchmarks clauses with boxes are uncommon and quantified formulas are usually unit-boxes (e.g., quantifiers range over entire disjunctions). A prototype without this simplification did not perform better on these benchmarks than the simplified version.

4.1   Indexing and Unification Without Skolemization

A key element to execute quantifier simplification, as shown in the algorithm in Fig. 2, is the lookup of the unit-box $\forall \bar{x}. \psi_1$ from the index I. The trimmed matrix of this box must be unifiable with the trimmed matrix of the quantified subformula $Q\bar{y}. \psi_2$. To implement the search for unifiable formulas efficiently we use a term index. We use non-perfect discrimination trees [21]. Non-perfect means that the lookup is an over-approximation: some returned terms are not unifiable with the query term and must be removed by a full unification step.

For each unit-box $\forall \bar{x}. \psi_1$ (of I in the algorithm in Fig. 2) the index stores **trim**(ψ_1) together with **pol**(ψ_1). For each possible subformula $Q\bar{y}. \psi_2$ the implementation uses **trim**(ψ_2) as a query term and retrieves unification candidates and their polarity. Afterwards, it performs a full unification to construct the substitution σ when possible. If, however, the quantifier of $Q\bar{y}. \psi_2$ is strong, the subformula should be Skolemized.

To handle variables that would be replaced by Skolem terms, the lookup process is enhanced: while normal variables are replaced by a variable placeholder that can match any term, variables to be Skolemized act like constants and can not match any other term. This embeds Skolemization into indexing, since

Skolem terms start with fresh function symbols that can never match indexed terms.

After the index returns a filtered set of possible premises $\mathbf{trim}(\psi_1)$ with their polarities $\mathbf{pol}(\psi_1)$ from I, the implementation must use full unification [19] to eliminate false positives and to build the unifier σ. It has to solve the unification problem between $\mathbf{trim}(\psi_1)$ and $\mathbf{trim}(\psi_2)$, where $\mathbf{trim}(\psi_2)$ can contain variables that must be Skolemized.

To handle Skolemized variables during unification, our implementation deviates from the standard version in two ways. First, similarly to the term index, it handles Skolemized variables as constants. Second, it considers a Skolemized variable as an occurrence of all the variables its Skolem term would depend on.

The resulting unifier σ cannot substitute a Skolem term into the quantified variables $x_{n+1}, \ldots, x_m$ of the box that is simplified. Hence, the conclusion $\varphi[b]\sigma$ is free of any Skolem terms, and no Skolem term has ever to be constructed. Overall, restricting quantifier simplification by unification to not simplify formulas below multiple nested quantifiers allows for this elegant implementation.

5 Evaluation

This section presents an empirical evaluation of quantifier simplification by unification and its variants as implemented in veriT.[1] The default variant of quantifier simplification solves more benchmarks than the default configuration of veriT, while losing few benchmarks. This justifies the activation of our quantifier simplification method in the default configuration. Almost all other variants also solve more benchmarks than the default configuration. veriT exposes a wide range of options to fine-tune the instantiation module. A specific configuration is a *strategy*. Quantifier simplification solves benchmarks not solved by any veriT strategy without this technique (Sect. 5.1).

In order to fully benefit from the strategies available, veriT can use strategy schedules. We generated strategy schedules with and without quantifier simplification and evaluated their performance. The strategies with quantifier simplification are an integral component of the generated schedules and increase the number of solved benchmarks. They are especially useful for short timeouts (Sect. 5.2).

We performed the experiments on the benchmarks from the SMT-LIB benchmark release 2021 [5]. Since quantifier simplification is only relevant for first-order formulas, we used the SMT-LIB logics supported by veriT which use quantifiers, uninterpreted functions, or arrays. Those are the SMT-LIB logics UF, UFLRA, UFLIA, UFIDL, ALIA, AUFLIA, and AUFLIRA. Since veriT is purely refutational, we removed benchmarks known to be satisfiable from the analysis.[2] Overall, the SMT-LIB contains 41 129 benchmarks using these logics.

---

[1] The raw data is available on Zenodo [1].

[2] Benchmarks known to be satisfiable can identify soundness problems. Hence, we included them in the experiments, but removed them from the data.

Table 1. Comparison with the default strategy and the theoretical best solver on 39 923 benchmarks.

vs. Default (solves 31 690)	N	E	S	Nd	Ed	Sd	Total
Solved	31 927	31 772	31 928	31 733	21 405	21 823	32 151
	+237	+82	**+238**	+43	−10 285	−9 867	+461
Gained	282	**315**	285	291	115	255	475
Lost	**45**	233	47	248	10 400	10 122	14
vs. Theoretical Best (solves 32 633)							
Gained	83	80	85	**86**	32	76	**125**

Of those, 1206 benchmarks are known to be satisfiable. This leaves 39 923 relevant benchmarks. We used the 2021.06-rmx release of veriT.

To interpret the numbers, the reader should keep in mind that veriT has no array solver. It treats the functions of the SMT-LIB theory of arrays as uninterpreted functions. Since veriT is restricted to refute benchmarks, this approach is sound. Nevertheless, veriT can fail to solve easy benchmarks that require array reasoning.

All experiments have been performed on computers with one Intel Xeon Gold 5220 processors with 18 cores and 96 GiB RAM. We ran one instance of veriT per available core and used a memory limit of 6 GiB per instance.

5.1   Baseline Comparison

Table 1 shows the number of benchmark solved within a timeout of 180 s in comparison to the default strategy. The standard version of quantifier simplification by unification is denoted N, eager simplification is denoted E, and the solitary variable heuristic is denoted S. A suffix d denotes the deletion of simplified clauses. Benchmarks are "Gained" if they are not solved by the default strategy and "Lost" if they are solved by the default strategy, but not by the variant. The column "Total" reports the union of the benchmarks solved by all variants.

The normal variant shows a good improvement by solving 237 benchmarks more. Most other variants solve more benchmarks not solved by the default strategy, but also lose many more. While the normal variant does not have the highest gain, the small loss justifies enabling it in the default strategy of veriT. The huge number of lost benchmarks for the variants that use clause deletion with either eager simplification or the solitary variable heuristic is not surprising: since most input assertions can be simplified in some way, clause deletion removes much of the original problem. The result is often an unsolvable problem.

Compared to the union of benchmarks solved by *any* existing veriT strategy (Theoretical Best), quantifier simplification by unification shows good improvement. We used a list of 43 strategies which are also used by veriT in the SMT competition.[3] The default configuration of veriT is on this list. Overall, the

---

[3] Competition website: https://smt-comp.github.io/.

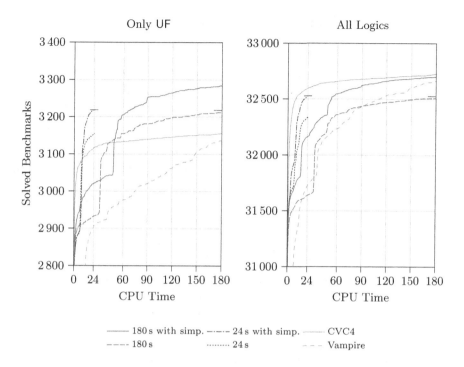

Fig. 3. CDF of different schedules on UF only and all logics.

variants together are able to solve 125 benchmarks that veriT could not solve before. While eager simplification solves only 80 more, 18 of those are not solved by any other quantifier simplification variant. Here, the two variants with clause deletion that have a huge loss are somewhat redeemed: together they solve eight benchmarks not solved by the theoretical best solver and the other quantifier simplification variants.

To perform the quantifier simplification, veriT does not need much time: for the normal variant, we measured a median runtime of 0.5 ms and mean of 3 ms.

5.2 Strategy Scheduling

Since quantifier instantiation relies on heuristics, veriT exposes parameters that can be set by the user in a strategy. Most benchmarks are solved by an appropriate strategy within a short timeout. Hence, it is sensible to execute many strategies for short time intervals one after another in a schedule.

To evaluate the quantifier simplification technique within a strategy schedule, we generated schedules with and without strategies extended with quantifier simplification. An optimal schedule is the set of strategy–timeout pairs which solves the most benchmarks. The list of possible strategies and timeouts is hand-crafted. We use integer programming to solve this optimization problem. veriT itself uses the logic of the problem to select a schedule.

To build strategies with quantifier simplification we picked six strategies from the strategy list of 43 strategies: the default strategy, the strategy that solved the most benchmarks overall, and four complementary strategies. The four complementary strategies were selected by finding a pair of strategies that together with the best strategy maximize the number of solved benchmarks. We searched such a pair on all logics and on first-order logic with equality (UF) alone. We then extended these six strategies with the six variants of quantifier simplification. This resulted in 36 new strategies.

We generated schedules optimized for timeouts of 180 s and 24 s. The short 24 s timeout allows us to evaluate the value of quantifier simplification for applications such as interactive theorem provers, which require a short timeout. It corresponds to the timeout used by the SMT competition to evaluate solvers for this purpose. The longer 180 s timeout was arbitrarily chosen.

Figure 3 shows the number of benchmarks solved within a time limit on UF alone and on all logics. On all logics, the schedule with quantifier simplification solved 193 benchmarks more after 24 s than the original 24 s schedule. For the 180 s timeout, the 180 s schedule with quantifier simplification solves 191 more than the one without. The 24 s schedule with quantifier simplification solves 18 benchmarks more than the 180 s schedule after 180 s. Hence, quantifier simplification is very useful for short timeouts. Since the form of quantified lemmas that quantifier simplification by unification eliminates appear in problems generated by interactive theorem provers, it is especially useful for this application.

To provide context the plots contain the results of two other systems: the state-of-the-art SMT solver CVC4 and the superposition prover Vampire [13]. We used the official builds of version 1.8 of CVC4 and version 4.5.1 of Vampire. Vampire includes the SMT solver Z3, which aids theory reasoning. Since CVC4 has no scheduler optimized for 24 s or 180 s, we ran the default strategy.[4] For Vampire we used the SMT-COMP scheduler with a timeout of 180 s.[5] We discarded all "satisfiable" results. Overall, CVC4 solves 70 benchmarks more than veriT with quantifier simplification after 24 s and 26 after 180 s. veriT with quantifier simplification after 180 s solves 595 benchmarks not solved by CVC4, of which 107 are also not solved by veriT without quantifier simplification. Surprisingly, Vampire solves fewer benchmarks than any other system on UF. This is due to the nature of typical SMT benchmarks: they usually require little quantifier reasoning and are hence easier to solve for instantiation-based systems.[6] This confirms that restricted methods, such as quantifier simplification by unification, are useful for SMT problems.

Figure 4 visualizes the schedules for the logic UF. Grey cells are strategies that use quantifier simplification. Cells with the same number use the same base strategy. Some base strategies appear both in the schedules with and without

---

[4] Using: -L smt2.6 --no-incremental --no-type-checking --no-interactive --full-saturate-quant.

[5] Using: -t 180s -m 6000 --mode portfolio --schedule smtcomp --input_syntax smtlib2 -om smtcomp -p off.

[6] This has been confirmed to us by the Vampire team in conversations.

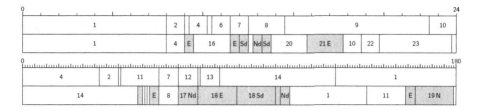

Fig. 4. Visualization of optimized UF schedules. The bottom rows are the schedules with quantifier simplification. The numbers denote the base strategies.

quantifier simplification. The strategies with quantifier simplification tend to be used for shorter time slices than the variants without.

6   Conclusion

We presented a new unification-based simplification technique for instantiation-based SMT solvers. Its design is motivated by limitations of modern instantiation methods, and it is efficient. Problems where formulas can be simplified are often solved much faster, despite the method creating new quantified formulas. We plan to enable quantifier simplification by unification by default in the next veriT release. The release will also produce machine-checkable proofs for simplifications performed by quantifier simplification by unification.

We believe that the technique implemented here within veriT can be ported easily into any instantiation-based SMT solver, and we are confident that it would also enable mainstream solvers to tackle problems outside of reach with other current strategies. We will investigate its potential in other solvers.

Our method is a step towards using techniques inspired by resolution-based theorem provers within SMT solvers. It is currently only used as a preprocessing technique, but we plan to investigate novel quantifier instantiation techniques which can directly handle nested strong quantifiers.

Acknowledgments. We are grateful to Haniel Barbosa, Jasmin Blanchette, Antoine Defourné, Daniel El Ouraoui, Mathias Fleury, Martin Riener, and Athénaïs Vaginay for many fruitful discussions and suggestions to improve the text. We thank the anonymous reviewers for many good suggestions to improve the text. The second author has received funding from the European Research Council (ERC) under the European Union's Horizon 2020 research and innovation program (grant agreement No. 713999, Matryoshka). Experiments presented in this paper were carried out using the Grid'5000 testbed, supported by a scientific interest group hosted by Inria and including CNRS, RENATER and several Universities as well as other organizations (see https://www.grid5000.fr).

References

1. Quantifier Simplification by Unification in SMT. Zenodo, July 2021. https://doi.org/10.5281/zenodo.5088868

2. Baaz, M., Egly, U., Leitsch, A., Goubault-Larrecq, J., Plaisted, D.: Chapter 5 - normal form transformations. In: Robinson, A., Voronkov, A. (eds.) Handbook of Automated Reasoning, pp. 273–333. North-Holland, Amsterdam (2001). https://doi.org/10.1016/B978-044450813-3/50007-2

3. Barbosa, H., Fontaine, P., Reynolds, A.: Congruence closure with free variables. In: Legay, A., Margaria, T. (eds.) TACAS 2017. LNCS, vol. 10206, pp. 214–230. Springer, Heidelberg (2017). https://doi.org/10.1007/978-3-662-54580-5_13

4. Barrett, C., et al.: CVC4. In: Gopalakrishnan, G., Qadeer, S. (eds.) CAV 2011. LNCS, vol. 6806, pp. 171–177. Springer, Heidelberg (2011). https://doi.org/10.1007/978-3-642-22110-1_14

5. Barrett, C., Fontaine, P., Tinelli, C.: The SMT-LIB Standard: Version 2.6. Technical report, Department of Computer Science, The University of Iowa (2017). www.SMT-LIB.org

6. Barrett, C., Tinelli, C.: Satisfiability modulo theories. In: Handbook of Model Checking, pp. 305–343. Springer, Cham (2018). https://doi.org/10.1007/978-3-319-10575-8_11

7. Bonacina, M.P., Lynch, C., de Moura, L.: On deciding satisfiability by theorem proving with speculative inferences. J. Autom. Reason. **47**, 161–189 (2011). https://doi.org/10.1007/s10817-010-9213-y

8. Bouton, T., Caminha B. de Oliveira, D., Déharbe, D., Fontaine, P.: veriT: an open, trustable and efficient SMT-solver. In: Schmidt, R.A. (ed.) CADE 2009. LNCS (LNAI), vol. 5663, pp. 151–156. Springer, Heidelberg (2009). https://doi.org/10.1007/978-3-642-02959-2_12

9. Detlefs, D., Nelson, G., Saxe, J.B.: Simplify: a theorem prover for program checking. J. ACM **52**(3), 365–473 (2005). https://doi.org/10.1145/1066100.1066102

10. Ekici, B., et al.: SMTCoq: a plug-in for integrating SMT solvers into Coq. In: Majumdar, R., Kunčak, V. (eds.) CAV 2017. LNCS, vol. 10427, pp. 126–133. Springer, Cham (2017). https://doi.org/10.1007/978-3-319-63390-9_7

11. Ge, Y., Barrett, C., Tinelli, C.: Solving quantified verification conditions using satisfiability modulo theories. In: Pfenning, F. (ed.) CADE 2007. LNCS (LNAI), vol. 4603, pp. 167–182. Springer, Heidelberg (2007). https://doi.org/10.1007/978-3-540-73595-3_12

12. Ge, Y., de Moura, L.: Complete instantiation for quantified formulas in satisfiabiliby modulo theories. In: Bouajjani, A., Maler, O. (eds.) CAV 2009. LNCS, vol. 5643, pp. 306–320. Springer, Heidelberg (2009). https://doi.org/10.1007/978-3-642-02658-4_25

13. Kovács, L., Voronkov, A.: First-order theorem proving and VAMPIRE. In: Sharygina, N., Veith, H. (eds.) CAV 2013. LNCS, vol. 8044, pp. 1–35. Springer, Heidelberg (2013). https://doi.org/10.1007/978-3-642-39799-8_1

14. de Moura, L., Bjørner, N.: Efficient E-matching for SMT solvers. In: Pfenning, F. (ed.) CADE 2007. LNCS (LNAI), vol. 4603, pp. 183–198. Springer, Heidelberg (2007). https://doi.org/10.1007/978-3-540-73595-3_13

15. de Moura, L., Bjørner, N.: Engineering DPLL(T) + saturation. In: Armando, A., Baumgartner, P., Dowek, G. (eds.) IJCAR 2008. LNCS (LNAI), vol. 5195, pp. 475–490. Springer, Heidelberg (2008). https://doi.org/10.1007/978-3-540-71070-7_40

16. de Moura, L., Bjørner, N.: Z3: an efficient SMT solver. In: Ramakrishnan, C.R., Rehof, J. (eds.) TACAS 2008. LNCS, vol. 4963, pp. 337–340. Springer, Heidelberg (2008). https://doi.org/10.1007/978-3-540-78800-3_24

17. Reynolds, A., Barbosa, H., Fontaine, P.: Revisiting enumerative instantiation. In: Beyer, D., Huisman, M. (eds.) TACAS 2018. LNCS, vol. 10806, pp. 112–131. Springer, Cham (2018). https://doi.org/10.1007/978-3-319-89963-3_7

18. Reynolds, A., Tinelli, C., de Moura, L.: Finding conflicting instances of quantified formulas in SMT. In: FMCAD 2014, pp. 195–202. IEEE (2014). https://doi.org/10.1109/FMCAD.2014.6987613

19. Robinson, J.A.: A machine-oriented logic based on the resolution principle. J. ACM **12**(1), 23–41 (1965). https://doi.org/10.1145/321250.321253

20. Schurr, H.-J., Fleury, M., Desharnais, M.: Reliable reconstruction of fine-grained proofs in a proof assistant. In: Platzer, A., Sutcliffe, G. (eds.) CADE 2021. LNCS (LNAI), vol. 12699, pp. 450–467. Springer, Cham (2021). https://doi.org/10.1007/978-3-030-79876-5_26

21. Sekar, R., Ramakrishnan, I.V., Voronkov, A.: Term Indexing, pp. 1853–1964. Elsevier Science Publishers B. V., Amsterdam (2001). https://doi.org/10.5555/778522.778535

22. Voronkov, A.: AVATAR: the architecture for first-order theorem provers. In: Biere, A., Bloem, R. (eds.) CAV 2014. LNCS, vol. 8559, pp. 696–710. Springer, Cham (2014). https://doi.org/10.1007/978-3-319-08867-9_46

Verification

Algorithmic Problems in the Symbolic Approach to the Verification of Automatically Synthesized Cryptosystems

Hai Lin[1] , Christopher Lynch[1] , Andrew M. Marshall[2]([✉]) ,
Catherine A. Meadows[3], Paliath Narendran[4], Veena Ravishankar[2]([✉]) ,
and Brandon Rozek[2]

[1] Clarkson University, Potsdam, NY, USA
[2] University of Mary Washington, Fredericksburg, VA, USA
{amarsha2,vravisha}@umw.edu
[3] Naval Research Laboratory, Washington, DC, USA
[4] University at Albany–SUNY, Albany, NY, USA

Abstract. Automated methods can be used to generate cryptosystems by combining the primitives in an arbitrary fashion, to weed out insecure cryptosystems, and to prove the security of those that survive. In this paper, we study several algorithmic problems arising from the verification of automatically synthesized cryptosystems built from block ciphers, in a theory that includes $ACUN$. One of these is static equivalence to an algorithm that produces a sequence of random terms. The other is invertibility, the problem of determining whether, given an automatically synthesized cryptosystem, built from block ciphers, and the ability to compute inverses, is it always possible to compute the original plaintext from the ciphertext? We show that static equivalence to random in this theory is undecidable in general. In addition, we identify a reasonable special case for which there is a decidable condition implying security, along with an algorithm for verifying it. For invertibility, we identify a reasonable class of cryptosystems for which invertibility is equivalent to a simple syntactic condition that can be easily verified.

Keywords: Cryptographic modes of operation · Symbolic reasoning · Equational theories · Unification

1 Introduction

In this paper we address symbolic analysis problems that arise from the automatic generation and verification of cryptosystems. In this approach one starts with a class of cryptosystems that use a fixed set of functions to combine a fixed set of primitives. Automated methods can be used to generate cryptosystems by

---

This work was funded by ONR Code 311. The work of Lin, Lynch, Marshall, Narendran, Ravishankar, and Rozek, was funded via NRL grant number N00173-19-1-G012.

B. Konev and G. Reger (Eds.): FroCoS 2021, LNAI 12941, pp. 253–270, 2021.
https://doi.org/10.1007/978-3-030-86205-3_14

combining the primitives in an arbitrary fashion, to weeding out insecure cryptosystems, and proving the security of those that survive. Symbolic techniques have proved particularly helpful in this process, because they give a compact representation of cryptosystems that is amenable to automated analysis.

In this paper we apply a technique we are developing for the synthesis and analysis of *cryptographic modes of operation*. Basic encryption algorithms such as AES are generally *block ciphers* that map λ-bit blocks to λ-bit blocks. A mode of operation combines multiple computations of block cipher encryption to encrypt longer messages securely. We model this block cipher approach by defining a protocol modeling the interaction between an adversary and an encryptor. In this model the adversary sends plaintext blocks, which the encryptor then processes according to some pre-determined method, e.g., the method of a particular cipher. When there are multiple actions that the encryptor can take, the choice is made by the adversary. The encrypted blocks are then sent back to the adversary based on some schedule, e.g. as soon as possible, or only after all the plaintext has been received. It is shown in [6,12], that both the processing method and the schedule are relevant to the security of the cryptosystem.

We consider two symbolic properties. The first is static equivalence [2], between a protocol in which a plaintext-adaptive adversary interacts with a real encryptor, and one in which it interacts with a random encryptor that sends randomly generated blocks. A plaintext-adaptive adversary is one that uses ciphertext it has received previously from an encryptor to construct new plaintext. Static equivalence between two symbolically defined protocols, roughly speaking, requires that, for any trace of one protocol, there is a trace of the other protocol such that any adversarial-computable equation satisfied by the first trace is satisfied by the other, and vice versa. Static equivalence to random may be thought of as the symbolic analog of IND$-CPA security [12], which requires that the cipher text received by the adversary be indistinguishable from a string of random bits.

The second symbolic property, invertibility, requires that a principal able to compute f (the block encryption function) and its inverse be able to retrieve plaintext from ciphertext.

Given one of the above symbolic properties, we can divide the questions we ask about it into two classes. In the first case, given a description of a class of ciphertexts, one can ask whether or not any member has that property. In the second, given a cryptosystem, one can ask whether all ciphertexts produced by that cryptosystem have that property. In this paper we focus on the second, more general, property.

Both questions about static equivalence to random are known to be undecidable for arbitrary convergent term rewriting systems [1,3]. In [8] Lin and Lynch present an algorithm that can be used to answer the first type of question for the class of cryptosystems discussed in this paper. In this paper we devote ourselves to the second type of question: given a mode, whether or not every possible sequence of ciphertext produced by it satisfies static equivalence to random. In Sect. 5.1 we show that this problem is undecidable for cryptographic modes of operation in general. Then, in Sect. 5.2 we give a class of cryptosystems for which there is a decidable property implying static equivalence to random, and we give an algorithm for deciding that property.

The rest of the paper is organized as follows. Section 2 provides the necessary background material. Section 3 defines $MOO_\oplus$-programs, which we use for symbolic specification of modes of encryption using the $\oplus$ (xor) function. In Sect. 4 we identify a simple syntactically checkable condition for a class of recursively defined modes of encryption, which we show is equivalent to every ciphertext produced by the mode being invertible. Section 5 considers the decision problems described above. Finally, Sect. 6 concludes the paper and describes some open problems.

1.1   Implementation

We are currently developing a new tool designed to manipulate and analyze Cryptographic Modes of Operation. The goal of this new tool is broad, to develop not only a usable analysis tool for a broad family of cryptographic algorithms but to also develop the underlying libraries which could be used in further analysis or in other symbolic analysis tools (https://symcollab.github.io/CryptoSolve/). As part of that tool, several of the algorithms developed in this paper have been implemented. More details of each implementation are given below as appropriate.

2   Preliminaries

2.1   Terms and Substitutions

Given a first-order signature Σ, a countable set of variables N bound by ν, and a countable set of variables X (s.t. $X \cap N = \emptyset$), the set of terms constructed in the normal recursive manner from X, N, and Σ, is denoted by $T(\Sigma, N \cup X)$. The set of free variables in a term t is denoted by $fv(t)$ and the set of bound variables in t is denoted by $fn(t)$. A term t is *ground* if $fv(t) = \emptyset$. In this paper, we follow the convention of the applied pi calculus [2] and use variables bound by ν to stand for randomly chosen bitstrings. For any position p in a term t (including the root position ϵ), $t(p)$ denotes the symbol at position p, $t|_p$ denotes the subterm of t at position p, and $t[u]_p$ denotes the term t in which $t|_p$ is replaced by u. The size of a term t is denoted by $|t|$ and defined in the usual [2] way as follows: $|f(t_1, \ldots, t_n)| = 1 + \sum_{i=1}^{n} |t_i|$ if f is a n-ary function symbol with $n \geq 1$, $|c| = 1$ if $c \in N$, and $|x| = 0$ if $x \in X$.

A substitution σ is an endomorphism of $T(\Sigma, N \cup X)$ mapping free variables to terms, with only finitely many variables not mapped to themselves, denoted by $\sigma = \{x_1 \mapsto t_1, \ldots, x_m \mapsto t_m\}$. Application of a substitution σ to a term t is written $t\sigma$. Given two substitutions θ and σ, the composition $\sigma \circ \theta$ is the substitution denoted here by $\theta\sigma$ and defined such that $x(\theta\sigma) = (x\theta)\sigma$ for any $x \in X$. The domain of σ is $Dom(\sigma) = \{x \in X \mid x\sigma \neq x\}$. The range of σ

is $Ran(\sigma) = \{x\sigma \mid x \in Dom(\sigma)\}$. When θ and σ are two substitutions with disjoint domains and only ground terms in their ranges, then $\theta\sigma = \theta \cup \sigma$. Given a substitution σ and a finite set of free variables $V \subseteq X$, the restriction of σ to V is the substitution denoted by $\sigma_{|V}$ such that $x\sigma_{|V} = x\sigma$ for any $x \in V$ and $x\sigma_{|V} = x$ for any $x \in X\backslash V$.

2.2 Equational Theories

Given a set E of Σ-axioms (i.e., pairs of Σ-terms, denoted by $l = r$), the *equational theory* $=_E$ is the congruence closure of E under the law of substitutivity. For any Σ-term t, the equivalence class of t with respect to $=_E$ is denoted by $[t]_E$. Since $\Sigma \cap N = \emptyset$, the Σ-equalities in E do not contain any bound variables in N. A theory E is *trivial* if $x =_E y$, for two distinct variables x and y. In this paper, all the considered theories are assumed non-trivial.

The Xor Equational Theory. In this paper we will primarily be concerned with the equational theory of Xor, $E_\oplus$. This theory can be represented as a combination of a rewrite system, $R_\oplus$, and an associative and commutative equational theory, AC. $E_\oplus = R_\oplus \cup AC$: $R_\oplus = \{x \oplus x \to 0,\ x \oplus 0 \to x\}$, $AC = AC(\oplus)$, over the signature, $\Sigma_\oplus = \{\oplus, f, 0\}$. We will often use $MOO_\oplus$-term to denote a term over $\Sigma_\oplus$.

A rewrite rule $\ell \to r$ is applied to a term t by finding a subterm s of t and a match σ of l and s, i.e., a unifier of l and s that leaves s unchanged, and then replacing s with $r\sigma$. We say that a term is in *normal form* if no rewrite rule can be applied. We note that any term in the $E_\oplus$ theory is reducible via a finite set of rewrite rules to a normal form term that is unique up to AC equivalence. If S is finite and $S \subset T_{E_\oplus}(\Sigma_\oplus, N \cup X)$, and $t \in T_{E_\oplus}(\Sigma_\oplus, N \cup X)$ we say that $S \oplus t$ if t can be derived by $\oplus$ summing elements of S. In the remainder of this paper, we assume that all $E_\oplus$ terms mentioned are in normal form, unless explicitly noted otherwise.

3 Modes of Operation

Most symmetric key ciphers are block ciphers that encrypt only fixed-length plaintext. In order to encrypt plaintexts longer than that fixed length, the encryptor divides it into a sequence of fixed-length blocks and then encrypts it using a *cryptographic mode of operation*. This is a sequence of recursively defined functions on plaintext blocks of fixed length so that each function returns a block of cipher text. To give an example, we demonstrate cipher block chaining (CBC) in Fig. 1, where the block C_0 returned by the encryptor is a random initialization vector iv, and block $C_i = E_K(m_i \oplus C_{i-1})$ for $i > 0$, where E_K is the block encryption method with key K.

We will be using part of the symbolic framework developed for the applied π-calculus [2]. In this calculus, messages exchanged in a protocol are defined over a term algebra $T_E(\Sigma, N \cup X)$, where X is a set of free variables, and N

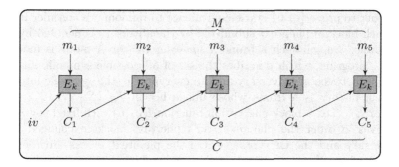

Fig. 1. An example of a cryptographic mode of operation: cipher block chaining

is a set of variables bound by the quantifier ν, standing for randomly chosen bitstrings. Protocols are defined using *processes* that describe communication between principals. A sequence of messages produced by a protocol is described using *frames*. A frame is a substitution ϕ from a set of free variables $x_1, \ldots, x_k$, to $T_E(\Sigma, N \cup X)$, i.e., $x_i\phi$ describes the i'th message sent in the frame. We may also denote a frame ϕ as $\nu R.[t_1, \ldots, t_k]$, where $t_i = x_i\phi$ and R is set of bound variables in $Ran(\phi)$.

Static equivalence in the applied π-calculus is used to describe the case in which the adversary cannot distinguish between two frames. Since all the adversary can do is combine terms via function symbols and check for equality, static equivalence is defined in terms of those actions. In our case, we have to generalize the definition slightly because, in the applied *pi* calculus it is assumed that the adversary can apply any function symbol in Σ, while in our case the adversary cannot compute f.

Definition 1. *Let $\Xi \subseteq \Sigma$. We say that two closed frames ϕ and ψ with range $T_E(\Sigma, N)$ are Ξ-statically equivalent, if $Dom(\phi) = Dom(\psi)$ and, for all terms M and N in $T_E(\Xi, N)$ that share no bound variables, $M\phi =_E N\phi$ if and only if $M\psi =_E N\psi$. We say that two closed processes (that is, two processes that produce only closed frames) are Ξ-statically equivalent if any closed frame produced by one is Ξ-statically equivalent to some frame produced by the other.*

For example, consider $\Sigma_\oplus$, and $\Xi = \{\oplus, 0\}$. Then $\phi = \nu r_1.r_2.r_3[r_1, r_2, r_3]$ is Ξ-statically equivalent to $\phi = \nu s_1.s_2.s_3[s_1, s_2, s_2 \oplus s_3]$. However it is not Ξ-statically equivalent to $\phi' = \nu s_1.s_2[s_1, s_2, s_1 \oplus s_2]$, because in ψ' the third term is the exclusive-or of the first two, but the same does not hold for ϕ. Similarly, ϕ is $\{\oplus, 0\}$-equivalent to $\rho = \nu u_1.u_2[u_1, u_2, f(u_1 \oplus u_2)]$, but it is not $\Sigma_\oplus$-statically equivalent to ρ.

Note that, for the purpose of proving or disproving static equivalence, it is enough to identify processes with the sets of frames they produce. Thus, for cryptographic modes of operation that use exclusive-or, we define a $MOO_\oplus$-process as the set of closed frames that describe all possible interactions between an adversary and an encryptor in a given mode of operation.

In order to prove $\{\oplus, 0\}$-static equivalence to random, we consider frames in which each block of plaintext submitted by the adversary is denoted by a fresh free variable. We call such a frame a *symbolic history*. A mode is modeled as a $MOO_\oplus$-program, which describes the set of all possible symbolic histories of interaction between an adversary and an encryptor in the symbolic interaction. Each such history is a frame whose image lies in $T_{E_\oplus}(\Sigma_\oplus, N \cup X)$ where f stands for E_K (i.e., a block encryption function $E_K(m)$ with fixed key K). This frame gives in order the plaintext and ciphertext blocks exchanged between the adversary and the encryptor, where the plaintext blocks are represented by free variables. For example, the following symbolic history describes the use of the CBC mode of encryption to encrypt a two-block message: $\nu r[r, x_1, f(r \oplus x_1), x_2, f(x_2 \oplus f(r \oplus x_1))]$. Each x_i models a plaintext block sent by the adversary, and all others are terms sent by the encryptor. We also note that a symbolic history can represent the interleaving of several sessions between the adversary and an encryptor, in which a session represents the interaction between the adversary and the encryptor necessary to encrypt a single message.

The set of symbolic histories that can be produced by a mode does not by itself give us a complete description of the closed frames that can be produced by it. For that we need to specify what closed substitutions the adversary can make. For this, we need the following definition:

Definition 2. *Let H be a symbolic history, and let x be a free variable sent by the adversary in H, i.e. $H = H_1, x, H_2$ where x does not appear in any term in H_1.*

1. *We define $KN_{H,x}$ to be the set of terms in H (including free variables sent by the adversary) sent before the adversary sent x, i.e. $KN_{H,x} = \{t \mid t \in H_1\}$.*
2. *We say that $x >_H t$ if $KN_{H,x} \vdash_\oplus t$.*
3. *We say that a substitution σ on the free variables of H is computable, if for each free variable x, $x\sigma = t\sigma$ such that $t <_H x$.*

The restriction to computable substitutions captures the fact that, since the adversary cannot predict the output of f on a given input, or the choice of a random string generated by the encryptor, it can only use such outputs that it has already seen when constructing its substitutions. Note that we do not include bound variables the adversary has generated itself. Although these can be represented in the applied π calculus, they turn out not to be necessary to proving security (See Lemma 1).

Example 1. Consider the CBC mode of encryption illustrated in Fig. 1. The initial cipher block is the iv, $C_0 \mapsto r$ where r is a random nonce, and the second cipher block is the term $C_1 \mapsto f(x_1 \oplus C_0)$. So at this point, the symbolic history, H, contains just two blocks, C_0 and C_1, and $KH_{H,x}$ is $\{r, f(x_1 \oplus C_0)\}$. Continuing, the next block is added to H, $C_2 \mapsto f(x_2 \oplus f(x_1 \oplus C_0))$. We are able to unify C_1 and C_2 with the *computable substitution* $\sigma = \{x_1 \mapsto C_0, x_2 \mapsto f(0)\}$. Notice that the adversary has seen C_0 before x_1, thus $C_0 <_H x_1$ and by using this mapping can compute $f(0)$ before seeing x_2.

We now formally define a property, symbolic security, and show that it is equivalent to $\{\oplus, 0\}$-statically equivalent to random. *Symbolic security is the property we will be proving in this paper.*

Definition 3. *We say that a mode is* symbolically secure *if, for any symbolic history H, and any computable closed substitution σ on the free variables of H, there is no subset S of the set of ciphertext blocks returned by the encryptor such that $\sum_{t \in S} \oplus t =_\oplus 0$.*

Lemma 1. *A mode is symbolically secure if and only if it is $\{\oplus, 0\}$-statically equivalent to random.*

Proof (Sketch). Consider a mode M_{real}. Let $\phi : y_1, \ldots y_k \to T_{E_\oplus(\Sigma, N \cup X)}$. be a symbolic history from M_{real}. Let $P\text{-}Dom(\phi)$ be the set of variables in $Dom(\phi)$ mapped to variables standing for plaintext blocks, and let $C\text{-}Dom(\phi)$ be the set of variables in $Dom(\phi)$ mapped to terms standing for ciphertext blocks. Let ψ be such that $Dom(\psi) = Dom(\phi)$ and $y_i\psi$ is a fresh bound variable if $y_i \in C\text{-}Dom(\phi)$, and a fresh free variable if $y_i \in P\text{-}Dom(\phi)$. We define M_{ran} to be the mode whose symbolic histories consist of all such ψ. Thus M_{ran} is a mode in which the encryptor always returns fresh random strings.

We note that, for any computable frame $\sigma\phi$ from M_{real} there is a computable frame $\sigma\psi$ from M_{ran} constructed as above, and any computable frame from M_{ran} can be obtained this way. It is clear from the definitions that if $\sigma\phi$ and $\sigma\psi$ are $\{\oplus, 0\}$-statically equivalent then $\sigma\phi$ is symbolically secure. We now show that for any such $\sigma\phi$ and $\sigma\psi$ that, if $\sigma\phi$ is symbolically secure then $\sigma\phi$ and $\sigma\psi$ are $\{\oplus, 0\}$-statically equivalent. For that, it is enough to show that, if M and N are the exclusive-or of elements of $(Dom(\phi))$, then 1) $M\sigma\phi =_{\Sigma_\oplus} N\sigma\phi$ if and only if 2) $M\sigma\psi =_{\Sigma_\oplus} N\sigma\psi$. We note that 2) is true if and only if each ciphertext terms appears an even number of times as a summand of $M\sigma\psi \oplus N\sigma\psi$, and since by hypothesis, the ciphertext terms returned by M_{real} satisfy no nontrivial $\oplus$ equation, the same conditions apply to 1).

We now consider the case in which the adversary may include bound variables, generated by itself, as summands of the plaintext. In the applied π calculus this is done by prepending to the frame the sequence of bound variables generated by the adversary. It is then straightforward to reduce this to the computable case with no adversary-generated bound variables. □

Given a cryptographic mode of operation, we can define several instances of the security problem, based on combination of different factors. These include the schedule (e.g. are ciphertext blocks returned by the encryptor only after all plaintext blocks are received (messagewise schedule), or as soon as the encryptor can compute them (blockwise schedule)), and the bounds on session length and number of sessions. We will use the following modes of operation as examples.

- Cipher Block Chaining (CBC) : The ith plain text is a ground $MOO_\oplus$-term p_i. The initial cipher block, the iv, is modeled by a bound variable, r. The ith block of cipher text, C_i, is modeled by the term $f(C_{i-1} \oplus p_i)$. This is secure in the messagewise schedule, but not in the blockwise.

- Cipher Feedback (CFB) : The ith plain text is modeled by a ground $MOO_\oplus$ term p_i. The initial cipher block, the iv, is modeled by a bound variable, r. The ith cipher block, C_i, is modeled by the term $f(C_{i-1}) \oplus p_i$. This is secure under both schedules.
- Similarly, Propagating Cipher Block Chaining $(PCBC)$: $C_1 = f(p_1 \oplus IV)$, $C_i = f(p_i \oplus p_{i-1} \oplus C_{i-1})$. This is secure under the messagewise schedule but not under the blockwise schedule.

4   The Invertibility Problem

A natural requirement of any cryptographic algorithm is that it be *invertible*; that is, one can find the original plaintext using the ciphertext and decryption key. While this property would normally be "built-in" to a mode of operation, it is not guaranteed to exist for all possible modes that can be automatically generated, even if these modes have other desirable properties such as symbolic security. Therefore in the automatically generated setting, we will need methods for checking if the invertibility property holds for any particular $MOO_\oplus$-program. This leads to two different questions.

- The first is, given a set S of $MOO_\oplus$-terms with subterms designated as plain text, can we tell if S is invertible? This bounded version of the problem follows from the Abadi and Cortier's [1] results on the decidability of deducability in various equational theories and
- The second is: given a $MOO_\oplus$-program, can we tell if an arbitrary cipher block is invertible? We explore this un-bounded version of the problem in this section.

Let $\mathcal{C} = \{C_0, C_1, \ldots, C_n\}$ represent the ciphertext blocks, C_i, produced by the encryptor in the $MOO_\oplus$-program. We instantiate the variables representing plaintext in $\mathcal{C}$ to bound variables p_i. Let $P = \{p_0, p_1, \ldots, p_n\}$ be the set representing the plaintext messages during a run of the $MOO_\oplus$-program. We introduce a new symbol, f^{-1}, where f is the symbolic encryption function, i.e., $f = enc(\_, K)$, for some key K, and let f^{-1} model decryption, $f^{-1} = dec(\_, K)$, s.t. $f^{-1}(f(M)) = M$. Then $E^{-1} = E_\oplus \cup \{f^{-1}(f(x)) = x\}$.

Lemma 2. *Let t be a closed term over $f, \oplus, 0$ and let $c \in fn(t)$. Let S be a set of terms consisting of t and every bound variable in t other than c. Then c can be deduced from S if and only if c appears exactly once in t.*

Proof. We first prove the "if" part. If $|t| = 1$, then $t = c$. Assume c is deducible for terms whose size is k or less. When size $|t| = k + 1$, the term either contains an $\oplus$ or f at the root, i.e., either $t = f(t')$ for some t', or $t = t_1 \oplus t_2$ for some t_1, t_2 where $t_1 \oplus t_2$ cannot be further simplified. When $t = f(t')$, we remove the f symbol by applying f^{-1}. Then $|t'| = k$, and t' contains c. By the induction hypothesis c can be deduced for terms up to size k, i.e., from set S. When $t = t_1 \oplus t_2$, without loss of generality we can assume that c appears exactly once in t_1, thus t_2 is known. The size of $t_1 \leq k$ and by induction hypothesis c can be derived from t_1. The "only if" part follows from the fact that given a known term $t_1 \oplus t_2$, neither t_1 nor t_2 can be deduced from it unless one of t_1 or $t_2 \in S$. □

Definition 4. *Consider recursive definitions which satisfy the following restrictions:*

1. *The base case, C_0, is the initial random nonce and the only nonce, i.e., a bound variable that is computed by the encryptor.*
2. *C_i contains the ith plaintext p_i, represented by a bound variable.*
3. *p_i appears only once in C_i.*

Directly from Lemma 2 and Definition 4 we obtain the following.

Theorem 1. *Cryptosystems defined using Definition 4 are invertible, i.e., for all $i \geq 0$, p_i can be deduced from $\{C_0, \ldots, C_i\}$.*

4.1   Implementation

Invertibility has been implemented via an algorithm based on Theorem 1. The algorithm is restricted to the set of $MOO_\oplus$-programs of Definition 4. The benefit of this algorithm is that it doesn't require the production of actual $MOO_\oplus$-terms, but can be applied directly to the recursive definition of the cryptosystem.

5   Decision Problems for Symbolic Security

In this section we prove results concerning decidability of symbolic security. For this we concentrate on modes of operation in which ciphertext blocks are of the form $x \oplus G$, where x is a free variable, and G contains no free variables. For such a mode, proving symbolic security reduces to proving that there is no symbolic history H containing a sequence $x_1 \oplus G_1, \ldots, x_k \oplus G_k$ such that $\sum_{i=1}^{k} \oplus G_i =_{E_\oplus} 0$. It is interesting to note that the problem is undecidable even when G_i contains no free variables, which means deciding it only requires checking for equality, not performing unification. Indeed, not only is the problem undecidable, but it is undecidable even when we bound some of the parameters, e.g. the number or length of sessions. We use an approach similar to that of Küsters and Truderung in [7], in which the security of recursive protocols defined in a term algebra that is a superset of ours is shown to be undecidable.

5.1   Undecidable Decision Problems for Block Ciphers

Due to space we consider just one type of decision problem here, those with sessions of an arbitrary or unbounded length but for which the number of sessions is bounded. That is, we do not assume a bound on the length of the interaction between the adversary and encryptor. However, we do assume a finite bound on the number of possible interleaved sessions the adversary may create. In fact, since a single session is sufficient to obtain the undecidability results we will just consider that case.

There are then two sub-cases of these unbounded length but bounded number of sessions problems. The cases are based on whether the $MOO_\oplus$-program is modeled by a non-deterministic function or a deterministic function. In this section we examine the non-deterministic case, where a session may have non-deterministic choice points, and the adversary chooses which path is taken. The second, deterministic case, and several additional related problems can be proven in a similar manner.

Definition 5. *Let α be a string $a_0 a_1 \ldots a_m$ and let C be a block. Then, $F(\alpha \bigoplus C) = f(a_0 \oplus f(a_1 \oplus \ldots f(a_m \oplus C) \ldots))$.*

We will use the following method for constructing ciphertext blocks. The construction encodes possible solutions to the Post Correspondence Problem (PCP).

Definition 6. *Let $PCP = (\frac{\alpha_0}{\beta_0}), (\frac{\alpha_1}{\beta_1}), \ldots, (\frac{\alpha_n}{\beta_n})$. Let $L = j_0, j_1, \ldots, j_k$ be a sequence of integers such that $0 \le j_i \le n$, and let $L_i = [j_{k-i}, \ldots, j_k]$. (Thus, $L_0 = [j_k]$ and $L_k = L$.) For $k \ge i > 0$ let $E_{i,L_i} = [f(r_i \oplus C_{i,L_i,1}) \oplus x_{i,1}, f(r_i \oplus C_{i,L_i,2}) \oplus x_{i,2}], 0 \le j \le n$, $C_{i,L_i,1} = F(\alpha_{j_i} \bigoplus C_{i-1,L_{i-1},1})$, and $C_{i,L_i,2} = F(\beta_{j_i} \bigoplus C_{i-1,L_{i-1},2})$. Where each r_i is a fresh bound variable, and $C_{0,L_0,1} = F(\alpha_{j_0} \bigoplus 0)$, $C_{0,L_0,2} = F(\beta_{j_0} \bigoplus 0)$.*

Essentially, the definition encodes any sequence of PCP blocks. Each E_{i,L_i} contains two strings. The first string encodes a sequence of α strings, from the tops of the PCP blocks, and the second string encodes a sequence of β strings, from the bottoms of the PCP blocks. Thus, any solution to the PCP problem can be encoded into a sequence of mode of encryption style cipher blocks (see Example 2).

Based on the non-deterministic system of Definition 6 we can define the following $MOO_\oplus$-program, which produces two equal cipherblocks which sum to zero iff the adversary finds a solution to the PCP.

Definition 7. *Denote the following $MOO_\oplus$-program as PCP_{NDMOO_1}. The program works as follows:*

- *The adversary non-deterministically picks a possible solution to the PCP, $[L = j_0, j_1, j_2, \ldots, j_k]$.*
- *At the adversary's i^{th} turn, it sends index j_{k-i} of the solution to the encryptor, as well as two plaintext blocks, $x_{i,1}$ and $x_{i,2}$.*
- *At i^{th} step the encryptor's i^{th} turn encodes a pair of ciphertext blocks $E_{i,L_i} = [f(r_i \oplus C_{i,L_i,1}) \oplus x_{i,1}, f(r_i \oplus C_{i,L_i,2}) \oplus x_{i,2}]$, according to Definition 6 and returns the pair to the adversary.*
- *After receiving each E_{i,L_i}, the adversary sums $f(r_i \oplus C_{i,L_i,1}) \oplus x_{i,1}$ with $x_{i,1}$ and $f(r_i \oplus C_{i,L_i,2}) \oplus x_{i,2}$ with $x_{i,2}$ to obtain the blocks $f(r_i \oplus C_{i,L_i,1})$ and $f(r_i \oplus C_{i,L_i,2})$.*

– *The program stops if $f(r_i \oplus C_{i,L_i,1}) = f(r_i \oplus C_{i,L_i,2})$ or the adversary stops sending input to the encryptor.*

Example 2. Consider the following PCP:

$$\underbrace{\left(\frac{ba}{baa}\right)}_{\text{tile 1}}, \quad \underbrace{\left(\frac{ab}{ba}\right)}_{\text{tile 2}}, \quad \underbrace{\left(\frac{aaa}{aa}\right)}_{\text{tile 3}}$$

One solution to this problem is $[1,3]$. Let's trace a run of the $MOO_\oplus$-program PCP_{NDMOO_1} where the adversary guesses the solution $[1,3]$. In the first step the adversary sends 3 to the encryptor and receives: $E_{0,[3]} = [f(r_0 \oplus C_{0,[3]1}) \oplus x_{0,1}, f(r_0 \oplus C_{0,[3],2}) \oplus x_{0,2}]$, $C_{0,[3],1} = F(\alpha_3 \bigoplus 0) = (f(a \oplus f(a \oplus f(a \oplus 0))))$, $C_{0,[3],2} = F(\beta_3 \bigoplus 0) = f(a \oplus f(a \oplus 0))$.

At the second step the adversary sends a 1 to the encryptor and receives the following in return. $E_{1,[1,3]} = [f(r_1 \oplus C_{1,[1,3],1}) \oplus x_{1,1}, f(r_1, C_{1,[1,3],2}) \oplus x_{1,2}]$, $C_{1,[1,3],2} = F(\alpha_1 \bigoplus C_{0,[3],1}) = f(b \oplus f(a \oplus C_{0,[3],1}))$, $C_{1,[1,3],2} = F(\beta_1 \bigoplus C_{0,[3],2}) = f(b \oplus f(a \oplus f(a \oplus C_{0,[3],2})))$.

Notice that now after step 2 the adversary has two ciphertext blocks, $C_{1,[1,3],1}$ and $C_{1,[1,3],2}$, which are equal and therefore their sum will be equal to zero. $C_{1,[1,3],1} = f(b \oplus f(a \oplus f(a \oplus f(a \oplus f(a \oplus 0)))))$, $C_{1,[1,3],2} = f(b \oplus f(a \oplus f(a \oplus f(a \oplus f(a \oplus 0)))))$.

Lemma 3. *A given PCP problem has a solution if and only if there is a sequence L of indices of that problem such that the $MOO_\oplus$-program PCP_{NDMOO_1} is symbolically secure.*

Proof (Sketch). Since each block returned by the encryptor is the sum of an f-rooted term and a free variable, symbolic security is violated if and only if two of these f-rooted terms are unified. Assume that two such terms are found to be equal. Due to the random r_i at each step the only blocks that are possibly equal are blocks from the same step, C_{i,L_i1} and $C_{i,L_i,2}$. If these blocks are equal then there is a solution to the PCP. Conversely, suppose that $[i_1, i_2, \ldots, i_m]$ is a solution to the PCP. Notice that during the mth step that the blocks $C_{m,[],1}$ and $C_{m,[],2}$ will fully encode this solution. □

Directly from Lemma 3 we obtain the following.

Theorem 2. *Assume M is an arbitrary non-deterministic $MOO_\oplus$-program. The problem of determining if M, executing with a bounded number of sessions and unbounded session lengths, is symbolically secure is undecidable.*

Several additional undecidability results can be proven using a similar reduction. These cases include deterministic unbounded session length, both deterministic and non-deterministic unbounded number of sessions with bounded session length.

5.2   An Algorithm for Checking Symbolic Security

While the question of symbolic security of modes of operation is undecidable in general, this section explores a sufficient condition for symbolic security, and gives an algorithm for checking symbolic security of modes of operation.

Let M be any mode of operation. Let H be a symbolic history of M, which can be an interleaving of multiple sessions, each of which is used to encrypt a single message of some plaintext blocks. M is defined inductively as $\mathbb{C}_{p,i} = t_{ind}, \mathbb{C}_{p,0} = t_0$. We call $\mathbb{C}_{p,i}$ a *ciphertext variable*, and use it to denote the ith ciphertext block from the pth session. We call $x_{p,i}$ a *plaintext variable*, and use it to denote the ith plaintext block from the pth session. If we *unfold* $\mathbb{C}_{p,i}$, we get t_{ind}. We assume that t_{ind} is a $MOO_\oplus$-term of the form $f(t_1) \oplus \ldots \oplus f(t_m) \oplus x_{p,i}$. We use *top-f-terms*($\mathbb{C}_{p,i}$) to denote $\{f(t_1), \ldots, f(t_m)\}$. Each $f(t_j)$ $(1 \le j \le m)$ is called an *f-rooted summand* of $\mathbb{C}_{p,i}$. We define $size_f(\mathbb{C}_{p,i})$ to be the number of f-rooted summands of $\mathbb{C}_{p,i}$.

Let t_1 and t_2 be two $MOO_\oplus$-terms. If $t_1\sigma =_\oplus t_2\sigma$, then we say that t_1 and t_2 are *$\oplus$-unifiable* under σ, or $\{t_1 \stackrel{?}{=} t_2\}$ is *$\oplus$-unifiable* under σ. Let Γ be a set of equations. If each equation in Γ is $\oplus$-unifiable under σ, then we say that Γ is $\oplus$-unifiable under σ.

Example 3. We use M_{CBC} to denote Cipher Feedback Mode, where
$\mathbb{C}_{p,i} = f(\mathbb{C}_{p,i-1}) \oplus x_{p,i}$, $\mathbb{C}_{p,0} = r_p$
(1) Here is a possible symbolic history of M_{CBC}:
$H = [r_1, r_2, x_{1,1}, f(r_1) \oplus x_{1,1}, x_{2,1}, f(r_2) \oplus x_{2,1}, x_{1,2}, f(f(r_1) \oplus x_{1,1}) \oplus x_{1,2}]$.
(2) Here is a computable substitution on H:
$\sigma = \{x_{1,1} \mapsto 0, x_{2,1} \mapsto f(r_1), x_{1,2} \mapsto f(r_1) \oplus r_2\}$.
$H\sigma = [r_1, r_2, 0, f(r_1), f(r_1), f(r_2) \oplus f(r_1), f(r_1) \oplus r_2, f(f(r_1)) \oplus f(r_1) \oplus r_2]$.

Note that, in the above example, there are no ciphertext blocks in $H\sigma$ such that they sum to 0. Here is the intuition. Let S be the set of all f-rooted summands of $MOO_\oplus$-terms in H. So $S = \{f(r_1), f(r_2), f(f(r_1) \oplus x_{1,1})\}$. No two $MOO_\oplus$-terms in S are unifiable under any computable substitution of H. We formalize this observation using the following Definition 8.

Definition 8. *Let M be a mode of operation. Consider any symbolic history H of M. Let $\mathbb{C}_{p,i}$ and $\mathbb{C}_{q,j}$ be any two ciphertext blocks in H. M satisfies the uniqueness property if for any two distinct $MOO_\oplus$-terms $t_1, t_2 \in$ top-f-terms($\mathbb{C}_{p,i}$) $\cup$ top-f-terms($\mathbb{C}_{p,j}$), there does not exist any computable substitution σ of H s.t. $t_1\sigma =_\oplus t_2\sigma$.*

The following lemma states that the uniqueness property implies symbolic security.

Lemma 4. *Let M be any mode of operation. If M satisfies the uniqueness property, then M is symbolically secure.*

Proof. Let M be a mode of operation. Consider any symbolic history H of M and any computable substitution σ. Let $S : \mathbb{C}_{p_1,i_1}, \ldots, \mathbb{C}_{p_m,i_m}$ be a subsequence of H. By the uniqueness property, $\sum_{k=1}^{m} \oplus \mathbb{C}_{p_k, i_k} \sigma = top\text{-}f\text{-}terms(\mathbb{C}_{p_m, i_m}) \sigma \oplus t$ for some t.   □

Let M be a mode of operation, H be any symbolic history of M. The following Definition 9 defines the notion of a *crucial pair* of H. Intuitively, a crucial pair is the earliest unifiable pair of f-rooted $MOO_\oplus$-terms in H. In order to show that M satisfies the uniqueness property, we show that M does not admit any symbolic history, where a crucial pair exists.

$$\frac{\Gamma \cup \{f(t) \overset{?}{=} 0\}}{\Gamma} \; Elim_f$$

$$\frac{\Gamma \cup \{\mathbb{C}_{p,m} \oplus \mathbb{C}_{q,n} \overset{?}{=} 0\}}{\Gamma} \; Elim_C$$

where $i \neq j$ implies $m \neq n$.

$$\frac{\Gamma \cup \{\mathbb{C}_{p,m} \oplus f(t) \overset{?}{=} 0\}}{\Gamma} \; Occurs\_check$$

where $\mathbb{C}_{p,m}$ is a subterm of t.

$$\frac{\Gamma \cup \{f(t_1) \oplus \ldots \oplus f(t_n) \overset{?}{=} 0\}}{\Gamma \cup \{t_k \oplus t_1 \overset{?}{=} 0\} \cup \ldots \{t_k \oplus t_{k-1} \overset{?}{=} 0\} \cup \{t_k \oplus t_{k+1} \overset{?}{=} 0\} \cup \ldots \cup \{t_k \oplus t_n \overset{?}{=} 0\}} \; Pick_f$$

where k is chosen nondeterministically between 1 and n.

$$\frac{\Gamma \cup \{\mathbb{C}_{p,m} \oplus f(t_1) \oplus \ldots \oplus f(t_n) \overset{?}{=} 0\}}{\Gamma \cup \{t'_u \overset{?}{=} t_1\} \cup \ldots \{t'_u \overset{?}{=} t_n\}} \; Pick_C$$

where (1) $f(t'_u)$ is an f-rooted summand of $\mathbb{C}_{p,m}$. (2) $size_f(\mathbb{C}_{p,m}) \leq n$. (3) $\mathbb{C}_{p,m} \in C\_Var(tm) \cup C\_Var(tm')$.

$$\frac{\Gamma \cup \{\mathbb{C}_{p,m} \oplus f(t_1) \oplus \ldots \oplus f(t_n) \overset{?}{=} 0\}}{\Gamma} \; Pick_{fail}$$

where $size_f(\mathbb{C}_{p,m}) > n$.

Fig. 2. Inference system $\mathcal{I}_{i,j,tm,tm'}$

Definition 9. *Let M be a mode of operation, H be any symbolic history of M.*

(1) Suppose that t_1 is an f-rooted summand of $\mathbb{C}_{p,i}$, t_2 is an f-rooted summand of $\mathbb{C}_{q,j}$.
- *If $\mathbb{C}_{p,i}$ appears no later than $\mathbb{C}_{q,j}$ in H, then $t_1 \preceq t_2$.*
- *If $\mathbb{C}_{p,i}$ appears earlier than $\mathbb{C}_{q,j}$ in H, then $t_1 \prec t_2$.*

(2) t_1 and t_2 are a crucial pair of H w.r.t (i, j, σ) if
- *There exist some $\mathbb{C}_{p,i}$ and $\mathbb{C}_{q,j}$ in H s.t. t_1 is an f-rooted summand of $\mathbb{C}_{p,i}$, t_2 is an f-rooted summand of $\mathbb{C}_{q,j}$.*
- *σ is a computable substitution of H, and $t_1\sigma =_\oplus t_2\sigma$.*

- If $t_1' \prec t_1$ and $t_2' \preceq t_2$, or $t_1' \preceq t_1$ and $t_2' \prec t_2$, then for any computable substitution σ of H, $t_1'\sigma \neq_\oplus t_2'\sigma$.

In order to show that no crucial pair exists in a symbolic history H, we take any two ciphertext blocks $\mathbb{C}_{p,i}$ and $\mathbb{C}_{q,j}$ in H. We then consider two different f-rooted summands tm and tm' of $\mathbb{C}_{p,i}$ and $\mathbb{C}_{q,j}$. We assume that tm and tm' are a crucial pair of H, and try to derive a contradiction using the inference rules in $\mathcal{I}_{i,j,tm,tm'}$ (Fig. 2), starting from an initial set of equations $\{tm \oplus tm' \stackrel{?}{=} 0\}$. Note that $\mathcal{I}_{i,j,tm,tm'}$ is parameterized by i, j, tm and tm', which are referred to by $Elim_C$ and $Pick_C$. We use $\mathcal{I}_{i,j,tm,tm'}^k(\{tm \oplus tm' \stackrel{?}{=} 0\})$ to represent the set of equations that we get after the kth inference step. We use $\mathcal{I}_{i,j,tm,tm'}(\{tm \oplus tm' \stackrel{?}{=} 0\})$ to represent the final result. We maintain the following invariant: If we get a set of equations Γ at any step, and tm and tm' are unifiable under some computable substitution, then at least one of the equations in Γ must hold. Intuitively, each equation in Γ represents a possibility that tm and tm' are unifiable under a computable substitution, and Γ represents the set of all possibilities. Our goal is to derive a contradiction, which is to make Γ empty.

The $Elim_f$ rule allows us to remove the possibility that an f-rooted $MOO_\oplus$-term is 0. The $Elim_C$ rule allows us to remove the possibility that we somehow find an earlier pair of unifiable terms. Unification of $\mathbb{C}_{p,m}$ with a $MOO_\oplus$-term strictly containing it is impossible by the $Occurs\_check$ rule. If the xor of some f-rooted terms is 0, the $Pick_f$ rule nondeterministically picks one of them and list all the possibilities that it can cancel with some other f-rooted $MOO_\oplus$-term. If the number of f-rooted summands of $\mathbb{C}_{p,m}$ is greater than the number of f-rooted terms in an equation, the $Pick_{fail}$ rule applies. The $Pick_C$ rule first unfolds $\mathbb{C}_{p,m}$, then picks an f-rooted summand of $\mathbb{C}_{p,m}$ and cancels it with some f-rooted term. Note that the $Pick_C$ rule rules out the possibility that two f-rooted summands of $\mathbb{C}_{p,m}$ can cancel with each other. In order to apply the $Pick_C$ rule, $\mathbb{C}_{p,m}$ must be a ciphertext variable of either tm or tm'. We need this condition for termination.

Algorithm 1. Checking Symbolic Security of Modes of Operation

---

Input: a recursive description of some mode of operation M.

$\Gamma = \textit{top-f-terms}(\mathbb{C}_{p,i}) \cup \textit{top-f-terms}(\mathbb{C}_{q,j})$
for each pair of distinct terms tm and tm' in Γ **do**
    if $\mathcal{I}_{i,j,tm,tm'}(\{tm \oplus tm' \stackrel{?}{=} 0\}) \neq \emptyset$ **then**
        return "unknown"
    end if
end for
return "secure"

Definition 10. *Given a* $MOO_\oplus$*-term* t, $C\_Var(t)$ *denotes the set of ciphertext variables occurring in* t. *More formally,*

(1) $C\_Var(\mathbb{C}_{p,i}) = \{\mathbb{C}_{p,i}\}$, if $\mathbb{C}_{p,i}$ is a ciphertext variable. (2) $C\_Var(x_{p,i}) = \emptyset$, if $x_{p,i}$ is a plaintext variable. (3) $C\_Var(f(t)) = C\_Var(t)$. (4) $C\_Var(t_1 \oplus t_2) = C\_Var(t_1) \cup C\_Var(t_2)$.

The following Lemma 5 describes an important invariant of $\mathcal{I}_{i,j,tm,tm'}$, which implies the soundness of Algorithm 1.

Lemma 5. *Let M be a mode of operation, H be any symbolic history of M. Suppose that tm and tm' are a crucial pair of H w.r.t. (i, j, σ). For all k, if $\mathcal{I}^k_{i,j,tm,tm'}(\{tm \oplus tm' \overset{?}{=} 0\}) = \Gamma$, at least one equation in Γ must be $\oplus$-unifiable under σ.*

Proof (Sketch). We prove this lemma by induction on k. When $k = 0$, the lemma holds trivially. Assume that the lemma holds when $k = l - 1$. We want to show that the lemma also holds when $k = l$. Consider the lth inference step.

If $Elim_f$, $Elim_C$, $Occurs\_check$ or $Pick_{fail}$ is used, an impossible case is removed. For example, if $Elim_C$ is used, $\{\mathbb{C}_{p,m} \oplus \mathbb{C}_{q,n} \overset{?}{=} 0\}$ is impossible, since it contradicts with the assumption that tm and tm' are a crucial pair of H w.r.t. (i, j, σ). If $Pick_f$ or $Pick_C$ is used, we nondeterministically guess an f-rooted term and list all the possibilities that it can cancel with some other term. □

Theorem 3 (Soundness). *For any mode of operation M, if Algorithm 1 returns "secure", then M is symbolically secure.*

Proof. Given a mode of operation M, if Algorithm 1 returns "secure", then for each pair of distinct terms tm and tm' in $top\text{-}f\text{-}terms(\mathbb{C}_{p,i}) \cup top\text{-}f\text{-}terms(\mathbb{C}_{q,j})$, $\mathcal{I}_{i,j,tm,tm'}(\{tm \oplus tm' \overset{?}{=} 0\}) = \emptyset$. By Lemma 5, no pair of terms tm and tm' are a crucial pair of H. This means that the uniqueness property holds for M. Therefore, by Lemma 4, M is symbolically secure. □

To prove termination of Algorithm 1, we define the following relations: $\prec_E$ and $\preceq_E$ are partial order relations on equations, $\prec_S$ is a partial order on sets of equations.

Definition 11. *Let eq be an equation of the form $t_1 \oplus \ldots \oplus t_m \overset{?}{=} 0$, where each t_i $(1 \le i \le m)$ is either f-rooted or a bound variable. Let eq' be an equation of the form $t'_1 \oplus \ldots \oplus t'_n \overset{?}{=} 0$, where each t'_i $(1 \le i \le n)$ is either f-rooted or a bound variable. We say that $eq \prec_E eq'$ if for all $1 \le i \le m$, there exists j such that t_i is a strict subterm of t'_j. We say that $eq \preceq_E eq'$ if $eq \prec_E eq'$ or eq is the same as eq'.*

Let $\Gamma = \{eq_1, \ldots, eq_m\}$, $\Gamma' = \{eq'_1, \ldots, eq'_n\}$. We say that $\Gamma \prec_S \Gamma'$ if for all $1 \le i \le m$, there exists j such that $eq_i \preceq_E eq'_j$, and at least one of the following conditions is true: (1) $|\Gamma| < |\Gamma'|$. (2) There exists i, j, s.t. $eq_i \prec_E eq'_j$.

Let Γ be a set of equations, let t and t' be two $MOO_\oplus$-terms. We define the following set. $C\_Var_{t,t'}(\Gamma)$ is the set of ciphertext variables that must occur in Γ, and also occur in either t or t'.

$$C\_Var_{t,t'}(\Gamma) = \{\mathbb{C}_{u,v} \mid \mathbb{C}_{u,v} \in C\_Var(t) \cup C\_Var(t'), \mathbb{C}_{u,v} \text{ occurs in } \Gamma\}.$$

Theorem 4 (Termination). *For any mode of operation M, Algorithm 1 always terminates.*

Proof. We show that for each tm and tm', $\mathcal{I}_{i,j,tm,tm'}$ always terminates. Consider some inference step. Suppose that we apply $\mathcal{I}_{i,j,tm,tm'}$ to Γ and get Γ'. There are 2 cases to consider.

Case 1: If $Pick_C$ is used, $|C\_Var_{tm,tm'}(\Gamma')| < |C\_Var_{tm,tm'}(\Gamma)|$.

Case 2: If $Elim_f, Elim_C, Occurs\_check, Pick_f$ or $Pick_{fail}$ is used, then $|C\_Var_{tm,tm'}(\Gamma')| = |C\_Var_{tm,tm'}(\Gamma)|$ and $\Gamma' \prec_S \Gamma$.

So either $|C\_Var_{tm,tm'}(\Gamma')| < |C\_Var_{tm,tm'}(\Gamma)|$, or $|C\_Var_{tm,tm'}(\Gamma')| = |C\_Var_{t,t'}(\Gamma)|$ and $\Gamma' \prec_S \Gamma$. For each tm and tm', $\mathcal{I}_{i,j,tm,tm'}$ always terminates. Therefore, Algorithm 1 always terminates. $\square$

Here is an example of checking symbolic security using Algorithm 1.

Example 4. Let M be Cipher Feedback Mode, where: $\mathbb{C}_{p,i} = f(\mathbb{C}_{p,i-1}) \oplus x_{p,i}$, $\mathbb{C}_{p,0} = r_p$. According to Algorithm 1, $\Gamma = \{f(\mathbb{C}_{p,i-1}), f(\mathbb{C}_{q,j-1})\}$. Apply the inference system $\mathcal{I}_{i,j,f(\mathbb{C}_{p,i-1}),f(\mathbb{C}_{q,j-1})}$ to $\{f(\mathbb{C}_{p,i-1}) \oplus f(\mathbb{C}_{q,j-1}) \overset{?}{=} 0\}$.

$$\frac{\{f(\mathbb{C}_{p,i-1}) \oplus f(\mathbb{C}_{q,j-1}) \overset{?}{=} 0\}}{\{\mathbb{C}_{p,i-1} \oplus \mathbb{C}_{q,j-1} \overset{?}{=} 0\}} Pick_f \qquad \frac{\{\mathbb{C}_{p,i-1} \oplus \mathbb{C}_{q,j-1} \overset{?}{=} 0\}}{\emptyset} Elim_C$$

Algorithm 1 returns "secure".

5.3 Implementation

The CryptoSolve tool can check for symbolic-security in several ways. The first, and most exhaustive, is via the P-unification approach [8]. In this approach, cipher blocks of the MOO-program under consideration are generated and the appropriate P-unification is used to check security (see [11]). The difficulty with this approach is that it can be time consuming in practice, due to the need to continually generate, then check new cipher blocks. However, the algorithm specified in Sect. 5.2 doesn't require the explicit generation of cipher blocks, but only requires us to compare. This approach is not complete but works for many cases. Thus, we are implementing it as a first pass symbolic security check.

6 Conclusions

We have investigated two algorithmic problems arising from the symbolic analysis of cryptographic modes of operation built using block ciphers and exclusive-or: symbolic security and invertibility. We have given algorithmic results for both. We also believe that we have learned something from treating the problems separately from each other. For example, one might ask if the restrictions imposed by invertibility might narrow the class of cryptosystems to ones for which IND$-security is decidable. Our results on undecidability of symbolic show that they do not, because our embedding of the Post Correspondence Problem all produce invertible cryptosystems.

There are many ways these results can be extended. We can, as mentioned in the introduction, investigate algorithms for deciding combinations of properties. We can investigate larger classes of modes that use additional primitives and functions, such as hash functions, field operations, concatenation, block ciphers with tweaks, and the successor function, the latter two of which have already been studied in [5,9] for the messagewise schedule. In addition, we can investigate other classes of modes built using the same or similar primitives, e.g. hash functions (studied in [10]), hash-based signatures, garbled circuits (studied in [4]), and message authentication codes (studied in [5]). We also intend to determine what other cryptosystems or classes of cryptosystems are amenable to symbolic analyses and study them if feasible.

References

1. Abadi, M., Cortier, V.: Deciding knowledge in security protocols under equational theories. Theoret. Comput. Sci. **367**(1–2), 2–32 (2006)
2. Abadi, M., Fournet, C.: Mobile values, new names, and secure communication. In: Proceedings of the 28th ACM SIGPLAN-SIGACT Symposium on Principles of Programming Languages, POPL 2001, pp. 104–115. ACM, New York (2001). https://doi.org/10.1145/360204.360213
3. Borgström, J.: Static equivalence is harder than knowledge. In: Baeten, J.C.M., Phillips, I.C.C. (eds.) Proceedings of the 12th Workshop on Expressiveness on Concurrency, EXPRESS 2005, San Francisco, CA, USA, 27 August 2005, pp. 45–57. Electronic Notes in Theoretical Computer Science, Elsevier (2005). https://doi.org/10.1016/j.entcs.2006.05.006
4. Carmer, B., Rosulek, M.: Linicrypt: a model for practical cryptography. In: Robshaw, M., Katz, J. (eds.) CRYPTO 2016. LNCS, vol. 9816, pp. 416–445. Springer, Heidelberg (2016). https://doi.org/10.1007/978-3-662-53015-3_15
5. Hoang, V.T., Katz, J., Malozemoff, A.J.: Automated analysis and synthesis of authenticated encryption schemes. In: Proceedings of the 22nd ACM SIGSAC Conference on Computer and Communications Security, pp. 84–95. Association for Computing Machinery, New York (2015). https://doi.org/10.1145/2810103.2813636
6. Joux, A., Martinet, G., Valette, F.: Blockwise-adaptive attackers revisiting the (in)security of some provably secure encryption modes: CBC, GEM, IACBC. In: Yung, M. (ed.) CRYPTO 2002. LNCS, vol. 2442, pp. 17–30. Springer, Heidelberg (2002). https://doi.org/10.1007/3-540-45708-9_2
7. Küsters, R., Truderung, T.: On the automatic analysis of recursive security protocols with XOR. In: Thomas, W., Weil, P. (eds.) STACS 2007. LNCS, vol. 4393, pp. 646–657. Springer, Heidelberg (2007). https://doi.org/10.1007/978-3-540-70918-3_55
8. Lin, H., Lynch, C.: Local XOR unification: definitions, algorithms and application to cryptography. IACR Cryptol. ePrint Arch. 2020, 929 (2020). https://eprint.iacr.org/2020/929
9. Malozemoff, A.J., Katz, J., Green, M.D.: Automated analysis and synthesis of block-cipher modes of operation. In: 2014 IEEE 27th Conference on Computer Security Foundations Symposium (CSF), pp. 140–152. IEEE (2014)

10. McQuoid, I., Swope, T., Rosulek, M.: Characterizing collision and second-preimage resistance in Linicrypt. In: Hofheinz, D., Rosen, A. (eds.) TCC 2019. LNCS, vol. 11891, pp. 451–470. Springer, Cham (2019). https://doi.org/10.1007/978-3-030-36030-6_18

11. Meadows, C.A.: Symbolic and computational reasoning about cryptographic modes of operation. IACR Cryptol. ePrint Arch. 2020, 794 (2020). https://eprint.iacr.org/2020/794

12. Rogaway, P.: Nonce-based symmetric encryption. In: 11th International Workshop on Fast Software Encryption, FSE 2004, Delhi, India, 5–7 February 2004, Revised Papers, pp. 348–359 (2004). https://doi.org/10.1007/978-3-540-25937-4_22

Formal Analysis of Symbolic Authenticity

Hai Lin$^{(\boxtimes)}$ and Christopher Lynch

Clarkson University, Potsdam, NY, USA
{hlin,clynch}@clarkson.edu

Abstract. Authenticated encryption schemes are ways of encrypting messages which simultaneously assure the secrecy and authenticity of data. Designing authenticated encryption schemes can be error-prone. In this paper, we consider the authenticity of authenticated encryption schemes . We introduce the notion of symbolic authenticity, and present two inference systems for verifying symbolic authenticity. The first inference system works for authenticated encryption schemes for messages of fixed length. It is sound, complete and terminating. The second one works for authenticated encryption schemes for messages of arbitrary length. It is sound, terminating, and complete under some condition. These inference systems can be used to automatically synthesize authenticated encryption schemes.

Keywords: Unification · Authenticated encryption · Formal methods

1 Introduction

Authenticated encryption (AE) schemes (e.g. CCM [4], XCBC [5], OTR [12], OCB [14], etc.) are ways of encrypting messages which simultaneously assure the secrecy and authenticity of data. It is a nontrivial task to construct AE schemes. Automated techniques have been used to verify and synthesize AE schemes [6]. In this paper, we are interested in the authenticity property. Roughly speaking, an AE scheme satisfies authenticity if an adversary cannot forge any new valid ciphertext message after observing some valid ciphertext messages. We consider two versions of AE schemes: a restricted version (*fixed-length AE schemes*), which handle messages of a fixed length, and *general AE schemes*, which handle messages of arbitrary length.

Motivated by the original work in [11], we propose to reason about authenticity symbolically. For each version of the AE schemes, we define a notion of symbolic authenticity in terms of a new unification problem, and give an inference system for checking symbolic authenticity. The idea is that we use function symbols to model cryptographic operations (e.g. tweakable block cipher, exclusive-or, etc.), use terms to model message blocks, and use an equational theory to capture the properties of cryptographic operations and the properties that valid ciphertext messages must satisfy.

The work is supported by NRL under contract N00173-19-1-G012.

B. Konev and G. Reger (Eds.): FroCoS 2021, LNAI 12941, pp. 271–286, 2021.
https://doi.org/10.1007/978-3-030-86205-3_15

Formal methods have been used to analyze various cryptosystems, including cryptographic modes of operation, authenticated encryption schemes, signature schemes, garbled circuits, etc. [1–3,6–8,10]. In the literature, [6] is the closest to our work. In [6], Hoang et al. consider AE schemes constructed from *tweakable block ciphers* [9]. An AE scheme is viewed as a directed acyclic graph, and a type system is developed. Hoang et al. show that "well-typed" graphs define secure AE schemes. However, no completeness result is given. Our inference system for fix-length AE schemes is sound, terminating and complete. Our inference system for general AE schemes is sound, terminating and complete under some condition.

The rest of this paper is organized as follows. In Sect. 2, we introduce the basics of tweakable block ciphers and authenticated encryption schemes. In Sect. 3, we consider symbolic authenticity of fixed-length AE schemes. In Sect. 4, we consider symbolic authenticity of general AE schemes. We conclude and discuss future work in Sect. 5.

2   Preliminaries

In cryptography, a *tweakable block cipher* [9] on λ-bit strings with tweak space $\mathcal{T}$ and key space $\mathcal{K}$ is a map $E: \mathcal{K} \times \mathcal{T} \times \{0,1\}^\lambda \rightarrow \{0,1\}^\lambda$ s.t. $E_K(T, \cdot)$ is a permutation on $\{0,1\}^\lambda$ for any $K \in \mathcal{K}$ and $T \in \mathcal{T}$. Each combination of a key and a tweak leads to a totally independent permutation. In this paper, we consider some tweakable block cipher with a fixed key K, which is not known to the adversary.

An authenticated encryption scheme Π is a tuple $(\mathcal{E}, \mathcal{D}, \mathcal{V})$ with key space $\mathcal{K}$, tweak space $\mathcal{T}$ and tag space $\mathcal{G}$, where $\mathcal{E}$ is an encryption algorithm, $\mathcal{D}$ is a decryption algorithm and $\mathcal{V}$ is a verification equation, which checks authenticity of ciphertext messages. l denotes the number of message blocks that Π handles. $\mathcal{E}$ maps $(K, Tk, M) \in \mathcal{K} \times \mathcal{T} \times \{0,1\}^{\lambda \times l}$ to a ciphertext message $(Tk, C, Tg) \in \mathcal{T} \times \{0,1\}^{\lambda \times l} \times \mathcal{G}$. A ciphertext message (Tk, C, Tg) is *valid* if and only if $\mathcal{V}_K(Tk, C, Tg)$ returns true. $\mathcal{D}$ maps $(K, Tk, C, Tg) \in \mathcal{K} \times \mathcal{T} \times \{0,1\}^* \times \mathcal{G}$ to either a message $M \in \mathcal{M}$ if (Tk, C, Tg) is valid or an error otherwise. In this paper, we only consider authenticated encryption schemes constructed from tweakable block ciphers, and the tag is the output of some tweakable block cipher.

Security Game. In order to check if an AE scheme satisfies authenticity, we consider a game between an adversary A and an encryption oracle $\mathcal{E}_K(\cdot, \cdot)$. The adversary queries the encryption oracle with plaintext messages, and gets back valid ciphertext messages. The adversary can choose plaintext messages adaptively based on previous queries. They can have as many rounds of interaction as they want. The adversary wins the game if and only if (s)he can forge a new ciphertext message (Tk, C, Tg) s.t. $\mathcal{V}_K(Tk, C, Tg) = True$. An authenticated encryption scheme satisfies authenticity if and only if the adversary can only win the game with negligible probability.

We consider a first-order signature $\Sigma = \{e/2, d/2, n/1, \oplus/2, 0/0\}$, and e models encryption using a tweakable block cipher with some fixed key. d models decryption using the same tweakable block cipher with the same key. In tweakable block cipher, each tweak can only be used to process a single block. If tk is the tweak for processing the ith block of some message, then $n(tk)$ is the tweak for processing the $i+1^{th}$ block of the same message. We use $n^k(t)$ as a shorthand for applying n to t for k times. 0 represents a block of all 0's.

In this paper, we consider two versions of AE schemes: fixed-length AE schemes, which handles messages of fixed length; general AE schemes, which handles messages of arbitrary length. Figure 1 illustrates the syntax of terms considered in this paper. T denotes a set of terms, modelling the fixed-length AE schemes. N represents the set of all *constants*, X represents the set of all *variables*, and T_{tk} represents the set of all *tweaks*. A term can be built up from constants, variables, and tweaks using $e, d, \oplus$. We say that a term is f-*rooted* if it is of the form $f(t_1, \ldots, t_u)$. The first argument of an e-rooted term or a d-rooted term has to be a tweak. We use the convention that variables start with upper-case letters and constants start with lower-case letters.

$$
\begin{aligned}
T &:= N \mid X \mid e(T_{tk}, T) \mid d(T_{tk}, T) \mid T \oplus T \\
N &:= N_{tk} \mid N_c \mid N_{tg} \mid N_{meta} \\
N_{tk} &:= tk_1 \mid tk_2 \mid \ldots \mid tk_i \mid \ldots \\
N_c &:= c_{1,1} \mid c_{1,2} \mid \ldots \mid c_{i,1} \mid c_{i,2} \mid \ldots \\
N_{tg} &:= tg_{1,1} \mid tg_{1,2} \mid \ldots \mid tg_{i,1} \mid tg_{i,2} \mid \ldots \\
X &:= X_C \mid Tk \mid Tg \\
X_C &:= C_1 \mid C_2 \mid \ldots \mid C_i \mid \ldots \\
T_{tk} &:= N_{tk} \mid Tk \mid n(T_{tk}) \\[4pt]
T^+ &:= N \mid X \mid e(T_{tk}, T^+) \mid d(T_{tk}, T^+) \mid T^+ \oplus T^+ \mid Y \\
Y &:= Y_1 \mid Y_2 \mid \ldots \mid Y_j \mid \ldots \\[4pt]
T_{meta} &:= N_{meta} \mid e(T_{meta\_tk}, T^+) \mid d(T_{meta\_tk}, T^+) \mid e(T_{tk}, T_{meta}) \mid d(T_{tk}, T_{meta}) \mid T \oplus T_{meta} \\
T_{meta\_tk} &:= tk_i \mid n(T_{meta\_tk}) \\
N_{meta} &:= tg_{i,1} \mid tg_{i,2} \mid \ldots \mid c_{i,1} \mid c_{i,2} \mid \ldots \mid c_{i,j} \mid \ldots
\end{aligned}
$$

Fig. 1. Syntax of terms

There are three types of constants: *tweak constants* (denoted by N_{tk}), *ciphertext constants* (denoted by N_c) and *tag constants* (denoted by N_{tg}). For all $i, j \in \mathcal{N}$, tk_i is a tweak constant, denoting the tweak for processing the first block of the ith message, $tg_{i,j}$ is a tag constant, denoting the tag of the ith ciphertext message of length j, $c_{i,j}$ is a ciphertext constant, denoting the jth block of the ith ciphertext message. There are three types of variables: Tk denotes a tweak, Tg denotes a tag, and C_i denotes the ith block of a message.

In Fig. 1, T^+ represents a set of terms, modelling the general AE schemes. T^+ augments T by some $Y_1, Y_2, \ldots$. $\forall j \in \mathcal{N}, Y_j$ represents some accumulative state after encrypting the jth block of a message. For example, Y_j may be the exclusive-or of the first j ciphertext blocks. In order to model general AE schemes, we define Y_j inductively in terms of Y_k's $(k < j)$ and C_k's $(k \leq j)$. If the ith message has l blocks, then the tag attached to that message is $e(n^l(tk_i), Y_l)$.

If a term t contains (at least) a subterm with variable indices, t is called a *meta-term*. In Fig. 1, we use T_{meta} to represent the set of all meta-terms. N_{meta} represents the set of all *meta-constants*. T_{meta_tk} represents the set of *meta-tweak-constants*. We can instantiate meta-terms. For example, $c_{i,1}$ is a meta-term representing the 1st block of some i^{th} ciphertext message. If we instantiate i by 1, then $c_{i,1}$ represents the 1st block of the 1st ciphertext message.

A *substitution* is a map: $X \to T - T_{meta}$. We use id to denote the identity substitution. A *meta substitution* is a map: $X \to T_{meta}$. Throughout the rest of this paper, ω_i^l denotes the following meta-substitution.

$$\omega_i^l = \{Tk \mapsto tk_i, C_1 \mapsto c_{i,1}, C_2 \mapsto c_{i,2}, \dots, C_l \mapsto c_{i,l}\}$$

We can instantiate meta-substitutions. Let γ_1 and γ_2 be two meta-substitutions. $\gamma_1\gamma_2$ denotes the composition of γ_1 and γ_2. For example,

(1) $\omega_i^2 = \{Tk \mapsto tk_i, C_1 \mapsto c_{i,1}, C_2 \mapsto c_{i,2}\}$
(2) $\omega_1^2 = \{Tk \mapsto tk_1, C_1 \mapsto c_{1,1}, C_2 \mapsto c_{1,2}\}$
(3) $\omega_i^2\{C_3 \mapsto c_{i,3}\} = \{Tk \mapsto tk_i, C_1 \mapsto c_{i,1}, C_2 \mapsto c_{i,2}, C_3 \mapsto c_{i,3}\}$

3   Formal Analysis of Symbolic Authenticity of Fixed-Length AE Schemes

In this section, we consider fix-length AE schemes, which handle messages of exactly l blocks, where l is a fixed integer. In Sect. 3.1, we show how such schemes can be modelled symbolically. In Sect. 3.2, we introduce the notion of *symbolic authenticity* for such schemes, and define symbolic authenticity in terms of a new unification problem, which can be solved using the inference rules presented in Sect. 3.3. We also give an algorithm for checking symbolic authenticity for fixed-length AE schemes in Sect. 3.3.

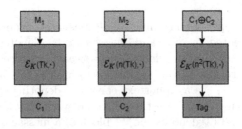

Fig. 2. A fixed-length AE scheme Π_1

3.1   Modelling Fixed-Length AE Schemes

Any fixed-length AE schemes can be modelled symbolically. We use the following example to illustrate the idea.

Example 1. Consider the authenticated encryption scheme Π_1 in Fig. 2. $\Pi_1 = (\mathcal{E}, \mathcal{D}, \mathcal{V})$, where
$\mathcal{E}_K(Tk, (M_1, M_2)) := (Tk, e(Tk, M_1), e(n(Tk), M_2), e(n^2(Tk), C_1 \oplus C_2)).$
$\mathcal{V}_K(Tk, (C_1, C_2), Tg) := (e(n^2(Tk), C_1 \oplus C_2) == Tg)$
$$\mathcal{D}_K(Tk, (C_1, C_2), Tg) := \begin{cases} (d(Tk, C_1), d(n(Tk), C_2)) & \text{if } \mathcal{V}_K(Tk, C_1, C_2, Tg) \text{ is } True \\ \bot & otherwise \end{cases}$$

Suppose that there are some rounds of interaction between an adversary A and an encryption oracle $\mathcal{E}_K(\cdot, \cdot)$. At round i: The adversary A queries the oracle with $(m_{i,1}, m_{i,2})$. $\mathcal{E}_K(\cdot, \cdot)$ replies with a valid ciphertext message $(tk_i, c_{i,1}, c_{i,2}, tg_{i,2})$.

There are many ways, in which the adversary can choose plaintext messages adaptively. Here is one possible way, $m_{2,1}$ is chosen as $c_{1,1}$, $m_{2,2}$ is chosen as $c_{1,1} \oplus c_{1,2}$. We have the following set of equations: $E_\oplus$, E_1 and E_2. $E_\oplus$ captures the properties of exclusive-or. E_1 captures the fact that the ciphertext messages, which A receives, are valid. E_2 captures the fact that the adversary can choose plaintext messages adaptively.

$E_\oplus = \{t \oplus t = 0, t \oplus 0 = t\} \cup AC(\oplus)$
$E_1 = \{e(n^2(tk_1), c_{1,1} \oplus c_{1,2}) = tg_{1,2}, e(n^2(tk_2), c_{2,1} \oplus c_{2,2}) = tg_{2,2}, \ldots\}$
$E_2 = \{d(tk_2, c_{2,1}) = c_{1,1}, d(n(tk_2), c_{2,2}) = c_{1,1} \oplus c_{1,2}\}$

After the above two rounds of interaction, the adversary can output a new valid ciphertext message: $(tk_1, c_{1,1} \oplus c_{1,2}, 0, tg_{1,2})$. Therefore, Π_1 does not satisfy authenticity.

3.2   Symbolic Authenticity for Fixed-Length AE Schemes

In this section, we introduce a new unification problem over terms in T, and define the notion of *symbolic authenticity* in terms of this new unification problem.

First we define VE^l, which is the set of verification equations that verify the validity of messages containing l blocks. The "Consistency" property holds since in tweakable block cipher, each tweak can only be used to process a unique message block.

Definition 1. *Let V be an equation over T, $V \in VE^l$ if (1) V is of the form $e(n^l(Tk), t) = Tg$. (lhs(V) denotes $e(n^l(Tk), t)$.) (2) no C_k $(k > l)$ occurs in V. (3) V satisfies the following "Consistency" property.*

(Consistency) *(I) For all terms $e(s, s')$ and $e(t, t')$ that occur in V, if $s = t$, then $s' = t'$. (II) For all terms $d(s, s')$ and $d(t, t')$ that occur in V, if $s = t$, then $s' = t'$.*

We then formalize the notion of an *FAE (Fixed-length Authenticated Encryption) theory* w.r.t. some $V \in VE^l$ using the following definition. The idea is that the adversary can take advantages of the equations in an *FAE* theory while trying to forge a new valid message. An *FAE* theory contains two subsets of equations: The first subset captures the fact that the ciphertext messages, which the adversary receives in the security game, are valid. The second subset captures the fact that the adversary can choose plaintext messages adaptively. In Example 1, $E_1 \cup E_2$ is an example of an *FAE* theory w.r.t. $e(n^2(Tk), C_1 \oplus C_2) == Tg$.

Definition 2. *Consider any $V \in VE^l$. A set of equations E_V over terms in T is an FAE theory w.r.t. V if the following properties hold:*

1. *(**Validity**) $\forall i \in \mathcal{N}, V(\omega_i^l \cup \{Tg \mapsto tg_{i,l}\}) \in E_V$.*
2. *(**TBC_PRP**) $\forall t \in E_V$, if $lhs(V)\sigma =_\oplus t\sigma$, then $\exists i$ s.t. $Tk\sigma = tk_i$.*
3. *(**Consistency**) (1) For all $e(s, s')$ and $e(t, t')$ that occur in E_V, if $s = t$, then $s' = t'$. (2) For all $d(s, s')$ and $d(t, t')$ that occur in E_V, if $s = t$, then $s' = t'$.*
4. *(**Stability**) No equation in E_V is of the form $n(t) = t'$.*

We assume that, in the security game described in Sect. 2, the adversary receives the following messages.

$(tk_1, c_{1,1}, \ldots, c_{1,l}, tg_{1,l})$
$(tk_2, c_{2,1}, \ldots, c_{2,l}, tg_{2,l})$
$\ldots \ldots$

In Definition 2, the "Validity" property says that all the above messages are valid. The "Stability" property says that the tweaks are irreducible in E_V. We assume that the tag attached to any ciphertext message is the output of some tweakable block cipher (TBC), and tweakable block ciphers are pseudorandom permutations (PRP). The "TBC_PRP" property says that if the adversary wants to generate a valid message, (s)he has to choose one of the tweaks in the messages that (s)he receives. (Otherwise, the tag is totally random to the adversary, and (s)he has negligible probability of guessing it correctly.)

The following Definition 3 defines a new unification problem, called $(\oplus, E_V)$-*unification*, where $V \in VE^l$ and E_V is an *FAE* theory w.r.t. V. In Definition 4, we then introduce the notion of *symbolic authenticity* based on this new unification problem.

Definition 3. *σ is a computable substitution if it maps Tk to a term in T_{tk}, and maps each C_i to the exclusive-or of terms in $N \cup X$.*

Let V be an equation in VE^l, and E_V be an FAE theory w.r.t. V. Consider two terms $t_1, t_2 \in T$ s.t. $t_1\omega_i^l = t_2$. t_1 and t_2 are $(\oplus, E_V)$-unifiable under σ if (1) $t_1\sigma =_{\oplus, E_V} t_2$, and (2) σ is a computable substitution.

σ is called a $(\oplus, E_V)$-meta-unifier of t_1 and t_2. σ^* is the most general $(\oplus, E_V)$-meta-unifier of t_1 and t_2 if for any $(\oplus, E_V)$-meta-unifier σ of t_1 and t_2, there exists some meta-substitution σ' s.t. $\sigma = \sigma^*\sigma'$. Let P be a set of equations over terms in T. σ is called a $(\oplus, E_V)$-meta-unifier of P if σ is a $(\oplus, E_V)$-meta-unifier of each equation in P.

To produce a valid message $m : (Tk, C, Tg)$, the adversary needs to compute some substitution σ s.t. $V(Tk\sigma, C\sigma, Tg\sigma)$ returns true. Due to the "Validity" property, the adversary can pick σ to be $\omega_i^l \cup \{Tg \mapsto tg_{i,l}\}$ ($\forall i \in \mathcal{N}$). But that does not produce a new message, it is the ith message that the adversary receives from the encryption oracle. Therefore, the adversary tries to find some other $(\oplus, E_V)$-meta-unifier σ' of $lhs(V)$ and $lhs(V)\omega_i^l$. If the adversary succeeds, $(Tk\sigma', C\sigma', tg_{i,l})$ ($\forall i \in \mathcal{N}$) is a new valid message. That is the idea behind the following definition.

Definition 4. *Let S be a fixed-length AE scheme with verification equation $V \in VE^l$. S is symbolically authentic if ω_i^l is the only $(\oplus, E_V)$-meta-unifier of $lhs(V)$ and $lhs(V)\omega_i^l$, where E_V is any FAE theory w.r.t. V.*

If an authenticated encryption scheme is symbolically authentic, there is no way for the adversary to forge a new valid message symbolically.

3.3   Inference system

In this section, we present a sound, complete and terminating inference system $\mathcal{I}_B$ for solving the $(\oplus, E_V)$-unification problem over terms in T. The difficulty

---

Decompose

$$\{f(s_1,\ldots,s_u) \overset{?}{=} f(t_1,\ldots,t_u)\} \cup \Gamma; \sigma \Longrightarrow \{s_1 \overset{?}{=} t_1,\ldots,s_u \overset{?}{=} t_u\} \cup \Gamma; \sigma$$

where $f \neq \oplus$, and u can possibly be 0.

Decompose$_n$

$$\{n^u(s) \overset{?}{=} n^u(t)\} \cup \Gamma; \sigma \Longrightarrow \{s \overset{?}{=} t\} \cup \Gamma; \sigma$$

Elim$_C$

$$\{C_{j_1} \oplus \ldots \oplus C_{j_u} \overset{?}{=} c_{i,j_1} \oplus \ldots \oplus c_{i,j_u}\} \cup \Gamma; \sigma \Longrightarrow \Gamma\sigma'; \sigma\sigma'$$

where $\sigma' = \{C_{j_1} \mapsto C_{j_2} \oplus \ldots \oplus C_{j_u} \oplus c_{i,j_1} \oplus \ldots \oplus c_{i,j_u}\}$.

Elim$_{Tk}$

$$\{Tk \overset{?}{=} tk_i\} \cup \Gamma; \sigma \Longrightarrow \Gamma\sigma'; \sigma\sigma'$$

where $\sigma' = \{Tk \mapsto tk_i\}$.

Split

$$\{s_1 \oplus f(n^u(s_2), s_3) \overset{?}{=} t_1 \oplus f(n^u(t_2), t_3)\} \cup \Gamma; \sigma$$
$$\Longrightarrow \{s_1 \overset{?}{=} t_1, f(n^u(s_2), s_3) \overset{?}{=} f(n^u(t_2), t_3)\} \cup \Gamma; \sigma$$

where f is either e or d.

Fig. 3. Inference system $\mathcal{I}_B$

for designing such an inference system is that E_V has an unbounded number of equations.

The inference rules of $\mathcal{I}_B$ are listed in Fig. 3. The *Decompose* rule is standard as in [13]. The *Decompose*$_n$ rule is an optimization rule: If we have an equation of the form $n^u(s) \stackrel{?}{=} n^u(t)$, instead of applying the *Decompose* rule u times, we can apply the *Decompose*$_n$ rule once. The *Variable Elimination* rule in [13] may not lead to computable substitutions. Instead, we have the $Elim_C$ rule and the $Elim_{Tk}$ rule, which always lead to computable substitutions. The *Split* rule is the key rule in $\mathcal{I}_B$. The following example illustrates the idea behind the *Split* rule.

Example 2. Let V be an equation in VE^2, and E_V be an FAE theory. Consider the following inference steps:

- $\{C_1 \oplus e(tk_1, C_2) \stackrel{?}{=} c_{1,1} \oplus e(tk_1, c_{1,2})\} \stackrel{Split}{\Longrightarrow} \{C_1 \stackrel{?}{=} c_{1,1}, e(tk_1, C_2) \stackrel{?}{=} e(tk_1, c_{1,2})\}$
  The first thing to observe is that: $\{C_1 \mapsto e(tk_1, C_2) \oplus c_{1,1} \oplus e(tk_1, c_{1,2})\}$ is not a computable substitution. If $(C_1 \oplus e(tk_1, C_2))\sigma =_{\oplus, E_V} c_{1,1} \oplus e(tk_1, c_{1,2})$, there are two cases to consider:
  (1) $(e(tk_1, C_2))\sigma =_\oplus e(tk_1, c_{1,2})$
  (2) $(e(tk_1, C_2))\sigma =_\oplus t$, where $t \in E_V$. Due to the "Validity" property, $e(tk_1, c_{1,2})$ occurs in E_V. Due to the "Consistency" property, $e(tk_1, c_{1,2})$ is the only term in E_V s.t. its first argument is tk_1.
  In both cases, $e(tk_1, C_2) =_\oplus e(tk_1, c_{1,2})$, which implies that $C_1 =_\oplus c_{1,1}$.
- $\{C_1 \oplus e(tk_i, C_2) \stackrel{?}{=} c_{i,1} \oplus e(tk_i, c_{i,2})\} \stackrel{Split}{\Longrightarrow} \{C_1 \stackrel{?}{=} c_{i,1}, e(tk_i, C_2) \stackrel{?}{=} e(tk_i, c_{i,2})\}$
  The justification for the above inference step can be generalized, and applies to this inference step.

A *unification state* is of the form $P; \tau$, where P is a set of equations and τ is a meta-substitution. Given $t_1, t_2 \in T$, to check if t_1 and t_2 are $(\oplus, E_V)$-unifiable, we start from the initial state: $\{t_1 \stackrel{?}{=} t_2\}; id$, where id is the identity substitution. We then apply the inference rules in $\mathcal{I}_B$. We use $\mathcal{I}_B^r(\{t_1 \stackrel{?}{=} t_2\}; id)$ to denote the result after the rth inference step. In particular, we use $\mathcal{I}_B^0(\{t_1 \stackrel{?}{=} t_2\}; id)$ to denote the initial state. $\mathcal{I}_B(\{t_1 \stackrel{?}{=} t_2\}; id) = \tau^*$ if and only if there exists q s.t. $\mathcal{I}_B^q(\{t_1 \stackrel{?}{=} t_2\}; id) = \emptyset; \tau^*$.

The inference rules in $\mathcal{I}_B$ can be applied in a "don't-care" nondeterministic fashion. Given $t_1, t_2 \in T$, $\mathcal{I}_B(t_1 \stackrel{?}{=} t_2; id)$ always returns the most general $(\oplus, E_V)$-meta-unifier of t_1 and t_2. Algorithm 1 checks symbolic authenticity of fixed-length AE schemes. The following theorems state that Algorithm 1 is sound, complete and terminating.

Theorem 1 (Completeness). *Let S be a fixed-length AE scheme. If S is symbolically authentic, then Algorithm 1 returns "authentic".*

Theorem 2 (Soundness). *Let S be a fixed-length AE scheme. If Algorithm 1 returns "authentic", then S is symbolically authentic.*

Theorem 3 (Termination). *Algorithm 1 always terminates for fixed-length AE schemes.*

Example 3. The verification equation of Π_1 (Fig. 2) is the following:

$$e(n^2(Tk), C_1 \oplus C_2) = Tg$$

According to Algorithm 1, we compute the most general $(\oplus, E_V)$-meta-unifier of $e(n^2(Tk), C_1 \oplus C_2)$ and $e(n^2(tk_i), c_{i,1} \oplus c_{i,2})$ using the following inference steps:

$$\{e(n^2(Tk), C_1 \oplus C_2) \stackrel{?}{=} e(n^2(tk_i), c_{i,1} \oplus c_{i,2})\}; id$$
$$\Longrightarrow \{n^2(Tk) \stackrel{?}{=} n^2(tk_i), C_1 \oplus C_2 \stackrel{?}{=} c_{i,1} \oplus c_{i,2}\}; id \quad (Decompose)$$
$$\Longrightarrow \{Tk \stackrel{?}{=} tk_i, C_1 \oplus C_2 \stackrel{?}{=} c_{i,1} \oplus c_{i,2}\}; id \quad (Decompose_n)$$
$$\Longrightarrow \{C_1 \oplus C_2 \stackrel{?}{=} c_{i,1} \oplus c_{i,2}\}; \{Tk \mapsto tk_i\} \quad (Elim_{Tk})$$
$$\Longrightarrow \emptyset; \{C_1 \mapsto C_2 \oplus c_{i,1} \oplus c_{i,2}, Tk \mapsto tk_i\} \quad (Elim_C)$$

$\{C_1 \mapsto C_2 \oplus c_{i,1} \oplus c_{i,2}, Tk \mapsto tk_i\} \neq \omega_i^2$. Therefore, S is not symbolically authentic. In fact, instantiating i using any natural number leads to a valid new ciphertext message. For example, $(tk_1, C_2 \oplus c_{1,1} \oplus c_{1,2}, C_2, tg_1)$ is a valid new ciphertext message, where C_2 can be an arbitrary message block, and C_1 is $C_2 \oplus c_{1,1} \oplus c_{1,2}$.

Algorithm 1. Checking Symbolic Authenticity of Fixed AE Schemes

Input: a fixed-length AE scheme S, whose verification function is of the form $e(n^l(Tk), t) = Tg$.

if $\mathcal{I}_B(\{e(n^l(Tk), t) \stackrel{?}{=} e(n^l(Tk), t)\omega_i^l\}, id) == \omega_i^l$ **then**
   return "authentic"
else
   return "inauthentic"
end if

---

4 Formal Analysis of Symbolic Authenticity of General AE Schemes

In this section, we consider general AE schemes, which handles messages of l blocks (l is not fixed). In Sect. 4.1, we show how such schemes can be modelled symbolically. In Sect. 4.2, we introduce the notion of *symbolic authenticity* for general AE schemes, in terms of a unification problem, which can be solved using the inference system given in Sect. 4.3. We also give an algorithm for checking symbolic authenticity for general AE schemes in Sect. 4.3.

4.1 Modelling General AE Schemes

In order to model general AE schemes, we consider the set of terms T^+ described in Fig. 1. Any general AE scheme can be modelled symbolically, we use the following example to illustrate the idea.

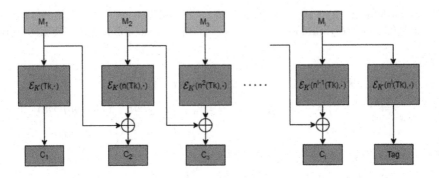

Fig. 4. A general AE scheme Π_2

Example 4. Consider the general AE scheme in Fig. 4. $\Pi_2 = (\mathcal{E}, \mathcal{D}, \mathcal{V})$, where

- $\mathcal{E}_K(Tk, (M_1, M_2, \ldots, M_l))$:=
  $(Tk, e(Tk, M_1), e(n(Tk), M_2) \oplus M_1, \ldots, e(n^{l-1}(Tk), M_l) \oplus M_{l-1}, e(n^l(Tk), M_l))$
- $\mathcal{V}_K(Tk, (C_1, \ldots, C_l), Tg) := (e(n^l(Tk), Y_l) == Tg)$, where
  - $Y_1 = d(Tk, C_1)$
  - $Y_j = d(n^{j-1}(Tk), C_j \oplus Y_{j-1})$ $(j > 1)$
- $\mathcal{D}_K(Tk, (C_1, \ldots, C_l), Tg)$:=
  $\begin{cases} (M_1, \ldots, M_l) & \text{if } \mathcal{V}_K(Tk, (C_1, \ldots, C_l), Tg) == True \\ \bot & otherwise \end{cases}$

As we discussed in Sect. 2, Y_j $(j \in \mathcal{N})$ represents some accumulative state after encrypting the jth block of a message. In this example, $Y_j = M_j$. But in general, this may not be the case. We will show that Π_2 satisfies symbolic authenticity.

4.2 Symbolic Authenticity for General AE Schemes

In this section, we introduce a unification problem over terms in T^+, and define the notion of symbolic authenticity of general AE schemes in terms of this unification problem. Let S be any general AE scheme, we use V_R to denote its verification equation. We assume that V_R is of the following form.

$e(n^l(Tk), Y_l) = Tg$, where Y_l is defined by the following set of equations R:

- $Y_1 = tm_1, \ldots, Y_r = tm_r$ (No Y_i occurs in $tm_1, \ldots, tm_r$.)

- $Y_j = tm_j[Y_{j-r}, \ldots, Y_{j-1}]$ $(j > r)$

$\forall j \in \mathcal{N}$, Y_j is a term that can be unfolded. We can apply a meta-substitution to a term $t \in T^+$ in the usual way, except that we require the following:

$$\forall j, \sigma. \, Y_j\sigma = Y_j^\sigma.$$

The idea is that we remember that if we unfold Y_j later on, we need to apply σ to the unfolding of Y_j.

Consider a term $t \in T^+$. $unfold_R(t)$ unfolds all the occurrences of Y_i's in t, based on R. We can unfold an equation by unfolding terms on both sides of the equation. We can also unfold a set of equations by unfolding all the equations in the set. We require the following.

$$\forall j, \sigma. \, unfold_R(Y_j^\sigma) = unfold_R(Y_j)\sigma$$

Example 5. Consider the general AE scheme in Fig. 4. Let $\sigma = \{C_1 \mapsto c_{i,1}, C_2 \mapsto c_{i,2}\}$

(1) $Y_1 = d(Tk, C_1)$
(2) $Y_2 = d(n(Tk), C_2 \oplus Y_1)$
(3) $Y_2\sigma = d(n(Tk), c_{i,2} \oplus Y_1^\sigma)$
(4) $unfold_R(Y_2\sigma) = d(n(Tk), c_{i,2} \oplus d(Tk, c_{i,1}))$

Next we define VE, which is the set of verification equations that verify the validity of messages of arbitrary length, and a GAE theory using the following definitions.

Definition 5. *Let V_R be an equation of the form $e(n^l(Tk), Y_l) = Tg$, where Y_l is defined by the following set of equations R:*

- $Y_1 = tm_1, \ldots, Y_r = tm_r$ *(No Y_i occurs in $tm_1, \ldots, tm_r$.)*
- $Y_j = tm_j[Y_{j-r}, \ldots, Y_{j-1}]$ $(j > r)$

$V_R \in VE$ if and only if the following "Consistency" property holds:
*(**Consistency**) (I) $\forall l \in \mathcal{N}$, if $e(s, s')$ and $e(t, t')$ both occur in $unfold_R(Y_l)$, and $s = t$, then $s' = t'$. (II) $\forall l \in \mathcal{N}$, if $d(s, s')$ and $d(t, t')$ both occur in $unfold_R(Y_l)$, and $s = t$, then $s' = t'$.*

Definition 6. *Let $V_R \in VE$. A set of equations E_{V_R} over terms in T^+ is a GAE (General Authenticated Encryption) theory w.r.t. V_R if the following properties hold:*

1. *(**Validity**) $\forall i, l \in \mathcal{N}$, $unfold_R(e(n^l(Tk), Y_l) = Tg)(\omega_i^l \cup \{Tk \mapsto tk_{i,l}\}) \in E_{V_R}$.*
2. *(**TBC_PRP**) $\forall l \in \mathcal{N}$, $t \in E_{V_R}$, if $unfold_R(e(n^l(Tk), Y_l))\sigma =_\oplus t\sigma$, then $Tk\sigma = tk_i$.*

3. (**Consistency**) (1) For all $e(s, s')$ and $e(t, t')$ that occur in E_{V_R}, if $s = t$, then $s' = t'$. (2) For all $d(s, s')$ and $d(t, t')$ that occur in E_{V_R}, if $s = t$, then $s' = t'$.

4. (**Stability**) No equation in E_{V_R} is of the form $n(t) = t'$.

We assume that, in the security game described in Sect. 2, the adversary receives the following messages.

$(tk_1, c_{1,1}, tg_{1,1}), (tk_1, c_{1,1}, c_{1,2}, tg_{1,2}), \ldots \ldots$
$(tk_2, c_{2,1}, tg_{2,1}), (tk_2, c_{2,1}, c_{2,2}, tg_{2,2}), \ldots \ldots$
$\ldots \ldots$

In Definition 6, the "Validity" property says that all the above messages are valid. The "TBC_PRP", "Consistency" and "Stability" properties are similar to those in Definition 2, except that equations and terms are now over T^+, and we unfold terms in T^+.

Definition 7. Let $V_R \in VE$, and E_{V_R} be a GAE theory w.r.t. V_R. Consider two terms $t_1, t_2 \in T^+$ s.t. $t_1 \omega_i^l = t_2$. t_1 and t_2 are $(\oplus, E_{V_R})$-unifiable under σ if (1) $t_1 \sigma =_{\oplus, E_{V_R}} t_2 \sigma$, and (2) σ is a computable substitution.

σ is called a $(\oplus, E_{V_R})$-meta-unifier of t_1 and t_2. σ^* is the most general $(\oplus, E_{V_R})$-meta-unifier of t_1 and t_2 if for any $(\oplus, E_{V_R})$-meta-unifier σ of t_1 and t_2, there exists some meta-substitution σ' s.t. $\sigma = \sigma^* \sigma'$. Let P be a set of equations over terms in T^+. σ is called a $(\oplus, E_{V_R})$-meta-unifier of P if σ is a $(\oplus, E_{V_R})$-meta-unifier of each equation in P.

Given some general AE scheme, to produce a valid ciphertext message m : (Tk, C, Tg), the adversary needs to compute some substitution σ s.t. $V(Tk\sigma, C\sigma, Tg\sigma)$ returns true. Due to the "Validity" property, we can pick σ to be $\omega_i^l \cup \{Tg \mapsto tg_{i,l}\}$. But that does not give us a new message. Therefore, the adversary tries to find some other $(\oplus, E_V)$-meta-unifier σ' of $e(n^l(Tk), Y_l)$ and $e(n^l(Tk), Y_l)\omega_i^l$. If the adversary succeeds, $(Tk\sigma', C\sigma', tg_{i,l})$ is a new valid message. So we have the following definition.

Definition 8. Let S be a general AE scheme with verification equation $V_R \in VE$. S is symbolically authentic if for all l, ω_i^l is the only $(\oplus, E_{V_R})$-meta-unifier of $unfold_R(e(n^l(Tk), Y_l)$ and $unfold_R(e(n^l(Tk), Y_l)\omega_i^l$, where E_{V_R} is any GAE theory w.r.t. V_R.

If a general AE scheme is symbolically authentic, the adversary cannot forge any new valid ciphertext message symbolically.

4.3 Inference System

In this section, we present a sound, complete and terminating inference system $\mathcal{I}_U$ for solving the $(\oplus, E_{V_R})$-unification problem over T^+. The difficulty for designing such an inference system is that E_{V_R} has an unbounded number of equations. In addition, the terms being unified may contain Y_j's, which we cannot fully unfold.

The inference rules of $\mathcal{I}_U$ are listed in Fig. 3. Compared with $\mathcal{I}_B$, $\mathcal{I}_U$ contains two new rules: the $Cancel_Y$ rule and the $Split_Y$ rule. The $Split_Y$ rule can be considered as a generalization of the $Split$ rule. A term is *splittable* if and only if it is the exclusive-or of some e-rooted terms and d-rooted terms. Note that a term t in T^+ is splittable if and only if $unfold_R(t)$ is splittable. The $Cancel_Y$ rule cancels Y_u and $Y_u^{\omega_i^j}$, assuming that ω_i^u is the only $(\oplus, E_V)$-meta-unifier of $unfold_R(Y_u)$ and $unfold_R(Y_u^{\omega_i^j})$. We can have this assumption for the reason described in the following paragraph.

Decompose

$$\{f(s_1, \ldots, s_u) \overset{?}{=} f(t_1, \ldots, t_u)\} \cup \Gamma; \sigma \Longrightarrow \{s_1 \overset{?}{=} t_1, \ldots, s_u \overset{?}{=} t_u\} \cup \Gamma; \sigma$$

where $f \neq \oplus$, and u can possibly be 0.

Decompose$_n$

$$\{n^u(s) \overset{?}{=} n^u(t)\} \cup \Gamma; \sigma \Longrightarrow \{s \overset{?}{=} t\} \cup \Gamma; \sigma$$

Elim$_C$

$$\{C_{j_1} \oplus \ldots \oplus C_{j_u} \overset{?}{=} c_{i,j_1} \oplus \ldots \oplus c_{i,j_u}\} \cup \Gamma; \sigma \Longrightarrow \Gamma\sigma; \sigma\sigma'$$

where $\sigma' = C_{j_1} \mapsto C_{j_2} \oplus \ldots \oplus C_{j_u} \oplus c_{i,j_1} \oplus \ldots \oplus c_{i,j_u}$

Elim$_{Tk}$

$$\{Tk \overset{?}{=} tk_i\} \cup \Gamma; \sigma \Longrightarrow \Gamma\sigma'; \sigma\sigma'$$

where $\sigma' = \{Tk \mapsto tk_i\}$.

Cancel$_Y$

$$\{Y_u \overset{?}{=} Y_u^{\omega_i^j}\} \cup \Gamma; \sigma \Longrightarrow \Gamma\omega_i^u; \sigma\omega_i^u$$

where $j > u$.

Split$_Y$

$$\{s \oplus Y_r \overset{?}{=} t \oplus Y_r^{\omega_i^j}\} \cup \Gamma; \sigma \Longrightarrow \{s \overset{?}{=} t, Y_r \overset{?}{=} Y_r^{\omega_i^j}\} \cup \Gamma; \sigma$$

where $unfold_R(Y_r)$ is splittable.

Split

$$\{s_1 \oplus f(n^u(s_2), s_3) \overset{?}{=} t_1 \oplus f(n^u(t_2), t_3)\} \cup \Gamma; \sigma$$
$$\Longrightarrow \{s_1 \overset{?}{=} t_1, f(n^u(s_2), s_3) \overset{?}{=} f(n^u(t_2), t_3)\} \cup \Gamma; \sigma$$

, where f can be either e or d.

Fig. 5. Inference system $\mathcal{I}_U$

Given some general AE scheme S, our goal is to show that S is symbolically secure. By Definition 8, we need to show that, for all l, ω_i^l is the only $(\oplus, E_{V_R})$-meta-unifier of $unfold_R(e(n^l(Tk), Y_l)$ and $unfold_R(e(n^l(Tk), Y_l)\omega_i^l$. Here is the overall idea. We prove this by induction. As the base case, we show that, ω_i^k is the only $(\oplus, E_{V_R})$-meta-unifier of $unfold_R(e(n^k(Tk), Y_k)$ and $unfold_R(e(n^k(Tk), Y_k)\omega_i^k$ $(1 \leq k \leq r)$. As the inductive case, we show that, ω_i^j is the only $(\oplus, E_{V_R})$-meta-unifier of $unfold_R(e(n^j(Tk), Y_j)$ and $unfold_R(e(n^j(Tk), Y_j)\omega_i^j$ $(j > r)$, assuming that for all $u < j$, ω_i^u is the only $(\oplus, E_{V_R})$-meta-unifier of $unfold_R(e(n^u(Tk), Y_u)$ and $unfold_R(e(n^u(Tk), Y_u)\omega_i^j$. This assumption implies that ω_i^u is the only $(\oplus, E_{V_R})$-meta-unifier of $unfold_R(Y_u)$ and $unfold_R(Y_u^{\omega_i^j})$ $(u < j)$.

Recall from Sect. 3.3 that a unification state is of the form $P; \tau$, where P is a set of equations and τ is a meta-substitution. Given two terms $t_1, t_2 \in T^+$, to compute the most general $(\oplus, E_{V_R})$-meta-unifier of $unfold_R(t_1)$ and $unfold_R(t_2)$, we start from the initial state: $\{t_1 \overset{?}{=} t_2\}; id$, where id is the identity substitution. We then apply the inference rules in $\mathcal{I}_U$. We use $\mathcal{I}_U^r(\{t_1 \overset{?}{=} t_2\}; id)$ to denote the result after the rth inference step. In particular, we use $\mathcal{I}_U^0(\{t_1 \overset{?}{=} t_2\}; id)$ to denote the initial unification state. $\mathcal{I}_U(\{t_1 \overset{?}{=} t_2\}; id) = \tau^*$ if and only if there exists q s.t. $\mathcal{I}_U^q(\{t_1 \overset{?}{=} t_2\}; id) = \emptyset; \tau^*$.

The inference rules in $\mathcal{I}_U$ can be applied in a "don't-care" nondeterministic fashion, and $\mathcal{I}_U(t_1 \overset{?}{=} t_2; id)$ returns the most general $(\oplus, E_{V_R})$-meta-unifier of t_1 and t_2 in T^+. Algorithm 2 checks symbolic authenticity of general AE schemes.

Algorithm 2. Checking Symbolic Authenticity of General AE Schemes

---

Input: a general AE scheme S, whose verification function is of the form $e(n^l(Tk), Y_l) = Tg$, where
$Y_1 = tm_1, \ldots, Y_r = tm_r$
$Y_j = tm_j[Y_{j-r}, \ldots, Y_{j-1}]$ $(j > r)$

$cond_1 := (\mathcal{I}_U(\{e(n(Tk), tm_1) \overset{?}{=} e(n(Tk), tm_1)\omega_i^1\}; id) == \omega_i^1)$ **and** $unfold_R(Y_1)$ is splittable
$\ldots\ldots$
$cond_r := (\mathcal{I}_U(\{e(n^r(Tk), tm_r) \overset{?}{=} e(n^r(Tk), tm_r)\omega_i^r\}; id) == \omega_i^r)$ **and** $unfold_R(Y_r)$ is splittable
$cond := (\mathcal{I}_U(\{e(n^j(Tk), tm_j) \overset{?}{=} e(n^j(Tk), tm_j)\omega_i^j\}; id) == \omega_i^j)$ **and** $unfold_R(Y_j)$ is splittable

if $cond_1$ **and** $\ldots$ **and** $cond_r$ **and** $cond$ **then**
    return "authentic"
else
    return "inauthentic"
end if

The following theorems state that Algorithm 2 is sound, terminating and complete under some condition.

Theorem 4 (Completeness). *Let S be a general AE scheme with a verification equation $e(n^l(Tk), Y_l) = Tg$, where Y_l is defined recursively using a set of equations R. If $\forall l \in \mathcal{N}$, $unfold_R(Y_l)$ is splittable, and S is symbolically authentic, then Algorithm 2 returns "authentic".*

Theorem 5 (Soundness). *Let S be a general AE scheme. If Algorithm 2 returns "authentic", then S is symbolically authentic.*

Theorem 6 (Termination). *Let S be a general AE scheme. Algorithm 2 always terminates.*

Example 6. Consider the general AE scheme Π_2 in Fig. 4. The verification equation of Π_2 is $e(n^l(Tk), Y_l) = Tg$, where
(1) $Y_1 = d(Tk, C_1)$ (2) $Y_j = d(n^{j-1}(Tk), C_j \oplus Y_{j-1})$ $(j > 1)$.
1. The most general $(\oplus, E_{V_R})$-meta-unifier of $d(Tk, C_1)$ and $d(tk_i, c_{i,1})$ is ω_i^1, according to the following inference steps:

$$\{d(Tk, C_1) \stackrel{?}{=} d(tk_i, c_{i,1})\}; id$$
$$\implies \{Tk \stackrel{?}{=} tk_i, C_1 \stackrel{?}{=} c_{i,1}\}; id$$
$$\implies \{C_1 \stackrel{?}{=} c_{i,1}\}; \{Tk \mapsto tk_i\}$$
$$\implies \emptyset; \{Tk \mapsto tk_i, C_1 \mapsto c_{i,1}\}$$

2. The most general $(\oplus, E_{V_R})$-meta-unifier of $e(n^j(Tk), d(n^{j-1}(Tk), C_j \oplus Y_{j-1}))$ and $e(n^j(tk_i), d(n^{j-1}(tk_i), c_{i,j} \oplus Y_{j-1}^{\omega_i^j}))$ is ω_i^j, according to the following inference steps:

$$\{e(n^j(Tk), d(n^{j-1}(Tk), C_j \oplus Y_{j-1})) \stackrel{?}{=} e(n^j(tk_i), d(n^{j-1}(tk_i), c_{i,j} \oplus Y_{j-1}^{\omega_i^j}))\}; id$$
$$\implies \{n^j(Tk) \stackrel{?}{=} n^j(tk_i), d(n^{j-1}(Tk), C_j \oplus Y_{j-1}) \stackrel{?}{=} d(n^{j-1}(tk_i), c_{i,j} \oplus Y_{j-1}^{\omega_i^j})\}; id$$
$$\implies \{Tk \stackrel{?}{=} tk_i, d(n^{j-1}(Tk), C_j \oplus Y_{j-1}) \stackrel{?}{=} d(n^{j-1}(tk_i), c_{i,j} \oplus Y_{j-1}^{\omega_i^j})\}; id$$
$$\implies \{d(n^{j-1}(tk_i), C_j \oplus Y_{j-1}) \stackrel{?}{=} d(n^{j-1}(tk_i), c_{i,j} \oplus Y_{j-1}^{\omega_i^j})\}; \{Tk \mapsto tk_i\}$$
$$\implies \{n^{j-1}(tk_i) \stackrel{?}{=} n^{j-1}(tk_i), C_j \oplus Y_{j-1} \stackrel{?}{=} c_{i,j} \oplus Y_{j-1}^{\omega_i^j}\}; \{Tk \mapsto tk_i\}$$
$$\implies \{tk_i \stackrel{?}{=} tk_i, C_j \oplus Y_{j-1} \stackrel{?}{=} c_{i,j} \oplus Y_{j-1}^{\omega_i^j}\}; \{Tk \mapsto tk_i\}$$
$$\implies \{C_j \oplus Y_{j-1} \stackrel{?}{=} c_{i,j} \oplus Y_{j-1}^{\omega_i^j}\}; \{Tk \mapsto tk_i\}$$
$$\implies \{C_j \stackrel{?}{=} c_{i,j}, Y_{j-1} \stackrel{?}{=} Y_{j-1}^{\omega_i^j}\}; \{Tk \mapsto tk_i\}$$
$$\implies \{Y_{j-1} \stackrel{?}{=} Y_{j-1}^{\omega_i^j}\}; \{Tk \mapsto tk_i, C_j \mapsto c_{i,j}\}$$
$$\implies \emptyset; \{Tk \mapsto tk_i, C_1 \mapsto c_{i,1}, \ldots, C_{j-1} \mapsto c_{i,j-1}, C_j \mapsto c_{i,j}\}$$

Both Y_1 and Y_j are splittable. Therefore, Algorithm 2 returns "authentic".

5   Conclusions and Future Work

In this paper, we propose to model AE schemes symbolically. For fixed-length AE schemes, we give a decision procedure for checking symbolic authenticity.

For general AE schemes, we give an inference system for checking symbolic authenticity, which is sound, terminating and complete under some condition.

As future work, we will connect the symbolic world and the computational world by showing that all AE schemes satisfy symbolic authenticity if and only if they satisfy authenticity computationally. We will also consider the secrecy property of AE schemes. Our goal is to develop methods that can synthesize secure AE schemes automatically based on unification techniques.

References

1. Akinyele, J.A., Green, M., Hohenberger, S.: Using SMT solvers to automate design tasks for encryption and signature schemes. In: Sadeghi, A.-R., Gligor, V.D., Yung, M. (eds.) 2013 ACM SIGSAC Conference on Computer and Communications Security (CCS 2013), Berlin, Germany, November 4–8 2013, pp. 399–410. ACM (2013)
2. Ambrona, M., Barthe, G., Schmidt, B.: Automated unbounded analysis of cryptographic constructions in the generic group model. In: Fischlin, M., Coron, J.-S. (eds.) EUROCRYPT 2016. LNCS, vol. 9666, pp. 822–851. Springer, Heidelberg (2016). https://doi.org/10.1007/978-3-662-49896-5_29
3. Carmer, B., Rosulek, M.: Linicrypt: A model for practical cryptography. In: 36th Annual International Cryptology Conference, pp. 416–445 (2016)
4. Dworkin, M.: Recommendations for block cipher modes of operation: The CCM mode for authentication and confidentiality (2007)
5. Gligor, V.D., Donescu, P.: Fast encryption and authentication: XCBC encryption and XECB authentication modes. In: Matsui, M. (ed.) FSE 2001. LNCS, vol. 2355, pp. 92–108. Springer, Heidelberg (2002). https://doi.org/10.1007/3-540-45473-X_8
6. Hoang, V.T., Katz, J., Malozemof, A.J.: Automated analysis and synthesis of authenticated encryption schemes. In: Proceedings of the 22nd ACM SIGSAC Conference on Computer and Communications Security, pp. 84–95 (2015)
7. Li, B., Micciancio, D.: Equational security proofs of oblivious transfer protocols. In: Abdalla, M., Dahab, R. (eds.) PKC 2018. LNCS, vol. 10769, pp. 527–553. Springer, Cham (2018). https://doi.org/10.1007/978-3-319-76578-5_18
8. Li, B., Micciancio, D.: Symbolic security of garbled circuits. In: 31st IEEE Computer Security Foundations Symposium (CSF 2018), Oxford, UK, July 9–12, 2018, pp. 147–161. IEEE Computer Society (2018)
9. Liskov, M., Rivest, R.L., Wagner, D.: Tweakable block ciphers. Adv. Cryptol.-Crypto **2002**, 31–46 (2002)
10. Malozemoff, A.J., Katz, J., Green, M.D.: Automated analysis and synthesis of block-cipher modes of operation. In: Computer Security Foundations Symposium (CSF), pp. 140–152 (2014)
11. Meadows, C.: Symbolic security criteria for blockwise adaptive secure modes of encryption. IACR Cryptol. ePrint Arch. **2020**, 794 (2020)
12. Minematsu, K.: Parallelizable rate-1 authenticated encryption from pseudorandom functions. In: Nguyen, P.Q., Oswald, E. (eds.) EUROCRYPT 2014. LNCS, vol. 8441, pp. 275–292. Springer, Heidelberg (2014). https://doi.org/10.1007/978-3-642-55220-5_16
13. Robinson, A., Voronkov. A.: Handbook of Automated Reasoning (2001)
14. Rogaway, P., Bellare, M., Black, J., Krovetz, T.: OCB: a block-cipher mode of operation for efficient authenticated encryption. In: 8th ACM Conference on Computer and Communications Security (CCS), pp. 196–205 (2001)

Formal Verification of a Java Component Using the RESOLVE Framework

Laine Rumreich$^{(\boxtimes)}$ and Paolo A. G. Sivilotti

The Ohio State University, Columbus, OH, USA
rumreich.1@osu.edu, paolo@cse.ohio-state.edu

Abstract. A Binary Decision Diagram (BDD) is an efficient representation of a Boolean formula with many applications in model checking, SAT solving, networking, and artificial intelligence. This paper uses the RESOLVE specification and reasoning framework to formally verify the functional correctness of a Java implementation of a BDD component. RESOLVE uses rich mathematical abstractions and clean value-based semantics for modular reasoning of assertive code. Java, on the other hand, includes many language features that are inconsistent with this notion of clean semantics and modular reasoning. Aliases, in particular, are easily created via assignment, parameter passing, and iterators, so reference-based semantics and points-to analysis are usually necessary when reasoning about Java code. This paper demonstrates the combination of these two paradigms. The implementation uses Java, but in a disciplined way and layered on a component catalog expressly designed to support modular reasoning. The assertional aspects of the code use RESOLVE, but are tailored to Java syntax and language constructs. In the development of the correctness proof for the BDD component, several errors in the original Java implementation were discovered and corrected. These errors were present despite the implementation passing an extensive test suite, exhibiting the value of the proof. The verification also exposed a limitation in the more general component design pattern related to unreachable code.

Keywords: Formal verification · Value semantics · Modularity · Binary Decision Diagram

1 Introduction

In order to be tractable, software verification must be modular. That is, the correctness of the entire system must follow from the correctness of its individual components. Modularity allows for components to be verified in isolation and for the cost of this verification to be amortized over the re-use of these components across multiple systems.

The work presented in this paper uses the RESOLVE (REusable SOftware Language with Verifiability and Efficiency) framework [34], which is both an integrated implementation and verification system as well as a design discipline

© Springer Nature Switzerland AG 2021
B. Konev and G. Reger (Eds.): FroCoS 2021, LNAI 12941, pp. 287–305, 2021.
https://doi.org/10.1007/978-3-030-86205-3_16

aimed to promote component re-use by easing client-side reasoning. The implementation notation uses assertional code with value semantics and the associated verification system uses extendable mathematical theories with custom decision procedures for automated verification. The discipline prescribes principles for interface design, the tenets of which reduce overall software cost and improve quality [40]. While the RESOLVE discipline is typically applied to software components written in the RESOLVE language, elements of the discipline could, in principle, also be adapted for use with industry-standard programming languages such as Java. This combination of Java and RESOLVE would leverage the strengths of both: the robust full-functional verification possible in RESOLVE and the practicality of an industry-standard programming language such as Java. This paper considers the feasibility of such a combination.

The primary contribution of this work concerns the careful construction of a proof that formally establishes the correctness of a Java-based Binary Decision Diagram component, the implementation of which is layered on top of a RESOLVE-style component library with RESOLVE specifications. Because industry-standard languages such as Java and C were not designed with verification in mind, they include many features that challenge the soundness of modular reasoning, including: aliasing-by-default, reference semantics, ubiquitous side-effects, and concurrency. Because of these challenges, the verification of software written in these languages is often restricted to subsets of properties of interest (*e.g.*, race detection) or limited in generality (*e.g.*, reasoning over memory locations rather than abstract mathematical values).

In contrast, the verification effort described in this paper entails both full-functional correctness and value-based reasoning. As a result of this verification, several errors were identified in the original BDD component implementation. In addition, we present several observations related to the success of adapting RESOLVE for application in the context of the Java programming language.

2   Background

2.1   Previous Work

While the RESOLVE discipline is typically applied to programs written in the RESOLVE programming language, there exists a substantial library of RESOLVE-style components written in the Java programming language. None of these components have been formally verified, however, despite their adherence to the discipline. This paper describes the verification of one of these components, BooleanStructure, which implements a Binary Decision Diagram (BDD). BDDs are frequently used and versatile data structures that represent Boolean formulas. BDDs have unique features that make them preferable to other common representations of Boolean formulas such as truth tables and propositional formulas. These features improve the efficiency of BDDs and make them more useful than other common representations for solving complex problems with many variables. In 2018, Asim [2,3] developed a Binary Decision Diagram software component in the Java programming language. Unlike existing BDD components, this BDD was developed with verification in mind, including behavioral specifications. This component was carefully constructed following the RESOLVE discipline, including the definition of an abstract mathematical model of state, an interface supporting observability and controllability, and a layered implementation that separates core functionality from secondary operations. This software component has been formally verified in this work and is accessible on GitHub [35].

2.2 Existing BDD Implementations

Existing software packages with implementations of the BDD data structure are available for commonly used programming languages such as Java, C, and Python, including BuDDy [25], CuDD [37], CacBDD [28], SableJBDD [31], JDD [38], Sylvan [11], and BeeDeeDee [27]. Of these packages, SableJBDD and JDD are Java-based. None of these packages have been formally verified or include formal specifications, however, so correctness guarantees cannot be made and the formal verification of these components would require substantial effort.

2.3 Applications of BDDs

BDDs are useful data structures in a variety of contexts, including disciplines where correctness is critical. Some examples of these disciplines include Boolean satisfiability, circuit design [24], formal verification, symbolic model checking, network analysis [39], and artificial intelligence [23,26].

BDDs have commonly been used in formal verification and model checking, which are highly relevant to this work due to their strict correctness requirements. Symbolic model checking based on BDDs was originally used in hardware model checking but was later extended to the domain of software verification. Prior to the introduction of BDD-based symbolic model checking, practical hardware verification via model checking was limited to models with less than 10^6 reachable states [9]. BDDs enabled practical verification of industrial systems with state spaces of more than 10^{20} [8], which also allows for software verification. Since they were popularized, BDDs have been frequently used in formal software verification and symbolic model checking, including in the Berkeley package HSIS for formal verification [4].

Despite the popularity and frequent use of the data structure, existing BDD components have not been formally verified. Thus, guarantees about their correctness cannot be made. This is particularly relevant for formal verification and symbolic model checking applications because the tools being used for verification purposes are not verified themselves.

2.4 Object-Oriented and Automatic Verification

This work concerns the verification of a Java software component consisting of two interfaces, an abstract base class, and a concrete derived class. A substantial barrier to this verification process and to reasoning about Java programs in general is the presence of aliases. Reasoning about software with aliases is well-known as a challenging problem [18]. Many techniques to control aliasing in object-based languages have been proposed, including notions of ownership and borrowing as in Rust [20], adding additional annotations just for aliasing [1], and the use of separation logic [7]. Another approach is to modify the language to prevent aliases altogether, such as requiring pointers to be unique [29] or using swapping to avoid aliasing [22]. The RESOLVE discipline, which is used in the component verified in this project, uses the notions of swapping and clean semantics to avoid problems related to aliasing [21]. This paper demonstrates some of the additional complexities of reasoning about aliasing in Java rather than the RESOLVE programming language.

Considerable research exists in the area of automatic software verification toward the goal of eliminating programming errors. Despite significant advances in automated theorem provers, SAT solvers, and SMT solvers, the construction of a fully automatic verifying compiler remains a long-term challenge in computer science. Challenges including aliasing, side-effects, fixed-width number representations, and concurrency make verification of object-oriented languages especially challenging. There has been relative success in this area using custom programming languages explicitly designed with verification in mind. Verification engines for such languages have been built using Dafny [15], RESOLVE [33], Why3 [12], and Whiley [30]. These verifying compilers leverage formal reasoning constraints built into the programming language to simplify automatic verification. Some of these languages, such as RESOLVE and Why3, can be translated to other languages such as C, Java, or Ada, but require that the program is first developed in the language designed for formal verification. However, these verifiers cannot be used for the BDD implementation because they were not designed for components written in Java.

Advancement in the area of a verifying compiler for industry-standard programming languages is also considerable but incomplete [6]. An influential verifying compiler for the Java programming language is the Extended Static Checker for Java (ESC/Java) [13]. Other successful prototype verifying compilers for Java, C#, and C are the KeY prover [14], VeriFast [19], Spec# [5], and VCC [10]. However, these verifying compilers use unique specification notations and thus cannot be used for the BDD component. For example, the KeY prover uses Java Modeling Language (JML) for specifications. To use these tools with the BDD component, the formal specifications would need to be reconstructed to match the required notation. Additionally, all of the library components used in the BDD component that were developed in the RESOLVE discipline would need to be replaced or modified to use the formal specifications of the new verifier. Another challenge is that many of these specification notations lack the clean semantics, full modularity, and comprehensibility of the RESOLVE framework, all of which ease verification.

3   Combining Value and Reference Semantics

3.1   RESOLVE and Value-Based Semantics

At the center of this project is the RESOLVE design philosophy and discipline
for software components that allows for ease of use by clients, reusability of software, and the ability to formally verify both the software itself and the client
code that uses it. This discipline describes the principles to design and compose high-quality component-based software systems. RESOLVE is also an integrated specification and programming *language* designed for building verified,
component-based software. It is imperative and object-based and has a collection of components such as those found in the standard libraries for C++, C#,
and Java. Programs written in RESOLVE can be verified with an automated
prover. Figure 1 illustrates this automated verification on a List component for
the Reverse procedure.

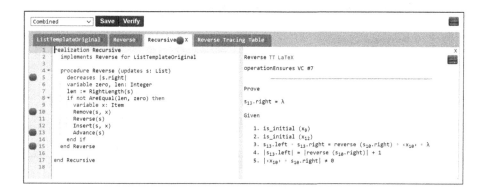

Fig. 1. A screenshot of the RESOLVE web IDE

Parameter Modes. An important construct in the RESOLVE discipline is the
definition of *parameter modes* for arguments in method contracts. Parameter
modes are used to define the modification frame of a method or loop. That is,
they define whether a method or loop body can change the value of a formal
parameter or variable. There are four parameter modes:

- **Clears:** The parameter is cleared to an initial value of its type
- **Updates:** The parameter can change value and the behavior of the method
  can depend on the parameter's (initial) value
- **Replaces:** The parameter can change value and the behavior of the method
  does not depend on the parameter's (initial) value
- **Restores:** (Default) The parameter's final value is the same as its initial
  value

Mathematical Model. A mathematical model is an abstract definition of a component's state space. It is implementation-independent and defines a precise mathematical type that the client can use to reason about the component's behavior. A mathematical model is written in terms of base types or mathematical subtypes. Math base types are either basic types such as integers or booleans or composite types such as tuples, sets, or strings (*i.e.*, sequences). Math subtypes are defined in terms of other math subtypes and base types. Math types are related to types in Java but are not equivalent. For example, the math type integer is infinite, but a Java int is bounded.

The math model for BooleanStructure is based on the mathematical type BOOLEAN_STRUCTURE. Clients use this math type to reason about the BooleanStructure component regardless of which implementation is used. The formal definition for this math type, shown in Listing 1.1, defines BOOLEAN_STRUC-TURE as a pair containing a set of ASSIGNMENTs named *sat* and a string of integers named *vars*.

Listing 1.1. BooleanStructure Mathematical Model

```
1   /**
2    * @mathsubtypes
3    * ASSIGNMENT is finite set of integer
4    *
5    * BOOLEAN_STRUCTURE is (sat: finite set of ASSIGNMENT,
6    *                       vars: string of integer)
7    *
8    * @mathmodel type BooleanStructureKernel is modeled by
         BOOLEAN_STRUCTURE
9    */
```

Correspondence and Convention. The correspondence, which is also referred to as the abstraction relation, defines how a particular implementation's specific representation, and similarly its convention, relates to the math model that applies to the general component interface that all implementations are based on. This relationship between the math model of the component and the mathematical representation of the concrete implementation allows a client to ignore the details of the implementation and reason about the component using only the mathematical model. Implementers are then able to reason about the implementing class using the mathematical representation that relates to the implementation details.

The convention, also referred to as the concrete invariant, defines constraints on a specific implementation. The convention for the BooleanStructure implementation verified in this work, shown in Listing 1.2, shows that the component has two constraints. The first is that the concrete field $this.sat does not contain any variables other than the ones in the field $this.vars. Note that the symbol "$" is used as a prefix to *this* to form $this when referring to the concrete state, in contrast to the abstract state which simply refers to this. The second constraint is that the $this.vars field does not contain any duplicates.

The `correspondence` for this component is trivial because it maps the concrete representation consisting of two fields, `$this.sat` and `$this.vars`, to the math model consisting of a tuple containing *sat* and *vars*.

Listing 1.2. `BooleanStructure` Convention and Correspondence

```
 1  /**
 2   * @mathdefinitions
 3   *    NO_EXTRANEOUS_VARIABLES (
 4   *      s: set of ASSIGNMENT, t: string of integer
 5   *    ) : boolean satisfies
 6   *    for all a: ASSIGNMENT where ( a is in s )
 7   *      ( a is subset of entries(t) )
 8   *
 9   *    NO_DUPLICATES_IN_VARS (
10   *      t: string of integer
11   *    ) : boolean satisfies
12   *    | t | = | entries(t) |
13   *
14   * @convention
15   *      NO_EXTRANEOUS_VARIABLES($this.sat, $this.vars) and
16   *      NO_DUPLICATES_IN_VARS($this.vars) and
17   *
18   * @correspondence this = ($this.sat, $this.vars)
19   */
```

3.2 RESOLVE with Object-Oriented Languages

The RESOLVE discipline defines guidelines for developing high-quality and verifiable software and applies when reasoning about the behavior of programs. However, these discipline guidelines must be modified for use in practical programming languages such as Java or C++. For instance, the Java constructs of interfaces and classes are leveraged to accommodate the separation of abstract and concrete representations of a component necessary for the RESOLVE discipline [36]. Java components that use this discipline also commonly have more than one implementing class in the component, each with different time and space performance profiles but otherwise interchangeable from a client's perspective. In this way, each implementing class can have different concrete implementations, but the client reasons about them in the exact same way using the abstract representation, or math model, of the component. Another change to the discipline is necessary because of the risks introduced by the presence of inheritance in the Java programming language, since RESOLVE does not allow this capability. This change is the separation of component methods into *kernel* and *secondary* methods. Kernel methods are the minimal set of operations that allow the client to give a variable of the type any allowable value (controllability) and determine the value of a variable of the type (observability). Kernel methods must be re-implemented for every implementing class in the component. Conversely, secondary layered methods are "layered" on top of kernel methods in an abstract class and are implemented as a client of the component, so they only need to be implemented once but apply to all implementing classes. An illustration of the RESOLVE component design pattern that separates the kernel and secondary methods of the BDD component is shown in Fig. 2. This illustration also demonstrates the use of Java interfaces and classes to separate abstract and concrete elements of the component. The methods of the `BooleanStructure` component are also shown.

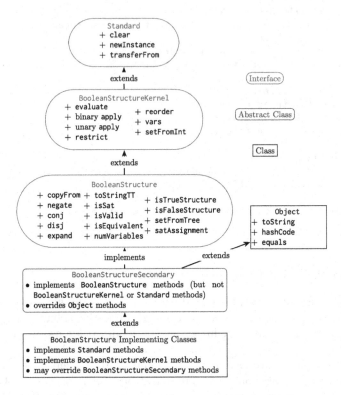

Fig. 2. `BooleanStructure` component diagram

The RESOLVE programming language has additional restrictions that are not present in Java and must also be accommodated. For example, RESOLVE uses *call-by-swapping* for parameter passing, unlike Java which allows references. RESOLVE also lacks an assignment operator, which prohibits aliasing, so formal verification in a Java component must verify that any aliases generated by the use of the assignment operator do not disrupt the soundness of the verification. The `BooleanStructure` component and all of the libraries used in it that follow the RESOLVE discipline attempt to avoid the pitfalls of the assignment operator by implementing the methods `transferFrom` and `copyFrom`. These methods are used in place of the assignment operator to transfer and copy objects while avoiding the complexities of aliasing. The BDD implementation of the `transferFrom` method assigns the concrete private fields of the BDD to those of the source BDD. The `copyFrom` method builds a copy of the source BDD by making copies of primitive types to avoid aliasing.

4 Formal Verification of the BDD Component

The full formal verification of a component involves the generation of loop invariants, reasoning tables, and proofs based on both the abstract and concrete components of the software. The goal of each proof in this work is to verify the correctness of a method in the `BooleanStructure` component. This verification requires proving that each method meets the requirements of its postcondition and eventually terminates. Details of the proof of correctness for this component are in [32].

4.1 Loop Invariants and Iteration

The construction of loop invariants allows loops to be traced in a verification proof without knowledge of how many times a loop will iterate during code execution. A special case of loop invariants is when they involve iterators, which require extra consideration in the verification process. An example of the for-each syntax in Java with a loop invariant can be seen in Listing 1.3. The loop in this example builds a duplicate of the sequence `this.vars` called `newOrder`. Correspondingly, the invariant for this loop maintains that the variable `newOrder` is always equal to the items in the collection `this.vars` that have already been iterated over. For verification purposes, the elements of the iterator that have been *seen* and *unseen* at a particular point in the loop can be accessed using the "$\sim$" operator, such as in $\sim$`this.vars.seen`. The parameter mode for the variable $\sim$`this.vars` is *updates* because the seen and unseen elements are changing each iteration.

Listing 1.3. Example for-each Loop With Iterator

```
1  /**
2   * @updates newOrder, ~this.vars
3   * @maintains newOrder = ~this.vars.seen
4   * @decreases |~this.vars.unseen|
5   */
6  for (int elt : this.vars) {
7      newOrder.add(newOrder.length(), elt);
8  }
```

However, this for-each loop syntax requires additional effort in the construction of proofs. An example of the challenge associated with loops in the for-each format is that the loop body in Listing 1.3 cannot be used to prove that the value of |$\sim$`this.vars.unseen`| decreases from one loop iteration to the next because the value of |$\sim$`this.vars.unseen`| is never explicitly updated through a call to an iterator's `next` method. Similarly, $\sim$`this.vars.seen` is never explicitly updated within the loop. However, the behavior of a for-each loop dictates that the first operation of each loop iteration is to update this variable. Now, in the first line of the reasoning table for this loop, the value of ∼this.vars.seen must simultaneously be its value before and after the update from an implicit call to next, which is undesirable.

To solve this problem, a strategy that maintains a close similarity to the source code but still allows for proofs of the loop invariant and progress metric is used, which is shown in Listing 1.4. This strategy is to add a comment containing a call to the iterator's next method at the beginning of the loop. This comment solves the problem of the .seen variable having two simultaneous values because in the reasoning table, .seen is updated after the commented call to next in line 7 of the listing. Thus, before line 7, the loop invariant is guaranteed to still hold, but after line 7 this is no longer a guarantee and the value of the seen and unseen elements of the collection have been updated.

Listing 1.4. Example for-each Loop With Iterator: Proof Equivalent

```
1  /**
2   * @updates newOrder, ~this.vars
3   * @maintains newOrder = ~this.vars.seen
4   * @decreases |~this.vars.unseen|
5   */
6  for (int elt : this.vars) {
7      // elt = this.vars.next();
8      newOrder.add(newOrder.length(), elt);
9  }
```

Due to the additional complexity of iterators, it is generally more desirable to use libraries of verified components with built-in functionality to perform tasks such as the one shown in Listing 1.3, which is to copy an object. These library components help avoid the dangers involved with iteration, such as the creation of aliases during iteration, but in this case the use of an iterator was unavoidable. Iteration over containers with immutable types, as in this example, does not threaten the validity of the proof, however.

4.2   Reasoning Tables and Proofs

A reasoning table is a method of organizing the facts and obligations, otherwise known as verification conditions, generated from the implementation body of a method. The facts and verification conditions are generated directly from specifications, the implementation, and the mathematical model, and the facts are used to confirm that the required verification conditions are met. The techniques employed in the production of the reasoning tables in this work use "natural reasoning" formulated by Heym [16] to aid in comprehensibility and usability. This reasoning technique is based on generating a sequence of facts that can be combined to form new facts to prove verification conditions. An example of a reasoning table for the BooleanStructure method apply, which applies the unary operator *not*, can be seen in Table 1. Note that the initial facts in the reasoning table are the convention and correspondence from Listing 1.2. Other facts and verification conditions in the table are generated directly from pre- and postconditions of other component methods. The final verification conditions in the table are generated from the method postcondition, shown in Listing 1.5, and the restoration of the convention. The specification in Listing 1.5 refers to #this, where the "#" symbol refers to the state of the object before the method call and this refers to the final state.

Table 1. Unary apply sample reasoning table

State	Path	Facts	Obligations
	`public void apply(UnaryOperator op) {`		
0		$this = (\$this.sat, \$this.vars)$ $NO\_EXTRANEOUS\_VARIABLES(\$this.sat_0, \$this.vars_0)$ $NO\_DUPLICATES\_IN\_VARS(\$this.vars_0)$	
	`if (op == UnaryOperator.NOT) {`		
1		$op = NOT$	
	`Set<Set<Integer>> newSat = new Set2<Set<Integer>> ();`		
2		$op = NOT$ $newSat_2 = \{\}$	$|\$this.vars_0| = |entries(\$this.vars_0)|$
	`PowerStringElements allAssignments = new PowerStringElements(this.vars());`		
3		$op = NOT$ $allAssignments = \$this.vars_0$ $\sim allAssignments.seen * \sim allAssignments.seen$ $= POWER\_STRING(allAssignments)$ $\sim allAssignments.seen_3 = <>$	$entries(\sim allAssignments.seen_3) \quad \setminus \quad \$this.sat_0 = newSat_2$
	`/**` `* @updates newSat, ~allAssignments` `* @maintains entries(~allAssignments.seen) \   $this.sat = newSat` `* @decreases	~allAssignments.unseen|` `*/`		
	`for (Set<Integer> a : allAssignments) {`		
4	$op = NOT$ $| \sim allA...unseen_4| > 0$	$entries(\sim allAssignments.seen_4) \quad \setminus \quad \$this.sat_0 = newSat_4$	$| \sim allAssignments.unseen_4| > 0$
5	`// a = allAssignments.next()` $op = NOT$	$\sim allAssignments.seen_5 = \sim allAssignments.seen_4 * <a>$ $<a> * \sim allAssignments.unseen_5 = \sim allAssignments.unseen_4$	$NO\_EXTRANEOUS\_VARIABLES(\$this.sat_0, \$this.vars_0)$ $NO\_DUPLICATES\_IN\_VARS(\$this.vars_0)$
	`if (!processAssignment(this.sat, this.vars, a)) {`		
6	$op = NOT$ `not(a intersection...)`		
	`newSat.add(a);`		
7	$op = NOT$ `not(a intersection...)`	$newSat_7 = newSat_4 \text{ union } \{a\}$	
	`} // end if`		
8	$op = NOT$	$a \text{ intersection } entries(\$this.vars_0) \text{ is in } \$this.sat_0$ $implies\ newSat_8 = newSat_4$ $not(a \text{ intersection } entries(\$this.vars_0) \text{ is in } \$this.sat_0)$ $implies\ newSat_8 = newSat_7$	$entries(\sim allAssignments.seen_5) \quad \setminus \quad \$this.sat_0 = newSat_8$ $| \sim allAssignments.unseen_5| < | \sim allAssignments.unseen_4|$
	`} // end for`		
9	$op = NOT$	$| \sim allAssignments.unseen_9| = 0$ $entries(\sim allAssignments.seen_0)\ \$this.sat_0 = newSat_9$	$NO\_EXTRANEOUS\_VARIABLES(\$this.sat_9, \$this.vars_0)$
	`this.sat.transferFrom(newSat);`		
10	$op = NOT$	$\$this.sat_{10} = newSat_9$ $newSat_{10} = \{\}$	
	`} // end if`		
11		$op = NOT\ implies\ \$this.sat_{11} = \$this.sat_{10}$ $op\ /= NOT\ implies\ \$this.sat_{11} = \$this.sat_0$ $\$this.vars_{11} = \$this.vars_0$	$this.vars_{11} = this.vars_0$ $for\ all\ p:\ ASSIGNMENT\ where\ (\ p\ is\ subset\ of\ entries(this.vars_{11})\ )$ $(\ p\ is\ in\ this.sat_{11}\ iff$ $(\ (\ if\ op = NOT\ then$ $not(p\ intersection\ entries(this.vars_0)\ is\ in\ this.sat_0)\ )\ and$ $(\ if\ op = IDENTITY\ then$ $(p\ intersection\ entries(this.vars_0)\ is\ in\ this.sat_0)\ )\ )\ )$ $NO\_EXTRANEOUS\_VARIABLES(\$this.sat_{11}, \$this.vars_{11})$ $NO\_DUPLICATES\_IN\_VARS(\$this.vars_{11})$
	`} // end unary_apply`		

Proofs of the verification conditions in the reasoning tables were constructed in a custom format but follow the general structure of a direct proof, otherwise known as a proof by construction. Facts taken directly from a reasoning table are the proof assumptions. A sequence of small, carefully justified steps using these facts and mathematical axioms were used to construct new factual statements or lemmas. These steps are small enough to be mechanically checkable. This sequence eventually results in the verification condition for the proof.

Proofs of each verification condition for the `BooleanStructure` component were constructed to form a single proof of correctness for the entire component.

Listing 1.5. Unary apply Specification

```
 1   /**
 2    * Apply the unary operator {@code op} to {@code this}
 3    * without changing the total order of the variables of
 4    * {@code this}.
 5    *
 6    * @param op
 7    *    the unary operation to be applied on this
 8    * @updates this
 9    * @ensures
10    *    this.vars = #this.vars and
11    *    for all p: ASSIGNMENT where ( p is subset of
12          entries(this.vars) )
13    *      ( p is in this.sat iff
14    *        ( ( if op = NOT then not EVALUATION(#this, p) ) and
15    *          ( if op = IDENTITY then EVALUATION(#this, p) ) ) )
16    */
17   void apply(UnaryOperator op);
```

5   Limitation in the Component Design Pattern

The Java component design pattern discussed in Sect. 3 is used in a sizeable component library which includes the BDD component verified in this work. During the process of verifying this BDD component, a shortcoming in the testing capabilities of this design pattern was discovered. This limitation was discovered in a component library used to teach thousands of computer science students since 2012 and was previously never discovered. This lack of detection indicates it is not an easily discoverable or obvious flaw. Additionally, it is likely that Java component design patterns similar to the one used in the `BooleanStructure` component also suffer from this testing limitation.

This limitation is related to how the design pattern uses abstract classes and overridden methods. Note that a component following the design pattern used in the `BooleanStructure` component may contain any number of implementing classes. For example, the BDD implementation illustrated in Fig. 3 contains `BooleanStructure1` and `BooleanStructure2`. Also note that these implementing classes extend a single shared abstract class, `BooleanStructureSecondary`, containing the layered method implementations.

The component design pattern is organized so that implementing classes are interchangeable from a client's perspective. Further, implementing classes may override any number of the layered methods that are in the component's abstract class. This is a desirable quality because overriding these methods allows their performance to be improved by leveraging direct access to concrete representation fields.

However, an undesirable consequence of this design pattern occurs when *every* implementing class overrides a particular layered method. Figure 3 illustrates this issue by listing which secondary methods are implemented in each class of the `BooleanStructure` component. Notice how four layered methods in `BooleanStructureSecondary`, including `expand`, `isTrueStructure`, `isFalseStructure`, and `satAssignment`, are overridden by all implementing classes of `BooleanStructure`. Since abstract classes cannot be instantiated directly, only instantiations of implementing classes can be tested by the test suite. As a consequence, if all of the implementing classes override a particular layered implementation, then that implementation never has the opportunity to be tested. This flaw is not critical because this untested code is by definition never used by any implementing classes so clients have no access to it. However, it is still undesirable to have untested and unreachable code in a component. Further, a future modification to the component may result in a new implementing class that does not override a previously hidden layered method, thus exposing the untested code and potentially an error.

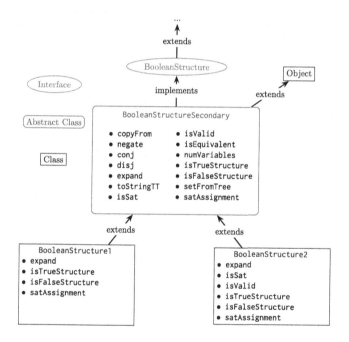

Fig. 3. `BooleanStructure` secondary method implementations

To correct this limitation in the `BooleanStructure` component, the implementation was modified to include a new reference class that does not override any secondary methods. This design pattern limitation is an interesting example of the challenges associated with verification using a language like Java that

allows inheritance and does not have the strict limitations of the RESOLVE
language.

6 Corrections to the Component

The unmodified BDD implementation contained 314 unit test cases in a test suite
with 96.3% code coverage. Despite the high quality of this test suite, two implementation errors were discovered during the verification process. The detection
of these errors despite a rigorous test suite demonstrates the relevance of the formal verification process. This also demonstrates how the verification process can
be practically carried out on a Java component with RESOLVE specifications.

Additionally, many errors in the specifications were discovered in this process.
Errors of this variety could lead to mistakes in client code due to a misrepre-
sentation of BooleanStructure behavior. The errors of this type were also not
revealed by the test suite.

copyFrom Runtime Exception. An error in the behavior of the copyFrom
method, which is shown in Listing 1.6, was discovered in the verification process.
This error was likely not discovered previously because the method appears to
be correct and passed many test cases with one-hundred percent code coverage.
The copyFrom method is a secondary layered implementation, so it is not based
on the underlying implementation of the component. In the original method
implementation, a runtime exception occurs when there are no satisfying assignments in the method argument BooleanStructure x but the number of variables is nonzero. An example of a Boolean formula with this quality is $x_1 \wedge \neg x_1$
because it has no possible satisfying assignments but it is over a nonzero number of variables. In this scenario, the precondition for the reorder method that
VARIABLES(newExp) = entries(newOrder) cannot be satisfied because the conditional block after if (x.evaluate(t)) never executes when x.sat is empty.
Thus, the variables in newExp remain in the initial empty state, causing a runtime
exception in line 28 in the call to reorder.

Listing 1.6. copyFrom Original Implementation With Error

```
1   public void copyFrom(BooleanStructure x) {
2       // Generate a false structure with the same vars as x
3       BooleanStructure newExp = this.newInstance();
4       newExp.negate();
5       Sequence<Integer> order = x.vars();
6
7       // Take the disjunction of every assignment in x.sat
8       PowerStringElements allAssignments = new
            PowerStringElements(order);
9       for (Set<Integer> t : allAssignments) {
10          if (x.evaluate(t)) {
11              // Conjunct terms in t and negations in not(t)
12              BooleanStructure term = this.newInstance();
13              for (int v : order) {
14                  BooleanStructure vExp = this.newInstance();
```

```
15              vExp.setFromInt(v);
16              if (!t.contains(v)) vExp.negate();
17              term.conj(vExp);
18            }
19            newExp.disj(term);
20          }
21        }
22
23        // Reorder variables in new structure to match x's order
24        Sequence<Integer> newOrder = new Sequence1L<Integer>();
25        for (int v : order) {
26            newOrder.add(newOrder.length(), v);
27        }
28        newExp.reorder(newOrder);
29
30        this.transferFrom(newExp);
31  }
```

toStringTT Violation of Postcondition. The need for an additional constraint in a method precondition was revealed when the formal verification of the method toStringTT could not be completed. This method constructs a truth table representation of the BDD. The original implementation of this method performed a left bit shift operation based on the number of variables in the structure. However, since the long type in Java is limited to 64 bits, the method produced an erroneous result and violated the postcondition if the number of variables exceeded this limit. The added constraint in the precondition of the method requires that the number of variables is less than 64.

Inconsistent isEquivalent Math Definition. The specification for the isEquivalent method, which compares the logical equivalence of two BDDs, had to be modified because the implementation and specification were inconsistent. The original specification compared the satisfying assignments and variables of the BDDs to check for equality. A modification to the specification was required because it did not consider logically equivalent BDDs with different variables to meet the specification, but the implementation did.

Missing newOrder Specifications. The original newOrder private method, which constructs a variable ordering that is compatible with two input orderings, had a postcondition that was too weak to be useful. It required that the new ordering was compatible with the original two, but did not require anything about the order entries. This is clearly too weak because an empty sequence would always satisfy this postcondition. To correct this, additional postcondition requirements were added to require that the new ordering variables are the union of the input variables. Further, the method required a strengthened precondition to prove a compatible ordering requirement of the original postcondition. In fact, a correct implementation of the specification without this precondition is impossible because a nontrivial compatible ordering of the result and the two inputs is impossible if the two inputs are not already compatible.

7   Conclusion

A contribution of this work is the identification of a limitation of the testing capabilities of the Java component design pattern used in the BDD implementation. The current structure of this design pattern allows for the possibility that all implementing classes of a component override the layered implementations of secondary methods, thus leaving these layered implementations unreachable and untested. This limitation demonstrates one of the challenges associated with combining an industry-standard language such as Java with formal verification.

A second outcome is the construction of a proof that formally verifies the correctness of a reference implementation of a Java-based BDD component. The resulting formally verified BDD component can now be used with a high level of confidence by clients. A third outcome resulting from the formal verification of the BDD component is the identification and correction of errors. Errors were discovered in both the specifications and implementation of the BDD component. The errors discovered in the implementation are particularly notable because they were not discovered by the comprehensive test suite. These errors were discovered only in the formal verification process, which indicates how critical formally verifying software is for error-resistant software development.

An expansion of this work is to develop an automated theorem prover to automate the verification process of a Java-based component with RESOLVE specifications. This verifier would be uniquely practical and useful because of the use of an industry-standard programming language with a specification notation that is particularly well-suited to client reasoning and modularity. This project lays some groundwork for an automated prover of this type because it provides a carefully constructed example of valid inputs and a corresponding ideal expected output. A verifier for a Java-based component with RESOLVE specifications would require the construction of a tool to automate the generation of verification conditions in a modular fashion. Existing RESOLVE verifiers [17,33] could then be leveraged with only slight modifications to discharge a substantial proportion of the verification conditions in an automated way.

Acknowledgement. The authors would like to acknowledge Saad Asim for his development of the original BDD code base. Additionally, this work has benefited from extensive discussions with other the members of the Reusable Software Research Group.

References

1. Aldrich, J., Kostadinov, V., Chambers, C.: Alias annotations for program understanding. SIGPLAN Not. **37**(11), 311–330 (2002). https://doi.org/10.1145/583854. 582448
2. Asim, S.: An exercise in design: the binary decision diagram. SIGSOFT Softw. Eng. Notes **43**(3), 19 (2018). https://doi.org/10.1145/3229783.3229801
3. Asim, S.: The binary decision diagram: abstraction and implementation. Master's thesis, The Ohio State University (2018)

4. Aziz, A., et al.: HSIS: a BDD-based environment for formal verification. In: 1994 31st Design Automation Conference, Los Alamitos, CA, USA, pp. 454–459. IEEE Computer Society (1994). https://doi.org/10.1145/196244.196467

5. Barnett, M., Fähndrich, M., Leino, K.R.M., Müller, P., Schulte, W., Venter, H.: Specification and verification: the Spec# experience. Commun. ACM **54**(6), 81–91 (2011). https://doi.org/10.1145/1953122.1953145

6. Beyer, D.: Advances in automatic software verification: SV-COMP 2020. In: TACAS 2020. LNCS, vol. 12079, pp. 347–367. Springer, Cham (2020). https://doi.org/10.1007/978-3-030-45237-7_21

7. Brookes, S.: A semantics for concurrent separation logic. In: Gardner, P., Yoshida, N. (eds.) CONCUR 2004. LNCS, vol. 3170, pp. 16–34. Springer, Heidelberg (2004). https://doi.org/10.1007/978-3-540-28644-8_2

8. Burch, J., Clarke, E., McMillan, K., Dill, D., Hwang, L.: Symbolic model checking: 10^{20} States and beyond. Inf. Comput. **98**(2), 142–170 (1992). https://doi.org/10.1016/0890-5401(92)90017-A

9. Chaki, S., Gurfinkel, A.: BDD-based symbolic model checking. In: Clarke, E., Henzinger, T., Veith, H., Bloem, R. (eds.) Handbook of Model Checking, pp. 219–245. Springer, Cham (2018). https://doi.org/10.1007/978-3-319-10575-8_8

10. Cohen, E., et al.: VCC: a practical system for verifying concurrent C. In: Berghofer, S., Nipkow, T., Urban, C., Wenzel, M. (eds.) TPHOLs 2009. LNCS, vol. 5674, pp. 23–42. Springer, Heidelberg (2009). https://doi.org/10.1007/978-3-642-03359-9_2

11. van Dijk, T., van de Pol, J.: Sylvan: multi-core framework for decision diagrams. Int. J. Softw. Tools Technol. Transf. **19**, 675–696 (2016). https://doi.org/10.1007/s10009-016-0433-2

12. Filliâtre, J.-C., Paskevich, A.: Why3—where programs meet provers. In: Felleisen, M., Gardner, P. (eds.) ESOP 2013. LNCS, vol. 7792, pp. 125–128. Springer, Heidelberg (2013). https://doi.org/10.1007/978-3-642-37036-6_8

13. Flanagan, C., Leino, K.R.M., Lillibridge, M., Nelson, G., Saxe, J.B., Stata, R.: Extended static checking for Java. SIGPLAN Not. **37**(5), 234–245 (2002). https://doi.org/10.1145/543552.512558

14. Hähnle, R., Menzel, W., Schmitt, P.H.: Integrierter deduktiver software-entwurf. Künstliche Intell. **12**(4), 40–41 (1998)

15. Herbert, L., Leino, K.R.M., Quaresma, J.: Using Dafny, an automatic program verifier. In: Meyer, B., Nordio, M. (eds.) LASER 2011. LNCS, vol. 7682, pp. 156–181. Springer, Heidelberg (2012). https://doi.org/10.1007/978-3-642-35746-6_6

16. Heym, W.: Computer program verification: improvements for human reasoning. Ph.D. thesis, Ohio State University (1995)

17. Hoffman, D.: Techniques for the specification and verification of enterprise applications. Ph.D. thesis, Ohio State University (2016)

18. Hogg, J., Lea, D., Wills, A., deChampeaux, D., Holt, R.: The Geneva convention on the treatment of object aliasing. SIGPLAN OOPS Mess. **3**(2), 11–16 (1992). https://doi.org/10.1145/130943.130947

19. Jacobs, B., Smans, J., Philippaerts, P., Vogels, F., Penninckx, W., Piessens, F.: VeriFast: a powerful, sound, predictable, fast verifier for C and Java. In: Bobaru, M., Havelund, K., Holzmann, G.J., Joshi, R. (eds.) NFM 2011. LNCS, vol. 6617, pp. 41–55. Springer, Heidelberg (2011). https://doi.org/10.1007/978-3-642-20398-5_4

20. Klabnik, S., Nichols, C.: The Rust Programming Language. No Starch Press, San Francisco (2018)

21. Kulczycki, G., Sitaraman, M., Ogden, W., Leavens, G.: Preserving clean semantics for calls with repeated arguments. Technical report RSRG-04-01, Department of Computer Science, Clemson University (2003). http://www.cs.clemson.edu/~resolve

22. Kulczycki, G., Vasudeo, J.: Simplifying reasoning about objects with Tako. In: Proceedings of the 2006 Conference on Specification and Verification of Component-Based Systems, SAVCBS 2006, pp. 57–64. Association for Computing Machinery, New York (2006). https://doi.org/10.1145/1181195.1181207

23. Kurai, R., Minato, S., Zeugmann, T.: N-gram analysis based on zero-suppressed BDDs. In: Washio, T., Satoh, K., Takeda, H., Inokuchi, A. (eds.) JSAI 2006. LNCS (LNAI), vol. 4384, pp. 289–300. Springer, Heidelberg (2007). https://doi.org/10.1007/978-3-540-69902-6_25

24. Lee, C.Y.: Representation of switching circuits by binary-decision programs. Bell Syst. Tech. J. **38**(4), 985–999 (1959). https://doi.org/10.1002/j.1538-7305.1959.tb01585.x

25. Lind-Nielsen, J.: BuDDy - A Binary Decision Diagram Package (2003). http://vlsicad.eecs.umich.edu/BK/Slots/cache/www.itu.dk/research/buddy/

26. Loekito, E., Bailey, J., Pei, J.: A binary decision diagram based approach for mining frequent subsequences. Knowl. Inf. Syst. **24**(2), 235–268 (2010). https://doi.org/10.1007/s10115-009-0252-9

27. Lovato, A., Macedonio, D., Spoto, F.: A thread-safe library for binary decision diagrams. In: Giannakopoulou, D., Salaün, G. (eds.) SEFM 2014. LNCS, vol. 8702, pp. 35–49. Springer, Cham (2014). https://doi.org/10.1007/978-3-319-10431-7_4

28. Lv, G., Su, K., Xu, Y.: CacBDD: a BDD package with dynamic cache management. In: Sharygina, N., Veith, H. (eds.) CAV 2013. LNCS, vol. 8044, pp. 229–234. Springer, Heidelberg (2013). https://doi.org/10.1007/978-3-642-39799-8_15

29. Minsky, N.H.: Towards alias-free pointers. In: Cointe, P. (ed.) ECOOP 1996. LNCS, vol. 1098, pp. 189–209. Springer, Heidelberg (1996). https://doi.org/10.1007/BFb0053062

30. Pearce, D.J., Groves, L.: Designing a verifying compiler: lessons learned from developing whiley. Sci. Comput. Program. **113**, 191–220 (2015). https://doi.org/10.1016/j.scico.2015.09.006. Formal Techniques for Safety-Critical Systems

31. Qian, F.: SableJBDD: A Java Binary Decision Diagram Package (2004). http://www.sable.mcgill.ca/~fqian/SableJBDD/

32. Rumreich, L.: The binary decision diagram: formal verification of a reference implementation. Master's thesis, The Ohio State University (2021)

33. Sitaraman, M., et al.: Building a push-button RESOLVE verifier: progress and challenges. Formal Aspects Comput. **23**(5), 607–626 (2011). https://doi.org/10.1007/s00165-010-0154-3

34. Sitaraman, M., Weide, B.: Component-based software using RESOLVE. ACM SIGSOFT Softw. Eng. Notes **19**(4), 21–22 (1994). https://doi.org/10.1145/190679.199221

35. Sivilotti, P., Asim, S., Rumreich, L.: BDD: A Binary Decision Diagram Software Component (2021). https://github.com/osu-rsrg/BDD

36. Sivilotti, P.A., Lang, M.: Interfaces first (and foremost) with Java. In: Proceedings of the 41st ACM Technical Symposium on Computer Science Education, SIGCSE 2010, pp. 515–519. Association for Computing Machinery, New York (2010). https://doi.org/10.1145/1734263.1734436

37. Somenzi, F.: CUDD: CU decision diagram package release 3.0.0 (2015). http://vlsi.colorado.edu/fabio/CUDD/

38. Vahidi, A.: JDD: a pure Java BDD and Z-BDD library (2019). https://bitbucket.org/vahidi/jdd/src/master/
39. Xing, L.: An efficient binary-decision-diagram-based approach for network reliability and sensitivity analysis. IEEE Trans. Syst. Man Cybern. Part A Syst. Hum. **38**(1), 105–115 (2008). https://doi.org/10.1109/TSMCA.2007.909493
40. Zweben, S.H., Edwards, S.H., Weide, B.W., Hollingsworth, J.E.: The effects of layering and encapsulation on software development cost and quality. IEEE Trans. Softw. Eng. **21**(3), 200–208 (1995). https://doi.org/10.1109/32.372147

Author Index

Printed in the United States
by Baker & Taylor Publisher Services